Management Science

introductory concepts and applications

david heinze

Associate Professor
of Management Science
School of Business
Virginia Commonwealth University
Richmond, Virginia

M38

Published by

SOUTH-WESTERN PUBLISHING CO.

CINCINNATI   WEST CHICAGO, ILL.   DALLAS   PELHAM MANOR, N.Y.   PALO ALTO, CALIF.

PREFACE

Management science has demonstrated itself to be a powerful decision making approach in a wide variety of managerial contexts. This quantitative approach to decision making is the focus of this introductory text. The primary objectives of this text are

1. To familiarize the reader with the vocabulary of management science.
2. To acquaint the reader with some of the capabilities of management science in various types of managerial situations.
3. To develop in the reader an ability to construct and analyze simple management science models for the sake of making good decisions.

In order to achieve these objectives, a wide assortment of management science models are presented. Applications are taken from finance, marketing, production, advertising, real estate development, small business operations, banking, transportation, health care, and public administration.

The development of the material in this text is decidedly oriented toward an intuitive, practical approach. Since beginning students learn most readily through the use of examples, illustrations and examples play a prominent role in the process of communicating the concepts of management science to the reader. In view of the importance of the illustrations and examples, considerable effort has been devoted to avoiding the usual insipid examples which do little to stir the reader's interest.

Chapter 2 gives the algebra and probability prerequisites in something of a "self-teaching" form. The reader will find that the algebra and probability used in the text does not go beyond that introduced in Chapter 2 except in a few places. In these cases the new mathematical technique is fully explained at its initial point of use. Even with much of the algebra and probability covered in Chapter 2, another explanation of the same is given at the point of its first use in later chapters.

Monte Carlo simulation is used in several chapters for the sake of analyzing certain decision situations which might otherwise require a mathematical model which is too complex. Through the construction of a simulation model the reader can readily see the relationships among many of the variables and can experiment by making changes in the controllable variables. This serves to give the mathematically naive reader something of a fuller insight into the method of management science.

With regard to the chapters that might be covered in a course, a few suggestions should be made. After the introductory material of Chapter 1 and the review of Chapter 2, it is *important* that Sections 3.1 through 3.6 of Chapter 3 be covered. The decision theory model gives the reader an understanding of the typical elements of a management science model and the primary means of reaching a decision on the basis of the model. After this there is considerable flexibility in the sequencing of chapters. Since simulation models are used in Chapter 6 on inventory models, in Chapter 10 on queueing models, and in

Chapter 11 in regard to replacement models, Chapter 5 on Monte Carlo simulation should precede these chapters. The following diagram indicates the wide latitude in the sequencing of chapters.

Finally, I would like to express my appreciation and thanks to Jay Heizer, my chairman at Virginia Commonwealth University, for his guidance and encouragement and I wish also to thank Daniel Brooks of Indiana University for his considerable effort in writing the last two chapters.

D.C.H.

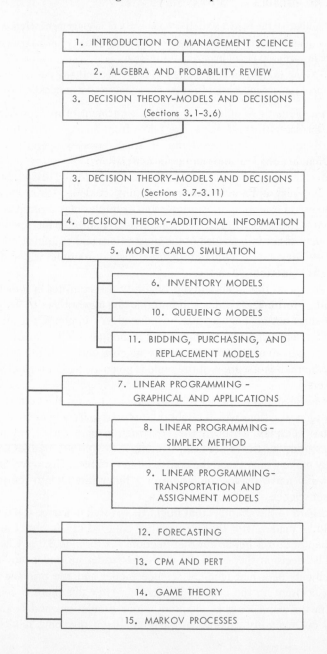

CONTENTS

1 Introduction to Management Science

1.1 SKETCHES

For the sake of introducing management science, several brief sketches of decision situations will be given which are representative of those where management science can make a significant contribution to decision making.

Kearfott Case

A large aerospace company has been awarded the contract to build a new mobile ICBM. The company is not in a position to develop and produce the guidance system for the missile due to the sophisticated nature of this system and because of time constraints. This missile, when launched from any spot in the northern hemisphere, must "read" the stars as it ascends thereby determining its precise location; then it must guide itself to the predetermined target. As the aerospace company is unable to develop this guidance system, it has decided to award a contract for the system to the lowest bidder. Among the several subcontractors which might be expected to bid for the stellar guidance system contract is Kearfott.

Ernesto Carlos is Kearfott's executive who is responsible for the preparation and submission of a bid for this stellar guidance system contract. What are some of the difficulties facing Carlos in this situation? For one, there is the matter of determining the cost of developing and producing the guidance system. While the R&D, engineering, and production departments can all estimate their respective costs for such a project, Carlos must determine the reliability of such estimates. If one of these departments significantly underestimates costs and if Kearfott gets the contract, it is obvious that serious consequences for the profitability of the contract will follow. Thus, considerable attention must be devoted for the sake of accurately projecting costs.

Even if Carlos knew with certainty the costs to perform this contract, there is also the matter of determining the actual bid. If the estimated costs were $10 million, should Kearfott bid $10.1 million or $12 million for the guidance system contract? A low bid would offer a good chance of obtaining the contract. But if such a bid were submitted and subsequently won, it would only offer Kearfott a small profit. A bid of $12 million, on the other hand, would offer a substantial profit but would be less likely to win against the bids of the other companies which are competing for the contract. Thus, Carlos is beset with various difficulties in attempting to prepare a bid for the guidance system.

It will be seen in Chapter 11 that management science offers a concrete, logical method of grappling with a bidding situation such as Kearfott faces.

Port of San Francisco Authority Case

The George Washington Bridge extends from San Francisco to Alcatraz Island which is the financial center of western civilization. As the George Washington Bridge is a toll bridge, visitors to Alcatraz must pay a toll of 50¢ upon crossing it and then another toll of 50¢ upon returning to San Francisco. The other way to get to the island from San Francisco is through the Holland Tunnel which had been dug by the Mole Man of Alcatraz. The Holland Tunnel, like the bridge, bears a one-way toll of 50¢. With economic woes besetting the city of San Francisco, the city put pressure on the Port of San Francisco Authority to cut the costs of operating the bridge and tunnel while keeping the toll revenues stable. The story of how this was done is one of the great monuments to human ingenuity; only the great pyramids of Egypt or perhaps the hanging gardens of Babylon surpass it in the catalog of great wonders.

Wilbur Wright and his brother Orville were retained by the Port Authority to expend their genius for the accomplishment of the cost-cutting task. It was Wilbur who said on that occasion, "What goes up must come down." The quick-of-mind Orville took hold of this profound pronunciation and adapted it to the situation at hand: "What goes out (to Alcatraz Island) must come back." Through this astute comprehension of the situation, the Port Authority dismissed half of its toll-takers and retained only those who collected the tolls from the travelers going to the island via the bridge or the tunnel. The new toll, of course, was $1. Toll revenues remained the same, and the travelers were pleased in having to pay a toll once instead of twice. Thus, the payroll for toll-takers was cut in half and the Port Authority was successful in cutting costs.

The city administrators were impressed with this cost reduction and with the ease with which it was accomplished. Nevertheless they felt more could be done. At this point, therefore, the Port Authority had to consider the possibility of reducing the number of toll-takers who serviced the travelers crossing to the island. (Remember that the toll-takers servicing the travelers returning to San Francisco had already been eliminated.) As the residents of San Francisco were tiring of great social experiments, the Port Authority was afraid to experimentally alter the number of toll-takers in order to see the effects on the waiting time of the travelers crossing the bridge or tunnel to the island. The Port Authority was therefore forced to undertake an extensive "theoretical" study. Through this "theoretical" study, consulting management scientists were able to predict how much extra waiting on the part of travelers would result if the number of toll-takers were reduced by varying amounts. The Port Authority and the consultants then were able to decide how many toll-takers could safely be dismissed without causing undue line-ups by the cars crossing to the island.

In Chapter 10 management science techniques which deal with decisions concerning service and waiting lines will be explored. These sorts of models were employed by the consulting management scientists working for the Port Authority.

Colemans Case

Colemans is a large department store. As with many other large retail establishments, Colemans has replaced the old standard cash registers with computerized registers. While performing the traditional cash register functions, the computerized register also serves as a component in the inventory system. When a customer purchases a harvest gold electric popcorn popper, for example, the clerk types into the register the inventory identification number for this specific product. The computer to which the cash register is tied then automatically accounts for the sale of one harvest gold popper. When the number of harvest gold poppers in inventory falls below a certain prescribed number, the computer which is keeping track of inventory prints out this fact or might even print an order to replenish the supply of harvest gold poppers.

To operate this elaborate system, Colemans must specify two numbers for the harvest gold poppers. First, a reorder level must be determined. The reorder level is the level of inventory, like three harvest gold poppers, which triggers the computer to print a request or order for the replenishing of the harvest gold poppers. Should this reorder level be a low number, like 3, or a high number like 6? Quite obviously if Colemans reorders a shipment of harvest gold poppers when inventory falls to a relatively high number like 6, it is not likely that they will run out of poppers while waiting for the new shipment to arrive. Letting the inventory level fall to 3 before reordering, however, runs the risk of selling out the poppers before the new shipment arrives. A customer seeking a harvest gold popper would therefore be unable to purchase one in this predicament. Thus, it would seem that a customer-oriented store like Colemans ought always to use a high reorder level so that they will never have to turn away customers seeking harvest gold poppers.

High reorder levels, however, have some unpleasant ramifications. With the higher reorder level Colemans will end up carrying extra harvest gold poppers in inventory. Then, of course, if a higher reorder level is used for harvest gold poppers, it should for the same reason also be used for avocado poppers, white poppers, aluminum poppers, and poppy red poppers. In fact, the higher reorder level should also prevail, in order to be consistent, for all Colemans products, that is, for newborn disposable diapers, toddler disposable diapers, 3' chain link fencing, 4' chain link fencing, 4 H.P. rototillers, 5 H.P. rototillers, gold curtain rods, white curtain rods, and so on. Quite obviously Colemans, in uniformly using higher reorder levels, will be forced to carry a huge inventory. This means money that could have been used elsewhere will be tied up in inventory, and more storage space will be required. Thus, there are disadvantages to high reorder levels as well as disadvantages with low levels.

Assuming that Colemans could optimally set reorder levels for each product sold, the second problem concerns the size of the order that Colemans should place for the sake of replenishing inventory. Should Colemans order 10 or 30 harvest gold poppers? The matter of determining reorder levels and order sizes is a problem which is best handled through a management science approach. Management science has made a substantial contribution in the area of inventory control. Chapter 6 will deal with some inventory models which are helpful in the management of inventory.

McGookin, Chickie, Buzard Bait, & Louie Case

McGookin, Chickie, Buzard Bait, & Louie is an advertising agency out of Philadelphia which puts together packages of television commercials. MCBBL buys television time from stations all over the United States. One day the makers of Acnil, an unknown but promising new acne skin creme, approached MCBBL with the intent of hiring MCBBL to put together a national televison promotion for Acnil. The makers of Acnil were quite specific in communicating to MCBBL how many young people, old people, middle income people, women, men, and so forth should be exposed to Acnil commercials by the television promotion. Since MCBBL had information as to how many persons in each of these groups were watching various television programs, it was now up to MCBBL to put together a minimum cost television campaign for the makers of Acnil which met all of the requirements. In other words, MCBBL needed to purchase a wide assortment of television spots for as little as possible which would expose the desired number of viewers in the various categories as specified by the makers of Acnil. Acnil ads, as a result of MCBBL's efforts, appeared during many programs such as Hogan's Hoboes, Little House in the Swamp, and Police Boy.

How did MCBBL put together this minimum cost television campaign? A management science technique known as linear programming was used to select the set of television programs which would meet the manufacturer's requirements while keeping costs to a minimum. Linear programming has many sorts of applications in various disciplines. It is presented in Chapters 7 through 9.

1.2 DEFINITION OF MANAGEMENT SCIENCE

In attempting to define or describe something, there are two possible approaches that may be taken. A definition can be given, or, some examples can be given. If you were called upon to describe a stone to someone unfamiliar with the same, you could turn to the dictionary which states that a stone is "concreted earthy or mineral matter." Such a definition might prove to be less than informative. A more promising method of communication would be to display to the person an assortment of stones of various sizes, colors, and shapes. This would be a more effective method of communication.

In attempting to define or describe management science, there are also these two alternative approaches. In this chapter an attempt will be made to define management science according to the dictionary approach. Realizing that the most effective and interesting way to communicate the character of management science is through the use of examples, excessive time will not be spent laboring to define management science according to the dictionary approach. For the sake of understanding management science, the succeeding chapters of this text will serve as the display of management science in its various "sizes, colors, and shapes." The four cases outlined in the first section serve to give a preliminary glimpse into the variety of situations with which management science deals.

The term *management science* suggests that this discipline has something to do with management and something to do with science. Consider first the management aspect. Decision making is the very heart of management. Convinced of the centrality of decision making to management, it would correctly be concluded that "management" science is concerned with decision making. It is further recognized that the management process is indigenous to all kinds of organizations. Management is not confined to profit-making corporations; it is common to every organization whether that organization be a hospital, a university, a governmental agency, or a business. The organization lives, moves, and adapts only through the implementation of decisions. Not only is the management process operating in all types of organizations, it is also present at the various levels in the hierarchies of these organizations. Thus, it would also be correctly concluded that "management" science could be expected to have a wide spectrum of application.

One of many definitions of management science is that it is a scientific approach to making decisions in a managerial context. A word should now be said concerning the "science" of management science. The term science connotes a couple of ideas, each of which are relevant to management science. In the first place, we think of science as being an explicit, systematic undertaking. The ideas of structure and system come to mind in thinking about science. So it is that management "science" is a systematic, explicit, and well-structured approach to decision making. In the second place, the term science brings to mind the ideas of hypothesis, observation, and experimentation. In management science alternative courses of action (hypotheses) are evaluated. This evaluation is accomplished through the method of experimenting with a model. Just as the aerodynamic engineer uses a model or replica of a plane in the wind tunnel for experimentation purposes, the management scientist uses a model of the decision situation in order to evaluate the choices that can be made. In this sense also management science becomes a scientific approach to making decisions.

Having given a definition of management science, some of its predominant characteristics should be noted. Besides having a decision-making orientation, management science is particularly concerned with decisions which have economic ramifications or consequences. Therefore, in management science there is abundant mention of revenues, costs, and profits. The fact that economic consequences are relatively easy to quantify leads to the second characteristic of management science. As with most sciences, there is the liberal use of mathematics in management science as an efficient way to describe managerial decision situations. This is not to say, however, that management science is a branch of mathematics. As Bertrand Russell has argued in *Principia Mathematica*, mathematics is an extension of logic.[1] Thus, in using mathematics, the management scientist is applying a powerful form of logic in order to assist in making decisions.

1.3 GENESIS AND DEVELOPMENT OF MANAGEMENT SCIENCE

How long has management science been in use? The answer to this question depends on how strictly management science is defined. Most observers agree that management science as a well-defined discipline arose during World War II. However, its roots go back much further. People have been faced with problems which admit to management science solutions since the beginning of history. Consider Joseph (Genesis 41) who predicted the famine and then as prime minister under Pharoah proceeded to accumulate a massive inventory of food in anticipation of the famine. The determination of inventory size, for example, is therefore not a new problem. However, though decision problems within the purview of management are not new, the management science approach to making decisions is relatively new.

Coming to the late 19th century, Frederick W. Taylor became the father of scientific management. Taylor scientifically evaluated various shop operating methods at the Midvale Steel works in Philadelphia and later was a consultant for Bethlehem Steel. As a result of his efficiency studies, Taylor determined, for example, optimal methods of handling ore and iron. Taylor also used the team approach to study problems, which approach became quite common in management science as it later developed. Taylor and other pioneers such as Henry Gantt and the Gilbreths can be considered as the forerunners of the modern management scientists.

Prior to World War II there were several accomplishments which were germane to the later development of management science. In 1917, for example, A. K. Erlang published a work based on his studies of telephone exchanges. Erlang's work became the foundation for waiting line or queueing models. In the 1920s several inventory models were developed thus constituting the beginnings of a very important area of management science.

In World War II management science became established through a number of successes. The British used management science in devising various logistic and war strategies. In this regard the British instituted the team approach where management science problems were solved by a team of specialists which might include military personnel, engineers, psychologists, mathematicians, physicists, and the like. In these formative years of World War II, management

[1] Bertrand Russell and Alfred N. Whitehead, *Principia Mathematica* (Cambridge University Press).

science was known as operations research. The term operations research, though bearing military overtones, is still widely used today even though operations research is no longer confined to military problems.

After World War II, operations research or management science found its way into the decision processes of business, non-profit, and government organizations. New techniques under the rubric of management science continued to be developed. The development, for example, by George Dantzig in 1947 of the simplex method for the solution of linear programming models opened the door to many new applications. Such advances along with the development of the computer made management science all the more powerful. Other work, such as that of John Von Neumann and Oscar Morganstern in decision and game theory, also gave added momentum to the development of management science. Yet a more recent development worthy of note was that of PERT. PERT was developed by the Special Projects Office of the U.S. Navy in the late 1950s. It was first used in the Polaris Weapons System project as a method of planning and controlling the numerous activities associated with the Polaris project. At about the same time a similar planning technique called the *critical path method* was developed at DuPont. Thus, though management science is comparatively new, its influence is both pervasive and substantial.

1.4 APPROACH OF MANAGEMENT SCIENCE

The management science approach to decision making can be described as a four-step process. These four steps are (1) problem recognition, (2) model construction, (3) analysis and decision, and (4) enrichment and/or implementation. Each will now be considered and briefly illustrated.

Problem Recognition

In the first place, a problem requiring a decision must exist and be recognized. Sometimes such a problem is forced on the manager as when a piece of equipment breaks or workers go on strike. In other situations management deliberately creates the problem as when, for example, management decides to explore new markets for its products. After the problem has been identified, it is imperative that the decision makers become saturated with the various aspects of the decision situation being faced. Objectives must be identified, alternative courses of action must be isolated, and critical elements must be determined.

Debbie Krahn Products is a competitor of Avon in the door-to-door perfume market. Currently Debbie Krahn is operating only in the Southwest. However, a tentative decision has just been made to go national and this decision has precipitated a number of problems. One problem concerns the method of manufacturing the line of Debbie Krahn perfumes. Should Debbie Krahn begin manufacturing its own perfumes, or should the company continue to purchase them from the independent manufacturer which has been supplying the perfumes till now? Quite obviously Debbie Krahn wishes to make a choice in favor of that alternative which will minimize costs and thus maximize profits.

Notice that the first step of the management science approach has been accomplished. The problem of how to supply or manufacture its product has appeared and been recognized. With considerable attention spent in deliberating about the problem, two courses of action have been determined. The two alternatives are:

a_1: Manufacture by independent
a_2: Manufacture by Debbie Krahn

In this context the objective of cost minimization has also been identified. After the problem has been recognized and studied, the second step in the management science process may take place.

Model Construction

What is a model? Everyone is familiar with model planes and model trains. A model plane which serves as a child's toy is simply a representation of a real plane. It has many of the features of a real plane. However, there are numerous characteristics of the real plane which are not common to the model plane. The model is a simplified representation of the real. A toy plane is called a physical model since it has the same physical appearance as the real. Models may become more abstract, however. A road map, for example, is a somewhat more abstract model. It is a model of a highway system where the lines on the map represent the actual configuration of the roads. Such a model is not too abstract since the physical lines on the map represent physical roads. Nevertheless, someone who had never seen a map would not automatically associate it with a highway system as they would a toy plane with a real plane.

An organization chart is an example of a model at yet a higher level of abstraction. In a road map the connecting lines represent connecting roads which are real physical entities. However, the typical organization chart with its connecting lines emanating from the president and proceeding to the various vice-presidents and so on does not represent a physical relationship between the officers. The lines in the organization chart represent the flow of authority and responsibility within the organization.

The most abstract type of model is a mathematical model. The uninformed person would never guess what

$$P = rX - c$$

represents. Each of the symbols, P, $=$, r, X, $-$, and c, as well as the syntax must be defined before this mathematical model can communicate any meaningful information or be used for the sake of making decisions. Management science primarily uses such mathematical models as they have proved to be the most versatile and powerful for decision-making purposes.

Having introduced the idea of a model, attention can now be directed to the second step in the management science approach to decision making.

After the decision maker has recognized the problem and studied it, a model of the decision situation is constructed. This model will not incorporate extraneous elements just as a road map does not incorporate extraneous details like fences. The decision maker should incorporate those elements of the decision situation which are deemed especially critical. In the first half of Chapter 3 which deals with decision theory, the primary components of a management science model are examined in detail and illustrated. Then in the remainder of the text a wide assortment of specific types of models are presented. For the sake of a preliminary glimpse into the nature of one kind of model, recall the Debbie Krahn case. What might the model look like in this situation?

The first component of the model is composed of the two courses of action as already given. Debbie Krahn can continue to purchase from the independent manufacturer, a_1, or can begin to make its own products, a_2. Next, the possible volume of sales must be considered. Debbie Krahn anticipates that either 1.0 million or 1.5 million bottles of its perfume will be sold. In particular, management feels that there is a 50–50 chance that 1.0 million bottles will be sold and a 50–50 chance that 1.5 million will be sold. The set of possible events, 1.0 or 1.5 million bottles, constitutes the second component of the model. Finally, the cost consequences must be determined. The current supplier is willing to produce an unlimited supply of perfume at a cost of \$.80 per bottle. This means that the total cost if a_1 is selected will be

$$T_1 = .80B$$

where B equals the number of bottles manufactured (sold). If Debbie Krahn, on the other hand, were to manufacture the perfume itself, a plant must be purchased for \$500,000. Once this plant has been purchased, bottles of perfume can be turned out at a cost of \$.20 each. Therefore, the total cost if a_2 were implemented would be

$$T_2 = .20B + 500,000$$

where B again equals the number of bottles manufactured (sold). A model of Debbie Krahn's situation has now been constructed. It is:

a_1: Manufacture by independent
a_2: Manufacture by Debbie Krahn

Let B = number of bottles manufactured
$P(B=1,000,000) = .50 \qquad P(B=1,500,000) = .50$

Total Cost with a_1: $\qquad T_1 = .80B$
Total Cost with a_2: $\qquad T_2 = .20B + 500,000$

Before moving to the next step or phase of the management science approach, another comment pertaining to model construction should be made. It is usually advantageous to initially construct a simple model rather than attempt to compose a complicated model which mirrors all the complexities and intricacies of the real situation. The analyst may too easily get lost in details by beginning with a complicated model. With a simple model the manager is able to get an overall perspective of the problem. The simple model can then be enriched as necessary till a suitable model has been developed. Many times, however, a simple model is sufficient for the decision-making purpose at hand.

Analysis and Decision

In the management science approach the model becomes the center of attention. By means of the model the manager analyzes and evaluates the alternative courses of action. Through the model each alternative is measured in terms of its contribution to the objectives at hand. In this manner a decision is made in favor of the alternative with the optimal consequences. Thus, the third step is essentially the activity of "solving" the model which has already been constructed.

Consider again the Debbie Krahn model. If sales are $B = 1,000,000$ bottles and if an independent manufacturer were used to supply the perfume, then the total cost would be

$$T_1 = (.80)(1,000,000)$$
$$= \$800,000$$

If, on the other hand, the product had been manufactured internally, then the total cost would be

$$T_2 = (.20)(1,000,000) + 500,000$$
$$= \$700,000$$

Thus, the internal manufacture of the perfume, a_2, is less costly for the lower sales figure. If sales instead were $B = 1,500,000$ bottles, then

$$T_1 = (.80)(1,500,000)$$
$$= \$1,200,000$$

and,

$$T_2 = (.20)(1,500,000) + 500,000$$
$$= \$800,000$$

Again it is less expensive to manufacture the perfume internally. Therefore, no matter whether $B = 1,000,000$ or $B = 1,500,000$ bottles are sold, manufacturing the perfume rather than purchasing from outside is less costly. It follows that Debbie Krahn should purchase the manufacturing plant and proceed to produce its own perfume; this course of action will minimize costs.

In this simple case the model has been solved quite easily. Through the analysis a decision has been made in favor of a_2. Though the Debbie Krahn case was quite easy to analyze, in many decision situations the advantage of one course of action over the others is not so obvious. In such cases this third step of "analysis and decision" can be quite challenging.

Enrichment and/or Implementation

Upon completing the foregoing analysis, the manager's decision may be that the current model does not sufficiently describe the decision situation. If the model does not constitute a suitable basis for making a decision, it must be enriched or modified so that it becomes an adequate image of reality. This means that the first three steps would have to be repeated in a more thorough fashion. On the other hand, the manager might be quite satisfied with the current model and is thus willing to implement the course of action prescribed.

CHAPTER 1

In the Debbie Krahn case the initial model was quite simplistic. No attempt was made, for example, to incorporate the salvage value of the plant into the model. Also, management did not incorporate the fact that a_2 (manufacture by Debbie Krahn) would require a substantial outlay of $500,000 whereas the other alternative allowed for the costs to be deferred till production actually takes place. These factors are important considerations and might be incorporated in a second model. However, Debbie Krahn's management decided that because of the considerable advantage of a_2 over a_1 on the basis of the simple model, the incorporation of these other factors would not prove to change the advantage from a_2 to a_1. In other words, management was sure that a complex model would yield the same choice favoring a_2. Thus, the analysis of the simple model was accepted and no enrichment was deemed necessary. Debbie Krahn therefore implemented the decision to manufacture the perfume itself.

Having sketched the steps of the management science approach, how does it differ from the classical management decision-making process? The classical approach could best be described as being intuitive. With the management science approach the problem is organized and structured into the form of a model. On the other hand, the intuitive approach is likely to be informal and somewhat piecemeal lacking a complete, systematic integration of the critical elements. With the classical approach the manager might also augment the experience-based intuitive judgment and piecemeal analyses with rules of thumb and the opinions of others who have dealt with similar problems.

In claiming the superiority of the management science approach over the informal, intuitive approach, it is not to be inferred that the intuitive approach leads to poor results. Managers have and continue to get along quite well without the advantages of management science. However, the performance of these managers could be enhanced with reference to certain types of problems if management science were utilized.

1.5 SIMPLE MODELS AND PEDAGOGY

The objectives of this text are to:

1. Familiarize the reader with the vocabulary of management science.
2. Acquaint the reader with some of the capabilities of management science in various types of managerial decision situations.
3. Develop in the reader a capability to construct and analyze simple management science models for the sake of making good decisions.

To this end, a wide assortment of simple models are presented. Occasionally students react unfavorably to the study of the simplified world of elementary models. However, the models in a text like this must be kept simple for at least three reasons. First, the text is addressed to readers who have a minimal background in mathematics. Since many complex models require sophisticated mathematics, they obviously cannot be considered in an elementary text. Second, even though an actual decision situation is complex, it is good management science procedure to begin the analysis with a simple model. It is with simple models that even the sophisticated analyst begins. Only if the simple model proves inadequate will it be enriched in an effort to evolve a suitable model upon which to base a decision. Simple models therefore do play an important role in management science. In the third place, if complex models were considered it would be impossible to sample the multitude of applications afforded by management science. Only a relatively few complex models could be adequately covered in a single course. Therefore, simple models can form the foundation of a meaningful course in management science.

In attempting to reach the objectives stated above, a further word is appropriate in anticipation of the remainder of this text. The development of the material is decidedly oriented toward a practical approach to management science which does not rely on rigorous, step-by-step mathematical substantiation. This does not mean, however, that the approach is non-mathematical; mathematical models are essential to management science. Furthermore, since beginning students learn most readily through the use of concrete examples, illustrations and examples play a prominent role in the process of unfolding and communicating management science to the reader in this text. In other words, expect an approach which leans toward the inductive in that the presentation typically begins with specific examples rather than with the general. Hopefully a text written in this manner will yield optimal results in moving toward the stated objectives.

1.6 PREVIEW

Management science models may be categorized or classified in various ways. One method of classification is by discipline or application. In such a case, for example, all the models for marketing applications or for inventory applications are grouped together. Management science models may also be classified according to their mathematical form or structure. The chapters in this text tend to follow this latter classification scheme.

There are two broad categories of mathematical forms in management science models. The two are probabilistic models and deterministic models. Under each of these there are subcategories. Probabilistic models include in the actual model the uncertainty which may be inherent in a decision situation. This is done through the introduction of a probability distribution. Deterministic models, on the other hand, do not formally incorporate the notion of uncertainty into the model. For example, in inventory management the decision maker might assume that the demand for a product in the next month will be 100 units. If this monthly demand figure of 100 units is the only one incorporated in the inventory model, the resulting model would be deterministic. However, if the manager perceives that demand could be 80, or 90, or 100, or 110 units next month, and if these figures with their respective probabilities were formally included in the model, then the model would be probabilistic.

In studying deterministic models one must be conversant with algebra; with probabilistic models the analyst must also have an understanding of probability. In Chapter 2 the algebra and probability prerequisites for this text are given. The reader will find that the algebra and probability used in the text does not go beyond that reviewed in Chapter 2. In some situations the mathematics that would be required goes beyond the prerequisites of this text. In order to still study these decision situations, a solution technique known as Monte Carlo simulation is used. In using simulation the difficult mathematics can be skirted. Thus, the mathematics can be kept simple while allowing the reader to study certain decision situations which are of interest yet more complicated. It is therefore important that Chapter 5, which describes Monte Carlo simulation, be read since simulation is subsequently used for certain probabilistic situations in Chapter 6 (Inventory Models), Chapter 10 (Queueing Models), and Chapter 11 (Bidding, Purchasing, and Replacement Models).

The applications in this text cover such diverse fields as finance, marketing, production, advertising, real estate development, and small business operations. However, as stated earlier, the text is organized in a manner where all of the various applications for a given model of specific mathematical form are placed together. Therefore, marketing applications, for example, are scattered throughout the text rather than being concentrated in one special chapter. Consider briefly now the principal topics covered.

Decision theory, Chapters 3 and 4, concerns the broadest approach to solving problems. Decision theory forms a foundation upon which the other models stand. As might be expected, decision theory models have numerous applications. Inventory models are presented in Chapter 6. Recall the Colemans Department Store sketch of Section 1.1; this is an example of an inventory problem. Linear programming is covered in Chapters 7, 8, and 9. This extremely important type of deterministic modeling approach may be applied to all sorts of problems. Recall the McGookin, Chickie, Buzard Bait, & Louie sketch of Section 1.1. In this case linear programming was used to allocate the advertising budget among television programs. Queueing models (see Chapter 10) deal with situations where waiting lines arise as in the Port of San Francisco Authority sketch. Bidding models, Chapter 11, concern situations where competitive bidding takes place as in the Kearfott sketch. Purchasing models are designed to aid management in the timing of the purchase of commodities whose prices vary. Replacement models deal with the optimal replacement frequency of items, such as machines, which wear out or break. In Chapter 12 various forecasting techniques are examined. Many of the models in management science rely on forecasts or predictions of one sort or another; thus, a consideration of forecasting is extremely important. The planning methods known as CPM and PERT are presented in Chapter 13. Through these techniques management is able to plan and coordinate, for example, all of the activities going into the completion of a major project. In game theory, Chapter 14, decision situations where there is a direct confrontation between competitors is considered. Finally, Chapter 15 concerns Markov models which have many applications. To take only one, with Markov analysis the future market shares of several competing companies can be estimated.

Though there are other specialized types of models in the domain of management science, the ones mentioned above constitute most of the important types. Let us now ride forward into the hosts of management science models and examine them more closely.

PROBLEMS

1-1. The following parts concern the sketches of Section 1.1.
  (a) In the Kearfott case, what is the advantage and disadvantage of submitting a high bid for the stellar guidance system?
  (b) In the Port Authority case, what will be the impact on the city and the travelers if the number of toll-takers is further reduced?
  (c) In the Colemans case, what would be the advantages and disadvantages of placing large orders for the replenishment of the harvest gold poppers?
  (d) In the MCBBL case, what are the sorts of things the makers of Acnil must specify before an advertising campaign using television can be put together?

1-2. Give a definition of management science.

1-3. When did management science come into its own as a recognized approach to decision making?

1-4. Briefly identify the contributions of the following to management science: F. W. Taylor, A. K. Erlang, G. Dantzig, Von Neumann, Special Projects Office of the U.S. Navy.

1-5. List the four steps in the management science approach to decision making and describe each in a paragraph.

1-6. In the Debbie Krahn case, if only 600,000 bottles of perfume would be sold, which alternative would be the better?

1-7. Contrast the management science and the classical approaches to decision making.

1-8. Why might certain modern managers be reluctant to use management science? (The reasons are not given in the text.)

1-9. Why are simple models appropriate for a first course in management science?

1-10. Why will Monte Carlo simulation be occasionally used in this text?

1-11. What is the difference between a probabilistic model and a deterministic model?

1-12. What are the objectives of this text in relationship to the study of management science?

2 Algebra and Probability Review

2.1 INTRODUCTION

In this chapter particular algebraic techniques and probability basics are covered which will subsequently be used in later chapters. Three points should be made for the sake of defining the nature of this chapter. First, a complete survey of algebra and probability is not intended. Only those topics which will actually be used in later chapters are covered. The material in this chapter therefore becomes a prerequisite to the remainder of the text. It will generally be assumed that the reader is somewhat familiar with the material of this chapter. In a few places in the text a specific algebra or probability topic not presented in this chapter will be explained at the point of its use. Second, this chapter is intended to be a review. The assumption is that the reader has previously been exposed to these topics; therefore, the material will be sketchy in places. Third, this chapter contains questions and answers immediately after most sections. These enable readers to test their understanding of the material while progressing through the review. While studying a later chapter the reader may wish to review a particular topic like the normal distribution. In such a case the reader can come back to the appropriate section in this chapter and find in one unit a review of the topic along with supporting questions and answers.

2.2 NOTATION

Students often get bogged down in mathematics because of the notation. In this text the notation is kept as simple as possible. Two types of notation, though used infrequently, will be reviewed here.

Subscripted Variables

An economist interested in measuring the unemployment rate in each state might choose to let letter symbols denote the various state-by-state unemployment rates. For example, X might represent the unemployment rate in Alabama,

Y the rate in Alaska, Z the rate in Arizona, and so forth. Quite obviously the economist will run out of letters. Instead of then going to the Greek alphabet for more letters, the economist could instead use subscripted variables. For example, X_1 could represent the unemployment rate in Alabama, X_2 the rate in Alaska, and so on. The same economist wishing also to denote the personal incomes for the residents of each state could then let, for example, Y_1 denote the personal income for Alabama, Y_2 the personal income for Alaska, and so on. The benefit of such a notation system should be obvious. The presence of subscripted variables should not be construed as a complication but as a simplification once the variables have been defined. Only on rare occasions, however, will there be a need for subscripted variables in this text.

Summation Notation

The capital sigma, Σ, means "sum up." Therefore, ΣX means sum up the values of X. Summation notation is used in statistics, for example, where the mean of a set of n observations is defined as

$$\overline{X} = \frac{\Sigma X}{n}$$

Suppose a set of four observed X values, where X is a variable referring to the weights of persons, are 100, 180, 160, and 120. Then,

$$\Sigma X = 100 + 180 + 160 + 120$$

and

$$\overline{X} = \frac{\Sigma X}{n} = \frac{100 + 180 + 160 + 120}{4}$$
$$= 140$$

The mean of data which is presented in a grouped frequency distribution is

$$\overline{X} = \frac{\Sigma f X_m}{n}$$

where f is the class frequency and X_m is the midpoint of the class. In Table 2.1 a frequency distribution is given for ten automobiles whose speeds have been clocked. The mean speed is therefore

$$\overline{X} = \frac{(3)(45 \text{ mph}) + (5)(55 \text{ mph}) + (2)(65 \text{ mph})}{10}$$
$$= 54 \text{ mph.}$$

Notice that each term in the numerator is $(f)(X_m)$.

TABLE 2.1
Frequency Distribution

Speed	Frequency
40.01 — 50	3
50.01 — 60	5
60.01 — 70	2
	10

Before continuing, work the following problems.

For the following three pairs of observations,

X	Y
2	10
4	20
6	30

Find:
1. ΣX
2. $\overline{X}$
3. $\overline{Y}$
4. ΣXY
5. ΣX^2

Answers: 12, 4, 20, $(20 + 80 + 180 = 280)$, 56.

2.3 MAXIMUMS AND MINIMUMS BY GRAPHING

Suppose that the cost C to operate a system is a function of its capacity K

$$C = K^2 - 40K + 500$$

where K cannot fall below 5. What is the optimal value for K, that is, what value of K will yield the minimum cost? By systematic trial and error coupled with graphing, the optimal value for K may be isolated. Begin by selecting several values for K for the sake of determining the resulting cost. For example, if $K = 5$, then

$$C = 5^2 - (40)(5) + 500 = 325$$

If $K = 10$, then

$$C = 10^2 - (40)(10) + 500 = 200$$

If $K = 20$, then $C = 100$, and if $K = 30$, then $C = 200$.

Of the values for K tried, $K = 20$ yields the lowest cost. The values for C corresponding to $K = 5, 10, 20,$ and 30 are next plotted as in Figure 2.1, page 18, where C is shown on the vertical axis and K on the horizontal axis. By fitting a curved line by sight through these points it becomes apparent that the minimum value for C is achieved by a K in the region of 20. Values of $K = 19$ and $K = 21$ might next be tried to see if they yield a lower cost. As they do not it can be concluded that $K = 20$ or some value very near is the optimal value for K. The company would therefore do well to install a system with a capacity of 20.

The profit P a company makes is a function of its advertising expenditure A:
$$P = 120A - A^2$$
Find the optimal value of A.
Answer: 60 which yields $P = \$3600$

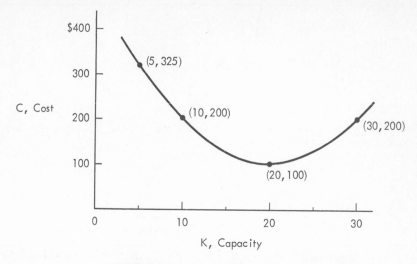

FIGURE 2.1   Graph of C = K² − 40K + 500

2.4 SIMULTANEOUS LINEAR EQUATIONS

In certain management science topics such as decision theory, linear programming, game theory, and Markov analysis it is necessary to solve several linear equations simultaneously. For the cases to be encountered in this text, the substitution method is an adequate solution technique.

Consider the following two linear equations:

$$-2X + 7Y = 700$$
$$5X + 14Y = 300$$

What values, if any, for X and Y will satisfy both of these equations? According to the substitution method of solving such equations, select either of the equations and solve for one variable in terms of the other. For example, take the first equation

$$-2X + 7Y = 700$$

and solve for Y

$$7Y = 700 + 2X$$
$$Y = \frac{(700 + 2X)}{7}$$

Now substitute this value for Y in the other equation

$$5X + 14Y = 300$$
$$5X + 14 \left[\frac{(700 + 2X)}{7} \right] = 300$$

Solve this equation, which has only one unknown, for X

$$5X + (2)(700+2X) = 300$$
$$5X + 1400 + 4X = 300$$
$$9X = -1100$$
$$X = \frac{-1100}{9}$$
$$X = -122.22$$

Now substitute this value for X in either of the original linear equations and solve for Y

$$-2X + 7Y = 700$$
$$-2(-122.22)+7Y = 700$$
$$244.44 + 7Y = 700$$
$$7Y = 455.56$$
$$Y = 65.08$$

Therefore the solution to this problem is ($X=-122.22$, $Y=65.08$). This solution should be checked by substituting it into the original equations:

$$(-2)(-122.22) + (7)(65.08) = 700$$
$$(5)(-122.22) + (14)(65.08) = 300$$

In solving two linear equations, what is achieved graphically? The solution is actually the point where the two graphs of the linear equations intersect. This is seen in Figure 2.2. Thus, the intersection of two straight lines is determined by simultaneously solving their algebraic equations.

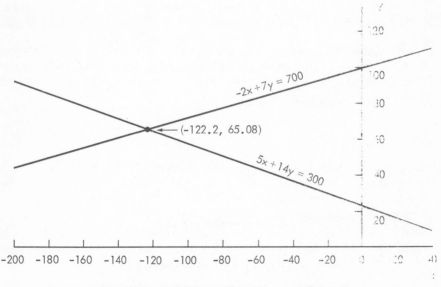

FIGURE 2.2 Two Linear Equations and Point of Intersection

1. Solve for G and p:
$$G = 5p - 3$$
$$G = 4 - 5p$$

2. Solve for X and Y:
$$2X + Y = 10$$
$$X + 3Y = 12.5$$

Answers: $(p=.7, G=.5)$, $(X=3.5, Y=3)$

2.5 SIMPLE, JOINT, AND CONDITIONAL PROBABILITIES

A group of one hundred stocks which are traded on the New York Stock Exchange were classified as in Table 2.2, on page 21. Suppose one stock is to be randomly selected from these one hundred. What is the probability that the stock is an industrial? Since there are 60 industrials and a total of 100 stocks, there are 60 chances out of 100 that the stock will be an industrial. Therefore, the probability is

$$P(I) = \frac{60}{100}$$

What is the probability that the selected stock is a poor performer? Since there are 20 poor performers in the 100, this probability is

$$P(P) = \frac{20}{100}$$

This type of probability is called a *simple*, or *marginal*, or *unconditional* probability. The other simple probabilities are $P(U) = .30$, $P(T) = .10$, $P(H) = .45$, and $P(M) = .35$. A simple probability gives the probability of the occurrence of a single event with no reference to other events.

What is the probability that a stock selected from the group is both a utility and a moderate performer? Since 15 of the 100 stocks are utilities which are moderate performers, the probability is

$$P(U,M) = \frac{15}{100}$$

This type of probability is called a *joint* probability. Joint probabilities involve the simultaneous or successive occurrence of two or more events. Some of the other joint probabilities are $P(I,H) = .30$, $P(T,P) = .70$, and $P(I,M) = .20$.

Suppose a stock has been selected which is an industrial. Given that it is an industrial, what is the probability it is a high performer? There are 60 industrials and of these 30 are high performers. Therefore, the probability of the stock being a high performer given that it is an industrial is

$$P(H|I) = \frac{30}{60}$$

TABLE 2.2
One Hundred Stocks

	Industrial I	Utility U	Transportation T	
High Performance H	30	12	3	45
Moderate Performance M	20	15	0	35
Poor Performance P	10	3	7	20
	60	30	10	100

The vertical slash is read "given that" in the symbolism above. This sort of probability is known as a *conditional* probability. It gives the probability of a certain event assuming that another event has already occurred. As another example of a conditional probability, what is the probability that a stock is a transportation given that it is a moderate performer? Since there are 35 moderate performers of which none are transportation stocks, the probability is $P(T|M) = 0/35$. Other conditional probabilities are $P(U|H) = 12/45$, $P(P|T) = 7/10$, and $P(P|I) = 10/60$.

The discussion of simple, joint, and conditional probabilities will be continued in the next sections.

Consider the following table which is analogous to that of Table 2.2.

	A	B	C
J	5	0	10
K	10	5	1
L	12	3	4

Find the following probabilities:

$$P(B), P(J), P(K,C), P(A,J),$$
$$P(B|L), P(K|C)$$

Answers: 8/50, 15/50, 1/50, 5/50,
3/19, 1/15.

2.6 INDEPENDENCE

Two events are said to be statistically independent if the occurrence of one of them gives absolutely no information as to the altering of the probability of the other. With this definition, are the following two events independent?

Event A: Heads on the first flip of a coin
Event B: Heads on the second flip of a coin

If it is reported that on the first flip a head occurs, this is of no help in guessing whether a head will occur on the second flip. Regardless of what occurs on the first flip, the probability of a head on the second is .50. Hence the occurrence of A gives no information as to the occurrence (or probability thereof) of B and thus the two events are independent. In terms of probabilities, $P(B) = .50$ and the probability of B is still .50 given that A has occurred; that is, $P(B|A) = .50$.

Suppose now that a bag has two marbles, a red marble and a green marble. Now let

Event A: Get red marble on first draw
Event B: Get red marble on second draw

Assume that the marble drawn on the first draw is not replaced in the bag. Not knowing the outcome of the first draw, the probability of getting a red on the second is .50, that is, $P(B) = .50$. However, if you are advised that a red marble was drawn on the first draw, then it is impossible that a red will be drawn on the second since only a green remains. Symbolically, $P(B|A) = 0$. In this example the occurrence (or non-occurrence) of A enables one to predict perfectly the outcome of the second draw. Hence A and B are not independent; in this case they are dependent.

Now suppose a person is to be randomly selected from a crowd. Let

Event A: Person weighs over 200 pounds
Event B: Person is a female

Without any weight information given, the probability that the selected person is a female is .50, that is, $P(B) = .50$. But what if it is known that event A has occurred and the person selected weighs over 200 pounds. What now is the probability that the selected person is a female? Since very few women weigh more than 200 pounds, you would now say that it is unlikely that the selected person is a female. For example, perhaps the probability is .02, that is, $P(B|A) = .02$. Notice that the occurrence of A gives information regarding the occurrence of B since the probability of B changes from .50 to .02 if A occurs. According to the definition this means that A and B are not independent; they are dependent. Notice that there does not need to be perfect dependence in order for two events to not be independent.

Mathematically speaking, two events A and B are said to be independent if

$$P(B|A) = P(B)$$

If the conditional probability does not equal the simple probability of the event, then the events are dependent.

From your general knowledge, which of the following pairs of events are independent?
1. Blue eyes and male.
2. High temperature in Dallas and decline in Dow Jones Industrial Index.
3. Big car and foreign-made car.
4. High grade average and win scholarship.

From your general knowledge, which of the following pairs of variables are independent?

5. Eye color and sex.
6. Temperature and stock market performance.
7. Hair color and race.
8. Height and weight.
9. Lung cancer and cigarette smoking.

Use the mathematical definition of independence to determine if, in Table 2.2, the following events are independent.

10. H and U
11. T and P

Answers: I,I,D,D, I,I,D,D,D, D,D

2.7 LAWS OF PROBABILITY

Three common laws of probability will now be reviewed.

Complement Law

The complement law states

$$P(A) = 1 - P(\bar{A})$$

where A is any event and $\bar{A}$ refers to the event "not A" which is also called the complementary event. On the roll of a die if A is defined as the event of getting 3, 4, 5, or 6 dots, then $\bar{A}$ is the event of getting 1 or 2 dots. By the complement law,

$$\begin{aligned} P(A) &= 1 - P(\bar{A}) \\ &= 1 - 2/6 \\ &= 4/6 \end{aligned}$$

To take another example, suppose that the probability that a company's sales will fall below one million units is .3, then by the complement law,

$$P\left(\begin{array}{c}\text{Sales of one million} \\ \text{or more}\end{array}\right) = 1 - P\left(\begin{array}{c}\text{Sales under} \\ \text{one million}\end{array}\right)$$
$$= 1 - .3$$
$$= .7$$

Addition Law

If two events A and B are mutually exclusive (that is, both cannot occur together), the addition law states

$$P(A \text{ or } B) = P(A) + P(B)$$

On the roll of a die let A be the event of getting 3, 4, 5, or 6 dots and B be the event of getting 1 dot. Since A and B are mutually exclusive events,

$$P(A \text{ or } B) = 4/6 + 1/6$$
$$= 5/6$$

To take another example, if the probability that sales will be from 1 to 2 million units is .2 and the probability that sales are from 2 to 3 million units is .1, then by the addition law,

$$P\left(\begin{array}{c}\text{Sales from 1 to 3}\\ \text{million units}\end{array}\right) = P\left(\begin{array}{c}\text{Sales from 1 to 2}\\ \text{million units}\end{array}\right) + P\left(\begin{array}{c}\text{Sales from 2 to 3}\\ \text{million units}\end{array}\right)$$

$$= .2 + .1$$
$$= .3$$

Multiplication Law

The multiplication law states

$$P(A,B) = P(A|B)\, P(B)$$

or,

$$P(A,B) = P(B|A)\, P(A)$$

Let A be heads on the first flip of a coin and B be heads on the second flip. What is the probability of getting two heads in a row, that is, what is $P(A,B)$? By the multiplication law,

$$P(A,B) = P(B|A)\, P(A)$$
$$= (.5)(.5)$$
$$= .25$$

Remember that $P(B|A) = .5$ since B and A are independent events. When events A and B are independent the multiplication law is more concisely stated as $P(A,B) = P(A)\, P(B)$.

When randomly selecting a stock from those of Table 2.2, what is $P(I,H)$? By the multiplication law this joint probability may be determined as follows:

$$P(I,H) = P(H|I)\, P(I)$$
$$= (30/60)(60/100)$$
$$= .30$$

As a final short example, consider the following. If there is a .40 probability that a product will enjoy high sales, and if there is a .70 probability that a product will produce high profits given that it has high sales, what is the probability that a product will have both high sales and high profits? Symbolically, what is $P(\text{High Sales, High Profits})$? It was given that $P(\text{High Sales}) = .40$ and $P(\text{High Profits} \mid \text{High Sales}) = .70$. Using the multiplication law the required joint probability may be found:

$$P(HS, HP) = P(HP|HS)\, P(HS)$$
$$= (.70)(.40)$$
$$= .28$$

Use the multiplication law to compute the following from Table 2.2.

1. $P(H,T)$
2. $P(M,P)$
3. $P(I|M)$
4. $P(I|U)$

5. If $P(S_2) = .4$ and $P(I|S_2) = .9$, what is $P(I,S_2)$?
6. If 20% of a store's customers have a credit card, and if 60% of those having a credit card make a purchase, find P(Has credit card, Makes purchase).
7. If a company receives a favorable tax ruling, there is a probability of .70 that a substantial profit will be made. The probability of a favorable tax ruling is .6. What is the probability of receiving a favorable tax ruling and making a substantial profit?
8. What is the probability of getting heads on the flip of a coin and an even number of dots on a die if the coin and die are tossed simultaneously?
9. The probability that a component is defective is .1. What is the probability that the component is not defective?
10. With respect to 9, what is the probability that three components will all be good?

Answers: .03, 0, 20/35, 0, .36, .12, .42, .25, .9, .729

2.8 RANDOM VARIABLES AND PROBABILITY DISTRIBUTIONS

A *random variable* is a variable such that the value it takes on is determined by chance. The value of a random variable therefore varies from occasion to occasion according to chance. Consider the variable D which represents the weekly tire sales by a particular service station. One week D may equal 1 tire, another week D may equal 4 tires, and so forth. Since the number of tires that will be sold next week is assumed to be determined by chance, D is a random variable. Let T represent the time it takes to process a bank customer. T may be 10 minutes, or 2.40 minutes, or 5.5 minutes, and so on. T is also a random variable since its value, from customer to customer, varies randomly according to chance.

A *probability distribution* consists of a pairing of the values of a random variable with the probability of each value or group of values. In Table 2.3, page 26, examples of probability distributions for D and T are given. Notice that the sum of the probabilities equals 1. Such is the case for every probability distribution. From the distribution of D, for example, it can be seen that the probability that the service station will sell 4 tires next week is .2, that is, $P(D=4) = .2$. From the distribution of T it is seen that there is a 30 percent chance that the next customer will require from 0 through 5 minutes to be processed, that is, $P(0 \leq T \leq 5) = .30$.

One distinction between random variables such as D and T should be noted here. D is called a *discrete* random variable because there are a limited number

TABLE 2.3
Two Probability Distributions

D	P(D)	T	P(T)
0 tires	.1	0 — 5 minutes	.3
1	.3	5.01 — 10	.5
2	.2	10.01 — 30	.2
3	.2		1.0
4	.2		
	1.0		

of particular values which D may take on. D may only take values such as 0, 1, 2, 3, ... D cannot take on values such as 3.44267 tires or 0.1129 tires. T, on the other hand, is a *continuous* random variable in that it may take any value along a continuum. A customer could take 1 or 2 or 3 minutes but also could take 3.44267 or 0.1129 minutes. There are therefore an infinite number of values which T can take on. Because of this the probability that T will take on any precise value such as 2.540000000... minutes is zero. When dealing with continuous random variables, probabilities are associated with ranges of values.

Identify each of the following random variables as being either discrete or continuous.
1. R = monthly runoff in the Colorado River watershed
2. X = daily usage of electricity in Escondido
3. G = weekly number of automobiles sold by General Motors dealers
4. W = hourly wage of a plumber
5. F = fuel sold by a service station
6. N = number of computer breakdowns in a week

Answers: C, C, D, D, C, D

2.4 EXPECTED VALUE, VARIANCE, AND STANDARD DEVIATION

The expected value or mean of a probability distribution represents a center of the distribution. For a discrete random variable like X, the *expected value* or *mean* is defined as

$$E(X) = \mu = \Sigma X P(X)$$

For example, the expected value of D whose distribution is given in Table 2.3 is

$$E(D) = (0)(.1) + (1)(.3) + (2)(.2) + (3)(.2) + (4)(.2)$$
$$= 2.1 \text{ tires}$$

If the distribution is given in grouped form such as that for T in Table 2.3, the expected value is determined as before with the exception that X represents the midpoint of each class and $P(X)$ is the probability for each class. For example,

$$E(T) = (2.5)(.3) + (7.5)(.5) + (20)(.2)$$
$$= 8.5 \text{ minutes}$$

Notice that 2.5 is the midpoint of the 0-5 minute class, 7.5 is the midpoint of the next class, and 20 is the midpoint of the last class in the distribution.

The variance and standard deviation measure the dispersion of the probability distribution. The *variance* of the random variable X is defined as

$$\sigma_X^2 = \Sigma(X - \mu)^2 \, P(X)$$

For example, the variance of D would be

$$\sigma_D^2 = (0 - 2.1)^2(.1) + (1 - 2.1)^2(.3) + \ldots + (4 - 2.1)^2(.2)$$
$$= 1.69$$

The variance of T would be

$$\sigma_T^2 = (2.5 - 8.5)^2(.3) + (7.5 - 8.5)^2(.5) + (20 - 8.5)^2(.2)$$
$$= 37.75$$

The *standard deviation* is the square root of the variance, hence the standard deviation is denoted by σ_X. For the examples above, $\sigma_D = 1.3$ tires and $\sigma_T = 6.14$ minutes.

Compute the expected value, variance, and standard deviation of Y.

Y	P(Y)
2	.3
5	.4
8	.3

Answers: 5, 5.4, 2.32

2.10 PARTIAL EXPECTED VALUES

In the presentation of purchasing models (Chapter 11), partial expected values will be used. The computation of partial expected values will now be demonstrated. Suppose Taylor is thinking about buying a mule next week. Table 2.4, page 28, gives the probability distribution of the price of a mule for next week. If Taylor is committed to the purchase of a mule, the expected price that will be paid is merely the expected value of the distribution:

$$E(M) = (\$80)(.2) + (\$85)(.3) + (\$90)(.3) + (\$95)(.2)$$
$$= \$87.50$$

Suppose now that Taylor will only buy if the price per mule is $87.50 or less, what is the expected amount of money Taylor will pay? There is a .20 probability that Taylor will pay $80 and a .30 probability of paying $85. However, if the price proves to be $90 or $95, Taylor will not buy. Thus, there is a .3 and .2

TABLE 2.4
Mule Prices

M	P(M)
$80	.2
85	.3
90	.3
95	.2

probability of not purchasing (paying nothing). Putting these payouts and probabilities together yields a partial expected value

Partial expected value
when M is limited to $= (80)(.2) + (85)(.3) + (0)(.3) + (0)(.2)$
$87.50

$$= \$41.50$$

If Taylor's limit had been $82.50, the partial expected value would be ($80)(.2) or $16. If Taylor's limit had been $91, the partial expected value would be $68.50. If Taylor's limit had been $M = \$100$, then the partial expected value would be the same as the expected value since none of the values of the random variable would be excluded.

Find the partial expected value if M is limited to $25, if M is limited to $45. What is $E(M)$?

M	P(M)
$10	.1
20	.1
30	.2
40	.3
50	.3

Answers: 3, 21, 36

2.11 EXPECTED VALUE OF A FUNCTION

Suppose the random variable X, which denotes sales in units, has the distribution of Table 2.5(a), page 29. Furthermore, suppose that the profit a company makes is a function of sales, namely,

$$P = 3X - 800$$

Notice that this profit function is a linear equation. By the definition given in an earlier section, the expected value of sales or expected sales can be computed as

$$E(X) = (200)(.3) + (300)(.4) + (400)(.3)$$
$$= 300 \text{ units}$$

What might be the expected value of profits or expected profits? One method of determining $E(P)$ which is of general applicability begins by computing the profit corresponding to each value of the random variable X. For example, if $X = 200$, then $P = (3)(200)-800$ or $P = -\$200$. If $X = 300$ units, then $P = \$100$, and if $X = 400$, then $P = \$400$. From this a probability distribution for P is derived as in Table 2.5(b).

TABLE 2.5
Distributions of X and P
($P=3X-800$)

(a)

X	Probability
200	.3
300	.4
400	.3

(b)

X	P	Probability
200	-$200	.3
300	100	.4
400	400	.3

The expected profit can now be computed from this distribution of P

$$E(P) = (-200)(.3) + (100)(.4) + (400)(.3)$$
$$= \$100$$

This approach to finding the expected value of a function can be used if the function is linear or nonlinear.

There exists a theorem which provides a quicker method of computing the expected profit if the function is linear. In particular, the theorem states that

If $Y = aX + b$ and if $E(X)$ is the expected value of X, then the expected value of Y is $E(Y) = aE(X) + b$.

Since $P=3X-800$ is a linear function and $E(X) = 300$ units, it follows from this theorem that the expected profit is

$$E(P) = 3\,E(X) - 800$$
$$= (3)(300) - 800$$
$$= \$100$$

This approach is only valid for linear functions. If a function is nonlinear, then the earlier method of first constructing a distribution for P must be used.

The random variable R has the following probability distribution:

R	P(R)
2	.5
6	.5

1. Find $E(G)$ if $G = 3R^2$. Notice that G is not a linear function of R.
2. Find $E(F)$ if $F = 3R - 5$. Notice that F is a linear function of R.

Answers: 60, 7

2.12 CUMULATIVE DISTRIBUTIONS

In Table 2.6(a) a probability distribution is given for S where S is a random variable representing the number of typewriters a retail dealer sells in a week. In Table 2.6(b) the cumulative form of this distribution is given which gives the

TABLE 2.6
Non-cumulative and Cumulative Distributions

	(a)		(b)
S	P(S)	S	P(S$\leq$C)
0	.1	0	.1
1	.2	1	.3
2	.2	2	.5
3	.3	3	.8
4	.2	4	1.0

probability of selling C or fewer typewriters. The cumulative form is an equivalent way to express a probability distribution. The first cumulative probability is the probability of selling 0 or fewer typewriters. This probability is .1 since from the original distribution it is seen that the probability of selling exactly 0 typewriters is .1. Therefore, $P(S\leq0) = .10$. The probability of selling 1 or less is

$$P(S\leq1) = P(S=0) + P(S=1)$$
$$= .1 + .2$$
$$= .3$$

In like manner it follows that $P(S\leq2) = .5$, $P(S\leq3) = .8$, and $P(S\leq4) = 1.00$.

Just as a cumulative distribution can be determined from a non-cumulative distribution, a non-cumulative distribution can be derived from a cumulative distribution. If, for example, the cumulative distribution of Table 2.6(b) were given alone, how could $P(S=2)$ be found? Since $P(S\leq2) = .5$ and $P(S\leq1) = .3$, it follows that $P(S=2) = .2$. Likewise,

$$P(S=4) = P(S\leq4) - P(S\leq3)$$

In this way any non-cumulative probability can be found.

General Statics is going to bid for the contract to build a new submarine. Based on our study of General Statics' bidding behavior, we believe that the following distribution of Table 2.7(a) depicts the likelihoods of their bid. The

TABLE 2.7
General Statics' Bids

	(a)		(b)	
B		P(B)	B	P(B$\leq$C)
	300.01 — 400	.20	300	0
	400.01 — 500	.25	400	.20
	500.01 — 600	.30	500	.45
	600.01 — 700	.15	600	.75
	700.01 — 800	.10	700	.90
			800	1.00

random variable representing the bid, in millions of dollars, is *B*. In Table 2.7(b) the corresponding cumulative distribution is given. Notice, for example, that the probability of General Statics' bidding 600 million or less is .75.

It is sometimes desirable to portray graphically a probability distribution. Figure 2.3 gives a histogram or graph of a non-cumulative distribution. Notice that the height of the columns above each class denotes the probability that *B* will fall within the class. In Figure 2.4, page 32, an ogive or graph of a cumulative distribution is given for the bids. Such a graph is drawn by first plotting the cumulative probabilities associated with the values of *B* in the cumulative distribution. These are represented by the six dots on the graph. Then these dots are connected by straight lines (or sometimes by curved lines). From this graph various cumulative probabilities can be read. Select a value for *B* and then move vertically to the graph and then horizontally to read the appropriate cumulative probability. For example, the probability of a bid of 600 or less is .75, the probability of a bid of 550 or less is .60, and $P(B \leq 375) = .15$.

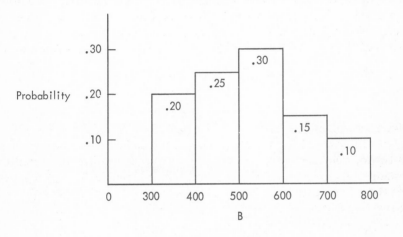

FIGURE 2.3   Histogram

Refer to the distribution of *D* as given in Table 2.3.
1. What is $P(D \leq 1)$?
2. What is $P(D \leq 2)$?
3. What is $P(D \leq 3)$?
4. What is $P(D \leq 8)$?
Refer to Figure 2.4. Then find:

5. $P(B \leq 450)$
6. $P(B \leq 750)$
7. $P(B \leq 350)$

8. $P(350 \leq B \leq 750)$
9. $P(B > 450)$
10. $P(B > 750)$

Answers: .4, .6, .8, 1.0, about .33, about .95, about .1, .85, .67, .05

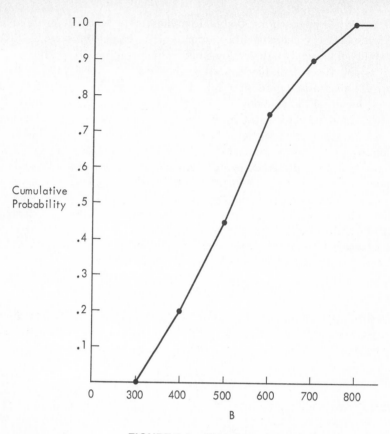

FIGURE 2.4 Cumulative Distribution

2.13 NORMAL DISTRIBUTION

The most important continuous probability distribution is the normal distribution. The normal distribution has the familiar bell-shape as illustrated in Figure 2.5. A particular normal distribution is identified or determined by its mean, μ, and standard deviation, σ. Since the normal distribution is a continuous distribution, probability is represented by the area under the curve rather than by the height of the curve. The total area under the normal curve is therefore 1.

Finding probabilities for a normally distributed variable is merely a matter of finding areas under sections of the normal curve. This will now be illustrated. Southern California Edison has found that the daily usage of electricity in Escondido is normally distributed with a mean of 100 megawatts and a standard deviation of 20 megawatts (assume that "megawatt" means megawatt hour). This normal distribution is pictured in Figure 2.5(a) where the random variable x represents daily electricity usage. Knowing that x varies from day to day according to this normal distribution, several probabilities can be computed. The probability that tomorrow's usage will be 100 megawatts or more is .50, that is,

$$P(x \geq 100) = .50$$

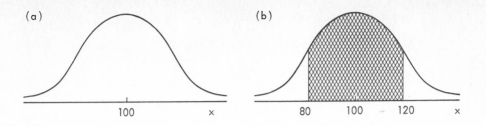

(a)   (b)

100   x   80   100   120   x

FIGURE 2.5   Daily Electricity Usage in Escondido
(μ = 100, σ = 20)

This is because the normal distribution is symmetrical around its mean and thus half of its area (probability) is to the right of 100. In like manner,

$$P(x \leq 100) = .50$$

Remember that with *any* continuous distribution, the probability that the random variable equals a single number is zero. For example, the probability that in a day Escondido will use exactly 100.0000000... megawatts is zero, that is,

$$P(x = 100) = 0$$

Because of this the following is true:

$$P(x \leq 100) = P(x < 100)$$

Now suppose the probability of tomorrow's usage falling between 80 and 120 megawatts is desired. The area between 80 and 120 in Figure 2.5(b) gives this probability. Roughly speaking, it looks like about 2/3 of the area under the curve lies between 80 and 120 and therefore the probability of x being between 80 and 120 is about 2/3.

In order to precisely find probabilities like $P(x > 130)$, there must be an accurate way to measure areas under the normal curve. A way to do this does exist. It is based on the following theorem.

All normal distributions are alike in terms of areas (probabilities) when considered in standard deviation units.

What exactly does this theorem imply? Without forgetting about the Escondido example, turn your attention to the daily usage of electricity in Mechanicsville. Virginia Electric Power says the daily usage, y, of electricity in Mechanicsville is normally distributed with a mean of 50 and a standard deviation of 5 megawatts. See Figure 2.6 on page 34. The value of $y = 55$ megawatts is exactly one standard deviation above the mean. With reference to the Escondido example, $x = 120$ megawatts is also exactly one standard deviation above the mean since the mean is 100 and the standard deviation is 20. Now the theorem above implies that the area above $y = 55$ in the Mechanicsville normal distribution is equal to

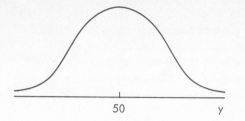

50   y

FIGURE 2.6   Daily Usage of Electricity in Mechanicsville
($\mu = 50$, $\sigma = 5$)

the area above $x = 120$ in the Escondido distribution since both of these respective values are exactly one standard deviation above their means. Hence,

$$P(x>120) = P(y>55)$$

It can also be maintained that

$$P(x\geq60) = P(y\geq40)$$

This is because $x = 60$ is two standard deviations below the mean of 100 and $y = 40$ is two standard deviations below the mean of 50. The points $x = 60$ and $y = 40$ therefore are in relatively the same places on their respective normal distributions and thus the same area is to the right of each.

Before continuing the review of the normal distribution, answer the following questions.

In view of the foregoing discussion and keeping in mind that the normal distribution is symmetrical, answer "true" or "false."
1. $P(x>120) = P(x<80)$
2. $P(y<50) = P(y>60)$
3. $P(y<45) = P(x<80)$
4. $P(y>55) = P(x<80)$
5. $P(50<y<55) = P(100<x<120)$
6. $P(x>140) = P(y>60)$
7. $P(x<60) = P(y<45)$

Give numerical answers to the following if it is known that the total area (probability) under every normal curve is 1, and it it is known that $P(x>120) = .16$.
 8. What is $P(y>55)$?
 9. What is $P(x\leq80)$?
10. What is $P(y<45)$?
11. What is $P(100<x<120)$?
12. What is $P(45\leq y\leq55)$?

It might be helpful to draw pictures of the normal distributions for Escondido and Mechanicsville for the sake of answering these questions.

Answers: T, F, T, T, T, T, F, .16, .16, .16, .34, .68

It is important in working with the normal distribution that the analyst be able to convert values of the random variable to standard deviation units. As has already been seen with the Escondido example, $x = 120$ is one standard deviation above the mean, $x = 140$ is two standard deviations above the mean, and $x = 80$ is one standard deviation below the mean. Likewise, $x = 130$ is 1.5 standard deviations above the mean and $x = 95$ is .25 standard deviations below the mean. The following relationship can be used to quickly convert values of the random variable into standard deviation units. Letting z denote the equivalent standard deviation units,

$$z = \frac{\text{Value} - \text{Mean}}{\text{Standard Deviation}}$$

Therefore, if the value is $x = 120$, the equivalent reading in standard deviation units is

$$z = \frac{120 - 100}{20}$$

$$z = 1$$

If $x = 95$, then the equivalent reading in standard deviation units is

$$z = \frac{95 - 100}{20}$$

$$z = -.25$$

Convert each of the following values for y into standard deviation units. Remember that y is the random variable describing the daily usage in Mechanicsville. This normal distribution has a mean of 50 and a standard deviation of 5.

1. $y = 50$
2. $y = 55$
3. $y = 60$
4. $y = 40$
5. $y = 47.5$
6. $y = 58$

Answers: 0, 1, 2, −2, −.5, 1.6

In the Appendix, areas (probabilities) for the normal distribution where the random variable is expressed in standard deviation units, z, are given. In particular, the areas (probabilities) under the normal curve from the mean or center to various values of z are given. For example, the area under the normal curve from $z = 0$ to $z = 1.00$ is .3413 and the area from $z = 0$ to $z = 2.25$ is .4878. In terms of probabilities this means

$$P(0 \leq z \leq 1.00) = .3413$$
$$P(0 \leq z \leq 2.25) = .4878$$

In Figure 2.7 several areas (probabilities) of the normal distribution are shown by the crosshatched region. Each of these areas can be determined by using Table 2 in the Appendix. Refer first to the crosshatched area in Figure 2.7(a). Reading directly from Table 2 for $z = 1.65$ shows the area to be .4505, that is,

$$P(0 \leq z \leq 1.65) = .4505$$

Because the normal distribution is symmetrical, .4505 is also the area in (d). Now refer to (b). To find the area beyond $z = 1.65$, it must first be recognized that the total right half of the normal distribution has an area of .5000. Since the area from $z = 0$ to $z = 1.65$ is .4505, the area beyond $z = 1.65$ must equal .5000 − .4505 or .0495. Hence,

$$P(z > 1.65) = .0495$$

Because of symmetry this is also the area in (e). Finally consider (c) where the area from 1.00 standard deviations to 1.65 standard deviations must be found.

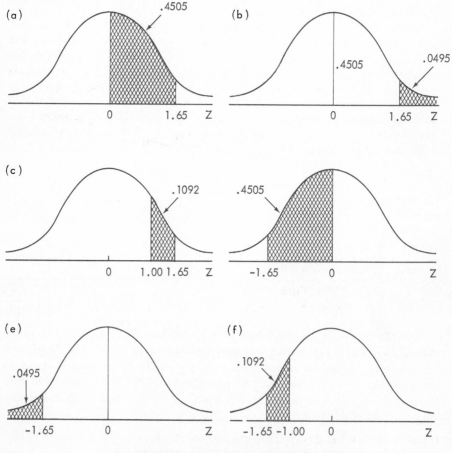

FIGURE 2.7   Areas Under the Normal Curve

According to Appendix Table 2 the area from $z = 0$ to $z = 1.00$ is .3413. It has already been seen that the area from $z = 0$ to $z = 1.65$ is .4505. Therefore the area between 1.00 and 1.65 must be .4505 — .3413 or .1092. Hence,

$$P(1.00 \leq z \leq 1.65) = .1092$$

which means the probability of z falling between 1.00 and 1.65 standard deviations on any normal curve is .1092. By symmetry this is also the area indicated in (f).

Find the following probabilities (areas). It may be helpful to draw a picture of the normal distribution for the sake of finding these areas.

1. $P(0 \leq z \leq 2.22)$
2. $P(z > 2.22)$
3. $P(z < -2.22)$
4. $P(-2.22 \leq z \leq 2.22)$
5. $P(1.05 \leq z \leq 2.22)$

Answers: .4868, .0132, .0132, .9736, .1337

With the capability of finding areas or probabilities when the normal variable is expressed in standard deviation units z, and being able to convert into standard deviation units, probabilities can now be found for any normal distribution. Returning to the Escondido electricity example, if x equals the daily usage what is the probability that tomorrow's usage will be from 100 to 110 megawatts? In other words, what is $P(100 \leq x \leq 110)$?

To answer this, first convert to standard deviation units. For $x = 100$,

$$z = \text{(Value — Mean)/Standard Deviation}$$
$$= (100 - 100)/20$$
$$= 0$$

For $x = 110$,

$$z = (110 - 100)/20$$
$$= .5$$

Therefore,

$$P(100 \leq x \leq 110) = P(0 \leq z \leq .5)$$

From Appendix Table 2 this probability is .1915.

To take another example, what is $P(75 \leq x \leq 95)$? Converting to z means

$$P(75 \leq x \leq 95) = P(-1.25 \leq z \leq -.25)$$

The corresponding area of the normal distribution is found by

$$
\begin{array}{rcr}
P(-1.25 \leq z \leq 0) = & & .3944 \\
- \quad P(-.25 \leq z \leq 0) = & - & .0987 \\
\hline
P(-1.25 \leq z \leq -.25) = & & .2957
\end{array}
$$

If this is unclear you should draw a picture of this area on the normal distribution in order to see that it is analogous to that of Figure 2.7(f).

Since x is normally distributed with a mean of 100 and a standard deviation of 20, find the following probabilities.

1. $P(80 \leq x \leq 100)$
2. $P(80 \leq x \leq 120)$
3. $P(70 \leq x \leq 100)$
4. $P(x < 70)$
5. $P(112 \leq x \leq 120)$

Answers: .3413, .6826, .4332, .0668, .1156

In some uses of the normal distribution a question of the following sort is asked: What is C such that $P(z > C) = .10$? Pictorially this is analogous to finding the value for C in Figure 2.8 which has ten percent of the area to the right. If an

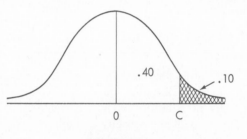

FIGURE 2.8

area of .10 is to the right of C, then the area of .40 must be between $z = 0$ and $z = C$. Symbolically, $P(O \leq z \leq C) = .40$. Look for an area or probability of .40 in Appendix Table 2 and then note the corresponding value of z; this value for z is the value of C. According to Table 2, C must equal 1.28 in order to make $P(O \leq z \leq C) = .40$ true. Since z is in standard deviation units it can be said for *any* normal distribution that if you go 1.28 standard deviations above the mean there will be only ten percent of the area further out. In the Escondido case this means that since 125.6 megawatts is 1.28 standard deviations above the mean, there is only a .10 probability that daily usage will exceed 125.6 megawatts. Notice that 125.6 is computed by

$$125.6 = \text{Mean} + (1.28)(\text{Standard Deviation})$$
$$= 100 + (1.28)(20)$$

Answer the following.

1. Find C such that $P(O \leq z \leq C) = .45$
2. Find C such that $P(z > C) = .05$
3. In the Escondido case, there is a five percent chance that tomorrow's electricity usage will exceed how many megawatts?

Answers: 1.65, 1.65, 133

3 Decision Theory – Models and Decisions

3.1 INTRODUCTION

It is appropriate to begin a study of management science with a consideration of decision theory. The many management science models which will follow in later chapters are nothing more than special designs woven into the fabric of decision theory. Decision theory serves as a unifying basis for all of management science since in decision theory the most general kind of decision model is utilized. In a decision model the various choices confronting the decision maker are set forth along with various consequences of these choices. The consequences of a given choice may be known with certainty or they may be determined by chance and thus described by a probability distribution. With a little reflection one can be convinced that every decision situation encountered essentially conforms to this sort of decision model. This does not mean, however, that every decision situation can easily be structured in the form of a quantitative decision model. In most actual situations it is difficult if not impossible to construct an adequate quantitative model. Nevertheless genuine benefits are afforded to the manager who is willing to approach a decision situation by means of a decision model. At the very least the model will enable the manager to organize the complex situation and will point to the areas of critical importance.

In this chapter several types of decision situations will be considered where the decision model in its most elementary form is applicable. More difficult situations of a wide variety will be studied in the remainder of the text. Regardless of the complexity, each management science model to be studied bears the marks of the elementary model of this chapter. There is always a choice to be made from among competing alternatives with differing sets of consequences.

3.2 MATRIX FORM OF THE DECISION MODEL

A decision model is composed of four distinct yet related components. First there are the *acts* or *alternative courses of action* from which the manager must make a choice. The acts in a decision model are typically denoted as a_1, a_2, a_3, ..., a_n. Sometimes there are simply two acts. Such is the case where the marketing manager must decide whether or not to introduce a new product:

a_1: Introduce

a_2: Don't introduce

Sometimes there are many acts. A production manager may be faced with several alternative production mixes in a context where several products are manufactured. In Chapter 7 on linear programming, for example, a producer of mining equipment must decide among:

a_1: Produce 4 rockers and 0 sluice boxes

a_2: Produce 4 rockers and 2 sluice boxes

a_3: Produce 3.5 rockers and 3 sluice boxes

a_4: Produce 0 rockers and 4.17 sluice boxes

Service managers must make decisions as to what level of service to provide for customers. After this a decision must be made to determine how to achieve this level of service at a minimum cost. Decision situations like this will be encountered in Chapter 10 on queueing models.

Inventory managers, as will be seen in Chapter 6, must make decisions as to how many units of product should be stocked. Aware of the dangers of stocking too many or too few, the manager must select an act, for example, from among the following:

a_1: Stock 200 units each month

a_2: Stock 250 units each month

a_3: Stock 300 units each month

The contractor bidding on a job, as in Chapter 11, must make a decision as to how high a bid to submit. Other decision makers are concerned with the optimal replacement of plant and machinery. All of these sorts of situations present management with a common element: a set of options or acts from which a choice must be made.

The second component in the decision model is called the *states of nature* or simply the *states*. The states of nature represent the various events that can occur in the context of the decision situation. More particularly, the states of nature set forth the diverse manifestations of the uncontrollable elements of the decision situation. For the marketing manager who has decided to introduce the new product, the states of nature might be:

S_1: Low Sales

S_2: Medium Sales

S_3: High Sales

For the inventory situation mentioned above, the states might be:

S_1: Customers demand 200 units in a month

S_2: Customers demand 250 units in a month

S_3: Customers demand 300 units in a month

Notice that the level of demand is beyond the control of the manager; demand is an uncontrollable variable. The states of nature as listed above systematically set forth various levels of this uncontrollable variable.

The states in any decision model must be mutually exclusive and exhaustive. Being mutually exclusive means that if one of the states occurs, then none of the others have occurred. If sales for the new product are low, S_1, then they are not medium, S_2, or high, S_3. Thus S_1, S_2, and S_3 are mutually exclusive states. Being exhaustive means that one of the states must occur, i.e., the states listed must cover the whole waterfront. Sales for the new product will either be low, medium, or high; there is no other possibility. Thus, these three states are also exhaustive. However, in the inventory situation cited above, demand could be 210 which is not included in any of the three listed states. Thus, these three states would not be exhaustive unless sales were only in bundles of fifty units and sales always seem to be 200, 250, or 300. When there are a large number of states, it is often wise (in the interest of keeping things simple) to merely work with a few representative states. These representative states would then be assumed to be exhaustive.

The third component of the decision model is the *probability* that each state will occur. The marketing manager may subjectively assign the following probabilities to each state: $P(S_1) = .35$, $P(S_2) = .45$, and $P(S_3) = .20$. In the inventory situation it may have been found that historically the demand was for 200 units about fifty percent of the time, 250 units about thirty percent of the time, and 300 units about twenty percent of the time. Hence the probabilities for these three states would be $P(S_1) = .50$, $P(S_2) = .30$, and $P(S_3) = .20$.

Notice that since the states are mutually exclusive and exhaustive, the probabilities of the states must add to one. When management is sure or just assumes that a particular state will occur, then the probability of this state is one and the probabilities for the remaining states are zero. In this case the resulting model is deterministic rather than probabilistic. The states which have probabilities of zero are not incorporated into the model.

The fourth and final component of the basic decision model is the *consequences* or *payoffs*. What is the resulting consequence if the marketing manager introduces the new product, a_1, and sales turn out to be high, S_3? The consequence of S_3 occurring after a_1 has been selected might be a profit of ten million dollars. For each combination of an act and a state there will be a consequence or payoff. If there are two acts and three states there would be six consequences that must be considered. In the inventory situation, if the manager stocked 200 units, a_1, and 300 were demanded, S_3, the consequence might be a profit of \$500. However, along with this monetary consequence there might well be customer ill will since many of the customers would not be able to get the product they demanded.

These four components are combined into a matrix which becomes the decision model. In Table 3.1, page 42, a hypothetical decision matrix is given for the marketing manager to whom allusion has been made. Notice that the acts are listed along the top, the states and their respective probabilities down the left side, and the consequences or payoffs are given in the boxes which are formed by the intersection of the acts and the states. As indicated earlier, there are six payoffs in this model. A more detailed example of a decision model will be given in the next section.

TABLE 3.1
A Decision Model

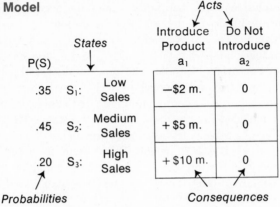

3.3 A DECISION MODEL EXAMPLE

With the llano estacado stretching before him, Big Al Conely contemplates the prospects of drilling another wildcat well. Conely holds an option on a piece of property near Lubbock, Texas, and must reach a decision soon regarding his plans. Conely is confronted with four alternatives or acts:

a_1: Don't drill
a_2: Drill with no partners
a_3: Drill with the Andersen syndicate as partner
a_4: Drill with the Lazaar syndicate as partner

The last two alternatives will be described in detail later.

For practical purposes, Conely thinks in terms of three possible states. Underneath the parcel of West Texas land there is either:

S_1: No oil
S_2: 100,000 barrels of recoverable oil
S_3: 500,000 barrels of recoverable oil

Based on a familiarity with the area and his previous drilling experience, Conely feels that there are 90 chances in 100 that there is no oil, 8 chances in 100 that there are 100,000 bbls, and 2 chances in 100 that there are 500,000 bbls. Therefore, the probabilities of the states are $P(S_1) = .90$, $P(S_2) = .08$, and $P(S_3) = .02$.

A decision matrix is presented in Table 3.2 which lists the four acts, three states, and their respective probabilities.

Conely must now determine the various consequences or payoffs if the decision matrix is to be completed. If Conely does not drill, a_1, then the profit that will be derived is zero regardless of what lies beneath the surface. Thus, a zero is entered in each box under a_1. If a hole is to be drilled, there will be costs and

TABLE 3.2
Conely Decision Model
(Payoff in Thousands of Dollars)

P(S)		a_1 Don't Drill	a_2 Drill, No Partner	a_3 Drill with Andersen	a_4 Drill with Lazaar
.90	S_1 No Oil	0	−100	−50	0
.08	S_2 100,000 bbls.	0	560	280	60
.02	S_3 500,000 bbls.	0	3360	1680	460

there may be revenues. The cost of drilling a well is $100,000. If and only if oil is discovered, an extra $40,000 must be spent on equipment such as pipes and pumps. Finally, oil at the well head can be sold for $7 a barrel. With this information the consequences of a_2, a_3, and a_4 can be determined.

Under a_2 Conely would go it alone. Suppose that S_1 occurs, that is, there is no oil. Conely would experience a loss of $100,000 which is the cost of drilling the dry hole. The extra $40,000 would not be spent since there is no need for pipes and pumps; futhermore, there would be no revenues. Therefore −100 should be placed in the decision matrix of Table 3.2 under a_2 across from S_1. If S_2 occurs, a 100,000 barrel well, then Conely will reap revenues in the amount of $700,000 since a barrel sells for $7. From these revenues must be subtracted the $100,000 drilling cost and the $40,000 equipment cost. This yields a payoff of $560,000. Finally, if S_3 occurs there will be revenues of $3,500,000 from which must be subtracted $140,000. The net gain here would be $3,360,000. Thus, each of the consequences for a_2 have been determined.

Conely has the opportunity to drill in partnership with the Andersen syndicate, which is a_3. The Andersen syndicate has offered to participate 50-50 with Conely in both losses and gains. This means that if S_1 occurred, Conely would lose only $50,000. However, if S_2 or S_3 occurred, Conely would make only half as much as with a_2. These consequences are listed under a_3 in the decision matrix.

Conely also has the opportunity to drill in partnership with the Lazaar syndicate. Under this arrangement Conely would pay only for the well equipment if needed, and would receive $1 per barrel of oil recovered. The syndicate would take care of the drilling costs and would receive the other $6 for each barrel. Under this arrangement, if S_1 occurred Conely would not lose a cent since the well equipment need not be puchased for a dry hole. If S_2 occurred, Conely would receive $1 for each of the 100,000 barrels. From this must be subtracted the cost of the well equipment leaving Conely with a gain of $60,000. If S_3 occurred, Conely's revenue would be $500,000 from which $40,000 must be subtracted leaving a net gain of $460,000. These consequences are also listed in Table 3.2. Notice that the payoffs under a_4 are only those for Conely. What the Lazaar syndicate gets or loses is of no importance to Conely.

The decision matrix of Table 3.2 presents Conely's decision situation in a clear, structured fashion. Conely can see at a glance the situation he faces and can easily make comparisons among the four acts. The next step in the decision theory process is that of selecting an act. Several methods of selecting an act will now be studied, then one of them will be employed by Conely to choose an act.

3.4 PRINCIPLES OF CHOICE

After a decision model has been constructed, one of the acts must be selected. Different decision makers will exhibit differing preferences in making a decision. Nevertheless, certain patterns of decision making are discernible. No decision maker would select a_1 in the Conely decision matrix. The reason is that a_4 is as good as or better than a_1 no matter what state occurs. Thus, it is said that a_4 dominates a_1. However, some decision makers could quite rationally prefer a_2 and others could prefer a_3 or a_4. Which of these acts is in fact the optimal act? Actually, none of these acts can be said to be the universally best act. One may be best for one decision maker while another is best for someone else. Asking which act is best is akin to asking what tastes better, apple pie or pumpkin pie. The answer is an individual or personal matter. In Section 3.7 and 3.8 of this chapter, the problem of finding the best act for a specific person will be explored in detail. In this section three techniques for selecting an act will be presented. The last of these three has been found to be appropriate in most corporate decision-making situations and will therefore be used throughout this text.

Principles of choice are criteria which guide in the selection of an act from among a set of competing acts. The three principles of choice to be considered are the *maximin* principle, the *aspiration level* principle, and the *expectation* principle. Others exist but these are the most important.

Maximin or Minimax Principle

The maximin and minimax principles are, in concept, identical principles. If the decision matrix has the consequences stated in terms of gains or profits, then the maximin principle is applied. If the consequences are stated in terms of losses or costs, then the minimax principle is applied.

With the maximin principle the minimum gain or payoff for each act is first found. In Table 3.3 a decision matrix is given and at the bottom the minimum gain for each act is given. The maximin principle requires that the decision maker consider only these minimum gains for each act. Maximin then selects the act which has the greatest or maximum of these minimum gains. Thus, a_2 would be selected since it guarantees a gain of at least 40 which is more of a gain than any other act can guarantee.

If the consequences are stated as costs or losses, minimax requires that the maximum cost for each act be first determined. Then the act which has the least or minimum of these maximum costs is chosen. If the matrix of Table 3.3 were stated in terms of costs, then a_3 would be selected by minimax since the maximum cost with a_3 would be 54 and this is less than the maximum cost for either a_1 or a_2 which are 200 and 61, respectively.

TABLE 3.3
Decision Matrix

		a_1	a_2	a_3
.25	S_1	200	52	20
.15	S_2	100	40	54
.60	S_3	30	61	54
Minimum Gain:		30	40	20

The maximin (minimax) principle would be utilized by a decision maker who always fears for the worst. This is because only the worst consequence for each act enters into the decision-making process. A very pessimistic decision maker might feel comfortable with this criterion. The meaningful managerial applications of this principle are quite limited. The primary application of this principle is in game theory, Chapter 14, where a competitor determines which of the states will occur. In this type of situation the state which the competitor forces on the decision maker is one which is to the competitor's advantage and to the decision maker's disadvantage.

Aspiration Level Principle

Suppose you were faced with the decision matrix of Table 3.4. The two states represent the outcomes of a flip of a coin, hence each has a probability of .5. If you select a_1 you will receive $30 if S_1 occurs and $900 if S_2 occurs. If you select a_2 you will receive $37 no matter what happens. Which would you select? Without giving it much thought, most people would select a_1. In fact, most would also be willing to defend a_1 as being far suprior to a_2. Contrary to common opinion, however, it is not necessarily superior to a_2. Read on.

TABLE 3.4
Decision Matrix

		a_1	a_2
.50	S_1 Heads	$30	$37
.50	S_2 Tails	$900	$37

You have just awoken to find yourself abandoned in a desolate desert region. Nothing is within sight in this barren wilderness except sand. Checking your belongings you find that your wallet is missing and all that remains is a note. The terse message of the note informs you that you are in the middle of Nevada and the closest settlement is over a hundred miles in an unnamed direction. As the sun reaches its full August intensity you reckon that your days are numbered. At this moment a plane appears in the horizon and finally lands on the packed sand near you. It is an Air West jetliner. From the plane emerges a slumped figure with four-inch fingernails bearing the initials H.H. He asks you if you want a ride to Reno which is the next scheduled stop. You answer in the affirmative. He asks for your ticket. You have none. He says he'll sell you one for $37. You say you have no money. He says "tough." You ask for credit. He says "tough." He walks toward the plane. You are about to jump him, then you spot the machine gun in the door. In desperation you blurt out, "I like your fingernails!" He turns around and with a paternal smile offers you a deal. He will flip a silver dollar. You can choose a_1 or a_2 before the flip. If you choose a_1 you get $30 if heads turns up and $900 if tails (see Table 3.4). If you choose a_2 you get $37 no matter what happens, heads or tails. Reread the last two sentences of the previous paragraph.

In this situation the decision maker, you, had an aspiration level of $37 which was the price of a ticket. That act was selected which offered the best chance of reaching or exceeding the aspiration level. Such is the essence of the aspiration level principle. In particular, if A is the aspiration level of a decision maker, the aspiration level principle stipulates that the act which offers the maximum probability of achieving A should be selected. In the decision matrix of Table 3.3 where the consequences are assumed to be expressed in profits, a_3 should be selected if A were 53. Why? With a_1 the aspiration level of 53 would be achieved only if S_1 or S_2 occurred; the probability of achieving A is therefore .25 + .15 or .40 for a_1. With a_2 the probability of achieving $A = 53$ is .6, that is, only when S_3 occurs would A be achieved. With a_3 the probability of achieving 53 or better is .15 + .60 or .75. Thus, a_3 is optimal with the aspiration level of 53. If A had been 50, then a_2 would be optimal. If A had been 65 then a_1 would be optimal according to the aspiration level principle.

Sometimes a variation of the aspiration level principle is used. Here the aspiration level is used to sort out unacceptable acts leaving a set of acceptable acts from which a selection is to be made by means of another principle of choice. Management might, for example, specify that only those acts which offer a .50 probability of making a profit of at least 50 are to be considered. Referring to the decision matrix of Table 3.3, a_1 offers the decision maker only a probability of .25 + .15 or .40 of making a profit of 50 while both a_2 and a_3 offer more than a 50 percent chance of making at least 50. Thus, a_1 is eliminated from further consideration and another principle of choice then might be used to choose between a_2 and a_3.

Does the aspiration level principle in either of its forms have any application to the real world of managerial decision making? The answer is an unequivocal yes. Managers have many kinds of aspiration levels which play an important role in the selection of alternative courses of action. A company might have an aspiration level in terms of a market share. Only acts which offer a high probability of maintaining or increasing their current market share might be considered. Here the aspiration level principle might be used to eliminate certain acts, then another principle of choice would be used to select an act from among the remaining. Another company might have an aspiration level in terms of liquidity. The company prides itself in never having missed or decreased a dividend in fifty years. Hence it will only consider projects and programs which will generate funds sufficient for dividend purposes. Again another principle of choice might then be employed to choose one act or project from among the ones that have not been eliminated by the aspiration level. A project which might have produced the best profits yet would have left the company short of liquid funds for the next two years might be one of these eliminated by the aspiration level principle.

Aspiration levels also play a role in decision making which relates to corporate social responsibility. The company might set forth aspiration levels in terms of pollution control, minority hiring, employee benefits, and the like which might eliminate certain plans or acts which would otherwise yield optimal profits or minimal costs.

Expectation Principle

The expectation principle is a principle of choice which is widely accepted among management scientists as the best criterion for most corporate decision making. It may be used after several acts have been eliminated by means of the aspiration level principle in order to find the optimal act or it can be used apart from the aspiration level principle. The expectation principle as it is presented in this section would not be particularly applicable in truly major decisions at the corporate level nor would it always be applicable to some of the decision making in a smaller business enterprise. It can be modified, however, through the use of the concept of utility. When so modified the expectation principle is applicable to an extremely wide variety of decision situations. This concept of utility will be discussed in a later section of this chapter.

With the expectation principle, the act which has the highest expected profit or lowest expected cost is selected. Computing the expected profit or cost for an act, once the decision matrix has been constructed, is an easy operation. The expected profit for each act Conely faces (see Table 3.2) will now be computed. The expected profit is merely a weighted average of the payoffs for an act where the weights are the probabilities of the respective states. For example, the expected profit for a_2 is

$$
E(P_2) = \begin{pmatrix} \text{Payoff} \\ \text{Associated} \\ \text{with } S_1 \end{pmatrix} \begin{pmatrix} \text{Probability} \\ \text{of } S_1 \end{pmatrix} + \begin{pmatrix} \text{Payoff} \\ \text{Associated} \\ \text{with } S_2 \end{pmatrix} \begin{pmatrix} \text{Probability} \\ \text{of } S_2 \end{pmatrix}
$$

$$
+ \begin{pmatrix} \text{Payoff} \\ \text{Associated} \\ \text{with } S_3 \end{pmatrix} \begin{pmatrix} \text{Probability} \\ \text{of } S_3 \end{pmatrix}
$$

$$
\begin{aligned}
E(P_2) &= (-100,000)(.90) + (560,000)(.08) + (3,360,000)(.02) \\
&= -90,000 + 44,800 + 67,200 \\
&= \$22,000
\end{aligned}
$$

For a_3,

$$
\begin{aligned}
E(P_3) &= (-50,000)(.90) + (280,000)(.08) + (1,680,000)(.02) \\
&= \$11,000
\end{aligned}
$$

For a$_4$,

$$E(P_4) = (0)(.90) + (60,000)(.08) + (460,000)(.02)$$
$$= \$14,000$$

The expected profit of a$_1$ is zero since zero appears in each box under a$_1$. By the expectation principle it can be concluded that a$_2$ is optimal since it yields the highest expected profit.

If the decision matrix of Table 3.2 were that of Exxon or Mobil, it could be stated with little reservation that a$_2$ is the best act. But with a lone wildcatter like Conely, it might be that a loss of \$100,000 would spell bankruptcy and therefore Conely might not be willing to go with a$_2$. Thus, Conely might not feel comfortable with the expectation principle as a guide to decision making. However, with the introduction of utility, as in Sections 3.7 and 3.8, the expectation principle will work for even a half-broke Conely.

The expectation principle, being preeminent among the principles of choice, will be utilized in many of the management science models which follow in subsequent chapters.

3.5 ALGEBRAIC FORM OF THE DECISION MODEL

Sometimes a given decision situation might require a fairly large decision matrix. There may be an extremely large number of acts and/or a large number of states. In these situations it might be more useful to express the model algebraically. Even if the decision matrix were not particularly cumbersome, it might be advantageous to express the model algebraically as this often permits a more rapid application of one of the principles of choice such as the expectation principle.

In this section consideration will be given to a decision situation where the consequences of each act can be expressed by a linear equation. An example will be used to present this type of model.

Arid Wonder Land Company has purchased a large piece of desert land along the Colorado River north of Yuma, Arizona. The company has developed this property by establishing roads, club houses, and marinas along the Colorado. Being in a remote region, Yucca Yuma is suffering from a lack of public exposure. Thus, sales of lots have not been particularly brisk. To remedy this situation the company has undertaken an enormous publicity ploy. The company has purchased the Brooklyn Bridge and has reconstructed it at Yucca Yuma. Since this happened sales have picked up dramatically; nevertheless, the developer would still like to get more people out to this paradise.

It was then that Arid Wonder Land struck upon the idea of flying potential land buyers to Yucca Yuma on a complimentary basis. Actually the idea was not that novel as a competing land developer some miles to the north had already been doing the same with success. Arid Wonder Land therefore began to consider the advisability of offering to potential land buyers a free flight with two nights and a day at Yucca Yuma. The natural place to make the offer would be the New York City area. Arid Wonder Land found that a DC-7 could be leased for a round-trip flight from New York City to Yuma for \$10,000. This plane could carry 100 passengers. When at Yucca Yuma, it would cost the developer about $50 per head to feed and lodge the potential buyers.

What could Arid Wonder Land expect in the way of sales from such a promotion? Each lot sold in Yucca Yuma nets the developer a profit of $1,200. It is quite obvious that if each potential buyer on the plane bought ten lots, then Arid Land would gross $1,200,000. From this the cost of the flight, meals, and lodging would have to be subtracted. But, could Arid Land sell an average of ten lots per potential buyer? Probably not. How many on the average could be sold per potential buyer? Arid Land's management is not too sure about the answer to this important question. In consulting with the developer upstream who has the London Bridge, Arid Land came to the conclusion that the average number of lots that could be sold per person is .1, .2, .3, or .4 lots. Letting the variable L denote the number of lots that could be sold per person, Arid Land subjectively determined the probability distribution for L of Table 3.5. (See the first half of Chapter 12 which deals with the method of making such a subjective forecast.) From this distribution it is seen, for example, that there is a .45 probability that .1 lots on the average will be sold to each of the 100 potential buyers making the flight from New York. There is only a .05 probability that an average of $L = .4$ lots would be sold per person.

TABLE 3.5
Distribution of Lots Sold
per Person

L	P(L)
.1 lots	.45
.2	.35
.3	.15
.4	.05
	1.00

With the information that has been supplied, Arid Land can now formulate a decision model. The two acts are:

a_1: Don't offer the free flight
a_2: Offer the free flight

The states refer to the various possible values for L which is the average number of lots sold per person making the flight. Arid Land has limited the values of L to four, namely, .1, .2, .3, and .4. In reality the average number of lots sold per person could be something like .25. However, in limiting the values of L to these four, no great damage is done since they represent the realistic range for L. Hence the four states are:

S_1: L = .1 lots per person
S_2: L = .2 lots per person
S_3: L = .3 lots per person
S_4: L = .4 lots per person

The third component of the model is the probabilities of the states, which are given in Table 3.5.

Finally the consequences or payoffs must be determined. Instead of forming a decision matrix to express the various consequences for each of the two acts, the consequences will be expressed algebraically. Let G denote the gain which accrues to Arid Land in this decision situation. If a_1 is selected there is no flight, no costs, no revenues, and thus no gain or loss. That is,

$$G_1 = 0$$

for a_1. If a_2 is implemented, a flight is made. Arid Land's gain in this case will equal

$$G_2 = \text{Revenues} - \text{Costs}.$$

The total costs in this situation are:

Lease of the DC-7	$10,000
Food & Lodging for 100 persons at $50 per head	5,000
Total Costs	$15,000

The total revenues are dependent on the average number of lots that will be sold per person. If L is the average number sold per person, then $100L$ is the total number of lots that would be sold since there are 100 persons making the flight. Then the total revenue would be $(100L)(\$1,200)$ or $\$120,000L$ since $\$1,200$ is the net profit per lot sold in Yucca Yuma. This means that the algebraic expression for the gain with a_2 is

$$G_2 = 120,000L - 15,000$$

With the consequences of each act expressed algebraically, an act can be selected by the application of the expectation principle. The expectation principle dictates the selection of the act with the highest expected gain $E(G)$. For a_1 the equation for the gain is simply $G_1 = O$, hence the expected gain for a_1 is zero. But what is the expected gain for a_2? In Section 2.11 of Chapter 2 it was shown that if one random variable is a linear function of another, such as

$$Y = aX + b$$

where a and b are constants, and if the expected value of the variable X is $E(X)$, then the expected value of Y will be

$$E(Y) = a\,E(X) + b$$

This may be applied in order to find the expected gain of a_2 since G_2 is a linear function of L.

First the expected value of L must be determined. From the probability distribution of Table 3.5, the expected value of L may be computed as

$$E(L) = (.1)(.45) + (.2)(.35) + (.3)(.15) + (.4)(.05)$$
$$= .18 \text{ lots}$$

Therefore, the expected value of G_2 will be

$$E(G_2) = 120{,}000\ E(L) - 15{,}000$$
$$= (120{,}000)(.18) - 15{,}000$$
$$= \$6{,}600$$

Since the expected value of a_2 is greater than that of a_1, Arid Land should institute the DC-7 flight.

The selection of a_2 has been made using the expectation principle without the aid of a decision matrix. A decision matrix could have been constructed however. The appropriate decision matrix for Arid Land is given in Table 3.6. Notice, for example, that the consequence of a_2 if S_2 occurs is a gain of \$9,000. This gain is computed by

$$\text{Gain} = \text{Revenues} - \text{Costs}$$

where the revenues are (.2 lots per person)(100 persons)(\$1200 per lot) or \$24,000 and the total costs are \$15,000. Alternately this payoff could have been determined by substituting a value of .2 for L in the profit equation for G_2 yielding

$$G_2 = 120{,}000L - 15{,}000$$
$$= (120{,}000)(.2) - 15{,}000$$
$$= \$9{,}000$$

Other consequences in the decision matrix are similarly determined.

TABLE 3.6
Decision Matrix for
Arid Wonder Land Company

P(S)	States	Don't Offer Flight a_1	Offer Flight a_2
.45	S_1 .1 lots	0	−$3000
.35	S_2 .2 lots	0	$9000
.15	S_3 .3 lots	0	$21,000
.05	S_4 .4 lots	0	$33,000

Finally the expectation principle could be directly applied to the decision matrix showing

$$E(G_1) = (0)(.45) + (0)(.35) + (0)(.15) + (0)(.05)$$
$$= \$0$$

and,

$$E(G_2) = (-3000)(.45)+(9000)(.35)+(21000)(.15)+(33000)(.05)$$
$$= \$6,600$$

which confirms the result obtained earlier.

3.6 EXPECTATION AND BREAK EVEN

Natano Computer Inc. is a producer of auxiliary computer components. Natano has developed a new component which it intends to market and must now come to a decision as to how to manufacture it. Natano's production engineers have suggested two manufacturing alternatives:

a_1: Use automated production system
a_2: Use semiautomated production system

Both systems of production will produce components of equal quality. The difference lies in costs. With the automated system the cost to produce a component is \$300 while the direct cost per component with the semiautomated system is \$400. If both systems cost the same amount to install there would be no difficulty in selecting a_1. However, the automated system costs \$120,000 whereas the semiautomated system can be installed for \$90,000. Which system should Natano use?

Of critical importance to this decision is the information concerning the number of components Natano expects to produce. If a very large number of components will be produced, then the automated system will prove to yield the lesser total costs because of the lower per unit direct costs. If a relatively few will be produced, then the semiautomated system would be preferred. The marketing manager for Natano is unsure of sales. This uncertainty is due in part to the very competitive nature of this market. When pressed for a prediction of sales, the marketing manager forecasted that sales would be normally distributed with a mean of 450 and a standard deviation of 100 components. (See the first half of Chapter 12 where the method of making such a subjective forecast is described in detail.) Figure 3.1 depicts this sales forecast for the Natano component. All the possible sales figures represent the numerous states.

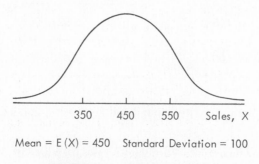

Mean = E (X) = 450   Standard Deviation = 100

FIGURE 3.1   Sales Forecast

Natano is now ready to construct a decision model. Because sales could be ..., or 250, or 251, or 252, ..., or 608, or 609, or 610, or ..., there are an extremely large number of states facing Natano. Hence an algebraic model should be constructed if possible. Letting X equal the number of components to be produced (and sold), the total cost to produce them with the automated system, a_1, will be

$$C_1 = \text{Variable Costs} + \text{Fixed Costs}$$
$$C_1 = 300X + 120{,}000$$

Recall that the per component cost is \$300 and the cost to install the system is \$120,000. The cost function for the semiautomated system will be

$$C_2 = 400X + 90{,}000$$

Which system should be installed?

Using the expectation principle, the act with the least expected cost should be selected. Following the procedure of the preceding section, $E(C_1)$ and $E(C_2)$ can be computed quite easily once $E(X)$ which is the expected number of components to be produced is known. This is because the two cost functions are linear. The marketing manager has forecasted sales, X, already. The mean of the normal distribution of Figure 3.1 is the same as the expected value of X, thus $E(X) = 450$. Knowing the expected value of X, it follows that

$$E(C_1) = 300\, E(X) + 120{,}000$$
$$= (300)(450) + 120{,}000$$
$$= \$255{,}000$$

and

$$E(C_2) = 400\, E(X) + 90{,}000$$
$$= (400)(450) + 90{,}000$$
$$= \$270{,}000$$

By the expectation principle, a_1 should be selected because the expected cost for the automated system is less than that for the semiautomated system.

Notice that the fact that the distribution of sales was normal, and that it had a standard deviation of 100 did not enter into the analysis. When the expectation principle is used and the payoffs are expressed with linear equations, only the mean or expected value of the random variable is important in coming to a decision. If the cost functions were nonlinear this would not be the case.

Although a decision has been reached using the expectation principle, another approach is possible which yields the same conclusion. In Figure 3.2, page 54, the cost functions for a_1 and a_2 are graphed. Notice that if sales fall below 300, then a_2 yields the lesser costs. If X exceeds 300, then a_1 yields the lower costs. The value of $X = 300$ is known as the *break-even point* and is designated by X_b. It is found by setting the two cost equations equal to each other and solving. This procedure determines the point of intersection of the two lines. In the Natano case, the break-even point may be found by

$$C_1 = C_2$$
$$300X + 120,000 = 400X + 90,000$$
$$30,000 = 100X$$
$$X = 30,000/100$$
$$X_b = 300$$

If the break-even point is known, the expectation principle can be easily applied to determine the optimal act. The expected value, $E(X)$, is identified on the horizontal axis. In this case $E(X) = 450$ is marked in Figure 3.2. The decision maker then assumes that $E(X)$ represents the actual number of components that will be sold and thereby chooses the act which yields the corresponding lesser costs. If sales were 450, it is apparent from Figure 3.2 that a_1 would be preferable since it yields a lower cost than a_2 for that value of X. If $E(X)$ had been something like 260, then a_2 would have been the choice of Natano. In summary, if $E(X)$ is below X_b, then a_2 is optimal; if $E(X)$ is greater than X_b, then a_1 is optimal.

In any decision situation with linear payoff functions, the expectation principle can be applied as in the Natano case by comparing the expected value of the variable to the break-even point. If, for example, the two linear payoff functions were the profit functions of Figure 3.3 and if $E(S)$ were 40, then a_1 would be the optimal choice since it yields a higher profit for a sales figure of 40. In this case a_1 is optimal as long as $E(S)$ is less than the break-even point S_b. The analyst must always be cognizant as to whether the linear functions represent costs or

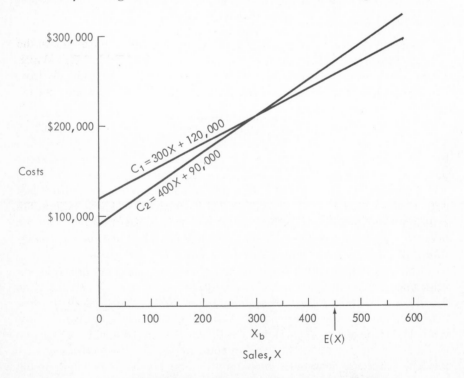

FIGURE 3.2   Linear Cost Functions for Natano

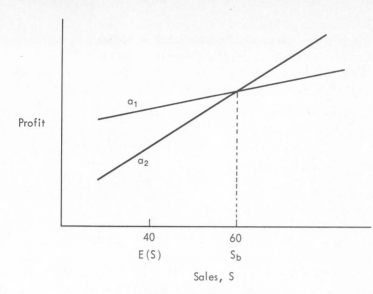

FIGURE 3.3   Linear Functions

profits. If the two lines of Figure 3.3 were cost functions, then a_2 would have been optimal assuming expected sales were 40.

3.7 UTILITY

Assume that you have the opportunity to select either a_1 or a_2 where the payoffs of these two acts are given in the decision matrix of Table 3.7(a). Which act would you select? Given your current circumstances, you undoubtedly have chosen a_2. If you had relied upon the expectation principle for guidance, the expected profits would be

$$E(P_1) = (\$1)(.5) + (\$1)(.5)$$
$$= \$1$$
and
$$E(P_2) = (\$200)(.5) + (0)(.5)$$
$$= \$100$$

and a_2 would be selected as it has the higher expected profit. Thus, you find yourself in complete agreement with the expectation principle.

TABLE 3.7
Decision Matrix

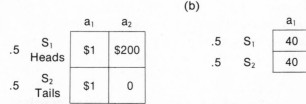

(a)

		a_1	a_2
.5	S_1 Heads	$1	$200
.5	S_2 Tails	$1	0

(b)

		a_1	a_2
.5	S_1	40	60
.5	S_2	40	0

Again assume that you have the opportunity to select either a_1 or a_2, but now the payoffs are stated in millions of dollars. In choosing a_1 you would be assured of receiving $1 million. With a_2 there is a probability of .5 that you would receive $200 million and a probability of .5 that you would receive nothing. (Assume this is all tax-free money.) Which act would you select? If you turn to the expectation principle you will find that the expected value of a_1 is $1 million and the expected value of a_2 is $100 million, therefore a_2 should be selected. However, very few people would in fact prefer a_2 over a_1 when the payoffs are in millions of dollars. Hence the expectation principle cannot always be relied upon to give satisfactory advice in the selection of an act.

Why is it that most people prefer a_2 when the payoffs of Table 3.7(a) are in dollars but a_1 when in millions of dollars? Certainly it is not because the expected monetary value is greater for a_2 when the payoffs are in dollars and greater for a_1 when in millions of dollars. Evidently people do not necessarily attempt to maximize their expected monetary gain; if they did, they would always select a_2. Rather, people choose the act which maximizes personal satisfaction. It might be that for a given decision maker, $1 million brings 40 units of satisfaction, $200 million brings 60 units of satisfaction, and a gain of $0 will bring 0 units of satisfaction. Without quibbling over the origin or precise meaning of these units of personal satisfaction, it would make sense for the decision maker facing the matrix of Table 3.7(a) to convert the monetary payoffs into units of satisfaction. Then a decision could be made on the basis of expected personal satisfaction. In Table 3.7(b) the decision maker has in fact replaced the monetary payoffs with their equivalent units of satisfaction.

Now the decision maker can use the expectation principle to select the act with the greater expected satisfaction. The expected satisfaction for a_1 would be

$$\text{Expected Satisfaction for } a_1 = (40)(.5) + (40)(.5)$$
$$= 40 \text{ units}$$

and for a_2,

$$\text{Expected Satisfaction for } a_2 = (60)(.5) + (0)(.5)$$
$$= 30 \text{ units}$$

Therefore, this decision maker who is interested in maximizing personal satisfaction will select a_1 according to the expectation principle when applied to satisfaction rather than money. This is in perfect agreement with the actual preference of this decision maker for a_1. By converting to units of satisfaction this decision maker can utilize the expectation principle whereas the expectation principle was an inadequate guide when applied to monetary payoffs.

The satisfaction a person derives from a gain of a given amount of money is called *utility*. Attempts have been made to find, for example, the true satisfaction or utility that is inherent in $100. It should be obvious that there is no inherent utility in $100 because this amount of money brings different satisfaction to different people. John Von Neumann and Oscar Morgenstern approached the subject of utility in a novel way which did not define utility as being some characteristic which inherently resides in a particular amount of money. The concept of utility which they developed can be used with advantage by decision makers faced with a risk situation. The utilization of the Von Neumann-Morgenstern utility will be the focus of the remainder of this section.

After a particular decision maker has found personal utility for various amounts of money according to the Von Neumann-Morgenstern technique, these utilities should replace the monetary payoffs in the decision matrix. Then the decision maker should select the act with the greatest expected utility. (In the section to follow the Von Neumann-Morgenstern technique for determining utilities will be given.)

The easiest way to display a person's utility for each of a variety of monetary values is through the medium of a *utility curve*. Figure 3.4 presents a utility curve for a particular decision maker. Every decision maker will have a uniquely personal utility curve since each decision maker has unique attitudes toward wealth and risk. Consider now this decision maker's utility curve. It is seen, for example, that for this decision maker the utility of $200,000 is about 61 and the utility of $70,000 is about 39 (units of satisfaction). Notice also the shape of the curve. The utility of $200,000, for example, is not much greater than the utility of $150,000. A utility curve of this shape is quite common indicating that extra amounts of money bring relatively less additional satisfaction. The shapes of utility curves will be further discussed in the next section.

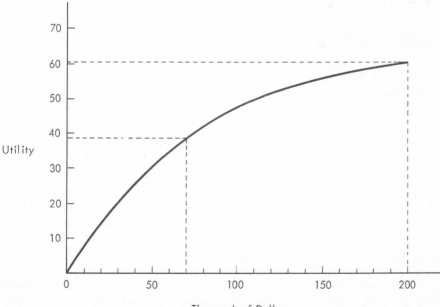

FIGURE 3.4   Utility Curve for Decision Maker of Table 3.8

TABLE 3.8
Monetary Payoffs and Utilities

(a)		a_1	a_2
.2	S_1	$200,000	$60,000
.3	S_2	$150,000	$70,000
.5	S_3	0	$80,000

(b)		a_1	a_2
.2	S_1	61	35
.3	S_2	56	39
.5	S_3	0	42

Suppose now that this decision maker is facing the decision model of Table 3.8(a) where the consequences are in profits. If the expectation principle were applied to these monetary payoffs, a_1 would be selected since the expected profit for each act is

$$E(P_1) = (200,000)(.2) + (150,000)(.3) + (0)(.5)$$
$$= \$85,000$$
$$E(P_2) = (60,000)(.2) + (70,000)(.3) + (80,000)(.5)$$
$$= \$73,000$$

This analysis, of course, does not take into account utility.

It has already been stated that a decision maker really wants to maximize satisfaction and this may not be the same as the maximization of profits. The decision maker should therefore convert each of the monetary payoffs of Table 3.8(a) into a utility. This is done in Table 3.8(b). From the utility curve in Figure 3.4, the utility of $200,000 is about 61. Symbolically this may be expressed as

$$U(\$200,000) = 61$$

Therefore, the monetary payoff of $200,000 under a_1 should be replaced with a utility of 61. Likewise, every other monetary payoff is replaced with the corresponding utility.

Now the expectation principle should be applied to the decision matrix of Table 3.8(b) in order to find the act with the maximum expected utility. The expected utility for a_1 is

$$E(U_1) = (61)(.2) + (56)(.3) + (0)(.5)$$
$$= 29.0 \text{ units}$$

and that for a_2 is

$$E(U_2) = (35)(.2) + (39)(.3) + (42)(.5)$$
$$= 39.7 \text{ units}$$

Therefore, the optimal act for this decision maker is a_2 and not a_1.

3.8 CONSTRUCTING A UTILITY CURVE

Decision makers may exhibit varying attitudes toward a risk situation. There are primarily three broad categories of attitudes toward risk: risk averse, risk neutral, and risk preferring. A simple decision model as in Table 3.9 can be used to demonstrate the choices of decision makers with these three attitudes. Notice

TABLE 3.9
A Simple Decision Matrix

		a₁	a₂
.5	Heads	$5,000	$10,000
.5	Tails	$5,000	0

that in the decision matrix of Table 3.9 the expected gain for both acts is $5,000. Hence the expectation principle when applied to monetary payoffs would conclude that a_1 and a_2 are equally desirable. If, however, a decision maker facing this simple decision matrix would prefer a_1, then that decision maker is exhibiting a risk averse attitude. This decision maker prefers $5,000 for sure rather than the risky situation of a_2. If the decision maker were indifferent between a_1 and a_2, then the decision maker is said to be risk neutral. Such a decision maker is guided solely by the expected monetary value criterion taking the act with the greater expected profit. If the expected profits are the same, the risk neutral person is indifferent between the acts. Finally, if the decision maker would prefer a_2 even though it has the same expected gain as a_1, then the decision maker is risk preferring. This decision maker likes the risky situation of a_2. With large quantities of money at stake, most decision makers tend to be risk averse. For this reason most people would purchase fire insurance for their home even if it were not required in order to secure a mortgage. However, some people who buy fire insurance (risk averse behavior) also purchase lottery tickets (risk preferring behavior). This means that it is not always possible to categorize a person as being simply risk averse, risk neutral, or risk preferring.

In Figure 3.5 three utility curves are presented. Each is representative of the type of utility curve which results from the three general attitudes toward

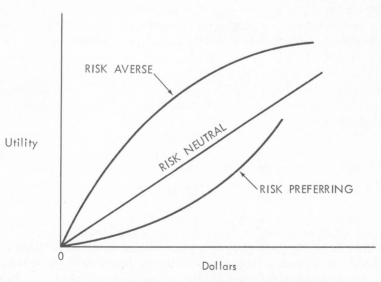

FIGURE 3.5   Three Types of Utility Curves

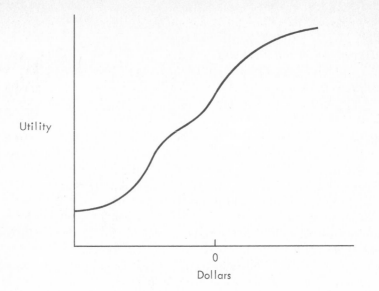

FIGURE 3.6   A Utility Curve

risk. As already indicated, though these are the general types of utility curves, a particular person may have a utility curve which is some combination of these. For example, the utility curve of Figure 3.6 is representative of that of some people.

Being somewhat acquainted with the three basic types of utility curves, a decision maker can proceed to construct a personal utility curve. To begin, the range of monetary values which the utility curve will cover must be determined. In Figure 3.4, for example, the utility curve gives a utility for each monetary value from $0 to $200,000. The decision maker must choose lower and upper monetary limits which will encompass all of the payoffs in the decision matrix. Conely the wildcatter, for example, would need a utility curve from −$100,000 to $3,360,000 since this is the range of the payoffs in his decision matrix of Table 3.2. Let B denote the lower or bottom limit and T the upper or top limit. B must be as low as, or lower than, any payoff and T must be as high as, or higher than, any payoff; thus, Conely could let B equal −$100,000 and T equal $4,000,000 in order to work with round figures. With these limits established, the utility curve can be constructed.

For illustrative purposes, suppose that a decision maker named Joyce wants to construct her utility curve for monetary values between $B = -\$10,000$ and $T = \$50,000$. To begin, let the utility of B be 0 and the utility of T be 100:

$$U(B) = U(-\$10,000) = 0$$
$$U(T) = U(\$50,000) = 100$$

Such an assignment of a utility value for B and T is arbitrary as long as $U(B)$ is less than $U(T)$. In other words, the construction of a utility curve could be accomplished just as easily if Joyce began by letting the utility of −$10,000 be 50 and the utility of $50,000 be 1000. For the sake of simplicity, in this text the utility of B will always be selected as 0 and the utility of T will always be put at 100.

This practice may be followed regardless of the decision maker or the values of B and T.

Next the decision maker constructs an artificial decision matrix such as that of Table 3.10(a). Notice that the probabilities of both states are .5 and that the values for B and T are placed under a_1. For a_2 the two consequences are designated by M. With a_2 the payoff is M dollars no matter what state occurs. The decision maker must decide what value for M will make her perfectly indifferent between a_1 and a_2. Suppose that Joyce, after giving it some thought, says that if M were \$3,000 she would be perfectly indifferent between a_1 and a_2. By this she is saying that getting \$3,000 for sure, a_2, is just as good (or bad) as a 50 percent chance of losing \$10,000 and a 50 percent chance of winning \$50,000. If in fact she is perfectly indifferent between a_1 and a_2 where $M = \$3,000$, then she should prefer a_1 if M were \$2900 and should prefer a_2 if M were \$3,100. Having come to this conclusion concerning the value of M which makes a_1 and a_2 of equal desirability, the theory underlying the construction of utility curves enables us to conclude that the utility of \$3,000 (which is M) is 50. That is,

$$U(M) = 50$$
$$U(\$3,000) = 50$$

Whatever the decision maker determines M to be, its utility will automatically be 50.

TABLE 3.10
Three Artificial Decision Matrixes
for the Construction of a Utility Curve

(a)

			a_1	a_2
.50	S_1	B =	−\$10,000	M
.50	S_2	T =	\$50,000	M

(b)

			a_1	a_2
.25	S_1	B =	−\$10,000	N
.75	S_2	T =	\$50,000	N

(c)

			a_1	a_2
.75	S_1	B =	−\$10,000	L
.25	S_2	T =	\$50,000	L

After this the decision maker constructs yet another artificial decision situation as represented in Table 3.10(b). Here S_1 has a probability of .25 and S_2 has a probability of .75. The decision maker must now ask herself what value for N would make her perfectly indifferent between a_1 and a_2. Suppose Joyce says that the value for N which makes her indifferent is $14,000. It can then be concluded that the utility of $14,000 (which is N) is 75, that is,

$$U(N) = 75$$
$$U(\$14,000) = 75$$

In the procedure being outlined, the utility of N is always 75 regardless of the decision maker and values for B and T. Of course the actual value of N itself varies depending on B, T, and who the decision maker is.

Finally the decision maker sets up the artificial decision situation of Table 3.10(c). Notice that S_1 has a probability of .75 now. The decision maker must subjectively determine the value for L which would make her perfectly indifferent between a_1 and a_2. Joyce claims to be indifferent between the two acts if L is −$5,000. The utility of L is always 25, therefore the utility in this case of −$5,000 is 25:

$$U(L) = 25$$
$$U(-\$5,000) = 25$$

The decision maker has now assessed the following:

$$
\begin{aligned}
U(B) &= U(-\$10,000) = 0 \\
U(L) &= U(-\$5,000) = 25 \\
U(M) &= U(\$3,000) = 50 \\
U(N) &= U(\$14,000) = 75 \\
U(T) &= U(\$50,000) = 100
\end{aligned}
$$

The same information is presented in Table 3.11. In Figure 3.7 the decision maker, or anyone else, plots the five points from Table 3.11 where the vertical axis represents utility and the horizontal axis represents money. Then a line is smoothed through these five points. This line becomes the decision maker's personal utility curve. The decision maker may use this utility curve in order to convert monetary consequences in a decision model to utilities. Then the expectation principle would be applied to find the act with the highest expected utility as was done in the last section. In this manner the optimal act for this decision maker is determined.

TABLE 3.11
Monetary Values
and their Corresponding Utilities
for Joyce

Money	Utility
−$10,000	0
− 5,000	25
3,000	50
14,000	75
50,000	100

In concluding this section and the last, a couple of points should be noted which bear upon the use of utility for decision-making purposes. If the decision maker is risk neutral (straight line utility curve) then the expectation principle as applied to monetary values is a perfectly adequate criterion. That is, there is no need to convert the payoffs to utilities if the decision maker is risk neutral since such a decision maker concurs with the expectation principle when applied to monetary payoffs. It is also not necessary to convert to utility if the payoffs in the model are relatively close to each other in size. Notice that the utility curve of Figure 3.7 is essentially a straight line for the region from −$5,000 to $3,000, or from $0 to $10,000. This means that if all the consequences in a decision model ranged from −$5,000 to $3,000 or from $0 to $10,000, the decision maker would be essentially risk neutral (straight utility line) in this situation and need not convert to utilities. However, with greater ranges of payoffs the utility curve is not straight and the conversion to utility is necessitated.

A decision maker acting in behalf of a large corporation would have a utility curve which is essentially a straight line for great ranges of monetary values. This means that corporate decision makers at all but the highest levels of the organization would not be making decisions with consequences that vary in magnitude enough to make utility conversion necessary. Only when there are relatively huge differences in monetary consequences would the large corporation be concerned with behavior which is other than risk neutral. Of course the smaller the corporation, the smaller the decision which might require the use of utilities. Since most operational and unique, small-scale decisions within the corporate framework do not involve relatively large differences in the magnitudes

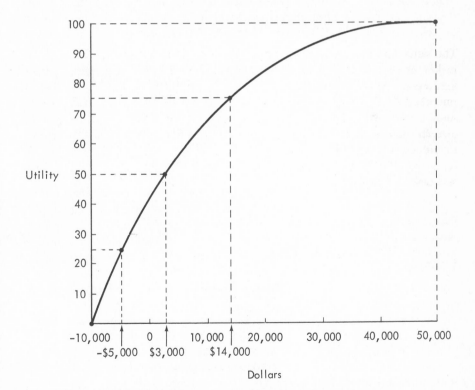

FIGURE 3.7   Joyce's Utility Curve

of the payoffs, utility will not be incorporated into the analyses of remaining chapters. However, with the background in utility given in this chapter, the reader has a working knowledge of how utility might be used in the process of decision making.

3.9 DECISION TREES

The decision situations that have been encountered in this chapter have required the manager to select a single act from among a set of competing acts. The decision matrix proved to be an adequate modeling device for this sort of situation. Many times, however, the manager is called upon to make a series of related decisions. An initial choice must be made, then several other choices must follow. In these multistage situations another modeling vehicle is desirable.

The *decision tree* or *decision diagram* is a modeling technique especially useful in multistage situations. In Figure 3.8 a decision tree is given as an alternate model to the decision matrix of Table 3.2 for the wildcatter Conely. This is not a model of a multistage decision situation, yet it exhibits the principal components of a decision tree.

A decision tree is composed of connected forks and branches. The branches emanating from a square constitute an *act fork*. The decision maker must deliberately select the branch (act) which emanates from an act fork. In the Conely decision tree, Conely must ultimately choose either branch a_1, or branch a_2, or branch a_3, or branch a_4. The other kind of fork is a chance fork. A *chance fork* is represented by branches emanating from a circle. With this type of fork, chance determines which branch is selected. In the Conely decision tree, chance determines whether no oil, 100,000 barrels, or 500,000 barrels will be struck. Attached to each branch from a chance fork is the probability of that state or branch occurring.

Below each branch is placed the monetary consequence resulting directly from that act or state. Under the a_1 branch a zero is placed indicating that no cost is involved if a hole is not drilled. Under a_2 is placed −100 indicating that if Conely drills alone he will have to pay the entire cost of $100,000 for the hole. Under a_3 is placed −50 since with this act Conely shares the drilling expense with Andersen. Under a_4 there is no cost as Lazaar pays the entire drilling cost. Concentrating on the chance fork which follows a_2, the monetary consequence of S_1 is zero since no oil is found. Under S_2 is recorded 660. This is based on a revenue of ($7 per bbl.)(100,000 bbls.) or $700,000 from which is subtracted the equipment cost of $40,000. The monetary consequences under all the other branches in Figure 3.8 may be similarly determined from the information given in Section 3.3.

At the *end positions* of the decision tree (to the far right) the total net consequences are recorded. Each is equal to the sum of the monetary consequences of the branches along the path leading from the beginning of the tree to that end position. For example, if a_2 is selected and S_3 occurs, then Conely will end up with −100 + 3460 or $3,360,000. This value is recorded at the appropriate end position. For analytic purposes, only the payoffs at the end positions are

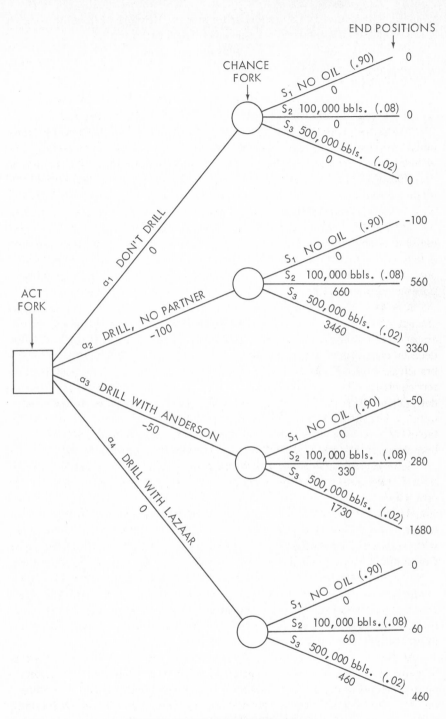

END POSITIONS

CHANCE
FORK

S_1 NO OIL (.90) — 0
0

S_2 100,000 bbls. (.08) — 0
0

S_3 500,000 bbls. (.02) — 0
0

a_1 DON'T DRILL
0

ACT
FORK

a_2 DRILL, NO PARTNER
−100

S_1 NO OIL (.90) — −100
0

S_2 100,000 bbls. (.08) — 560
660

S_3 500,000 bbls. (.02) — 3360
3460

a_3 DRILL WITH ANDERSON
−50

S_1 NO OIL (.90) — −50
0

S_2 100,000 bbls. (.08) — 280
330

S_3 500,000 bbls. (.02) — 1680
1730

a_4 DRILL WITH LAZAAR
0

S_1 NO OIL (.90) — 0
0

S_2 100,000 bbls. (.08) — 60
60

S_3 500,000 bbls. (.02) — 460
460

**FIGURE 3.8 Conely Decision Tree
(In Thousands of Dollars)**

required. The monetary values along the branches leading to the end positions may be deleted once the end position values have been obtained.

A multistage decision situation will now be illustrated. Then a method of applying the expectation principle to the decision tree will be employed in order to select the optimal act.

Masutro Ltd. must decide whether to pursue the development of an organically synthesized food coloring which will be free of toxic effects. It will cost $100,000 to complete the research relating to this proposed product. By means of this research Masutro will be able to determine whether the food coloring can or cannot be developed and produced. Masutro's scientists maintain that as things look now, there is an eighty percent chance of developing the desired food coloring. If the food coloring can be developed, the activity of competitors in this area will be of prime interest to Masutro. Presently no company has developed such a food coloring; Masutro believes that there are three chances in ten that a competitor will have introduced such a product by the time Masutro would be ready to produce it (assuming that Masutro could develop such a food coloring). Depending on whether or not a competitor will have synthesized such a food coloring, Masutro would then have to make a final "Go" or "No Go" decision.

It is projected that it would cost about $150,000 to install the production equipment necessary for the manufacture of the food coloring. If the food coloring is produced and a competitor has already introduced such a product, there is a .2 probability that Masutro sales will be high, a .3 probability that sales will be medium, and a .5 probability that sales will be low. The profits corresponding to each level of sales, after overhead and direct costs have been subtracted, would be $500,000, $300,000, and $100,000, respectively. These figures do not account for research costs and the cost to install the production equipment. If the food coloring is produced and there is no competition, the probabilities for high, medium, and low sales are .4, .5, and .1, respectively. The net profits, not including research and installation expenses, would be $500,000, $300,000, and $100,000, respectively.

If Masutro should decide not to pursue the research and development of the organically synthesized food coloring, it can use its resources for the implementation of an alternative project which will yield a net profit of $25,000. What should Masutro do?

The decision situation faced by Masutro is too complex to analyze without the aid of a model. A decision matrix would not be adequate for modeling purposes as there are several sets of decisions to be made. Masutro must first decide between the pursuit of the food coloring through research and the alternative project which would net $25,000. If the research is undertaken and the food coloring is developed, then another decision would have to be made as to whether or not it should be produced. Because of this complexity a decision tree should be used for modeling purposes.

In Figure 3.9 a decision tree for Masutro is given. Read through the paragraphs above which describe Masutro's situation and see how the decision tree follows the logical and chronological flow of the problem. Notice that the square

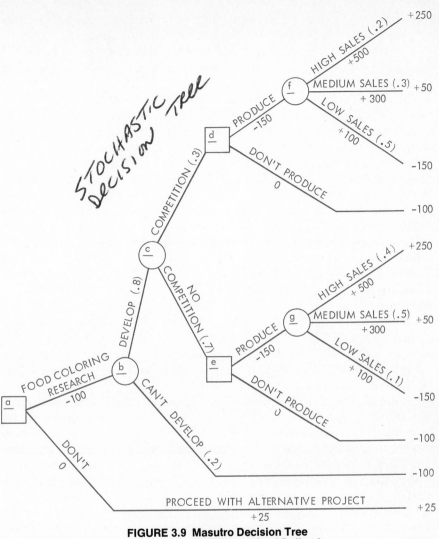

**FIGURE 3.9 Masutro Decision Tree
(In Thousands of Dollars)**

forks, a, d, and e, are act forks and the circle forks, b, c, f, and g, are chance forks. Under each branch a monetary consequence is placed if such a consequence is directly associated with the branch. After the word of description attached to each branch, the probability of the branch occurring if it is a chance branch is given. Finally, the consequences along the branches from the initial square, square a, to each end position are summed. These sums are recorded at each end position. For example, the following sequence of acts and events might occur: Research-Develop-Competition-Produce-High Sales. This sequence would net $-100 - 150 + 500$ or \$250,000. The sequence of Research-Develop-Competition-Produce-Medium Sales might instead occur. This would yield a profit of \$50,000.

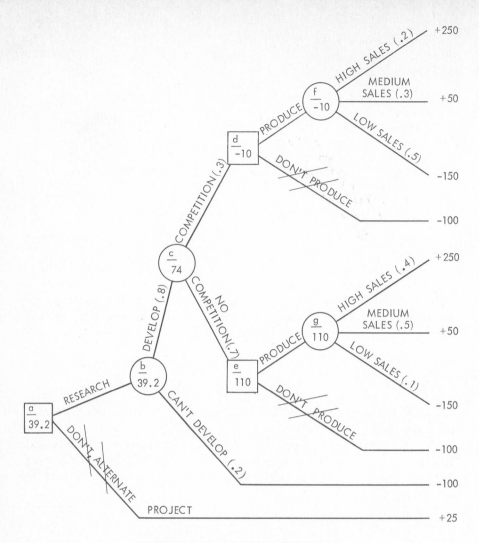

FIGURE 3.10   Decision Tree Analysis

3.10 BACKWARD INDUCTION

With the decision tree of Masutro constructed, the expectation principle can be applied to determine the optimal acts. The expectation principle is applied to a decision tree by means of a technique known as *backward induction*. It is important to note that the expectation principle and backward induction are applied only to the payoffs found at the end positions. Once the payoffs for each end position have been determined, the monetary values associated with the branches should be deleted or crossed out. In Figure 3.10 a decision tree for Masutro is given without these intermediate monetary values. This decision tree will be used for analytic purposes. For the time being, disregard the numbers found in the squares and circles.

Backward induction is accomplished by repeating a two-step process after a decision tree has been constructed and the payoffs at each end position determined:

1. Select a fork which has all of its branches leading directly to an end position.
2. If the fork is an act fork, select that branch or act which has the highest payoff. Then cross out the other branches emanating from that fork. Place the payoff of the selected branch in the square of the act fork.

   If the fork is a chance fork, compute the expected payoff. Place the expected payoff in the circle of the chance fork.

   The square or circle of the fork is now considered to be an end position and the value inside is the payoff for that end position.

These steps will now be illustrated by means of the Masutro decision tree of Figure 3.10.

First, a fork is to be chosen which has all of its branches leading directly to an end position. There are only two such forks, namely, f and g. Either may be selected, thus f is arbitrarily chosen. Fork f is a chance fork as shown by the circle. Thus, by the second step of backward induction, the expected value of the payoffs emanating from this fork must be computed:

$$\text{Expected Payoff at Fork } \underline{f} = (250)(.2) + (50)(.3) + (-150)(.5)$$
$$= -10$$

This expected profit of −10,000 is then placed in circle f and circle f is considered to be an end position.

Having completed the two-step process once, it must now be repeated. Presently there are two forks which lead directly to end positions, namely, g and d. Select g. Since g is a chance fork, the expected payoff for it must be computed:

$$\text{Expected Payoff at Fork } \underline{g} = (250)(.4) + (50)(.5) + (-150)(.1)$$
$$= 110$$

The expected profit of $110,000 is placed in circle g and g is now considered to be an end position.

There are now two forks whose branches lead directly to end positions, d and e. Figure 3.11, page 70, depicts the relevant part of the decision tree as it now stands. Select d. Notice that the top branch emanating from d leads directly to circle f which is considered to be an end position with a payoff of −10. The lower branch leads directly to an end position with a payoff of −100. Fork d is an act fork; therefore, the decision maker should select whichever branch has the highest payoff. The "Produce" branch has the higher payoff and thus the "Don't Produce" branch must be crossed out. The payoff for "Produce" which is −10 is then entered in square d. Square d is now considered as an end position. (Keep referring to Figure 3.10. Figure 3.11 and those to follow are given only to clarify what is happening in Figure 3.10.)

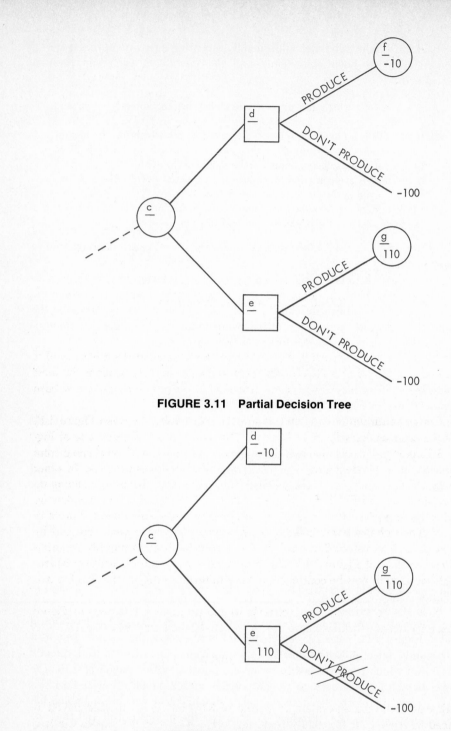

FIGURE 3.11   Partial Decision Tree

FIGURE 3.12   Partial Decision Tree

There is now only one fork, e, which has all of its branches leading directly
to an end position. Figure 3.12 shows the current situation with the decision

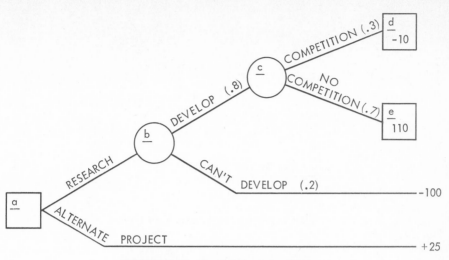

FIGURE 3.13   Partial Decision Tree

tree. Since $\underline{e}$ is an act fork, the branch or act with the most desirable payoff is selected and the other is crossed out. Then the value of 110, which is the most desirable payoff, is placed within the $\underline{e}$ square. The decision tree has now been reduced to that of Figure 3.13.

Before continuing, pause to consider the relationship between Figure 3.13 and the original decision tree of Figure 3.10. The reduced decision tree of Figure 3.13 is actually equivalent to the original. Forks $\underline{f}$ and $\underline{e}$ of the original were replaced by equivalent single values of −10 and 110, respectively. In other words, the risk situation of fork $\underline{f}$ where there was a .2 probability of ending up with 250, a .3 probability of ending up with 50, and a .5 probability of ending up with −150 is equivalent to a profit of −10 because −10 is the expected profit of fork $\underline{f}$. Through backward induction, successive forks have been replaced by single equivalent values. The result of this process has been to simplify the original tree to that of Figure 3.13. This process of replacing forks with equivalent single values will now be continued in order to further simplify the decision tree of Figure 3.13.

Now the only fork leading directly to end positions is $\underline{c}$ as seen in Figure 3.13. $\underline{c}$ is a chance fork and therefore its expected payoff must be computed:

$$\begin{array}{r} \text{Expected Payoff} \\ \text{at Fork } \underline{c} \end{array} = (-10)(.3) + (110)(.7)$$
$$= 74$$

Fork $\underline{c}$ is therefore equivalent to a gain of $74,000. This expected payoff is placed in circle $\underline{c}$. It is actually replacing fork $\underline{c}$ with a single payoff. Circle $\underline{c}$ now becomes an end position.

Figure 3.14, page 72, now depicts the reduced decision tree. Fork $\underline{b}$ has all of its branches leading directly to an end position. As it is a chance fork, the expected payoff must be computed:

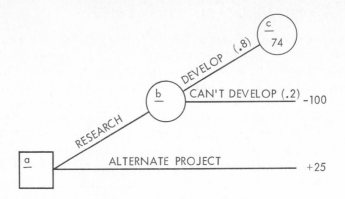

FIGURE 3.14   Partial Decision Tree

$$\begin{array}{c} \text{Expected Payoff} \\ \text{at Fork } \underline{b} \end{array} = (.8)(74) + (.2)(-100)$$
$$= 39.2$$

This expected payoff is placed in circle $\underline{b}$ and $\underline{b}$ becomes an end position (see Figure 3.15).

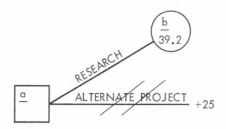

FIGURE 3.15   Partial Decision Tree

There remains one fork in Figure 3.15, the act fork $\underline{a}$. Since "Research" carries an expected profit of $39,200 and "Alternate Project" carries a profit of $25,000, Masutro should commit itself to the research and development of the food coloring. Considering again the tree of Figure 3.10, Masutro should initially go the "Research" route. Then if the food coloring can be developed, Masutro should produce it regardless of the presence of competition. This is because the "Don't Produce" acts of forks $\underline{d}$ and $\underline{e}$ have already been crossed out in the early stages of backward induction.

In Figure 3.10 the results of the step-by-step process of backward induction are shown where an equivalent single value for each fork replaces the fork. Again it should be noted that all of the reduced decision trees of Figures 3.11 through 3.15 need not be drawn in applying backward induction. The original decision tree may be exclusively used by placing the equivalent values in the various squares and circles as the analysis takes place by moving from the right to the left.

3.11 BACKWARD INDUCTION WITH UTILITIES

Suppose a risk averse decision maker were confronted with a multistage decision situation where the monetary consequences were of considerable magnitude and varied over a wide range. How could this decision maker bring utility to bear upon the analysis of this situation? Once the decision tree has been constructed with the monetary payoffs placed at the end positions, the conversion to utility is extremely simple. The decision maker need only convert each of the end position payoffs to utility. The utility of each monetary payoff is determined by the decision maker's utility curve. Then backward induction is applied to the decision tree exactly as before except that the utilities are used rather than the monetary payoffs.

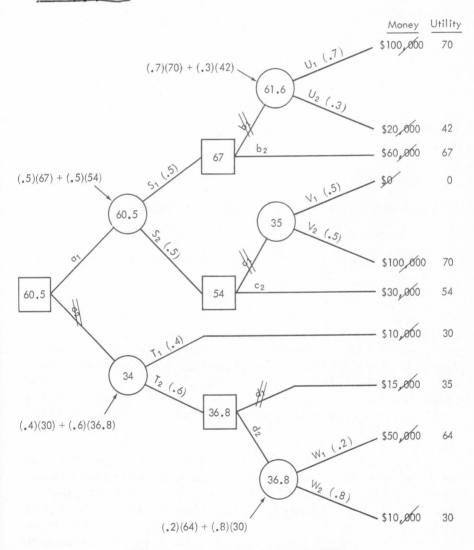

FIGURE 3.16   A Decision Tree with Utilities

A decision tree is given in Figure 3.16, page 73, with the monetary payoffs given at the end positions. These payoffs have been crossed out and replaced by the decision maker's utilities (the utility curve is not given). For example, the utility of $100,000 is 70, hence 70 replaces $100,000. This decision maker has completed the analysis by backward induction as is evidenced by the utilities found in the squares and circles. It is seen that the decision maker should initially select a_1 rather than a_2 since it has an expected utility of 60.5. Then, if S_1 occurs the decision maker should select b_2. On the other hand, if S_2 occurs, then c_2 should be selected. This is the optimal strategy.

In closing it should be emphasized that the payoffs must be converted to utilities first, then the process of analysis by backward induction may begin.

PROBLEMS

3-1. Consider the following decision matrix where the payoffs are expressed as profits.

		a_1	a_2	a_3
.2	S_1	40	90	80
.5	S_2	60	50	10
.3	S_3	30	20	70

(a) Which act is optimal if maximin is used? a_1
(b) Which act is optimal by the expectation principle? a_2
(c) With an aspiration level of 55, which act is optimal? $a_1 \mbox{ } a_3$

3-2. Assume that the payoffs in the decision matrix of Problem 3–1 are costs rather than profits.
(a) Which act is optimal if minimax is used? a_1
(b) Which act is optimal by the expectation principle? a_3
(c) With an aspiration level of 45, which act is optimal? $a_1 \mbox{ } a_3$

3-3. A manager must decide which project to select from among six. The decision matrix below gives the consequences for each act. In the upper left of each box the profit is given while in the lower right the market share is given. If a_1 were selected, for example, and S_1 occurred, then a profit of 120 would result along with a market share of 50%.

		a_1		a_2		a_3		a_4		a_5		a_6	
.2	S_1	120		100		110		130		110		100	
			50%		30%		40%		45%		40%		30%
.3	S_2	130		140		110		120		115		110	
			45%		60%		50%		55%		40%		30%
.3	S_3	140		120		110		100		115		120	
			40%		50%		30%		25%		40%		40%
.2	S_4	100		110		100		100		105		130	
			20%		40%		25%		25%		35%		50%

(a) Any project (act) which might possibly leave the company with a market share of less than 30% is unacceptable. With this stipulation, use the expectation principle to select an act from among the acceptable projects. *a₂*

(b) If instead it had been stipulated that a project must offer at least a .50 probability of a market share of 45% or more, what projects would have to be eliminated from further consideration? *a₃, a₅, a₆*

3-4. Travis Dynamics has developed a new device which should make the internal combustion engine more efficient. Travis is faced with three alternatives in regard to this device. Travis can proceed to manufacture and market the device itself; in this case Travis would make a profit of $2 for each device sold. As a second choice, Travis can sell the patent outright to another company for $1 million. In the third case, Travis can sell the patent for $.3 million and receive a royalty of $1.00 per device sold. Which is the optimal choice using the expectation principle if there is a .50 probability that sales of the device would be .2 million units, a .40 probability of sales of .8 million units, and if there is a .10 probability of 1.4 million units being sold. Set up a decision matrix before applying the expectation principle. *a₁*

3-5. Perry Insurance has just sold another fire insurance policy to a homeowner. The premium is $200 per year. $30 of the premium goes to commissions and home office expenses. The home for which the policy has been purchased is insured for $40,000. The probability of no fire is .99, the probability of a small fire causing damage of $5,000 is .008, and the probability of a large fire causing $40,000 in damage is .002. What is the expected profit to the insurance company of this policy? *$50*

3-6. Casey Electrical must decide if a bid should be submitted for the electrical work on the Gila Dam. Casey's bid will be one of the following:

> a₁: Bid $.25 million
> a₂: Bid $.28 million
> a₃: Bid $.31 million
> a₄: Don't Bid

Assume that the probability distribution of the lowest bid by another contractor is: *a₂*

	Bid	P(Bid)	a₁	a₂	a₃	a₄
S₁	$.23 million	.1	0	0	0	0
S₂	.26	.3	.03	0	0	0
S₃	.29	.4	.03	.06	0	0
S₄	.32	.2	.03	.06	.09	0

Casey can do the work for $.22 million. By the expectation principle, which bid should Casey submit. (Clarification: if Casey submitted a bid of $.28 million and the lowest bid were $.26 million, then Casey would not get the job. If the lowest bid had been $.29 million, then Casey would get the job.)

3-7. Mopoostri Motors has sold a fleet of huge dump trucks to a mining company operating in the Mesabi Range of Minnesota. Mopoostri has agreed to service these trucks. In the event of a breakdown, Mopoostri can send either an engine mechanic or a gear/suspension mechanic. There are three general types of problems that can develop with these big trucks: minor problem, engine problem, gear/suspension problem. The probabilities of these three problems in the event of a breakdown are .3, .4, and .3, respectively.

The cost to send the engine mechanic for purely diagnostic purposes is $200. If there is a minor problem, the engine mechanic can fix it for $300. If there is an engine problem, the engine mechanic can fix it for $900. If there is a gear/suspension problem, the engine mechanic cannot fix it and the gear/suspension mechanic must be sent. It will then cost $1,000 to fix the problem.

The cost to initially send the gear/suspension mechanic for a diagnosis is $100. If there is a minor problem, this mechanic can fix it for $200. If there is a gear/suspension problem, this mechanic can go on to fix it for an additional $700. If there is an engine problem the engine mechanic must come and it will cost $1100 to fix it. Set up a decision matrix where the two acts are:

a_1: Send the engine mechanic first
a_2: Send the gear/suspension mechanic first

Then determine the optimal act by using the expectation principle. (Note: Each consequence or payoff in the decision matrix will consist of the sum of the diagnostic cost and the repair cost.)

3-8. Fremont Publishing Company has the opportunity to publish a management science manuscript. After market research, Fremont is convinced that sales over the lifetime of the first edition of the text would be either 20,000 or 40,000 copies. The probabilities of these two states are .6 and .4, respectively. There are three alternatives for Fremont:

a_1: Don't publish
a_2: Publish, initial printing of 20,000 copies
a_3: Publish, initial printing of 40,000 copies

The economic details relating to this decision follow. It would cost $40,000 to get the manuscript ready for the printer, including editorial and production expenses. If 20,000 copies are printed at a time, the cost per copy is $9. If 40,000 are printed at a time, the printer charges only $7 per copy. The text would sell competitively at $15 per copy. The author would receive a royalty of $2 per copy sold. Fremont would spend an additional $25,000 on the promotion of the text. Set up a decision matrix and then use the expectation principle to select the optimal act.

3-9. Cappy Shorty manufactures strollers. There are two possible manufacturing methods that can be employed. With the first, the fixed costs are $40,000 and the variable cost per stroller is $10. With the second, the fixed costs are $70,000 and the cost per stroller is $8. Cappy Shorty would sell the strollers to dealers for $14 each. If sales have been forecasted to be normally distributed with a mean of 12,000 and a standard deviation of 3,000 strollers, find the optimal method of manufacturing using the expectation principle. Be sure to set up a profit function for each method.

3-10. The captain of a tuna boat working out of San Diego must decide whether to hire

a_1: Small Crew
a_2: Large Crew

Important to this decision is the density, D, of tuna to be encountered. If D is high, a_2 would be optimal; if D is low then a_1 would be optimal. The profit functions for the two acts are:

$$P_1 = 40D - 800$$
$$P_2 = 60D - 1400$$

On past fishing trips, a high tuna density $(D=40)$ has been encountered 40% of the time, a medium density $(D=30)$ has been encountered 50% of the time, and a low density $(D=10)$ has been encountered 10% of the time.

(a) Using the expectation principle, which act should be selected?

(b) If instead D were normally distributed with a mean of 35 and a standard deviation of 10, which act should be selected?

3-11. Kampgrounds of Kanada is seeking to determine the advisability of leasing a campground on the Alcan Highway which has just been constructed. KOK would lease the campground for $5,000 per year. It would cost KOK an additional $8,000 to keep the campground open for a summer. 10,000 vehicles pass the campground each summer. The proportion, p, of vehicles which would stop and spend the night is unknown. KOK feels that p will be either .2, .3, or .4. The probabilities of these values are .55, .35, and .10, respectively. Each stopping vehicle would pay the typical KOK overnite rate of $5 per vehicle. Should KOK lease the campground? Set up the profit functions for "Lease" and "Don't Lease" and then use the expectation principle.

3-12. Weiland & Company is developing a new copying machine and must decide on the method of servicing it in the Los Angeles area. Two alternatives are being considered:

a_1: Company Service Center

a_2: Service by Independent Service Company

If Weiland selects a_1, a service office must be established in Los Angeles at an annual cost of $100,000. This figure includes the salaries of office personnel, the service engineers' salaries, and the lease and other overhead expenses. A machine can be repaired at a cost of $20 per machine under this arrangement. If a_2 is selected, Weiland contracts out all of the repair work to an independent service company. The independent company will do the work at an average of $130 per machine. The annual number of repairs required in the Los Angeles area is given by the following distribution:

R	P(R)
800	.4
1000	.3
1200	.2
1400	.1

Which act should be selected?

(a) Determine the cost function for each act.

(b) Find the break-even point.

(c) Select the optimal act using the expectation principle.

3-13. Construct your own utility curve for monetary values from $0 to $40,000.

3-14. A decision maker claims to be indifferent between a_1 and a_2 in each of the following situations. From this information, construct a utility curve for this decision maker.

		a_1	a_2
.75	S_1	$10,000	$20,000
.25	S_2	$80,000	$20,000

		a_1	a_2
.50	S_1	$10,000	$30,000
.50	S_2	$80,000	$30,000

		a_1	a_2
.25	S_1	$10,000	$45,000
.75	S_2	$80,000	$45,000

3-15. A decision maker is facing the following decision matrix.

		a_1	a_2	a_3
.5	S_1	$80,000	$20,000	$18,000
.4	S_2	−10,000	10,000	18,000
.1	S_3	0	90,000	18,000

a_1
a_2

(a) If the decision maker were risk neutral, which act should be selected?
(b) If instead the decision maker had the utility curve below, which act should be selected?

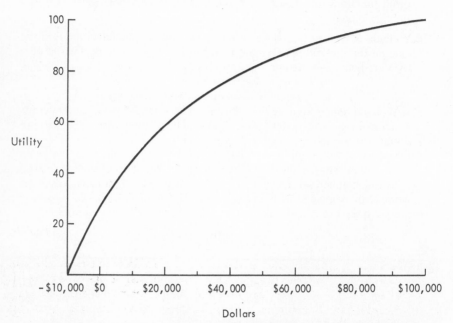

Dollars

3-16. Scott-Seplak Motor Lines has a fleet of 100 trucks which operate in the Chicago area. Two companies have offered to provide tires and emergency tire service for these trucks. Goodmonth will keep the trucks in tires and make emergency repairs for a flat fee of $80,000 per year. Firerock will charge Scott-Seplak according to the formula

$$C = 300 \sqrt{M}$$

where M equals the average annual miles driven per truck. Because of uncertain economic conditions, Scott-Seplak is unsure as to the average mileage of their trucks next year. If M has the following distribution,

M	P(M)
40,000	.2
62,500	.6
90,000	.2

$E(C_1) = 80,000$

$E(C_2) = 75,000$

FIRE ROCK IS OPTIMAL

what is the optimal choice if Scott-Seplak is risk neutral?

3-17. Consider the decision tree below.

a_1 (a) Use backward induction to determine the optimal strategy based on a consideration of monetary payoffs only.

(b) Use backward induction based on utilities if the decision maker has the

a_1 utility curve as given in Problem 3-15.

3-18. An analyst for El Paso Gas is attempting to use a decision tree for the sake of modeling a drilling situation. The tree the analyst has constructed is shown at the top of page 80. Assuming the monetary consequences were also added and assuming that only three states are possible, why is this tree still totally inadequate as a model?

3-19. For the decision tree shown on page 81, (a) find the monetary values for each end position, and (b) find the optimal strategy by using backward induction. a_3

3-20. Poohmer Modules is going to manufacture modular kitchens which can be installed as a single unit by the home builder. Initially Poohmer must decide whether to build a large plant, a_1, or a small plant, a_2. There is a .6 a_1

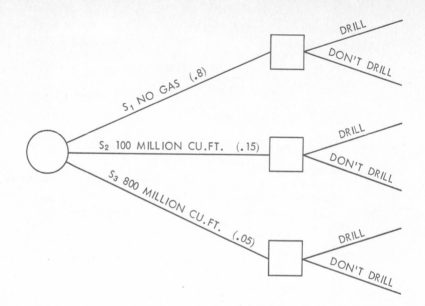

probability that demand for this modular kitchen will be strong and a .4 probability that demand will be weak. If Poohmer has a large plant and demand is strong, a profit of $20 million will result. If demand is weak with a large plant, profits will be $2 million. If the small plant were in operation and demand is weak, Poohmer would make $8 million. If a small plant is in operation and demand is strong, then Poohmer will want to notice the presence of competition. There is a 50–50 chance that competition will exist at that time. If competition exists it would be advantageous for Poohmer to build a separate small plant in another locality. The profit to Poohmer of "Small Plant-Strong Demand-Competition Exists-Separate Plant" would be $12 million. If there were no competition, it would be best to add on to the small plant already in existence. The net profit of "Small Plant-Strong Demand-No Competitition-Add On" is $15 million.

(a) Draw a decision tree for Poohmer.

(b) Use backward induction to determine the optimal strategy.

3-21. Chapman, Inc., produces mass transportation equipment and wishes to enter the European market. Chapman has three initial choices:

a_1: Build equipment in U.S., ship to Europe.

a_2: Build equipment in Europe through a wholly owned subsidiary.

a_3: Build equipment in Europe through a fifty percent owned subsidiary.

If a_1 is selected, Chapman's profits are quite uncertain due to tariffs and European reaction to a U.S. product. There is a .6 probability of a profit of $20 million and a .4 probability of a profit of $0 million. If a_2 is selected, Chapman might receive a very unfavorable tax status; the probability of this is .50 and hence the probability of receiving a favorable tax status under a_2 is also .50. If a_2 is followed by an unfavorable tax status, Chapman will have to sell out to a European investor. There is a 30% chance that

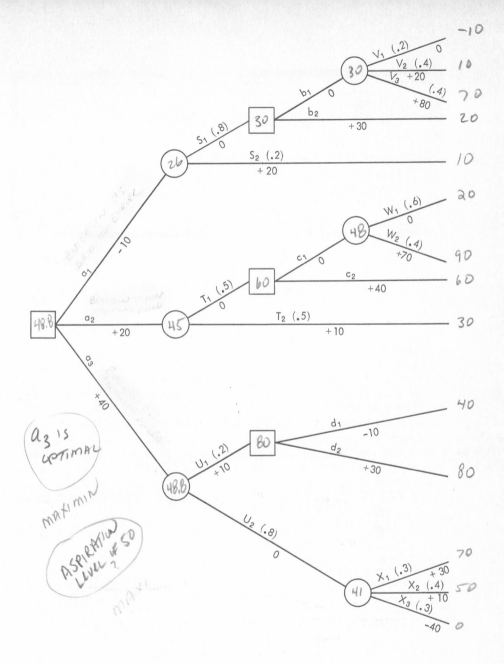

Chapman could sell out at a profit of $5 million and a 70% chance that selling out would result in a loss of $3 million. On the other hand, if a_2 is followed by a favorable tax status, Chapman would make a profit of $30 million. If a_3 were selected initially, the chance of an unfavorable tax status is .1 and Chapman would then make $2 million. If a favorable tax status were achieved after a_3, Chapman would make $10 million. Draw a decision tree and then use backward induction to determine Chapman's optimal strategy.

4 Decision Theory– Additional Information

4.1 INTRODUCTION

In Chapter 3 the construction of a decision model and the subsequent choice of an act were the principal topics of consideration. In this chapter another dimension of decision theory will be explored.[1] A simple illustration will now be given for the sake of introducing this new dimension of decision theory.

The Webbs have just been informed by the obstetrician that a child will be born to them in a few months. Upon hearing the good news, Aunt Sarah offers the Webbs a choice of two gifts. The Webbs may choose either a_1 or a_2 where the decision matrix of Table 4.1 defines these two alternatives or gifts. The Webbs must make a choice within a month. Which alternative should the Webbs select?

Since Aunt Sarah sent the decision matrix in a letter there is no need to construct this model. Furthermore, there is no need to alter this decision matrix as it perfectly depicts the decision situation which the Webbs currently face. All the Webbs have to do is choose either a_1 or a_2. Turning to the expectation principle for guidance, the Webbs find the expected gain for a_1 and a_2 to be

$$E(P_1) = (10,000)(.5) + (0)(.5)$$
$$= \$5,000$$
$$E(P_2) = (0)(.5) + (8,000)(.5)$$
$$= \$4,000$$

Therefore, a_1 should be chosen. The Webbs would then receive \$10,000 if its a girl and \$0 if it's a boy. When questioned regarding this matter, the Webbs readily agreed that a_1 is the better of the two acts. In other words, the Webbs are in agreement with the expectation principle.

---

[1] For a more comprehensive treatment of decision theory, see David Heinze, *Statistical Decision Analysis for Management* (Columbus, Ohio: Grid, Inc., 1973).

TABLE 4.1
The Webbs' Decision Matrix

		a_1	a_2
.5	Girl	$10,000	0
.5	Boy	0	$8,000

In agreeing that a_1 is optimal, however, the Webbs were quick to point out that the choice of a_1 might prove to be a very disappointing choice. Such, of course, would be the case if a boy were born. This caused the Webbs to hestitate in making a choice. Rather than immediately selecting a_1, the Webbs decided to seek additional information which might be of value to them in making their choice. Clearly, the only kind of information that would prove valuable is information concerning the sex of the child. The Webbs returned to the obstetrician and asked if the sex of the child could be determined. The obstetrician replied that she would listen to the fetal heartbeat. She then went on to explain that if the heartbeat is fast, the baby is more likely to be a boy. If it is slow, a girl is more likely.

The Webbs then asked for a more precise answer. The obstetrician then stated: "The probability of the child being male given that it has a fast heart rate is .55, and, the probability of it being male if it has a slow rate is .47." Symbolically these conditional probabilities may be expressed as

$$P(\text{Boy} \mid \text{Fast}) = .55$$
$$P(\text{Boy} \mid \text{Slow}) = .47$$

Given these it follows that

$$P(\text{Girl} \mid \text{Fast}) = .45$$
$$P(\text{Girl} \mid \text{Slow}) = .53$$

The Webbs acknowledged that knowing the fetal heart rate was of some value, but not much.

Before continuing, notice that this extra information (fetal heart rate) if obtained would be reflected by a change in the probabilities of the states. For example, if the obstetrician reported a fast heart rate, then the matrix of Table 4.2 would replace the former decision matrix. The Webbs could then again apply the expectation principle to find the optimal act.

TABLE 4.2
The Webbs' Decision Matrix
After Fast Fetal Heartbeat

		a_1	a_2
.45	Girl	$10,000	0
.55	Boy	0	$8,000

Seeing that the Webbs were unimpressed with the fetal heart rate information, the obstetrician indicated that for $2,000 a sample of amniotic fluid could be taken and analyzed. This analysis would be a perfectly reliable indicator of the sex of the child. That is, if this information were purchased, the Webbs would know with certainty what the sex of the child is.

The possibility of obtaining the amniotic information brings to focus an important aspect of the Webbs' decision situation. Assuming that information (which will change the probabilities of the states) can be purchased for a given price, is it worth it? Most readers would agree that if perfect information regarding the sex could be purchased for $2,000, it would be worth it to the Webbs in view of Aunt Sarah's offer. But, would this perfect information be worth $3,000? $4,000? $5,000? $6,000?

In this chapter the value of information in the context of a decision situation will be considered. It will be possible to determine, for example, the precise value of the amniotic information. After an analysis of the value of information, the technique of formally incorporating additional information into the decision model will be outlined. Decision theory is greatly enhanced as a useful decision making approach if the manager is capable of determining the value of additional information and then is able to formally include additional information in the decision-making process.

4.2 EXPECTED VALUE OF PERFECT INFORMATION

In the last section perfect information regarding the sex of the unborn child could be purchased for $2,000. What is the actual value of such information? In this section the method of determining the value of perfect information will be studied. A business example will be employed for the sake of demonstrating the method of finding the value of perfect information.

Pessner Solar of Colorado has designed a solar heat and electricity system for home use. Pessner has two alternatives for the production of the system. Pessner can manufacture it, a_1, or another company can manufacture the system for Pessner, a_2. In either case Pessner retains the design rights and will market the system. The decision matrix for the Pessner situation is given in Table 4.3.

By means of the expectation principle, Pessner should have the system manufactured by another company, a_2, since

$$E(P_1) = (0)(.5) + (100,000)(.3) + (300,000)(.2)$$
$$= \$90,000$$
$$E(P_2) = (70,000)(.5) + (120,000)(.3) + (170,000)(.2)$$
$$= \$105,000$$

Pessner, though agreeing with the optimality of a_2, is bothered by the possibility of S_3 occurring in which case a_1 would have been a much more desirable choice. Faced with this situation Pessner was reluctant to actually implement a_2. Rather, Pessner wanted to get a clearer picture of sales.

Before summoning a market research firm to conduct a study of sales potential, Pessner wants to know the value of this sort of information. If a market research firm could, for a fee of $50,000, tell Pessner with certainty what state

TABLE 4.3
Pessner's Decision Matrix
(Profits in Thousands of Dollars)

			a_1	a_2
.5	S_1	(Low Sales)	0	70
.3	S_2	(Medium Sales)	100	120
.2	S_3	(High Sales)	300	170

would occur, should Pessner buy the services of the firm? Pessner must have some idea as to the value of such information before negotiating with a market research firm. In particular, Pessner needs to know the expected value of perfect information since the market research firm is offering Pessner perfect information as to which state will occur. If Pessner found the expected value of perfect information to be $26,000, then it would obviously be a mistake to pay $50,000 for such information. On the other hand, if the *EVPI* were $80,000, then Pessner would do well to purchase this information for $50,000. The method of actually determining the *EVPI*, expected value of perfect information, must now be considered.

It has already been seen that Pessner has an expected profit of $105,000 if a_2 is implemented. What could Pessner expect if perfectly reliable information concerning the states would become available? In other words, if a market research firm could conduct a study which would determine with certainty which state would occur, what expected profit would result if Pessner could select an act based on this forthcoming information? If the market research firm concluded that S_1 (Low Sales) would occur, Pessner would select a_2 and reap a profit of $70,000. If the market research firm concluded that S_2 (Medium Sales) would occur, Pessner would again select a_2 and make a profit of $120,000. If instead the market research firm concluded that S_3 (High Sales) would occur, then Pessner would select a_1 and make a profit of $300,000. This is the way Pessner would react to the perfect information which would be forthcoming from the market research firm. Pessner would make either $70,000, $120,000 or $300,000 depending on what the firm found about the market for the solar heat and electricity system.

Now it might be asked what is the probability that the market research firm would conclude with certainty that S_1 will occur? As far as Pessner is concerned, there is a .5 probability that S_1 will in fact occur. Therefore, it could be said that there is a .5 probability that the market research firm will conclude that S_1 will occur. Likewise there is a .30 probability that the firm will conclude that S_2 will occur, and a .20 probability that it would conclude that S_3 will occur. Linking these probabilities with the gains mentioned in the previous paragraph, there is a .5 probability that Pessner would make $70,000, a .3 probability that Pessner would make $120,000, and a .2 probability of making $300,000. This, of course, is assuming that Pessner can act on the basis of the perfect information concerning sales which the market research firm would supply. Therefore the expected profit on the basis of forthcoming perfect information is:

$$\text{EPFPI} = (.5)(70{,}000) + (.3)(120{,}000) + (.2)(300{,}000)$$
$$= \$131{,}000$$

That is, with the services of an infallible market research firm, Pessner has an expected profit of \$131,000. Table 4.4 summarizes the determination of the expected profit on the basis of forthcoming perfect information.

TABLE 4.4
Computing the Expected Profit on the Basis of Forthcoming Perfect Information

Infallible Market Research Firm Concludes:	Probability That M. R. Firm Will So Conclude	Optimal Act on Basis of Perfect Info.	Profit Based on Optimal Act
S_1 (Low Sales)	.5	a_2	\$70,000
S_2 (Medium Sales)	.3	a_2	120,000
S_3 (High Sales)	.2	a_1	300,000

$$\text{EPFPI} = (.5)(70{,}000) + (.3)(120{,}000) + (.2)(300{,}000) = \$131{,}000$$

Recall that Pessner's expected profit using a_2 is \$105,000. With perfect information the expected profit is \$131,000. Therefore, the expected value of perfect information is \$131,000 − \$105,000 or \$26,000. In other words, by using the service of an infallible market research firm, Pessner boosts its expected profit by \$26,000. Hence the expected value of the infallible market research firm's services (which provides perfect information) is \$26,000. Since the *EVPI* is \$26,000, Pessner should pay no more than this for perfect information. (Another method of computing *EVPI* will be given in the next section.)

Hearing that Pessner Solar might be interested in purchasing the services of a market research firm, the firm of Berry & Solomon approached Pessner with an offer to conduct such a study. Berry & Solomon claims that for \$30,000 it can tell Pessner with ninety percent reliability what state will occur. Should Pessner commission Berry & Solomon to make this study? As has just been seen, the expected value of *perfect* information is only \$26,000. Thus, Pessner should not spend \$30,000 to purchase imperfect (though good) information. If instead Berry & Solomon put the price tag at \$20,000 for their ninety percent reliable information, it might be difficult to advise Pessner. There exists a more advanced form of analysis in decision theory which can be used to find the expected value of imperfect information; such an analysis, though not presented here, could be used to determine if \$20,000 were a good price. (For a discussion of the expected value of imperfect or sample information, see the reference footnoted at the beginning of the chapter.) To take one more possibility, suppose Berry & Solomon offered their services for \$5,000. Although Pessner does not know the precise value of this imperfect information, a decision can be made. Knowing that the *EVPI* is \$26,000 and that the imperfect information is very good (ninety percent reliable), Pessner might well surmise that the information is worth more than \$5,000 and therefore Berry & Solomon should be retained. In other words, if perfect information is worth \$26,000, information which is almost perfect should be worth much more than \$5,000 and therefore should be purchased if offered for \$5,000.

In this way a knowledge of *EVPI* can be helpful even in the decision to purchase imperfect information. In no circumstance is a decision maker warranted to spend more than the *EVPI* in the acquisition of additional information. *EVPI* serves to fix an upper bound on all such information gathering expenditures.

4.3 EXPECTED OPPORTUNITY LOSS AND EVPI

In this section an alternate approach to determining the optimal act by the expectation principle will be considered. The advantage of this new method of applying the expectation principle will afterwards be explained.

Suppose a manager is faced with the decision matrix of Table 4.5 where the payoffs are expressed in terms of profits. The expectation principle could be easily applied to find the optimal act:

$$E(P_1) = (80)(.3) + (20)(.4) + (0)(.3) = 32$$
$$E(P_2) = (10)(.3) + (60)(.4) + (60)(.3) = 45$$
$$E(P_3) = (30)(.3) + (-10)(.4) + (90)(.3) = 32$$

Hence a_2 is optimal.

TABLE 4.5
Decision Matrix
(Payoffs in Profits)

		a_1	a_2	a_3
.3	S_1	80	10	30
.4	S_2	20	60	−10
.3	S_3	0	60	90

Another approach, however, is possible which is based on what is known as an opportunity loss table. The nature of an opportunity loss and an opportunity loss table will now be considered. For the moment, assume that the manager of Table 4.5 had selected a_1. If subsequently S_1 occurred, would this manager have any regrets over having selected a_1? No! The manager would make a profit of 80 in such a case; if a_2 had been selected a profit of only 10 would have been made and if a_3 had been selected a profit of only 30 would have been made. Thus, the manager who selects a_1 and finds that S_1 occurs is a manager with no regrets. It is therefore said that the regret or opportunity loss in this situation is 0.

But what if S_2 occurred, would this manager then have any regrets? Having selected a_1 the manager would gain a profit of 20. However, if the manager had instead selected a_2 a gain of 60 could have been achieved. (Notice that 60 is the best payoff that can be achieved if S_2 were to occur.) The difference between the actual gain, 20, and what could have been gained, 60, is the regret or opportunity loss in this situation. Thus, the opportunity loss in this case is 40. Finally, if S_3 instead occurred, would the manager have any regrets? Yes. The manager would regret that a_3 had not been selected. The opportunity loss would be 90 −0 or 90. These opportunity losses for a_1 are recorded in Table 4.6 on page 88.

TABLE 4.6
Opportunity Loss Table

		a_1	a_2	a_3
.3	S_1	0	70	50
.4	S_2	40	0	70
.3	S_3	90	30	0

Now assume that the manager had instead initially selected a_2. If S_1 occurs the manager would regret that a_2 was selected and would wish that a_1 had been selected. Why? 10 is made with a_2 and 80 could have been gained with a_1 assuming S_1 were to occur. Hence the opportunity loss is $80 - 10$ or 70. The opportunity loss is merely the difference between what could have been gained and what was gained. If S_2 occurred, however, the selection of a_2 would result in no regrets as 60 is better than 20 or -10. The opportunity loss is therefore 0. Finally, the opportunity loss if S_3 occurred is 30 which is $90 - 60$.

In the last place, assume that a_3 had been initially selected. If S_1 subsequently occurred there would be a regret or opportunity loss of $80 - 30$ or 50. If S_2 occurred there would be an opportunity loss of $60 - (-10)$ or 70. And, if S_3 occurred there would be no opportunity loss. These opportunity losses are recorded in Table 4.6.

Before proceeding with the use of the opportunity loss table, an analogous method for constructing this table will be presented. If the payoffs in the original decision matrix are gains or profits,

1. Select a row in the decision matrix.

2. Isolate the greatest payoff in the selected row and then enter an opportunity loss of zero in the corresponding position in the opportunity loss table.

3. Subtract each of the other payoffs in the selected row from the greatest payoff (which was isolated in the previous step). This gives the opportunity loss corresponding to each of these payoffs. They should be entered in the opportunity loss table.

4. Repeat steps 1 through 3 for another row.

If the original payoff matrix is expressed in terms of costs, then proceed in an analogous fashion, realizing that the opportunity loss will be zero in the case of the least cost in a row. Regardless of whether the original decision matrix involves profits or costs, opportunity losses are *never* negative numbers. In Table 4.7 a decision matrix is expressed in costs and the corresponding opportunity loss table is given.

Having discussed the method of constructing an opportunity loss table, the use of this table in decision analysis may be considered. The expectation principle may be applied to the opportunity loss table instead of to the original payoff table to find the optimal act. The following theorem is of importance.

The act with the minimum expected opportunity loss is the act with the maximum expected gain (or minimum expected cost), and vice versa.

TABLE 4.7
Cost Matrix and Opportunity Loss Table

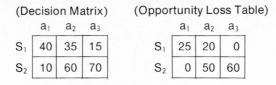

	(Decision Matrix)				(Opportunity Loss Table)		
	a_1	a_2	a_3		a_1	a_2	a_3
S_1	40	35	15	S_1	25	20	0
S_2	10	60	70	S_2	0	50	60

According to this theorem the optimal act may be found by computing the expected opportunity loss, *EOL*, for each act and then selecting the act with the minimum *EOL*. Referring to the example of Tables 4.5 and 4.6, the expected opportunity loss for each of the acts is:

$$EOL_1 = (0)(.3) + (40)(.4) + (90)(.3) = 43$$
$$EOL_2 = (70)(.3) + (0)(.4) + (30)(.3) = 30$$
$$EOL_3 = (50)(.3) + (70)(.4) + (0)(.3) = 43$$

Since a_2 has the minimum expected opportunity loss, it is the optimal act. This is in agreement with the conclusion reached earlier in this section which showed a_2 to be optimal since it had the maximum expected profit of 45.

What is the advantage of using the *EOL* rather than the expected profit in order to determine the optimal act? The advantage is set forth by the following theorem:

> The expected opportunity loss of the optimal act equals the expected value of perfect information.

This means that the *EOL* method of applying the expectation principle kills two birds with one stone. The optimal act is determined and the *EVPI* is automatically found. No further calculations are required to find the *EVPI*. Thus, in the example at hand the *EVPI* is 30 since 30 is the *EOL* of the optimal act, a_2.

In the Pessner Solar example of Table 4.3, it was found that a_2 is optimal and the *EVPI* is \$26,000. This will now be confirmed by the *EOL* approach. The opportunity loss table corresponding to Pessner's decision matrix of Table 4.3 is given in Table 4.8 on page 90. The *EOL* of each act is

$$EOL_1 = (70,000)(.5) + (20,000)(.3) + (0)(.2) = 41,000$$
$$EOL_2 = (0)(.5) + (0)(.3) + (130,000)(.2) = 26,000$$

Since the expected opportunity loss of a_2 is the lesser, a_2 is optimal. Also, the *EVPI* is \$26,000 since this is the *EOL* of this optimal act.

4.4 BAYES' THEOREM

To this point the value of information to the decision maker who is faced with a particular decision situation has been considered. Assuming that information is purchased, how can this information be utilized in the decision-making process? In the introductory section of this chapter it was indicated that the incorporation of new information regarding the states is reflected in a change in

TABLE 4.8
Opportunity Loss Table for Pessner
(In Thousands of Dollars)

		a_1	a_2
.5	S_1	70	0
.3	S_2	20	0
.2	S_3	0	130

the probabilities of the states in the model. In the Webb illustration, the probability of the child being a boy, S_1, was initially .50. If the information that the child had a fast heart rate were then acquired, the probability of S_1 would be revised to .55. Thus, the heartbeat information has an effect on the probabilities of the states and in this manner is introduced into the decision model.

Bayes' Theorem is a law of probability which is often useful in the task of incorporating additional information into the decision-making process. In particular, Bayes' Theorem provides a way of revising or changing the probabilities of the states on the basis of new information that becomes available. Suppose, for example, that in a given decision model there are three states with their three probabilities of $P(S_1)$, $P(S_2)$ and $P(S_3)$. It has already been shown how the manager could use the model which incorporates these probabilities in order to make a decision by some principle of choice like the expectation principle. These initial or original probabilities of the states will be called the prior probabilities. Perhaps the manager now seeks some additional information regarding which state will occur. Let I denote the information that is obtained. This information I will typically alter the prior probabilities. Having obtained I, some of the states might now be more likely and some less likely. The manager could designate these new probabilities which take into account I as $P(S_1|I)$, $P(S_2|I)$, and $P(S_3|I)$. These conditional probabilities are called the posterior probabilities since they are determined *after* and are influenced by the information I which has been obtained. (See Section 2.5 of Chapter 2 for a discussion of conditional probabilities.)

Before seeing how Bayes' Theorem fits into the picture, recall the case of Big Al Conely, the wildcatter of Section 3.3 in the last chapter. Conely's decision matrix is given in Table 3.2. Conely initially concluded that the probabilities of the states are

$$P(S_1) = .90 \qquad \text{where } S_1: \text{No Oil}$$
$$P(S_2) = .08 \qquad \qquad S_2: \text{100,000 bbls. well}$$
$$P(S_3) = .02 \qquad \qquad S_3: \text{500,000 bbls. well}$$

These are the prior probabilities and based on them Conely decided to select a_2 which was to drill with no partner.

It might be, however, that Conely would want to put off a final decision till more information concerning the states could be obtained. Conely could, for example, purchase a seismic test. (In a seismic test an explosive is detonated underground at the potential drilling site and its shock waves are measured at various surrounding locations. By an analysis of the shockwaves, something of the rock formations below can be determined. Certain formations are more likely to hold oil than others.) Suppose that Conely did purchase a seismic test and the test turned out positive, that is, there is a rock formation which is of the oil-bearing variety. Let this information be denoted by I, that is,

I: Positive Seismic Results

With this new information Conely would want to revise his prior probabilities. For example, the revised or posterior probabilities might prove to be something like

$$P(S_1 \mid I) = .83$$
$$P(S_2 \mid I) = .13$$
$$P(S_3 \mid I) = .04$$

These posterior probabilities, which add to one like the priors, would now replace the prior probabilities in Conely's decision model.

Bayes' Theorem is used to blend or combine the prior probabilities of the states with the information I in order to get the posterior probabilities. The mathematical form of Bayes' Theorem when there are three states is

$$P(S_i|I) = \frac{P(I|S_i)\,P(S_i)}{P(I|S_1)\,P(S_1) + P(I|S_2)\,P(S_2) + P(I|S_3)\,P(S_3)}$$

where I is the information obtained, S_i is the ith state, $P(S_i)$ is the prior probability of the ith state, $P(I|S_i)$ is the conditional probability of I given S_i, and $P(S_i|I)$ is the posterior probability of the ith state. The conditional probabilities of the form $P(I|S_i)$ are often called the likelihoods. Bayes' Theorem will now be applied to the Conely situation.

In the Conely case the prior probabilities have already been given. The other ingredients in Bayes' Theorem are the likelihoods. The likelihoods, $P(I|S_i)$, are used to link the information and the states. For example, the following relationships between positive seismic results, I, and the states have been found over years of testing. Of all the wells which have no oil, S_1, forty percent have yielded positive seismic results. Hence,

$$P(I|S_1) = .40$$

Of all the wells drilled in the past which have produced 100,000 bbls. of oil, S_2, seventy percent had positive seismic results.

$$P(I|S_2) = .70$$

Finally, based on past experience, the probability of a 500,000 bbl. well producing positive seismic results is .90, that is,

$$P(I|S_3) = .90$$

These likelihoods show how various types of wells (states) respond to seismic tests. Conely can now use Bayes' Theorem to find the posterior probabilities.

The posterior probability of S_1 based on the fact that Conely's seismic test was positive is

$$P(S_1|I) = \frac{P(I|S_1)\,P(S_1)}{P(I|S_1)\,P(S_1) + P(I|S_2)\,P(S_2) + P(I|S_3)\,P(S_3)}$$

$$= \frac{(.40)(.90)}{(.40)(.90) + (.70)(.08) + (.90)(.02)}$$

$$= .83$$

The posterior probability of S_2 is

$$P(S_2|I) = \frac{(.70)(.08)}{(.40)(.90) + (.70)(.08) + (.90)(.02)}$$

$$= .13$$

Notice that the denominator is the same in each case. The posterior of S_3 is

$$P(S_3|I) = \frac{(.90)(.02)}{(.40)(.90) + (.70)(.08) + (.90)(.02)}$$

$$= \frac{.018}{.434}$$

$$= .04$$

Notice that originally there was a 90 percent chance of no oil but now that the positive seismic reading has been acquired there is only a .83 chance of no oil. Conely should use the posterior probabilities of .83, .13, and .04 instead of the prior probabilities in his decision model. Each of the acts should be evaluated by the expectation principle then to determine the optimal act.

There exists another format for computing the posterior probabilities by means of Bayes' Theorem. This tableau format is shown in Table 4.9. The states are listed in column 1, the prior probabilities are given in column 2, and the likelihoods are given in column 3. From here on the remainder of the columns are based on columns 2 and 3. The entries in column 4 are found by multiplying the corresponding entries of columns 2 and 3. Then these joint probabilities of column 4 are added; in this case their sum is .434. Finally the posterior probabilities are found by dividing each of the joint probabilities by the sum of the joint probabilities. Thus the posterior for S_1 is $.360/.434 = .83$. In like manner each of the other posterior probabilities are found. The same approach can be used whether there are merely two states or whether there are a dozen.

4.5 POSTERIOR ANALYSIS

Earlier in this chapter (see Table 4.3) the case of Pessner Solar was presented. Pessner's optimal act was found to be a_2 since it had an expected profit of $105,000 as compared to $90,000 for a_1. Upon further analysis, the expected value of perfect information proved to be $26,000. The use of *EVPI* in determining the advisability of collecting more information was also discussed. In view of

TABLE 4.9
Finding Posterior Probabilities
by Bayes' Theorem

(1) States S	(2) Prior Probabilities P(S)	(3) Likelihoods P(I|S)	(4) Joint Probabilities P(I,S)	(5) Posterior Probabilities P(S|I)
S_1	.90	.40	.360	.360/.434 = .83
S_2	.08	.70	.056	.056/.434 = .13
S_3	.02	.90	.018	.018/.434 = .04
			.434	

its situation, Pessner decided to seek further information regarding sales. The market research firm of Trebbi & Fritzsche agreed to do a study of potential sales for a fee of $6,000.

Trebbi & Fritzsche offered the following comments concerning the type and reliability of their anticipated market research findings. First of all, the market researchers would come to one of only two conclusions. Trebbi & Fritzsche would either predict "Good Sales" or "Poor Sales." Based on past experience and exposure to Pessner's situation, Trebbi & Fritzsche convinced Pessner of the following. The probability of reaching a "Good Sales" conclusion given that sales would actually be low is .25. If the informational event "Good Sales" were denoted by I_G, this probability could be stated as $P(I_G|S_1) = .25$ since S_1 denotes low sales in the Pessner model. Letting I_P represent the informational event "Poor Sales," it could also be stated that $P(I_P|S_1) = .75$. Next, the probability of predicting "Good Sales" when in fact sales would be medium is .55. This could be stated as $P(I_G|S_2) = .55$. This implies, by the complement law of probability, that $P(I_P|S_2) = .45$. Finally, Trebbi & Fritzsche said that in cases where sales prove to be high, the prediction of "Good Sales" would have been previously made about 85 percent of the time; that is, $P(I_G|S_3) = .85$. This means that $P(I_P|S_3) = .15$.

The conditional probabilities just given are the likelihoods which link the states and the two sorts of informational conclusions. The likelihood $P(I_P|S_3) = .15$, for example, says that in 15 percent of the cases when sales are high, the market research study had concluded that sales would be poor. These likelihoods are necessary to give meaning to the market research conclusions.

With Pessner's approval, Trebbi & Fritzsche begin their study. On the basis of their market research, Trebbi & Fritzsche subsequently make a prediction of "Poor Sales." Pessner, having the likelihoods and the prior probabilities of the states, is now ready to determine the posterior probabilities of the three states.

Using Bayes' Theorem in the tableau format, Pessner computed the posterior probabilities as in Table 4.10 on page 94.

It is seen that the probabilities of the three states are now .69, .25, and .06. Pessner should now replace the prior probabilities of the original decision matrix of Table 4.3 with these posterior probabilities which are based on the market research results. Table 4.11, page 94, gives Pessner's new model.

TABLE 4.10
Finding Posterior Probabilities
for Pessner Solar

States S	Prior Probabilities P(S)	Likelihoods P(I_P|S)	Joint Probabilities P(I_P,S)	Posterior Probabilities P(S|I_P)
S_1: Low	.5	.75	.375	$.375/.54 = .69$
S_2: Medium	.3	.45	.135	$.135/.54 = .25$
S_3: High	.2	.15	.030	$.030/.54 = .06$
			.540	

TABLE 4.11
Pessner Decision Matrix
with Posterior Probabilities
(Profits in Thousands)

		a_1	a_2
.69	S_1	0	70
.25	S_2	100	120
.06	S_3	300	170

Just as was done initially, Pessner should now apply the expectation principle to determine the optimal act. The expected profits for the acts are

$$E(P_1) = (0)(.69) + (100,000)(.25) + (300,000)(.06)$$
$$= \$43,000$$
$$E(P_2) = (70,000)(.69) + (120,000)(.25) + (170,000)(.06)$$
$$= \$88,500$$

Therefore, a_2 is still the optimal act. Pessner, as a result of the market research, is quite sure that S_3 will not occur and thus would proceed to implement a_2 with little reservation. There is not much chance that Pessner will experience the large opportunity loss which will occur if S_3 happens.

This process of computing the posterior probabilities and then using them in the place of the priors to make a decision is called posterior analysis. It should be noted in closing that the decision maker could collect still more information concerning the states. Such an action would be taken in view of the new *EVPI* which would be computed on the basis of the posterior probabilities. If it were economically justifiable to purchase yet additional information, this information would be used to revise the previously obtained posterior probabilities Therefore, a new set of posterior probabilities would be computed where the former posteriors would take the place of the prior probabilities in Bayes' Theorem.

PROBLEMS

4-1. For the decision situation which follows where the payoffs are given in terms of profits,

		a₁	a₂	a₃
.1	S_1	70	90	20
.3	S_2	10	−20	0
.6	S_3	30	80	50

$E(P)$ 28 51 32

(handwritten table, headers a_1 a_2 a_3)

a_1	a_2	a_3
20	0	70
0	30	10
50	0	30

EOL 32   9   28

(a) Find the expected profit for each act and the optimal act.
(b) Construct an opportunity loss table.
(c) Find the expected opportunity loss for each act and thereby select the optimal act.
(d) Determine the *EVPI*. 9

4-2. For the decision situation which follows where the payoffs are given in terms of costs,

		a₁	a₂	a₃	a₄
.4	S_1	400	200	100	500
.3	S_2	400	900	300	500
.3	S_3	400	600	700	400

$E(C)$ 400   530   340   470

(handwritten table, headers a_1 a_2 a_3 a_4)

a_1	a_2	a_3	a_4
300	100	0	400
100	600	0	200
0	200	300	0

150   280   90   220

(a) Find the expected cost for each act and the optimal act.
(b) Construct an opportunity loss table.
(c) Find the *EOL* for each act and thereby select the optimal act.
(d) Determine the *EVPI*. 90

(handwritten, right margin) OL: A_1 A_2
45 | 0 | 10,500
8,00 | 0

4-3. For the example of the Webbs as given in Section 4.1, find the *EVPI*. What is the maximum that the Webbs should be willing to pay for the amniotic information after a fast fetal heart beat has been detected? *EVPI $4,400*

4-4. There are three states in a manager's decision model with prior probabilities of $P(S_1) = .2$, $P(S_2) = .1$, and $P(S_3) = .7$. Information I has been obtained. If $P(I|S_1) = .3$, $P(I|S_2) = .4$, and $P(I|S_3) = .5$, find the posterior probabilities of the three states.

4-5. The Connecticut Rubin Insurance Company has found that ten percent of the applicants for auto insurance are poor drivers, S_1, and ninety percent are good drivers, S_2. Of all the poor drivers, thirty percent have received a speeding ticket. Of all the good drivers, five percent have had a speeding ticket. An applicant for auto insurance has just appeared. *$P(T|P)=.3$ $P(T|G)=.1$ $P(P)=.1$*
(a) What is the probability that the applicant is a poor driver? a good driver? *.9 = $P(G)$*
(b) If it is subsequently learned that the applicant has received a speeding ticket, what is the probability that the applicant is a poor driver? a good driver? *.4, .6*
(c) If instead it were found that the applicant had never received a speeding ticket, what is the probability that the applicant is a poor driver? a good driver? *.08 .92*

4-6. Stevenson Sterling is engaged in silver plating. With a certain process, 98 percent of the items plated are perfect and 2 percent have plating defects. Stevenson has an inspection station where each newly plated item is scanned. Of perfect items, ten percent get diverted to the rejection bin. Of all the imperfect items (defectives), ninety-nine percent get diverted to the rejection bin.

$P(P) = .98$
$P(D) = .02$ $P(R'|P)=.9$
$P(R|P)=.1$
$P(R|D)=.99$ $P(R'|D)=.01$

	$P(S)$	$P(R\|S)$	$P(R,S)$	$P(S\|R)$		$P(R'\|S)$	$P(R',S)$	$P(S\|R')$
P	.98	.1	.098	.33		.9	.8820	.9998
D	.02	.99	.198	.67		.01	.0002	.0002
			.296					

$P(P\|R) = .33$
$P(D\|R) = .67$
$P(P\|R') = .9998$
$P(D\|R') = .0002$

(a) Of all the items in the rejection bin, what proportion are defective and what proportion are perfect? (Use Bayes' Theorem in the tableau format)

(b) Of all the items which do not get rejected, what proportion are defective and what proportion are perfect?

4-7. Ten percent of the people entering a new car showroom are seriously interested in purchasing a new car. A salesperson, seeking to identify the serious customer, has made the following observation. In the past, of all those who have purchased a new car, 80 percent drove up in a recently washed used car (probably the customer wanted the used car spruced up in order to get the top trade-in dollar). Only 40 percent of the non-serious customers drove up in recently washed used cars. A person has just arrived at the new car showroom. What is the probability that the person is a serious customer if that person's car has been recently washed?

$P(S\|W) = \dfrac{P(S) = .08}{.08 + .36}$

4-8. A marketing manager faces the new product decision as described in the decision matrix below.

		a_1 Introduce Product	a_2 Don't Introduce
.5	High Sales	1,000	0
.5	Low Sales	−800	0

(a) Find the optimal act.

a_1

(b) How much should the marketing manager be willing to spend for the sake of acquiring perfect information concerning sales?

$500 - 100 = 400$

(c) Before making a final decision, the marketing manager test markets the product. The test market results are eighty percent reliable, that is,

$P(\text{Test Market says High} \mid \text{High Sales}) = .80$
$P(\text{Test Market says Low} \mid \text{High Sales}) = .20$
$P(\text{Test Market says High} \mid \text{Low Sales}) = .20$
$P(\text{Test Market says Low} \mid \text{Low Sales}) = .80$

The test market actually indicated that sales would be low. Find the posterior probabilities of the two states. Then determine the optimal act.

$P(S)$
$S \quad P(L\|S) \qquad P(S\|L)$
$H \quad .5 \quad .2 \qquad .1 \qquad .2$
$L \quad .5 \quad .8 \qquad .4 \qquad .8$

4-9. The owner of the Chicago White Sox must decide between

a_1: No stadium improvements
a_2: Minor stadium improvements
a_3: Major stadium improvements

The decision matrix facing the owner has the states of

S_1: Bad season
S_2: Mediocre season
S_3: Winning season

The probabilities of these states occurring are based on the manager's feelings about the team in the upcoming year. The resulting decision matrix in terms of profits is

		a_1	a_2	a_3
.3	S_1	10	5	0
.5	S_2	15	15	10
.2	S_3	30	40	60

(handwritten)

$P(s)$	$P(z\|s)$	$P(s)P(z\|s)$	$P(s\|z)$
.3	.1	.03	.1
.5	.3	.15	.5
.2	.6	.12	.4
		.30	

(a) What act is optimal?

(b) What is the *EVPI*?

(c) The owner puts off the decision till spring training has begun. The White Sox win their first five spring training games. Looking over past records, the owner noticed that of the times the White Sox had a bad season, they had done well in spring training about <u>ten percent</u> of the time. When the team proved to have a mediocre season, <u>thirty percent</u> of the previous spring performances were good. When the team had a winning season, <u>sixty percent</u> of the spring performances had been good. Incorporate the information in the decision making process that the White Sox are having a good spring performance. Based on the posterior probabilities, which act is optimal?

4-10. Thornburg Packing is faced with a decision situation where the price of beef next year is of critical importance. In forty percent of recent years beef prices have been relatively high, and in sixty percent of the years low prices have prevailed. The decision matrix for Thornburg is (payoff in profits)

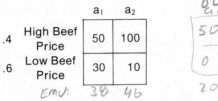

		a_1	a_2
.4	High Beef Price	50	100
.6	Low Beef Price	30	10

EMV: 38 46

(handwritten)

OL

	a_1	a_2
	50	0
	0	20
	20	12

EVPI = 12

Before making a decision Thornburg wishes to seek more information concerning next year's beef prices.

(a) What is the most that Thornburg should pay for perfect information concerning beef prices?

(b) Thornburg believes that the number of young cattle grazing in open land might be a valuable indicator of subsequent beef prices. Thornburg finds that during those years when prices were high, in 80 percent of the preceeding years there were few young cattle in open lands. Also, *P*(Few Cattle in open lands | Low prices a year later) = .3. Thornburg has just found that there are many young cattle grazing in open lands. Based on this information, what are the posterior probabilities and what is the optimal act?

(handwritten)

	$P(s)$	$P(many\|s)$	$P(many, s)$	$P(s\|many)$
HIGH PRICE S_1	.4	.2	.08	.16
LOW PRICE S_2	.6	.7	.42	.84
			.5	

5 Monte Carlo Simulation

5.1 INTRODUCTION

Simulation is a method of analyzing a system by experimentally duplicating its behavior. The aeronautical engineer seeking to evaluate the performance of a new wing constructs a model of the wing and then experiments with the model wing in a wind tunnel. In the wind tunnel the engineer duplicates the performance of the wing through a series of experiments on the model. By simulating the behavior of the wing in the wind tunnel, the engineer is able to make inferences about the performance of a real wing of the proposed design.

In like manner, the management scientist may be able to make meaningful inferences concerning the operation of some real world system by constructing a model of the system and then experimenting with the model. If the model is an adequate representation of the real system, a study of the responses of the model to various decisions will give considerable insight into the effects of implementing such decisions in the real system.

There are numerous forms of simulation or types of simulation techniques. The type of simulation which will be discussed and utilized in this text is *Monte Carlo simulation.* In Monte Carlo simulation the behavior of at least some components of the model are probabilistically determined. With the presentation of examples beginning in the next section, the nature of Monte Carlo simulation will become apparent.

Simulation techniques are of value to the manager in solving certain problems which are not easily solved by a so-called analytic mathematical technique. In succeeding chapters, methods of making decisions on the basis of the mathematical analysis of models will be studied. It may be, however, that the real world situation is so complex that such mathematical analysis becomes too difficult. In these cases the simulation approach may provide an alternative mode of analysis. In the study of inventory models, for example, analytic mathematical techniques will be used to make decisions in simple real world situations.

However, Monte Carlo simulation will be used in a more complicated inventory management situation. Likewise, Monte Carlo simulation will be employed in the queueing chapter and in the chapter concerned with replacement models.

5.2 RANDOM NUMBER TABLE

Suppose a bag contains ten identical chips. On one chip a zero is then imprinted, a 1 is imprinted on the second, a 2 on the third, ..., and a 9 is imprinted on the tenth chip. Now the chips are returned to the bag and mixed. You then begin the following process:

1. Reach into the bag with eyes closed and take one chip out.
2. Record the number imprinted on the chip.
3. Return the chip to the bag and mix well. Then go to step 1 and repeat.

In following this procedure a collection or table of random numbers could be generated. The first ten numbers in the table might be, for example, 0, 3, 2, 1, 4, 0, 3, 6, 9, and 8. Roughly speaking, there would be about as many one's in a large table of random numbers as there are zero's or eight's or three's or .... Furthermore, there would be no patterns evident in the table. For example, low numbers would not typically be followed by high numbers and even numbers would not be typically followed by odd numbers. A table of random numbers is given in the Appendix.

The use of randomly generated numbers is central to the process of Monte Carlo simulation. A series of examples will now be given which demonstrate how these random numbers are used in the simulation of some phenomenon or system. It will be seen that a sequence of numbers is taken from a table of random numbers in every Monte Carlo simulation. It should be noted that these numbers can be selected according to any fixed selection procedure. For example, the successive numbers in a row could be used, or every other number in a row could be used, or every fourth number in a column or on a diagonal could be used.

5.3 TWO ELEMENTARY EXAMPLES OF SIMULATION

Suppose you wished to determine the results of simultaneously tossing ten coins on the floor. You find, however, that you have no coins. With nothing but a table of random numbers, how could you simulate the simultaneous tossing of ten coins? Let the odd numbers, 1, 3, 5, 7, and 9, represent "Heads" and the evens, 0, 2, 4, 6, and 8, represent "Tails." For any *one* coin, $P(\text{Heads}) = .5$ and $P(\text{Tails}) = .5$. Also, if a random number were selected from a table of random numbers, $P(\text{Odd Number}) = .5$ and $P(\text{Even Number}) = .5$. Because the probability of "Heads" and "Odd Number" are identical, and the probability of the events "Tails" and "Even Number" are identical, selecting ten numbers from a random number table and recording each as being "Odd' or "Even" is just like tossing ten coins and recording each as being "Heads" or "Tails." Since tossing coins and selecting numbers from a table of random numbers can be viewed as being probabilistically identical, select ten numbers from the table of random numbers instead of tossing ten coins simultaneously. Assume the ten numbers as chosen from Table 1 in the Appendix are

$$6, 4, 0, 9, 3, 1, 1, 7, 2, 7$$

These ten are

$$\text{Even, Even, Even, Odd, Odd, Odd, Odd, Odd, Even, Odd}$$

Since "Odd" represents "Heads" and "Even" represents "Tails," this simulation trial yields

$$\text{T, T, T, H, H, H, H, H, T, H}$$

One toss of ten coins has therefore been simulated.

Of course there is no reason why "Heads" should always be associated with odd numbers and "Tails" with even numbers. Instead the correspondence could be

Event	Random Numbers
Heads	$0 - 4$
Tails	$5 - 9$

Then if the following numbers were taken from the random number table,

$$1, 8, 9, 8, 3, 2, 8, 3, 9, 2$$

the simulated result would be

$$\text{H, T, T, T, H, H, T, H, T, H}$$

Table 5.1 gives the results of four more simulation trials of the tossing of ten coins. The last two columns in Table 5.1 are used to summarize the simulated results.

TABLE 5.1
Simulating the Toss of Ten Coins

Event	Random Numbers
Heads	$0 - 4$
Tails	$5 - 9$

Simulation Trial	Random Numbers	Simulated Result	Number of Heads	Number of Tails
1	1898328392	HTTTHHTHTH	5	5
2	6147133175	THHTHHHHTT	6	4
3	4742255591	HTHHHTTTTH	5	5
4	2413381724	HHHHHTHTHH	8	2
5	6725369995	TTHTHTTTTT	2	8

A slightly more complex Monte Carlo simulation will now be conducted. Conovaloff Electronics has received a shipment of cathode ray tubes from a new supplier. Unwilling to accept the shipment without testing it, Conovaloff has proceeded to sample and test several tubes from the shipment. As a result of the test there is a .20 probability that the shipment is of high quality, a .50 probability it is of fair quality, and a .30 probability it is of poor quality. Conovaloff must decide between

> a_1: Accept the shipment.
> a_2: Reject the shipment and reorder
> from another supplier.

The decision matrix of Table 5.2 presents the payoffs in costs to Conovaloff. What should Conovaloff do?

TABLE 5.2
Conovaloff Electronics
Decision Matrix

		a_1	a_2
.2	S_1: High Quality	10	60
.5	S_2: Fair Quality	40	60
.3	S_3: Low Quality	90	60

This problem is easily solved by the analytic or mathematical technique of decision theory. The expected cost for a_1 is

$$E(C_1) = (10)(.2) + (40)(.5) + (90)(.3)$$
$$= 49$$

and the expected cost for a_2 is 60. Thus, the optimal act is a_1 by the expectation principle.

A simulation approach to the solution of this problem is comparatively cumbersome. However, for instructional purposes the simulation approach will be presented. The element of chance in the Conovaloff situation pertains to the quality of the shipment of cathode ray tubes. As seen in Table 5.2, there is a .20 probability of the shipment being "High Quality." When selecting a number from a table of random numbers there is a .20 probability of getting a 0 or 1. Getting a 0 or 1 in a table of random numbers could therefore represent, in a simulation, the occurrence of a high quality shipment. This is because

$$P(\text{High Quality}) = .2 = P(0 \text{ or } 1)$$

In like manner, let "Fair Quality" be represented by the numbers 2, 3, 4, 5, and 6 since

$$P(\text{Fair Quality}) = .5 = P(2 \text{ or } 3 \text{ or } 4 \text{ or } 5 \text{ or } 6)$$

Finally, let "Low Quality" be represented in the simulation by the numbers 7, 8, and 9.

A simulation work sheet is now constructed in Table 5.3; this work sheet will be used to display the simulation of the arrival of ten successive shipments of cathode ray tubes. Column 1 identifies these shipments. In Column 2 single digit random numbers are recorded; they are taken from a table of random numbers according to some fixed selection scheme. In Column 3 the state or quality of the shipment, corresponding to each random number, is given. Column 4 gives the cost if a_1 had been the selected act; these costs are based on the decision matrix of Table 5.2. Finally, Column 5 gives the cost with a_2; the cost is always 60 regardless of the quality of the shipment.

TABLE 5.3
Conovaloff Simulation

	State	Random Numbers		
	High Quality	$0-1$		
	Fair Quality	$2-6$		
	Low Quality	$7-9$		

(1)	(2)	(3)	(4)	(5)
	Random		Cost if	Cost if
Shipment	Number	Quality	a_1	a_2
1	3	Fair	40	60
2	5	Fair	40	60
3	3	Fair	40	60
4	1	High	10	60
5	7	Low	90	60
6	1	High	10	60
7	3	Fair	40	60
8	3	Fair	40	60
9	5	Fair	40	60
10	2	High	90	60
		AVERAGE:	44	60

For the first simulated shipment, the random number is 3, which represents a fair quality shipment. The quality of the shipment is recorded in Column 3. Such a shipment will yield a cost of 40 if a_1 had been selected. The cost would have been 60 if a_2 instead had been implemented. For the second shipment, the random number is 5. Since 5 represents a fair quality shipment, this fact is stated in Column 3. With a_1 a fair quality shipment yields a cost of 40; this cost is recorded in Column 4. The cost if a_2 had been used is 60 as shown in Column 5. This process is repeated ten times in Table 5.3 which represents ten simulation trials.

What conclusion can be drawn from the simulation of Table 5.3? On the basis of the ten trials the average cost per shipment under a_1 is 44 which is better than the average of 60 per shipment under a_2. Therefore, one might be inclined to conclude that a_1 is optimal. Though this is the correct approach to evaluate a_1 and a_2, a conclusion should not be drawn till many more shipments have been simulated. It is easy to be misled by the results of a simulation with an insufficient number of trials. Another hundred simulation trials were performed for the Conovaloff case. On the basis of this relatively reliable simulation, the average cost for a_1 was 49.4 and that for a_2 was 60. These results demonstrate that a_1 is optimal. In the last section of this chapter the problem of determining an adequate number of simulation trials will be considered. Till then attention will be centered on setting up simulation work sheets and conducting simulations.

5.4 PACKAGE DELIVERY SIMULATION

Greypooch Bus Lines has claimed it can offer exceptionally fast delivery on small packages to be shipped within the region east of the Mississippi. Table 5.4, page 104, gives the probability distribution for delivery time in days which Greypooch offers. There is a .3 probability that a package would arrive within 1 day (24 hours), a .6 probability that a package would get to its destination in 2 days, and a .10 chance it would arrive in 3 days. Also the delivery times for air freight are given in Table 5.4. For example, fifty percent of the packages shipped via air freight arrive in a day. From this information, what is the probability that a package shipped by air freight would arrive at its destination before a package shipped by Greypooch?

Though this problem could easily be solved mathematically through probability theory, a simulation approach will be used. First, random numbers must be assigned to each event. Since the probability of 1-day service with Greypooch is .3, a set of random numbers with a .3 probability of occurring must be specified to represent this event. Therefore, let the numbers 0, 1, and 2 represent the event of 1-day delivery with Greypooch. Notice that

P(1-day delivery with Greypooch) $= .3$
P(0 or 1 or 2 from table of random numbers) $= .3$

Random numbers are assigned in Table 5.4 to each of the other delivery times for Greypooch. In the simulation to follow, if a random number from 3 through 8 comes up, this would represent a 2-day delivery time. If 9 comes up, this would mean the package took 3 days.

In like manner random numbers are assigned for the air freight delivery times. If a random number from 5 through 7 appeared, for example, then the air freight delivery time would be 2 days for simulation purposes.

Ten "races" between a package shipped by Greypooch versus a package shipped by air freight will not be simulated. The simulation work sheet of Table 5.4 will be used. First, use the table of random numbers in the Appendix to fill up the two columns of random numbers in the work sheet. These random numbers are enclosed in parentheses. The first race may now begin.

One package is delivered to the Greypooch station and one is delivered to the air freight terminal. The Greypooch package takes 3 days since the random number is 9. The random number for air freight is 0 which means that the air freight package arrived in 1 day. Therefore air freight wins the first race. In the second race (see the second row in the work sheet) the Greypooch package takes 2 days because the random number is 4 and the air freight package takes 1 day because the corresponding random number is 2; therefore, air freight wins again. Eight more races are then simulated in the work sheet.

TABLE 5.4
Greypooch vs. Air Freight Simulation

Distribution of Greypooch Delivery Times in Days			Distribution of Air Freight Delivery Times in Days		
Days	Probability	RN	Days	Probability	RN
1	.3	(0–2)	1	.5	(0–4)
2	.6	(3–8)	2	.3	(5–7)
3	.1	(9)	3	.2	(8–9)

Simulation Work Sheet

Race	Greypooch (RN)	Greypooch Delivery Time	Air Freight (RN)	Air Freight Delivery Time	Air Freight Wins	Air Freight Ties	Air Freight Loses
1	(9)	3	(0)	1	Win		
2	(4)	2	(2)	1	Win		
3	(7)	2	(8)	3			Lose
4	(2)	1	(3)	1		Tie	
5	(3)	2	(5)	2		Tie	
6	(5)	2	(5)	2		Tie	
7	(8)	2	(3)	1	Win		
8	(5)	2	(0)	1	Win		
9	(9)	3	(7)	2	Win		
10	(4)	2	(9)	3			Lose

Although ten simulation trials are not enough, a conclusion will nevertheless be drawn in order to demonstrate how the results of such a simulation might be used. Since the air freight package arrived sooner (win) on five of the ten occasions, it could be concluded that fifty percent of the time, air freight packages would arrive before Greypooch packages. In other words, a conclusion is reached on the basis of the observed frequencies in the simulation work sheet. If the work sheet of Table 5.4 had been extended to simulate several hundred races, the proportion of air freight wins would come close to .38. This is the true proportion of wins which can be determined through probability theory.

5.5 AMBULANCE SIMULATION

The Ambulator Ambulance Company is seeking to evaluate alternative locations for its new ambulance station. A map of the metropolitan area served by Ambulator is given in Figure 5.1. The metropolitan area has been divided into four distinct zones; the hospital is located in Zone 4. One possible site for the ambulance station is adjacent to the hospital in Zone 4. This site is marked on the map.

Of critical importance in the selection of a site is the quality of service made possible by ambulances originating at the site. In particular, Ambulator must select a site which keeps the total time, from the receipt of a patient call to the delivery of the patient to the hospital, to a minimum. The ambulance station site in Zone 4 will now be examined by Monte Carlo simulation.

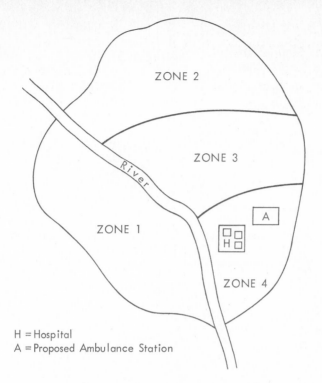

ZONE 2

ZONE 3

River

A

H

ZONE 1

ZONE 4

H = Hospital
A = Proposed Ambulance Station

FIGURE 5.1   Metropolitan Area Map

Quite obviously there are a number of factors which will influence how long it takes to get a patient to the hospital from the time a call is received requesting an ambulance. In this analysis only three factors which influence the total time will be considered. They are: (1) the location of the patient who requires the ambulance, (2) the traffic density, and (3) the problems of getting the patient into the ambulance. Consider for a moment how each of these factors will influence the total time in getting the patient to the hospital.

If the patient is at a great distance, say Zone 2, it will typically take more time for the ambulance to make the round trip from the station to the patient and back to the hospital. Also, if the call comes at rush hour the ambulance will typically be slowed by the heavy traffic. Finally, the condition of the patient will influence the amount of time it takes to get the patient into the ambulance. If the patient is located on the twentieth floor of a large apartment building, or is pinned under a wrecked automobile it will take longer to get the patient into the ambulance.

Ambulator has collected a good bit of information concerning these three factors and has constructed several probability distributions which describe various possibilities. Consider probability distribution II in Table 5.5, page 106. This distribution describes the origin or location of patients who call for an ambulance. It is seen that 20 percent of the calls come from patients in Zone 1, 30 percent from Zone 2, 35 percent from Zone 3, and 15 percent from Zone 4. In

TABLE 5.5
Ambulance Simulation
Probability Distributions

<table>
<tr><th colspan="3">II
Location of Call</th><th colspan="3">III
Traffic Density</th></tr>
<tr><th>Zone</th><th>Probability</th><th>(RN)</th><th>Density</th><th>Probability</th><th>(RN)</th></tr>
<tr><td>1</td><td>.20</td><td>(00–19)</td><td>Light</td><td>.3</td><td>(0–2)</td></tr>
<tr><td>2</td><td>.30</td><td>(20–49)</td><td>Moderate</td><td>.5</td><td>(3–7)</td></tr>
<tr><td>3</td><td>.35</td><td>(50–84)</td><td>Heavy</td><td>.2</td><td>(8–9)</td></tr>
<tr><td>4</td><td>.15</td><td>(85–99)</td><td></td><td></td><td></td></tr>
</table>

IV
One-way Travel Times from Ambulance Station
to Patient

LIGHT TRAFFIC

					Zone				
Time	1	(RN)	2	(RN)	3	(RN)	4	(RN)
10 min.	.1	(0)	0	—	.2	(0–1)	.8	(0–7)
20	.8	(1–8)	.4	(0–3)	.6	(2–7)	.2	(8–9)
30	.1	(9)	.6	(4–9)	.2	(8–9)	0	—

MODERATE TRAFFIC

					Zone				
Time	1	(RN)	2	(RN)	3	(RN)	4	(RN)
10	.1	(0)	0	—	.2	(0–1)	.6	(0–5)
20	.7	(1–7)	.3	(0–2)	.5	(2–6)	.4	(6–9)
30	.2	(8–9)	.7	(3–9)	.3	(7–9)	0	—

HEAVY TRAFFIC

					Zone				
Time	1	(RN)	2	(RN)	3	(RN)	4	(RN)
10	0	—	0	—	.1	(0)	.5	(0–4)
20	.6	(0–5)	.2	(0–1)	.5	(1–5)	.5	(5–9)
30	.4	(6–9)	.8	(2–9)	.4	(6–9)	0	—

V
Time at Patient's Location

Time	Probability	(RN)
5	.5	(0–4)
10	.5	(5–9)

order to simulate the origin of a call, random numbers have been attached to each zone according to the probability for that zone. Since the probability of Zone 1 is .20, the random numbers 00—19 have been assigned. When taking a two-digit number from a random number table, there is a probability of exactly .20 that the two-digit number will be from 00 through 19. Thus 00–19 adequately represents Zone 1. In a like manner, two-digit numbers have been assigned to each other zone according to their probabilities.

Probability distribution III indicates the traffic density. There is, for example, a .3 probability that a call comes when light traffic conditions prevail. Single-digit random numbers are assigned to each traffic density according to the probabilities. The numbers 0, 1, and 2, for example, represent light traffic. Notice that

$$P(0 \text{ or } 1 \text{ or } 2) = .3 = P(\text{Light Traffic})$$

The probability distributions under IV give one-way travel times in minutes. There is a set of distributions for each of the three types of traffic conditions. Suppose a call comes from Zone 1 when light traffic prevails, how long will it take the ambulance to get to the patient? Find the probability distribution for light traffic and under that for Zone 1. From this particular distribution it is seen that there is a .1 probability that it would take 10 minutes, a .8 probability that it would take 20 minutes, and a .1 probability that it would take 30 minutes to get to the patient.

Notice that the appropriate random numbers are assigned to each of these times according to the respective probabilities. Suppose instead a call comes from Zone 3 during heavy traffic. How long will it take for the ambulance to get to the patient? You should be able to confirm that there is a .1 probability that it would take 10 minutes, a .5 probability that it would take 20 minutes, and a .4 probability that it would take 30 minutes.

Finally, probability distribution V shows the time it would take to get the patient into the ambulance once the ambulance has arrived. There is a .5 probability it would take 5 minutes and a .5 probability it would take 10 minutes. Notice again that appropriate random numbers have been attached to each of these events.

Now the simulation work sheet must be constructed. Table 5.6, page 108, presents a work sheet for the Ambulator case. Take a moment to read the column headings of this work sheet. The entries which will occur in columns II through V will be determined by chance according to the probability distributions of Table 5.5. The best way to understand the work sheet is to begin the actual simulation process.

Ten calls for the ambulance will be simulated; therefore, ten rows in the work sheet will be required. It is a good idea to initially enter ten random numbers under each of columns II, III, IV, and V; this will make it possible to avoid the constant turning to the Appendix. Notice that two-digit random numbers are entered in column II, in parentheses, and single-digit random numbers are required in the other columns. The two-digit number is needed in column II because of the random number assignments made in probability distribution II of Table 5.5.

Having entered all the random numbers for ten simulation trials, the simulation process may begin. Consider the first call for an ambulance. The random number in column II is 04 which when compared to probability distribution II in Table 5.5 reveals that this patient is located in Zone 1. Therefore, enter a 1

TABLE 5.6
Ambulance Simulation Work Sheet

I	II		III		IV		V		VI	VII
	Origin of Call		Traffic Density		Travel Time to Patient		Time at Patient's Location		Travel Time to Hospital	Total Time
Call	(RN)	Zone	(RN)	Density	(RN)	Time	(RN)	Time		
1	(04)	1	(2)	Light	(5)	20	(3)	5	20	45
2	(77)	3	(5)	Moderate	(2)	20	(7)	10	20	50
3	(89)	4	(6)	Moderate	(1)	10	(2)	5	10	25
4	(30)	2	(9)	Heavy	(4)	30	(1)	5	30	65
5	(48)	2	(6)	Moderate	(1)	20	(1)	5	20	45
6	(51)	3	(2)	Light	(6)	20	(6)	10	20	50
7	(13)	1	(2)	Light	(8)	20	(7)	10	20	50
8	(52)	3	(6)	Moderate	(0)	10	(9)	10	10	30
9	(87)		(9)		(0)		(0)			25
10	(14)		(0)		(5)		(3)			45
									Average:	43

under column II in the work sheet. The random number 2 in column III represents the traffic density. Looking at probability distribution III in Table 5.5 reveals that traffic is light since the random number 2 has previously been associated with light traffic. Enter "Light" under column III. How long will it take for the ambulance to get to this patient in Zone 1 if light traffic prevails? The random number in column IV is 5, which when compared to the distribution under IV in Table 5.5 reveals that the time is 20 minutes. (Notice that for light traffic with a destination of Zone 1, the random numbers from 1 through 8 correspond to 20 minutes.) Therefore, enter a 20 under column IV. How long will it take to get the patient into the ambulance? The random number of 3 in column V when compared to probability distribution V reveals that it takes 5 minutes. Therefore, enter a 5 under column V in the work sheet. How long will it take to return to the hospital? Since the ambulance station is adjacent to the hospital, it will be assumed that the return trip takes the same time as the trip out, or 20 minutes. Enter a 20 under column VI. The entry in column VI will always be the same as that in column IV. Finally, the total time is computed by adding the entries of columns IV, V, and VI. For the first call the total time is 20 + 5 + 20 or 45 minutes.

Before going further, the reader should confirm the entries in the work sheet for at least the next two calls. Also, the reader should use the random numbers as supplied for the ninth and tenth calls to confirm that in these two cases the total times are 25 and 45 minutes, respectively.

What conclusions can Ambulator draw concerning the ambulance station site in Zone 4? Because there are only ten simulation trials, any conclusions drawn would be unreliable. More calls should be simulated. Nevertheless, the simulation results as they appear in Table 5.6 will be used to illustrate the method of analysis which would follow a simulation involving many trials.

By averaging the total times of column VII, it appears that the average total time when the station site adjacent to the hospital is used is 43 minutes. Some probabilistic statements could also be made based on the times in column VII. For example, in nine out of ten calls the total time was 50 minutes or less. Therefore, one might conclude that there is a .90 probability that the total time would be 50 minutes or less. Again remember that such a statement is unreliable because of the small number of simulation trials.

How can this type of simulation analysis be used to help Ambulator select a site? The same type of simulation could be conducted for a proposed site in Zone 3, for example. Then the average total time for this site in Zone 3 could analogously be computed or the probability of the total time being 50 minutes or less could be determined. With this information Ambulator could determine which of the two sites is better. It might be, for instance, that the site in Zone 3 has a slightly lower average total time, but the time savings is not great enough to offset the advantage of having the station located near the hospital in Zone 4. Following the general type of simulation procedure outlined, Ambulator could also simulate the results of having two stations, one in Zone 4 and one somewhere else. In this manner Ambulator can use Monte Carlo simulation for the sake of making decisions.

5.6 RISK ANALYSIS SIMULATION

Greek Inc. is contemplating the introduction of a sophisticated, computer-augmented X-ray unit. Before making a final decision, Greek Inc. wishes to determine the various possible profit consequences of such an action. The chief financial officer for Greek has constructed the following equation which expresses the profit for this project

$$P = \left[S - (C_m + C_s)\right] mI - F$$

where

P = profit
S = selling price
C_m = manufacturing cost per unit
C_s = selling cost per unit
I = total industry sales of this type of equipment
m = Greek's market share
F = fixed costs

Each of the variables in this profit equation is a random variable with its own probability distribution.

The selling price, S, of the equipment will be either $10,000, $11,000, or $12,000. The selling price will largely be dictated by the prices established by other competitors who sell similar equipment. The probability distribution for these prices is given in Table 5.7. The probability distributions for C_m, C_s, and F are also given in Table 5.7. The total industry sales, I, for this type of equipment are anticipated to be either 10,000 or 12,000 units. If $I = 10,000$, Greek's market share will be .20, .30, or .40 with probabilities of .4, .4, and .2, respectively. If $I = 12,000$, m will be .20, .30, or .40 with probabilities .3, .5, and .2 respectively. These conditional distributions of m are also shown in Table 5.7 as is the distribution of I.

In the face of this uncertainty or risk with regard to the variables, what kind of profit might Greek experience if such equipment is manufactured? Through Monte Carlo simulation Greek can obtain a description of possible profits. Consider the simulation work sheet of Table 5.8, page 112. Each of the variables comprising the profit equation appears in a separate column. Ten single-digit random numbers are placed in each of the first six columns. By comparing these random numbers to the distributions of Table 5.7, values for the variables can be determined.

Consider the first simulation trial which is represented by the first row in the work sheet. The first random number is 5 which when compared to the selling price distribution of Table 5.7 reveals that the selling price is $S = \$11,000$. The second random number, 6, means that the manufacturing cost per unit is $C_m = \$5,000$. The third random number, 8, means that the selling cost per unit is $C_s = \$2,000$. The fourth random number, 8, indicates total industry sales to be $I = 12,000$ units. The fifth random number, 9, must be compared to the conditional distribution for m where I equals 12,000. The resulting market share is .40 or 40

TABLE 5.7
Probability Distributions
for Greek's Risk Analysis

Selling Price

S	P(S)	RN
$10,000	.3	(0–2)
11,000	.5	(3–7)
12,000	.2	(8–9)

Manufacturing Cost per Unit

C_m	$P(C_m)$	RN
$4,000	.4	(0–3)
5,000	.6	(4–9)

Total Industry Sales

I	P(I)	RN
10,000 units	.5	(0–4)
12,000	.5	(5–9)

Selling Cost per Unit

C_s	$P(C_s)$	RN
$1,000	.4	(0–3)
2,000	.6	(4–9)

Market Share if I = 10,000

m	P(m‖I = 10,000)	RN
.20	.4	(0–3)
.30	.4	(4–7)
.40	.2	(8–9)

Fixed Costs

F	P(F)	RN
$6,000,000	.3	(0–2)
8,000,000	.5	(3–7)
10,000,000	.2	(8–9)

Market Share if I = 12,000

m	P(m‖I = 12,000)	RN
.20	.3	(0–2)
.30	.5	(3–7)
.40	.2	(8–9)

percent. Finally, fixed costs are F = $8,000,000 since the random number is 7. Using the financial officer's profit equation,

$$P = \left[S - (C_m + C_s)\right] mI - F$$

the profit for the first simulation trial may be computed

$$P = \left[11,000 - (5,000 + 2,000)\right](.40)(12,000) - 8,000,000$$
$$= \$11.2 \text{ million}$$

In like manner nine more trials are simulated in the work sheet. The simulated profits could be averaged for the sake of estimating Greek's expected profit from the project. This type of simulation gives another sort of valuable information. Greek can determine the range of profits that might be experienced. In Figure 5.2 on page 113 a frequency distribution of profits based on fifty simulation trials is shown. From this frequency distribution Greek can draw a variety of conclusions. For example, the expected profit can be estimated by finding the average profit from the frequency distribution. As reviewed in Section 2.2 of Chapter 2, the mean or average of grouped data is

$$\text{Average} = \frac{\Sigma(\text{Class Frequency})(\text{Class Midpoint})}{\text{Total Number of Observations}}$$

TABLE 5.8
Greek's Simulation Work Sheet

Selling Price per Unit (RN)	S	Manufacturing Cost per Unit (RN)	C_m	Selling Cost Per Unit (RN)	C_s	Industry Sales (RN)	I	Market Share (RN)	m	(RN)	Fixed Costs F	Profit $[S-(C_m+C_s)]mI-F$ P	Trial
(5)	$11,000	(6)	$5,000	(8)	$2,000	(8)	12,000	(9)	.40	(7)	$8,000,000	$11.2 million	1
(0)	10,000	(2)	4,000	(5)	2,000	(7)	12,000	(4)	.30	(5)	8,000,000	6.4	2
(3)	11,000	(1)	4,000	(5)	2,000	(4)	10,000	(1)	.20	(4)	8,000,000	2.0	3
(2)	10,000	(8)	5,000	(5)	2,000	(0)	10,000	(1)	.20	(6)	8,000,000	−2.0	4
(6)	11,000	(3)	4,000	(2)	1,000	(9)	12,000	(6)	.30	(2)	6,000,000	15.6	5
(7)	11,000	(1)	4,000	(4)	2,000	(4)	10,000	(6)	.30	(7)	8,000,000	7.0	6
(3)	11,000	(2)	4,000	(2)	1,000	(9)	12,000	(7)	.30	(5)	8,000,000	13.6	7
(8)		(0)		(2)		(4)		(3)		(8)		4.0	8
(7)		(5)		(2)		(1)		(8)		(3)		12.0	9
(0)		(2)		(9)		(3)		(5)		(9)		2.0	10

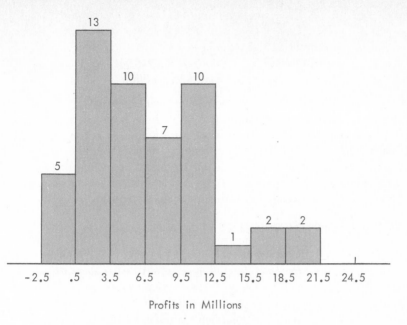

CHAPTER 5

FIGURE 5.2   Frequency Distribution of Profits
(Greek's Simulation)

Therefore, from Figure 5.2 the expected or average profit is

$$\text{Expected Profit} = \frac{(5)(-1 \text{ million}) + (13)(2 \text{ million}) + \dots + (2)(20 \text{ million})}{50}$$

$$= \$6.5 \text{ million}$$

If Greek's decision maker had a nonlinear utility function, the expected utility instead of the expected profit could be determined. The utilities of each of the possible profit figures represented by the class midpoints (namely, −$1 million, $2 million, …, and $20 million) would first be determined by using the utility curve. (See Sections 3.7 and 3.8 of Chapter 3 for a discussion of utility.) Suppose, for example, that $U(-\$1 \text{ million}) = 0$, $U(\$2 \text{ million}) = 400$, …, and $U(\$20 \text{ million}) = 1000$. Then the expected utility of the proposed project would be:

$$\text{Expected Utility} = \frac{(5)(0) + (13)(400) + \dots + (2)(1000)}{50}$$

or,

$$E(U) = (5/50)(0) + (13/50)(400) + \dots + (2/50)(1000)$$

In this manner, then, utility analysis may be incorporated.

Also from Figure 5.2 certain probabilistic estimates can be made. For example, since in 5 cases out of 50 trials the profit was $.5 million or less, one might conclude that with the implementation of the project Greek has a probability of 5/50 that profit will fall below $.5 million. Some other probabilistic statements are:

$$P(\text{Profit} \leq \$3.5 \text{ million}) = 18/50$$
$$P(\text{Profit} \leq \$12.5 \text{ million}) = 45/50$$
$$P(\$.5 \text{ million} \leq \text{Profit} \leq \$12.5 \text{ million}) = 40/50$$

Thus, by Monte Carlo simulation a manager can construct a probabilistic profile of the outcomes of some project. In such analyses risk is not suppressed (as would be the case if the market share, for example, were fixed at 30%, I fixed at 10,000 units, etc), but rather is expressed in its effect on profit. This analytic method, called risk analysis, is a valuable method of assessing the consequences of alternative projects. Simulation makes risk analysis relatively simple, thereby making this approach readily available to the decision maker.

5.7 THE COMPUTER AND STATISTICS

The situations that have been simulated in this chapter were on a scale which permitted a non-computerized approach. In each example a simulation trial could be conducted by hand calculations in a short amount of time. If an analyst were required to conduct even a hundred trials, the time required would not be great even though the task would quickly become boring. Many Monte Carlo simulation models, however, are quite complex and it would take considerable time to conduct the simulation by hand. In these cases the computer is most helpful.

By means of the computer an analyst can execute many simulation trials for even complex models in a relatively short time. There are a number of computer programming languages which have been specifically designed for Monte Carlo simulation. Among these are *SIMSCRIPT, GPSS,* and *GASP.* With these languages the analyst is able to instruct the computer to perform simulation trials. The results of the simulation can then be summarized on the computer printout.

In the examples given in this chapter the matter of determining an adequate number of simulation trials has been frequently noted. How many simulation trials should be conducted in order to get reliable conclusions? There is no magic number which can be given in answer to this question. The answer depends on the degree of reliability desired, the type of information needed, and the amount of variability in the simulation results from trial to trial.

The simulation results, such as the profit figures in the work sheet of Table 5.8, should be viewed as sample data taken from the output of the simulated system. Since this is a random sample, statistical techniques should be used to interpret the reliability of the results. Likewise, statistical methods should be used for the sake of determining an adequate number of simulation trials just as statistics are used to determine sample size when sampling from a population. Typically speaking, the problem of finding an adequate number of simulation trials is not a difficult problem. However, since the purpose of this text is neither to present nor review statistics, this problem will not be further discussed. In subsequent chapters where Monte Carlo simulation is used for the sake of managerial decision making, the emphasis will be on the construction of a simulation model and the implementation of several trials. No attempt will be made to present the statistical details of determining an adequate number of simulation trials. Furthermore, the simulations will be conducted by hand rather than by computer.

PROBLEMS

5-1. Using random numbers from Table 1 in the Appendix,
- (a) Simulate ten more races between Greypooch and air freight. See Table 5.4.
- (b) Simulate five more ambulance calls. See Tables 5.5 and 5.6.
- (c) Simulate three more profit results in the Greek risk analysis case. See Tables 5.7 and 5.8.

5-2. The profit that Meo Farms will make this season is given by the following profit function:

$$P = 20X - F + R/B$$

where X measures produce prices, F is fixed costs, R is rainfall, and B measures bug infestation. If these variables have the following distributions, simulate five seasons for the sake of determining profits for Meo Farms.

X	P(X)	F	P(F)	R	P(R)	B	P(B)
.40	.3	10	.6	30	.4	0.5	.6
.50	.5	15	.4	40	.4	1.0	.3
.60	.2			50	.2	2.0	.1

5-3. An instructor has constructed a twenty-question, multiple-choice test with five choices for each question. If a student were to randomly select answers, how many questions would be answered correctly? Simulate five times.

5-4. The firm of SBC-DCH is building a dam which requires the completion of three major activities: Foundation, Concrete, and Electrical. The last two activities may be performed simultaneously and cannot begin till the Foundation is completed. The diagram below pictures the situation.

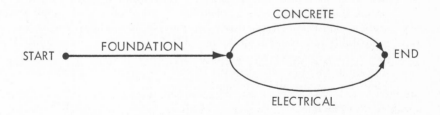

If the following distributions give the time in months to complete each of these major activities, simulate ten dam constructions in order to ascertain the total project time for the dam. (Average the total times from the ten trials.)

Foundation		Concrete		Electrical	
Time	Probability	Time	Probability	Time	Probability
5	.3	9	.2	8	.3
6	.4	10	.4	10	.4
7	.2	11	.3	12	.3
8	.1	12	.1		

Note that if the foundation took 6 months, the concrete 10 months, and the electrical 8 months, the total project time would be 6 + 10 or 16 months.

5-5. Each batter for the N.Y. Yankees has the first probability distribution below and each batter for the Cleveland Indians has the second. Simulate one nine-inning game. (Assume that there are no double-plays, sacrifice outs, etc.)

New York Yankees' Batter		Cleveland Indians' Batter	
Outcome	Probability	Outcome	Probability
Out	.70	Out	.65
Single	.20	Single	.25
Double	.04	Double	.08
Triple	.01	Triple	0
Home Run	.05	Home Run	.02

5-6. Wyatt Inc., Casey Ltd., and Byrd Co. are three independent electrical contractors who typically bid for jobs in Southern Arizona. The bidding behavior for an upcoming Fort Huachuca job may be described by the following distributions:

Wyatt		Casey		Byrd	
Bid	P(Bid)	Bid	P(Bid)	Bid	P(Bid)
$40,000	.2	$38,000	.4	$39,000	.3
45,000	.3	43,000	.4	44,000	.4
50,000	.5	48,000	.2	49,000	.3

Simulate ten bidding competitions. What proportion of the time did Casey get the contract?

5-7. The racing route at Monte Carlo is given on page 117. The route is divided into three stretches: I, II, and III. The time it takes to get through a stretch varies and is given by the probability distribution below. There are two traffic lights as shown; if a driver hits a red light 5 minutes will be lost. The probability of a traffic light being red is .5. There is a .3 probability that a racer will experience tire failure during a lap; if this occurs an additional 15 minutes will be added to the racer's time. A race consists of five laps. Simulate one race and give the racer's total time.

Stretch I		Stretch II		Stretch III	
Time	P(Time)	Time	P(Time)	Time	P(Time)
40 min.	.3	90 min.	.1	60 min.	.2
50	.5	100	.4	70	.4
60	.2	110	.3	80	.4
		120	.2		

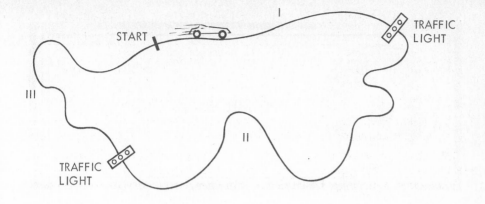

START

I

TRAFFIC
LIGHT

III

II

TRAFFIC
LIGHT

6 Inventory Models

6.1 INTRODUCTION

Management science has made a significant contribution toward better decision making in the area of inventory policy. Inventories consist of resources such as raw materials, partially completed products, and finished goods which are temporarily idle. Retail stores hold inventories in order to supply immediately the goods which are demanded by their customers, since a delay in satisfying customer demand would result in a loss of goodwill and perhaps the loss of sales. In manufacturing, if the product produced has a strong seasonal sales pattern, inventories must be held by the company if it wishes to operate with a fairly constant production rate. For example, Kodak experiences substantial film sales in the summer months and in December; in order to keep a stable labor force large inventories must be accumulated during the winter months and early spring as well as during the fall. If inventories were not so used, the labor force would have to be increased and subsequently decreased with changes in sales, and this would entail all sorts of difficulties.

For an organization faced with a fairly constant demand rate there is an incentive to carry inventories beyond that of immediately satisfying customer demand. Acquisition costs may be minimized if larger purchases are made from the manufacturer or wholesaler in that paper work and handling are reduced by making fewer purchases. Furthermore, quantity discounts are sometimes available to the buyer willing to place a large order. Whereas there are benefits in carrying inventories, there are also costs associated with inventories. The product or material held in inventory requires storage space, it may need to be insured, deterioration and spoilage may take place, and funds which could be invested elsewhere are tied up in this asset called inventory. It is the purpose of this chapter to construct models which are useful in inventory management decision making. These models and the strategies which are based on them will take into account the diverse effects and costs associated with maintaining inventories.

6.2 A SIMPLE DETERMINISTIC INVENTORY MODEL

Consider the situation where a company periodically acquires a shipment of some item to be held in inventory until demanded. Let the following costs be defined:

C_a = Acquisition cost per order
C_h = Holding cost per unit of inventory per unit of time

Typically, the *acquisition cost* per order is the cost of placing an order and then processing the paper work which goes along with the receipt of the order or shipment. If the supplier charges a fixed fee for filling an order regardless of its size, this also would be an acquisition cost. The *holding cost* per unit of inventory held over a unit of time includes storage and insurance costs. Often the most significant holding cost is an opportunity cost associated with the amount of money that is invested in the inventory. The money invested in inventory could have been invested in a government security where it would gain interest income. This foregone interest income can be considered as a "cost" of investing money in inventory and thus a holding cost.

A company which orders often will have high yearly aquisition costs but low holding costs as only a small inventory is maintained which is frequently being replenished. At the other extreme, a company which places a few large orders will have low yearly acquisition costs while annual holding costs will be relatively high. In both cases the frequency of ordering is inversely related to the size of the order placed. The goal of inventory management is to find a strategy which minimizes the total of acquisition plus holding costs. As depicted in Figure 6.1, $n°$ is the optimal number of orders to be placed annually if total costs are to be minimized.

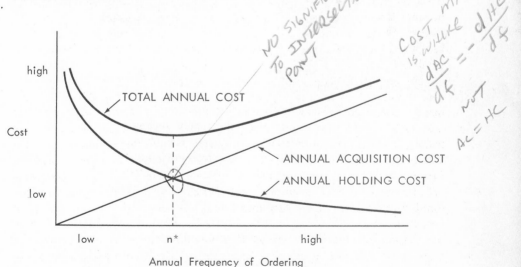

FIGURE 6.1   Inventory Costs

Consider an example where a policy of a low annual frequency of ordering is contrasted with a policy of a high annual frequency of ordering. In the first case, suppose a company places an order only twice a year. If the aquisition cost per order is $50, then the annual acquisition cost will be $100. The company, however, will have a high average inventory level because the orders it receives will necessarily have to be large. Assume that the annual holding cost is $500. This means that the total annual cost will be $100 + $500 or $600 for this company which follows a policy of ordering infrequently. If, on the other hand, the company placed smaller monthly orders, then the annual acquisition cost would be $50 times 12 or $600. The annual holding costs, because of the low level of inventory carried, might be only $200. Hence the total annual cost would be $600 + $200 or $800. Considering *only* these two strategies, the two orders per year policy is better. However, a strategy where orders are placed quarterly, for example, might produce the lowest total annual cost. In Figure 6.1 the quarterly ordering might be represented by $n°$ (i.e., $n° = 4$ per year); then the first case cited above would correspond to a "low" annual frequency of ordering and the second would correspond to a "high" ordering frequency. Both of these would yield a higher total annual cost than $n°$. This is apparent from the total annual cost curve of Figure 6.1 which is at its minimum value above $n°$.

In Figure 6.1 the acquisition cost line is linear because it is assumed that the cost to process an order is constant, therefore if one order costs $50 to process, ten will cost $500 and fifteen will cost $750. The annual holding cost line declines because more frequent ordering permits smaller orders and hence smaller average inventories. Small inventories imply small holding costs.

A simple inventory situation will now be studied where a company orders a quantity of some product. When the shipment of the product arrives it is held in inventory till sold. When the product has been sold it is replaced by a new shipment which is also eventually sold. In this situation answers to the following questions will be sought: How large should the orders be? When should orders be placed? What is the cost of maintaining the inventory? In order to answer these questions an inventory model will be employed.

To facilitate the construction of an inventory model, consider Figure 6.2 and the following definitions. Let

M = Maximum level of inventory
Q = Size of the order or shipment received
t_0 = Time of the receipt of an order or shipment, also the time when inventory is at its maximum level.
t_1 = Time of the receipt of the second order, also the time when the inventory has been reduced to zero.
D = Rate of demand per unit of time.

The company, for example a retailer, receives a shipment of items at time t_0. The size or quantity of the shipment is Q items, which brings the level of inventory items to its maximum level of M. As time passes customers purchase or

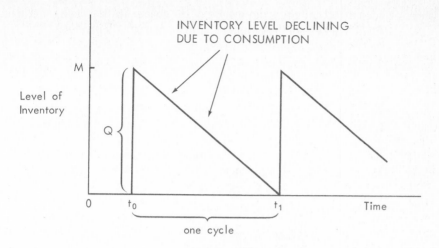

FIGURE 6.2   Inventory Level

consume the items held in inventory at a rate of D units per unit of time, steadily decreasing the quantity of product held in inventory. At time t_1 all the items have been sold and a new shipment of size Q arrives to replenish the stock bringing the inventory level to its maximum again. This process will now be illustrated.

As the aspen in the Colorado Rockies turn to hues of yellow, Dan Brooks and the recluse Howard Hues steal into the darkness of the Moffat Tunnel. Brooks is running the Rocky Mountain Coal Co. of Denver which supplies coal to residents of Denver and the nearby inhabitants of the old mining camps just west of Denver. Hues, the owner of Rocky Mountain Coal, used the cloak of darkness to direct Brooks toward more effort in the matter of inventory management. Though the necessity for such secrecy in the issuance of this directive was beyond Brooks, he immediately hurried back to Denver to formulate plans for stocking coal for this winter's demand.

The circumstances surrounding Rocky Mountain Coal Company's coal inventory problem are relatively simple. Brooks initially considered the annual cost of maintaining a ton of coal in inventory. RMCC has a special agreement with the Denver-Rio Grande Railroad whereby the railroad, which delivers the coal, will store the coal on some of its property along a siding. Denver-Rio Grande charges RMCC $1 to store a ton of coal for a year on this property. RMCC buys the coal for $20 per ton; therefore, if a ton of coal is kept in inventory for a year, Brooks does not have the use of the $20 invested in that ton. What could be done with the $20? Brooks could invest it in high grade bonds which yield 10 percent interest per annum, hence Brooks is foregoing the opportunity to make $2 interest on the money tied up in each ton for a year. These, storage and interest, are the only costs which can be considered holding costs. Thus, $C_h = \$3$ per ton per year. Acquisition costs amount to $C_a = \$140$ per order of coal. This includes the expense of telegraphing the order to Rocky Mountain Coal Company's supplier, $8, the cost of the associated paper work and the time involved in documenting the receipt of the coal at the rail siding, $32, and paying a fee of $100 which the supplier charges as a coal order handling fee.

In order to design an optimal inventory policy for Rocky Mountain Coal Company, return to a consideration of Figure 6.2. One inventory cycle, from shipment to shipment, has a length of $t_1 - t_0$ units of time. At the start of the cycle when the shipment of size Q arrives, the inventory level is M; M in this case equals Q. The inventory level then uniformly declines to 0 by the end of the cycle. This means that the average amount of product stored in inventory is $M/2$ over any cycle. The total holding cost over an inventory cycle may easily be found if the average inventory level for the cycle, $M/2$, is known and if the length of the cycle is known. Since the span of a cycle is $t_1 - t_0$ units of time and since the holding cost has been defined to be C_h per unit of inventory held over a unit of time, the total holding cost over one cycle is

$$\text{Total holding cost over one inventory cycle} = C_h(M/2)(t_1 - t_0) \tag{6-1}$$

For example, if the holding cost is $C_h = \$.25$ per ton per month, and if an inventory cycle lasts for 5 months, and if the average inventory level is 200 tons, then the total holding cost over an inventory cycle is $(\$.25)(200)(5) = \$250$.

Since there is only one acquisition cost associated with each cycle, the total inventory cost for a cycle will equal the sum of the acquisition cost and the total holding cost over the cycle, or

$$C_{total} = C_a + C_h(M/2)(t_1 - t_0) \tag{6-2}$$

As an inventory cycle covers a period of $t_1 - t_0$ units of time, the average inventory cost per unit of time will be

$$C_{avg} = C_{total}/(t_1 - t_0) \tag{6-3}$$
$$= \frac{C_a + C_h(M/2)(t_1 - t_0)}{(t_1 - t_0)} \tag{6-4}$$

It is now desirable to express Equation 6–4 in a different, yet equivalent, form. To do this first notice that

$$t_1 - t_0 = M/D$$

where M is the total amount of inventory at the beginning of a cycle, D is the amount demanded per unit of time, and $t_1 - t_0$ is the number of units of time in a cycle. The truth of this relationship may be seen by the following example. Suppose the amount of inventory at the beginning of a cycle is $M = 100$ units and that customers demand the product at a rate of $D = 20$ units per month. How long will an inventory cycle last under these circumstances? Quite obviously a cycle will last M/D months or $100/20 = 5$ months. Therefore $t_1 - t_0$, which is the length of a cycle, is 5 months or M/D. Since M/D is equivalent to $t_1 - t_0$, M/D may then be substituted for $t_1 - t_0$ in Equation 6–4 thereby yielding an alternate expression for the average inventory cost per unit of time:

$$C_{\text{avg}} = \frac{C_a + C_h(M/2)(M/D)}{(M/D)} \tag{6-5}$$

It has already been noted that in this inventory situation the maximum inventory level M equals Q which is the size of the order. By substituting Q for M in Equation 6–5 and simplifying, another expression for C_{avg} is derived:

$$C_{\text{avg}} = \frac{C_a + C_h(Q/2)(Q/D)}{(Q/D)}$$
$$= [C_a + C_h(Q/2)(Q/D)][D/Q]$$
$$C_{\text{avg}} = C_a(D/Q) + C_h(Q/2) \tag{6-6}$$

The expression for the average inventory cost per unit of time as given in Equation 6–6 can be interpreted as follows. D/Q represents the number of acquisitions per unit of time. For example, if $D = 20$ units per month and $Q = 100$ units, then there is an average of $20/100$ or $.2$ acquisitions per month. Multiplying D/Q by the acquisition cost per order yields $C_a(D/Q)$ which gives the average acquisition cost per unit of time (e.g., per month). $Q/2$, which is the same as $M/2$, is the average inventory level per unit of time. Thus $C_h(Q/2)$ gives the average holding cost per unit of time. When $C_a(D/Q)$ and $C_h(Q/2)$ are added, the result is the total average cost per unit of time.

Having constructed a model of average inventory costs, it is the immediate objective to develop an optimal inventory management strategy. In particular, the order size Q which will yield the minimal average inventory cost, C_{avg}, is sought. This resultant minimal cost of maintaining the inventory will shortly be determined and in a later section the timing of orders will be considered (see Section 6.5).

In a given situation C_h as well as C_a will be known and the rate of demand D will be known, therefore determining the optimal order size is solely a matter of selecting the value of Q which will minimize C_{avg} as given in Equation 6–6. This optimal value of Q will be denoted by Q°. How can this Q° be found which makes possible the lowest C_{avg}? One approach uses systematic trial-and-error, that is, try an assortment of Q values in Equation 6–6 computing the C_{avg} of each. Then try some more Q values in the region of the one which initially yielded the lowest C_{avg}. Following such an approach the Q yielding the minimum C_{avg} can be isolated. This approach will be illustrated later in this section. A quicker and more accurate technique to find Q° is to use the differential calculus. Through the application of differential calculus[1] the optimal order size

---

[1] In order to find that value of Q which minimizes C_{avg}, where $C_{\text{avg}} = C_a(D/Q) + C_h(Q/2)$, take the first derivative of C_{avg} with respect to Q:

$$\frac{dC_{\text{avg}}}{dQ} = -C_a(D/Q^2) + \frac{C_h}{2}$$

Set this equal to zero and solve for Q:

$$0 = -C_a(D/Q^2) + \frac{C_h}{2}$$
$$0 = -DC_a + Q^2\left(\frac{C_h}{2}\right)$$
$$Q^2 = 2DC_a/C_h$$
$$Q = \sqrt{2DC_a/C_h}$$

has been determined to be

$$Q^\circ = \sqrt{2DC_a/C_h} \tag{6-7}$$

This Q° in turn yields the minimum average inventory cost of

$$C_{avg}^\circ = C_h(Q^\circ/2) + C_a(D/Q^\circ) \tag{6-8}$$

Equation 6–8 is found by merely replacing Q with Q° in Equation 6–6. An equivalent expression for C_{avg}° which may be easier to compute is

$$C_{avg}^\circ = \sqrt{2DC_aC_h} \tag{6-9}$$

Finally, the length of the inventory cycle where Q° items are stocked will be

$$t_1 - t_0 = Q^\circ/D \tag{6-10}$$

Returning to the Rocky Mountain Coal Company example, it has already been stated that

$$C_a = \$140 \text{ per order}$$
$$C_h = \$\ \ 3 \text{ per year per ton.}$$

Before going further let holding costs be stated on a monthly basis, that is,

$$C_h = \$.25 \text{ per month per ton}$$

since Brooks wishes to use the month as a unit of time. From past records Brooks determines that the average coal demanded in the winter is 2,000 tons per month, or

$$D = 2,000 \text{ tons per month}$$

How much coal should Rocky Mountain Coal Company order each inventory cycle in order to achieve the minimum average inventory costs? First, the systematic trial-and-error technique will be utilized to answer this question. Table 6.1 computes the average cost per month C_{avg}, for orders of $Q = 500$, 1000, 1500, 2000, and 4000 tons. Of the Q values tried, $Q = 1500$ yields the lowest average inventory cost per month. With the data of Table 6.1 plotted in Figure 6.3 it is apparent that the C_{avg} line has the same shape as the total cost line of Figure 6.1. Furthermore it appears that the optimal order size will be close to 1500. As the next step in the systematic trial-and-error technique, several other values of Q around 1500 might be tried to see if any would reduce the average cost. In this manner Q° could be isolated.

TABLE 6.1
Order Sizes and Average Inventory Costs

Order Size, Q	Average Cost, C_{avg}
500	$622
1000	405
1500	374
2000	390
4000	570

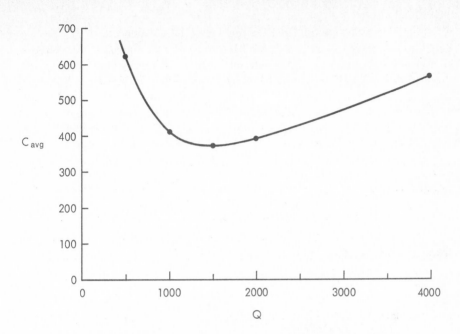

FIGURE 6.3   Order Sizes and Average Inventory Costs

Instead of pursuing the trial-and-error approach, it is possible to apply Equations 6–7, 6–9 and 6–10 to find $Q°$, $C_{avg}°$, and t_1-t_0.

$$Q° = \sqrt{2DC_a/C_h}$$
$$= \sqrt{2(2000)(140)/.25} = 1497 \text{ tons}$$

Having determined the optimal order size, the average cost of a policy utilizing this order size of 1497 tons will be

$$C_{avg}° = \sqrt{2DC_aC_h}$$
$$= \sqrt{2(2000)(140)(.25)} = \$374 \text{ per month.}$$

and the inventory cycle will last

$$t_1-t_0 = Q°/D$$
$$= 1497/2000 = .75 \text{ months}$$

With these values Brooks is on his way to an optimal inventory management policy. Nevertheless, some other aspects of this situation must still be explored.

6.3 SENSITIVITY ANALYSIS

It is often quite difficult to ascertain the exact values for C_a and C_h, the acquisition and holding costs. The relative sizes of these variables are extremely important to the determination of $Q°$. It is therefore advisable to see how sensitive $Q°$ and in turn $C_{avg}°$ are to differing values for C_a and C_h.

In the Rocky Mountain Coal Company case Brooks concedes that C_a is not necessarily \$140 but could vary from \$120 to \$160 even though \$140 is still his best estimate. Regarding C_h, the interest rates on high grade bonds are not always 10 percent and for that matter why shouldn't the interest rate of medium grade bonds be used instead? Also the Denver-Rio Grande occasionally gives Rocky Mountain Coal some other services beside coal storage for \$1 per ton per year. Brooks therefore sees C_h as varying between \$2.60 to \$3.40 per ton per year, or from \$.22 to \$.28 per month per ton. Table 6–2 gives the optimal order size Q° and the ensuing average cost C_{avg}° for the extreme combinations of C_a and C_h within the ranges specified by Brooks. For example, if C_h were \$.22 and C_a were \$120, then

$$Q^\circ = \sqrt{2(2000)(120)/.22} = 1477 \text{ tons}$$
$$C_{avg}^\circ = \sqrt{2(2000)(120)(.22)} = \$325 \text{ per month}$$

The average cost could also have been computed using Equation 6–8, that is

$$C_{avg}^\circ = C_h(Q^\circ/2) + C_a(D/Q^\circ)$$
$$= .22(1477/2) + 120(2000/1477) = \$325$$

TABLE 6.2
Sensitivity Analysis

C_a	C_h	Q^*	C_{avg}^* (Based on Q^*)	C_{avg} (Based on Q = 1497)
120	.22	1477	325	325
120	.28	1309	367	370
160	.22	1706	375	378
160	.28	1512	423	423

It has just been shown what Brooks should do if $C_a = \$120$ and $C_h = \$.22$. He should order $Q^\circ = 1477$ tons and this strategy will yield an average monthly cost of \$325. But what if Brooks had acted as if $C_a = \$140$ and $C_h = \$.25$ as *originally* specified? He would have then stocked 1497 tons, that is, he would have ordered 20 tons too many by assuming the original acquisition and holding costs were valid when in fact they are not. Ordering 1497 tons in the situation where in reality $C_h = \$.22$ and $C_a = \$120$ would yield an average cost of

$$C_{avg} = C_h(Q/2) + C_a(D/Q)$$
$$= .22(1497/2) + 120(2000/1497)$$
$$= \$325 \text{ per month}$$

The average cost is the same (after rounding) as the average cost under a policy of $Q^\circ = 1477$, therefore the average cost in this situation is not sensitive to the error in Q. Ordering 1497 tons when 1477 should be ordered has no discernable effect on costs.

In Table 6.2 the numbers in the last column are the average costs under the prevailing conditions if Brooks had ordered 1497 tons as suggested under the original assumptions concerning C_a and C_h. It is clear that these average costs of the last column do no deviate very much from the optimal average costs given in the C_{avg}° column, thus Brooks can implement orders of 1497 without worrying about pinpointing C_a and C_h. C_{avg}° is not very sensitive to changes in C_a and C_h of the magnitude Brooks has considered.

6.4 QUANTITY DISCOUNTS

In the inventory situation which has been studied the supplier did not offer the purchaser any sort of price discount if the purchase was of considerable size. In the Rocky Mountain Coal example the supplier did not offer to reduce the $20 a ton price if Rocky Mountain Coal would place an exceptionally large order for coal. Although there are many cases where quantity discounts are not available, it is not unusual for a buyer to be offered a quantity discount. In other cases there might not be a price break for large orders, but the product may be transported with less expense per unit if shipped in large quantities. The net effect in such a case is the same as receiving a quantity price discount from the supplier. Where quantity discounts prevail the model as constructed in Section 6.2 is not directly applicable, however this model may still be used to ascertain the advisability of increasing the order size to benefit from a discount in price.

The quantity discount situation may be analyzed by the following procedure where Q_d denotes the minimum order size which qualifies the buyer for a price discount:

1. Use the model of Section 6.2, assuming there are no quantity discounts, to determine Q° and C_{avg}°. Recall that Q° is the optimal order size and C_{avg}° is the average inventory cost per unit of time resulting from placing orders of size Q°.
2. Assuming that Q° is less than the order size required for a quantity discount, Q_d, compute C_{avg} for Q_d. This C_{avg} based on the quantity discount sized order will be greater than C_{avg}°. (Equation 6–6 may be used to compute the C_{avg}.) Then from the C_{avg} based on the Q_d subtract the price savings afforded by taking the quantity discount; the price savings must be expressed in the same unit of time as C_{avg}. If C_{avg}–Savings is less than C_{avg}° then the quantity discount should be taken, that is, place an order of size Q_d instead of Q°.

This entire procedure will now be illustrated for the Rocky Mountain Coal Company case.

Rocky Mountain Coal Company's supplier has just announced that any buyer who purchases 4,000 tons or more at a time will get a $.20 discount per ton. Should Rocky Mountain Coal take advantage of this quantity discount and order 4,000 tons at a time? First Rocky Mountain should determine Q° and C_{avg} assuming there were no discounts. Recall that in Section 6.2 the following were given: $C_a = \$140$ per order, $C_h = \$.25$ per ton per month, and $D = 2,000$ tons per month. Q° was found to be 1497 tons and $C_{avg}^\circ = \$374$ per month. The discount quantity, $Q_d = 4,000$ tons, is considerably greater than $Q^\circ = 1497$ tons. With an order of 4,000 tons Rocky Mountain Coal would have an average cost of

$$C_{avg} = C_h(Q/2) + C_a(D/Q)$$
$$= (.25)(4,000/2) + (140)(4,000/2,000) \qquad (6\text{--}11)$$
$$= \$570 \text{ per month}$$

Though average inventory costs increase from \$374 to \$570 per month, how much is saved because of the \$.20 per ton price cut? Since $D = 2,000$ tons per month are used, the price savings per month will be $(2,000)(\$.20) = \$400$. This \$400 savings far offsets the rise of $\$570-\$374 = \$196$ in inventory costs caused by an order of 4,000 tons, therefore Rocky Mountain Coal should order 4,000 tons at a time instead of 1497 tons.

6.5 REORDER LEVEL

In the simple deterministic inventory model under consideration the optimal order size has been determined. It yet remains to determine when the order of size Q° should be placed. The *reorder level* is that level of current inventory which when reached signals the need to place an order for the sake of replenishing the inventory. If the demand rate is 50 units per day and if it takes 4 days for a shipment to arrive, then the reorder level should be 200 units since demand will equal 200 units during the time it takes to get another shipment. The *lead time* is the time it takes from placing an order to the actual receipt of the shipment. In general, the reorder level R equals the demand rate D times the lead time L where D and L are stated in terms of the same unit of time. When the inventory on hand falls to the reorder level R an order for Q° items should be placed. This order will then arrive at the time when the inventory on hand has just been reduced to zero.

It has been the assumption to this point that the demand rate D and lead time L are known constants. This assumption will now be partially relaxed. Suppose that D is constant but that the lead time L may vary. In the Rocky Mountain Coal Company example, the manager Dan Brooks had always figured the lead time to be 5 days, which was the time the Denver-Rio Grande Railroad claimed it takes to deliver a shipment after receipt of a telegraphed order. As monthly demand is 2,000 tons, which is about 66 tons per day, Brooks has always worked with a reorder level of $R = (5 \text{ days})(66 \text{ tons per day}) = 330$ tons. It has become increasingly apparent however that lead time is not always 5 days. The probability distribution of Table 6.3 represents the actual relative frequencies of lead times encountered by Rocky Mountain Coal in dealing with the Denver-Rio Grande Railroad.

TABLE 6.3
Distribution of Lead Time

L	P(L)
3 days	.05
4	.15
5	.60
6	.15
7	.05

When the lead time is 6 days Rocky Mountain Coal finds itself out of coal for one day. The customers may be persuaded to wait another day or so, or, Rocky Mountain may lose the sale of the 66 tons demanded that day or some portion thereof. In either case there is likely to be the loss of goodwill which in turn may have some adverse effects on future sales. Likewise if the lead time were 7 days there would be the same sort of ramifications or "costs." It is usually difficult to determine the economic impact of lost sales; the cost will be at least equal to the immediate foregone profits. Rather than attempting to measure the cost to Rocky Mountain Coal of being short a ton of coal, Brooks has decided to follow what is known as a *service level policy*. He has decided that he wishes to provide a quality of service such that there is no more than a .10 chance of running out of coal each time he places an order. In the situation as detailed above this means that he better allow for a lead time of 6 days, then in only 5 percent of the ordering situations will he be caught without coal. With $L = 6$ the new reorder level will be $R = (6)(66) = 396$ tons. Such an action is not taken without cost to Rocky Mountain Coal; in the most common or modal situation where $L = 5$ days, Rocky Mountain Coal will have 66 tons on hand when the new shipment of $Q°$ arrives. This means that typically the minimum inventory will be 66 tons during an inventory cycle and the maximum inventory level will be 66 tons in excess of $Q°$. In essence Rocky Mountain Coal is carrying a safety stock of 66 tons when acting as if the lead time were 6 days. With a holding cost of about $.25 per month per ton the safety stock of 66 tons costs $16.50 per month.

Another real life possibility would have the lead time fixed but the demand variable during the lead time. With a service level policy of taking no more than a .10 chance of being short during any lead time, Rocky Mountain Coal may, as was just done, determine the appropriate reorder level. Suppose that the lead time is fixed at $L = 5$ days and that demand over this five-day period is normally distributed with a mean of 330 units and a standard deviation of 50 units. With the random variable d representing the demand during this five day interval, Rocky Mountain wishes to fix the reorder level R so that $P(d \geq R) = .10$. Figure 6.4 depicts R in relation to the normal distribution of d. From the standard normal distribution, Appendix Table 2, it is seen that a point which is 1.28 standard deviations above the mean will have 40 percent of the area under the normal curve

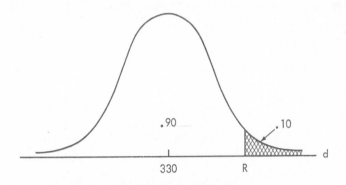

FIGURE 6.4   Distribution of Demand During Lead Time

TABLE 6.4
Standard Deviations above the Mean
Corresponding to Various Service Levels

Service Level*	Standard Deviations above the Mean, z
.005	2.58
.01	2.33
.025	1.96
.05	1.65
.10	1.28
.20	.84
.30	.53
.40	.25
.50	.00

*Service Level refers to the probability of running out of product before the arrival of the next shipment

between it and the mean. (See Section 2.13 of Chapter 2 for a review of the normal distribution.) This implies that there would be a total of 90 percent of the area under the curve to the left of 1.28 standard deviations above the mean and 10 percent to the right. Therefore, for a service level policy of .10 the reorder level must be 1.28 standard deviations above the mean of 330. Since a standard deviation is 50 units it follows that $R = 330 + (1.28)(50) = 394$ tons. With a reorder level of 394 tons Rocky Mountain Coal will have no more than 10 percent of the coal orders arriving after the stock has been reduced to zero.

For the situations where demand is normally distributed during the lead time, Table 6.4 gives the number of standard deviations by which R must exceed the mean demand in order to yield the desired service level. For example, .005 of the area under any normal curve lies beyond 2.58 standard deviations above the mean, and, .05 of the area lies in the tail beyond 1.65 standard deviations above the mean. These areas or probabilities are determined through the use of Table 2 in the Appendix. The reorder level corresponding to a predetermined service level may then be found by

$$R = \bar{d} + z\, s_d \tag{6-12}$$

where $\bar{d}$ equals the mean demand during the lead time

z equals the number of standard deviations above the mean corresponding to some service level

s_d equals the standard deviation of demand during the lead time.

In determining an appropriate service level the manager should realize that in the situations where shortages have lesser consequences in terms of lost sales and the loss of goodwill, then service levels might tend toward .50. When shortages have a serious negative impact, then the service level should be fixed toward the .005 level.

6.6 AN INVENTORY-PRODUCTION MODEL

In the model outlined in Section 6.2 inventory was replenished by the receipt of a shipment of goods, thus inventory was brought to its maximum level instantaneously (see Figure 6.2). Now attention will be focused on the situation where the goods are produced by the same organization which holds them in inventory for later use or sale.

Figure 6.5 depicts the situation where the goods are produced at a rate of P per unit of time and are used at a rate of D per unit of time. More particularly, at time t_0 production begins and continues till t_1 at which time the production process is shut down. The product is being consumed at a constant rate of D per unit of time throughout the inventory cycle from t_0 to t_2, however, since the production rate is greater than the consumption rate inventory builds during the t_0 to t_1 interval. After t_1 there is no production so the inventory level declines till time t_2 when production is again resumed.

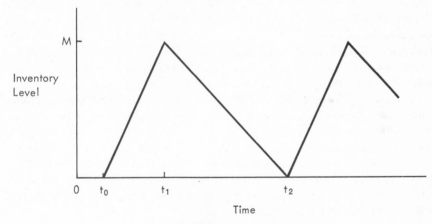

FIGURE 6.5 Inventory Level

With reference to the model above, let

t_0 = Time of the beginning of the inventory cycle, also the time at which production begins

t_1 = Time of cessation of production, also the time of maximum inventory level

t_2 = Time of the end of the inventory cycle, also the time when the inventory level equals zero and production is again resumed

D = Demand or consumption rate

P = Production rate

M = Maximum inventory level

Q = Size of a production run

C_a = Set-up or acquisition cost

C_h = Holding cost per unit of time

Over an inventory cycle the average inventory level will be $(M+0)/2$ or $M/2$. The total holding cost over a cycle will then be equal to the product of the average inventory, the holding cost per unit of time, and the number of units of time in a cycle.

$$\text{Total holding costs over one cycle} = (M/2)(C_h)(t_2-t_0) \tag{6-13}$$

Since the set-up cost per cycle is C_a (this is the cost to set up the production facilities for the sake of making a production run), the total cost for a cycle is

$$\text{Total costs over one cycle} = (M/2)(C_h)(t_2-t_0) + C_a \tag{6-14}$$

and the average cost per unit of time is

$$C_{avg} = \frac{C_h(M/2)(t_2-t_0) + C_a}{(t_2-t_0)} \tag{6-15}$$

For a lengthier discussion on the development of these costs review Section 6.2 which describes an analogous situation.

It is next desired to find the production run size Q which will yield the minimum C_{avg}. C_{avg} as given in Equation 6-15 does not, however, appear to be a function of Q. This equation may be altered by replacing M and t_2-t_0 with equivalent expressions involving Q, P, and D. The resulting equivalent form for C_{avg} is

$$C_{avg} = C_h \frac{Q(P-D)}{2P} + C_a \frac{D}{Q} \tag{6-16}$$

By means of the differential calculus[2] the optimal value of Q, that is, the value of Q which will minimize C_{avg}, is found to be

[2] The derivative of C_{avg} as expressed by Equation 6-16 is taken with respect to Q:
$$\frac{dC_{avg}}{dQ} = C_h\left[(P-D)/2P\right] - DC_a(1/Q^2)$$

After setting the derivative equal to zero, solve for Q:
$$0 = C_h[(P-D)/2P] - DC_a(1/Q^2)$$
$$DC_a = [Q^2C_h(P-D)]/2P$$
$$Q^2 = [2PDC_a]/[C_h(P-D)]$$
$$Q = \sqrt{\left[\frac{2D}{1-D/P}\right]\left[\frac{C_a}{C_h}\right]}$$

$$Q^\circ = \sqrt{\left(\frac{2D}{1-D/P}\right)\left(\frac{C_a}{C_h}\right)} \qquad (6\text{--}17)$$

When this Q° is substituted into Equation 6–16 the minimum average inventory cost per unit of time becomes

$$C_{avg}^\circ = C_h \frac{Q^\circ(P-D)}{2P} + C_a \frac{D}{Q^\circ} \qquad (6\text{--}18)$$

which may be equivalently expressed as

$$C_{avg}^\circ = \sqrt{2DC_aC_h(1-D/P)} \qquad (6\text{--}19)$$

In other words, Equation 6–19 gives the minimum average inventory cost per unit of time which results from a policy of producing Q° units per production run.

The time span of the production run under optimal conditions where Q° is produced each run will be

$$t_1-t_0 = Q^\circ/P \qquad (6\text{--}20)$$

and the maximum inventory level that will be achieved is

$$M^\circ = (Q^\circ/P)(P-D) \qquad (6\text{--}21)$$

Finally, the time span of the total inventory cycle will be

$$t_2-t_0 = Q^\circ/D \qquad (6\text{--}22)$$

This model will now be illustrated.

Abus Copper has been engaged in open pit mining near Bisbee, Arizona for some time. Not only is Abus mining in the great Purple Pit, but Abus owns concentration and smelting facilities in nearby Cochise. The copper ore Abus mines is about one percent copper; this ore is crushed, ground, and then introduced into flotation cells where a frothing agent and collector is added to the water. In the flotation cell the copper sulfide adheres to the air bubbles and the resulting froth is dried and sent to the smelter. Abus has had some difficulty in purchasing adequate supplies of the frothing agent and collector. This problem along with volatile prices has led to the decision to adapt some of Abus' facilities for the manufacture of the frothing agent and collector, FAC. These production facilities are also used in the production of other chemicals that Abus uses and markets. Abus now wishes to determine the size of the optimal FAC production run.

The adapted production facilities have a capacity to produce $P = 25,000$ gallons of FAC per month. This far exceeds Abus' need which is $D = 10,000$ gallons per month. It costs approximately $1,000 to set up the production facilities in order to make a batch of FAC, thus $C_a = \$1,000$. Holding costs are estimated to be \$.60 per year or \$.05 per month per gallon of FAC. With this information Abus proceeds to describe the optimal inventory-production situation. The optimal production run size will be, based on Equation 6–17,

$$Q° = \sqrt{\left(\frac{(2)(10,000)}{1-(10,000/25,000)}\right)\left(\frac{1,000}{.05}\right)}$$

$$= 25,807 \text{ gallons}$$

This $Q°$ will yield an average cost per month of, based on Equation 6–19,

$$C°_{\text{avg}} = \sqrt{(2)(10,000)(1,000)(.05)(1-10,000/25,000)}$$
$$= \$775$$

The time it will take to produce $Q° = 25,807$ gallons is

$$t_1-t_0 = Q°/P = 25,807/25,000 = 1.03 \text{ months}$$

At the end of the production run the inventory level will have risen to

$$M° = (Q°/P)(P-D) = \frac{25,807}{25,000}(25,000-10,000)$$
$$= 15,450 \text{ gallons}$$

Finally, one production-inventory cycle will last

$$t_2-t_0 = Q°/D = 25,807/10,000 = 2.58 \text{ months}$$

6.7 A PROBABILISTIC INVENTORY MODEL WITH NO REORDERING

In the two inventory models studied the business situation was one where there was a continual, ongoing need for the product held in inventory. In the first model this meant that inventory would periodically be replenished by executing a new order when the inventory level reached the predetermined reorder level. Also, if inventory were not zero at the time of the arrival of a new order, the old inventory could be sold in the ensuing inventory cycle. In the inventory-production model new batches of the product would have to be periodically manufactured, and anything produced would eventually be used. A contrasting model will be studied in this section where there will be a one-time only need for the product to be carried in inventory. In no event will excess inventory be saved for a later time. A couple of examples will now be presented to demonstrate more specifically the nature of the model for this "one shot" inventory predicament.

An Example with a Discrete Distribution

Der Heintzel Tours of Dusseldorf has begun the promotion of a new tour to the United States. Attempting to capitalize on Western Europe's infatuation with Western Americana, Der Heintzel has put together a tour which has as its main attraction, Deadwood, South Dakota. As many Europeans have dreamed of seeing the final resting place of Wild Bill (not Kaiser Bill) and Calamity Jane, Der Heintzel has experienced a gratifying subscription response in the three months it has been advertising the Deadwood Tour. As it is now one month before the tour begins, Der Heintzel must make reservations with Transatlanta Airways to transport the tourists to America. Transatlanta gives Der Heintzel a special charter rate for these tours; however, there is a substantial amount of inflexibility built into the arrangement Der Heintzel has with Transatlanta. In particular, Der Heintzel must irrevocably "buy" the round trip seats on the flight one month prior to takeoff. A round trip seat costs Der Heintzel $200. With one month till departure 50 eager eyed Europeans have signed up already for the trip, thus Der Heintzel will buy at least 50 seats from Transatlanta. However, during the last month more Europeans are likely to sign up for the tour. If only 50 seats had been purchased these extra would-be tourists will have to be turned away. For every tourist turned away from the Deadwood Tour, Der Heintzel must forego the opportunity to make a profit of $100. Of course if Der Heintzel bought more than 50 seats and no one else subscribed to the tour, then $200 is lost for each unused seat purchased as Transatlanta will not refund the purchase price of an unused seat or ticket. In this predicament how many seats should Der Heintzel buy?

Before attempting to advise Der Heintzel, attention should be directed to the essential nature of this situation. The problem Der Heintzel is faced with is an inventory problem. The item which is held in inventory is a round trip seat on the flight. As this tour is offered only once there is no consideration of reordering the item in inventory, only one order is placed and this order fixes the amount of inventory available. Finally, the demand for the item is not known but is rather described by a random variable. That is, the actual quantity which is demanded may be represented by a variable whose value is determined by chance. (See Section 2.8 of Chapter 2 for a review of "random variables.") Conceptually the Der Heintzel situation is identical to the dilemma of the newspaper vendor selling papers on the street corner. The vendor can place only one order for a given day's edition and faces the possibility of either having ordered too few papers (and passing up the chance to make a little more money) or too many (in which case good money was spent for papers which must be discarded).

Der Heintzel realizes that the decision as to how many seats more than 50 to purchase depends on what the demand for the tour is likely to be in the last month. Upon reviewing last month subscriptions for their previous tours to the Sheep Ranches of New Zealand (a big winner), Gold Rush California, Gorilla Habitats in Borneo, and the like, and by subjectively assessing the excitement of the European community for the present Deadwood Tour, Der Heintzel has constructed a probability distribution for the number of subscriptions for the Deadwood Tour in the last month. Table 6.5, page 136, gives the distribution of last month subscriptions. Before analytically determining the optimal number of seats to purchase, Der Heintzel submits the situation to an intuitive analysis. As it costs $200 for every excess seat Der Heintzel ends up with, and it costs $100 in foregone profit for every seat Der Heintzel is short, it is relatively more desirable to be caught with too few seats. One might therefore guess that the optimal solution would entail the purchase of only 2 or 3 more seats for possible last month subscribers.

TABLE 6.5
Distribution of Last Month Subscriptions

D	P(D)
1	.05
2	.10
3	.15
4	.20
5	.25
6	.17
7	.08
	1.00

The two kinds of costs faced in this sort of inventory problem are *underage* costs and *overage* costs. An underage cost, C_u, refers to the cost of being one unit under or short of the quantity actually demanded. In the Der Heintzel case the underage cost is $100 since Der Heintzel foregoes a $100 profit for each seat that is demanded but which is not available. The overage cost, C_o, is the cost of having one unit of inventory left over. In the present case this overage cost is $200 as each unused seat costs $200 and Transatlanta Airways does not reimburse Der Heintzel for unused seats. If, for example, Transatlanta did rebate Der Heintzel something like $50 for each unused seat, then the overage cost would be $150.

This sort of inventory situation can efficiently be analyzed by means of an incremental approach. Der Heintzel can initially ask the question: "Should 1 extra seat be purchased?" This question may be answered by utilizing the decision theory approach of Chapter 3 where the alternative acts are:

$$a_1 = \text{Buy the first seat}$$
$$a_2 = \text{Don't buy the first seat}$$

and where the two possible states of nature are:

$$S_1 = \text{First seat is demanded}$$
$$S_2 = \text{First seat is not demanded}$$

Remember that this first seat which is being considered is in reality the 51st seat; there is no question as to whether the first 50 seats should be purchased as Der Heintzel has that many people signed up for the tour already. The resulting decision matrix with payoffs expressed in terms of profits is given in Table 6.6.

TABLE 6.6
Profit Matrix

		a_1: Buy First	a_2: Don't Buy
S_1	First is Demanded	$100	0
S_2	Not Demanded	− $200	0

Alternately, the decision matrix may be expressed in terms of opportunity losses as in Table 6.7. In order to complete the decision matrix or model, the probabilities of the two states must be determined. What is the probability that S_1 will occur, that is, what is the probability that the first extra seat will be demanded in the last month? By taking a look at the distribution of demand D as given in Table 6.5, it is apparent that the demand in the last month will be either 1, or 2, or 3, ... , or 7 seats. In no case will the demand in the last month be zero. Therefore since D will be at least 1, Der Heintzel is certain that at least 1 extra seat will be demanded. Since the first extra seat is certain to be demanded, it follows that $P(S_1) = 1$ and hence that $P(S_2) = 0$. Note also that the probability of S_1 may be expressed as $P(S_1) = P(D \geq 1) = 1$ and the probability of S_2 is $P(S_2) = P(D \leq 0) = 0$. These probabilities appear in the decision model of Table 6.7.

TABLE 6.7
Opportunity Loss Matrix

$P(S_i)$		a_1 Buy the First Seat	a_2 Don't Buy the First Seat
1	S_1 First Demanded	0	100
0	S_2 First Not Demanded	200	0

According to the expectation principle, the act with the maximum expected profit or minimum expected opportunity loss is optimal. From the opportunity loss matrix of Table 6.7 the expected opportunity loss for each act may be computed:

$$E(L_1) = (200) \, P(S_2)$$
$$= (200)(0) = 0$$
$$E(L_2) = (100) \, P(S_1)$$
$$= (100)(1) = 100$$

Since the expected opportunity loss of a_1 is less than that of a_2, Der Heintzel should purchase at least the first extra seat.

If the first extra seat should be purchased, one might next wonder if another or the second extra seat should also be purchased. Table 6.8, page 138, gives the opportunity loss matrix and model for this decision. Now S_1 refers to the event or state where the second seat is demanded. The probability that the second seat will be demanded is the probability that demand D will equal 2 or more seats. That is, if 2 or more seats are demanded then the second seat will be demanded for sure. The probability that D will be greater than or equal to 2 is .95, which is seen in Table 6.5. Since $P(S_1) = P(D \geq 2) = .95$, it follows that $P(S_2) = .05$. For the decision regarding the second, the expected opportunity loss for a_1 is $E(L_1) = (200)(.05) = 10$ and that for a_2 is $E(L_2) = (100)(.95) = 95$. As the EOL for a_1

TABLE 6.8
Opportunity Loss Matrix
for the Decision to Buy the Second Seat

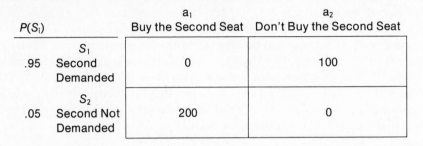

$P(S_i)$		a_1 Buy the Second Seat	a_2 Don't Buy the Second Seat
.95	S_1 Second Demanded	0	100
.05	S_2 Second Not Demanded	200	0

is the lesser it follows that a_1 is optimal and thus Der Heintzel should purchase or "stock" the second extra seat.

Should the third extra seat be purchased? The decision model of Table 6.8 pertains to this decision if the word "second" is replaced by "third" and if the probability of S_1 is given as .85 and $P(S_2) = .15$. As the EOL of a_1 is then 30 and that of a_2 is 85, Der Heintzel should select a_1 which means the third extra seat should be purchased.

Should the fourth seat be purchased? In this case $P(S_1) = P(D \geq 4) = .70$ and $P(S_2) = .30$. The resulting expected opportunity losses are: $E(L_1) = 60$ and $E(L_2) = 70$. This means that the fourth seat should be purchased.

Should the fifth extra seat be purchased? Here the probability that the fifth would be demanded is $P(S_1) = P(D \geq 5) = .50$. The probability that the fifth would not be demanded is $P(D < 5) = .50$. The expected losses are $E(L_1) = (.50)(200) = 100$ and $E(L_2) = (.50)(100) = 50$. Since the EOL of a_2 is the lesser, a_2 is optimal which is "Don't buy the fifth extra seat." The conclusion of the whole matter is then that the purchase of 4 extra seats or a total of 54 seats is the optimal decision for Der Heintzel.

Although the method of analysis just completed was not exceptionally tedious in the Der Heintzel example, it might be in other problems where there are many more values for the demand random variable. It would therefore be worthwhile to attempt to distill a more efficient solution technique from the procedure outlined. The opportunity losses of Tables 6.7 and 6.8 are nothing more than the underage and overage costs mentioned earlier in this section. Generalizing these tables so that the decision concerns the purchase of the kth unit, Table 6.9 results. The kth unit should be purchased if the expected opportunity loss of a_1 is less than the EOL of a_2, that is, if

$$E(L_1) < E(L_2) \qquad (6\text{--}23)$$

or

$$[P(D < k) \, C_o] < [P(D \geq k) \, C_u] \qquad (6\text{--}24)$$

Recognizing that $P(D < k) = 1 - P(D \geq k)$ by the complement law of probability, Inequality 6-24 may be equivalently expressed as

$$[(1 - P(D \geq k)) \, C_o] < [P(D \geq k) \, C_u] \qquad (6\text{--}25)$$

TABLE 6.9
Opportunity Loss Matrix
for the Decision to Buy the kth Seat

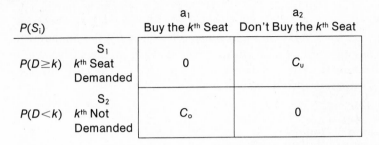

		a_1 Buy the kth Seat	a_2 Don't Buy the kth Seat
$P(D \geq k)$	S_1 kth Seat Demanded	0	C_u
$P(D < k)$	S_2 kth Not Demanded	C_o	0

column header: $P(S_i)$

As long as Inequality 6–25 holds true, the kth item or seat should be purchased since this inequality is equivalent to 6–24. By means of some algebraic manipulations Inequality 6–25 may be stated in a more useful form:

$$[(1 - P(D \geq k)) \, C_o] < [P(D \geq k) \, C_u]$$
$$[C_o - C_o \, P(D \geq k)] < [C_u \, P(D \geq k)]$$
$$C_o < [C_o \, P(D \geq k) + C_u \, P(D \geq k)]$$
$$C_o < [(C_o + C_u) \, P(D \geq k)]$$
$$[C_o/(C_o + C_u)] < P(D \geq k) \tag{6–26}$$

Because Inequality 6–26 is equivalent to Inequality 6–25, the following theorem holds true:

The kth unit should be purchased if the following inequality is satisfied,

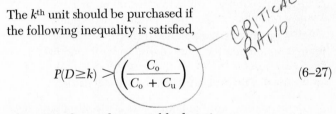

CRITICAL RATIO

$$P(D \geq k) > \left(\frac{C_o}{C_o + C_u} \right) \tag{6–27}$$

where D is the random variable denoting demand, C_o is the overage cost, and C_u is the underage cost.

In Inequality 6–27 the ratio $C_o/(C_o + C_u)$ is known as the *critical ratio*. Inequality 6–27 is true if and only if the expected opportunity loss of "Buy the kth Item" is less than the EOL of "Don't Buy the kth Item." With the probability distribution of D given and with the values of C_o and C_u fixed, it is now quite easy to determine the optimal purchase or stocking quantity in this sort of inventory situation. The theorem associated with Inequality 6–27 will now be applied to the Der Heintzel example.

In the Der Heintzel case $C_o = \$200$ and $C_u = \$100$, therefore the critical ratio of $C_o/(C_o + C_u)$ equals $200/(200 + 100) = .67$. The kth seat should be purchased if and only if $[P(D \geq k)] > .67$ according to the theorem. The distribution of D as originally given in Table 6.5 is reproduced in Table 6.10. Also the cumulative distribution of D is given in Table 6.10. From this cumulative distribution it appears that for $k = 3$, $P(D \geq k)$ equals .85 and therefore since this probability exceeds the critical ratio of .67, at least 3 seats should be purchased. For $k = 4$, $P(D \geq 4) = .70$ and since this also exceeds .67, at least 4 extra seats should be bought. For $k = 5$, $P(D \geq 5) = .50$ which is less than .67; this implies that the EOL of "Buy the Fifth Seat" is greater than the EOL of "Don't Buy the Fifth Seat." Therefore, the fifth seat should not be purchased. The final conclusion is that only 4 extra seats should be purchased.

TABLE 6.10
**Distributions of Demand
and Relationship to Critical Ratio**

D,k	$P(D)$	$P(D \geq k)$		$C_o/(C_o + C_u)$
1	.05	1.00	>	.67
2	.10	.95	>	.67
3	.15	.85	>	.67
4	.20	.70	>	.67
5	.25	.50	<	.67
6	.17	.25	<	.67
7	.08	.08	<	.67

Purchase $k = 4$ is optimal

By listing the appropriate cumulative distribution of D along with the value of the critical ratio (as in the fourth column in Table 6.10), the optimal purchase quantity may be picked out rapidly. The point where the inequality sign switches its sense is the point marking the optimal order or purchase quantity. Again it is seen that the optimal decision is to purchase 4 extra seats, or 54 in all.

An Example with a Continuous Distribution

In the case where the demand D is a continuous random variable the same approach to finding the optimal order or stocking quantity may be used; the only difference is that the probability distribution of D is no longer discrete.

Havasupai Canyon is a tributary canyon leading into the south rim of the Grand Canyon. In a wide spot at the bottom of Havasupai Canyon lives the Havasupai Tribe. One of the young bucks left the idyllic way of life there in the isolated canyon and after many years of school found himself at the ASU Business School. Sitting Bull, for the young buck had been named after a famous chief of another tribe, while roaming through the university library found an old document issued by the U.S. Government entitling the Havasupai Tribe to run a small business along any of the trails leading to the bottom of the Grand Canyon. This unanticipated discovery came during a semester when Sitting was enrolled in an MBA course where the intricacies of inventory models were being studied. After the semester ended Sitting left for the Canyon and trekked down the popular Bright Angel Trail. As this well-traveled trail lies wholly within the

National Park there are no small businesses extant along its way; however, Sitting found a spot along a switchback where the so-called pre-cambrian stratum begins and commenced to set up a fast food stand where he would sell sopaipillas. Each morning before sunrise Sitting would make a batch of sopaipillas and carry them down on a mule to his stand. Sitting would then sit in the stand till a hungry hiker or mule rider came along wanting a sopaipilla. The selling price for a sopaipilla is $.75. Sitting makes them each morning for $.35 each. If any sopaipillas are left at the end of the day Sitting can sell them cold to the park rangers upon climbing out of the canyon in the evening; he gets $.10 for a cold and slightly dusty sopaipilla. How many sopaipillas should Sitting take down the canyon on a given day?

Let us now consider Sitting's approach. Sitting took an abundant supply of sopaipillas down the canyon and found out that he sells an average of one sopaipilla for every person that passes his stand. Therefore, in order to determine the distribution of demand, Sitting must try to determine how many people will be coming down the Bright Angel Trail on a given day. Sitting put together a forecasting model where the number of people entering the park the day before and the weather forecast were used to predict the number of persons making the trip down the canyon (consult Chapter 12 on forecasting for a complete description of Sitting's forecasting model). Using his forecasting model for tomorrow's demand, Sitting considered the number of sopaipillas demanded to be normally distributed with a mean of 200 and a standard deviation of 40. With this normal distribution of demand D, Sitting was able to determine the optimal number of sopaipillas to take down the canyon on the morrow.

The underage cost, C_u, facing Sitting is $.75 - $.35 = $.40 per sopaipilla. That is, for every sopaipilla Sitting cannot supply he loses the profit of $.40. The overage cost, C_o, or cost of having one sopaipilla left over is $.35 - $.10 = $.25; this is because one sopaipilla costs $.35 to make but if it is unsold at the end of the day the park ranger will buy it for $.10. From this the critical ratio is $C_o/(C_o + C_u) = .25/(.25 + .40) = .385$. According to the theorem developed earlier in this section, Sitting should stock the kth sopaipilla as long as

$$P(D \geq k) > .385$$

This implies that on the normal distribution, the optimal stocking amount k is the point where the area to the right of k is .385. This optimal value of k is denoted by the point k° in Figure 6.6, page 142. From Appendix II it is determined that k° must be .29 standard deviations above the mean if it is to have an area of .385 to its right and .615 to its left. Therefore the optimal quantity to be stocked is .29 standard deviations above the mean of 200 where a standard deviation is 40 sopaipillas. Equivalently,

$$k^\circ = 200 + (.29)(40) = 211.6 \text{ sopaipillas}$$

Notice that this value for k° is intuitively plausible since the underage cost per unit is greater than the overage cost; Sitting would prefer to err on the side of having too many sopaipillas.

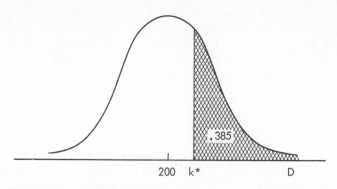

FIGURE 6.6 **Optimal Stocking Quantity and the Distribution of Demand**

6.8 SENSITIVITY ANALYSIS

In this section sensitivity analysis will be considered in the context of the probabilistic model with no reordering of the last section. The "Sitting Bull and the Sopaipilla" example will be further developed in order to illustrate sensitivity analysis.

Sitting much prefers selling sopaipillas at the bottom of the canyon to pushing the pencil at the top for the sake of deriving optimal inventory policies. He knows that the cost to make a sopaipilla may easily change. In view of this possibility, Sitting wants to determine what effect changes in the overage and underage costs will have on $k°$, the optimal quantity to be stocked. The model developed in Section 6.7 indicates that the kth unit should be stocked if

$$P(D \geq k) > [C_o/(C_o + C_u)] \qquad (6\text{--}28)$$

It is quite apparent that changes in C_o and/or C_u will affect the critical ratio and thereby may change $k°$. Sitting thought that he might construct a table with an assortment of values for C_o and C_u and the corresponding $k°$. For example, if $C_o = \$.25$ and $C_u = \$.25$, then the critical ratio would equal .50 and $k°$ would be 200 if demand were normally distributed as before. Of course there are an extremely large number of combinations of C_o and C_u that Sitting might want to examine if he wished to assure himself that he would never have to return to the use of the model again to compute $k°$. How can Sitting accomplish his task with a minimum of effort? Remember, Sitting wants to construct a table which has the optimal quantity to be stocked each morning, $k°$, corresponding to any pair of overage and underage costs. If lard were to escalate in price meaning that it would cost Sitting $\$.45$ to make a sopaipilla instead of $\$.35$, the result would be that $C_o = \$.35$ instead of the previous $\$.25$ and $C_u = \$.30$ instead of $\$.40$ as in Section 6.7. With his table Sitting would only have to find this new combination of C_o and C_u and then read off the new $k°$.

With the thoughts of the day on his mind, Sitting slipped into sleep. Soon he was caught up in a dream where Red Cloud was standing before him. From the venerable old chief's lips spilled these words: "What is over belongs over what is under." Rousing from his sleep, Sitting immediately proceeded to place overage costs over underage costs getting what he called the Red Cloud Ratio

$$\frac{C_o}{C_u} \tag{6-29}$$

Then with a spark of brilliant illumination, Sitting was able to translate the critical ratio into a new form which utilizes the Red Cloud Ratio.

$$\text{Critical Ratio} = \frac{C_o}{C_o + C_u} \tag{6-30}$$

By dividing both numerator and denominator by C_u, Sitting got

$$\text{Critical Ratio} = \frac{C_o/C_u}{(C_o + C_u)/C_u} \tag{6-31}$$

Then simplifying the denominator,

$$\text{Critical Ratio} = \frac{C_o/C_u}{C_o/C_u + 1} \tag{6-32}$$

Sitting immediately realized the ramifications for sensitivity analysis of this new form of the critical ratio which used the Red Cloud Ratio. In essence, the individual values of C_o and C_u are not important, rather their ratio is the determinant of $k°$.

With the new expression for the critical ratio, Sitting constructed Table 6.11 which gives $k°$ (the optimal stocking quantity) corresponding to various values of the C_o/C_u ratio. For example, if $C_o/C_u = .1$, then $k°$ is the largest k value which satisfies

TABLE 6.11
Optimal Stocking Quantity
Corresponding to the Ratio of Overage to Underage Costs

C_o/C_u	Critical Ratio	k^*
.1	.091	253.2
.2	.167	238.8
.3	.231	229.6
.4	.286	222.8
.6	.375	212.8
.8	.444	205.6
1.0	.500	200.0
1.5	.600	190.0
2.0	.667	182.8
3.0	.750	173.2
5.0	.833	161.2
10.0	.909	146.8

$$P(D \geq k) > \frac{C_o/C_u}{C_o/C_u + 1} \qquad (6\text{–}33)$$

$$> \frac{.1}{.1 + 1}$$

$$> .091$$

With demand D distributed normally with a mean of 200 and a standard deviation of 40 sopaipillas, the optimal quantity that Sitting should take down the canyon is

$$k^\circ = 200 + (1.33)(40) = 253.2$$

Sitting next graphed the data of Table 6.11 letting C_o/C_u be represented on the horizontal axis and k° on the vertical. Smoothing a line through this data resulted in the graph of Figure 6.7. This graph enables the analyst to immediately determine k° for any C_o/C_u ratio and thereby shows how sensitive k° is to changes in C_o/C_u. As long as the distribution of demand for sopaipillas remains the same, Sitting can use the graph of Figure 6.7 to determine the optimal number to take down the canyon.

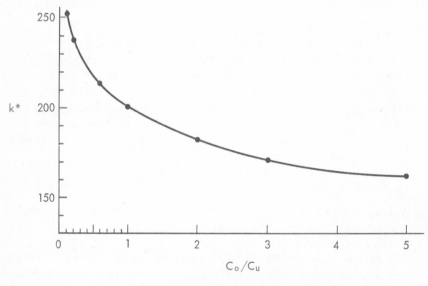

FIGURE 6.7 k^* Plotted Against C_o/C_u

6.9 A PROBABILISTIC INVENTORY MODEL WITH REORDERING

In this final section on inventory models a more complex sort of inventory situation will be considered. Here there will be variable demand for the product held in inventory, the inventory function will be ongoing thus necessitating the reordering of inventory, and there will be variability in the lead time. With increased complexity it is often preferable to analyze the decision situation by means of simulation rather than through the mathematical analysis of a formal model as has been done in the earlier sections of this chapter. A simulation model will therefore be presented for this more complex inventory situation.

In the middle of the nineteenth century many an American left the security of the East for the mining camps of California in hope of striking it rich. Some of the gold seekers did strike it rich, although most were sorely disappointed. On the heels of the great western gold migration came an astute Virginian, Timotheus Charles. Timotheus correctly surmised that the surefire way to get rich in California would be in supplying food to the booming population. Timotheus thus set up his company, Timotheus Wholesale Foodstuffs, on the American River near present-day Sacramento. One item of inventory Timotheus carried was flour. Each day Timotheus would receive 0, 1, or 2 orders for flour; these orders would amount to 5, 10, 15, or 20 sacks each. When Timotheus' inventory dropped to the reorder level R he would place an order with a mill located further north in California, which was supplied with grains from Washington, Oregon, and Utah. The lead time or time from the placing of the order to the receipt of the shipment of flour was either 3, 4, or 5 days. Table 6.12 displays the probability distribution for each of the variables mentioned.

TABLE 6.12
Three Distributions

A	P(A)	S	P(S)	L	P(L)
0	.2	5	.2	3	.2
1	.5	10	.3	4	.6
2	.3	15	.3	5	.2
	1.0	20	.2		1.0
			1.0		

where
  A = Number of customer orders per day,
  S = Size of a customer order in sacks,
  L = Lead time in days.

Timotheus figured the holding cost of a sack of flour to be C_h = $.05 per day. The mill which supplies the flour charges $50 to make a delivery; other acquisition costs amounted to $20 making the total acquisition cost per order to be C_a = $70. The foregone profit of being a sack short is $8; this is the underage cost. Since the wholesale food business is an ongoing business and since the flour does not become worthless if not sold during an inventory cycle but may be sold later, there are no overage costs. In the circumstances Timotheus finds himself, the two decision variables which must be optimized are the size of an order Q and the reorder level R. A simulation procedure will now be outlined for the sake of evaluating the economic impact of any (Q,R) combination which Timotheus might consider. In so doing the optimal values for Q and R can be isolated.

What might be a reasonably good choice for Q and R in this probabilistic situation? A plausible approach to roughly approximate optimal values of Q and R would be to assume that the situation here encountered was deterministic and proceed accordingly. In particular, let a deterministic simplification be made where the number of customer orders per day equals the expected number of customer orders per day as derived from the distribution of A in Table 6.12. The mean or expected value of A is

$$E(A) = (0)(.2) + (1)(.5) + (2)(.3)$$
$$= 1.1 \text{ customer orders per day}$$

Let the size of an order equal the expected value of S, namely,

$$E(S) = (5)(.2) + (10)(.3) + (15)(.3) + (20)(.2)$$
$$= 12.5 \text{ sacks per customer order}$$

This implies that the daily demand rate, assuming this deterministic simplification, is the product of 1.1 customer orders per day and 12.5 sacks per order or 13.75 sacks per day. With a constant demand rate and with $C_h = \$.05$ per day and $C_a = \$70$, the deterministic model of Section 6.2 may be employed to find the optimal order size that Timotheus should place with the mill for the deterministic simplification:

$$Q^\circ = \sqrt{2DC_a/C_h} \qquad (6\text{--}34)$$
$$= \sqrt{(2)(13.75)(70)/.05}$$
$$= 196$$

What should the reorder level be? If the lead time be considered as equal to the expected lead time, that is,

$$E(L) = (3)(.20) + (4)(.60) + (5)(.20)$$
$$= 4 \text{ days}$$

and with a demand rate of 13.75 sacks per day, then the reorder level should be $(4)(13.75) = 55$ sacks. It is with this Q of 196 and R of 55 sacks derived from a simplification of the real probabilistic situation that the simulation procedure will initially be run. After evaluating costs with this (Q,R) combination, other combinations may be run in an attempt to isolate the optimal order size Q and reorder level R.

Before turning to the simulation procedure and work sheet, a few more observations and clarifications should be made. Whenever Timotheus cannot fill an entire order, it is assumed that the customer will accept lesser amounts. Also, Timotheus will place an order to the mill at the end of the day. If, for example, he places an order at the end of Day 2 and if the lead time were 3 days, it is further assumed that the order will arrive from the mill at the *beginning* of Day 6 and will be available for sale on Day 6.

Table 6.13 presents a simulation work sheet adequate to the simulation problem being studied. The values in columns 2, 3, 4, and 10 are determined randomly according to the probability distributions of Table 6.12. As the method of selecting values from probability distributions for the sake of Monte Carlo simulation has been discussed in detail in Chapter 5 and illustrated subsequently, this procedure will not again be discussed here. The step-by-step procedure for simulating the Timotheus Wholesale Foodstuffs flour inventory problem will now be considered.

TABLE 6.13
Inventory Simulation Work Sheet
with R = 55 and Q = 196

Day (1)	No. of Cust. Orders, A * (2)	Size of First Order, S * (3)	Size of Second Order, S * (4)	Total Daily Demand (5)	Beginning Inventory Level, I_b (6)	Ending Inventory Level, I_e (7)	Lost Sales (8)	Reorder at end of day? 0 = no, 1 = yes (9)	Lead Time, L * (10)	Arrival Date of Order from Mill (11)
1	2	10	20	30	196	166	0	0		
2	0				166	166	0	0		
3	2	20	20	40	166	126	0	0		
4	1	15		15	126	111	0	0		
5	1	10		10	111	101	0	0		
6	2	15	15	30	101	71	0	0		
7	0				71	71	0	0		
8	1	5		5	71	66	0	0		
9	2	20	10	30	66	36	0	1	5	15
10	1	15		15	36	21	0	0		
11	2	5	15	20	21	1	0	0		
12	0				1	1	0	0		
13	2	10	20	30	1	0	29	0		
14	1	10		10	0	0	10	0		
15	1	15		15	196	181	0	0		
16	2	10	10	20	181	161	0	0		
Column sums:					1510	1279	39	1		

*The entries in these columns are determined randomly using the probability distributions which are given in Table 6.12

It will be assumed that Timotheus starts Day 1 with an inventory of 196 sacks which is the Q value derived from the deterministic simplification. Therefore, in Column 6 a value for I_b of 196 should initially be entered.

Day 1: (Enter 1 in Column 1)
1. Randomly select a value for A, the number of customer orders, and enter into Column 2. In this example, $A = 2$ customer orders was randomly selected according to the distribution of Table 6.12. This means that on this day Timotheus will receive two separate orders for flour from customers.
2. Randomly select the size S of the first customer order, assuming there is a first customer order in the day, and enter into Column 3. In this example the first customer ordered $S = 10$ sacks of flour; this was selected randomly according to the S distribution of Table 6.12.
3. Randomly select the size S of the second order, assuming there is a second customer order in the day, and enter into Column 4. The second customer ordered $S = 20$ sacks of flour from Timotheus. This value for S was again selected from Table 6.12 by a random technique.
4. Add Columns 3 and 4 and place the total in Column 5. On Day 1 there was a total demand of $10 + 20 = 30$ sacks of flour. This appears in Column 5.
5. Subtract the total demand of Column 5 from the beginning inventory level of Column 6. If the difference is greater than or equal to zero then record this difference in Column 7; if the difference is less than zero then enter 0 in Column 7 and the absolute value of the negative number in Column 8. In this example the total demand of 30 sacks was subtracted from the beginning inventory of 196 yielding a difference of 166 which is nonnegative. Since 166 is nonnegative it is entered into Column 7. In other words, Timotheus is ending the day with 166 sacks of flour in inventory and no sales were lost because of a shortage.
6. If Column 7 is equal to or below the reorder level of $R = 55$ sacks, place a 1 in Column 9 indicating that an order for $Q = 196$ is being placed with the mill. No reordering is then permitted until this order arrives. If the ending inventory is above $R = 55$, then enter 0 in Column 9 to indicate that no order is being placed. In the case of Day 1 the ending inventory is 166 as found in Column 7 and as this is well above the reorder level a 0 is entered in Column 9.
7. If a 1 appears in Column 9 randomly select the lead time L for the mill order from the distribution of L in Table 6.12 and enter L in Column 10. Since there was no order sent to the mill at the end of Day 1, Column 10 is left blank.
8. If a value appears in Column 10 denoting the lead time, take this value and add to it the value found in Column 1 plus 1; enter this sum in Column 11. In other words, the entry in Column 11 will be equal to the value in Column 1 plus the value in Column 10 plus 1; this gives the arrival date of the mill order. In the case of Day 1 there was no value to begin with in Column 10, therefore Column 11 is left blank.
9. If a value appears in Column 11 enter $Q = 196$ in Column 6 of the arrival date found in Column 11. This step merely records the future arrival of the shipment from the mill.
10. Go to the next day (next row) by first determining its beginning inventory level. This is done by adding the ending inventory of the previous day to

any entry representing the receipt of a mill order which is already found in Column 6 of the new day and placing their sum in Column 6 for the new day. In this example 166 is placed in Column 6 for the new day which is Day 2.

A review of the illustrative values of the simulation work sheet in Table 6.13 for Day 2 through Day 16 will now be presented more concisely. It should not be too difficult to get the "feel" for filling out this simulation work sheet.

Day 2: (Enter 2 in Column 1)
    The beginning inventory level taken from the ending inventory of Day 1 is 166 as found in Column 6. There were no orders received by Timotheus on this day as indicated by the random selection of 0 for Column 2. This means that the ending inventory level in Column 7 is 166.
Day 3: (Enter 3 in Column 1)
    The beginning inventory level for Day 3 is 166, which is found in Column 6. During Day 3, $A = 2$ customer orders are received, each being for 20 sacks of flour. The total demand equals 40 sacks of flour, reducing the inventory level to 126 sacks at the end of the day. No reorder is necessary as 126 is in excess of $R = 55$.
Day 4: (Enter 4 in Column 1)
    The beginning inventory is 126 sacks, one order is received and it is for 15 sacks thus reducing the inventory to 111 sacks.
Day 5:
    The beginning inventory is 111 sacks, one order for 10 sacks is filled reducing inventory to 101. No reordering from the mill is necessary.
Day 6:
    The beginning inventory is 101 sacks, two orders are received during the day for 15 sacks each making a total demand of 30 sacks. Ending inventory is 71 sacks.
Day 7:
    No orders are received. Ending inventory is 71 sacks.
Day 8:
    The beginning inventory is 71, one order is received for 5 sacks thereby reducing the inventory to 66 sacks.
Day 9:
    The beginning inventory is 66 sacks; two customer orders are received for a total demand of 30 sacks, thereby reducing the ending inventory to 36 sacks. Since 36 is less than the reorder level of $R = 55$, Timotheus must place an order of $Q = 196$ with the mill. The lead time is randomly selected and turns out to be $L = 5$ days, hence this is recorded in Column 10. Notice also that a 1 appears in Column 9 indicating that a mill order is being placed. The arrival date will be (as described in step 8 under Day 1) determined as $9 + 5 + 1$ or Day 15. The 196 sacks is then entered in Column 6 for the row representing Day 15, indicating its arrival on the morning of Day 15.
Day 10:
    The beginning inventory is 36 sacks, one order is received for 15 sacks reducing the ending inventory to 21 sacks. There are no lost sales, see Column 8. Even though the ending inventory of 21 is below the reorder level, no reordering is permitted as a shipment from the mill is already on its way to Timotheus.

Day 11:
Beginning inventory is 21 sacks. Two orders for a total of 20 sacks are received bringing ending inventory to 1 sack. No sales are lost.

Day 12:
Beginning inventory is 1 sack, no orders from customers are received.

Day 13:
The beginning inventory is 1 sack. Two orders are received from customers for a total of 30 sacks. The 1 sack in inventory is sold leaving Timotheus unable to fill the remaining order for 29 sacks. Thus 29 is entered in Column 8 representing lost sales, and, the ending inventory is 0.

Day 14:
Beginning inventory is 0 sacks. One order for 10 sacks is thus unfilled causing lost sales of 10 sacks.

Day 15:
Beginning inventory equals the new shipment from the mill of 196 sacks plus the ending inventory of 0 sacks from the day before. One customer order is received for 15 sacks reducing the ending inventory to 181 sacks. No sales are lost and no mill order is placed.

Day 16:
The beginning inventory of 181 is reduced to 161 because of two customer orders for a total of 20 sacks.

The simulation of this policy of $Q = 196$ and $R = 55$ might be continued for an entire year and then be repeated for several more years in order to determine its economic implications. It should be apparent that the computer would be quite useful in quickly performing a highly structured simulation as this one. In Section 5.7 of Chapter 5 the role of computers in simulation is noted; also comments are made in Section 5.7 regarding the length of the period which should be simulated. The simulation of the Timotheus inventory situation will not be carried beyond sixteen days as the pattern of the simulation has been sufficiently demonstrated. Attention will now be turned toward the determination of the economic impact in terms of holding, acquisition, and underage costs of the $Q = 196$ and $R = 55$ policy for the sixteen simulated days.

With a simulation work sheet completed as in Table 6.13 the various costs may be easily computed. Holding costs were initially given as $C_h = \$.05$ per sack per day held in inventory. By averaging Columns 6 and 7 over the time span of the simulation, the average inventory level may be found. When this average inventory level is multiplied by C_h, the average daily holding cost results. In the Timotheus Wholesale Food Stuffs example of Table 6.13 the simulation covers $n = 16$ days. The average daily holding cost is therefore

$$\text{Average Daily Holding Cost} = (\text{Average Inventory Level})(C_h)$$

$$= \left(\frac{\Sigma(6) + \Sigma(7)}{2n} \right)(C_h) \tag{6–35}$$

where $\Sigma(6)$ denotes the sum of Column 6, $\Sigma(7)$ denotes the sum of Column 7, and n refers to the number of days. In particular, since the sums of Columns 6 and 7 are shown in Table 6.13,

$$\text{Average Daily}\atop\text{Holding Cost} = \left(\frac{1510 + 1279}{(2)(16)}\right)(.05)$$

$$= \$4.36$$

By summing Column 9 the number of acquisitions during the time span is determined. The product of the number of acquisitions and $C_a = \$70$ gives the total acquisition costs over the simulated period. Dividing this product by the number of days yields the average acquisition cost per day. In this example,

$$\text{Average Daily}\atop\text{Acquisition Cost} = \frac{(\text{Number of acquisitions})(C_a)}{n}$$

$$= \frac{[\Sigma(9)][C_a]}{n} \qquad\qquad (6\text{--}36)$$

$$= \frac{(1)(70)}{16}$$

$$= \$4.38$$

Summing Column 8 reveals the number of lost sales over the period simulated. When lost sales are multiplied by the underage cost of $C_u = \$8$ per sack and then divided by the number of days, the average daily underage cost is found. In particular,

$$\text{Average Daily}\atop\text{Underage Cost} = \frac{(\text{Lost sales})(C_u)}{n}$$

$$= \frac{[\Sigma(8)][C_u]}{n} \qquad\qquad (6\text{--}37)$$

$$= \frac{(39)(8)}{16}$$

$$= \$19.50$$

The total economic impact of the inventory policy of $Q = 196$ and $R = 55$ would therefore be estimated as the sum of the three average daily costs resulting from the simulation. That is,

$$\text{Average Daily}\atop\text{Total Cost} = {\text{Average Daily}\atop\text{Holding Cost}} + {\text{Average Daily}\atop\text{Acquisition Cost}} + {\text{Average Daily}\atop\text{Underage Cost}}$$

$$= \$4.36 + 4.38 + 19.50$$

$$= \$28.24$$

By simulating several years of experience with this Q and R, Timotheus would have an accurate picture of the total average costs. By changing Q, R, or both systematically and then simulating with the new pairs of values, Timotheus could converge on that combination of Q and R which yields the minimum average total cost. This (Q,R) combination or strategy would constitute the optimal solution to the inventory problem. As a general rule the order quantity Q may stray from the optimal value of $Q°$ without drastic cost consequences; in other words, average total cost is not too sensitive to small changes in Q. In the model for Timotheus Food Stuffs, changes in the reorder level R are apt to have greater effects on cost. Timotheus would do well to run the next simulation by keeping

Q at 196 sacks and using a reorder level of 70 or more in his search for the optimal inventory strategy. Larger values for R will permit Timotheus to reduce the average daily underage cost which was comparatively great.

6.10 ANOTHER INVENTORY MODEL.

In this chapter a varied assortment of inventory models and analysis techniques have been studied. In this text one more sort of inventory model will be presented. The modeling and analysis of this other inventory situation differs markedly from the approaches considered in this chapter. As the model is a "linear programming" model its presentation and consideration will be deferred until Chapter 7 where linear programming is introduced.

PROBLEMS

6-1. If in a simple deterministic model with instantaneous acquisitions, the following are known:

$$D = 50 \text{ per month}$$
$$C_a = \$100 \text{ per order}$$
$$C_h = \$2 \text{ per item per month}$$

(a) Find the optimal order size, the average inventory cost per month, and the length of an inventory cycle.

(b) Plot a graph as in Figure 6.3 which shows average inventory cost as a function of order size.

6-2. Webster Appliance sells television sets at a rate of 80 per month. Holding costs for a television set amount to $2 per month. It costs $20 to process an order for more sets. Find the optimal order size, the average inventory cost per month, and the length of an inventory cycle.

6-3. Galloping Horse uses a chemical in the processing of its leather goods at a rate of 1000 gallons per year. The cost to place and receive an order of the chemical is $100. The chemical is purchased for $20 per gallon. Holding costs per year for a gallon of the chemical are considered to be 15 percent of its cost. Find the optimal order size, the average inventory cost per year, and the length of an inventory cycle.

6-4. In Problem 6-3, suppose C_a were $60, what is the new value for Q°? What is the new C_{avg}°? If the Q° found in Problem 6-3 had been used when C_a is the present $60, what would C_{avg} be?

6-5. In the Webster Appliance problem, 6-2, the supplier of the television sets announces that any dealer who purchases 100 sets at a time will get a discount of $.50 per television set. Should Webster order 100 sets in order to get this discount?

6-6. In the Galloping Horse problem, 6-3, the chemical supplier offers Galloping Horse a 1 percent discount on the price of a gallon if an order of 1000 gallons is placed. Should Galloping Horse order 1000 gallons at a time in order to get this quantity discount?

6-7. G. Scott is a manufacturer of cameras. Scott manufactures all of the components for their cameras except the lenses. The manufacturing process uses lenses at a rate of 1,000 per month. Acquisition costs per order are $60. The cost to hold a lens in inventory for a month is $.20. When an order is placed with a lens manufacturer, it takes 8 days for the order to arrive. Find the optimal order size, the average monthly inventory cost, the length of an inventory cycle, and the reorder level.

6-8. Lanter Office Machines sells calculators at a rate of 3 per day. When Lanter reorders calculators from its supplier, the lead time varies. The distribution of lead time is

L	P(L)
8 days	.30
9	.30
10	.20
11	.08
12	.07
13	.05

R = 36

need 12 DAY SUPPLY

Lanter has already found the optimal order size to be 80 calculators. What should the reorder level be if Lanter will take no more than a 10 percent chance of being out of calculators when an order is placed?

6-9. At the Torres-Canter Radiology Clinic a special type of X-ray film is used. The lead time to replenish the stock of this film is 4 days. The usage of this film during a four-day period is normally distributed with a mean of 20 and a standard deviation of 5. At the clinic a service level policy of .01 has been established for this type of film. What is a "service level policy of .01"? What should the reorder level be for such a policy?

R = 32

6-10. Find the optimal production run size, the average inventory cost, the maximum inventory level, and the length of an inventory-production cycle for the situation where $C_a = \$300$, $C_h = \$.10$ per month, $P = 4,000$ per month and $D = 2,000$ per month.

PRODUCTION PROBLEMS

6-11. Kipper Electronics produces semiconductors for use in a number of electronic components. Kipper can produce a particular semiconductor at the rate of 800 per week. The semiconductor is used at a rate of 300 per week. The cost to hold one semiconductor in inventory for a week is $.01. It costs Kipper $100 to convert their production facility for the production of the semiconductor in question. How large should a production run be? What is the average inventory cost? What is the maximum level of inventory for this semiconductor? What is the length of a production-inventory cycle?

6-12. A company is faced with a probabilistic inventory situation where no reordering is possible. The overage cost is $10 per unit while the underage cost is $5 per unit. The demand is given by the following distribution:

D	P(D)	P(D ≥ K)	10/15
6	.3	1	.67
7	.4	.7	.67
8	.2	.3	.67
9	.1	.1	.67
		0	

Co/Cu+Co

PROB INV — NO REORDER

How many units should be stocked?

6-13. Do Problem 6–12 if D had a normal distribution with a mean of 500 and a standard deviation of 100.   457

6-14. Barbara & Dolly operate the refreshments concession at VCU basketball games. They purchase cola for $.50 a liter and sell it to the fans for $1.50 per liter. Cola which is unsold is returned to the supplier who pays $.20 per liter for it. The demand, in liters, for cola at a game is given below. How many liters should the concessionaire stock for a game?

D	P(D)	$P(D \geq Q)$		.23
20	.10	1		
21	.15	.9	~	1|
22	.25	.75		
23	.25	.50		
→ (24)	.15	.25		
25	.10	~10		

6-15. Do Problem 6–14 assuming D had a normal distribution with a mean of 40 liters and a standard deviation of 10 liters.   47.4

6-16. Travis Publishing must decide on how many copies of a new book should be printed. Each copy costs $3.00 to produce. Travis sells the book to book dealers for $8.00 each. Any unsold books are considered worthless. If sales are normally distributed with a mean of 50,000 and a standard deviation of 20,000 copies, how many copies should be printed?

6-17. In Problem 6–16, plot the optimal quantity that should be printed, k°, as a function of the ratio of C_o / C_u.

6-18. Simulate 20 more days for the Timotheus Foodstuffs example of Section 6.9 beginning with Day 17. Compute the average daily total cost over the twenty-day simulated period.

6-19. Simulate 20 days for the Timotheus Foodstuffs example of Section 6.9 with $Q = 120$ and $R = 70$. Compute the average daily total cost based on this simulation.

6-20. The Meal-Bone Department Store sells cashews. The number of purchases, A, per day and the average size of the daily purchases, S, are distributed as follows:

A	P(A)	S	P(S)
10	.5	.5 lbs	.3
15	.5	1.0 lbs	.7

Cashews may be reordered at the end of each or any day. The lead time is either 2 or 3 days with probabilities of .8 and .2 respectively. Whenever Meal-Bone is out of cashews, there is a .50 chance that the customer will be satisfied with the purchase of another equally profitable nut. Set up a simulation work sheet and simulate 20 days of experience if the quantity ordered is 70 pounds and the reorder level is 20 pounds. Do not attempt to calculate costs. (Assume that the initial inventory is 70 pounds.)

Linear Programming– Graphical and Applications

7.1 INTRODUCTION TO LINEAR PROGRAMMING

Modern management is often faced with complex problems where there are numerous variables or conditions affecting the manager's success in dealing with these problems. Because of the complexity of the situation there are many different strategies a manager can pursue in an effort to get good results. The marketing manager, for example, is well aware of the many variables which may affect the sales success of a new product that is being introduced. The same manager is also cognizant of the many alternatives that are available in regard to the distribution, pricing, selling, and advertising of the product. Assuming that an advertising budget has been set, the manager still is faced with limitless alternatives as to how to allocate that budget among various advertising vehicles for the purpose of inducing the greatest sales volume. Many of the complex problems with numerous variables and limitless alternatives for action are conceptually similar and may be analyzed by means of linear programming. But what is linear programming? It might be described, somewhat technically, as an analytic procedure which shows how scarce resources should be allocated for the sake of achieving some goal like maximizing profits. This linear programming might aid the marketing manager in allocating an advertising budget among various advertising media in order to maximize sales. Before proceeding, a few more remarks concerning the nature of linear programming should be made.

The term "programming" in linear programming has nothing to do with the computer. Programming in the broad sense of the term refers to the orderly execution of a task or the systematic arrangement of material. The programmer at the local television station has the responsibility of selecting and arranging the programs so that a systematic, comprehensive schedule results. The computer programmer follows a logical, orderly procedure to instruct the computer what to do. Understanding the background of the term "programming," it would be a fair guess that linear programming involves an orderly, well-defined procedure for building and solving some sort of model. It might next be asked, "What kind of model is solved in this systematic fashion?" The term "linear" gives a clue. A linear programming model is a mathematical model which consists solely of linear equations and/or inequalities. However, all models composed of linear equations and/or inequalities are not necessarily linear programming models. The actual form of the linear programming model will now be demonstrated by means of examples; familiarity with these examples provides the best appreciation for the capabilities of linear programming.

7.2 A LINEAR PROGRAMMING MODEL—MAXIMIZATION

In the last section it was mentioned that linear programming can be used to solve some very complex problems which face management. A consideration of these complicated linear programming models is beyond the scope of an introductory text; however, with some simple examples the nature of linear programming can be suitably revealed.

Over a hundred years ago business was booming in San Francisco because of the gold rush. North of San Francisco was a Russian fort, Fort Ross, manned by a token force of soldiers among whom were the Brothers Karamazov. One of the brothers was a carpenter, the other a tinsmith. During their spare time the Brothers Karamazov would wander into San Francisco and were soon infected with gold fever. Upon returning to the fort the Brothers requested permission to pan in the gold fields. Their commander, General Aliotov, in a fit of bombast denied the Brothers their request. The Brothers then turned their attention toward some gainful occupation that might enable them to use their Saturday visits to San Francisco profitably while satisfying in some measure their urge to be embroiled in the gold pandemonium. In particular, the Brothers rented a shop in the Telegraph Hill area where they decided to make gold-mining equipment. Linear programming, which had not been invented then, was instrumental in the Brothers' quest for optimal profits.

The Brothers faced a production situation where there were scarce resources, namely, their time and certain materials. The carpenter can work only 12.5 hours on a Saturday; the tinsmith can only manage 10 hours of labor as years of drinking from his tin cups have dulled his propensity for work. The Brothers found their skills to be especially adapted to the construction of two special pieces of mining equipment, the rocker and the sluice box. The rocker was essentially a big gold pan on a cradle and was operated by two placer miners. The sluice box was a much larger device and was operated by several miners. The Brothers' objective was to find that production mix which would maximize their profits. Should they make only sluice boxes? only rockers? or some combination of each? The Brothers figured they could make a net profit of $30 for each rocker they produced and $20 for each sluice box. To make one rocker, one hour of the carpenter's time was required and two hours of the tinsmith's. To make a sluice box, three hours of the carpenter's time was required and only one hour of the tinsmith's. It was therefore obvious to the Brothers that since they had only a limited amount of time to devote to this occupation, only a limited number of rockers and sluice boxes could be produced each Saturday. The Brothers could get all the lumber and tin they needed; however, the iron runners used on the bottom of the rocker were in short supply. The Brothers' supplier could only let them have a maximum of eight of these runners each week; each rocker required two iron runners. How many rockers and sluice boxes should the Brothers Karamazov build each Saturday in order to make the most profit?

Building a linear programming model is essentially a three-step process. First there is the task of *defining the variables* or activities. What is it that the Brothers are trying to decide upon? They are trying to determine how many rockers and how many sluice boxes to make each Saturday. Therefore, let the following variables be defined:

X = the number of rockers to be made each Saturday
Y = the number of sluice boxes to be made each Saturday

The Brothers want to determine the best values for X and Y; that is, they are seeking that combination of (X, Y) which will yield the maximum profit for a Saturday's work. There are many possible solutions or combinations of X and Y. For example, the Brothers could make two of each which is represented symbolically by $X = 2$, $Y = 2$. They could make one rocker and three sluice boxes, that is, $X = 1$, $Y = 3$. Or perhaps they could make four rockers and seven sluice boxes, $X = 4$, $Y = 7$. Notice that the combinations of X and Y constitute possible solutions to the Brothers' dilemma.

The second step in constructing a linear programming model is the *writing of the objective function*. What is the goal the decision maker is seeking? Sometimes the goal is minimizing costs, sometimes it is maximizing sales or market share, or, sometimes it is the maximization of profits. The Brothers' goal is to maximize profits. Having determined the objective or goal, it is necessary to mathematically express the quantity (like profit) to be maximized or minimized as a function of the variables previously defined. This equation is called the objective function. Letting P represent profit, the Brothers will make a profit of

$$P = 30\,X + 20\,Y$$

if they produce X rockers and Y sluice boxes in a Saturday. For example, if they make $X = 2$ rockers and $Y = 3$ sluice boxes, then their profit will be

$$P = (\$30)(2) + (\$20)(3)$$
$$= \$120$$

since $30 is made for each rocker and $20 for each sluice box. With the objective function $P = 30\,X + 20\,Y$, it is obvious that as X and Y increase, the more profit will be made. However, there are limitations on the Brothers' capacity to produce the mining equipment and therefore the profit P that they can make will be limited. This brings us to the third step in the construction of the model.

Before considering the third step, it may be that the reader has forgotten many of the details of the Brothers' problem which was given at the beginning of this section. Instead of having to read the initial statement of the problem again and again to pick out the various pertinent details, it is helpful to summarize all the relevant information in table form for easy access. The construction of an information table (see Table 7.1, p. 158) permits the analyst to pick out the information needed at a glance. Notice that the two products are listed along the top and the resources are listed down the left side. The information in this table was taken directly from the paragraph describing the Brothers' problem.

TABLE 7.1
Brothers Karamazov Information Table

| | PRODUCT | | |
RESOURCE	Each Rocker requires:	Each Sluice Box requires:	Amount of Resource Available:
Carpenter	1 hour	3 hours	12.5 hours
Tinsmith	2 hours	1 hour	10.0 hours
Iron Runners	2	0	8 runners
Profit per Unit of product:	$30	$20	

The third step in constructing a linear programming model is the *writing of the constraints.* If there were no limitations on the Brothers' capacity they could produce an infinite number of rockers and/or sluice boxes thereby making an infinite profit. However, it has been indicated that the brother who is the carpenter has only 12.5 hours of time which he can devote to his work and the tinsmith has only 10 hours. In the parlance of linear programming, the time each brother has available is a resource. The Brothers wish to maximize profit P while faced with a scarcity of these two resources. Consider the carpentry time resource first. Recall from Table 7.1 that each rocker uses 1 hour of carpentry time and each sluice box uses 3 hours of carpentry time. Since the carpenter has only 12.5 hours available, it follows that $X=4$ rockers and $Y=4$ sluice boxes cannot be built in a Saturday. Why? It would take a total of

$$(4 \text{ rockers})(1 \text{ hour per rocker}) = 4 \text{ carpentry hours}$$

to build 4 rockers, and a total of

$$(4 \text{ sluice boxes})(3 \text{ hours per sluice box}) = 12 \text{ carpentry hours}$$

to build 4 sluice boxes for a grand total of 16 carpentry hours on a Saturday when only 12.5 are available. If this combination of $X=4$ rockers, and $Y=4$ sluice boxes is not feasible, what combinations or production mixes are feasible as far as the carpentry resource is concerned? An inequality will be given which expresses all the (X,Y) combinations which are feasible. Considering only the carpentry resource, any (X,Y) which satisfies the following inequality is permissible or feasible:

$$X + 3Y \leq 12.5 \qquad \text{(Carpenter Constraint)}$$

The left side of this inequality expresses the number of hours of carpentry time required by a production mix of X rockers and Y sluice boxes. This total must be less than or equal to 12.5 hours. In linear programming an inequality like this is called a *constraint.* Using this constraint it can be shown that the aforementioned production mix of $X=4$, $Y=4$ is not feasible since $4 + (3)(4) \nleq 12.5$. A production mix like $X=4$, $Y=1$ is possible since $4 + (3)(1) \leq 12.5$.

Another scarce resource is tinsmithing time which is limited to 10 hours. The constraint which mathematically expresses the production limitations with regard to this resource is

$$2X + Y \leq 10 \qquad \text{(Tinsmith Constraint)}$$

Since each rocker requires 2 hours of the tinsmith's time and each sluice box requires 1 hour of the tinsmith's time, then X rockers will require $2X$ hours and Y sluice boxes will require Y hours of the tinsmith's time. Therefore the left side of the constraint or inequality expresses the amount of tinsmithing time required to make X rockers and Y sluice boxes. The right side of this constraint gives the total available tinsmithing hours. Notice that the production mix, $X=3$ rockers, $Y = 2$ sluice boxes, is feasible, but the mix $X=4$, $Y=3$ is not since it would require 11 hours of the tinsmith.

In the initial statement of the Brothers Karamazov situation it was also noted that only 8 iron runners would be available each week. The sluice box does not use these runners but each rocker uses two. This means that under no circumstances could the Brothers build more than 4 rockers on a Saturday. This limitation on X may be expressed mathematically by the following constraint

$$2\,X \leq 8 \qquad \text{(Runners Constraint)}$$

The variable Y does not appear in this constraint since sluice boxes do not use iron runners.

It should be emphasized that any solution or production mix that might be considered by the Brothers *must* satisfy all three of the above constraints. For example, the mix of $X=2$ rockers, $Y=5$ sluice boxes satisfies the tinsmith constraint since such a mix would require only 9 hours from the tinsmith, and it would satisfy the runners constraint as only 4 runners would be used. Nevertheless, the (2,5) mix is not feasible since it also requires 17 hours from the carpenter who only has 12.5 hours available. If a production mix fails to satisfy even one constraint it must be discarded as being infeasible.

Finally, two extra constraints are added which eliminate the possibility of the Brothers making a negative quantity of some product. These two non-negativity constraints are

$$X \geq 0 \qquad\qquad Y \geq 0$$

All the parts of the linear programming model have now been considered. The model may now be expressed as one mathematical composite of variables, objective function, and constraints.

Maximize $P = 30X + 20Y$
Subject to:

$X + 3Y \leq 12.5$	(Carpenter Constraint)	
$2X + Y \leq 10$	(Tinsmith Constraint)	
$2X \leq 8$	(Runners Constraint)	
$X \geq 0$	(Nonnegativity Constraint)	
$Y \geq 0$	(Nonnegativity Constraint)	

The optimal solution or production mix (X, Y) is that mix which maximizes profit P while satisfying the constraints or limitations. This model will be solved in the following section in order to determine how many rockers and sluice boxes the Brothers Karamazov should make each Saturday.

7.3 A GRAPHICAL SOLUTION

In order to find the optimal solution which is some combination of values for X and Y, a coordinate system should be laid out on graph paper letting X be represented on one axis and the variable Y on the other axis. On this graph paper the constraints, which are usually inequalities, must be graphed. After the constraints have been graphed the optimal solution may be found. The method of graphing these constraints or inequalities will now be illustrated.

Before studying the procedure of graphing an inequality, it would be helpful to know what the graph of a linear inequality is supposed to look like. The graph of a linear equation is simply a straight line (see Figure 7.1). The graph of a linear inequality includes not only a straight line but also all of the points on one side of that straight line. In Figure 7.2 there is an example of a graph of an inequality. Notice that its graph consists of the straight line and all the shaded area to one side. Any point in the shaded area or on the line will satisfy the linear inequality. Now consider the technique of graphing a particular linear inequality such as $X + 3Y \leq 12.5$.

The first constraint in the Brothers Karamazov example was $X + 3Y \leq 12.5$. Such an inequality may be graphed in two steps.

1. Replace the inequality sign temporarily with an equal sign and then graph the resulting linear equation.
2. Restore the original inequality sign to the constraint. Then substitute into this inequality or constraint a point (X, Y) which is obviously on one side of the line which was graphed in the first step. If this point satisfies the

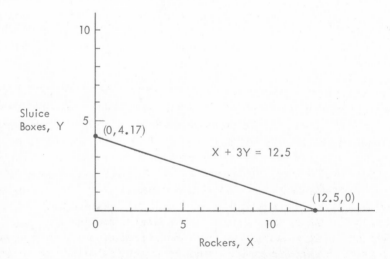

FIGURE 7.1   Graph of a Linear Equation

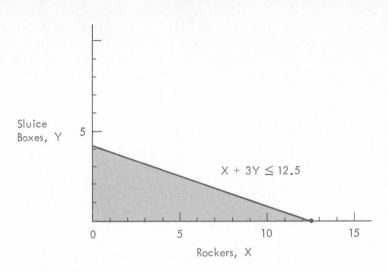

FIGURE 7.2   Graph of the Carpenter Inequality or Constraint

inequality, then every point which is on the same side of the line as this test point is the graph of the constraint (the line is also part of the graph). If the test point does not satisfy the inequality, then the points on the other side of the line and the line itself is the graph of the inequality or constraint. Shade the side of the line which represents the graph of the inequality.

In linear programming the constraints are always linear and therefore by means of the first step a linear equation will always result which has a straight line as its graph. In Figure 7.1 the equation $X + 3Y = 12.5$ is graphed.

Again referring to Figure 7.1, it is apparent that the point $X=0$, $Y=0$ is to the southwest of the line drawn in the first step. When (0,0) is substituted into $X + 3Y \leq 12.5$, it yields $0 + 0 \leq 12.5$ which is true. Therefore (0,0) satisfies this inequality. It then follows by the second step that every point of the southwest side of the line constitutes the graph of the carpentry constraint. This graph is presented as the shaded area of Figure 7.2.

In a similar manner the graph of the tinsmith constraint which is $2X + Y \leq 10$ may be drawn. Verify that any point selected which is on the line or in the shaded area of Figure 7.3, page 162, satisfies the tinsmith constraint. For example, the production mix of $X=3$ rockers, $Y=1$ sluice box falls in the shaded area and it satisfies the constraint since $(2)(3) + 1 \leq 10$. It can therefore be concluded that the production mix (3,1) does not use more than the available amount of tinsmith time. Notice that the shaded areas of both Figures 7.2 and 7.3 have been confined to the first quadrant because the nonnegativity constraints require that only nonnegative values of X and Y be considered.

Finally the runners constraint, $2X \leq 8$, is graphed in Figure 7.4, page 162. Considering this constraint alone, any point or production mix in the shaded area is permissible as each of those points represent production mixes where 4 rockers or less are built.

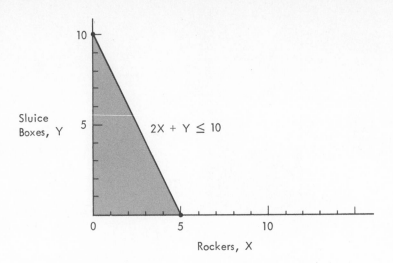

FIGURE 7.3   Graph of the Tinsmith Constraint

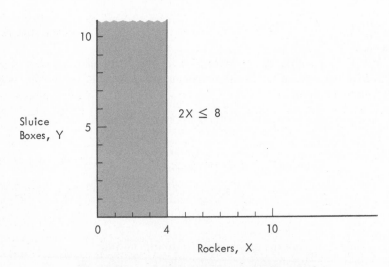

FIGURE 7.4   Graph of the Runners Constraint

It was emphasized in the last section that any production mix that is considered must satisfy all of the constraints. For example, $X=2$, $Y=5$ falls in the shaded area of Figures 7.3 and 7.4 thus indicating that the tinsmith and runners constraints are satisfied; however, it falls outside the shaded area of Figure 7.2 indicating that the carpenter constraint is not satisfied. This potential solution must therefore be discarded. Figure 7.5 presents all of the constraints simultaneously. The shaded area in this graph is only the shaded area which is common to all of the constraints. It may be concluded then that only points or production mixes which fall in this shaded area are feasible. In fact, in the terminology of

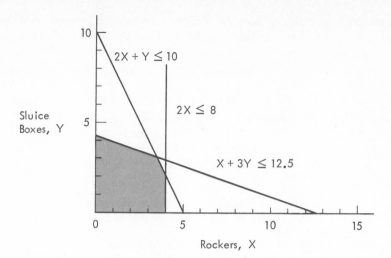

FIGURE 7.5   Feasible Solutions Represented by Shaded Area

linear programming, these points or production mixes represented by the shaded area in Figure 7.5 are called feasible solutions. Any point outside this shaded area is called infeasible.

Within the shaded area of Figure 7.5 there are an infinite number of points or feasible solutions. In the linear programming model the solutions are not limited to integer values for the variables or activities. That is, the solution represented by $X = 3.24$, $Y = 1.95$ must not be disqualified solely because the X and Y values are not integers. If this kind of noninteger solution is absolutely unpractical, linear programming may have to be abandoned in favor of "integer programming." In integer programming some or all of the variables may be specified to be integers.

In the Brothers Karamazov problem it should be asked if a noninteger solution is workable. It will appear later that the solution $X = 3.5$, $Y = 3$ will be among the front running feasible solutions in the Brothers' quest for an optimal feasible solution. Could the Brothers live with this solution if it were in fact optimal? The Brothers could build 3.5 rockers and 3 sluice boxes on a Saturday but they could only sell 3 rockers and 3 sluice boxes as there is no market for .5 or half a rocker. However, they could save this half-completed rocker till the next Saturday when it could be completed. On that Saturday they would end up with 4 rockers and 3 sluice boxes all of which could be sold. Therefore the noninteger solution poses no insuperable difficulty for the Brothers Karamazov.

With a collection or set of all the feasible solutions represented by the shaded area in Figure 7.5, the Brothers must now be advised as to which solution is optimal. That is, which of these solutions will yield the maximum profit? Recall that the objective function to be maximized in this linear programming model is

$$P = 30X + 20Y$$

The profit P is increased as X and/or Y increase in value. This means that the optimal solution will certainly not be represented by a point close to the origin in the shaded area of Figure 7.5. In Figure 7.6, which gives the same shaded area or set of feasible solutions as Figure 7.5, point F would certainly not be optimal since there are many points or solutions which have greater values for both X and Y. Even a point like G would not be optimal because there are points to its northeast which are composed of yet larger values of X and Y and hence would yield a larger profit P. With a little reflection on the matter one should conclude that the optimal solution (that which yields the maximum profit) will occur on the border of the shaded area. In fact, even a more specific statement or theorem can be given.

> The optimal solution in a linear programming model will occur at one of the corners of the border of the shaded area where the shaded area represents all of the feasible solutions.

A little later some evidence for the validity of this theorem will be presented. At this time it will be accepted as given and used for the sake of finding the optimal solution to the Brothers' problem.

In Figure 7.6 there are five corner points on the border of the shaded area. According to the theorem, one of these points A, B, C, D, or E will represent the optimal solution to the Brothers' problem. Since there are so few of these corners, the optimal solution could be found by checking each one of them to see what profit each would yield. That point, from among the five, which would yield the highest profit would then be the optimal solution to the Brothers' problem. This is exactly the procedure that will be followed. First, however, the coordinates of these five points must be found since the values of X and Y of the points represent the actual solutions.

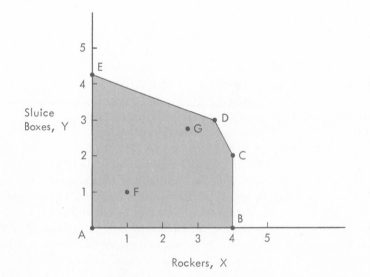

FIGURE 7.6 Feasible Solutions

The point A has the coordinates $(0,0)$ which means that this potential solution involves making $X=0$ rockers and $Y=0$ sluice boxes. The point or corner B (see Figure 7.7) is at the intersection of the $2X = 8$ line and the horizontal axis which has the equation $Y=0$. Therefore, the coordinates of this intersection at point B are $X=4$, $Y=0$. Point B represents the feasible solution of building $X=4$ rockers and $Y=0$ sluice boxes on a Saturday. Point C is at the intersection of the lines whose equations are $2X = 8$ and $2X + Y = 10$. These two equations may be solved simultaneously (review Section 2.4 of Chapter 2 for the method of solving two linear equations simultaneously). Dividing the equation $2X = 8$ by 2 yields $X=4$ as one coordinate of point C. Substituting $X=4$ into the equation $2X + Y = 10$ and solving for Y yields $Y=2$. Hence the coordinates of point C are $(4,2)$ representing the construction of 4 rockers and 2 sluice boxes on a Saturday. Point D is found by solving $2X + Y = 10$ and $X + 3Y = 12.5$ simultaneously since D lies at the intersection of these two lines. By the method of substitution, rewrite the first of these two equations as

$$Y = 10 - 2X$$

Then substitute $(10 - 2X)$ for Y in the second equation. That is,

$$X + 3Y = 12.5$$
$$X + 3(10-2X) = 12.5 \qquad \text{(by substitution)}$$

Then solve for X in the last equation:

$$X + 30 - 6X = 12.5$$
$$-5X = -17.5$$
$$X = 3.5$$

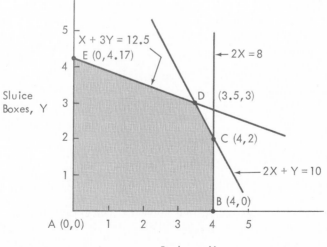

FIGURE 7.7   Feasible Solutions and Corner Solutions

Finally, substitute this $X = 3.5$ back into the first equation which was $Y = 10 - 2X$. This yields

$$Y = 10 - 2(3.5)$$
$$= 3$$

Therefore, the coordinates of point D are $X=3.5$, $Y=3$ which represents 3.5 rockers and 3 sluice boxes. The last of the five corners, point E, has the coordinates (0,4.17). The Y coordinate is found by substituting $X=0$ in the equation $X + 3Y = 12.5$ and solving for Y.

Now that the coordinates of the five corners have been determined, the theorem can be applied to find the optimal solution. Remember, the theorem states that the solution or production mix which yields the maximum profit will be found at a corner of the shaded area. Each corner will now be checked to see what profit it yields. The coordinates of corner A are (0,0) meaning that this production mix would yield a Saturday profit of

$$P = (30)(0) + (20)(0)$$
$$= 0$$

since the objective function is $P = 30X + 20Y$. The profit associated with corner B, where 4 rockers and 0 sluice boxes are made, is

$$P = (30)(4) + (20)(0)$$
$$= \$120$$

The profit for corner C is

$$P = (30)(4) + (20)(2)$$
$$= \$160$$

The profit for corner D is

$$P = (30)(3.5) + (20)(3)$$
$$= \$165$$

And the profit for the last corner, corner E, is

$$P = (30)(0) + (20)(4.17)$$
$$= \$83.40$$

Because of the theorem it may now be concluded with certainty that the optimal solution is represented by corner D since it yields the greatest profit, which is $165. The Brothers Karamazov should make 3.5 rockers and 3 sluice boxes each Saturday.

In the next section a topic which is related to the graphical solution of the linear programming problem will be presented. The objective function will be graphed. By seeing the graph of the objective function the validity of the theorem given in this section will become apparent. The graph of the objective function in conjunction with the graph of the constraints will also give a clearer insight into the linear programming model.

Before this section is concluded, the steps by which a graphical solution was achieved will be reviewed:

1. Graph each of the constraints or inequalities.
2. Find the area which is common to all the inequality graphs. In other words, shade in the area which represents the points which satisfy each of the constraints. This shaded area constitutes the set of feasible solutions.
3. Find the coordinates of each of the corners of the shaded area. The optimal solution will be found among these corner solutions.
4. Find the profit corresponding to each corner solution by substituting the corner's coordinates into the objective function.
5. The optimal feasible solution is that represented by the corner which yields the maximum profit.

7.4 THE GRAPH OF THE OBJECTIVE FUNCTION

The linear programming model of the Brothers Karamazov problem was given as

$$\text{Max } P = 30X + 20Y$$

Subject to:

$$X + 3Y \leq 12.5$$
$$2X + Y \leq 10$$
$$2X \leq 8$$
$$X \geq 0$$
$$Y \geq 0$$

In the section just completed this model was solved graphically. The graphical solution procedure outlined did not entail the graphing of the objective function. Though it is not necessary to graph the objective function, it is useful to do so as it permits several valuable insights.

Consider how the Brothers might make $90 on a Saturday. One way this profit could be achieved is by making 3 rockers and 0 sluice boxes since by the objective function

$$P = (30)(3) + (20)(0)$$
$$= \$90$$

Another way would be by making 1 rocker and 3 sluice boxes. Yet another way a profit of $90 could be made is by building 2 rockers and 1.5 sluice boxes. The production mix represented by $X=2.5$, $Y=.75$ would also yield $90. Since linear programming solutions are not confined to integer values, there are literally an infinite number of combinations of X and Y which yield $P = \$90$ when substituted into $P=30X+20Y$. All of these production mixes can be shown graphically by merely graphing the objective function with 90 substituted for P, that is, by graphing $90 = 30X + 20Y$. The graph of this equation where P is fixed is called an isoprofit line since every point of the line yields the same profit. In Figure 7.8, page 168, this graph or isoprofit line is expressed by a dotted line. Notice that $90 = 30X + 20Y$ is a linear equation and thus it is a straight line when graphed. To reiterate, the dotted line of Figure 7.8 is the graph of the objective function when profit is 90 in that it shows all the production mixes which will yield the same ("iso") profit of $90.

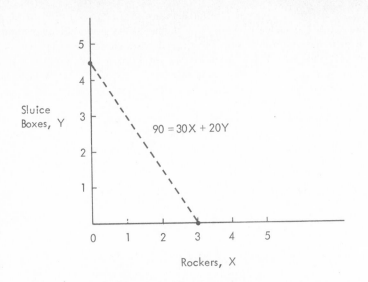

FIGURE 7.8   Objective Function (Isoprofit Line) Representing All Mixes Yielding Profit of $90

In Figure 7.9 several isoprofit lines are graphed. Each of them represents the production mixes which yield some particular profit. The second dotted line from the origin, whose equation is $150 = 30X + 20Y$, shows all the combinations of rockers and sluice boxes which would produce a profit of exactly $150. It is apparent that the isoprofit lines (which are objective function lines) represent higher profits as one moves to the northeast. Now since the Brothers want to maximize profits they would want to make some combination of rockers and sluice boxes which lies on the isoprofit line which is as far to the northeast as possible. Could the Brothers, for example, manufacture some combination as represented by the $P = 200$ isoprofit line? Six rockers and 1 sluice box would produce a profit of $200 but it must be recalled that there are some limitations or constraints on what the Brothers can do in a day! It takes 2 hours of the tinsmith's time to make a rocker; making 6 rockers would consume 12 hours of his time and he only has a total of 10 hours available. Therefore, the Brothers cannot make $200 in this manner because of the tinsmith constraint. No matter what point on the $P = 200$ line is tried, it will be found that it would use too much time and/or too many runners. In other words, none of the points on this isoprofit line satisfy all of the constraints, which means that none of the production mixes they represent are feasible. The Brothers must give up all hope of making $200 on a Saturday.

The dotted lines of the isoprofit lines tell us what mixes of rockers and sluice boxes will yield varying levels of profits, but unfortunately they do not tell which mixes are feasible. Recall that in Figure 7.5 or 7.6 all the feasible production mixes have already been given as shown by the shaded area. In Figure 7.10, page 170, this shaded area, which represents the feasible solutions, is superimposed on the isoprofit (objective function) lines of Figure 7.9. It now becomes

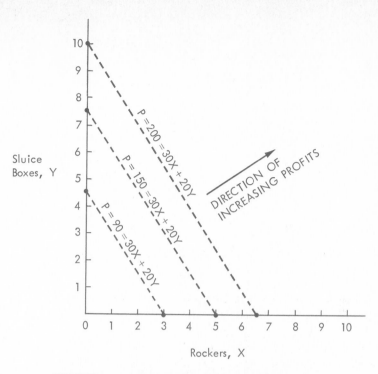

**FIGURE 7.9 Isoprofit Lines (Objective Functions)
Representing Various Profit Levels**

obvious that since the $P=200$ line lies entirely outside the shaded area, there is
no possibility of making a profit of $200. There are some production mixes or
points which yield $150 which fall within the shaded area; this means that the
Brothers can make a profit of $150. Note that some of the production mixes
which yield a profit of $150 are not feasible. Still looking at Figure 7.10, it
should be clear that if the Brothers can produce any mix of rockers and sluice
boxes represented by points in the shaded area, they can do better than 150 since
there are isoprofit lines which lie to the northeast of $P=150$ but which are still
partially in the shaded area (these lines are not shown). In Figure 7.11, page 170,
the isoprofit lines yielding profits of $160 and $165 are graphed. As $P=165$ is the
last isoprofit line to touch the shaded area (as one moves toward the northeast),
the point D must be the production mix which represents the maximum profit
and thus is optimal. This conclusion accords with that of the previous section.

Because the objective function is a straight line, and because the objective
function or isoprofit lines for greater and greater profits are parallel and further
out, the isoprofit line last to touch the shaded area when moving in the direction
(northeast) of increasing profit will touch the shaded area at a corner. This is because the corners jut out. This means that the optimal solution yielding the maximum profit will always be a corner solution. This insight lends support to the
theorem of the previous section which stated that the optimal solution will always occur at a corner of the shaded area of feasible solutions.

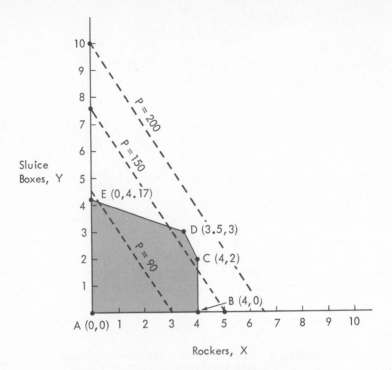

FIGURE 7.10   Isoprofit Lines and Feasible Solutions

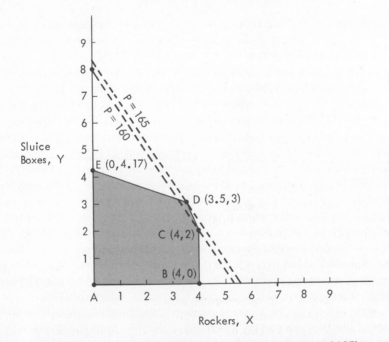

FIGURE 7.11   Optimal Solution at Corner D (Profit of $165)

7.5 A LINEAR PROGRAMMING MODEL—MINIMIZATION

In the Brothers Karamazov example the objective was to maximize profits. Other maximization problems might deal with maximizing rates of return, sales, market shares, and output. Yet in some cases the objective of management might be to minimize some quantity. Such an example will now be given.

Near Richmond, Virginia, is a large amusement park known as Tiger Country Safari. Tiger Country Safari boasts a large variety of "rides" along with a monorail ride through a wilderness area inhabited by tigers. Tiger Country Safari has experienced strong sales in the summer months but must close for the winter. The closing date in October is not too far off and the management is especially conscious of keeping up crowd size right up to the closing date. To keep attendance high, Tiger Country Safari is paying special attention to its advertising in the Richmond area because most of the crowd comes from Richmond in October. As a publicity ploy to end the year, one of the tigers has agreed to try to swallow the mayor of New York City whole. Tiger Country Safari wants to advertise this coming event through the Richmond newspaper and television. Consider now some of the details.

By its advertising program Tiger Country Safari (TCS) wishes to publicize the coming event by making 60,000 exposures among the young of Richmond. An exposure represents one time when a person is made aware of the coming event; if one person were exposed to the coming event by seeing a television ad once and then by seeing three different newspaper ads, this would count for four exposures. Therefore, making 60,000 exposures among the young does not mean that TCS requires that 60,000 different youngsters be exposed. Only 40,000 different youngsters might be exposed where some were exposed several times yielding the required 60,000 exposures. To repeat TCS's wish, the advertising program must make 60,000 exposures among the young of Richmond. As far as oldsters go, TCS has not set any particular minimum except that TCS wants to end up having twice as many exposures among oldsters as youngsters.

One television advertisement is known to make 10,000 exposures among the young and one newspaper advertisement will make 3,000 exposures among the young. A television ad will result in 10,000 exposures among the old and a newspaper ad will yield 9,000 exposures. In trying to determine the mix of televison and newspaper ads to use, TCS must bear in mind that it has a standing agreement with the Richmond newspaper that it will place at least 5 ads in the paper each week the amusement park is open. With respect to advertising costs, television ads cost $200 each while newspaper ads cost $100 each. Under these conditions what should be TCS's advertising mix if the various requirements are to be met at a minimum cost?

Before modeling the Tiger Country Safari situation, an information table is set up which summarizes the critical elements of this advertising problem. For this information table see Table 7.2, page 172.

In this problem the objective is to minimize advertising costs while at the same time satisfying the various stated requirements. The first step in constructing a linear programming model is *defining the variables*. Let

TABLE 7.2

Tiger Country Safari Information Table

	Exposures Made per Advertisement	
Audience	Television	Newspaper
Youngsters	10,000	3,000
Oldsters	10,000	9,000
Cost per ad:	$200	$100

Requirements:
　　At least 60,000 exposures among the young.
　　At least twice as many exposures among the old.
　　Must place at least 5 newspaper ads.

$$T = \text{the number of television ads}$$
$$N = \text{the number of newspaper ads}$$

The second step is the *formulation of the objective function* in terms of the variables defined. As the objective is to minimize advertising costs, let C represent total advertising costs and then the objective function may be stated as

$$\text{Minimize} \quad C = 200T + 100N$$

For example, if $T=3$ television ads are used and $N=4$ newspaper ads are placed, the total advertising cost would be

$$C = (200)(3) + (100)(4)$$
$$= \$1,000$$

since each television ad costs $200 and each newspaper ad costs $100.

Finally the *constraints must be written*. There must be at least 60,000 exposures among the young. Since each television ad makes 10,000 exposures and each newspaper ad makes 3,000 exposures, it follows that T television ads will make a total of $10,000T$ exposures and N newspaper ads will make a total of $3,000N$ exposures. The total number of exposures among the young from an advertising program of (T,N) will be $10,000T + 3,000N$. The total number of exposures here must equal at least 60,000; this is expressed mathematically by the constraint

$$10,000T + 3,000N \geq 60,000$$

This is the first constraint in the model.

In the second place it was stated that TCS wishes to have at least twice as many exposures among the old as among the young. As one television ad makes 10,000 exposures among the old and one newspaper ad makes 9,000 exposures among the old, the total number of exposures among the old from an advertising mix of (T television ads, N newspaper ads) will be $10,000T + 9,000N$. This total figure must be at least twice that of the exposures among the young which has already been shown to be $10,000T + 3,000N$. Equivalently,

(Exposures among the old) $\geq$ 2(Exposures among the young)

or,

$$10,000T + 9,000N \geq 2(10,000T + 3,000N)$$

This last inequality may be algebraically simplified resulting in the equivalent form

$$-10,000T + 3,000N \geq 0$$

This is the second constraint in the model.

Another requirement facing Tiger County Safari is the agreement to place at least 5 newspaper ads with the Richmond newspaper as long as the park is open. This requirement may be simply expressed as

$$N \geq 5$$

There are also two nonnegativity contraints which must be added

$$N \geq 0 \quad \text{and} \quad T \geq 0$$

The first of these is not really necessary since the constraint $N \geq 5$ has already appeared.

In summary, the linear programming model for Tiger Country Safari is:

Minimize $C = 200T + 100N$
   Subject to:

$10,000T + 3,000N \geq 60,000$	(Youngsters Constraint)
$-10,000T + 3,000N \geq 0$	(Oldsters Constraint)
$N \geq 5$	(Newspaper Constraint)
$T \geq 0$	(Nonnegativity Constraints)
$N \geq 0$	

The solution of this model will now be presented.

7.6 A GRAPHICAL SOLUTION

The procedure to solve a minimization problem is the same as that for a maximization problem except for a slight difference at the end. First the constraints are graphed. For the first constraint,

$$10,000T + 3,000N \geq 60,000$$

the inequality sign is replaced by an equal sign and the linear equation is graphed as in Figure 7.12, page 174. To determine which side of the line should be shaded, the point (0,0) which is on the southwest side of the line is tried in the constraint:

$$(10,000)(0) + (3,000)(0) \geq 60,000 \quad \text{False!}$$

Since (0,0) does not satisfy this constraint, the shaded area must be on the other (northeast) side of the line.

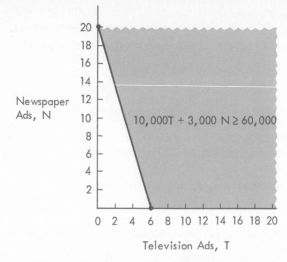

FIGURE 7.12   Graph of Youngsters Constraint

In Figure 7.13 the other two principal constraints are also graphed and only the shaded area which is common to all three constraints or inequalities is given. The little arrows coming off each line indicate the side of the line that should be shaded. The shaded area of Figure 7.13 represents all of the feasible solutions. For example, the point $T=3$, $N=20$ which is within the shaded area represents

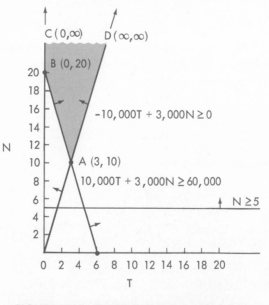

FIGURE 7.13   Feasible Solutions (Shaded) and Corner Solutions

an advertising program which will yield (10,000)(3) + (3,000)(20) or 90,000 exposures among the young, which is well above the required 60,000 and thus the first constraint is satisfied. This advertising mix will yield (10,000)(3) + (9,000)(20) or 210,000 exposures among the old which is more than twice the 90,000 among the young; hence the second constraint is satisfied by $T=3$, $N=20$. The third constraint which requires at least 5 newspaper ads is also amply satisfied. On the other hand, the advertising mix $T=1$, $N=10$ while satisfying the second and third constraints does not meet the first constraint because it represents an exposure of only (10,000)(1) + (3,000)(10) = 40,000 among the young thereby falling short of the required 60,000.

Which of the advertising mixes represented by the shaded area in Figure 7.13 is optimal or requires the minimum advertising cost? The theorem given in Section 7.3 will be of help in finding the optimal advertising mix. That theorem stated that the optimal point or mix will occur at a corner of the shaded area; this theorem holds whether the problem is one of maximization or of minimization. How many corners does the shaded area of Figure 7.13 have? Points A and B are certainly corners, but are there others? The shaded area in this problem is open-ended and therefore there are no more corners. However, one might consider that a corner lies at the "end" of the shaded area in the direction of C with coordinates of $T=0$, $N=\infty$. Likewise one might conceive of a corner in the direction of D with coordinates of (∞, ∞); more on this later.

The actual coordinates of corners A and B in Figure 7.13 must now be found. Point A lies at the intersection of the lines with equations $10,000T + 3,000N = 60,000$ and $-10,000T + 3,000N = 0$. Solving these two equations simultaneously shows the coordinates of A to be $T=3$, $N=10$. The coordinates of corner B are found by solving $10,000T + 3,000N = 60,000$ for N where $T=0$; this yields coordinates of (0,20).

With the coordinates of the corners found, each must now be examined to see what total advertising cost it represents. The advertising cost associated with corner A is found by substituting its coordinates of $T=3$ and $N=10$ into the objective function which was given as $C = 200T + 100N$. Therefore the cost is

$$C = (200)(3) + (100)(10)$$
$$= \$1600$$

The cost for corner B which has coordinates of $T=0$, $N=20$ is

$$C = (200)(0) + (100)(20)$$
$$= \$2,000$$

In the case of the "corners" C and D with coordinates of $(0,\infty)$ and (∞,∞), the resulting total advertising cost would be infinite and thus neither of these "corners" can possibly represent an optimal solution. Since corner A is the corner with the minimum cost, it represents the optimal advertising mix. Tiger Country Safari should place 3 television ads and 10 newspaper ads if it desires to minimize advertising costs while satisfying the constraints. The minimum or optimal advertising cost will be $1600.

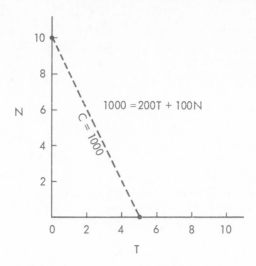

FIGURE 7.14   All Advertising Mixes Costing $1000 (Isocost Line)

Before leaving the Tiger Country Safari example, consider the graph of the objective function. In Figure 7.14 all the advertising mixes are given which cost a total of $1,000. This dotted line is merely the graph of the objective function with C equal to 1,000, that is, it is the graph of

$$1,000 = 200T + 100N$$

None of the points or advertising mixes on this isocost line will satisfy all of the requirements that Tiger Country Safari has set forth. This means that TCS cannot put on the kind of advertising program it desires for only $1,000. In Figure 7.15 several isocost or objective function lines are shown each representing a different total advertising cost. Notice that the lines closer to the origin (to the southwest) have the smaller costs. Since the objective in this problem is the minimization of costs, the dotted line closest to the origin which also touches the shaded area will represent the optimal cost. The dotted line denoting a cost of $1600 is the isocost line which is the closest to the origin while still touching the shaded area of feasible solutions. That place or point where it touches the shaded area is the optimal advertising mix. It is corner A which was already found to be $T = 3$, $N = 10$. The analysis using the isocost lines therefore produces the same optimal solution as before.

7.7 SPECIAL CONSIDERATIONS

Occasionally the analyst will run into some strange results while graphing the constraints and isolating the optimal corner or solution. In this section four such unusual occurrences will be studied.

Redundancy

Suppose a linear programming model has been constructed which uses the two variables X and Y. Suppose further that among the set of constraints are found the following two inequalities:

$$6X + 2Y \leq 80$$

and

$$12X + 4Y \leq 160$$

When these two inequalities are graphed it will be found that they have the same graph. Why? The two inequalities are actually the same since the second may be reduced to the first by dividing both of its sides by two. Sometimes it

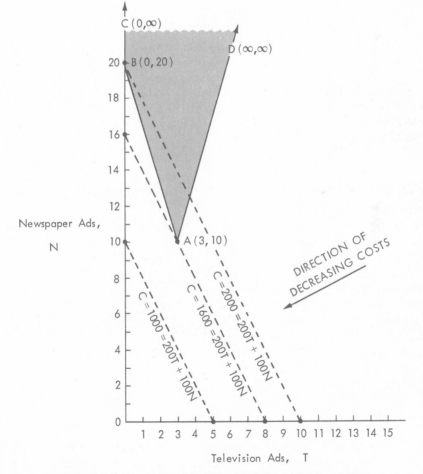

FIGURE 7.15   Optimal Solution Yielding a Cost of $1600

does not immediately seem that a couple of constraints are really the same but in fact they are. For example, the following two constraints are identical:

$$4X - 3Y \le 14$$
$$2X + 5Y \le 2(4Y - X + 7)$$

Whenever there are two constraints which are actually the same, it is said that redundancy exists or that there is a redundant constraint.

What if redundancy exists, what should be done about it? If redundancy is detected, merely strike out one of the two identical constraints and proceed as usual. Even if the redundancy is not detected there will be no harm done.

Unbounded Solution

In Figure 7.16 the shaded area representing the feasible solutions of a set of constraints is given. The shaded area is open-ended which in itself is no problem as this was the case in the Tiger Country Safari example of the last two sections. However, in Figure 7.16 it is seen that this is a maximization problem and the higher profits are associated with objective function or isoprofit lines (dotted) in the northeast direction. In this example there is no limit to the northeast direction so that isoprofit lines representing higher and higher profits still fall within the shaded area. There is no limit to the profit that can be made if the shaded area is open-ended as in this example. One might think of a "corner" existing at (∞,∞) and when this point is substituted in a profit function like $P = 2X + 3Y$, an infinite profit results. The linear programming problem in this case is said to be unbounded.

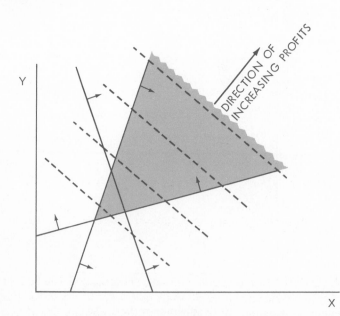

FIGURE 7.16 An Unbounded Solution

CHAPTER 7

What if a linear programming problem is unbounded, what should be done about it? The fact that it is unbounded should be stated; then the model builder should find the constraint which was overlooked which would have "capped off" the shaded area. With this overlooked constraint added, the analysis would proceed as usual since the shaded area would no longer be open-ended.

Alternate Optimal Solutions

In Figure 7.17 the shaded area of feasible solutions is given and the dotted isoprofit lines from the objective function are also displayed. The dotted line which lies furthest out and which yet touches the shaded area is the one which yields a profit of $P = 100$. Any isoprofit line further out does not touch the shaded area. The $P = 100$ isoprofit line runs along one side of the shaded area rather than touching at just one corner. Therefore, any point between corners A and B and including these two corners will yield the maximum profit of 100. As there are an infinite number of these points there are an infinite number of alternate optimal solutions, each one producing a profit of 100. Alternate optimal solutions occur when the objective function is parallel to the side of the shaded area it last touches. Alternate optimal solutions may just as easily occur in minimization problems.

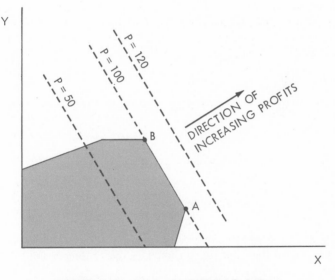

FIGURE 7.17 Alternate Optimal Solutions

What should be done if alternate optimal solutions exist? The fact that they exist should be noted and one of the alternate optimal solutions should be chosen for implementation. Usually one of the two optimal corners is selected rather than some point on the line between them.

Inconsistent Constraints

With the variables X and Y in use, suppose that a linear programming model has among its constraints the following two inequalities

$$X + Y \geq 10$$
$$X + Y \leq 5$$

It should be readily apparent that there does not exist, there cannot exist, two numbers X and Y which when added together are at the same time greater than or equal to 10 and less than or equal to 5. Therefore, these constraints are calling for a solution (X, Y) which does not exist. If the two constraints were graphed as in Figure 7.18, no common shaded area can be found (note the direction of the arrows coming off the lines to indicate which sides of the lines should be shaded). When no shaded area exists after the constraints are graphed, it can be concluded that the constraints are inconsistent or contradictory and hence no solution is possible. Upon examining the inequalities in Figure 7.19 one should conclude that in the (b) case the constraints are inconsistent. They are consistent in the (a) case as a shaded area can be found.

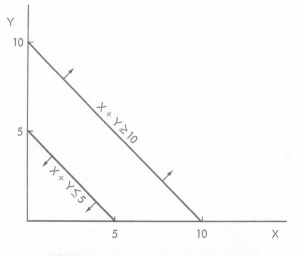

FIGURE 7.18   Inconsistent Constraints

Are sets of constraints ever written in real applications which contain inconsistencies? A glance at the want ads can convince one of the possibility:

Wanted—Chief executive for large corporation located in the Northwest. Applicant should have a college degree, be familiar with international business operations especially European and Australian, have a strong finance background, should have at least 20 years of top-level corporate experience, should have developed intimate familiarity with copper mining in Peru, should be conversant with FDA regulations, be an able spokesperson in behalf of liberalized patent laws, should have spent at least 3 years behind the wheel of a big highway rig, and be a devoted family person in their early thirties with a strong commitment to the geriatric business.

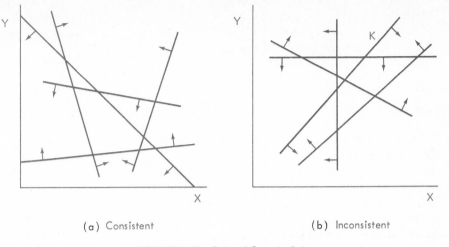

(a) Consistent (b) Inconsistent

FIGURE 7.19 Sets of Constraints

When a set of constraints are found to be inconsistent, care should be taken to see if there are any unintended constraints which could be eliminated. If all were intended then the model builder must decide which constraint(s) to eliminate or relax. In Figure 7.19(b) the constraint labeled K is one of several that might be eliminated or relaxed (moved).

7.8 MORE APPLICATIONS

In the remainder of this chapter several more applications of linear programming model building will be presented. There were only two variables used in the models for the Brothers Karamazov production mix example and the Tiger Country Safari advertising problem. When only two variables are used in a linear programming model the model can be solved graphically as was illustrated. When more variables are used the graphical approach becomes difficult or impossible, therefore some other technique must be utilized to solve such models. A technique known as the "simplex method" will be introduced in the next chapter which will make the solution of larger linear programming models possible. As the models in the remainder of this chapter will make use of more than two variables, they will not be solved graphically. The primary purpose of the rest of this chapter is in the study of the construction of linear programming models. A finance, a production-inventory, and a blending problem will be studied to round out the domain of linear programming applications at the elementary level.

7.9 A FINANCE APPLICATION

The Lone Star Bank has grown quite rapidly. In the midst of this growth the management has not, till present, paid too much attention to policies and objectives regarding the proportions of its monies it will make available for different types of loans. With 100 million dollars currently available for investment in loans, the management has sought to map out some policies and goals. The bank's management has set the objective of gaining the maximum return on the $100,000,000 available. However, this objective must be accomplished within the bounds established by government regulatory agencies and the bank's own directors. In particular, the investment alternatives are restricted by policies and regulations dealing with flexibility, security, and service.

The bank fears that there may be serious repercussions if it gets too heavily invested in long-term commitments. An increase in interest rates and/or a slowing or reverse in the bank's growth could stand the bank in undesirable circumstances. Therefore an investment profile containing short- and intermediate-term commitments is recommended to provide the necessary flexibility. Security is obviously another important factor to the bank. Signature loans, for example, cannot represent too great a proportion of the loans outstanding if security is to be preserved. Finally, service to the community is a significant factor in the bank's investment planning. The bank wants to be able to satisfy its customers by making automobile, mortgage, and signature loans as well as rendering service to the community through an assortment of business loans. The bank's management has been able to distill all the policies and regulations concerning flexibility, security, and service into five definitive investment statements. These five statements will be reviewed after some information is given concerning the types of loans the bank can make with their respective average rates of return.

The bank divides its loans into two categories, business and personal. There are three types of business loans and three types of personal loans. These six types of loans are listed in Table 7.3 with their annual rates of return.

TABLE 7.3
Lone Star Bank Loans
and Interest Rates

Type	Annual Rate of Return
BUSINESS	
Short-term	.10
Intermediate-term	.11
Long-term	.12
PERSONAL	
Signature	.14
Automobile	.12
Mortgage	.09

The five investment requirements which represent a distillation of the relevant regulations and bank policies are:

1. Business loans must not exceed 60 percent of the total amount invested in all loans.
2. Signature and autombile loans combined must not exceed 20 percent of total loans.

3. Mortgage loans must be at least 40 percent of personal loans.
4. Long-term and mortgage loans together must not exceed 30 percent of total loans.
5. There must be twice as much invested in short-term loans as in intermediate-term loans.

How should the Lone Star Bank apportion its $100,000,000 among the six types of loans if a maximum annual return is sought within the bounds stated?

The construction of the appropriate linear progamming model will follow the typical three-step process: define the variables, formulate the objective function, and write the constraints. To begin, let the following six variables be defined:

$$X_1 = \text{amount of money (in millions) invested in short-term loans}$$
$$X_2 = \text{amount invested in intermediate-term loans}$$
$$X_3 = \text{amount invested in long-term loans}$$
$$Y_1 = \text{amount invested in signature loans}$$
$$Y_2 = \text{amount invested in automobile loans}$$
$$Y_3 = \text{amount invested in mortgage loans}$$

It is the values for these six variables that the bank's management is seeking.

The maximization of return on the invested monies is management's stated objective. Letting R denote the annual return (in millions of dollars), the objective function may be written as

$$\text{Maximize } R = .10X_1 + .11X_2 + .12X_3 + .14Y_1 + .12Y_2 + .09Y_3$$

Suppose, for example, that $X_1 = 30$, $X_2 = 10$, $X_3 = 0$, $Y_1 = 10$, $Y_2 = 20$, and $Y_3 = 30$, then the total yearly interest return would be

$$R = (.10)(30) + (.11)(10) + (.12)(0) + (.14)(10) + (.12)(20) + (.09)(30)$$
$$= \$10.6$$

Of course, the solution just proposed might violate some of the restrictions that management has given. The constraints must next be written which express these restrictions.

Management's first requirement is that business loans must not exceed 60 percent of total loans. This restriction must be stated mathematically in the form of a constraint. Before doing this, a few preliminaries will be considered. The total amount of money invested in all loans will be $X_1 + X_2 + X_3 + Y_1 + Y_2 + Y_3$. The total value of business loans will be $X_1 + X_2 + X_3$, and the total amount of personal loans may be expressed simply as $Y_1 + Y_2 + Y_3$. By keeping the mathematical expressions of these three totals in mind, the formulation of the constraints becomes relatively simple. Again, the first requirement is that business loans must not exceed 60 percent of total loans. This may be written as

$$(\text{Total Business Loans}) \le .60(\text{Total Loans})$$

or

$$X_1 + X_2 + X_3 \le (.60)(X_1 + X_2 + X_3 + Y_1 + Y_2 + Y_3)$$

This first constraint could be rewritten as

$$X_1 + X_2 + X_3 \leq .6X_1 + .6X_2 + .6X_3 + .6Y_1 + .6Y_2 + .6Y_3$$

and then

$$.4X_1 + .4X_2 + .4X_3 - .6Y_1 - .6Y_2 - .6Y_3 \leq 0$$

In the next chapter it will be seen that this last form of the constraint is the most desirable where all the variables are neatly arranged on one side and the constant on the other side of the inequality. For the purposes of this chapter, however, the constraints will be left in their initial form.

In the second place, signature and automobile loans combined must not exceed 20 percent of total loans. This means that

$$(\text{Signature plus Automobile Loans}) \leq .20(\text{Total Loans})$$

or

$$Y_1 + Y_2 \leq .20(X_1 + X_2 + X_3 + Y_1 + Y_2 + Y_3)$$

Management's third restriction is that mortgage loans must be at least 40 percent of personal loans

$$(\text{Mortgage Loans}) \geq .40(\text{Total Personal Loans})$$
$$Y_3 \geq .40(Y_1 + Y_2 + Y_3)$$

The fourth restriction states that long-term and mortgage loans combined must not exceed 30 percent of total loans

$$(\text{Long-term plus Mortgage Loans}) \leq .30(\text{Total Loans})$$
$$X_3 + Y_3 \leq .3(X_1 + X_2 + X_3 + Y_1 + Y_2 + Y_3)$$

The fifth restriction states that there must be twice as much invested in short-term loans as in intermediate-term loans. Therefore,

$$(\text{Short-term Loans}) \geq 2(\text{Intermediate-term Loans})$$
$$X_1 \geq 2X_2$$

Since the bank has only 100 million to invest, this limitation must also be incorporated into the model

$$(\text{Total Loans}) \leq 100 \text{ million dollars}$$
$$X_1 + X_2 + X_3 + Y_1 + Y_2 + Y_3 \leq 100$$

There are also the usual non-negativity constraints to be added which specify that each variable cannot assume a negative value.

The completed linear programming model for the Lone Star Bank is

$$\text{Max } R = .10X_1 + .11X_2 + .12X_3 + .14Y_1 + .12Y_2 + .09Y_3$$
Subject to:
$$X_1 + X_2 + X_3 \leq (.6)(X_1 + X_2 + X_3 + Y_1 + Y_2 + Y_3)$$
$$Y_1 + Y_2 \leq (.2)(X_1 + X_2 + X_3 + Y_1 + Y_2 + Y_3)$$
$$Y_3 \geq (.4)(Y_1 + Y_2 + Y_3)$$

$$X_3 + Y_3 \leq (.3)(X_1 + X_2 + X_3 + Y_1 + Y_2 + Y_3)$$
$$X_1 \geq 2X_2$$

$$X_1 + X_2 + X_3 + Y_1 + Y_2 + Y_3 \leq 100$$
$$X_1, X_2, X_3, Y_1, Y_2, Y_3 \geq 0$$

Immediately after the objective function was written a potential solution was suggested. This solution returned $10.6 million to the bank. This potential solution was $X_1 = 30$, $X_2 = 10$, $X_3 = 0$, $Y_1 = 10$, $Y_2 = 20$, and $Y_3 = 30$. It will now be examined to see if it is a feasible solution. Substituting this potential solution into each of the constraints yields

$$30 + 10 + 0 \leq (.6)(30 + 10 + 0 + 10 + 20 + 30) \qquad \text{True!}$$
$$10 + 20 \leq (.2)(30 + 10 + 0 + 10 + 20 + 30) \qquad \text{False!}$$
$$30 \geq (.4)(10 + 20 + 30) \qquad \text{True!}$$
$$0 + 30 \leq (.3)(30 + 10 + 0 + 10 + 20 + 30) \qquad \text{True!}$$
$$30 \geq (2)(10) \qquad \text{True!}$$
$$30 + 10 + 0 + 10 + 20 + 30 \leq 100 \qquad \text{True!}$$

Because the second constraint is not satisfied, this potential solution is not feasible (does not fall within the shaded area) and must therefore be eliminated from consideration. Even if all the constraints were satisfied, it would not follow that the solution is optimal. Such would only indicate that it is one of many feasible solutions.

7.10 A PRODUCTION-INVENTORY APPLICATION

Navajo Enterprises out of Gallup, New Mexico, is in the business of producing and selling Navajo sand paintings to tourists. Navajo Enterprises is planning operations for the next year which is composed of four seasons (periods). The sand painters are not enthusiastic about working in the winter and also are somewhat reluctant to work in the summer. This is reflected in the production capacity of Navajo Enterprises for each of the seasons and it also influences the cost to produce a sand painting from season to season. In particular, Navajo Enterprises has a capacity to produce 10 paintings in the winter at a cost of $40 each, 30 paintings in the spring at a cost of $20 each, 20 paintings in the summer at a cost of $30 each, and 30 paintings in the fall at a cost of $20 each. The demand for sand paintings by tourists is quite seasonal being 5 in the winter, 15 in the spring, 35 in the summer, and 25 in the fall. Regardless of the time of purchase, Navajo Enterprises sells the paintings for $80 each.

Navajo Enterprises' problem is how many paintings to produce in each season (starting with the winter) so that costs can be held to a minimum while making sure that the demand for the paintings can be satisfied. Alternately the objective may be stated in terms of maximizing profits from the sale of the paintings. Navajo Enterprises would obviously like to produce paintings in the spring and fall as production costs are at their lowest during these two seasons. If paintings are produced in one season for sale in a later season, they must be stored in inventory during the interim. It costs $3 to store a painting from one season to the next; this inventory storage cost must be considered in any plan. In the context of the details outlined above, how many sand paintings should Navajo Enterprises produce in each season in order to maximize profits? Assume that Navajo Enterprises is to be in this business for only one year.

Before commencing with the construction of the linear programming model, an information table is given which summarizes the relevant details of this problem (see Table 7.4).

TABLE 7.4
Information Table for Navajo Enterprises

Period	Winter	Spring	Summer	Fall
Production Capacity	10	30	20	30
Demand	5	15	35	25
Production Cost/Unit	$40	$20	$30	$20
Selling Price/Unit	$80	$80	$80	$80

Storage Costs: It costs $3 to store a painting from
one season to the next.

The first task is that of defining the variables. One might be tempted to use only four variables in this problem, namely,

W = number of paintings produced in the winter
G = number of paintings produced in the spring
S = number of paintings produced in the summer
F = number of paintings produced in the fall

However, these variables would prove to be too general. Instead let the following more specific variables be defined:

W_w = number of paintings produced in the winter to be sold in the winter
W_g = number produced in the winter to be sold in the spring
W_s = number produced in the winter to be sold in the summer
W_f = number produced in the winter to be sold in the fall
G_g = number produced in the spring to be sold in the spring
G_s = number produced in the spring to be sold in the summer
G_f = number produced in the spring to be sold in the fall
S_s = number produced in the summer to be sold in the summer
S_f = number produced in the summer to be sold in the fall
F_f = number produced in the fall to be sold in the fall

These variables designate not only the time (season) of production but also the destined time (season) of sale. The subscript refers to the season of sale while the capital letter refers to the season of production. Notice that if $W_w = 5$, $W_g = 3$, $W_s = 0$, and $W_f = 0$, this would mean that the total production during the winter would be 8 paintings. Five of the 8 paintings would be destined to be sold during the same winter and three would be sold in the spring. If $S_s = 10$ and $S_f = 10$, this would mean that a total of 20 are produced in the summer and half of these are to be sold in the same summer and half are to be stored for sale in the fall. There is no variable such as S_g since Navajo Enterprises is in this business for only a year, and that year ends with the fall.

Instead of writing the objective function next, as is usually done, the constraints will first be considered. In this problem there are two types of constraints. The production constraints will insure that Navajo Enterprises never produces more paintings than is possible in a season. The demand constraints guarantee that the supply of paintings each season will equal the projected demand (as shown in Table 7.4).

There will be four production capacity constraints. It has been stated that the production capacity in the winter period is 10 sand paintings. In other words, Navajo Enterprises can produce no more than 10 paintings in the winter. The total winter production is simply $W_w + W_g + W_s + W_f$. This may be verified by recalling the definitions of these variables. The constraint on winter production will take the form

$$\text{(Total Winter Production)} \leq 10 \text{ paintings}$$

or

$$W_w + W_g + W_s + W_f \leq 10$$

Similarly, the constraint on spring production will be

$$\text{(Total Spring Production)} \leq 30 \text{ paintings}$$

or

$$G_g + G_s + G_f \leq 30$$

The production constraint for the summer will be

$$S_s + S_f \leq 20$$

Finally, the production capacity constraint for the fall is

$$F_f \leq 30$$

There are also four demand constraints. There must be 5 paintings available for sale in the winter since 5 is the number that will be demanded then. The only source of paintings for winter sales is from production in the same winter. W_w is the variable denoting the number of paintings produced in the winter for sale in the same winter. The first demand constraint is therefore

$$W_w = 5$$

Notice that this constraint is an equality rather than an inequality as has previously been the case. There is no reason why constraints cannot take the form of an equality even though inequality constraints are the most often encountered.

The demand constraint for the spring must guarantee that there will be 15 paintings available for sale in the spring. These 15 can originate from only two seasons, winter and spring. W_g refers to the number of paintings produced in the winter for sale in the spring, and G_g refers to the number of paintings produced in the spring which are also to be sold in the spring. Therefore the demand constraint for the spring will be

$$W_g + G_g = 15$$

Since exactly 35 paintings are required for the summer, and since these 35 must be produced in the winter, spring, and/or summer, the third demand constraint is

$$W_s + G_s + S_s = 35$$

Finally, the demand constraint for the fall will be

$$W_f + G_f + S_f + F_f = 25$$

The four production capacity constraints and the four demand constraints along with the nonnegativity constraints constitute the complete set of constraints for this linear programming model.

All that now remains is the formulation of the objective function where the objective is to maximize profits. In order to determine the total profit that will be achieved by any production pattern, the profits associated with each of the ten variables will be examined.

1. Profit associated with the W_w paintings which are produced in the winter to be sold in the winter.

Each painting produced during the winter has a production cost of $40 as shown in Table 7.4. If the painting is to be also sold the same winter there will be no storage costs, and the painting will sell for $80 thus yielding a net profit of $40. If W_w is the number of such paintings produced in the winter for sale in the winter, then the total profit from these paintings only will be 40W_w$. For example, if W_w were 5, then the net profit associated with those 5 paintings would be $(40)(5) = \$200$.

2. Profit associated with the W_g paintings which are produced in the winter and will be sold in the spring.

Each of these paintings costs $40 to produce since they are made in the winter. They must be stored for one season thus entailing a storage cost of $3 per painting. Finally, they are sold in the spring for $80 each thereby yielding a net profit of $80-40-3 = \$37$ per painting. As there are W_g of these paintings, the total profit here will be 37W_g$.

3. Profit associated with W_s.

Each of these paintings will net $80-40-6 = \$34$ where 80 represents the selling price, 40 the production cost, and 6 the storage cost for two seasons.

4. Profit associated with W_f.

Each of these paintings will net $80-40-9 = \$31$.

5. Profit associated with G_g.

Each of these paintings which are produced in the spring costs only $20 to produce. As they are sold in the same spring there are no storage costs and the net profit per painting is $80-20 = \$60$.

6. Profit associated with G_s.

Each of these paintings will net $80-20-3 = \$57$.

7. Profit associated with G_f.

Each of these paintings will net a profit of $80-20-6 = \$54$.

8. Profit associated with S_s.

Each of these will yield a net profit of $80-30 = \$50$.

9. Profit associated with S_f.

Each of these paintings which are produced in the spring for sale in the fall will yield a net profit of $80-30-3 = \$47$.

10. Profit associated with F_f.

Each of these paintings will yield a net profit of $80-20 = \$60$. Having examined the net profit associated with each of the ten variables, it may be concluded that a production plan of $(W_w, W_g, W_s, W_f, G_g, G_s, G_f, S_s, S_f, F_f)$ would produce a total profit of

$$P = 40W_w + 37W_g + 34W_s + 31W_f + 60G_g + 57G_s + 54G_f + 50S_s + 47S_f + 60F_f$$

As this equation expresses the total profit in terms of the variables, it is the objective function whose value is to be maximized.

The completed linear programming model for Navajo Enterprises is

$$\text{Max } P = 40W_w + 37W_g + 34W_s + 31W_f + 60G_g + 57G_s + 54G_f + 50S_s + 47S_f + 60F_f$$

Subject to:

$$
\begin{aligned}
W_w + W_g + W_s + W_f &\le 10 & &\text{(Winter Production Constraint)} \\
G_g + G_s + G_f &\le 30 & &\text{(Spring Production Constraint)} \\
S_s + S_f &\le 20 & &\text{(Summer Production Constraint)} \\
F_f &\le 30 & &\text{(Fall Production Constraint)}
\end{aligned}
$$

$$
\begin{aligned}
W_w &= 5 & &\text{(Winter Demand Constraint)} \\
W_g + G_g &= 15 & &\text{(Spring Demand Constraint)} \\
W_s + G_s + S_s &= 35 & &\text{(Summer Demand Constraint)} \\
W_f + G_f + S_f + F_f &= 25 & &\text{(Fall Demand Constraint)}
\end{aligned}
$$

$$W_w, W_g, W_s, W_f, G_g, G_s, G_f, S_s, S_f, F_f \ge 0$$

The optimal solution which yields the maximum profit could be determined by the simplex method of the next chapter or in this particular case it can be found by inspection. The optimal solution is $W_w = 5$, $G_g = 15$, $G_s = 15$, $S_s = 20$, and $F_f = 25$ with the other five variables equal to zero. Substituting these values into the model, the optimal profit is easily determined and it is further demonstrated that all of the constraints are satisfied.

$$
\begin{aligned}
P &= (40)(5) + 0 + 0 + 0 + (60)(15) + (57)(15) + 0 + (50)(20) + (60)(25) \\
&= \$4,455
\end{aligned}
$$

and,

$$
\begin{aligned}
5 + 0 + 0 + 0 &\le 10 \\
15 + 15 + 0 &\le 30 \\
20 + 0 &\le 20 \\
25 &\le 30
\end{aligned}
\qquad \text{Production Constraints}
$$

$$
\begin{aligned}
5 \quad\quad\quad &= 5 \\
0 + 15 \quad\quad &= 15 \\
0 + 15 + 20 \quad &= 35 \\
0 + 0 + 0 + 25 &= 25
\end{aligned}
\qquad \text{Demand Constraints}
$$

With regard to inventory ramifications, it should be noted that the optimal solution requires the carrying of an inventory of 15 paintings from the spring to the summer since $G_s = 15$. At no other times is inventory carried from season to season.

7.11 A BLENDING APPLICATION

As it became apparent to both the North and the South that the Civil War would not be ended quickly, General Broda of the Confederacy began laying plans for the continued support of his troops. The General well knew that an army marches on its stomach. It was the practice of the Union armies to take along beef on the hoof; it was Broda who pioneered taking along chicken on the claw for the supply of fresh meat for the rebel troops. Broda acquired a large number of chickens and now was concerned with the feeding of the same. Alpheno Chemical Company of Atlanta was chosen as a feed supplier for General Broda's chickens. Alpheno agreed to supply a certain number of "servings" of chicken feed. General Broda specified that each serving must contain at least 5 units of protein, 1 unit of calcium, 12 units of carbohydrates, .2 units of pituitary activator, and between 4 and 6 units of grit. Having received this contract, Alpheno set about to produce this chicken feed at a minimum cost.

At Alpheno's disposal were four ingredients from which the chicken feed could be made: acorns, seaweed, jojoba beans, and clamshells. The reader is familiar with all of these except the jojoba bean. A short departure from the main theme of model building is therefore warranted to describe the jojoba bean. *The Wall Street Journal* (page 48, Oct. 14, 1975) reports:

> Jojoba (pronounced ho-HO-buh) abounds in desert areas of the Southwest. The evergreen bushes, five to 10 feet tall, blend with majestic seguaro cactus in the otherwise bleak desert landscape. Jojobas always have provided a browse for deer and even cattle, and the Indians of the area still use the oily wax from jojoba seeds as a balm for wounds. . . . researchers are now talking about a host of new uses for jojoba oil. . . . A partial list of possible applications in a National Academy of Sciences report mentions, for openers: waterproofing compounds, leather softeners, paints, adhesives, linoleum, printing ink, medicines, low-calorie foods, food-shrinkage retardants, paper, textiles, insulating material, matches, soap, chalk, crayons . . .

Alpheno has to make a serving of chicken feed which meets General Broda's requirements. Table 7.5 gives information regarding the nutritional contents of acorns, seaweed, jojoba beans, and clamshells. For example, each pound of acorns has 4 units of protein, 0 units of calcium, 5 units of carbohydrates, 0 units of pituitary activator, and 1 unit of grit. Each pound of jojobas has 5 units of protein, .5 units of calcium, 7 units of carbohydrates, 3 units of pituitary activator, and 0 units of grit. At the bottom of the table the requirements in terms of these nutrients as stipulated by General Broda are given. Table 7.5 also indicates the current costs of the four ingredients. A pound of acorns costs $.40, seaweed costs $.10 per pound, jojobas cost $.90 per pound, and clamshells go for $.20 a pound.

TABLE 7.5
Information Table for Alpheno Chemical

		Nutrients per Pound of Ingredient				
Cost/lb.	Ingredient	Protein	Calcium	Carbo-hydrate	Pituitary Activator	Grit
$ .40	Acorns	4	0	5	0	1
.10	Seaweed	2	1	8	0	0
.90	Jojobas	5	.5	7	3	0
.20	Clamshells	0	9	0	0	6

REQUIREMENTS/SERVING:

minimum—		5	1	12	.2	4
maximum—		—	—	—	—	6

OTHER REQUIREMENTS:
Taste—Must be at least half seaweed.
Pollution—Jojobas must be at least 10 percent of acorn level.

Alpheno wishes to synthesize the chicken feed at a minimum cost while meeting the nutritional requirements. There are also two other restrictions that must be satisfied. Alpheno's research department has found that a chicken will not eat a blend of acorns, seaweed, jojobas, and clamshells unless there is more seaweed than all the other ingredients combined. As it was implicit in Alpheno's agreement with General Broda that the chickens would be willing to eat the feed supplied, this requirement is important. Furthermore, Alpheno's astute marketing manager perceives that if the chickens smell up the Confederate camps, maybe the troops would just as well forego the chicken in favor of something else. If this happened, Alpheno's lucrative contract for chicken feed would be terminated. The research department at Alpheno Chemical found that the acorns in the feed are chiefly responsible for the aroma. Also, it was discovered that if the ratio of the versatile jojoba bean to the acorns were 1 to 10 or greater, then the aroma would be quite tolerable (in fact, General Broda found it to be pleasing). In conclusion, the feed which Alpheno blends must meet the nutritional requirements as well as the "taste" and "pollution" requirements which were just mentioned.

As with each linear programming model, the first step in the construction process is the definition of the variables. In the Alpheno blending situation let

W = pounds of acorns in a serving of chicken feed
X = pounds of seaweed in a serving of chicken feed
Y = pounds of jojobas in a serving of chicken feed
Z = pounds of clamshells in a serving of chicken feed

Alpheno's objective is to produce the feed at a minimum cost. Letting C denote the cost of one serving of chicken feed, the objective function may be written as

$$\text{Minimize } C = .40W + .10X + .90Y + .20Z$$

The total cost, for example, of a serving composed of $W = .5$ pounds, $X = 1$ pound, $Y = 1$ pound, and $Z = .4$ pounds would be

$$C = (.40)(.5) + (.10)(1) + (.90)(1) + (.20)(.4) = \$1.28.$$

The final phase of model construction is the writing of the constraints. There will be a constraint for each of the five nutrients and the two extra restrictions associated with taste and pollution. Each serving of feed must contain 5 units of protein. Since a pound of acorns has 4 units of protein, then W pounds of acorns will have $4W$ units of protein. Similarly, X pounds of seaweed will contain $2X$ units of protein, Y pounds of jojobas will contain $5Y$ units of protein, and Z pounds of clamshells will contain 0 units of protein since there is no protein in clamshells as indicated in Table 7.5. Putting all of this together, a serving composed of W pounds of acorns, X pounds of seaweed, Y pounds of jojobas, and Z pounds of clamshells will have a total of $4W + 2X + 5Y$ units of protein. According to the protein requirement, there must be at least 5 units of protein per serving. This may be mathematically expressed by the constraint

$$\text{(Amount of Protein per Serving)} \geq 5 \text{ units}$$
$$4W + 2X + 5Y \geq 5 \qquad \text{(Protein Constraint)}$$

By following the same line of reasoning the constraints for the other four nutrients may be written. They are

$$1X + .5Y + 9Z \geq 1 \qquad \text{(Calcium Constraint)}$$
$$5W + 8X + 7Y \geq 12 \qquad \text{(Carbohydrate Constraint)}$$
$$3Y \geq .2 \qquad \text{(Pituitary Activator Constraint)}$$
$$1W + 6Z \geq 4 \qquad \text{(Grit Constraint)}$$

With regard to the grit, there must be one more constraint as there is to be a maximum of 6 units of grit per serving. This constraint may be written as

$$1W + 6Z \leq 6 \qquad \text{(Maximum Grit Constraint)}$$

The taste requirement stated that at least half of the feed by weight must be composed of seaweed. If this requirement is not met the chickens will not eat the feed. X equals the number of pounds of seaweed in a serving; the total weight of the other three ingredients in a serving is $W + Y + Z$. Since X must be at least half the weight of a serving,

$$\text{(Weight of Seaweed per Serving)} \geq \text{(Weight of Other Ingredients)}$$
$$X \geq W + Y + Z \qquad \text{(Taste Contraint)}$$

The pollution requirement states that the ratio of jojobas to acorns must be at least 1 to 10. In other words,

$$\frac{\text{Pounds of Jojobas}}{\text{Pounds of Acorns}} \geq .1$$

Since Y equals the number of pounds of jojobas in a serving and W equals the number of pounds of acorns in a serving, this constraint can be mathematically expressed as

$$Y/W \geq .1$$

Multiplying both sides of this inequality by W gives a preferable form of this constraint:

$$Y \geq .1W \qquad \text{(Pollution Constraint)}$$

The linear programming model in its entirety for the Alpheno chicken feed blending problem may now be given

$$\text{Minimize } C = .40W + .10X + .90Y + .20Z$$

Subject to:
$$4W + 2X + 5Y \geq 5$$
$$X + .5Y + 9Z \geq 1$$
$$5W + 8X + 7Y \geq 12$$
$$3Y \geq .2$$
$$W + 6Z \geq 4$$
$$W + 6Z \leq 6$$

$$X \geq W + Y + Z$$
$$Y \geq .1W$$

$$W, X, Y, Z \geq 0$$

Solving this model involves finding that ingredient combination (W,X,Y,Z) which costs the least while satisfying all of the constraints. The simplex method for the solution of such a problem will be presented in the next chapter.

PROBLEMS

7-1. With the feasible (shaded) area defined below, find the optimal solution if the objective function is:
(a) Max $P = 4X + 7Y$
(b) Max $P = 5X + 5Y$
(c) Min $C = 3X + 5Y$
(d) Min $C = -7X + 2Y$

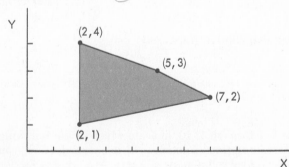

7-2. With the feasible (shaded) solutions defined below, find the optimal solution if the objective function is: (in each case graph the objective function.)
  (a) Max $P = X + Y$ *UNBOUNDED*
  (b) Min $C = -X - Y$ "
  (c) Min $C = 8X + Y$ (1,3)

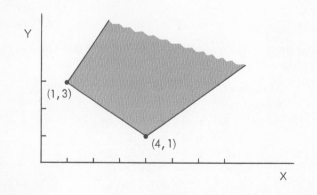

7-3. Graphically solve the following linear programming model. Plot the isoprofit lines.

$$\text{Maximize} \quad P = 4X + 2Y$$
$$\text{Subject to:} \quad X \le 7$$
$$2X + 3Y \le 18$$
$$X,\ Y \ge 0$$

$(7, 4/3)$

7-4. Graphically solve the following linear programming model. Plot the isoprofit lines.

$\left(\dfrac{7}{4},\ \dfrac{5}{4} \right)$

$$\text{Maximize} \quad P = 2X - Y$$
$$\text{Subject to:} \quad 5X + Y \le 10$$
$$X + Y \ge 3$$
$$Y \le 6$$
$$X, Y \ge 0$$

7-5. Find the optimal solution graphically:

$(600, 0)$

$$\text{Minimize} \quad C = 30X + 70Y$$
$$\text{Subject to:} \quad 2X + Y \ge 800$$
$$2X + 3Y \ge 1200$$
$$X, Y \ge 0$$

7-6 Find the optimal solution graphically:

$W = 0$
$Z = 10$

$$\text{Minimize} \quad T = 20W + 10Z$$
$$\text{Subject to:} \quad W + Z \le 30$$
$$W + Z \ge 10$$
$$W - Z \le 0$$
$$W, Z \ge 0$$

In Problems 7–7 through 7–10, indicate which of the following conditions prevails: (A) alternate optimal solutions, (B) unbounded, (C) inconsistent constraints, (D) single optimal solution.

7-7. Maximize $P = 14X + 9Y$
  Subject to:
  $$X - Y \leq 0$$
  $$X \geq 6$$
  $$X + Y \leq 8$$
  $$X, Y \geq 0$$

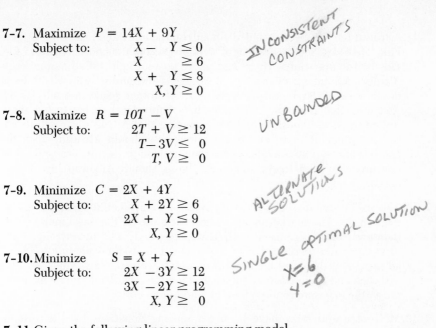

INCONSISTENT CONSTRAINTS

7-8. Maximize $R = 10T - V$
  Subject to:
  $$2T + V \geq 12$$
  $$T - 3V \leq 0$$
  $$T, V \geq 0$$

UNBOUNDED

7-9. Minimize $C = 2X + 4Y$
  Subject to:
  $$X + 2Y \geq 6$$
  $$2X + Y \leq 9$$
  $$X, Y \geq 0$$

ALTERNATE SOLUTIONS

7-10. Minimize $S = X + Y$
  Subject to:
  $$2X - 3Y \geq 12$$
  $$3X - 2Y \geq 12$$
  $$X, Y \geq 0$$

SINGLE OPTIMAL SOLUTION
$X = 6$
$Y = 0$

7-11. Given the following linear programming model,
  Maximize $6X + 5Y + 4Z$
  Subject to:
  $$10X + 20Y + 30Z \leq 1000$$
  $$20X + Y \geq 200$$
  $$Z \geq 10$$
  $$-X + Y + Z \leq 0$$
  $$X, Y, Z \geq 0$$

  which of the following potential solutions are feasible?
  (a) $(X = 10, Y = 0, Z = 10)$ *FEASIBLE*
  (b) $(20, 5, 15)$ *FEASIBLE*
  (c) $(80, 30, 20)$ *NOT FEASIBLE*

7-12. Jenny's Meatless Sausage is to be prepared from two ingredients, soy concentrate and corn meal. Each kilogram of soy concentrate contains 60 units of protein and 80 calories. Each kilogram of corn meal contains 30 units of protein and 80 calories. To satisfy nutritional requirements, each serving of sausage must contain at least 60 units of protein and at least 160 calories. If the cost of soy concentrate is $1.50 per kilogram and the cost of corn meal is $1.10 per kilo, find the minimum cost blend of soy concentrate and corn meal which satisfies the nutritional requirements for a serving of this sausage.

MIN: $1.5S + 1.1C$
S.T.
$60S + 30C \geq 60$
$80S + 80C \geq 16$
$\Rightarrow S = 0$
$C = 2$

7-13. Alunamun Aluminum Co. makes lawn chair frames and FM antennas. An antenna requires .5 hours of time on a tube bender and 1 hour of time on a drilling machine for its production. To produce a lawn chair frame, .5 hours is required on both the tube bender and the drilling machine. There are 4 hours available on the tube bender and 6 hours available on the drilling machine. If the profit is $6 per antenna and $4 per lawn chair frame, how many of each should be made in order to maximize profits?

MAX: $6A + 4L$
ST
$.5A + .5L \leq 4$
$A + .5C \leq 6$
$A, C \geq 0$
$A = 4$
$C = 4$

7-14. Altruism Inc. has been assigned a booth on the midway at the Illinois State Fair. There are 800 square feet of storage space in the booth. Altruism Inc. sells two items, stuffed tigers and music boxes. Each stuffed animal costs Altruism $2, takes 2 square feet of storage space, and sells for $3.50. Each music box costs $3, requires 1 square foot of storage space, and sells for $4. Assuming that once the fair opens it is impractical to try to get more stuffed tigers and music boxes, and assuming that Altruism can sell its entire inventory of tigers and music boxes, how should Altruism stock the booth if only $1200 is available for the purchase of the inventory? That is, how many stuffed tigers and music boxes should Altruism buy for its booth?

7-15. The Six-Twelve market wishes to advertise the availability of hot drinks at their stores. The market chain wishes to expose 60 thousand men and 40 thousand women by using local newspaper and radio advertising. Each newspaper ad exposes 6 thousand men and 4 thousand women. Each radio ad exposes 2 thousand men and 5 thousand women. Newspaper ads cost $70 each and radio ads cost $40 each. Find the advertising mix which will satisfy the exposure requirements at a minimum cost.

7-16. McGookin and Buzz have been out seeking donations for their Junior Achievement Mixed Nut Company. After a fortnight of tireless effort, they have accumulated 24 pounds of cashews, 64 pounds of peanuts, 8 pounds of almonds, 50 "Premium Mix" cans, and 40 "Economy Mix" cans (the cans are empty). A Premium Mix can must contain .5 pounds of peanuts, .3 pounds of cashews, and .2 pounds of almonds. The Economy Mix can must contain .8 pounds of peanuts and .2 pounds of cashews. If the Premium Mix can is hawked for $3 and the Economy Mix goes for $1.20 per can, how many of each should be made to optimize revenue?

In the remaining problems a linear programming model is to be constructed but not solved.

7-17. Armbrecht Steel supplies pipes for an oil pipeline. Armbrecht sets production schedules by a quarterly calendar. The demand for the pipes is quite variable being at a peak in the second and third quarters. The pipeline will be finished in a year, therefore Armbrecht is only planning for the next four quarters. Production costs vary from quarter to quarter due to a variety of reasons. The information table below sets forth all the relevant details of Armbrecht's situation.

Quarter:	I	II	III	IV
Demand	20 Pipes	90	70	10
Cost/Pipe	$1,000	$1,200	$1,500	$1,000
Plant Capacity	60 Pipes	60	60	60

Set up a linear programming model which will minimize total production costs while satisfying demand. There are no storage costs associated with pipes produced in one quarter which will be sold in a later quarter. (Hint: let W_I denote the number of pipes produced in the first quarter for sale in the first quarter. Also see Section 7.10 for a similar problem.)

7-18. The North Dakota Snow Bank has 10 million dollars to invest in loans. The types of loans NDSB makes and their annual rates of return and their security ratings are

Type	Annual Rate of Return	Security Rating
Snowmobile	15%	2 points/million
Mortgage	8%	8
Signature	18%	1
Business	12%	6

The NDSB wishes to maximize the return on the money it lends. However, the following restrictions must hold: business loans must equal at least 40% of the total amount lended; snowmobile loans must be no more than 20% of mortgage loans; the total number of safety points achieved must be at least 62. (Note: Regarding the security rating, each million dollars lended gets the number of safety points specified above according to the type of loan. For example, if 5 million dollars were invested in snowmobile loans this would yield $(5)(2) = 10$ safety points. If 5 million dollars were invested in mortgage loans, this would yield $(5)(8) = 40$ safety points.) Set up a linear programming model which would maximize annual return in the face of the restrictions imposed. (Hint: see Section 7.9).

7-19. Texas Dextrous is attempting to devise a minimum cost meal which meets the government's recommended nutritional standards. Each meal for an adult must contain 100 units of protein, 400 units of carbohydrates, 20 units of minerals, and 50 units of vitamins. Working with dried beans, milk, eggs, ground beef, carrots, and spinach which have the nutritional characteristics as listed below, set up a model which would yield the minimum cost meal.

Cost	Food	Protein	Carbohydrates	Minerals	Vitamins
$ .30	1 lb. beans	40 units	180	17	25
.40	1 qt. milk	70	190	27	35
.10	1 egg	20	50	7	5
1.00	1 lb. beef	90	80	19	25
.50	1 lb. carrots	5	30	13	55
.45	1 lb. spinach	6	40	9	65
Requirements/meal		100	400	20	50

7-20. Goose Marine produces rowboats, sailboats, and cabin cruisers. The profit for each of these boats is

Type	Profit/Boat
Rowboat	$ 40
Sailboat	$300
Cabin Cruiser	$500

Each boat must pass through three production centers known as the fiberglass center, mechanical center, and finishing center. The information table below indicates how long each type of boat must spend in each of these centers. Also the hours of operating time available in each of these centers is given for the planning period.

	Fiberglass	Mechanical	Finishing
Rowboat	3 hours	5 hours	2 hours
Sailboat	7	20	8
Cabin Cruiser	6	30	9
Available Hours:	800	1600	700

Goose can sell as many sailboats and cabin cruisers as can be produced; however, a maximum of 100 rowboats can be sold. Goose jealously guards its reputation as being a crafter of both power boats and sailboats, therefore it is specified that the number of sailboats cannot exceed twice the number of cabin cruisers made, and, the number of cabin cruisers cannot exceed twice the number of sailboats made. Set up a linear programming model for the objective of maximizing profits under the circumstances given.

7-21. Lana Fish Furs wishes to advertise a new line of coats in three fashion magazines: Vo-goo, Family Square, and Acquire. These three magazines reach different audiences, and, advertising costs differ by magazine. The information table below gives a number of details.

	Vo-goo	Family Square	Acquire
Cost per ad	$500	$300	$600
Number of exposures per ad	30,000	20,000	40,000
Number of exposures among the middle income group	25,000	10,000	30,000
Number of exposures among persons in cold climate	15,000	10,000	26,000
Maximum number of ads that can be placed in 3 months	6	12	3

(a) If Lana Fish Furs requires a total of 200,000 exposures, 150,000 exposures among middle income persons. 120,000 exposures among persons in cold climates, and must abide by the maximum limits on the number of ads to run in each magazine as noted, set up a model which would yield the minimum cost advertising mix.

(b) Forget about the entire information table except for the top two rows. Set up a model which would maximize the total number of exposures subject to a budget restriction of $10,000. That is, find the advertising mix which would produce the maximum number of exposures by spending no more than $10,000.

8 Linear Programming–Simplex Method

8.1 INTRODUCTION

In Chapter 7 linear programming was introduced. A graphical procedure to solve linear programming models containing only two variables was presented. The graphical approach becomes unwieldly if three variables are used and impossible if more than three are used. As most applications of any significance require a large number of variables in the LP model, another solution technique is needed. George Dantzig developed a technique to solve large linear programming problems algebraically, a technique known as the *simplex method*. With a computer programmed to perform the simplex method, even very large linear programming models can be easily solved. The primary intent of this chapter is to explain and illustrate the use of the simplex method.

The instructor who says "The simplex method can be accomplished with great speed" stands in the tradition of General Custer who said "I think them is friendly Indians on the other side of the hill." Though the simplex method is long, it is not difficult to learn and is easy to apply.

8.2 ALGEBRAIC PRELIMINARIES

Before the simplex method can be applied, the linear programming model with its objective function and constraints must be expressed in a standard form. In particular,

Initial Standard Form—Each constraint must be written in a manner such that all of the variables are on the left side of the inequality (or equality) sign and a nonnegative constant appears on the right side.

For example, the following three constraints are written in the standard form.

$$2X - 9Y \quad \leq 4$$
$$X - \quad Y + Z \geq 9$$
$$7X + 3Y - Z = 5$$

On the other hand, the next set of three constraints is not written in the initial standard form.

$$5X + 4Y \leq 2(X - Y)$$
$$X - Y - Z \leq -3$$
$$8 \leq 2X - 3$$

These last three constraints must be algebraically converted to the standard form. Each of them will now be so converted.

For the first unacceptable constraint, $5X + 4Y \leq 2(X-Y)$, the right side should be expanded by multiplication yielding

$$5X + 4Y \leq 2X - 2Y$$

By subtracting $2X$ and adding $2Y$ to each side, the equivalent inequality is

$$3X + 6Y \leq 0$$

This inequality is now in initial standard form.

For the second unacceptable constraint, $X-Y-Z \leq -3$, the problem resides in the fact that the constant on the right side is negative. By multiplying both sides by a -1 this situation may be rectified:

$$-X + Y + Z \geq 3$$

Notice that multiplying both sides of an inequality by a negative number *always* changes the sense or direction of the inequality.

For the third unacceptable constraint, $8 \leq 2X - 3$, subtract 8 and $2X$ from both sides which yields

$$-2X \leq -11$$

Then multiply by a -1; this results in the inequality being expressed in standard form.

$$2X \geq 11$$

Once the constraints have been expressed in the initial standard form with the variables on the left side and a nonnegative constant on the right side, the next requirement is

Conversion to Equalities—The constraints which are inequalities must be expressed as equalities by the appropriate introduction of slack or surplus variables.

The first constraint in the Brothers Karamazov model of the previous chapter (see Section 7.2) is

$$X + 3Y \leq 12.5 \qquad \text{(Carpenter Constraint)}$$

The production mix represented by $X = 3$ rockers, and $Y = 3$ sluice boxes satisfies this constraint since

$$3 + (3)(3) \leq 12.5$$
$$12 \leq 12.5$$

This production mix requires only 12 hours of the carpenter's time leaving him .5 extra hours on a Saturday. It could be said that there is .5 hours of slack time with this production mix. If slack time were denoted by the variable S_c, this variable could be formally incorporated into the constraint:

$$X + 3Y + S_c = 12.5 \quad \text{as long as } S_c \geq 0$$

This converts the inequality into an equation without damaging the constraint as long as the slack variable is not permitted to be negative. The slack variable S_c merely takes on the value necessary to bring the left side of the inequality up to the value of the right side. In no way has the character of the constraint been altered by the addition of a slack variable. A production mix of $X=3.5$, $Y=3$ satisfies the original carpenter constraint since

$$
\begin{aligned}
X + 3Y &\leq 12.5 \\
3.5 + (3)(3) &\leq 12.5 \\
12.5 &\leq 12.5
\end{aligned}
$$

and it also satisfies the equivalent equation $X + 3Y + S_c = 12.5$ if the slack variable is 0, that is, $3.5 + (3)(3) + 0 = 12.5$. For the production mix of $X=2$, $Y=3$ the slack variable would have a value of $S_c = 1.5$ since this mix uses only 11 hours of the carpenter's time. For $(2,1)$ the slack variable would be $S_c = 7.5$, for $(0,0)$ the slack would be $S_c = 12.5$ as a production mix of $(0,0)$ requires no time from the carpenter thus leaving him with 12.5 hours of slack time. The general condition requiring a slack variable to convert an inequality to an equation will be discussed after one more specific case.

Sometimes an inequality is in the form

$$10{,}000T + 3{,}000N \geq 60{,}000 \quad \text{(Youngsters Constraint)}$$

as was the case in the Tiger Country Safari illustration of the last chapter (see Section 7.5). If the advertising mix of $T=4$ television ads, $N=10$ newspaper ads were used, the total number of exposures among the young would be $10{,}000(4) + 3{,}000(10) = 70{,}000$ which satisfies the constraint requiring at least 60,000 exposures among the young. In such a case the advertising mix yields a surplus of 10,000 exposures among the young. Letting the variable U denote the number of surplus exposures among the young, the constraint could be written as

$$10{,}000T + 3{,}000N = 60{,}000 + U$$

or,

$$10{,}000T + 3{,}000N - U = 60{,}000$$

as long as U is not negative. An advertising mix of $T=10$, $N=0$ would yield a surplus of $U=40{,}000$ exposures among the young. With 40,000 inserted into the constraint equation, all is satisfied.

$$10{,}000(10) + 3{,}000(0) - 40{,}000 = 60{,}000$$

A mix of $(6,0)$ would yield a surplus of $U=0$. The introduction of a surplus variable, as with a slack, does not alter an inequality. Its introduction merely converts the constraint to an equivalent equation.

In summary, constraints which are expressed as inequalities in standard form must be expressed as equations in preparation for the simplex method. If the inequality is of the form

$$aX + bY + cZ \leq d$$

where a, b, c, and d are constants and d is nonnegative, then a slack variable must be added to the left side resulting in the equation

$$aX + bY + cZ + S = d$$

Each of the inequalities of this form in the set of constraints will need a different slack variable. If the inequality is of the form

$$aX + bY + cZ \geq d$$

where d is a nonnegative constant, then a surplus variable must be subtracted from the left side resulting in the equation

$$aX + bY + cZ - U = d$$

After the constraints of a linear programming model have been expressed as equations by the use of slack variables or surplus variables, the constraints and objective function must be written in a manner such that all the same variables are lined up vertically; this requirement will be explained by means of an example. The entire process of introducing slack variables and then lining up the variables will now be demonstrated for the Brothers Karamazov model. In Section 7.2 of the last chapter the Brothers Karamazov model was given as

$$
\begin{aligned}
\text{Maximize } P &= 30X + 20Y \\
\text{Subject to:} \quad X + 3Y &\leq 12.5 \quad \text{(Carpenter Constraint)} \\
2X + Y &\leq 10 \quad \text{(Tinsmith Constraint)} \\
2X &\leq 8 \quad \text{(Runners Constraint)} \\
X, Y &\geq 0 \quad \text{(Nonnegativity Constraints)}
\end{aligned}
$$

where X = number of rockers produced
Y = number of sluice boxes produced

For each of the constraints (disregarding the nonnegativity constraints) a slack variable must be added in order to convert them into equations:

$$
\begin{aligned}
X + 3Y + S_c &= 12.5 \\
2X + Y + S_t &= 10 \\
2X + S_r &= 8
\end{aligned}
$$

S_c represents slack time for the carpenter, S_t represents slack time for the tinsmith, and S_r represents slack or unused iron runners resulting from a given production mix. With reference to S_r, if $X = 3$ rockers were produced, then 6 iron runners would be used. Since 8 runners are available, there would be 2 runners which could have been used but were not. Hence S_r would take on a value of 2 in this case.

Finally the entire model with original variables and slack variables must be written in a fashion such that the variables line up vertically. Therefore

$$\text{Maximize} \quad P = 30X + 20Y$$
$$X + 3Y + S_c \qquad\qquad = 12.5$$
$$2X + Y \qquad + S_t \qquad = 10$$
$$2X \qquad\qquad\qquad + S_r = 8$$

where X, Y, S_c, S_t, $S_r \geq 0$. The model is now in final standard form; it is ready for the simplex method.

8.3 SIMPLEX METHOD—AN OVERVIEW

In the last chapter it was stated that the optimal solution to a linear programming problem will always occur at a corner of the shaded area of feasible solutions. When there are three variables in the model the set of feasible solutions is no longer a shaded area but rather a three-dimensional shaded space. One might picture this set of feasible solutions as a pyramid floating in space; any point in or on the pyramid is a feasible solution. The optimal solution in such a case will again occur at a corner. Regardless of the number of variables in the linear programming model, the optimal solution will always occur at a "corner." As with the graphical method, the simplex method is based upon this fact.

Essentially the simplex method for finding the optimal solution proceeds as follows. A corner of the shaded space or set of feasible solutions is found. The simplex then checks to see if that first corner happens to be the optimal corner. If it is not, the simplex jumps to another corner which will yield a solution just as good as or better (higher profit, for example) than the first corner. Then this second corner is checked. If it is not optimal the simplex takes another jump. The next jump is guaranteed to land on a corner which again represents a solution at least as good as that of its immediate predecessor, almost always it is better. Ultimately, since there are a limited number of corners the simplex will jump to the corner which has the optimal solution. When that corner is reached the simplex method is completed. Thus the simplex method is merely a mathematical technique of jumping from corner solution to corner solution in pursuit of the optimal corner. The simplex method is an iterative method in that the same type of procedure (jumping) is repeated again and again. The fact that the simplex is an iterative procedure accounts for its length but also makes it easy as there is a lot of repetition.

In the next sections the simplex method will be presented and illustrated. One iteration of the simplex will involve three steps:

Step 1: Examine the current corner solution to see if it is optimal. If it is, Stop. If it is not, go to Step 2.

Step 2: Find the next corner. This corner will represent a solution which is at least as good as the current corner solution.

Step 3: Jump to the next corner. Go to Step 1.

The Brothers Karamazov model will be used to illustrate the simplex method. Figure 8.1, page 204, is presented for reference purposes as it shows the feasible (shaded) solutions and the corner solutions. The progress of the simplex method can be studied in connection with this graph even though the simplex does not rely on a graph. Anticipating the simplex analysis, the first corner solution will occur at A with coordinates of $X=0$, $Y=0$ and yielding a profit of $P=0$. The first jump will be to Corner E which will yield a profit of about $P=83.40$. The second jump will be from Corner E to Corner D. The simplex will then advise that the optimal corner solution has been reached. It should also be noted that the simplex could just as easily have ended up at Corner D by jumping from A to B to C and then to D.

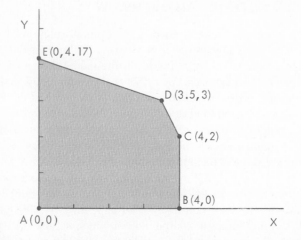

FIGURE 8.1   Feasible and Corner Solutions (Brothers Karamazov)

8.4 SIMPLEX METHOD—THE INITIAL CORNER SOLUTION

Having expressed the linear programming model in final standard form, it is now desirable to express the model in what is called tableau format. The Brothers Karamazov model was converted to final standard form with slack variables in Section 8.2 Adding some zero coefficients and rewriting the objective function, this model may be equivalently expressed as

$$\text{Maximize} \quad P - 30X - 20Y + 0S_c + 0S_t + 0S_r = 0$$
$$1X + 3Y + 1S_c + 0S_t + 0S_r = 12.5$$
$$2X + 1Y + 0S_c + 1S_t + 0S_r = 10$$
$$2X + 0Y + 0S_c + 0S_t + 1S_r = 8$$

In Table 8.1(a) some lines are drawn which merely set off parts of this model. Then in Table 8.1(b) the variable symbols are removed leaving only the constants; the variables are then placed at the top of their respective columns for identification purposes. The letter R is placed at the top of the column representing the right-hand sides of the equations. With one modification of Table 8.1(b) and some explanation, this tableau will be called the initial tableau for the simplex method. It will represent the first corner solution from which the simplex will begin jumping.

TABLE 8.1
Conversion to Tableau Format

(a)

P	$-30X - 20Y + 0S_c + 0S_t + 0S_r = 0$
	$1X + 3Y + 1S_c + 0S_t + 0S_r = 12.5$
	$2X + 1Y + 0S_c + 1S_t + 0S_r = 10$
	$2X + 0Y + 0S_c + 0S_t + 1S_r = 8$

(b)

	X	Y	S_c	S_t	S_r	R
P	-30	-20	0	0	0	0
	1	3	1	0	0	12.5
	2	1	0	1	0	10
	2	0	0	0	1	8

Before commencing with the actual simplex method, it is important to understand something of the nature of a corner solution. If there are m constraints in a linear programming model (disregarding nonnegativity constraints), a corner solution will have at most m non-zero variables. For example, in the Brothers Karamazov model there are 3 constraints and 5 variables; the variables are $X, Y, S_c, S_t,$ and S_r. Now since there are $m=3$ constraints, a corner solution will have no more than 3 non-zero variables. The rest of the variables will be equal to zero. The corner C, for example, in Figure 8.1 represents the following solution: $X=4$, $Y=2$, $S_c=2.5$, $S_t=0$, and $S_r=0$. Since C is a corner it is necessarily represented by a solution with only 3 non-zero variables which in this case are X, Y, and S_c. The fact that a corner solution will never use more than m non-zero variables is quite important to the simplex method. Because of its importance, this characteristic of corner solutions will now be stated as a theorem:

> In a linear programming model with m constraints, no more than m variables will be positive at a corner solution. The other variables will be zero.
> NON ZERO.

In the most typical case, exactly m variables will be positive for a corner solution. These m variables are called *basic* variables. All the other variables in the model are called *non-basic* variables and they have a value of zero. This theorem plays an important role in making sure that when a jump takes place, the landing is at a corner and not at some other point within the shaded space of feasible solutions.

To begin the simplex method, a corner solution is needed. It is certain because of the theorem just given, that a corner solution in the Brothers Karamazov case will have three $(m=3)$ basic variables. How can such a corner solution be found? It turns out that the algebraic preliminaries concluded in Section 8.2 have laid the groundwork for finding a corner solution with ease. The initial corner solution is always found by letting the original variables in the model (e.g., X and Y) take the value of zero. This forces the slack variables to assume positive values. Notice how this is achieved with the set of Brothers Karamazov constraints:

$$X + 3Y + S_c \qquad\qquad = 12.5$$
$$2X + 1Y \qquad + S_t \qquad = 10$$
$$2X \qquad\qquad\quad + S_r = 8$$

Now letting $X = Y = 0$,

$$S_c \qquad\qquad = 12.5$$
$$S_t \qquad = 10$$
$$S_r = 8$$

The solution $X = 0$, $Y = 0$, $S_c = 12.5$, $S_t = 10$, $S_r = 8$ not only satisfies the constraints but also is a corner solution having exactly 3 basic variables. This corner is represented by Corner A in Figure 8.1.

Having seen how an initial corner solution may easily be achieved, it is next necessary to express this solution in tableau format. Table 8.2 is derived from the tableau of Table 8.1(b). In Table 8.2 the 3 basic variables are identified and placed to the left. S_c is identified with Row 1 since it appears only in the first constraint. Likewise, S_t and S_r are identified with the second and third constraint rows. The values of the basic variables for the current corner solution are always read from column R. Notice that S_c equals 12.5, S_t equals 10, and S_r equals 8 as found in column R for this initial solution.

Every variable in the model which does not appear on the left side of the tableau is a non-basic variable and thus has a value of zero (X and Y are the non-basic variables in this initial corner solution). The entry under column R for Row 0 always gives the current value of the objective function. In Table 8.2 a 0 appears in this position indicating that the initial corner solution yields a profit of $P = 0$. This is true since $X = Y = 0$ and the profit function is $P = 30X + 20Y$.

A couple more observations might be made concerning a tableau which represents a corner solution. The values of the basic variables will never be negative (these values are found in Rows 1, 2, and 3 under Column R). If any of these became negative it would be in direct violation of the nonnegativity constraints which specify that no variable, whether it be an original variable or a slack variable or a surplus variable, may take on a negative value. The algebraic preliminaries of Section 8.2 guarantee that these values under the R column are not negative at the outset; the simplex method is so constituted that they never will become negative as jumps from corner to corner take place. It might also be noticed that the entries under the basic variable columns in Row 0 are always zero. Furthermore, the entire column for the basic variables (in this case, the columns under S_c, S_t, and S_r) are always composed of zeros and a 1. The values in Row 0 under the non-basic variables (in this case the non-basic variables are X and Y) may be negative, zero, or positive.

The initial corner solution as depicted in the tableau of Table 8.2 may now be summarized.

1. The initial corner solution is an all slack variable solution. As there are $m = 3$ constraints there will be three basic variables in any corner solution.

The basic variables are initially all slack variables. The values of the basic variables are $S_c = 12.5$, $S_t = 10$, and $S_r = 8$. These values are found in Column R. The other or non-basic variables, X and Y, are both zero. The zero value of the non-basic variables is not given in the tableau but it is always understood that the non-basic variables are zero.

2. The corner which the initial solution represents is Corner A in Figure 8.1.
3. The profit for the corner is read from Row 0 under Column R. The initial profit is 0. This may be confirmed by substituting $X = Y = 0$ into the profit function.

With a corner solution determined and then depicted in tableau format, the simplex method may be implemented.

TABLE 8.2
Initial Corner Solution Tableau

		X	Y	S_c	S_t	S_r	R	
	P	−30	−20	0	0	0	0	Row 0
Basic Variables	S_c	1	3	1	0	0	12.5	Row 1
	S_t	2	1	0	1	0	10	Row 2
	S_r	2	0	0	0	1	8	Row 3

Variable Columns

— current profit
— value of S_c
— value of S_t
— value of S_r

8.5 SIMPLEX METHOD—IMPLEMENTATION

Before proceeding, review the three steps of the simplex method in Section 8.3. With the initial tableau constructed as in Table 8.2, the simplex method may begin.

STEP 1: *Examine the current corner solution to see if it is optimal.*

Does the tableau of Table 8.2 represent the optimal solution? The Simplex Optimality Rule provides assistance in answering this question.

Simplex Optimality Rule—Scan all of the entries in Row 0 excluding that under Column R. If all the entries under the variable columns in Row 0 are zero or positive, then the current solution is optimal. On the other hand, if any of these entries are negative, then there is a better corner solution and thus the current solution is not optimal.

By examining all of Row 0 except the entry under Column R in the initial tableau, it appears that there are two negative entries. −30 appears under the X column and −20 appears under the Y column. Therefore, by the Simplex Optimality Rule it should be concluded that the current solution is not optimal and a better solution exists. There needs to be a jump to this better corner solution.

STEP 2: *Find the next corner which represents the better corner solution.*

A new corner solution will be represented by a new set of three basic variables. One of the current basic variables will be replaced by one of the current non-basic variables. When this replacement has taken place and the tableau has been adjusted, then the jump will have been consummated and the new corner solution will appear. (Notice that one variable will leave the set of basic variables but it is to be replaced immediately by a formerly non-basic variable. The net effect is to keep exactly $m = 3$ variables as basic which is required to make sure the solution will be a corner solution.)

As a new solution will come about when one of the basic variables in the tableau gets replaced, it must be determined which variable actually gets replaced and which variable takes its place. The Simplex Incoming Rule isolates the variable which is to become the new basic variable.

> *Simplex Incoming Rule*—Find a negative entry under a variable column in Row 0 of the tableau. The variable associated with this negative entry should be the new basic variable. If there are several negative entries in Row 0, arbitrarily select one. Then the variable associated with that arbitrarily selected negative entry in Row 0 will be the new or incoming basic variable.

In the initial tableau of Table 8.2 there are two negative entries in Row 0 under the variable columns, namely, -30 and -20. Let -20 be arbitrarily selected. This means that since -20 is in the Y column, Y will be the new basic variable.

Now that the incoming variable has been isolated, what basic variable must leave in order to preserve exactly 3 basic variables? The Simplex Outgoing Rule helps here.

> *Simplex Outgoing Rule*—Circle the entire column of the variable which is to become the new basic variable. Divide each entry in the R column (excluding that of Row 0) by the corresponding entry in the circled column unless the corresponding entry in the circled column is zero or negative. If it is zero or negative, do not form the ratio. The basic variable associated with the row which has the minimum ratio is the basic variable which is to be replaced. Circle the row associated with the outgoing basic variable.

In Table 8.3 the Y column is circled (do not pay attention to the circled row) as it is the column associated with the new basic variable. The ratio of the entries in Column R to the entries in this circled column are (disregarding Row 0):

$$
\begin{aligned}
&\text{For Row 1:} && 12.5/3 = 4.17 \\
&\text{For Row 2:} && 10/1 = 10 \\
&\text{For Row 3:} && \text{Do not form ratio since entry} \\
& && \text{in the circled column is zero}
\end{aligned}
$$

TABLE 8.3
**Initial Tableau with Column of Incoming Variable
and Row of Outgoing Variable Circled**

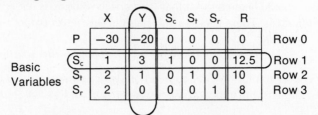

		X	Y	S_c	S_t	S_r	R	
	P	−30	−20	0	0	0	0	Row 0
Basic	S_c	1	3	1	0	0	12.5	Row 1
Variables	S_t	2	1	0	1	0	10	Row 2
	S_r	2	0	0	0	1	8	Row 3

Of the two ratios computed, the first has the minimum value which is 4.17. Therefore, the variable associated with Row 1, namely S_c, will be the outgoing basic variable. Row 1 is therefore circled (see Table 8.3).

The second step of the simplex method has now been completed in that the incoming and outgoing variables have been isolated. Essentially, the direction of the jump has now been fixed.

STEP 3: *Jump to the next corner.*

The jump to the next corner solution takes place by transforming the initial tableau. The outgoing variable is replaced by the incoming variable on the left side where the basic variables are designated; Y will therefore appear in the place of S_c in the new tableau. In Table 8.3, which gives the initial tableau, the entry at the intersection of the two circles is called the *pivot* entry. The pivot entry in this case is a 3. The Simplex Jump Rule enables the new tableau representing the new corner solution to be completed.

> *Simplex Jump Rule*—A new tableau representing a new corner solution may be determined from the entries of the former tableau by the following operations:
> OPERATION 1. Every entry in the circled row must be divided by the pivot entry. This yields the new row in the new tableau. (This is the row associated with the new basic variable.)
> OPERATION 2. The circled column will be filled from top to bottom with zeros except for the 1 which is in the pivot position. The columns for the basic variables which remained will be untouched and thus will be the same in the new tableau as they were in the former tableau.
> OPERATION 3. Every other entry in the former tableau can be updated by using the formula
>
> $$E' = E - \frac{R\,C}{P}$$
>
> where E' refers to the new entry, E refers to the former entry, R refers to the entry in the circled row which is in the same column as E, C refers to the entry in the circled column which is in the same row as E, and P represents the pivot entry in the former tableau. (The locations of E, R, C, and P are illustrated in Table 8.4.)

TABLE 8.4
Finding New Entry Using OPERATION 3

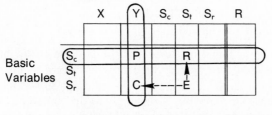

The entry that will replace E in the new tableau is computed by $E' = E - RC/P$.

The three parts of Table 8.5 demonstrate the three operations of the Simplex Jump Rule. In part (a) the entries were found by dividing each of the entries in Row 1 (circled) of Table 8.3 by the pivot entry which is 3. This is Operation 1. In part (b) the second operation of the Simplex jump rule is accomplished. The Y column is filled with zeros except for the 1 in the pivot position. The basic variables S_t and S_r did not leave the corner solution, hence their respective columns are the same as in the former tableau of Table 8.3.

TABLE 8.5
Jump to Second Corner Solution Using Simplex Jump Rule

(a)

		X	Y	S_c	S_t	S_r	R	
	P							
Basic Variables	Y	.33	1	.33	0	0	4.17	Row 1
	S_t							
	S_r							

(b)

		X	Y	S_c	S_t	S_r	R	
	P		0		0	0		Row 0
Basic Variables	Y	.33	1	.33	0	0	4.17	Row 1
	S_t		0		1	0		Row 2
	S_r		0		0	1		Row 3

(c)

		X	Y	S_c	S_t	S_r	R	
	P	−23.33	0	6.67	0	0	83.34	Row 0
Basic Variables	Y	.33	1	.33	0	0	4.17	Row 1
	S_t	1.67	0	−.33	1	0	5.83	Row 2
	S_r	2	0	0	0	1	8	Row 3

Finally, part (c) of Table 8.5 gives all the other updated entries as determined by Operation 3 of the Simplex Jump Rule. These were found using

$$E' = E - RC/P$$

For example, the entry in Row 0 under Column X is found by using the information of the initial tableau of Table 8.3 in the following manner:

$$E = -30, R = 1, C = -20, \text{ and } P = 3$$

thus,
$$E' = -30 - (1)(-20)/3$$
$$= -23.33$$

Note that the $R = 1$ was found by starting at the position of the entry $E = -30$ (which is to be updated) and moving vertically downward to the circled row. The entry encountered in the circled row is 1. The $C = -20$ was found by starting with the entry -30 and moving horizontally to the circled column. The entry in the circled column is -20. Refer to Table 8.4 for the general approach of finding E'.

The entries under the X column in Rows 2 and 3 are determined by

$$E' = 2 - (1)(1)/3 = 1.67 \qquad \text{For Row 2}$$
$$E' = 2 - (1)(0)/3 = 2 \qquad \text{For Row 3}$$

The three entries in the new tableau of part (c) under the S_c column are found by

$$E' = 0 - (1)(-20)/3 = 6.67 \qquad \text{For Row 0}$$
$$E' = 0 - (1)(1)/3 = -.33 \qquad \text{For Row 2}$$
$$E' = 0 - (1)(0)/3 = 0 \qquad \text{For Row 3}$$

The new entries under Column R are found by

$$E' = 0 - (12.5)(-20)/3 = 83.34 \qquad \text{For Row 0}$$
$$E' = 10 - (12.5)(1)/3 = 5.83 \qquad \text{For Row 2}$$
$$E' = 8 - (12.5)(0)/3 = 8 \qquad \text{For Row 3}$$

The jump to the new corner solution has now been completed in that the new tableau has been determined. This means that the third and final step of one simplex iteration has taken place. The new corner solution, as represented in Table 8.5(c), will now be examined. Then the three-step process of the simplex method will again be carried out.

The corner solution of Table 8.5(c) has as its three basic variables, Y, S_t, and S_r. The R column reveals their values to be $Y = 4.17$, $S_t = 5.83$, and $S_r = 8$. The non-basic variables automatically have a value of zero, that is, $X = S_c = 0$. Recall that the constraints in the final standard form for the Brothers Karamazov example were

$$
\begin{aligned}
X + 3Y + S_c &= 12.5 \\
2X + Y + S_t &= 10 \\
2X + S_r &= 8
\end{aligned}
$$

Substituting the values for the variables just given perfectly satisfies each of these constraints. The profit for this corner solution is shown in Row 0 under the R column, a profit of \$83.34. This profit figure can be verified by substituting the current corner solution into the profit function. This corner is Corner E in the graph of Figure 8.1. As promised by the Simplex Optimality Rule, it yields a profit at least as great as the initial solution (compare \$83.34 to \$0).

Does the corner solution of Table 8.5(c) represent the optimal solution?

STEP 1: *Examine the current corner solution to see if it is optimal.*

The Simplex Optimality Rule provides the basis for concluding that the current solution is not optimal. By checking Row 0 under the variable columns, a negative value of -23.33 is discovered under the X column. This means that a better solution exists.

STEP 2: *Find the next corner which represents the better solution.*

As the new corner solution will be represented by a change in the basic variables, it must be determined which variable will become the new basic variable and which basic variable will be replaced by the new one. The Simplex Incoming Rule specifies that a variable associated with a negative value in Row 0 should be the new basic variable. The negative value of -23.33 is associated with X, therefore X will be the new basic variable. But which variable will X replace? The Simplex Outgoing Rule states that the column of the incoming variable should be circled, see Table 8.6. Then the ratios of the values in Column R to the circled column should be formed. These ratios are

$$\text{For Row 1:} \quad 4.17/.33 = 12.64$$
$$\text{For Row 2:} \quad 5.83/1.67 = 3.5$$
$$\text{For Row 3:} \quad 8/2 = 4$$

The ratio for Row 2 is the minimum ratio, therefore according to the Simplex Outgoing Rule the basic variable associated with Row 2 must be replaced. This means that S_t is to be replaced. Circle Row 2 as in Table 8.6. Having determined the incoming and the outgoing variables, the direction of the jump to the next corner has been established.

TABLE 8.6
Second Tableau with Column of Incoming Variable and Row of Outgoing Variable Circled

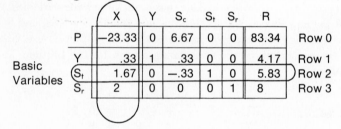

		X	Y	S_c	S_t	S_r	R	
	P	−23.33	0	6.67	0	0	83.34	Row 0
	Y	.33	1	.33	0	0	4.17	Row 1
Basic	S_t	1.67	0	−.33	1	0	5.83	Row 2
Variables	S_r	2	0	0	0	1	8	Row 3

STEP 3: *Jump to the next corner solution.*

The jump to the next corner takes place by transforming the tableau of Table 8.6. The outgoing variable S_t is replaced by X on the left side where the basic variables are designated. The pivot entry is at the intersection of the two circles in Table 8.6; it is 1.67. The three operations of the Simplex Jump Rule will now be applied in order to update the current tableau. In Table 8.7(a) Operation 1 is accomplished in that every entry in the circled row, Row 2, has been divided by the pivot entry. That is, 1.67, 0, −.33, 1, 0, and 5.83 or Row 2 in Table 8.6 have each been divided by 1.67 to yield 1, 0, −.2, .6, 0, and 3.5.

In Table 8.7(b) the second operation is accomplished. As Y and S_r remain as basic variables, the columns associated with these two variables are untouched and therefore are the same in Table 8.7(b) as in Table 8.6. The column of the new basic variable X is filled with zeros except for the 1 in the pivot position. This is in accordance with Operation 2 of the Simplex Jump Rule.

Finally the other entries of the tableau are found using $E' = E - RC/P$. Using the information from Table 8.6, the remaining entries for the S_c column are determined by

$$E' = 6.67 - (-.33)(-23.33)/1.67 = 2 \qquad \text{For Row 0}$$

TABLE 8.7
Jump to Third Corner Solution Using Simplex Jump Rule

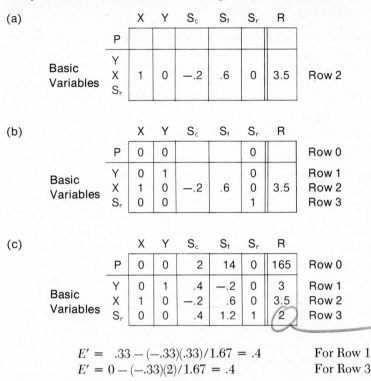

(a)

		X	Y	S_c	S_t	S_r	R	
	P							
Basic Variables	Y							
	X	1	0	−.2	.6	0	3.5	Row 2
	S_r							

(b)

		X	Y	S_c	S_t	S_r	R	
	P	0	0			0		Row 0
Basic Variables	Y	0	1			0		Row 1
	X	1	0	−.2	.6	0	3.5	Row 2
	S_r	0	0			1		Row 3

(c)

		X	Y	S_c	S_t	S_r	R	
	P	0	0	2	14	0	165	Row 0
Basic Variables	Y	0	1	.4	−.2	0	3	Row 1
	X	1	0	−.2	.6	0	3.5	Row 2
	S_r	0	0	.4	1.2	1	2	Row 3

$$E' = .33 - (-.33)(.33)/1.67 = .4 \qquad \text{For Row 1}$$
$$E' = 0 - (-.33)(2)/1.67 = .4 \qquad \text{For Row 3}$$

The remaining entries under the S_t column are determined by

$$E' = 0 - (1)(-23.33)/1.67 = 14 \qquad \text{For Row 0}$$
$$E' = 0 - (1)(.33)/1.67 = -.2 \qquad \text{For Row 1}$$
$$E' = 0 - (1)(2)/1.67 = 1.2 \qquad \text{For Row 3}$$

Then the remaining entries under the R column are found

$$E' = 83.34 - (5.83)(-23.33)/1.67 = 165 \qquad \text{For Row 0}$$
$$E' = 4.17 - (5.83)(.33)/1.67 = 3 \qquad \text{For Row 1}$$
$$E' = 8 - (5.83)(2)/1.67 = 2 \qquad \text{For Row 3}$$

With the completion of Table 8.7(c) the jump has been completed and the new corner solution achieved.

The corner solution represented in Table 8.7(c) is $X = 3.5$, $Y = 3$, $S_r = 2$, and $S_c = S_t = 0$. This solution yields a profit of \$165 as indicated by the entry in Row 0 under Column R. Looking back at Figure 8.1 it is evident that the simplex has now jumped to Corner D. Is this corner solution optimal?

STEP 1: *Examine the current corner solution to see if it is optimal.*

Scanning Row 0 of Table 8.7(c) under the variable columns reveals no negative entries. Therefore, by the Simplex Optimality Rule it may be concluded with certainty that the optimal solution is represented by the current corner solution. The solution of Table 8.7(c) is optimal. Having led to the optimal corner solution, the simplex method is finished.

8.6 SPECIAL CONSIDERATIONS

In Section 7.7 of the last chapter the conditions known as redundancy, unbounded solution, alternate optimal solutions, and inconsistent constraints were discussed. It would be well to review Section 7.7 at this time as the first three of these conditions will now be considered in the context of the simplex method. Other topics relating to the simplex method will also be considered in this present section.

Redundancy and Degeneracy

How does redundancy show up in the simplex method when it exists? If redundancy exists, it will appear in the simplex method by yielding a zero value for one of the basic variables (the zero would appear in Column R). It was pointed out in Section 7.7 that redundancy presents no problem and thus it follows that having a value of zero for one of the basic variables is no problem.

The usual cause of a zero-valued basic variable is redundancy. Whenever there is a zero-valued basic variable in a solution, the solution is said to be *degenerate*. When degeneracy exists the analyst should continue as usual. The only problem associated with degeneracy concerns the application of the Simplex Outgoing Rule. After the incoming variable has been determined and its column circled, the Simplex Outgoing Rule states that the ratios of the entries in Column R to those in the circled column are to be formed. Then the minimum of these ratios is isolated and the row with the minimum ratio is circled. The basic variable associated with the circled row is the basic variable which is to be replaced. When degeneracy exists it will be discovered that there is a tie for the minimum ratio. In this case which row should be circled? The easiest rule is to arbitrarily choose one of the rows with the minimum ratio and circle it, thereby deciding which variable will be replaced. Sometimes this arbitrary selection will result in making no progress toward the optimal solution—this will become apparent to the analyst as succeeding jumps take place and the profit does not increase or the whole process begins to repeat itself. If this does occur, go back to where the arbitrary selection was made at the point of the tied ratios and instead circle the other row. Then proceed as usual and all will be well.

The partial tableau of Table 8.8 illustrates the onset of degeneracy. To determine the outgoing variable, select Row 1 or Row 3 arbitrarily to be circled.

Alternate Optimal Solutions

According to the Simplex Optimality Rule, the optimal corner solution has been reached if under the variable columns in Row 0 there are no negative entries. However, if an entry in Row 0 in a non-basic variable column is zero while no negative entries exist elsewhere in Row 0, then alternate optimal solutions exist. Recall that the existence of alternate optimal solutions means that there is at

TABLE 8.8
Partial Tableau Illustrating the Onset of Degeneracy

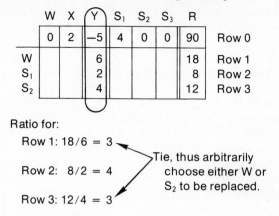

	W	X	Y	S_1	S_2	S_3	R	
	0	2	−5	4	0	0	90	Row 0
W			6				18	Row 1
S_1			2				8	Row 2
S_2			4				12	Row 3

Ratio for:

Row 1: 18/6 = 3

Row 2: 8/2 = 4

Row 3: 12/4 = 3

Tie, thus arbitrarily choose either W or S_2 to be replaced.

least one more corner which gives the same optimal objective function value. If the analyst wishes to find another optimal corner when one exists, all that is required is to replace one of the basic variables with the non-basic variable whose Row 0 entry was zero. This is achieved as before by circling the column of the incoming variable and then using the Simplex Outgoing Rule to determine which basic variable is to be replaced. Finally the tableau is updated (the jump takes place) using the Simplex Jump Rule as before.

In Table 8.9 part of a tableau is presented. Scanning Row 0, it is apparent that an optimal solution has been reached since none of the entries are negative. This means that 100 is the maximum profit which occurs at the corner represented by $X_2 = 7$, $S_1 = 8$, $S_3 = 9$ and $X_1 = X_3 = X_4 = S_2 = 0$.

TABLE 8.9
Partial Tableau Illustrating the Existence of Alternate Optimal Solutions

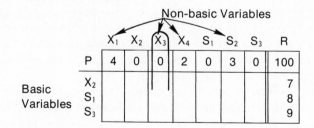

Non-basic Variables

		X_1	X_2	X_3	X_4	S_1	S_2	S_3	R
	P	4	0	0	2	0	3	0	100
Basic Variables	X_2								7
	S_1								8
	S_3								9

The basic variables will *always* have a zero entry in Row 0 no matter what corner solution is being represented. To determine if there are alternate optimal solutions the entries in Row 0 for the non-basic variables must be checked (the non-basic variables are X_1, X_3, X_4, and S_2). Notice that the entry in Row 0 under X_3, which is a non-basic variable, is zero. This means that alternate optimal solutions exist. To find another solution which yields a profit of 100, the X_3 column should be circled and then the simplex method followed as usual. X_3 would become a basic variable and one of the three current basic variables would be replaced. The profit for the new corner would still be 100.

When alternate optimal solutions exist it is desirable to note the fact but there is no need to find any of the other solutions since they are no better than the current one.

Unbounded Solution

According to the Simplex Outgoing Rule, the outgoing basic variable is found by determining the minimum ratio formed by dividing the entry in Column R by the corresponding entry in the circled column of the incoming variable. The Simplex Outgoing Rule also specifies that if a zero or negative entry exists in the circled column, then the ratio for that row should not be formed. Suppose that every entry in the circled column were zero or negative, what should be done? If this happens it means that the next jump, if taken, would be to infinity and the "corner" at infinity would represent a solution with infinite profit. In other words, the shaded area of feasible solutions is open-ended in the direction of increasing profits, thus an unbounded solution exists.

Table 8.10 gives part of a simplex tableau illustrating the predicament where all the entries in the circled column are zero or negative, thus indicating that an unbounded solution exists. When this condition occurs the simplex process is terminated and the fact that an unbounded solution exists should be stated. The analyst must then go look for the missing constraint which should have been part of the model which would have kept the solution from being unbounded.

TABLE 8.10
Partial Tableau Illustrating the Existence of an Unbounded Solution

	X_1	X_2	X_3	S_1	S_2	R
	0	0	−6	5	0	35
X_1			−2			3
X_2			−.5			4
S_2			0			5

Shadow Prices

The entries in Row 0 of the final tableau under the slack variables are sometimes called the shadow prices. If any of the slack variables are basic variables, then their shadow price is zero since the entry in Row 0 for any basic variable is always zero. Slack variables which are non-basic will typically have some positive valued entry under them in Row 0 of the final tableau representing the optimal solution. In the Brothers Karamazov example where the final tableau representing the optimal solution is given in Table 8.7(c), the shadow price associated with S_c is 2, that for S_t is 14, and that for S_r is 0. What is the significance of these shadow prices?

Each shadow price is associated with a particular slack variable, and each slack variable is associated with a particular constraint. The constraint associated with the greatest shadow price is the constraint which is most restrictive. What does this mean in the Brothers Karamazov situation? Suppose the Brothers could get 1 hour extra of carpentry time, or 1 hour extra of tinsmithing time, or 1 extra iron runner each week. Which of these three resources would be the best to acquire? Since the shadow price for the slack variable S_t is the greatest, it can be concluded that it would be best to add 1 extra hour of tinsmithing time. Adding more of the tinsmithing resource does the most for making greater profits possible. The fact that the shadow price for S_r is 0 implies that having 1 more iron runner available each week would be of no benefit to the Brothers in their quest for higher profits. This accords with the fact that in the optimal solution S_r has a value of 2, which means that with the optimal production mix all the eight available runners are not being used (only six are being used). If what is available is not being used, making yet another runner available will obviously be of no benefit.

In summary, the shadow prices enable management to spot excess resources (they have a shadow price of zero) as well as the resources which can be increased for the greatest benefit. In closing this discussion, a word of caution. Just because the tinsmithing resource has the greatest shadow price, namely 14, it does not follow that this resource can be continually augmented with the consequence of producing more and more profit. Ultimately a point will be reached where it would be better to increase one of the other resources. If 10 more hours of tinsmithing time were made available, there would be a shortage of iron runners and an excess of tinsmithing hours. Hence if the resources in a linear programming model can be increased substantially, a good deal more analysis is required beyond the inspection of shadow prices.

8.7 SIMPLEX FOR MINIMIZATON MODELS—PRELIMINARIES

In Section 8.5 the simplex for a maximization problem was illustrated. When the objective of the linear programming model is the minimization of some quantity like cost, and where some of the constraints are of the "greater than or equal to" variety (for example, $X + Y \geq 4$), then there are some difficulties which must be resolved before the simplex method can be used. In this section the minimization model will be converted in a way which will permit the application of the simplex method as described in Section 8.5. Then in the next section the actual simplex method will be performed for a converted minimization model.

The preliminary preparations for the typical minimization model will now be briefly summarized. Having expressed the constraints in initial standard form as defined in Section 8.2, then

1. Add slack variables to all the "$\leq$" constraints and introduce surplus variables in all of the "$\geq$" constraints thereby converting the inequalities to equalities.
2. Introduce an artificial variable to each of the constraints which formerly were "$\geq$" inequalities. (Artificial variables will be defined and explained later.)

3. Add the artificial variable(s) to the objective function.
4. Put all the variables on the left side of the objective function.
5. Remove the artificial variable(s) from the objective function by adding to the objective function an appropriate multiple of the constraint equation(s) containing the artificial variable(s).
6. Change the sign of every term in the objective function.
7. Place the resulting model in tableau format and solve it as if it were a maximization problem using the simplex rules of Section 8.5.

make into   ← [handwritten note]
petober

These preliminaries will now be illustrated and fleshed out by means of an example. Consider a model already in initial standard form:

$$\text{Minimize} \quad C = X + 2Y$$
$$\text{Subject to:} \quad X - Y \leq 0$$
$$X + Y \geq 10$$
$$X, Y \geq 0$$

Preliminary 1

Since the first constraint is of the "$\leq$" variety, a slack variable S will be added to its left side to convert it to an equality (Review Section 8.2 for the discussion of slack and surplus variables):

$$X - Y + S = 0$$

Since the second constraint is of the "$\geq$" variety, subtract the surplus variable U from the left side in order to convert it to an equality:

$$X + Y - U = 10$$

In the simplex method the first corner solution was determined by letting the original variables, X and Y in this example, equal zero thereby forcing the slack variables to take on some value to make the constraints true. In this example if $X = Y = 0$, then for the first constraint the slack variable S will take the value zero and all is satisfied as far as this constraint is concerned. However, for the second constraint when X and Y equal zero, the surplus variable U must equal -10 which violates the stipulation that the surplus variable must never be negative. In other words, the tentative solution $X = 0$, $Y = 0$ does not satisfy the second constraint which is $X + Y \geq 10$. This means that an initial corner solution represented by $X = 0$, $Y = 0$ is not feasible. The conclusion of the matter is that an initial corner solution cannot be found easily by letting X and Y equal zero as was done in Section 8.4 for the maximization model. However, since the simplex method can only start when a corner solution has been found, the search for a corner solution must continue.

In order to find a way out of this dilemma of not being able to easily find an initial corner solution from which to start, another variable called an artificial variable must be added to the model. The artificial variable is added solely to get the simplex method started. After the simplex is on its way the artificial variable(s) is discarded. The artificial variable could be likened to the battery in the automobile, it is needed to get the engine started but once the engine is running the battery is no longer needed.

Preliminary 2

An artificial variable must be introduced in each constraint which was formerly of the "≥" type. The constraint to which a surplus variable has already been introduced must now have an artificial variable added

$$X + Y - U + A = 10$$

Having introduced the artificial variable A, let the original variables along with the surplus variable equal zero. This forces S to take the value of zero and the artificial variable to take the value 10. In other words, if $X = Y = U = 0$, then in order to satisfy the modified constraints the slack S must equal 0 and A must equal 10. This is confirmed by substitution into the modified constraints

$$X - Y + S = 0$$
$$X + Y - U + A = 10$$

or,

$$0 - 0 + 0 = 0$$
$$0 + 0 - 0 + 10 = 10$$

Such a solution, while satisfying the modified constraints, does not satisfy the original constraints which were

$$X - Y \leq 0$$
$$X + Y \geq 10$$

since

$$0 - 0 \leq 0$$
$$0 + 0 \geq 10 \quad \text{False!}$$

Therefore, this initial solution is really not feasible. But since it is a solution which does not require negative values it will enable the simplex method to get started. Then after a few jumps a feasible corner solution will be reached and the artificial variable will be discarded. The objective function must next be modified in order to guarantee that the artificial variable will ultimately be discarded by the simplex.

The objective function calls for the minimization of cost C where $C = X + 2Y$. The optimal solution will be some pair of values for X and Y which are as small as possible thus yielding a small total cost C. Suppose the objective function were formulated as

$$\text{Minimize} \quad C = X + 2Y + 100A$$

Here the artificial variable has been introduced into the objective function. The coefficient of A was chosen to be an arbitrary large number. If in a solution A were to have a value of only 1 this would produce a large total cost. By so introducing A into the objective function with a large positive coefficient, there will be an irresistible incentive for the simplex to jump to a corner where A equals zero in order to achieve a minimum cost. This is the technique used to make sure that A will not appear in a solution but will drop out (become a nonbasic variable) as the simplex starts jumping from corner to corner. Hence the third preparation.

Preliminary 3

Add the artificial variable A to the objective function with a large arbitrary coefficient so that there will be an irresistible incentive for the simplex to jump to a corner solution where A will take on the value zero. This arbitrarily large coefficient should be well in excess of the other coefficients in the objective function. In the present example the coefficient of 100 will be used

$$\text{Minimize} \quad C = X + 2Y + 100A$$

Preliminary 4

Put all of the variables on the left side of the objective function. This means that the objective function in this example must be written as

$$\text{Minimize} \quad C - X - 2Y - 100A = 0$$

Preliminary 5

The artificial variable A is to be removed from the objective function by adding a multiple of one of the constraints to it. The reason for this action will be given after it is demonstrated. The model in its entirety currently has the form

$$
\begin{aligned}
\text{Minimize} \quad C - X - 2Y \qquad\qquad - 100A &= 0 \\
X - Y + S \qquad\qquad &= 0 \\
X + Y \quad - U + A &= 10
\end{aligned}
$$

By multiplying the last constraint by 100, an equivalent equation is found

$$100X + 100Y - 100U + 100A = 1000$$

Then add this equation to the objective function

$$
\begin{array}{r}
C - X - \quad 2Y \qquad\qquad - 100A = \quad 0 \\
+ \quad \underline{100X + 100Y - 100U + 100A = 1000} \\
C + 99X + \quad 98Y - 100U \qquad\qquad = 1000
\end{array}
$$
(New Objective Function)

The result of adding this multiple of the last constraint to the objective function is to produce an equivalent objective function which does not contain the artificial variable. The reason for this action is that the artificial variable will be a basic variable in the initial tableau. The entry in Row 0 under each basic variable must always be zero. This will now be the case in the current problem due to the process just completed.

Preliminary 6

Change the sign of every term of the objective function. Multiplying both sides of the objective function by -1 in this example yields

$$-C - 99X - 98Y + 100U = -1000$$

The Simplex Incoming Rule as given in Section 8.5 applies to maximization models only. As the model in this section is a minimization model, it must be altered according to Preliminary 6 in order to adapt the model to the Simplex Incoming Rule. Now the Simplex Incoming Rule can be used exactly as before.

The preliminary preparations have now been completed except for the expressing of the model in tableau format.

Preliminary 7

Place the resulting model in tableau format letting the slack and artificial variables be the initial basic variables. The model as it currently stands is

$$-C - 99X - 98Y \quad + 100U \quad = -1000$$
$$X - \quad Y + S \quad\quad\quad = \quad 0$$
$$X + \quad Y \quad - U + A = \quad 10$$

This model is expressed in tableau format in Table 8.11.

Initially the non-basic variables (those equal to zero) are X, Y, and U. The basic variables, S and A, will therefore equal 0 and 10 respectively as shown in Column R of Table 8.11. Notice that the slack variable S is identified with Row 1 since it appears only in the first constraint. The artificial variable is associated with Row 2 as it appears initially in the second constraint only. In the section to follow the simplex method will be used to solve the model beginning with the initial tableau solution of Table 8.11.

TABLE 8.11
Initial Tableau

		X	Y	S	U	A	R	
	−C	−99	−98	0	100	0	−1000	Row 0
Basic	S	1	−1	1	0	0	0	Row 1
Variables	A	1	1	0	−1	1	10	Row 2

8.8 SIMPLEX FOR MINIMIZATION MODELS—COMPLETION

In the previous section the minimization model

$$\text{Minimize} \quad C = X + 2Y$$
$$\text{Subject to:} \quad X - Y \le 0$$
$$X + Y \ge 10$$

was converted through the addition of slack, surplus, and artificial variables to a form suitable for the simplex method. The fruition of the conversion process came in the statement of the model in tableau format as shown in Table 8.11. Notice that the initial solution has S and A as the basic variables with values of 0 and 10 respectively. When these are substituted into the objective function as it was expressed in Preliminary 3 of the previous section, the result is a cost of 1000 as is indicated by the entry in Row 0 under Column R. That is,

$$\text{Min } C = X + 2Y + 100A$$
$$= 0 + 0 + (100)(10)$$
$$= 1000$$

It might be objected that the entry in Row 0 is −1000, not 1000. At the extreme left of Row 0 in Table 8.11 is a −C, hence −C equals −1000 or C equals 1000 as claimed.

The simplex method will now start from this initial corner solution as depicted in Table 8.11.

STEP 1: *Examine the current corner solution to see if it is optimal.*

By scanning the entries under the variable columns in Row 0, two of them are recognized to be negative. By the Simplex Optimality Rule it may therefore be concluded that the current solution is not optimal.

STEP 2: *Find the next corner which represents a better solution.*

By the Simplex Incoming Rule, any variable with a negative entry in Row 0 can become the new basic variable. As the entry in Row 0 under X is -99, circle the X column thus indicating that X is to be the new basic variable. (The Y column could instead have been circled as the entry under Y in Row 0 is also negative.) See Table 8.12.

What basic variable is to be replaced? The Simplex Outgoing Rule requires the formation of the ratios of the entries in Column R to those of the circled column. These two ratios are:

$$\text{For Row 1:} \quad 0/1 = 0$$
$$\text{For Row 2:} \quad 10/1 = 10$$

As the ratio for Row 1 is the minimum ratio, Row 1 should be circled indicating that S is the variable to be replaced by X. Remember that since there are only $m = 2$ constraints, there will be only two basic variables thus guaranteeing that corner solutions only are considered.

Having determined the incoming and outgoing variables, the direction of the jump has been established.

TABLE 8.12
Initial Tableau with Column of Incoming Variable
and Row of Outgoing Variable Circled

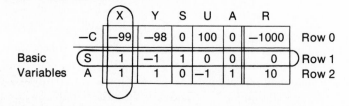

		X	Y	S	U	A	R	
	$-C$	-99	-98	0	100	0	-1000	Row 0
Basic	S	1	-1	1	0	0	0	Row 1
Variables	A	1	1	0	-1	1	10	Row 2

STEP 3: *Jump to the next corner.*

The jump to the next corner takes place by transforming or updating the initial tableau by means of the Simplex Jump Rule. S is replaced by X as a basic variable on the left side of the tableau; see Table 8.13. Operation 1 of the Simplex Jump Rule is accomplished by dividing every entry in Row 1 of Table 8.12 by the pivot entry which is 1. Dividing by 1 does not alter these entries and so Table 8.13(a) exhibits the same Row 1. In Operation 2 the X column which is the column of the incoming basic variables is filled with zeros except for the 1 in the pivot position. The column under A in Table 8.12 is unaffected as A remains as a basic variable, thus it is transported intact to Table 8.13(b). Table 8.13(b) is the result of the first two operations of the Simplex Jump Rule.

222

The remaining entries in Table 8.12 are updated and placed into Table 8.13(c) according to Operation 3. In particular, the new entry E' is found by

$$E' = E - RC/P$$

where E, R, C, and P come from the former tableau of Table 8.12. Using this formula the new entries as found in Table 8.13(c) under the Y column are

$$E' = -98 - (-1)(-99)/1 = -197 \qquad \text{For Row 0}$$
$$E' = 1 - (-1)(1)/1 = 2 \qquad \text{For Row 2}$$

The new entries under the S column are

$$E' = 0 - (1)(-99)/1 = 99 \qquad \text{For Row 0}$$
$$E' = 0 - (1)(1)/1 = -1 \qquad \text{For Row 2}$$

The new entries under the U column are

$$E' = 100 - (0)(-99)/1 = 100 \qquad \text{For Row 0}$$
$$E' = -1 - (0)(1)/1 = -1 \qquad \text{For Row 2}$$

Finally, the new entries under the R column are

$$E' = -1000 - (0)(-99)/1 = -1000 \qquad \text{For Row 0}$$
$$E' = 10 - (0)(1)/1 = 10 \qquad \text{For Row 2}$$

TABLE 8.13
Jump to Second Corner Solution Using Simplex Jump Rule

(a)

	X	Y	S	U	A	R	
X A	1	−1	1	0	0	0	Row 1

(b)

	X	Y	S	U	A	R	
−C	0				0		Row 0
X	1	−1	1	0	0	0	Row 1
A	0				1		Row 2

(c)

	X	Y	S	U	A	R	
−C	0	−197	99	100	0	−1000	Row 0
X	1	−1	1	0	0	0	Row 1
A	0	2	−1	−1	1	10	Row 2

It should be noticed that the solution of Table 8.13(c) has just as high a cost, 1000, as the initial solution. The first jump did not actually improve the cost situation; this occurred because of the temporary degeneracy present in the initial tableau. There is no cause for alarm here, and the simplex process should be continued.

Is the solution of Table 10.13(c) optimal?

STEP 1: *Examine the current corner solution to see if it is optimal.*

Through the application of the Simplex Optimality Rule it is concluded that the solution of Table 8.13(c) is not optimal since there is a negative entry under one of the variable columns in Row 0.

STEP 2: *Find the next corner which represents a better solution.*

By the Simplex Incoming Rule, the variable to become the new basic variable is Y since its entry in Row 0 is negative. This column should be circled as in Table 8.14. The Simplex Outgoing Rule stipulates the formation of the ratios of the R column entries to the circled column entries. These ratios are

For Row 1: Do not form ratio since entry in the circled column is negative

For Row 2: $10/2 = 5$

The minimum and only ratio is associated with Row 2 thus implying that A must be replaced. Circle Row 2.

TABLE 8.14
Second Tableau with Column of Incoming Variable and Row of Outgoing Variable Circled

		X	Y	S	U	A	R	
	−C	0	−197	99	100	0	−1000	Row 0
Basic	X	1	−1	1	0	0	0	Row 1
Variables	A	0	2	−1	−1	1	10	Row 2

STEP 3: *Jump to the next corner.*

All of the entries in the circled row, Row 2, are divided by the pivot entry which is 2. The new entries for Row 2 are shown in Table 8.15. The Y column is filled with zeros except for the pivot entry which is 1. Since the basic variable X was not replaced, the column under X in Table 8.14 is transported to Table 8.15. This concludes the first two operations of the Simplex Jump Rule.

TABLE 8.15
Third Corner Solution

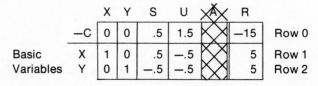

		X	Y	S	U	A	R	
	−C	0	0	.5	1.5		−15	Row 0
Basic	X	1	0	.5	−.5		5	Row 1
Variables	Y	0	1	−.5	−.5		5	Row 2

The remaining entries in Table 8.14 are updated according to Operation 3 of the Simplex Jump Rule. The corresponding new entries in Table 8.15 are found from those of Table 8.14 by using the relationship $E' = E - RC/P$. Specifically, the new entries under S in Table 8.15 are determined by

$$E' = 99 - (-1)(-197)/2 = .5 \qquad \text{For Row 0}$$
$$E' = 1 - (-1)(-1)/2 = .5 \qquad \text{For Row 1}$$

The new entries under U are

$$E' = 100 - (-1)(-197)/2 = 1.5 \qquad \text{For Row 0}$$
$$E' = 0 - (-1)(-1)/2 = -.5 \qquad \text{For Row 1}$$

The new entries under R are found by

$$E' = -1000 - (10)(-197)/2 = -15 \qquad \text{For Row 0}$$
$$E' = 0 - (10)(-1)/2 = 5 \qquad \text{For Row 1}$$

Finally, notice that in Table 8.15 the column under A has been marked out. Whenever an artificial variable is replaced by a new basic variable, that artificial variable has served its purpose and may be dropped from the analysis. Therefore, the column under A may be marked off.

The new corner solution represented by the tableau of Table 8.15 has X and Y as the basic variables each having a value of 5. The slack and the surplus variable are non-basic variables and thus have values of zero. The cost associated with this solution is $-C = -15$ or 15.

Is this solution optimal?

STEP 1: *Examine the current corner solution to see if it is optimal.*

Scanning Row 0 under the variables reveals no negative entries. By the Simplex Optimality Rule it may then be concluded that the solution represented by Table 8.15 is optimal. The minimum cost is therefore 15 which is achieved by $X = 5$ and $Y = 5$. Furthermore there are no alternate optimal solutions as none of the entries under the non-basic variables in Row 0 are zero.

8.9 SIMPLEX FOR MINIMIZATION MODELS— PRELIMINARIES AGAIN

In the minimization model concluded in the last section only one artificial variable was required. In this section the preliminary preparations of Section 8.7 will be briefly demonstrated for a more complex model where two artificial variables are required.

Suppose the following linear programming model were encountered

$$\begin{aligned}
\text{Minimize} \quad & C = 10X + 30Y \\
\text{Subject to:} \quad & 5X + 10Y \geq 15 \\
& X - Y \geq 8 \\
& X, Y \geq 0
\end{aligned}$$

This model will now be prepared for the simplex method.

Preliminary 1

Introduce a different surplus variable to each constraint as each is of the "≥" variety

$$5X + 10Y - U_1 \qquad = 15$$
$$X - \quad Y \qquad - U_2 = 8$$

Preliminary 2

Add an artificial variable to each constraint since both were formerly of the "≥" variety

$$5X + 10Y - U_1 \qquad + A_1 \qquad = 15$$
$$X - \quad Y \qquad - U_2 \qquad + A_2 = 8$$

Preliminary 3

Add the artificial variables to the objective function with large, arbitrarily chosen coefficients

$$C = 10X + 30Y + 500A_1 + 1000A_2$$

Preliminary 4

Put all of the variables on the left side of the objective function

$$C - 10X - 30Y - 500A_1 - 1000A_2 = 0$$

Preliminary 5

Remove the artificial variables from the objective function by adding to the objective function an appropriate multiple of the constraint equations containing the artificial variables. In particular, multiply the first constraint, which is

$$5X + 10Y - U_1 + A_1 = 15$$

by 500. This yields

$$2500X + 5000Y - 500U_1 + 500A_1 = 7500$$

When this equation is added to the objective function, the first artificial variable is removed from the objective function

$$
\begin{array}{l}
C - \quad 10X - \quad 30Y \qquad\qquad - 500A_1 - 1000A_2 = \quad 0 \\
+ \quad\quad 2500X + 5000Y - 500U_1 + 500A_1 \qquad\qquad = 7500 \\
\hline
C + 2490X + 4970Y - 500U_1 \qquad\qquad\quad - 1000A_2 = 7500
\end{array}
$$

Now multiply the second constraint, which contains A_2, by 1000. This yields

$$1000X - 1000Y - 1000U_2 + 1000A_2 = 8000$$

Add this equation to the most recent form of the objective function. This operation eliminates the second artificial variable yielding the following objective function

$$C + 3490X + 3970Y - 500U_1 - 1000U_2 = 15500$$

Preliminary 6

Change the sign of every term of the objective function by multiplying through by a -1

$$-C - 3490X - 3970Y + 500U_1 + 1000U_2 = -15500$$

Preliminary 7

Place the model in tableau format. This is accomplished in Table 8.16.

TABLE 8.16
Initial Tableau

	X	Y	U_1	U_2	A_1	A_2	R
$-C$	-3490	-3970	500	1000	0	0	-15500
A_1	5	10	-1	0	1	0	15
A_2	1	-1	0	-1	0	1	8

This series of preliminary preparations gives an initial tableau with A_1 and A_2 as the initial basic variables. The simplex process may now begin. For example, X might become the new basic variable replacing A_1. The simplex method will ultimately lead to the optimal corner solution.

8.10 ARTIFICIAL VARIABLES AND MAXIMIZATION MODELS

In Sections 8.7 through 8.9 minimization models which included constraints (in standard form) of the "$\geq$" variety were considered. In these cases a series of seven preliminaries were required in order to get the model ready for the simplex method. The "$\geq$" constraints often appear in maximization models also; when this occurs the maximization model also must be modified before the simplex method can be used.

The easiest way to modify a maximization model which has "$\geq$" constraints when in standard form is by following the same seven preliminaries given in Section 8.7; however, the maximization model must undergo one change before these seven preliminaries can be carried out. A maximization model must first be changed according to *Preliminary 0*. *Preliminary 0*, which is only used in the case of maximization models which have "$\geq$" constraints when in standard form, may be stated as

Convert the objective function, where a, b, c, ... are coefficients, from its original form of

$$\text{Maximize } P = aX + bY + cZ + ...$$

to

$$\text{Minimize } -P = -aX - bY - cZ - ...$$

After *Preliminary 0* has been performed, the seven preliminaries of Section 8.7 as outlined for minimization models must next be performed. After completing the seventh of these, the simplex method can be immediately applied to find the optimal solution. An example follows.

Suppose the following maximization model is given:

$$\text{Maximize} \quad P = 2X + 3Y - 4Z$$
$$\text{Subject to:} \quad X + Y + Z \le 45$$
$$8X + Y + Z \ge 60$$

Since a "$\ge$" constraint exists in this maximization model, *Preliminary 0* must first be performed.

$$\text{Maximize} \quad P = 2X + 3Y - 4Z$$

must be converted to

$$\text{Minimize} \quad -P = -2X - 3Y + 4Z$$

Therefore, the model may now be expressed as

$$\text{Minimize} \quad -P = -2X - 3Y + 4Z$$
$$\text{Subject to:} \quad X + Y + Z \le 45$$
$$8X + Y + Z \ge 60$$

The seven preliminaries of Section 8.7 then follow.

In performing the seven preliminaries, nothing is new when compared to the examples given in Sections 8.7 through 8.9. These preliminaries will therefore be presented here only in abbreviated fashion. In *Preliminary 1* slack and surplus variables are introduced in the constraints:

$$X + Y + Z + S = 45$$
$$8X + Y + Z - U = 60$$

An artificial variable is then added in the second constraint; this is *Preliminary 2*.

$$X + Y + Z + S = 45$$
$$8X + Y + Z - U + A = 60$$

In *Preliminary 3* the artificial variable is introduced into the objective function.

$$\text{Minimize} \quad -P = -2X - 3Y + 4Z + 100A$$

Then, *Preliminary 4*

$$\text{Minimize} \quad -P + 2X + 3Y - 4Z - 100A = 0$$

With *Preliminary 5* the artificial variable is eliminated from the objective function by adding a multiple (100) of the second constraint to the objective function. The resulting objective function is

$$\text{Minimize} \quad -P + 802X + 103Y + 96Z - 100U = 6000$$

The sign of every term in the objective function is then changed in *Preliminary 6*. This converts the model back to a maximization model.

$$\text{Maximize} \quad P - 802X - 103Y - 96Z + 100U = -6000$$

In *Preliminary 7* the model as it now stands is

$$\text{Maximize} \quad P - 802X - 103Y - 96Z \quad\quad + 100U \quad\quad = -6000$$
$$\text{Subject to:} \quad\quad X + \quad Y + \quad Z + S \quad\quad\quad\quad = \quad 45$$
$$\quad\quad 8X + \quad Y + \quad Z \quad - \quad\quad U + A = \quad 60$$

This is placed in tableau format. It may then be solved using the simplex method. The solution will give the values of X, Y, and Z which yield the maximal value of P.

8.11 EQUALITY CONSTRAINTS

So far, constraints in the form of an inequality have been treated. Occasionally there will be a constraint(s) in a linear programming model which is an equality rather than an inequality. When an equality constraint does appear, it can be converted into two inequalities. The two inequalities would then take the place of the single equality constraint in the model.

Assume, for example, that the following equality appears as a constraint

$$X + Y = 10$$

This equality is equivalent to the following pair of inequalities

$$X + Y \le 10$$
$$X + Y \ge 10$$

Any values for X and Y which satisfy $X + Y = 10$ will satisfy the two inequalities, and, every pair of values for X and Y which satisfy *both* inequalities will also satisfy $X + Y = 10$.

In view of the preceding discussion, the linear programming model

$$\text{Maximize} \quad P = 2X + 7Y$$
$$\text{Subject to:} \quad\quad X + \quad Y = 10$$
$$\quad\quad 5X - \quad Y \le 20$$

is equivalent to

$$\text{Maximize} \quad P = 2X + 7Y$$
$$\text{Subject to:} \quad\quad X + \quad Y \le 10$$
$$\quad\quad X + \quad Y \ge 10$$
$$\quad\quad 5X - \quad Y \le 20$$

This equivalent model may now be solved by the simplex method.

8.12 INCONSISTENT CONSTRAINTS

In Section 8.6 degeneracy, redundant constraints, alternate optimal solutions, and unbounded solutions were discussed as they relate to the simplex method. The case of inconsistent constraints was not considered. In Section 7.7 of Chapter 7, inconsistent or contradictory constraints were shown to represent a situation where no feasible solutions (shaded area) exist. If constraints are inconsistent, the simplex method signals the presence of this condition. In particular, if an artificial variable appears in the final tableau as a basic variable with a positive value, then the constraints are inconsistent and no solution exists.

For example, the final (partial) tableau of Table 8.17 signals the presence of inconsistent constraints. By the Simplex Optimality Rule, since all entries in Row 0 are zero or positive, the current "solution" is optimal. However, the artificial variable is a basic variable in this "solution" and has a positive value of

TABLE 8.17
Partial Final Tableau Illustrating Existence of Inconsistent Constraints ("A" Is an Artificial Variable)

	X	Y	Z	S_1	S_2	U	A	R
	0	4	6	0	7	1	0	200
X								40
S_1								10
A								5

$A = 5$. Because of the presence of this positive-valued artificial variable in the final tableau, no feasible solution exists and it is therefore concluded that the constraints in this model are inconsistent or contradictory.

The fact that an artificial variable remains at a positive value in the final tableau indicates that despite the jumping which has taken place according to the Simplex Jump Rule, a feasible corner solution was never found and in fact does not exist. Thus it follows that no *optimal* feasible corner solution can exist.

When inconsistent constraints are encountered in solving a linear programming model, the existence of this condition should be stated. Nothing more can be done until the contradiction within the system of constraints is resolved. See Section 7.7 where the matter of correcting contradictory constraints is considered.

8.13 SENSITIVITY ANALYSIS

Once the optimal solution for a linear programming model has been achieved, it may be necessary to make a small change in the objective function and/or the constraints. Will such a change affect the solution? Sensitivity analysis is the study of the effects of changes in a linear programming model. Though sensitivity analysis is beyond the purview of this text, a brief non-mathematical discussion of it is appropriate.

Recall the Brothers Karamazov model which was

Maximize $P = 30X + 20Y$
Subject to:

$X + 3Y \leq 12.5$	(Carpenter Constraint)
$2X + Y \leq 10$	(Tinsmith Constraint)
$2X \leq 8$	(Runners Constraint)
$X, Y \geq 0$	

where

$$X = \text{number of rockers produced}$$
$$Y = \text{number of sluice boxes produced}$$

By means of sensitivity analysis the following types of questions can be answered

1. Objective Function Changes—What would be the effect on the optimal solution if the Brothers could make $22 for each sluice box instead of $20 as originally given?
2. Resource Changes—What would be the effect of having an extra hour of carpentry time available? an extra iron runner? These two questions were partially answered in the discussion of shadow prices in Section 8.6.
3. Constraint Coefficient Changes—What would be the effect if it took the tinsmith only 1.8 hours to do the tin work on a rocker instead of the original 2 hours?
4. New Variable—What would be the effect if the Brothers could make a new product, the Georgia pan, which would yield a profit of $9 and would take 2 hours of the tinsmith's time and none of the carpenter's?
5. New Constraint—What would be the effect if General Aliotov told the Brothers that they must maintain a low profile in American business and that means that they can produce no more than five rockers and sluice boxes combined? The new constraint would be $X + Y \leq 5$.

Without sensitivity analysis these questions could be answered by reworking the entire problem with the indicated change incorporated. However, sensitivity analysis spares the analyst from having to do all this extra work of starting from the beginning again. Sensitivity analysis also provides the analyst with valuable insights into the model.

PROBLEMS

In Problems 1 through 6,
(a) Set up the initial tableau.
(b) Give the initial corner solution.
(c) Indicate the variable to become the new basic variable and determine which basic variable will be replaced.

8-1. Maximize $T = 40X - 10Y$

Subject to:
$$8 - 12X \geq 0$$
$$9X + 14Y \leq 10$$
$$-2X + Y \geq -6$$
$$X, Y \geq 0$$

8-2. Maximize $P = 10X + 20Y + 30Z$
$$2X - 4Y + 3Z \leq 5$$
$$4X - 5Y - 6Z \leq 9$$
$$X, Y, Z \geq 0$$

8-3. Minimize $C = 5X + 8Y$
$$-2X - 4Y \geq -10$$
$$X - Y \leq 4$$
$$X, Y \geq 0$$

(handwritten table)

	X	Y	S_1	S_2	R
-C	5	8	0	0	0
S_1	2	4	1	0	10
S_2	1	-1	0	1	4

INITIAL SOLUTION IS OPTIMAL

8-4. Minimize $C = 2V - 3W$
$$4V \leq 6 + 2W$$
$$-8W \leq 3V - 4$$
$$-2V + 7W \leq 5 - W$$
$$V, W \geq 0$$

(handwritten table)

	V	W	S_1	U	A	S_2	R
	-298	-803	0	100	0	0	-400
S_1	4	-2	1	0	0	0	6
A	3	8	0	-1	1	0	4
S_2	-2	8	0	0	0	1	5

8-5. Maximize $T = (.5)(10M + 20N)$
$$M + N \leq 8$$
$$M - 2N \geq 4$$
$$M, N \geq 0$$

(handwritten table)

	m	N	S_1	U	A	R
	-105	190	0	100	0	-400
	1	1	1	0	0	8
	1	-2	0	-1	1	4

8-6. Minimize $P = 2X - 3Y + 4Z$
$$X \leq 8$$
$$X + Y + Z \geq 3$$
$$Z \geq 25$$
$$X, Y, Z \geq 0$$

(handwritten table)

	X	Y	Z	S_1	U	U_2	A_1	A_2	R
	-98	-103	-196	0	100	100	0	0	-50
S_1	1	0	0	1	0	0	0	0	8
A_1	1	1	1	0	-1	0	1	0	3
A_2	0	0	1	0	0	-1	0	1	2

In Problems 7 through 15, solve using the simplex method. In certain cases there are alternate optimal solutions, inconsistent constraints, redundancy, and unbounded solutions.

8-7. Maximize $P = 10X + 5Y$
Subject to: $\quad 2X + Y \leq 10$
$$X \leq 4$$
$$X, Y \geq 0$$

ALTERNATE OPTIMAL SOLUTIONS

8-8. Maximize $K = 40X + 30Y$
Subject to: $\quad X + 2Y \leq 20$
$$X, Y \geq 0$$

X=20, Y=0, K=800

8-9. Minimize $T = 20W - 10Y$
$$W + Y \leq 30$$
$$W + Y \geq 10$$
$$W - Z \leq 0$$
$$W, Y, Z \geq 0$$

W=0, Y=30, T=-300, Z=0

(handwritten table)

	W	Y	Z	S_1	U	A	S_2	R
	-80	-110	0	0	-10	0	0	-1000
	1	1	0	1	0	0	0	30
	1	1	0	0	-1	1	0	10
	1	0	-1	0	0	0	1	0

8-10. Maximize $P = 14X + 9Y$
$$X - Y \leq 0$$
$$X \geq 6$$
$$X + Y \leq 8$$
$$X, Y \geq 0$$

INCONSISTENT CONSTRAINTS

(handwritten table)

	X	Y	S_1	U	A	S_2	R
	-114	-9	0	100	0	0	-600
	1	-1	1	0	0	0	0
	1	0	0	-1	1	0	6
	1	1	0	0	0	1	8

8-11. Maximize $L = 2M + N$
$$-M + N \leq 0$$
$$N \geq 6$$
$$M, N \geq 0$$

UNBOUNDED

(handwritten table)

	m	N	S	U	A	R
	-2	-101	0	100	0	-600
	-1	1	1	0	0	0
	0	1	0	-1	1	6

8-12. Maximize $P = 4X + 12Y$

$$10X + 20Y \le 100$$
$$2X + 4Y \le 20$$
$$X \le 30$$
$$X, Y \ge 0$$

8-13. Minimize $Q = 3X + Y - Z$

$$-X + 2Y + Z \le 6$$
$$-X - Y + 2Z \le 5$$
$$-3X - Y + 5Z \ge 20$$
$$X, Y, Z \ge 0$$

8-14. Maximize $W = X - Y + 2Z$

$$X + Y + Z + V \le 8$$
$$-X + 2Y \le 4$$
$$X, Y, Z, V \ge 0$$

8-15. Minimize $C = X + Y$

$$X + Y + Z + W \ge 10$$
$$-X + 2Y - W \ge 2$$
$$X, Y, Z, W \ge 0$$

8-16. Heizer Dynamics produces three products, A, B, and C. It costs \$10 to make a unit of A and it sells for \$15 a unit. B costs \$6 per unit and sells for \$8. C costs \$7 per unit and sells for \$9. Heizer has all the materials needed to produce these products, however there is a shortage of natural gas and labor. Product A consumes 1 unit of natural gas and takes 2 units of labor. Product B consumes 2 units of natural gas and uses only 1 unit of labor. Product C uses 3 units of natural gas and 1 unit of labor. If there are 300 units of natural gas and 240 units of labor available, how many of each product should Heizer make in order to maximize profits?

8-17. Set up the initial tableau for the following model.

$$\text{Minimize}\ \ C = 3X + 8Y$$
$$X + Y = 100$$
$$X \le 50$$
$$X, Y \ge 0$$

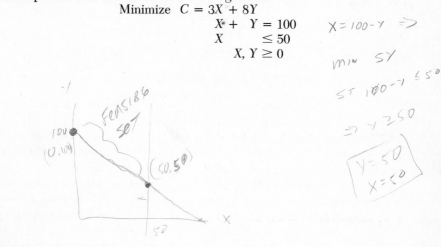

$X = 100 - Y \Rightarrow$

$\min\ 8Y$

$ST\ 100 - Y \le 50$

$\Rightarrow Y \ge 50$

$Y = 50$
$X = 50$

9 Linear Programming– Transportation and Assignment Models

9.1 INTRODUCTION

In this chapter a special type of linear programming model called the transportation model is studied. An example will first be given to illustrate the form of the transportation model. Then a technique of solving the transportation model will be presented. Since the transportation model is a linear programming model it could be solved by means of the simplex method. However, because of its special nature, more efficient solution procedures or algorithms have been devised to make the transportation model easier to solve than the typical linear programming model. Though there are several of these specialized solution techniques, only one of them, known as the "stepping-stone technique," will be considered here.

In the study of the transportation model it will become apparent that several varieties of this model exist. What are known as balanced and unbalanced models will be considered as well as a special model known as the "assignment model."

9.2 THE TRANSPORTATION MODEL

The typical transportation model describes a situation in which there are several sources of product such as manufacturing plants located in different regions which ship the product to various destinations such as warehouses located in other places. The management's objective in such situations is to minimize the transportation costs while shipping the required quantities of the product from the sources to the destinations. Such a transportation situation can be modeled successfully using a special form of linear programming. Whenever a linear programming model has this special form it is designated as a transportation model even though the model may not represent a situation in which goods are actually transported from one geographical location to another. An illustration of the most typical transportation model will now be given. Transportation models for decisions which do not actually involve the physical transport of goods will be shown later in the chapter as well as in the problems at the end of the chapter.

In the 1870s the cattle business was flourishing on the American plains and prairies. Enterprising cattle raisers were shipping their beef to England and Scotland as well as to the various American markets. As the British livestock industry could not compete with the cheap American cattle, the British decided to invest in ranches in America thereby affording them the opportunity to capitalize on the inexpensive production of beef made possible by the almost limitless sea of prairie grasses covering the region from Montana to Texas. The British had invested approximately $30 million in land thus controlling about 20 million acres in 1882. One of the British firms was the Prairie Cattle Company. Let us suppose that the Prairie Cattle Company owned three large ranches which were located in present-day Montana, Kansas, and Texas. The management of the Prairie Cattle Company is concerned with economically moving the cattle at these three ranches to three different market areas. Suppose that the three market areas are Chicago, New Orleans, and San Francisco. The cattle destined for New Orleans would be shipped overseas whereas the cattle arriving at Chicago and San Francisco would be consumed by the American public.

The Prairie Cattle Company had 200 head of cattle ready for market at the Montana ranch, 300 head at the Kansas ranch, and 500 head ready to go at the Texas ranch. Representatives of the company had made arrangements with buyers to supply 450 head to Chicago, 450 head to New Orleans, and 100 head of cattle to San Francisco. Getting the cattle to the markets in the 1880s involved driving the cattle overland on trails such as the Chisholm or Western to the railroads. Railroads such as the Union Pacific or the Santa Fe then carried the cattle on to the markets. The Prairie Cattle Company computed the cost to transport one head from each of the ranches (sources) to each of the markets (destinations). Included in these costs were the various costs associated with the cattle drives as well as the rail costs. Figure 9.1, page 236, shows these per head costs over each route from ranch to destination. For example, it would cost $6 to get one head from Montana to Chicago, it would cost $12 to get one head from Kansas to San Francisco, and it would cost $3 to get one head from Texas to New Orleans. How can the Prairie Cattle Company transport the cattle from the ranches to the markets at a minimum cost?

The Prairie Cattle Company situation may be modeled by means of a transportation tableau or more abstractly it may be algebraically modeled by the use of variables, objective function, and constraints. Both of these models will be presented. However, only the transportation tableau will be utilized for modeling and solution purposes in the remainder of the chapter.

The linear programming model for the transportation problem will be given first. Initially the variables must be defined. Let

M_c = number of cattle shipped from Montana to Chicago
M_n = number of cattle shipped from Montana to New Orleans
M_s = number shipped from Montana to San Francisco
K_c = number shipped from Kansas to Chicago
K_n = number shipped from Kansas to New Orleans

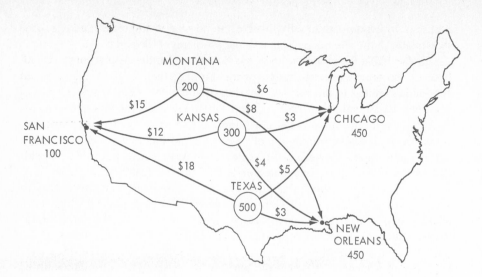

FIGURE 9.1   Prairie Cattle Company

K_s = number shipped from Kansas to San Francisco
T_c = number shipped from Texas to Chicago
T_n = number shipped from Texas to New Orleans
T_s = number shipped from Texas to San Francisco

A solution to the Prairie Cattle Company problem will consist of finding values for each of these variables.

The objective is to transport the cattle to the markets at a minimum cost. It costs, as shown in Figure 9.1, \$6 to move a head from Montana to Chicago. Therefore $6M_c$ would represent the total transportation cost incurred over the Montana-Chicago route since M_c is the actual number of head moved over this route and \$6 is the cost per head. Similarly, $8M_n$ represents the total transportation cost over the Montana-New Orleans route. There are nine possible routes. The overall transportation cost which takes account of all nine routes is

$$C = 6M_c + 8M_n + 15M_s + 3K_c + 4K_n + 12K_s + 5T_c + 3T_n + 18T_s$$

It is this cost which is to be minimized. A solution, for example, such as $M_c = 200$ head, $K_c = 250$, $K_n = 50$, $T_n = 400$, and $T_s = 100$ with the other variables equalling zero would incur a total transportation cost of:

$$C = (6)(200) + 0 + 0 + (3)(250) + (4)(50) + 0 + 0 + (3)(400) + (18)(100)$$
$$= \$5150$$

In all transporation models there are two distinct types of constraints. The *supply* constraints insure that the amount shipped from each source (ranch) equals the actual supply available at each of these sources. The *demand* constraints insure that the amount of product arriving at the destinations (cities) equals the actual quantity demanded at each of these destinations. There will be one supply constraint for each source and one demand constraint for each destination.

In the Prairie Cattle Company case there will be a supply constraint for each of the ranches since they are the sources. There are 200 head ready for market at the Montana ranch. Therefore, the number of cattle shipped out of Montana must equal exactly 200. M_c equals the number shipped from Montana to Chicago, M_n equals the number shipped from Montana to New Orleans, and M_s equals the number shipped from Montana to San Francisco. The total number shipped out of Montana is therefore $M_c + M_n + M_s$. Again, this amount must equal 200. This may be expressed by the first supply constraint:

$$M_c + M_n + M_s = 200 \qquad \text{(Montana Supply Constraint)}$$

Analogously the supply constraint for Kansas insures that exactly 300 head are shipped from this ranch:

$$K_c + K_n + K_s = 300 \qquad \text{(Kansas Supply Constraint)}$$

The supply constraint for Texas must stipulate that exactly 500 head will be shipped:

$$T_c + T_n + T_s = 500 \qquad \text{(Texas Supply Constraint)}$$

Next there will be a demand constraint for each of the destinations. Chicago must get 450 head. These cattle may come from Montana, Kansas, and/or Texas. The quantities shipped from these three sources to Chicago are M_c, K_c, and T_c, respectively. Thus the demand constraint for Chicago will be:

$$M_c + K_c + T_c = 450 \qquad \text{(Chicago Demand Constraint)}$$

This guarantees that 450 head will be received at Chicago. In a similar fashion the demand constraint for New Orleans will be:

$$M_n + K_n + T_n = 450 \qquad \text{(New Orleans Demand Constraint)}$$

since 450 head must be shipped there. Exactly 100 head are demanded at San Francisco. The constraint which insures that this requirement will be satisfied is:

$$M_s + K_s + T_s = 100 \qquad \text{(San Francisco Demand Constraint)}$$

The complete transportation model for the Prairie Cattle Company case is

Minimize $C = 6M_c + 8M_n + 15M_s + 3K_c + 4K_n + 12K_s + 5T_c + 3T_n + 18T_s$

Subject to:
$$
\begin{aligned}
M_c + M_n + M_s &= 200 \\
K_c + K_n + K_s &= 300 \qquad \text{Supply Constraints}\\
T_c + T_n + T_s &= 500 \\
M_c + K_c + T_c &= 450 \\
M_n + K_n + T_n &= 450 \qquad \text{Demand Constraints}\\
M_s + K_s + T_s &= 100 \\
M_c, M_n, M_s, K_c, K_n, K_s, T_c, T_n, T_s &\geq 0
\end{aligned}
$$

The simplex method could be used to solve this model. Since there are six constraints one would guess that there would be six basic variables which means that a corner solution (and hence the optimal solution) would never use more than six of the nine possible routes. In reality there is a complicated form of redundancy present in the constraints which means that in this transportation model the optimal solution (or any corner solution) will never use more than five routes. The number of routes in a corner solution will be one less than the number of constraints. As the simplex method is unduly laborious for transportation models, another solution procedure will be used to solve these models. Before modeling the Prairie Cattle Company situation by means of a transportation tableau which makes this more efficient solution procedure possible, a potential solution to the problem will be considered.

Suppose $M_c = 200$ head, $K_c = 250$, $K_n = 50$, $T_n = 400$, and $T_s = 100$ with the other variables all equal to zero. Is this a feasible solution? When the objective function was formulated for this model, it was shown that this potential solution would yield a total transportation cost of $5150. It must now be determined whether the solution satisfies the constraints. Substituting these values into the constraints yields

$$200 + 0 + 0 = 200 \qquad \text{(Montana Supply)}$$
$$250 + 50 + 0 = 300 \qquad \text{(Kansas Supply)}$$
$$0 + 400 + 100 = 500 \qquad \text{(Texas Supply)}$$

$$200 + 250 + 0 = 450 \qquad \text{(Chicago Demand)}$$
$$0 + 50 + 400 = 450 \qquad \text{(New Orleans Demand)}$$
$$0 + 0 + 100 = 100 \qquad \text{(San Francisco Demand)}$$

All of the constraints are perfectly satisfied, thereby demontrating that the proposed solution is feasible. The solution is not only feasible, it is also a corner solution. This is related to the fact that only five routes are used. Adding the number of sources to the number of destinations and subtracting 1 yields the number of routes typically utilized in a corner solution. In the Prairie Cattle Company case this figure is $3 + 3 - 1 = 5$ as stated earlier.

The linear programming model just constructed for the transportation problem will not be used in this chapter. Rather the transportation problem will be modeled by means of a transportation tableau. It should be emphasized at the start that this tableau is *not* the same type of tableau as was presented in Chapter 9 in connection with the simplex method. Table 9.1 pictures the beginnings of the transportation tableau for the Prairie Cattle Company example. The sources (ranches) are listed to the left with a source associated with each row. At the right the available supply at each of the sources is given. It is seen that 200 head are available for shipment from the Montana ranch, 300 are available at the Kansas ranch, and 500 from the Texas ranch. At the top of the tableau are listed the three destinations which are Chicago, New Orleans, and San Francisco. At the bottom are listed the quantities demanded at each of the destinations. For example, 450 head are required at both Chicago and New Orleans while 100 are required at San Francisco.

Each cell in Table 9.1 represents a route from a source to a destination. In the upper right corner of each cell is listed the cost to transport one head over that particular route. For example, the cell representing the Montana-Chicago

TABLE 9.1
Prairie Cattle Company
Transportation Tableau

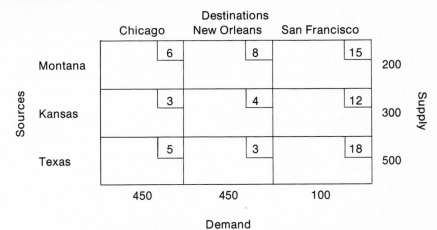

	Destinations			
	Chicago	New Orleans	San Francisco	Supply
Montana	6	8	15	200
Kansas	3	4	12	300
Texas	5	3	18	500
Demand	450	450	100	

route has a cost of $6. The cell representing the Kansas-San Francisco route has a per head cost of $12, and the Texas-New Orleans route has a per head cost of $3. These per head transportation costs were taken from Figure 9.1.

Numbers will ultimately be placed in the centers of five of the nine cells indicating which routes are used in a solution and how many cattle are shipped over these particular routes. For example, in Table 9.2(c), page 240, a corner solution is given. The value of 200 appears in the most northwesterly cell indicating that in this solution 200 head are to be shipped from Montana to Chicago. The value of 250 indicates that 250 head in this solution are to be shipped from Kansas to Chicago. Continuing, 50 head are to be shipped from Kansas to New Orleans, 400 from Texas to New Orleans, and finally 100 are to be shipped from Texas to San Francisco. Notice that this is a feasible solution since the values in each row add up to the supply given at the right of the rows and each column adds up to the demand given at the bottom. (This is the same corner solution which was discussed in relationship to the algebraic formulation of the linear programming model given earlier in this section.) All the blank cells are assumed to be unused routes.

It is next necessary to consider how a corner solution such as that in Table 9.2(c) can be found. Once an initial corner solution is determined, a solution procedure known as the "stepping-stone technique" will be used to find the optimal corner solution which is the solution showing how the cattle must be shipped to achieve the minimum total transportation cost.

Before continuing, consider again the essential nature of a transportation problem. There will be several sources from which a product will be shipped to any of several destinations. The total supply at the sources must equal the total demand at the destinations; when this is the case the model is said to be balanced. The objective is to transport the goods from the sources to the destinations in such a manner that total costs, time, distance or some such will be minimized. The optimal solution will precisely define how many units of product must be shipped over each of the routes (from source to destination) in order to achieve the minimum cost.

TABLE 9.2
Finding an Initial Solution by the Northwest Corner Rule

(a)

(b)
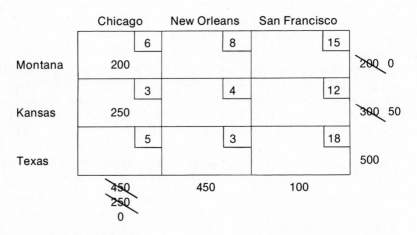

(c)
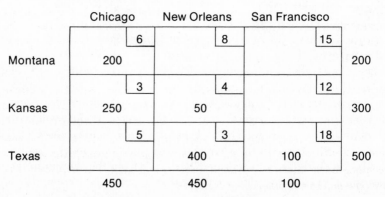

9.3 NORTHWEST CORNER RULE

As with the simplex method, an initial corner solution must be found before a solution procedure can begin. A particularly easy method of finding an initial corner solution is afforded by the "northwest corner rule." Beginning with the transportation tableau of Table 9.1, an entry in the cell in the northwest corner (representing the Montana-Chicago route) is made. This entry is to represent the number of cattle to be shipped over this route. As many cattle are shipped over this route as is possible without breaking the relevant supply or demand requirements. In Table 9.2(a) the entry of 200 is placed in this cell which represents the route from Montana to Chicago. A number larger than 200 head could not be placed in this cell since that would require the shipment of more cattle from Montana than are available in Montana. Shipping 200 head over this route completely depletes the supply in Montana, hence the 200 at the right of the Montana row is crossed out and replaced with a zero. Since 200 appears in this cell it means that Chicago will receive 200 head and now needs only $450 - 200 = 250$ head. The 450 at the bottom of the Chicago column has been replaced with 250.

According to the northwest corner rule, once a cell (route) has been filled, another cell must be filled which is either immediately to the right of or below the previous cell. In the example at hand, the cell to the right representing the Montana-New Orleans route would not be filled since the 200 head available from Montana have already been designated to go to Chicago thus reducing the supply in Montana to zero. Instead the cell immediately below representing the Kansas-Chicago route is to be filled with as large a number as practicable. Since there are 300 head available in Kansas, one might be tempted to put 300 in this cell. This cannot be done since this would mean that Chicago would be getting a total of $200 + 300$ or 500 head. Since Chicago is to get only a total of 450 head, only 250 should be shipped over this route (see Table 9.2(b)). This reduces the available Kansas supply to 50 and perfectly satisfies the Chicago demand. Thus the 300 at the right of the second row is reduced to 50 and the 250 at the bottom of the first column is reduced to zero.

Again, a cell either immediately to the right of or immediately below the previous cell must now be filled. In other words, either the cell representing the Kansas-New Orleans route or the cell representing the Texas-Chicago route must be filled with as large a number as possible. Since Chicago needs no more cattle and since Kansas has 50 head as of yet unassigned, the obvious cell would be the cell to the immediate right. 50 should be placed in this cell meaning that 50 head would be shipped from Kansas to New Orleans. This reduces the supply of Kansas cattle to zero and leaves a need or demand of 400 yet for New Orleans (see Table 9.2(c)).

Table 9.2(c) shows the completed transportation tableau with the initial solution as determined by the northwest corner rule. The analyst step-by-step fills cells with numbers as large as possible, moving always to the cell to the immediate right or just below until the entire tableau has been completed. Notice that all the rows sum up to the supply values at the right indicating that exactly the number available at each ranch are being shipped. Also the columns add up to the values at the bottom indicating that each of the cities or destinations will receive the number of cattle they demanded.

The solution of Table 9.2(c) is also a corner solution; the northwest corner rule always yields corner solutions. The number of routes used is five. Recall that the number of routes in a corner solution will equal the number of sources plus the number of destinations minus 1. Corner solutions are important as the optimal solution will be a corner solution.

9.4 STEPPING-STONE TECHNIQUE

A special procedure for solving transportation models was developed by A. Charnes and W. Cooper and is known as the *stepping-stone technique.* Although the simplex method can successfully be used to solve transportation models, the stepping-stone technique is preferred as it is more efficient. There are other solution procedures for transportation models, notably the MODI method, which are more efficient than the stepping-stone technique. However, the stepping-stone technique is the easiest to learn and gives a relatively clear picture of what is happening on the way to finding the optimal solution.

The stepping-stone technique is accomplished by repeating two steps or phases:

Phase 1: Determine if the current corner solution is optimal. If it is, Stop. If it is not, go to Phase 2.

Phase 2: Jump to a better (or at least as good) corner solution. Go to Phase 1.

These two phases will now be amplified as the stepping-stone technique is applied to the Prairie Cattle Company example whose initial solution is given in Table 9.2(c).

PHASE 1: *Check for Optimality*

In Table 9.3(a) the initial solution consisting of five routes is given. Is this solution optimal? If it is not optimal then there should be some shift in the routes used. The optimality of a solution is determined by examining each of the unused routes (cells). For example, might the Montana-New Orleans route be used in some way thus reducing the total transportation costs? To answer this question, suppose that one steer were to be shipped over this route. Since there are only 200 head available in Montana this necessitates shipping only 199 from Montana to Chicago; never can more cattle be shipped from a ranch than what are available. Of course shipping only 199 from Montana to Chicago (instead of the original 200 as shown in Table 9.3(a)) means that Chicago gets one less than what is needed in Chicago. This means that an extra head must be shipped to Chicago from somewhere else. That one extra head will be shipped along a route already in use, namely, the Kansas-Chicago route. Therefore ship 251 head from Kansas to Chicago. While taking care of Chicago there is now a problem in that Kansas is currently required to ship 251 + 50 or one more than what is available at that ranch. To remedy this, Kansas must ship one less (only 49) to New Orleans. In Table 9.3(b) this path of adjustments required to permit the shipment of one steer over the Montana-New Orleans route is traced. In Table 9.3(c) the actual adjustments are made. Notice that all the rows still add to the supplies available and the columns add to the demands required.

TABLE 9.3
Consideration of a New Route

(a)

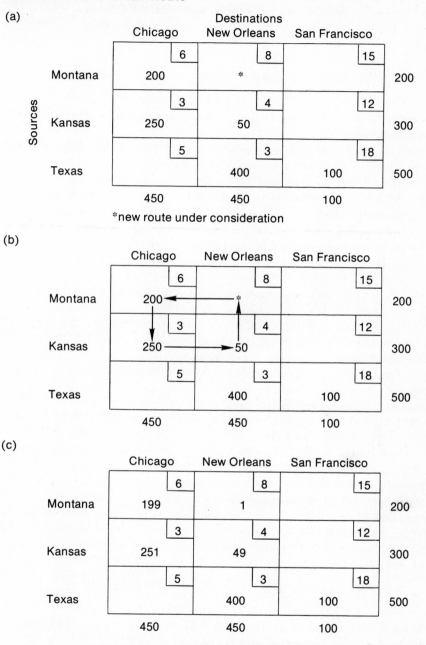

Destinations

	Chicago	New Orleans	San Francisco	
Montana	6 / 200	8 / *	15	200
Kansas	3 / 250	4 / 50	12	300
Texas	5	3 / 400	18 / 100	500
	450	450	100	

*new route under consideration

(b)

	Chicago	New Orleans	San Francisco	
Montana	6 / 200	8 / *	15	200
Kansas	3 / 250	4 / 50	12	300
Texas	5	3 / 400	18 / 100	500
	450	450	100	

(c)

	Chicago	New Orleans	San Francisco	
Montana	6 / 199	8 / 1	15	200
Kansas	3 / 251	4 / 49	12	300
Texas	5	3 / 400	18 / 100	500
	450	450	100	

Is the solution of Table 9.3(c) any better than that of Table 9.3(a)? By shipping one steer over the new route (Montana to New Orleans) a cost of $8 is incurred. Of course one less was of necessity shipped over the Montana-Chicago route saving $6. Then one more was shipped over the Kansas-Chicago route costing $3. Finally, one less was shipped over the Kansas-New Orleans route saving $4 since it costs $4 per head to ship over this route. The net effect is an extra cost of $1 since the extra costs are $8 and $3 but the savings are only $4 and $6. That is,

$$\text{Net Effect per head of using the Montana-New Orleans route} = +8 - 4 + 3 - 6 = +1$$

Therefore, it would not be advisable to use the Montana-New Orleans route in the fashion indicated.

If every one of the currently unused routes of Table 9.3(a) when submitted to this kind of analysis yielded a positive net effect (i.e., increased transportation costs), then it could be concluded that the current solution is optimal.

Consider now another one of the unused routes, namely, the Montana-San Francisco route which has a cost of $15 per head. Looking at Table 9.4(a), which is the same as Table 9.3(a) and which represents the initial solution, if one steer were shipped over this route then one less would have to be shipped from Montana to Chicago in order to insure that exactly 200 head are shipped out of Montana. The path traced in Table 9.4(b) indicates the various adjustments which would have to be made. One more would have to be shipped over the Kansas-Chicago route, one less over the Kansas-New Orleans route, one more over the Texas-New Orleans route, and one less over the Texas-San Francisco route. All these adjustments must be made (which occur at the corners of the path of adjustments) to satisfy the supply and demand requirements as shown in the margins of the tableau. The plus and minus signs in the cells at the corners of the path indicate whether the route should have one more or one less in order to preserve the supply and demand conditions. Table 9.4(c) shows all the adjustments of used routes which permit the one steer to be shipped over the Montana-San Francisco route.

Is the solution of Table 9.4(c) better than that of Table 9.4(a)? It would cost $15 to ship a steer over the new route. Shipping one less over the Montana-Chicago route would save $6. Shipping one more over the Kansas-Chicago route would cost an extra $3. Shipping one less over the Kansas-New Orleans route would save $4. Shipping one more over the Texas-New Orleans route would cost an extra $3. Finally, shipping one less over the Texas-San Francisco route would save $18. The net effect of this shuffle is a savings of $7, that is,

$$\text{Net Effect per head of using the Montana-San Francisco route} = +15 - 6 + 3 - 4 + 3 - 18 = -7$$

Therefore, the current solution is not optimal since by using the Montana-San Francisco route transportation costs can be cut.

Before Phase 2 is begun, more should be said concerning the construction of the path of adjustments. The path of adjustments, as illustrated in Tables 9.3(b) and 9.4(b), can be constructed quite mechanically. For illustrative purposes suppose that by the northwest corner rule the initial solution to a transportation

244

situation with three sources and four destinations has been found as shown in Table 9.5(a). If the route from C to W were to be evaluated (its net effect found) to see if it could be used to cut costs, the path of adjustments would be that of Table

TABLE 9.4
Consideration of a New Route

(a)

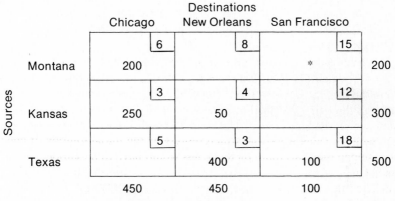

*new route under consideration

(b)

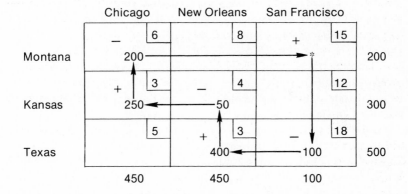

(c)

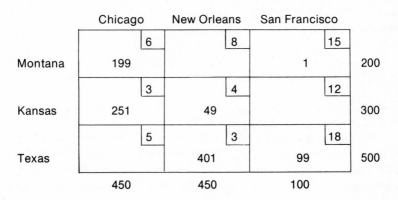

9.5(b). Picture the tableau of Table 9.5(a) as a pond having stones only in the cells with numbers. Beginning from an unused route such as the C-W cell, temporarily assume that you or one of your acquaintances is a frog that can jump *only* along rows or along columns. The idea is to start jumping from the initial unused cell such that you land *only* on stones. The ultimate intent is to return to the unused cell from whence you started. Furthermore, it is required to jump as few times as possible in accomplishing this round trip. Jumping over stones is permitted, diagonal jumping is not permitted. By following these rules the path of adjustments will be traced if you strap a crop dusting apparatus filled with chalk dust on your underside.

In Table 9.5(b) the frog takes off from the unused route represented by the C-W cell, which has an asterisk in it. The first jump takes the frog to cell C-Z where the frog lands on the stone. Remember that each cell with an entry in the center of the cell is assumed to be a stone. This first jump was toward the east and followed the bottom row. The second jump leaves the stone at cell C-Z and lands at B-Z. This was a legitimate jump as it was not in a diagonal direction. The next jump takes the frog to the stone of cell B-X. Notice that the frog jumped over the stone at cell B-Y. This is not only legitimate but mandatory if the frog is to make the round trip in as few jumps as possible. The next jump lands at A-X. Another jump takes the frog to A-W (to have a snort of root beer). Finally the frog jumps from the stone at A-W back to the original starting cell. By adjusting each of the entries at the stones the frog landed on, the integrity of the tableau can be maintained. If one unit is shipped over the unused route of cell C-W, then one less must be shipped over C-Z. Then one more must be shipped over B-Z, and one less over B-X, and one more over A-X and one less over A-W. In Table 9.5(c) a plus or a minus sign is attached to each stone which the frog landed on. Cells which the frog did not land on should not have a sign. Starting with a plus at the unused cell where the frog started, the signs alternate around the path of adjustments. The net effect of the new route is then mechanically determined by adding or subtracting the costs in the upper right corners of the stones (cells) the frog landed on according to whether there is a plus or minus sign in the cell. In the case of Table 9.5(c) the net effect per head is

$$\text{Net Effect of Using C-W route} = +4 - 5 + 1 - 6 + 3 - 8 = -11$$

Hence for every unit that can be diverted to this route the company would save $11 assuming the quantities shipped on the other routes were properly adjusted.

Having concluded this re-statement of finding paths of adjustments and the net effect of introducing an unused route, Phase 2 of the Prairie Cattle Company example will now be considered.

PHASE 2: *Find the New Solution*

In Phase 1 it was determined that the current solution as expressed in Table 9.4(a) is not optimal since by using the Montana-San Francisco route a savings of $7 per head shipped over that route can be achieved. Once a route is found whose use would result in a reduction of transportation costs, this route should

TABLE 9.5
Finding a Path of Adjustments

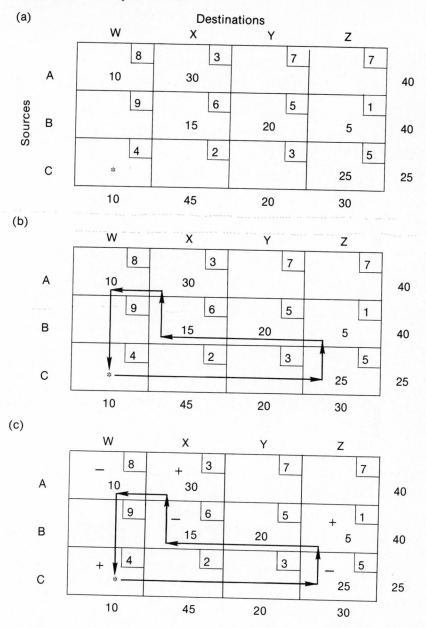

(a)

(b)

(c)

be introduced into the solution. (Some analysts prefer to compute the net effect for each of the unused routes and then introduce that route which has the greatest negative net effect.) How can the Montana-San Francisco route be utilized? If $7 can be saved by shipping a single steer over this route, it would make sense to ship as many over this new route as possible. Looking at the path of adjustments in Table 9.4(b) it appears that shipping cattle over the Montana-San Francisco route entails shipping fewer cattle over the Montana-Chicago, Kansas-New Orleans, and Texas-San Francisco routes, which are the routes with minus signs attached. If 100 head were shipped over the Montana-San Francisco route, then $200 - 100 = 100$ would have to be shipped over the Montana-Chicago route, $250 + 100 = 350$ over the Kansas-Chicago route, $50 - 100 = -50$ over the Kansas-New Orleans route. Now a problem becomes apparent. Shipping a negative quantity of cattle over a route is impossible (if it were possible it might be an effective way to convert steer chips to grass). This implies that 100 head cannot be shipped over the Montana-San Francisco route because doing so necessitates shipping a negative quantity over the Kansas-New Orleans route. That is, shipping 100 head as indicated requires an adjustment which is not feasible. Since 100 cannot be shipped over the Montana-San Francisco route, how many can?

The number of cattle that can be shipped over a new route will be equal to the smallest entry in the minus cells on the path of adjustments. In Table 9.4(b) there are minus signs attached to the Montana-Chicago, Kansas-New Orleans, and Texas-San Francisco routes as these are the routes over which the number of cattle would have to be diminished if cattle were to be diverted to the Montana-San Francisco route. The quantities of cattle presently shipped over these three routes are 200, 50, and 100, respectively. The smallest of these minus cell entries on the path of adjustments is 50, thus indicating that the new Montana-San Francisco route should be used to ship a maximum of 50 head.

In Table 9.6, 50 head are redirected over the Montana-San Francisco route and all the quantities of the other routes at the corners of the path of adjustments have been adjusted in order to preserve the supply and demand conditions. Notice that the quantity shipped over the Kansas-New Orleans has been reduced to zero. This means that there are still only five routes which are

TABLE 9.6
Second Solution
Prairie Cattle Company

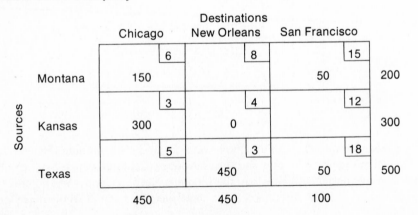

actually used. This suggests that the new solution is a corner solution. It is important that the solutions be corner solutions as the optimal solution will always be a corner solution. Table 9.7(a) gives this new solution with only five routes (and cells) used; the zero entry for the Kansas-New Orleans route has been deleted to keep only five cells in use.

TABLE 9.7
Consideration of a New Route

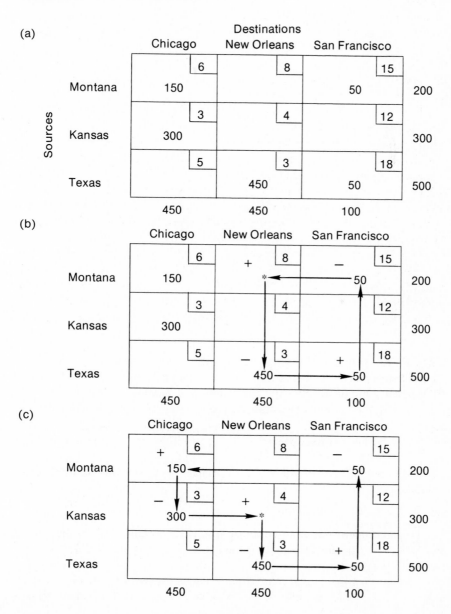

(d)

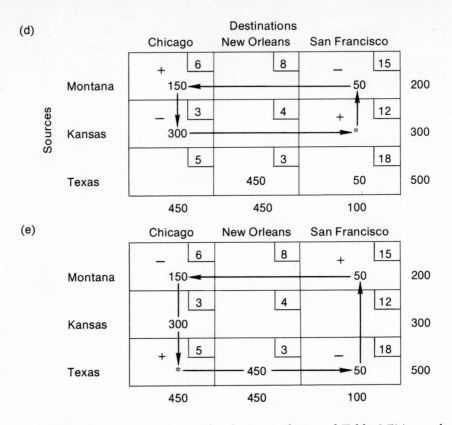

The total transportation cost for the new solution of Table 9.7(a) may be computed as

$$C = (6)(150) + (15)(50) + (3)(300) + (3)(450) + (18)(50)$$
$$= \$4800$$

This cost was computed by simply adding the products of the cell entries and the per head costs of the five routes in the solution of Table 9.7(a). The total cost for the first solution was $5150, thus a savings of $350 was effected by the introduction of the Montana-San Francisco route. The amount of this saving could also have been computed by realizing that the new route would save $7 per head, and 50 head were diverted to this route thus resulting in a savings of ($7)(50) = $350.

Is this new solution of Table 9.7(a) optimal? To answer this question return to Phase 1.

PHASE 1: *Check for Optimality*

To determine if the solution of Table 9.7(a) is optimal, each of the unused routes must be examined to see what the net cost effect would be if these routes were introduced.

Consider first the unused route from Montana to New Orleans which carries a per head transportation cost of $8. In Table 9.7(b) the path of adjustments is traced for this route. If one steer were shipped over this route then one less would have to be shipped over the Montana-San Francisco route, one more over the Texas-San Francisco route, and one less over the Texas-New Orleans route. The net effect per head of this change would be

$$\text{Net Effect of using} \atop \text{Montana-New Orleans route} = +8 - 15 + 18 - 3 = +8$$

Since the net effect would be to increase transportation costs at a rate of $8 per head diverted to this route, this route should not be introduced.

Consider the route from Kansas to New Orleans. Table 9.7(c) traces the path of adjustments. The net effect of introducing this route would be to increase costs by $7 per head for those shipped from Kansas to New Orleans. That is,

$$\text{Net Effect of using} \atop \text{Kansas-New Orleans route} = +4 - 3 + 18 - 15 + 6 - 3 = +7$$

Hence there is no benefit in using this route.

In Table 9.7(d) the path of adjustments for the introduction of the Kansas-San Francisco route is given. It can be verified that the net effect in this case is $+12 - 15 + 6 - 3$ or zero. Thus there is no benefit in terms of saving on transportation costs in introducing this route.

In Table 9.7(e) the path for the introduction of the Texas-Chicago route is given. The net effect of introducing this route is to reduce costs since

$$\text{Net Effect of using} \atop \text{Texas-Chicago route} = +5 - 18 + 15 - 6 = -4$$

Each head that can be diverted to this route will save the Prairie Cattle Company $4. Therefore, the solution of Table 9.7(a) is not optimal as a less expensive transportation plan exists.

What is this new plan or solution?

PHASE 2: *Find the New Solution*

If $4 can be saved for each steer diverted to the Texas-Chicago route, it would obviously be wise to divert as many as possible to this new route. Examine all of the cells of Table 9.7(e) which have a minus sign attached. There are two such cells. The quantities currently shipped over these two routes are 50 and 150 head. The minimum of these two numbers, 50, becomes the quantity to be shipped over the new route. Table 9.8, page 252, shows the new solution where the appropriate entries at the corners of the path have been adjusted. Notice that the value for the Texas-San Francisco route is now zero leaving exactly five routes in use. Table 9.9(a), page 253, depicts the new solution with the Texas-San Francisco route deleted.

Table 9.9(a) gives the new solution. The total transportation cost for this solution is

$$C = (6)(100) + (15)(100) + (3)(300) + (5)(50) + (3)(450)$$
$$= \$4600$$

TABLE 9.8
Third Solution
Prairie Cattle Company

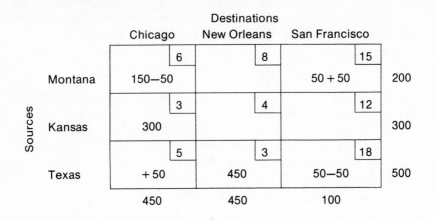

	Destinations			
	Chicago	New Orleans	San Francisco	
Montana	6 150—50	8	15 50 + 50	200
Kansas	3 300	4	12	300
Texas	5 + 50	3 450	18 50—50	500
	450	450	100	

This is a savings of $200 over the previous solution and represents shipping 50 head over the new route at a savings of $4 each.

Is the solution of Table 9.9(a) optimal?

PHASE 1: *Check for Optimality*

Each unused route of Table 9.9(a) must be examined to see if it would reduce transportation costs if introduced. Table 9.9(b) gives the path of adjustments for the Montana-New Orleans route which is unused in the current solution. The net effect in this case is $8 - 3 + 5 - 6 = +4$. Hence there would be no benefit in using this route at this time. Introducing the Kansas-New Orleans route would have a net effect of $+3$ and introducing the Texas-San Francisco route would have a net effect of $+4$ per head, thus none of these unused routes should be introduced. Table 9.9(c) traces the path for the unused Kansas-San Francisco route. The net effect for this route is $+ 12 - 15 + 6 - 3 = 0$. There will be no cost savings by introducing this route. It may therefore be concluded that the solution of Table 9.9(a) is optimal since none of the net effects for the four unused routes are negative. The Prairie Cattle Company should ship 100 head from Montana to Chicago, 100 head from Montana to San Francisco, 300 from Kansas to Chicago, 50 from Texas to Chicago, and 450 from Texas to New Orleans. The cost of this transportation plan has already been shown to equal $4600.

Alternate Optimal Solutions

The fact that the net effect of the introduction of the Kansas-San Francisco route was zero means that using this route would not cut costs but its use would also not increase costs. This route could be introduced and a new solution would be found having a cost of $4600 which is no different from the cost of the previous solution of Table 9.9(a). Hence an alternate optimal solution exists. There is another transportation plan which yields the same total costs.

252

TABLE 9.9
Consideration of a New Route

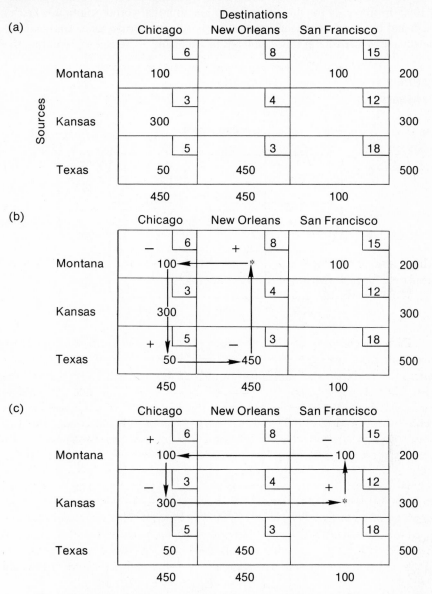

(a)

Destinations

Sources	Chicago	New Orleans	San Francisco	
Montana	6	8	15	200
	100		100	
Kansas	3	4	12	300
	300			
Texas	5	3	18	500
	50	450		
	450	450	100	

(b)

(c)

Alternate optimal solutions exist in the transportation problem when there are no negative net effects for the unused routes but when there is a net effect which is zero. There is no particular need to find the alternate optimal solution(s) if one exists. The fact of its existence should be stated however.

9.5 DEGENERACY

In this section several problems which may arise in connection with the transportation model and its solution will be considered.

Suppose that the transportation tableau for a problem were that of Table 9.10(a). In the quest for the optimal solution an initial corner solution is first to be found by some technique such as the northwest corner rule. Applying the northwest corner rule in this case leads to a difficulty. The cell representing the

TABLE 9.10
Degeneracy

(a)

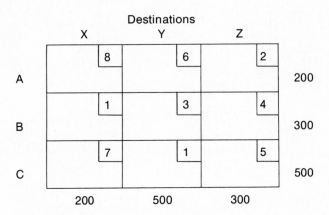

(b)

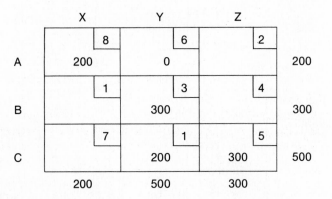

(c)

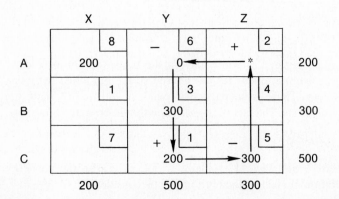

(d)

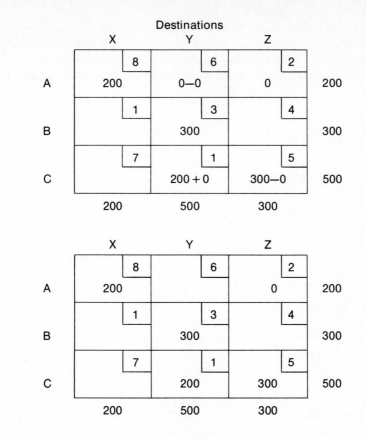

Destinations

	X	Y	Z	
A	8 200	6 0—0	2 0	200
B		1 300	3	4	300
C		7 200 + 0	1 300—0	5	500
	200	500	300	

(e)

	X	Y	Z	
A	8 200	6	2 0	200
B		1 300	3	4	300
C		7 200	1 300	5	500
	200	500	300	

A-X route which is located in the northwest corner is to be filled first with as large a quantity as practicable. As is shown in Table 9.10(b) this quantity is 200. This 200 simultaneously uses up the entire supply of source A and satisfies perfectly the demand at destination X. The northwest corner rule specifies that the next cell to be filled must be the one to the immediate right, A-Y, or the cell immediately below, B-X. In this case putting anything but zero in either of these two cells (routes) would destroy the supply or demand conditions stipulated. In such a case a zero should be placed in one of these two cells and then the analyst should proceed with the northwest corner rule. In this example the A-Y cell was chosen arbitrarily to contain the zero as shown in Table 9.10(b). Proceeding, the northwest corner rule requires the assignment of 300 to the B-Y route, and so on. In the end there are five cells or routes filled. This is necessary because a corner solution must employ five routes in this model where there are three sources and three destinations. Since the entry for route A-Y is zero this route is in reality not used. However, for the sake of implementing the stepping-stone algorithm it must be identified. Recall that when a basic variable in the simplex tableau had a value of zero, as found in the R column, then the solution was said to be degenerate. Likewise when one of the typically non-zero routes in a corner solution of the transportation tableau has a zero entry, that solution is said to be degenerate.

Continuing to focus attention on the solution of Table 9.10(b), it must be determined if the solution is optimal. By examining the unused route from A to Z, whose path of adjustments is traced in Table 9.10(c), it appears that the net effect of introducing a unit of product over this route is

$$\text{Net Effect of using A-Z route} = +2 - 6 + 1 - 5 = -8$$

Because there is a savings of \$8 for every unit that can be diverted to the A-Z route, the solution of Table 9.10(b) is not optimal.

By applying Phase 2 the entries associated with the cells with the minus signs along the path are examined. The two such entries in this case are 0 and 300 which are associated with routes A-Y and C-Z, respectively. The number of units to be shipped over the new route must equal the minimum of these two values. Therefore, zero units are to be shipped over the new route. Table 9.10(d) shows the adjustments necessary to incorporate the new A-Z route into the corner solution. Table 9.10(e) shows the result of this process. This is a corner solution (it has five cells filled) and it is also degenerate as one of the routes, namely A-Z, has a zero value. Thus the stepping-stone technique moved from one degenerate solution to another, which is quite acceptable. However since only zero units could be diverted to the new route, there will be no reduction in costs. By continuing the stepping stone technique the optimal solution will ultimately be reached.

Degeneracy may appear during the application of the stepping-stone technique even if it had not previously been present. This will occur when there is a tie for the minimum value at some of the minus cells along the path of adjustments. Consider the situation depicted in Table 9.11(a). Route F-U should be introduced as its net effect per unit is $+1 - 6 + 2 - 4 = -7$. How many units should be diverted to this new route? According to Phase 2 the entries in the minus cells of the path must be isolated. These are 100 and 100. The minimum of these two values is 100 and there is a tie. Shipping this minimum quantity over the F-U route brings about, after adjustments, the solution of Table 9.11(b). As only five routes must be designated, one of the zero cells (either E-U or F-W) must be erased leaving five cells filled. The zero in the F-W cell was arbitrarily selected to be deleted thus yielding the solution of Table 9.11(c), which is degenerate. The stepping-stone technique should still be applied and ultimately the optimal solution will be found. Whenever degeneracy exists the analyst should be extra cautious. There is no need, however, to abort the whole process as an optimal solution does exist and can be found.

9.6 UNBALANCED MODELS AND IMPOSSIBLE ROUTES

In each transportation model presented the sum of the supplies at the sources equalled the sum of the demands at the destinations. Such transportation models are said to be balanced. If in reality these two sums do not equal each other, then the model must be modified in order to permit the application of the

TABLE 9.11
Appearance of Degeneracy

(a)

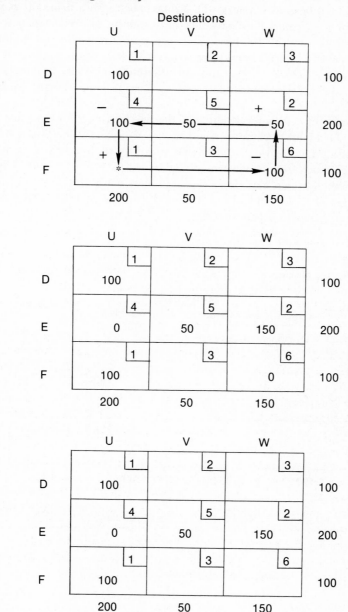

(b)

(c)

stepping-stone technique. There are two possibilities that must be considered. The first is when total supply exceeds total demand and the second is when the total demand exceeds the total supply, In both cases the transportation model is said to be unbalanced.

Supply Exceeds Demand

Returning to the Prairie Cattle Company example, assume that there proved to be 400 head available at the Kansas ranch rather than 300 as previously stated. With a market for only 1000 head as originally indicated, now the supply exceeds demand by 100 head. The northwest corner rule and stepping-stone technique both work from a transportation tableau where the sum of the supplies equals the sum of the demands. It is therefore necessary to modify the tableau or model if a solution is to be found by these techniques that have been discussed.

If the supply of cattle exceeds the total demand by 100, this means that 100 of the cattle should not be shipped. Another way of looking at the situation is to consider that all 1100 cattle at the ranches are shipped, but 100 of them are shipped to the ranch from which they originated. Of course if they are shipped to the same ranch from which they originated, they really were not shipped at all and the cost of so shipping a head is zero. The tableau of Table 9.12(a) is the same as that of Table 9.1 except that the supply for Kansas has been increased to 400 head, and a new destination denoted as F has been added which has a

TABLE 9.12
Supply Exceeds Demand

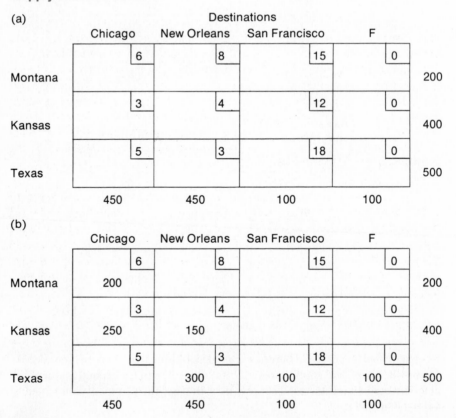

(a)

	Destinations				
	Chicago	New Orleans	San Francisco	F	
Montana	6	8	15	0	200
Kansas	3	4	12	0	400
Texas	5	3	18	0	500
	450	450	100	100	

(b)

	Chicago	New Orleans	San Francisco	F	
Montana	200 / 6	8	15	0	200
Kansas	250 / 3	150 / 4	12	0	400
Texas	5	300 / 3	100 / 18	100 / 0	500
	450	450	100	100	

demand of 100. This new destination is a fictitious destination in that it merely represents the cattle which are "shipped" to their own ranch. This fictitious destination has a demand just large enough to make the sum of the demands equal to the sum of the supplies; both now equal 1100 head. There is a cost of zero for each steer shipped over these routes since the cattle are not actually moved. In Table 9.12(b) the northwest corner rule is used to find an initial corner solution for this modified tableau. The presence of 100 in the Texas-Fictitious cell means that 100 of the Texas cattle stay home on the range. The fact that the Montana-Fictitious and Kansas-Fictitious routes are not used implies that none of the cattle in Montana or Kansas stay home; they are all shipped to the markets in this initial solution. The stepping-stone technique may now be used starting with the tableau of Table 9.12(b) in pursuit of the optimal solution.

In summary, if the total supply exceeds the total demand by some quantity, then create a fictitious destination with a demand for that destination equal to the difference between total demand and total supply. Each of the shipping costs per unit in the cells representing the routes to the fictitious destination is zero. In any solution, the entries in these cells represent the number of units of product which remain at the respective source.

Demand Exceeds Supply

Suppose now that the Prairie Cattle Company has only 1000 head as originally given but that the demand is for 1200 head. In particular, let the demand at Chicago be 600 instead of 450, and the demand at New Orleans be 500 instead of 450 as originally given. See Table 9.13(a), page 260. In such a situation it should be obvious that all the demand cannot be met; the supply falls 200 head short! In order to construct a transportation tableau which has the total supply equal to the total demand, create a fictitious ranch, the Willie Sol Ranch of Estes Park, which has a herd of 200 fictitious cattle. With Willie Sol's fictitious ranch supplying 200 head, the total supply now equals 1200 which is the total demand. The fictitious source is listed with the other sources in Table 9.13(a) and is denoted by the letter F.

The northwest corner rule is now applied yielding the initial solution of Table 9.13(b). In this solution New Orleans gets 100 of the fictitious cattle and San Francisco gets the other 100. The cost to ship one fictitious steer from Willie Sol's ranch to anywhere is zero, therefore the costs in the upper right corners in the fictitious row are all zero. Since New Orleans and San Francisco get the fictitious cattle in this initial solution, it is clear that if this solution were implemented then these two cities are the ones whose demand is not satisfied.

In summary, if the total amount demanded exceeds the total supply, create a fictitious source with a supply equal to the quantity by which the total supply falls short of the total demand. Each of the shipping costs from this fictitious source to each of the destinations is zero. In any solution, the entries in the cells of the fictitious source (row) refer to units of product which do not actually exist. Therefore destinations which receive these are not getting the full quantity they demanded.

TABLE 9.13
Demand Exceeds Supply

(a)

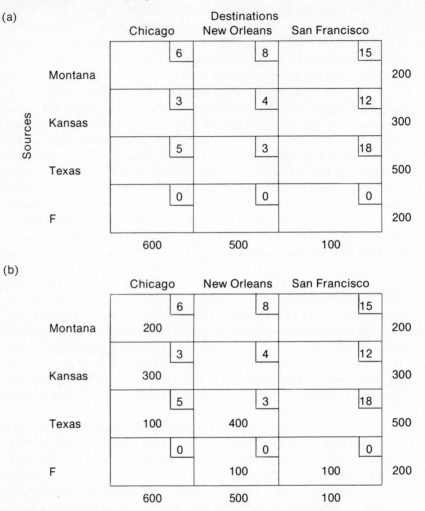

	Destinations		
Sources	Chicago	New Orleans	San Francisco	
Montana	6	8	15	200
Kansas	3	4	12	300
Texas	5	3	18	500
F	0	0	0	200
	600	500	100	

(b)

	Chicago	New Orleans	San Francisco	
Montana	6 / 200	8	15	200
Kansas	3 / 300	4	12	300
Texas	5 / 100	3 / 400	18	500
F	0	0 / 100	0 / 100	200
	600	500	100	

Impossible Routes

Sometimes certain of the routes set forth by the transportation model become impossible, that is, certain routes become unusable for one reason or another. If this is the case the transportation tableau must be modified so that the optimal solution will not utilize one of the impossible routes. A glance at the map of Figure 9.1 reveals that the route from Texas to San Francisco runs through Apache country. Geronimo has just informed the Prairie Cattle Company that he will not honor the cattle company's easement through his territory, thus the Texas-San Francisco route becomes an impossible route. Mathematically speaking, this route can be eliminated by changing its per head cost from the present \$18 to some extraordinarily large figure like \$18 million per head.

With this outlandish transportation cost for the Texas-San Francisco route, the stepping-stone technique will automatically avoid using this route in the optimal solution. If several routes become impossible the same procedure should be followed in each case, namely, increasing the cost associated with these routes to an extremely large arbitrary value. The northwest corner rule and stepping-stone technique are then applied as usual.

9.7 MORE APPLICATIONS

The transportation model has applications which do not involve the transporting of items from one location (the source) to another (the destination). Two "non-transportation" applications of the transportation model will now be briefly described. In both cases a transportation tableau like that of Table 9.1 will be constructed.

Exporting tremendous quantities of oil, the Shiekdom of Aridia has ample monetary resources for the recruitment of army personnel for its newly modernized army. The Shiek currently has need of 20,000 recruits for the infantry, 5,000 for the artillery, and 5,000 recruits for office work. Recruits exhibit a wide variety of personality types and they also vary according to educational background and job experience. In an effort to optimize the method of assigning various types of recruits to the three branches (infantry, artillery, and office) of the army, the Shiek's personnel advisor has classified each recruit into one of four different categories. The four categories or types of recruits are affectionately known as Barracuda, Mongoose, Roach, and Camel. The personnel advisor claims that each recruit falls quite naturally into one of these "personality types."

Presently there are 30,000 new recruits. They have been classified as follows. There are 3,000 Barracudas, 3,000 Mongeese, 15,000 Roaches, and 9,000 Camels.

The problem faced by the Shiek is how to assign these 30,000 recruits to the three branches of the army in order to optimize the army's performance. This problem may be viewed as a transportation problem if the four types of recruits are likened to four sources with supplies of 3,000, 3,000, 15,000, and 9,000 recruits. Then the three branches of the army may be likened to three destinations with demands of 20,000, 5,000, and 5,000 recruits. The "transportation tableau" of Table 9.14, page 262, shows the sources and destinations with their respective supplies and demands.

In the upper right corners of each cell a performance rating is given. A low performance rating indicates that that type of recruit can perform well in the corresponding branch of the army. For example, a Barracuda is especially suited to the infantry and thus receives a rating of 1. A Barracuda does poorly in the office as indicated by a rating of 9. A Roach (the mainstay of the Shiek's army) gets a 7 when performing in the infantry, a 9 when in the artillery, and an 8 when performing office work. The Shiek, therefore, wishes to allocate the recruits to the branches in a manner which will yield a minimum total performance rating. (Remember that a high rating indicates poor performance.) By the northwest corner rule an initial solution would be as seen in Table 9.14.

TABLE 9.14
Transportation Tableau for the
Allocation of Army Recruits

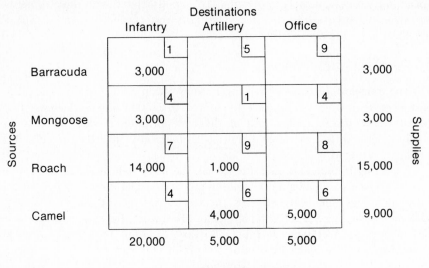

	Infantry	Artillery	Office	Supplies
Barracuda	1 / 3,000	5	9	3,000
Mongoose	4 / 3,000	1	4	3,000
Roach	7 / 14,000	9 / 1,000	8	15,000
Camel	4	6 / 4,000	6 / 5,000	9,000
Demands	20,000	5,000	5,000	

Allocate the 3,000 Barracudas to the infantry. (This is analogous to shipping 3,000 items from the "Barracuda" source to the "Infantry" destination.)
Allocate the 3,000 Mongeese to the infantry.
Allocate 14,000 Roaches to the infantry.
Allocate 1,000 Roaches to the artillery.
Allocate 4,000 Camels to the artillery.
Allocate 5,000 Camels to the office.

This would yield a total performance rating of

$$\text{Total Performance Rating} = (3,000)(1) + (3,000)(4) + (14,000)(7)$$
$$+ (1,000)(9) + (4,000)(6) + (5,000)(6)$$
$$= 176,000$$

The stepping-stone technique could then be used to reallocate recruits in order to get a lower and hence better total performance rating. In this manner, then, the transportation model may be used to solve this allocation problem.

In Chapter 7 several applications of linear programming were given. One of these, the production-inventory example of Section 7.10, may be viewed as a transportation problem. Recall that the problem in this example involved finding a production schedule for Navajo Enterprises, a company which produces sand paintings. Winter, Spring, Summer, and Fall may be considered as sources. The supplies available from each of these sources are the production capacities of these periods. Thus the supply for winter is 10 sand paintings since a maximum of 10 can be produced in that season. The four seasons may also be viewed as destinations with their respective demands. For example, there is a demand requirement of 35 for the summer. Figure 9.15 gives the appropriate "transportation tableau." Because the model is unbalanced, a fictitious destination has been added thereby making total demand equal total supply.

TABLE 9.15
Transportation Tableau for
Production Scheduling

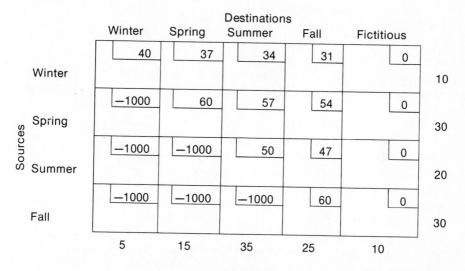

The entries in the upper right corners of each cell give the profits associated with producing sand paintings in various periods and then selling them in various periods. For example, as was shown in Section 7.10, a profit of 34 is realized on each sand painting produced in the winter and sold in the summer. Since it is impossible to produce a painting in the summer and sell it in the previous spring, a large negative profit of −1000 is entered in such cells. This assures Navajo Enterprises that a solution will not require the sale of a painting before it is produced. Profits of zero have been entered in the fictitious destination column as is appropriate.

The northwest corner rule can now be used to find an initial solution. Then the stepping-stone technique should be utilized to find the optimal production schedule. However, before the stepping-stone technique can be applied the model must be slightly altered since the goal is *maximization* (of profits) rather than minimization as was the case in the Prairie Cattle Company and the Shiekdom of Aridia examples. This alteration is considered in Section 9.10.

9.8 THE ASSIGNMENT MODEL

A special case of the transportation model is called the assignment model. In the assignment model the number of sources equals the number of destinations. Also, the supply at each source is one and the demand at each destination is one.

An illustration setting forth the essential nature of the assignment model and demonstrating an application will now be given.

As the Kansas Pacific Railroad pushed through Kansas just prior to the operation of the Prairie Cattle Company, it was necessary to build stations along the way where the livestock could be held till shipped. The Kansas Pacific planned such a facility at Abilene which was the northern terminus of the Chisholm Trail. There were four jobs associated with the construction of the station,

1. The well drilling and water storage job.
2. The timber job.
3. The adobe job.
4. The finishing job.

At this time there were four contractors working in the Abilene area: the James Bros., the Daltons, McKenzie, and Sioux-Zuki. The first three were domestic contractors whereas the last was an American Indian-Japanese outfit.

The Kansas Pacific asked each of the four contractors to submit a bid on each of the jobs even though each of the contractors was only big enough to handle one job. If a contractor were uninterested in one of the jobs, a very high bid would be submitted for that job. The James Bros.' bids for the well, timber, adobe, and finishing jobs were (in thousands) $22, $30, $41, and $18. The Daltons' bids were (in thousands) $20, $35, $40, and $15, respectively. McKenzie's bids were $24, $33, $42, and $19, respectively. Finally, Sioux-Zuki submitted bids of $23, $36, $42, and $18, respectively. The Kansas Pacific after examining all of the bids concluded that there had been no collusion and decided to award one job to each contractor. How should the Kansas Pacific assign contractors to jobs in order to minimize total construction costs?

The problem facing the Kansas Pacific could be considered as a transportation problem where the Kansas Pacific was concerned with "shipping" each contractor to a job. In Table 9.16(a) a transportation tableau is set up showing that the form of the model is that of the transportation model. Here the supply for each contractor is one, and the demand for each job is also one. An initial solution could be obtained by the northwest corner rule. For example, the James Bros. could be given the well job, the Daltons could be given the timber job, McKenzie could be given the adobe job, and Sioux-Zuki could be assigned the finishing job (see Table 9.16(b)). In this case each contractor would have exactly one job, and each job would be accomplished by exactly one contractor. The total cost to the Kansas Pacific would be 22 + 35 + 42 + 18 = $117,000. In this assignment model the bids take the place of the per unit transportation costs.

The stepping-stone technique or any method of solving the transportation model could now be applied in order to find the minimum cost assignment. However, a more efficient technique has been developed for solving the assignment model. This technique will be described in the next section.

In review, an assignment problem exists when there are X agents who must be assigned to X tasks. Each agent must be assigned to exactly one task and each task must have exactly one agent assigned to it. Under these conditions the assignments are to be made in a manner which will optimize some quantity like costs. Assignment models might be useful in assigning salespeople to sales territories, jobs to machines, repairers to jobs, detectives to cases, and research teams to projects.

TABLE 9.16
Kansas Pacific Assignment Model

(a)

Sources \ Destinations	Wells	Timber	Adobe	Finishing	
James Bros.	22	30	41	18	1
Daltons	20	35	40	15	1
McKenzie	24	33	42	19	1
Sioux-Zuki	23	36	42	18	1
	1	1	1	1	

(b)

	Wells	Timber	Adobe	Finishing	
James Bros.	22 — 1	30 — 0	41	18	1
Daltons	20	35 — 1	40 — 0	15	1
McKenzie	24	33	42 — 1	19 — 0	1
Sioux-Zuki	23	36	42 — 1	18	1
	1	1	1	1	

9.9 THE ASSIGNMENT METHOD

Assignment models may be efficiently solved by using the technique which will now be described. The assignment method will be illustrated by means of the Kansas Pacific construction example.

To begin, form a matrix where the entries in the cells are the values found in the upper right corners of the transportation tableau. The transportation tableau of Table 9.16(a) is converted to such a matrix in Table 9.17.

TABLE 9.17
Assignment Matrix

	Wells	Timber	Adobe	Finishing
James Bros.	22	30	41	18
Daltons	20	35	40	15
McKenzie	24	33	42	19
Sioux-Zuki	23	36	42	18

The assignment method is then accomplished by the following five steps:

STEP 1: Subtract the minimum value in each column from every entry in the same column.

The minimum value in the first column (wells column) is 20, therefore, 20 must be subtracted from every entry in the first column. This results in the entries found in the first column of Table 9.18(a). The minimum value in the second column (timber column) is 30, therefore 30 must be subtracted from every entry in the second column. See Table 9.18(a) for the new second column. In like manner, 40 is subtracted from every entry in the third column, and 15 is subtracted from each entry in the fourth column. The entire new matrix is given in Table 9.18(a).

STEP 2: With respect to the matrix resulting from Step 1, subtract the minimum value in each row from every entry in the same row.

In the first row of Table 9.18(a) the minimum value is zero, thus zero must be subtracted from every entry in the first row (see Table 9.18(b)). The minimum value in the second row is zero. When zero is subtracted from every entry in the second row nothing is affected. The minimum value in the third row is 2, thus 2 must be subtracted from every entry in the third row of Table 9.18(a). See Table 9.18(b) for the new third row. Similarly, the minimum value in the fourth row is 2 which when subtracted from every entry in that row yields the fourth row as given in Table 9.18(b).

STEP 3: Draw as few vertical and/or horizontal lines as possible through the rows and columns of the matrix in order to cross out each of the zero entries.

Restated, the object of this step is to draw straight lines on the matrix of Table 9.18(b), which are not diagonal, such that all of the zeros are crossed with the use of a minimum number of these lines. Table 9.19 shows one way this could be accomplished. A minimum of three lines are required even though these three lines might be drawn differently than in Table 9.19.

TABLE 9.18
Steps 1 and 2 of Assignment Method

(a)

	Wells	Timber	Adobe	Finishing
James Bros.	2	0	1	3
Daltons	0	5	0	0
McKenzie	4	3	2	4
Sioux-Zuki	3	6	2	3

(b)

	Wells	Timber	Adobe	Finishing
James Bros.	2	0	1	3
Daltons	0	5	0	0
McKenzie	2	1	0	2
Sioux-Zuki	1	4	0	1

TABLE 9.19
Step 3 of Assignment Method

	Wells	Timber	Adobe	Finishing
James Bros.	2	0	1	3
Daltons	0	5	0	0
McKenzie	2	1	0	2
Sioux-Zuki	1	4	0	1

STEP 4: If the minimum number of lines required in Step 3 equals the number of rows (or columns), then make an optimal assignment using only the cells in which there are zero entries. If the minimum number of lines required is less than the number of rows, proceed to the next step.

Three lines were required to cover the zeros of Table 9.19. As three is less than the number of rows (or columns), which is four, go to the next step.

STEP 5: Find the smallest entry which is not crossed by one of the lines of Step 3. Subtract this entry from every entry in the matrix that is not crossed, and add it to every entry which comes at an intersection of two of the lines of Step 3. Return to Step 3.

In Table 9.19 the smallest uncrossed entry is a 1 which is found in three different cells. This 1 is subtracted from every uncrossed entry in the matrix. It is also added to the entries, 1 and 0, which occur at the intersection of some of the lines. The result of Step 5 is given in Table 9.20(a). Now return to Step 3.

TABLE 9.20
Steps 5 and 3 of Assignment Method

(a)

	Wells	Timber	Adobe	Finishing
James Bros.	2	0	1 + 1	3
Daltons	0	5	0 + 1	0
McKenzie	2—1	1—1	0	2—1
Sioux-Zuki	1—1	4—1	0	1—1

(b)

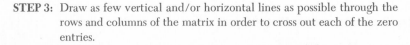

	Wells	Timber	Adobe	Finishing
James Bros.	2	0	2	3
Daltons	0	5	1	0
McKenzie	1	0	0	1
Sioux-Zuki	0	3	0	0

STEP 3: Draw as few vertical and/or horizontal lines as possible through the rows and columns of the matrix in order to cross out each of the zero entries.

It now takes a minimum of four lines to cross all of the zero entries in Table 9.20(a). These four lines are shown in Table 9.20(b). Since four lines are required and four is the number of rows, an optimal assignment can now be made by using only cells with zero entries according to Step 4.

How can the optimal assignment be made using only cells with zeros as given in Table 9.20? The transportation tableau which was the starting point for the assignment method is given in Table 9.21(a). Check marks have been placed in the cells of this transportation tableau which correspond to cells in the matrix of Table 9.20(b) which have zero entries. Since there are eight zero cells in Table 9.20(b), there are eight corresponding cells or routes of the transportation tableau which are checked. Using the tableau of Table 9.21(a), place 1's judiciously in only checked routes so that the supply and demand conditions are satisfied. That is, there must be a single 1 in each row and a single 1 in each column and these 1's must appear only in checked cells.

The tableau of Table 9.21(b) gives one such assignment which satisfies the stated requirements. The presence of a 1 in a cell indicates that the contractor associated with the row of the cell is assigned the job of the column in which that cell is found. According to the assignment of Table 9.21(b), the James Bros. get the timber job, the Daltons get the well job, McKenzie gets the adobe job, and Sioux-Zuki gets the finishing job. The total cost to the Kansas Pacific will be

$$C = 30 + 20 + 42 + 18$$
$$= \$110 \text{ thousand}$$

The checked cells of Table 9.21(a) could be used to produce another assignment where each contractor gets one job and each job gets exactly one contractor. Table 9.21(c), page 270, gives this alternate optimal solution which also has a cost of $110,000.

9.10 SPECIAL CONSIDERATIONS

In conclusion a short discussion concerning two problems which have not yet been considered will take place.

TABLE 9.21
Making Assignments

(a)

	Wells	Timber	Adobe	Finishing	
James Bros.	22	30 √	41	18	1
Daltons	20 √	35	40	15 √	1
McKenzie	24	33 √	42 √	19	1
Sioux-Zuki	23 √	36	42 √	18 √	1
	1	1	1	1	

(b)

	Wells	Timber	Adobe	Finishing	
James Bros.	22	30 1	41	18	1
Daltons	20 1	35	40	15	1
McKenzie	24	33	42 1	19	1
Sioux-Zuki	23	36	42	18 1	1
	1	1	1	1	

(c)

	Wells	Timber	Adobe	Finishing	
James Bros.	22	30 1	41	18	1
Daltons	20	35	40	15 1	1
McKenzie	24	33	42 1	19	1
Sioux-Zuki	23 1	36	42	18	1
	1	1	1	1	

Unbalanced Assignment Model

In the event that there are more agents than tasks, or more tasks than agents, the assignment problem becomes unbalanced. The situation may be rectified or balanced by the incorporation of either fictitious tasks or fictitious agents by following the type of procedure that was outlined in Section 9.6.

Maximization

In both the transportation and assignment models presented in this chapter the objective was to *minimize* costs. Suppose management were concerned with maximization instead of minimization, are the techniques of this chapter still applicable? Upon the completion of one modification, maximization models can be successfully converted to minimization models. To illustrate, suppose management were concerned with assigning research teams to projects with the objective of maximizing some measure of effectiveness. Of the three teams, Team 1 could accomplish the three projects designated by A, B, and C with effectiveness ratings of 40, 60, and 55, respectively. Team 2 could accomplish the three projects with ratings of 50, 65, and 50, respectively. Team 3 can accomplish the projects with ratings of 50, 70, and 60, respectively. Management wants to assign the teams to the projects in order to maximize the total ratings. This maximization model may be converted to a minimization model by changing the ratings to negative numbers with the goal of minimizing these negative ratings. For example, Team 1 can now be considered to accomplish the three projects with ratings of -40, -60, and -55. With the ratings for the other teams also converted, that assignment of teams to projects which gives the minimum (most negative) total rating is the same as that which would give the maximum total rating if the individual ratings were still positive. The assignment method can now be applied exactly as before to find the assignment plan which will produce the most negative total rating.

270

In summary, maximization models can be converted to minimization models by merely changing the sign on all the values in the upper right corner of the transportation tableau. After this transformation the stepping-stone technique or assignment method may be used in the manner in which they were presented.

PROBLEMS

9-1. Use the northwest corner rule to find an initial corner solution.

(a)

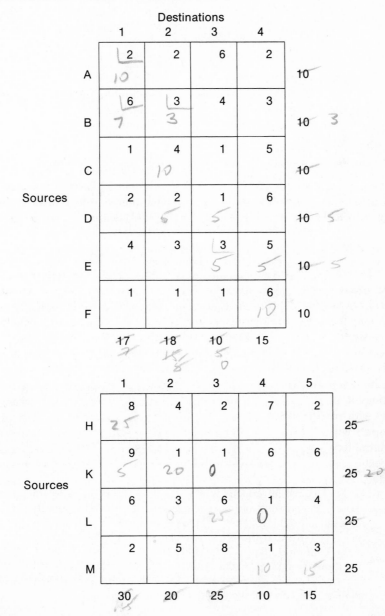

Destinations

Sources	1	2	3	4	
A	2 (10)	2	6	2	10
B	6 (7)	3 (3)	4	3	10 (3)
C	1	4 (10)	1	5	10
D	2	2 (6)	1 (5)	6	10 (5)
E	4	3	3 (5)	5 (5)	10 (5)
F	1	1	1	6 (10)	10
	17 (7)	18 (8)	10 (5)(0)	15	

(b)

Sources	1	2	3	4	5	
H	8 (25)	4	2	7	2	25
K	9 (5)	1 (20)	1 (0)	6	6	25 (20)
L	6 (0)	3 (25)	6 (0)	1	4	25
M	2	5	8	1 (10)	3 (15)	25
	30	20	25	10	15	

9-2. Up around Hibbing, Minnesota, there is a boom in low-grade iron ore mining. Taconite, the ore, is being mined from three big pits and is transported to four processing centers. The table below gives the distances from each of the pits to each of the processing centers. The Big Texas pit can produce 80 kilotons per day, the Little Meo can produce 30 kilotons per day, and the Moon Face can produce 50 kilotons per day. Processing Center 1 can handle 40 kilotons per day, Center 2 can handle 30 kilotons per day, Center 3 can handle 50, and Center 4 can handle 40.

		Processing Center			
		1	2	3	4
	Big Texas	2	3	5	4
Pit	Little Meo	3	5	5	7
	Moon Face	7	8	5	9

(a) Set this up as a linear programming model with objective function and constraints. The objective is to minimize the total daily ton-miles traveled.

(b) Beginning with the northwest corner rule, find the optimal solution using the stepping-stone technique.

(c) The county has notified the mining company that it cannot use the bridge on the route from the Big Texas to Processing Center 4. What is the optimal solution if this route is not allowed.

9-3. The U.S. Cavalry wants to assign new recruits to three western forts. Fort Mohave needs 200 dragoons, Fort Collins needs 300 dragoons, and Fort Leavenworth needs 400. There are 200 recruits waiting for assignment in Los Angeles, 350 in St. Louis, and 350 in New York City. The Cavalry wants to get the recruits to the forts with a minimum number of man-weeks of travel. The time in weeks to get a recruit from each of the cities to the forts is given in the table below. How should the recruits be transported to the forts?

	Fort Mohave	Fort Collins	Fort Leavenworth
Los Angeles	2	6	7
St. Louis	7	4	2
New York	9	6	5

9-4. Kadko has just introduced a new camera. The demand for the camera far exceeds the current supply. The camera is produced at facilities in Rochester and Colorado. Kadko ships the camera to five regional distribution centers. The output at the Rochester plant is 200,000 cameras and the output at the Colorado plant is 150,000 cameras. The demand at each of the distribution centers is 80,000 cameras. Transportation costs per thousand cameras are given in the table. Find the minimum cost transportation scheme. Who does not get all the cameras requested?

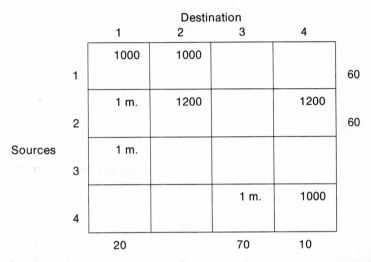

	Distribution Center				
	1	2	3	4	5
Rochester	8	6	4	3	.2
Colorado	3	2	5	7	9

9-5. Refer to the Armbrecht Steel situation of Problem 7–17. This problem may be formulated as a transportation model. Each quarter may be considered as a source, and each quarter may be considered as a destination. A partial, unbalanced transportation tableau for Armbrecht Steel is given below.

		Destination				
		1	2	3	4	
Sources	1	1000	1000			60
	2	1 m.	1200		1200	60
	3	1 m.				
	4			1 m.	1000	
		20		70	10	

(a) Why is the cost associated with routes such as 3–1 given as $1,000,000?

(b) Balance the model.

(c) Find the minimum cost production schedule.

9-6. Spencer Farm Machinery produces harvesters in three plants and ships the harvesters to four sales areas. In the table below the values given are the profits (in thousands of dollars) per harvester shipped over the designated route. The profits are affected by both transportation costs and differing manufacturing costs at the four plants. Find the transportation plan that will maximize profits.

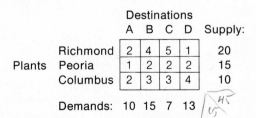

		Destinations				Supply:
		A	B	C	D	
	Richmond	2	4	5	1	20
Plants	Peoria	1	2	2	2	15
	Columbus	2	3	3	4	10

Demands: 10 15 7 13

9-7. Four trainees have worked on four different machines at Vernon Tool & Die. The number of defects per week each trainee was responsible for while working on the different machines are recorded in the table below. For example, Clay turned out 10 defects in a week while working on Machine A. What trainee should be permanently assigned to what machine in order to minimize the total number of weekly defectives?

Machine

		A	B	C	D
	Clay	10	25	5	4
	Joan	12	23	9	2
Trainee	Larry	14	20	8	1
	Christy	13	20	7	3

CLAY, C
JUAN, A
LARRY, D
CHRIS, B

Now assume, after answering the first question, that Christy leaves the company. What machine should be idled and how should the remaining three trainees be assigned?

9-8. Griggs is assigning faculty members to committees. Each faculty member has ranked the committees such that first preference is given a rank of 1 and the least desirable choice receives a rank of 6. Assign the faculty to the committees in a fashion which will yield the minimum total sum of ranks.

COMMITTEES

	Curriculum	Disciplinary	Social	Evaluation	Search	Advisory
Abdelsamad	4	3	1	2	5	6
Berry	1	6	2	3	5	4
Thornton	6	1	5	2	4	3
Haas	2	1	3	4	5	6
Johnston	1	2	3	4	5	6
Rimler	6	3	2	1	4	5

A, S
B, C
T, A
H, D
J, S
R, E

9-9. Scotland wishes to assign each salesperson to a different territory. The matrix below indicates how much each salesperson could sell in each territory. Find the assignment plan which will maximize total sales.

	Yukon	Tombstone	Eastern	Southern	International
Hope	20	15	30	40	25
Potter	15	30	25	17	19
Shuart	18	22	29	43	24
Carter	17	18	36	12	23
Begley	12	24	32	36	29

9-10. Trans-Pecos Airlines has five types of aircraft which it must assign to five different routes. Because of variations among the routes (distances, number of passengers, weather, airport facilities, etc.) the aircraft are not all equally adapted to each route. The cost over each of the routes for each aircraft is given in the table on the next page.

	Houston- Dallas	Del Rio- Cape Cod	El Paso- Gary	Lubbock- London	Waco- Berlin
DC 3	10	15	17	40	45
DC 7	8	12	20	38	43
F-27	7	14	18	34	37
727	6	13	12	30	32
B 24	9	12	21	42	41

(a) How should the aircraft be assigned to minimize total costs?

(b) If the DC 3 were eliminated from the fleet because of a collision with an English sparrow (on a flight to London), what should be the assignment plan?

Queueing Models

10.1 INTRODUCTION

Waiting lines or queues are ubiquitous. Cars line up to wait for the Staten Island Ferry. Students line up to get registration materials. Wedding guests line up to offer their best wishes. Shoppers line up behind cash registers at the supermarket. Planes circle above airports while waiting to land. Cars wait at the service station pumps. Patients wait for the physician. Inoperative computers in a city wait for the service engineer. Telephone calls wait at the switchboard. Auto mechanics wait for replacement parts at the parts window. Travelers wait to check their baggage at the airport terminal. Musical lovers wait for tickets at the box office. Certainly no one could be unfamiliar with waiting lines of one form or another.

When a waiting line is mentioned, most people picture something like a column of cars behind a toll booth or a line of shoppers at the cash register in the supermarket. However, there need not be an actual physical waiting line in order for a queueing situation to exist. The "line" may be the collection of plumbing problems located throughout a large building which are waiting for the appearance of the plumber. Regardless of the actual form of a waiting line situation, it is the object of this chapter to construct and utilize models of these situations for the sake of making decisions. The nature of these decisions will become apparent as the various elements of a waiting line situation are isolated and explained.

Whenever there are waiting lines there will be some kind of costs associated with these lines and the costs may be either monetary or nonmonetary. The two primary types of costs present in queueing situations are *waiting costs* and *service costs.* Waiting costs are those costs which are incurred because something or someone must spend time waiting for a service to be performed. An airline passenger circling above the airport is likely to experience the nonmonetary waiting costs such as anxiety about being late. The airline, whose plane is circling, at the same time faces monetary waiting costs such as excessive fuel consumption.

Service costs, on the other hand, are the costs of providing service. Monetary service costs are associated with the number of runways available since it takes financial resources to keep a runway open or to add a new one. Nonmonetary service costs might include the noise which must be endured by residents living near the airport.

In the typical situation, waiting costs can only be reduced by increasing service costs, and vice versa. The manager of a supermarket is confronted with these two types of costs in determining how many cashiers should be on duty. With a large number of cashiers on duty there will be high service costs as these employees draw wages. However, waiting costs will be minimal as customers will not have to wait for service. On the other hand, if few cashiers are on duty, then service costs would be low but waiting costs would be high. What are these waiting costs? Though the supermarket does not pay customers if they have to wait, still there is a cost to the market if customers are forced to wait too long. Some customers upon entering the store will immediately leave upon seeing the long queues. Though others will still shop despite the long lines, they will be prone to do their future business at stores which offer faster service. The reduction in sales volume and the concomitant customer ill-will constitute the waiting costs to the supermarket.

The general relationship between waiting costs and service rate is depicted by one of the lines in Figure 10.1. The service rate merely refers to the rate at which customers can be serviced. The relationship between service costs and service rate is also depicted in Figure 10.1. Notice that as the service rate increases, the waiting costs decrease. As the airport constructs additional runways (increased service rate) there are reductions in waiting costs. Notice also that as the service rate increases, the service costs increase. Opening more toll booths increases both the rate of service and the cost of operating the bank of toll

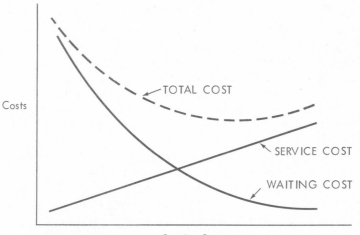

Costs

TOTAL COST

SERVICE COST

WAITING COST

Service Rate

FIGURE 10.1   Relationship Between Costs and Service Rate

booths. It is management's objective to find that service rate which will minimize total costs where total costs are composed of the sum of the waiting and service costs. The service rate directly below the lowest point on the total cost curve in Figure 10.1 is the optimal service rate since it yields the minimum total costs. In the remainder of the chapter, consideration will be given to the actual determination of the service costs and waiting costs realizing that these costs are dependent upon the service rate. By linking these costs to the service rate, the optimal service rate can then be determined.

10.2 QUEUEING MODEL COMPONENTS

In Figure 10.2 a queueing model with its various components is displayed. Each of these components will now be discussed. Notice that the term "queueing system" will apply only to the queue and the service mechanism; the queueing system is enclosed with a dotted line.

Input Source

The input source is the population or collection of people or things which generates the people or things found in the waiting line. The people or things entering the waiting line for the sake of obtaining service are designated as calling units. The input source may be finite or infinite. A company might have a fleet of ten trucks which are serviced by the company's own mechanic. This fleet is a finite input source in that there are only ten units which might require mechanical service. On the other hand, a service station operating along a superhighway is fed by an infinite input source. That is, there are thousands of automobiles using the highway, any of which might require service.

The type of input source has various ramifications in the construction of queueing models and thus has effects on the conclusions derived from the use of the models. For example, with a fleet of ten trucks the queue could never grow in length beyond ten. With an infinite input source there is no particular limit to the length of the queue. Not only are there implications with regard to line length, there are also implications with regard to the arrival of calling units. In the finite case recent past experience is apt to influence the generation of calling

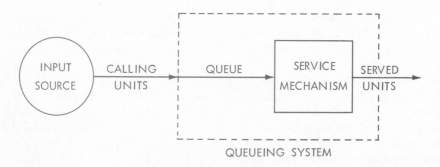

FIGURE 10.2 Queueing Model

units in the present. If the mechanic had just lubricated the ten trucks in the fleet last week, then there is little chance that a truck will need lubrication this week. With an infinite input source the experience of the immediate past is not likely to influence the current situation in the manner just described. In the superhighway example, lubricating ten automobiles last week at the service station will have no effect on the number seeking lubrication this week.

Calling Units

From the input source come the calling units which enter the queue to wait for service. The mode and the timing of the arrivals of calling units should be noted. In some queueing situations the calling units arrive in groups. Such is the case when a Greyhound bus traveling across the country stops at a restaurant. Suddenly a group of travelers converges on the restaurant forming two great queues. In contrast, at the truckstop restaurant the calling units (truck drivers) arrive one by one rather than in groups.

Having indicated two modes of arrival, the timing of the arrivals may be considered. Calling units may arrive uniformly in that the same amount of time separates each arrival. For example, partially completed appliances coming down the assembly line may arrive uniformly at an inspection station. In other cases the calling units may arrive randomly, that is, the interarrival times vary randomly. Automobiles, for example, arrive randomly at the auto teller's window at the bank. Unpredictable periods of time separate the arrivals of successive automobiles.

After specifying the details of the pattern of arrivals, the average rate of arrivals is often given. The superhighway service station might experience an average rate of 12 automobiles seeking a lubrication per week. This means that on average 12 automobiles seek a lubrication per week. Some weeks only 4 autos might seek this service and during some weeks as many as 25 might seek a lube. Nevertheless, the weekly average is 12. This average arrival rate serves as a measure of the frequency of arrivals. The Greek letter lambda, λ, is often used for the average arrival rate. For example, $\lambda = 12$ per week in the service station example just cited.

Queue

As the calling units arrive they form a queue or waiting line. Sometimes, however, the calling unit upon seeing a long line decides not to wait. This is called balking. Assuming that calling units are waiting in the queue, in what order are they to be served or serviced? There are several queue disciplines or rules for prescribing the order in which calling units waiting in line should be served. The most common is the "first-come, first-served" discipline. Another type of queue discipline is the priority system where those calling units with a high priority are served first regardless of when they entered the queue. Such a system is employed at the university computer center where certain types of users and jobs have higher priorities than others. High priority jobs are run ahead of low priority jobs even if the low priority jobs were submitted first.

The amount of time that calling units spend in the queue is the basis for determining the magnitude of waiting costs. In the supermarket example cited earlier, long waits in line will cost the supermarket a reduction in sales volume. The supermarket may have difficulty in actually measuring these costs even though there is no question as to their existence. In other situations these kinds of costs may be measured quite easily and thus management can accurately determine total waiting costs once the average waiting time per calling unit is determined.

Service Mechanism

The service mechanism consists of one or more servers or channels of service. A service station may have one mechanic on duty, an airport may have two parallel runways in use, and a bank might have three tellers on duty. The mechanic, the runways, and the tellers are the respective servers in each case. The calling units in these three cases would be automobiles, planes, and people, respectively. The units waiting in the queue are serviced when a channel becomes open. After the calling unit is served it departs from the queueing system as a served unit.

Focusing on a single server or channel of service, the server may be able to perform the service for each calling unit in the same amount of time. A worker on an assembly line can perform a task such as mounting the wheels on a tractor in a fixed amount of time since there is no variation in the task from tractor to tractor. On the other hand, the time to perform a service may vary randomly according to the specific need of the calling unit being serviced. The time it takes for a service engineer to repair a computer will vary from situation to situation due to a wide variety of problems that are encountered.

The service capacity of a server may be described either in terms of an average service time or in terms of an average service rate. A warehousing crew might be able to unload trucks on an average of 30 minutes each. Here the average service time per truck is 30 minutes. This could alternately be expressed as an average service rate by saying that the crew can unload trucks at an average rate of 2 per hour. The Greek letter mu, μ, is typically used to denote the service rate of a server.

Also associated with the service mechanism is the service cost. The service cost is the cost of providing the service which the calling units are seeking. In a supermarket where customers wait for cash register service, for example, the service cost includes the wages of the cashiers. The service rate may be increased by opening more channels or servers and/or by increasing the service rate of an individual server. Both the method used to increase the service rate and the particular details of the queueing situation will dictate the actual effects on service costs and the degree of the reduction in waiting costs.

10.3 A SINGLE-SERVER MODEL

A queueing situation where there is a single server and where calling units arrive randomly and require varying service times will now be considered. The assumptions upon which the ensuing model rests are three.

1. There is one server and one waiting line. The length of the waiting line is not limited.
2. Calling units arrive from an infinite input source according to a Poisson process at an average of λ arrivals per unit of time.
3. Served units depart from the service mechanism according to a Poisson process at an average of μ departures per unit of time assuming that there are calling units in the queueing system.

While the first assumption is self-explanatory, the second and third assumptions need explanation and amplification.

In the second assumption it is stated that the calling units arrive at the service facility according to a Poisson process. What is a Poisson process? The characteristics of a Poisson process will now be discussed. With a Poisson process the calling units arrive at the service mechanism randomly and independently. The fact that a calling unit has just arrived has no influence upon when another calling unit will arrive, and, the fact that no calling unit has recently arrived has no influence on when the next will arrive. In other words, the chance that a calling unit will arrive during one moment is not at all affected by what has happened in previous moments. This is what is meant by saying that arrivals of the calling units are independent. Sometimes it is said that a Poisson process has no memory in that what has happened in the past has no influence upon arrivals in the present. Regarding the probability of there being an arrival in any particular moment of time, with a Poisson process the chance of an arrival in any one moment of time is the same as in any other moment.

Consider an example of a Poisson process. Suppose that the telephone switchboard in a hotel is the service mechanism in a queueing situation and that the incoming telephone calls are the calling units. If we approach the switchboard at 2:36 p.m., would the fact that there have been eight incoming calls in the past ten minutes affect what will happen in the next minute? No! Calls made to the hotel are initiated independently of what has transpired in the past. A person places a call to the hotel with no thought as to how many telephone calls have recently been placed. The fact that there were eight, or fifteen, or two calls in the past ten minutes does not affect what the next caller is going to do. Furthermore, callers do not get together to plan their calls so they will arrive at the switchboard according to some neat pattern. Therefore, calls arrive at the switchboard in a random, haphazard fashion. Figure 10.3 displays a possible history of arrivals during one hour of operation of the switchboard.

FIGURE 10.3 Poisson Arrivals Along a Time Continuum

Even though calling units arrive randomly and independently under a Poisson process, the average number of arrivals per unit of time can be computed.

For the hotel switchboard illustration it might be found, for example, that during afternoons the average number of incoming calls is twenty-five per hour; this average is designated by the Greek letter lambda ($\lambda = 25$). Even though there is an average of twenty-five calls per hour, the fact that they arrive randomly means that some hours will have fewer and some hours will have more calls arriving. Nevertheless the overall average is twenty-five calls per hour. In summary, the second assumption in saying that arrivals follow a Poisson process implies that the calling units arrive randomly and independently at an average rate of λ such that the probability of an arrival in each moment is constant.

The third assumption is similar to the second except that it concerns the service rate rather than the arrival rate. The idea contained in the third assumption is that if there were a long line of calling units, thus guaranteeing that the server would always be busy, then the served units would pop out or depart from the service mechanism according to a Poisson process. That is, they would depart at random, haphazard times. The fact that there were quite a few departures from the service mechanism in the immediate past would give no information as to whether there will be relatively fewer or more in the next interval of time. Also, in the third assumption it is stated that μ represents the average number of calling units which can be serviced per unit of time. Because it takes a different amount of time to serve each calling unit, there may be many served units departing in some hours and relatively few departing in other hours. Nevertheless an average of μ calling units can be served.

The third assumption was stated in terms of service rates or departure rates. This assumption may alternately be given in terms of service times rather than rates. When this is done it is said that service times are "exponentially distributed." Without offering an explanation it will be asserted that a queueing model with exponential service times and Poisson arrivals is the same thing as the model discussed in this section which has Poisson departures and Poisson arrivals.

A number of conclusions can be drawn with respect to any real-life queueing situation which fits the three assumptions given. Before proceeding to these conclusions, briefly consider a waiting line situation which would appear to fit the three assumptions set forth. Automobiles arrive at the auto teller window of a bank. Suppose that there is only one auto teller and thus only one line of automobiles will form. These conditions serve to satisfy the first assumption. The automobiles (calling units) arrive from various quarters randomly and independently at the rate of six per hour, thus $\lambda = 6$. Hence the second assumption is satisfied. The amount of time it takes the teller (service mechanism) to process an auto customer varies due to the nature of the business each customer wishes to transact. Automobiles therefore depart from the teller window randomly and independently. The teller has the capability of processing ten customers per hour on the average, thus $\mu = 10$. Hence the third assumption is satisfied. In a nutshell this is the type of queueing situation to which the model of this section pertains.

If a queueing situation meets the three assumptions given, then several conclusions can be drawn. However, the statements or conclusions which follow are valid only after the queueing system has reached a state of equilibrium. After the queueing system begins operation, it takes a little while before the initial state of the system is no longer of any influence on what occurs. For example, if you rush into a grocery store at 9 a.m. in pursuit of a loaf of bread, you will not have to wait for service because upon opening at 9 a.m. none of the cashiers are busy. The initial state of the system (no customers at the cash registers at 9 a.m.) influences the kind of service you can expect. The probability of having to wait in line is zero if you enter the store when it first opens. After the store has been open for a while with customers randomly arriving, the queueing system comes into equilibrium or a state of "balance." If you rush in for the bread at 10 a.m. you might well have to wait in line. The fact that the store was empty (the initial state) at 9 a.m. has no influence on the customer entering at 10 a.m. The queueing system is therefore said to be in equilibrium at 10 a.m. With this additional assumption that the queueing system is in equilibrium (i.e., it has been in operation for a while), the following conclusions are warranted. First, let

λ = average arrival rate
μ = average service rate
n = number of calling units in the queueing system (the queueing system includes the queue and the service mechanism)

If μ is greater than λ, it follows that [1]

L = average number of calling units in the entire queueing system

$$L = \frac{\lambda}{\mu - \lambda} \qquad (10\text{--}1)$$

L_q = average number of calling units in the queue

$$L_q = \frac{\lambda^2}{\mu(\mu - \lambda)} \qquad (10\text{--}2)$$

W = average time a calling unit spends in the queueing system

$$W = \frac{1}{\mu - \lambda} \qquad (10\text{--}3)$$

W_q = average time a calling unit will spend waiting in the queue

$$W_q = \frac{\lambda}{\mu(\mu - \lambda)} \qquad (10\text{--}4)$$

$P(n)$ = probability of there being exactly n calling units in the queueing system

$$P(n) = \left(\frac{\lambda}{\mu}\right)^n \left(1 - \frac{\lambda}{\mu}\right) \qquad (10\text{--}5)$$

[1] These equations are derived in advanced texts such as Frederick Hillier & Gerald Lieberman, *Operations Research* (2d ed.; San Francisco: Holden-Day, 1974), Chapter 9.

$$P(n \geq k) = \text{probability of there being } k \text{ or more}$$
$$\text{calling units in the queueing system}$$

$$P(n \geq k) = \left(\frac{\lambda}{\mu}\right)^k \tag{10-6}$$

$$U = \text{utilization ratio, or proportion of time the}$$
$$\text{server is busy}$$

$$U = \frac{\lambda}{\mu} \tag{10-7}$$

The queueing model described will now be illustrated by an example. The example will then be carried through succeeding sections for the sake of ultimately demonstrating the economic implications and uses of a queueing model.

Uta Woo of Hong Kong has developed a special copying machine for introduction in the South American market. The machine, called the Gringo Machino, has been widely leased in South America. A large number of Gringo Machinos are in use in the populated area from Porto Alegre to Novo Hamburgo in southern Brazil. Uta Woo has been relying on Mañana Ltd. to service the Gringo Machinos of the Novo Hamburgo area. However, the lessees have been complaining about the poor service that Mañana has rendered and are threatening to lease copying machines from Xerox instead of Uta Woo. Uta Woo has therefore decided to take over the service of their own machines in the Novo Hamburgo area and is now trying to come to a decision as to the assignment of personnel to this area of operations.

Uta Woo is convinced that the situation faced is a single server queueing situation with Poisson arrivals and Poisson service. In particular, the calling units are the broken Gringo Machinos. The service mechanism is a service engineer who goes from broken machine to broken machine repairing them. Uta Woo, from records collected by Mañana, knows that these Gringo Machinos break down randomly at a rate of .20 machines per hour. In other words, $\lambda = .20$. Using another time frame, it could be said that there is an average of 1.6 breakdowns in an eight-hour day. There are a host of reasons for the breakdowns and thus each machine requires a different amount of time for repair. Uta Woo has only two service engineers that can be assigned to Novo Hamburgo. The number of engineers who can serve in this area is limited because the engineer must be somewhat conversant in two languages. The ace service engineer is El Nathan who can repair Gringo Machinos at an average rate of .30 machines per hour, that is, $\mu = .30$. The other service engineer, affectionately known as Slobbering Salivor, can repair Gringo Machinos at an average rate of .21 machines per hour. Uta Woo must ultimately decide which of these two will be the Novo Hamburgo service engineer. In succeeding sections the salaries of these two engineers and some of the details of Uta Woo's service contract with the lessees will be disclosed. At this point it is merely desired to determine waiting line lengths and waiting times if either of these two engineers were sent to Novo Hamburgo.

Equations (10–1) through (10–7) will now be employed to describe the results if Salivor were designated as the service engineer. These equations may be employed because the arrival rate of $\lambda = .20$ is less than the service rate of $\mu = .21$. Assuming Salivor had been on the job for some time, the following statements could be made with regard to the state of affairs. The average number of machines in the queueing system would be

$$L = \frac{\lambda}{\mu - \lambda}$$

$$= \frac{.20}{.21 - .20} = 20 \text{ machines}$$

The average number of machines actually waiting in the queue would be

$$L_q = \frac{\lambda^2}{\mu(\mu - \lambda)}$$

$$= \frac{.20^2}{(.21)(.21 - .20)} = 19 \text{ machines}$$

The average amount of time a machine spends in the queueing system (waiting line and service mechanism combined) is

$$W = \frac{1}{\mu - \lambda}$$

$$= \frac{1}{.21 - .20} = 100 \text{ hours}$$

This means that on the average it is 100 hours from the time the lessee reports a broken Gringo Machino to the time when Salivor has it operating. The average amount of time a machine spends in the queue is

$$W_q = \frac{\lambda}{\mu(\mu - \lambda)}$$

$$= \frac{.20}{(.21)(.21 - .20)} = 95.2 \text{ hours}$$

If Uta Woo were interested in knowing what the probability is of having exactly n machines in the queueing system, this could be found by

$$P(n) = \left(\frac{\lambda}{\mu}\right)^n \left(1 - \frac{\lambda}{\mu}\right)$$

$$= \left(\frac{.20}{.21}\right)^n \left(1 - \frac{.20}{.21}\right)$$

$$= (.95^n)(.05)$$

For example, the probability of there being $n = 0$ machines in the queueing system would be

$$P(0) = (.95^0)(.05) = .05$$

That is, there is a probability of .05 that no machine is waiting to be repaired or is actually being repaired. The probability that k or more machines are in the queueing system is given by

$$P(n \geq k) = \left(\frac{\lambda}{\mu}\right)^k$$
$$= \left(\frac{.20}{.21}\right)^k$$

Using this the probability of there being 5 or more machines in the queueing system at one time is

$$P(n \geq 5) = \left(\frac{.20}{.21}\right)^5 = .78$$

Finally, the utilization ratio with Salivor functioning as the service mechanism is

$$U = \frac{\lambda}{\mu}$$
$$= \frac{.20}{.21} = .95$$

This means that Salivor will be busy 95 percent of the time spent on the job.

El Nathan if assigned to the Novo Hamburgo job would service Gringo Machinos at an average rate of .30 per hour. El Nathan is about fifty percent faster than Salivor. Equations (10–1) through (10–7) yield the following when El Nathan functions as the service mechanism. The average number of breakdowns per hour is $\lambda = .20$ and the average number of machines that can be serviced per hour is $\mu = .30$. Then the average number of machines in the queueing system is

$$L = \frac{.20}{.30 - .20} = 2 \text{ machines}$$

The average number of machines in the queue is

$$L_q = \frac{.20^2}{(.30)(.30-.20)} = 1.33 \text{ machines}$$

The average amount of time a machine spends in the queueing system is

$$W = \frac{1}{.30-.20} = 10 \text{ hours}$$

The average amount of time a machine spends in the queue waiting for service is

$$W_q = \frac{.20}{(.30)(.30-.20)} = 6.66 \text{ hours}$$

The probability of exactly n machines being in the queueing system is

$$P(n) = \left(\frac{.20}{.30}\right)^n \left(1 - \frac{.20}{.30}\right)$$
$$= (.67^n)(.33)$$

For example, the probability of there being $n = 0$ machines in the system is

$$P(0) = (.67^0)(.33) = .33$$

The probability of there being k or more machines in the system is

$$P(n \geq k) = \left(\frac{.20}{.30}\right)^k$$

For example, the probability of there being 5 or more in the system with El Nathan as the engineer is

$$P(n \geq 5) = \left(\frac{.20}{.30}\right)^5 = .13$$

Finally, the utilization ratio is

$$U = \frac{.20}{.30} = .67$$

indicating that El Nathan would be busy 67 percent of the time spent on the job.

The results of assigning Salivor and El Nathan have now been detailed by means of Equations (10–1) through (10–7). As of yet economics have not been introduced into the picture; the queueing situations have been merely described in terms of queue lengths, waiting times, and the like. In the section to follow the economic implications will be introduced. In some queueing situations the waiting costs and service costs are difficult to determine. When this is the case management may wish to make a decision on the basis of the kind of information that has already been determined. For example, Uta Woo may establish a service level policy which stipulates that the average time a machine is in the system must not exceed two days (sixteen hours). If this policy had been extant it is obvious that Uta Woo must send El Nathan or someone who is only slightly slower. On the other hand, if it posed no problem in terms of customer relations if the average time in the system were two or three weeks, then Salivor could be sent.

Before examining the economic implications, something should be mentioned concerning the relationship between the utilization ratio U and the average number of units in the system which is L. Since U is λ/μ it should be apparent that the average number of calling units in the system would be small if U is relatively small. This is because U is only small when μ is much larger than λ. For example, if arrivals averaged 1 per hour and the service mechanism could service an average of 10 per hour, then U would be small and one would not expect much of a waiting line to build up thus resulting in a small L. In fact, the average number of calling units in the system would be $L = \lambda/(\mu-\lambda) = 1/(10-1) = .11$. In this case the utilization ratio is $U = \lambda/\mu = 1/10 = .1$. On the other hand, if there were an average of 9 arrivals per hour and service took place at an average of 10 per hour, then the average number of units in the system would be substantially increased. Here the utilization ratio is .9 and the average number of units in the system is $L = 9$. This demonstrates by example that L increases as U increases.

Analysts have found that L may be expressed in terms of U, that is, an alternative formula for L is

$$L = U/(1-U) \tag{10–8}$$

Using this formula, L can be found for any utilization ratio. In Figure 10.4 an assortment of values for U are given with the corresponding values for L. These are then graphed showing that the number of calling units in any queueing system of the variety being discussed is quite limited as long as the utilization ratio is below .8 or so. When U gets larger than .90 the average number of calling units in the system jumps dramatically. This graph provides a valuable insight into the management of queueing systems. If a queueing system is operating with a relatively small U, then decreasing this U by increasing the service rate μ will result in only a minimal reduction in the average number of units in the system. For example, reducing U from .4 to .3 reduces the average number in the system from .67 to .43 calling units. On the other hand, if the queueing system is operating with a U near unity, then any improvement in μ which in turn reduces U will have a dramatic effect in reducing the average number of units in the system. Witness that reducing U from .99 to .90 has the effect of reducing L from 99 to 9 calling units. As a rule of thumb it can be stated that when the utilization ratio is near unity, then it will pay to increase the service capability. When the utilization ratio is relatively small it is doubtful that it would be economically wise to increase the service rate μ.

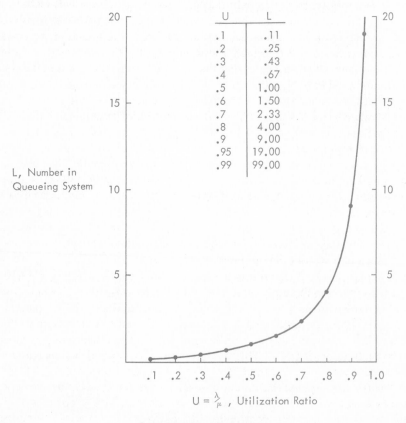

FIGURE 10.4   U versus L

CHAPTER 10

10.4 ECONOMIC IMPLICATIONS

In the Gringo Machino situation faced by Uta Woo the service costs and waiting costs are fairly easy to determine. The lessees in the Novo Hamburgo area have negotiated a service contract with Uta Woo which stipulates that Uta Woo must pay a lessee $5 for each hour during the working day its leased Gringo Machino is down. The lessees, who had been complaining about the service rendered by Mañana Ltd., believe that this kind of penalty inflicted upon Uta Woo will be sufficient incentive for Uta Woo to get the broken copying machines fixed in a reasonable amount of time. Notice that the penalty of $5 per hour applies only to the period of the eight working hours in a day. If a lessee reported an inoperative Gringo Machino at 4 p.m. and if the Uta Woo service engineer had it fixed by 10 a.m. the next morning, the total penalty would be only $10 as the machine would be down for only two hours during the standard working day which ends at 5 p.m. and begins at 9 a.m. The waiting costs can be easily determined with this service contract in force.

Before determining the waiting costs precipitated by a day's activity, consider the service costs. Salivor draws a salary from Uta Woo which amounts to $6 an hour. El Nathan's annual salary is equivalent to a wage of $12 per hour. Both service engineers are expected to be on duty for eight hours each day.

In attempting to select a service engineer for the Novo Hamburgo job, Uta Woo has decided to base the economic analysis on the happenings of an average day. Both service costs and waiting costs must be considered.

Service Costs for a Day of Operations

Since a working day consists of eight hours, the service cost for a day of operations when Salivor is the service mechanism is

$$\text{Daily Service Cost with Salivor} = (8 \text{ hours})(\$6 \text{ per hour}) = \$48$$

The service cost for a day of operations when El Nathan is functioning as the service mechanism is

$$\text{Daily Service Cost with El Nathan} = (8 \text{ hours})(\$12 \text{ per hour}) = \$96$$

If there were no waiting costs then it would obviously be advantageous to send Salivor since it only costs $48 a day to keep Salivor on duty in Novo Hamburgo.

Waiting Costs for a Day of Operations

In Section 10.3 it was stated that the Gringo Machinos break down at a rate of .20 machines per hour, that is, $\lambda = .20$. This means that these machines "arrive" at the service mechanism at a rate of .20 per hour, or equivalently, at a rate of 1.6 machines per eight-hour day. Also in Section 10.3 the average waiting time, W, in the queueing system for a broken machine was computed using Equation (10–3). The W for the case when Salivor was assumed to be the service mechanism or server proved to be 100 hours. The W for El Nathan was only 10 hours.

Focus now on the situation if Salivor were assigned to the Novo Hamburgo job. Since 1.6 broken machines "arrive" on the average each day, and since each broken machine spends an average of 100 "business day" hours in the queueing system, it follows that an average day of operation precipitates 160 hours of waiting time. The service contract stipulates that Uta Woo must compensate the lessees at the rate of $5 for every hour the lessee does not have the use of a machine during the 8-hour business day. This means that one day of operations with Salivor on duty generates ($5)(160) or $800 in waiting costs. In summary, the average waiting costs per day is found by

$$\begin{matrix} \text{Daily Average} \\ \text{Waiting Costs with} \\ \text{Salivor} \end{matrix} = \begin{pmatrix} \text{Average Number} \\ \text{of Arrivals} \\ \text{per day} \end{pmatrix} \begin{pmatrix} \text{Average Waiting} \\ \text{Time in System} \\ \text{per Arrival, } W \end{pmatrix} \begin{pmatrix} \text{Cost per} \\ \text{Hour of} \\ \text{Waiting} \end{pmatrix}$$

$$= (1.6)(100)(5)$$
$$= \$800$$

The same sort of analysis may now be performed with regard to El Nathan. With El Nathan on the job there are still an average of 1.6 breakdowns per day, and the service contract still stipulates a penalty of $5 per hour of waiting time. The only thing that differs is W which is 10 hours per machine when El Nathan is on duty as opposed to an average waiting time of 100 hours per machine for Salivor. Therefore, for El Nathan,

$$\begin{matrix} \text{Daily Average} \\ \text{Waiting Costs with} \\ \text{El Nathan} \end{matrix} = \begin{pmatrix} 1.6 \; \begin{matrix} \text{Arrivals} \\ \text{per day} \end{matrix} \end{pmatrix} \begin{pmatrix} 10 \; \begin{matrix} \text{Hours Wait} \\ \text{per arrival} \end{matrix} \end{pmatrix} \begin{pmatrix} \$5 \text{ per Hour} \end{pmatrix}$$

$$= \$80$$

Total Costs for a Day of Operations

From the foregoing analysis it is quite clear that the assignment of Salivor as service engineer would result in low service costs and high waiting costs while the assignment of El Nathan would produce relatively high service costs and low waiting costs. Refer back to Figure 10.1 and notice that with a low rate of service (as in the case of Salivor) one can expect low service costs and high waiting costs. Where a high rate of service exists (as in the case of El Nathan) the waiting costs are low and the service costs are high. A decision as to which engineer to assign must now be made on the basis of total costs.

Total costs are found by summing service costs and waiting costs. Hence,

$$\begin{matrix} \text{Daily Average Total} \\ \text{Costs with Salivor} \end{matrix} = \begin{matrix} \text{Daily Service Cost} \\ \text{with Salivor} \end{matrix} + \begin{matrix} \text{Daily Average Waiting} \\ \text{Costs with Salivor} \end{matrix}$$

$$= \$48 + \$800$$
$$= \$848$$

and,

$$\begin{array}{rl} \text{Daily Average Total} \\ \text{Costs with El Nathan} \end{array} = \begin{array}{l} \text{Daily Service Cost} \\ \text{with El Nathan} \end{array} + \begin{array}{l} \text{Daily Average Waiting} \\ \text{Costs with El Nathan} \end{array}$$
$$= \$96 + \$80$$
$$= \$176$$

Under the circumstances it would cost Uta Woo $848 per day to service the Gringo Machinos of Novo Hamburgo if Salivor were the service engineer, and $176 per day on the average if El Nathan were the service representative. Therefore, Uta Woo should assign El Nathan to this job.

Unfortunately the matter does not end here as the resourceful Salivor will come up with a plan in the next section which would seemingly indicate that he should get the desirable Novo Hamburgo assignment.

10.5 A TWO-SERVER QUEUEING MODEL

Figure 10.5 depicts a queueing situation where there are two servers or channels of service. Though there are two servers, there is only one queue or waiting line. Both servers are fed from the single queue. The assumptions upon which the conclusions of this section rest are essentially the same as those for the single-server model. Calling units arrive from the input source according to a Poisson process. The average rate of arrivals is denoted by λ. Each of the two servers has the capability of serving the calling units at the same rate. The service rate for each server is denoted by μ. Assuming the servers are kept busy, the served units depart from each of the servers according to a Poisson process. (With respect to the servers it may equivalently be said that the service times for each are exponentially distributed.)

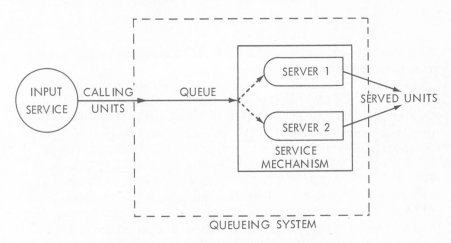

FIGURE 10.5   A Two-Server Queueing Model

From these assumptions a mathematical queueing model can be constructed. From this model several conclusions can be drawn. Let

$$\lambda = \text{average arrival rate}$$
$$\mu = \text{average service rate for a server}$$

After the two-server queueing system has been in operation for a while,

$$P_o = \text{probability that zero calling units are in the queueing system}$$

$$P_o = \cfrac{1}{\left[1 + \cfrac{\lambda}{\mu} + \cfrac{(\lambda/\mu)^2}{2-\lambda/\mu}\right]} \qquad (10\text{--}9)$$

$$L_q = \text{average number of calling units waiting in the queue}$$

$$L_q = \left[\frac{(\lambda/\mu)^3}{(2 - \lambda/\mu)^2}\right](P_o) \qquad (10\text{--}10)$$

$$L = \text{average number of calling units in the queueing system}$$

$$L = L_q + \frac{\lambda}{\mu} \qquad (10\text{--}11)$$

$$W_q = \text{average time a calling unit spends waiting in the queue}$$

$$W_q = \frac{L_q}{\lambda} \qquad (10\text{--}12)$$

$$W = \text{average time a calling unit spends in the queueing system}$$

$$W = \frac{L}{\lambda} \qquad (10\text{--}13)$$

These formulas serve to characterize the conditions which prevail in the two-server queueing model.

In the Uta Woo case of the two preceeding sections it was stated that there were only two potential candidates for the Novo Hamburgo service engineer job. That statement was not quite accurate. Salivor has an identical twin brother who can also service Gringo Machinos. Dili, who is the twin brother, can service Gringo Machinos at the rate of .21 per hour which is the same service rate that Salivor works at. Each twin also draws a salary of $6 per hour. Salivor told Dili of Uta Woo's decision to send El Nathan to Novo Hamburgo. Dili then suggested to Salivor the possibility of both the twins going to Novo Hamburgo instead of El Nathan. He reasoned that it would cost Uta Woo the same in wages to send them as it would to send El Nathan who draws $12 per hour. The Dalli Twins (Dalli is their surname) then approached Uta Woo's management with their idea.

In essence the Dalli Twins have suggested that the single-server system with El Nathan be replaced with a two-server system utilizing the twins as servers. The economic implications of the single-server system with El Nathan as server have already been studied. It was found that such a system would cost Uta Woo $176 per day. The two-server model will now be employed to analyze the new option that the Twins have suggested.

Equations (10–9) through (10–13) may be used to analyze the two-server system with Salivor and Dili acting as the two servers. The average hourly arrival rate or breakdown rate is still $\lambda = .20$. The average service rate for each of the twins is $\mu = .21$. The probability that no Gringo Machinos will be in the queueing system is

$$P_0 = \cfrac{1}{\left[1 + \cfrac{.20}{.21} + \cfrac{\left(\cfrac{.20}{.21}\right)^2}{\left(2 - \cfrac{.20}{.21}\right)} \right]}$$

$$= .355$$

The average number of machines waiting in the queue will be

$$L_q = \left[\cfrac{\left(\cfrac{.20}{.21}\right)^3}{\left(2 - \cfrac{.20}{.21}\right)^2} \right] (.355)$$

$$= .28$$

The average number of machines in the queueing system will be

$$L = L_q + \frac{\lambda}{\mu}$$

$$= .28 + \frac{.20}{.21}$$

$$= 1.23$$

The average amount of time a broken machine will spend waiting in the queue is

$$W_q = \frac{L_q}{\lambda}$$

$$= \frac{.28}{.20}$$

$$= 1.40 \text{ hours}$$

Finally, the average amount of time a machine will spend in the queueing system is

$$W = \frac{L}{\lambda}$$

$$= \frac{1.23}{.20}$$

$$= 6.15 \text{ hours}$$

What would be the cost of sending the Dalli Twins to Novo Hamburgo? Considering an average eight-hour day, the total service cost would equal

$$\text{Daily Service Cost with Twins} = (8 \text{ hours})(\$6 + \$6)$$
$$= \$96.00$$

since the twins each draw $6 an hour. The waiting costs would be

$$\text{Daily Average Waiting Costs with Twins} = \left(1.6 \frac{\text{Arrivals}}{\text{per Day}}\right) \left(6.15 \frac{\text{Hour Wait}}{\text{per Arrival}}\right) \left(\$5 \text{ per hour}\right)$$
$$= \$49.20$$

Hence the total daily costs would average to 96.00 + 49.20 or $145.20 with the two-server system. Recall that the average daily cost under the single-server system with El Nathan was $176. Cost conscious Uta Woo therefore is ready to install this two-server system instead of the single server system.

When El Nathan was advised that he would not be assigned to Novo Hamburgo, he dipped the tongs of cold logic into his great boiling cauldron of experience and pulled out a startling alternative. El Nathan reasoned that if he were given an unskilled assistant who was a native of Novo Hamburgo, this assistant (being familiar with the roads and able to offer limited help in the repair of machines) would increase El Nathan's service rate from .30 machines per hour to μ = .42. Such an assistant could be employed for the sum of $1.50 an hour. El Nathan brought this proposal to Uta Woo's headquarters.

When the Dalli Twins heard of El Nathan's proposal they snickered because they knew that El Nathan would not get the job. The Twins' reasoning went something like this. El Nathan's new single-server system has a service rate of μ = .42, and the combined wages of El Nathan and the assistant would be 12.00 + 1.50 or $13.50 per hour. If the Twins went, each contributes a service rate of μ = .21 which when added gives .42. Thus the Twins believed they could equal El Nathan in the domain of waiting costs. However, their total wages would be only 6 + 6 or $12 per hour. Since the Twins figured they could service machines as fast as El Nathan and since service costs with the Twins would be less, they were confident that the two of them would get the assignment. It will now be demonstrated that this reasoning is faulty.

A single-server system with λ = .20 and μ = .42 yields an average waiting time for a machine in the queueing system of

$$W = \frac{1}{\mu - \lambda}$$

See Equation (10–3). Therefore, the single-server team of El Nathan and assistant will yield a W of

$$W = \frac{1}{.42 - .20}$$
$$= 4.55 \text{ hours}$$

Notice that this is less than the W of the two-server queueing system using Salivor and Dili which was 6.15 hours!

The cost to keep El Nathan and assistant in the field for a day can now be determined. The service costs are

$$\text{Daily Service Cost with El Nathan \& Assistant} = (8 \text{ hours})(\$12.00 + \$1.50)$$
$$= \$108.00$$

The waiting costs are

$$\text{Daily Average Waiting Costs with El Nathan \& Assistant} = \left(1.6 \frac{\text{Arrivals}}{\text{per Day}}\right)\left(4.55 \frac{\text{Hour Wait}}{\text{per Arrival}}\right)(\$5 \text{ per Hour})$$
$$= \$36.40$$

Thus the total average daily costs for the El Nathan and assistant single-server system is 108.00 + 36.40 or $144.40. This figure is slightly less than the $145.20 average daily cost afforded by the two-server system. Therefore, El Nathan goes to Novo Hamburgo.

Before concluding this section a principle may be gleaned from the example given. A single-server system with a service rate of $\mu = .42$ causes less waiting in the queueing system than a two-server system where each server is half as fast ($\mu = .21$). Many people would have guessed that there would be no difference between these two systems. A company, for example, trying to decide between a fast computer or two slower computers each of which are half as fast as the first would do better to buy the first assuming the price of the first were twice that of the slower. The basis for the advantage of one fast server over two half-as-fast servers will now be explored.

Suppose that the MOD 100 computer can make 100 calculations in an hour and the MOD 50 can make 50 calculations in an hour. Let us see why one MOD 100 is better than a pair of MOD 50 computers. If there were two problems each requiring 100 calculations, a system with one MOD 100 would complete the two problems successively in a total of two hours. The pair of MOD 50's would work the two problems simultaneously and complete them in two hours also. In this situation the MOD 100 offers no speed advantage over the pair of MOD 50 computers. In fact, as long as there are two or more problems (calling units) in the system, the pair of MOD 50's will keep abreast of the MOD 100. However, what if there is only one problem requiring 100 calculations? The MOD 100 will complete it in an hour while the pair of MOD 50's will take two hours to complete it since the problem can be handled by only one of the two MOD 50's. Therefore, when one calling unit is in the system the MOD 100 is superior to the pair of MOD 50's. When zero or more than one calling units are in the system, the MOD 100 and pair of MOD 50's are equivalent. Since there are occasions when only one calling unit is in the system, it can be concluded that the MOD 100 is preferable. On the basis of this kind of reasoning, which is implicitly incorporated in the queueing model formulas, it turns out that assigning El Nathan and assistant to the Novo Hamburgo job is to be preferred over the assignment of the Dalli Twins. This is the case even when the service costs for El Nathan and assistant are slightly higher.

In conclusion, when managing a queueing system one should always be aware that there are two alternatives available for increasing the service rate. More servers can be added and/or the current server(s) can be made more efficient through the use of more training, assistance, or equipment. The models and mode of analysis presented in these sections makes possible the cost comparison of such methods for increasing service rates.

10.6 THE SIMULATION OF A QUEUEING SYSTEM

This chapter will be concluded with two examples where Monte Carlo simulation is used to analyze queueing problems. Very often the real situation management encounters does not satisfy all of the assumptions required by any of the numerous mathematical queueing models which have been developed. In these cases the analyst must resort to simulation in order to understand the operation of a queueing system. The simulated model then becomes the basis for guidance in making decisions. A simple simulation model will be considered in this section and then a slightly more complicated model will be presented in the last section of the chapter.

Vast expanses and the lack of highways necessitate the wide use of small planes in Alaska. Fairbanks North is a company which rents plane and pilot on a daily basis to traders, hunters, and business people. Currently Fairbanks North has two planes available for rental. Scott-Doolittle & Co. is a large aviation rental firm of which Fairbanks North is a subsidiary. Scott-Doolittle makes the two planes available to Fairbanks North for a period of forty days each year. This period coincides with the peak season for plane rentals in Alaska. Presently Fairbanks North rents bush pilot and plane for $300 per day plus fuel. Sometimes a renter appears but both of the planes have already been rented for the day. For such situations Fairbanks North has a policy of refunding to the renter the sum of $50 for each day the renter must wait before getting a plane. Thus a renter who would have to wait two days would have to pay merely $200 plus fuel.

The total daily cost to keep a single plane and pilot on hand or in operation is $100. In anticipation of another year of operations, Fairbanks North is interested in several matters. In particular,

1. How busy will the company be with just two planes available for rent?
2. What is the expected profit from the operation of two planes for a season of forty days?
3. Should another plane be added to the rental operation?

Before commencing with the simulation analysis leading to the answers to these questions, the various components of the ensuing queueing model must be identified. The calling units are the renters who need the use of a plane and pilot. Renters desiring the services of Fairbanks North arrive randomly at the Fairbanks airport. Here the renters wait in a queue till one of the planes becomes available. As Fairbanks North has two planes there are two servers in this situation. A renter begins service upon boarding the plane for the day's flight.

From a knowledge of the number of renters likely to show up in a day during the flying season, Fairbanks North has assessed a probability distribution for the number of renters which will seek their services in a day. (See Section 12.3 of Chapter 12 for the technique of assessing such a probability distribution.) This distribution of arrivals is given in Table 10.1. Notice, for example, that the probability of no renters requesting a plane on a given day is .10 while the probability of exactly three arrivals in a day is .30.

TABLE 10.1
Distribution of Arrivals
per Day

A	P(A)	RN
0	.10	00–09
1	.20	10–29
2	.30	30–59
3	.30	60–89
4	.10	90–99
	1.00	

The simulation of this queueing situation is quite easy. The entire season of forty days is simulated in the work sheet of Table 10.2. To begin, a set of random numbers is associated with each of the outcomes in the probability distribution of arrivals. These random number assignments are given in Table 10.1. This is in accord with the method of Monte Carlo simulation which was explained in detail in Chapter 5.

Turning to the work sheet of Table 10.2, one row is alloted for each day of the season. A random number (*RN*) is then placed in each row under Column (2). This random number will be used to determine the number of arrivals in a particular day. The process of simulation will now be illustrated on a day-by-day basis.

TABLE 10.2
Simulation of a Two-Server Queueing System

Day (1)	RN (2)	No. of Arrivals (Renters) (3)	No. of Renters Left from Yesterday (4)	Total No. of Renters Waiting (5)	No. of Renters Served Today (6)	No. of Renters Left for Later (7)
1	26	1	0	1	1	0
2	63	3	0	3	2	1
3	92	4	1	5	2	3
4	29	1	3	4	2	2
5	72	3	2	5	2	3

(continued)

Day (1)	RN (2)	No. of Arrivals (Renters) (3)	No. of Renters Left from Yesterday (4)	Total No. of Renters Waiting (5)	No. of Renters Served Today (6)	No. of Renters Left for Later (7)
6	36	2	3	5	2	3
7	02	0	3	3	2	1
8	95	4	1	5	2	3
9	63	3	3	6	2	4
10	34	2	4	6	2	4
11	53	2	4	6	2	4
12	16	1	4	5	2	3
13	46	2	3	5	2	3
14	38	2	3	5	2	3
15	69	3	3	6	2	4
16	58	3	4	7	2	5
17	95	4	5	9	2	7
18	44	2	7	9	2	7
19	59	2	7	9	2	7
20	89	3	7	10	2	8
21	87	3	8	11	2	9
22	59	2	9	11	2	9
23	73	3	9	12	2	10
24	19	1	10	11	2	9
25	45	2	9	11	2	9
26	57	2	9	11	2	9
27	68	3	9	12	2	10
28	01	0	10	10	2	8
29	07	0	8	8	2	6
30	86	3	6	9	2	7
31	47	2	7	9	2	7
32	86	3	7	10	2	8
33	74	3	8	11	2	9
34	16	1	9	10	2	8
35	34	2	8	10	2	8
36	57	2	8	10	2	8
37	92	4	8	12	2	10
38	19	1	10	11	2	9
39	64	3	9	12	2	10
40	57	2	10	12	2	10
41		0	10	10	2	8
42		0	8	8	2	6
43		0	6	6	2	4
44		0	4	4	2	2
45		0	2	2	2	0
					89	268

DAY 1

Column (1) is used to identify the day. In Column (2) is found the randomly selected number for each day. The *RN* for Day 1 is 26. When 26 is compared to the distribution of Table 10.1 it indicates that the number of arriving renters on the first day is to be 1. In Column (3) the number of arrivals is recorded. Column (4) gives the number of renters left from earlier days. These are renters that have not yet been served. Since there are no renters left from earlier days, a 0 is placed in Column (4). The total number of renters requiring service is recorded in Column (5). The entry in Column (5) is merely the sum of the new arrivals, from Column (3), and the leftovers, from Column (4). Fairbanks North has only two planes each of which can service only one renter in a day. Therefore the maximum number of services in a day will be 2. The entry in Column (6) records how many renters are serviced on the day in question. A 1 is placed in Column (6) since there is only one renter requiring service in Day 1. Finally, the number of renters still waiting to be served at the end of the day is recorded in Column (7). This quantity will equal the entry in Column (5) minus the entry of Column (6). For Day 1 there are no renters left unserviced.

DAY 2

The random number of 63 when compared to the distribution of arrivals indicates that there are 3 arrivals in Day 2. The number of renters left from Day 1 is 0 as is seen in Column (7) for Day 1. Thus enter 0 in Column (4). The total number of renters waiting is 3. The number of renters served is 2 which is the maximum that can be served in a day. Hence 1 renter is left for the next day.

DAY 3

Day 3 sees the arrival of 4 renters. As there was 1 renter left from Day 2, there are a total of 5 needing service. Only 2 renters can be serviced leaving 3 to be served at a later date.

The simulation process continues in like manner till the fortieth day when there are 2 arrivals. At the end of Day 40 there are 10 renters still waiting for service. Thus Fairbanks North must keep working for the next five days in order to reduce the queue to zero calling units. There are no arrivals in these last five days as the last renter came on Day 40 which was the close of the season.

From Table 10.2 it is quite apparent that the waiting line had a tendency to slowly grow. The fact that it got no longer than it did was due to the limit of forty days in the rental traveling season. The reason for this growth in the queue must lie in the relationship between the arrival rate and the service rate. Fairbanks North can provide service at the rate of 2 per day. However, the expected number of arrivals per day is 2.1 renters. This is determined by computing the expected value of A whose distribution is given in Table 10.1:

$$\begin{aligned} E(A) &= (0)(.10) + (1)(.20) + (2)(.30) + (3)(.30) + (4)(.10) \\ &= 2.1 \end{aligned}$$

where A is the random variable denoting the number of arrivals in a day. Since the average rate of arrivals exceeds the service rate, the queue will continue to grow as long as the queueing system is in operation.

Fairbanks North initially wished to know how busy the company would be with two planes available for rent. From the work sheet it is seen that for this simulation run they were working at capacity every day except the first. Knowing the relationship between the arrival rate and service rate, it would be unnecessary to execute more simulations in order to come to a general conclusion as to how busy they would be with two servers.

Consider next the economic implications of this two-server system. By summing Column (6) the total number of calling units served in the season is determined. The total revenue, at $300 per renter served, would be $26,700 which is the product of 89 and 300. Notice that there were 89 renters served. From this must be subtracted the operating costs and payments for delays. The operating costs are $100 per plane per day. Since there were two planes working for 45 days, the total service cost or total operating cost is

$$\begin{aligned} \text{Total Operating Cost} \atop \text{(Service Cost)} &= (45 \text{ Days})(2 \text{ Teams})(\$100 \text{ per Day}) \\ &= \$9,000 \end{aligned}$$

Fairbanks North paid a renter $50 for each day of waiting. The entries in Column (7) indicate how many renters were left waiting at the end of each day. The total of this column is 268 meaning that in 268 instances Fairbanks North had to remit a sum of $50 to a renter because of delays. The total waiting cost is therefore

$$\begin{aligned} \text{Total Delay Payments} \atop \text{(Waiting Costs)} &= (268)(\$50) \\ &= \$13,400 \end{aligned}$$

The resulting net profit for the simulated season of Table 10.2 is

Gross Revenue	$26,700
Less	
Total Operating Costs	− 9,000
Total Delay Payments	−13,400
Net Profit	$ 4,300

To get a good fix on the true expected net profit for a season with two servers, several more simulation runs should be performed. The net profit for these runs should then be averaged to provide Fairbanks North with a good estimate of net profits.

In the last place Fairbanks North had wondered if an extra plane should be added to the operation. By means of simulation a three-server system can easily be analyzed. In Table 10.3 the same random numbers as were used in Table 10.2 are used as the basis of a simulation with three planes. The number of renters that can be served in a day is now 3. A perusal of this work sheet indicates that on only 19 of the 40 days were all three planes used. Only 5 renters were delayed in this simulation run. An economic analysis similar to that performed for the two-server model reveals

TABLE 10.3
Simulation of a Three-Server Queueing System

Day (1)	RN (2)	No. of Arrivals (Renters) (3)	No. of Renters Left from Yesterday (4)	Total No. of Renters Waiting (5)	No. of Renters Served Today (6)	No. of Renters Left for Later (7)
1	26	1	0	1	1	0
2	63	3	0	3	3	0
3	92	4	0	4	3	1
4	29	1	1	2	2	0
5	72	3	0	3	3	0
6	36	2	0	2	2	0
7	02	0	0	0	0	0
8	95	4	0	4	3	1
9	63	3	1	4	3	1
10	34	2	1	3	3	0
11	53	2	0	2	2	0
12	16	1	0	1	1	0
13	46	2	0	2	2	0
14	38	2	0	2	2	0
15	69	3	0	3	3	0
16	58	3	0	3	3	0
17	95	4	0	4	3	1
18	44	2	1	3	3	0
19	59	2	0	2	2	0
20	89	3	0	3	3	0
21	87	3	0	3	3	0
22	59	2	0	2	2	0
23	73	3	0	3	3	0
24	19	1	0	1	1	0
25	45	2	0	2	2	0
26	57	2	0	2	2	0
27	68	3	0	3	3	0
28	01	0	0	0	0	0
29	07	0	0	0	0	0
30	86	3	0	3	3	0
31	47	2	0	2	2	0
32	86	3	0	3	3	0
33	74	3	0	3	3	0
34	16	1	0	1	1	0
35	34	2	0	2	2	0
36	57	2	0	2	2	0
37	92	4	0	4	3	1
38	19	1	1	2	2	0
39	64	3	0	3	3	0
40	57	2	0	2	2	0
					89	5

Gross Revenue, (89)(300)	$26,700
Less	
Total Operating Costs, (40)(3)(100)	−12,000
Total Delay Payments, (5)(50)	− 250
Net Profit	$14,450

Another few simulation runs would yield a good picture of what Fairbanks North could expect with three teams in action. Even without further simulations one would feel confident in recommending a three-server system over a two-server system. Since waiting costs are almost nonexistent with a three-server system, it would not be necessary to explore the economic ramifications of a four-server system.

10.7 ANOTHER QUEUEING SIMULATION

Inspector Colosse Incorporated runs a chain of automobile inspection stations in the state of New York. Each registered automobile must pass a safety inspection once each year. Typically the state inspections are performed at service stations. Motorists are often forced to wait in long lines to get their vehicles inspected at the service station since most service station operators view inspections as a low priority service. Inspector Colosse Inc. has therefore opened this chain of inspection stations which are dedicated to fast, honest inspections as there seems to be a substantial interest in such a service.

ICI is planning a new inspection station and must determine how to staff this facility. ICI advertises that there is only a ten percent chance that a motorist will have to wait more than five minutes before the inspection process is begun. Furthermore, ICI claims that after the inspection process is begun there will be no interruptions since the inspector will stay with the job till completed. ICI also offers minor repair services in connection with the inspection. If an automobile fails inspection for such reasons as defective wiper blades, improperly aimed headlights, and the like, ICI will make the repair at the time of inspection if the motorist so desires. How many inspectors should ICI employ for its new inspection/repair station if it wishes to live up to its advertised claims?

Based on previous experience, ICI feels that the distribution of time between the arrivals of motorists has the distribution given in Table 10.4. (Notice that in previous examples the arrival information was given in the form of "arrivals per time period." Here the times between arrivals, or interarrival times, are used to describe the manner in which calling units arrive. Both ways are legitimate methods of describing arrivals. However, the interarrival time approach is usually better adapted to simulating complex queueing systems.) According to this probability distribution of interarrival times, for example, there is a probability of .1 that the time between arriving automobiles seeking an inspection is 30 minutes. The probability is .1 that 0 minutes will separate two successive arrivals, this indicates that two vehicles arrive simultaneously. Random numbers have been associated with each of the interarrival times for the sake of the Monte Carlo simulation to follow.

TABLE 10.4
Interarrival Times for Vehicles

Time	Probability	Random Number
0 min.	.1	0
5	.1	1
10	.1	2
15	.1	3
20	.1	4
25	.1	5
30	.1	6
35	.1	7
40	.1	8
45	.1	9
	1.0	

Table 10.5 gives several probability distributions which have implications for service times. In Table 10.5(a) the distribution of inspection times is given. Here it is seen that it takes an inspector 10, 15, or 20 minutes to complete an inspection. The probabilities of these times are .4, .5, and .1, respectively. In Table 10.5(b) the probability of there being a minor problem with the inspected vehicle is given. The probability of no minor problems (which means that there is either no problem or a major problem) is .7. If a minor problem does not exist, ICI does nothing more than an inspection. The probability of a minor problem with the vehicle is .3. If an automobile has a minor problem, the motorist may or

TABLE 10.5
Distributions Related to Service

(a)

Inspection Time	Probability	RN
10 min.	.4	0–3
15	.5	4–8
20	.1	9
	1.0	

(b)

Minor Problem?	Probability	RN
None	.7	0–6
Yes	.3	7–9
	1.0	

(c)

Repair?	Probability	RN
Yes	.8	0–7
No	.2	8–9
	1.0	

(d)

Repair Time	Probability	RN
5 min.	.2	1–2
10	.2	3–4
15	.2	5–6
20	.2	7–8
25	.2	9–0
	1.0	

may not wish ICI to make the repair. Table 10.5(c) gives the probability that the motorist would want ICI to make any needed repair. If ICI is to make the repair, Table 10.5(d) gives the distribution of repair times. These repair times are in addition to the inspection times. Repairs take place immediately upon the completion of inspection; the customer is not asked to wait for the repairing to commence.

ICI suspects that the optimal number of inspectors for the new station is two. It is desired to simulate the operation of the inspection station to see if two inspectors being on duty will insure that a customer has no more than a ten percent chance of waiting more than five minutes.

Table 10.6 presents a simulation worksheet for the ICI queueing situation. For each motorist entering the inspection station there is the potential need of using all five distributions that are given in Tables 10.4 and 10.5. Therefore it will be shown that a random number composed of five digits may be required for a given customer if a simulation is to be performed. In each row under Column (1) of the worksheet is given this five-digit random number (*RN*). In this work sheet a row will represent a motorist or vehicle, hence there will be a five-digit number given for each row. The simulation process will now be explained by working through the work sheet on a vehicle-by-vehicle basis.

First Vehicle

The random number for the first vehicle is 63213. The first digit, 6, is compared to the interarrival time distribution of Table 10.4 from which is found that the first vehicle arrives 30 minutes after the previous vehicle. Since this is the first vehicle of the day there is no previous vehicle. Hence it is assumed that this first vehicle arrives 30 minutes after the inspection station opens. Thus a 30 is entered in Column (2). In Column (3), which records the time of arrival, it is indicated that 30 minutes have elapsed since the opening of the station. The second digit, 3, of the random number is compared to Table 10.5(a) where the inspection time of 10 minutes is found. 10 is thus entered in Column (4). The third digit, 2, when compared to the distribution of Table 10.5(b) shows that the first vehicle did not have a minor problem. This is recorded in Column (5). Since no minor repair is indicated for the first vehicle, the last two random digits are not used and Columns (6) and (7) are not used. Column (8) records the total time the vehicle must be in the station. This total is found by adding the value of Column (4) to that of Column (7). The total is 10 minutes in this case. Neither inspector is busy so the first vehicle can be inspected immediately upon arrival. The vehicle goes to Inspector 1 who begins the inspection at 30 minutes after opening and finishes at 40 minutes after opening. Columns (9) and (10) are used to record the time when service begins and ends. Column (13) indicates the waiting time till inspection begins. For the first vehicle this waiting time is 0.

Second Vehicle

The random number is 81278 for the second vehicle. The first digit, 8, indicates that the interarrival time is 40 minutes. This means that the second vehicle arrives 40 minutes after the first vehicle arrived. Hence the time of arrival is 70 minutes as shown in Column (3). The second digit, 1, indicates that the

TABLE 10.6
Two-Server Queueing Simulation Work Sheet

Random Digits (1)*	Inter-arrival Time (2)	Time of Arrival (3)	Inspection Time (4)	Minor Problem? (5)	Repair? (6)	Repair Time (7)	Total Time (8)	Inspector 1 Begins (9)	Inspector 1 Ends (10)	Inspector 2 Begins (11)	Inspector 2 Ends (12)	Waiting Time (13)**
63213	30	30	10	None	—	—	10	30	40			0
81278	40	70	10	None	—	—	10			70	80	0
44455	20	90	15	None	—	—	15	90	105			0
99678	45	135	20	None	—	—	20			135	155	0
52301	25	160	10	None	—	—	10	160	170			0
58968	25	185	15	Yes	Yes	20	35			185	220	0
07774	0	185	15	Yes	Yes	10	25	185	210			0
36988	15	200	15	Yes	No	—	15	210	225			10
15533	5	205	15	None	—	—	15			220	235	15
71718	35	240	10	Yes	Yes	20	30	240	270			0

*First random digit for interarrival time
Second random digit for inspection time
Third random digit for existence of a minor problem
Fourth random digit for repair decision (if appropriate)
Fifth random digit for repair time (if appropriate)

**Waiting time found by comparing beginning of service to time of arrival inspection time is 10 minutes. The third digit, 2, indicates that no minor repairs are required. The last two digits are not needed. The total time required is 10 minutes. The second vehicle goes to Inspector 2 (it could have gone to the other inspector) who is not busy, thus service begins at the time of arrival which is at 70 minutes after the station opened. Service ends at 80 minutes and there was no wait.

Third, Fourth, and Fifth Vehicles

None of these vehicles required repair service and none had to wait for service to begin. Rows 3, 4, and 5 of the worksheet give the details.

Sixth Vehicle

The random number for this vehicle is 58968. The first digit, 5, indicates the interarrival time to be 25 minutes. This vehicle arrives 25 minutes after the fifth making its time of arrival at 185 which is 160 + 25. The second digit, 8, indicates that the inspection time is 15 minutes. The third digit, 9, indicates when compared to Table 10.5(b) that this vehicle is in need of minor repair. This is stated in Column (5). The fourth digit, 6, when compared to Table 10.5(c) indicates that the motorist desires ICI to make the repair. Therefore "Yes" is written in Column (6). The last digit, 8, indicates that the repair time is 20 minutes. The total time, Column (8), is 35 minutes. This vehicle begins its inspection upon arrival at time 185 and is finished 35 minutes later at time 220. No wait was required.

Seventh Vehicle

As the interarrival time is 0 for this vehicle, it arrived simultaneously with the preceeding vehicle at time 185. It begins service with Inspector 1 at 185 and completes service at 210.

Eighth Vehicle

This vehicle arrives 15 minutes after the previous vehicle which means it arrives at time 200. The total time for the eighth vehicle is 15 minutes. It needs minor repair but the owner decided that ICI would not make the repair. Can this eighth vehicle be serviced upon its arrival at time 200? Look at Columns (10) and (12) and it will be seen that both inspectors are busy at time 200. At time 200 Inspector 1 is working with the seventh vehicle while Inspector 2 is working with the sixth vehicle. Inspector 1 will be free at time 210 and Inspector 2 will be free at time 220. Therefore, the eighth vehicle will have to wait till Inspector 1 has completed work on the seventh vehicle. The eighth vehicle will begin service at time 210 with Inspector 1 and will be done at time 225. Because this vehicle arrived at time 200, see Column (3), and began being serviced at time 210, see Column (9), there is a 10 minute wait. This wait is recorded in Column (13). The entry in Column (13) will always equal the difference between the time of arrival and the time of the beginning of service.

Ninth Vehicle

This vehicle arrives at time 205 but service is delayed till 220 thus necessitating a 15 minute wait.

Tenth Vehicle

This vehicle arrives at time 240 and enters service immediately.

The tenth automobile arrived at time 240 which is four hours into the day. If ICI wishes to get a good picture of the service that can be offered with two inspectors, many days ought to be simulated. This simulation will not be continued here as the process has been amply illustrated. Several conclusions can now be drawn with respect to ICI's success in achieving its stated service goals.

Ten vehicles have been served in the simulated half-day. According to Column (13) of Table 10.6, two or twenty percent of the vehicles had to wait more than five minutes. ICI guarantees that there will be no more than a ten percent chance of having to wait more than five minutes. Because only half of a day has been simulated it is impossible to determine if the use of two inspectors would meet this objective. Two inspectors may be more than adequate in the long run even though twenty percent of the vehicles had to wait during this short simulated period. After many days had been simulated, then ICI should check Column (13) to see what proportion of the automobiles had to wait more than five minutes.

Column (13) could also be used to determine the average waiting time per customer. Summing the values in Column (13) gives 25 minutes which when divided by ten vehicles means that the average wait was only 2.5 minutes.

After an adequate number of days had been simulated with two inspectors or servers on duty, ICI could then simulate the operation with one or three inspectors depending on the results of the simulation with two inspectors. In this manner the minimum number of inspectors required to satisfy ICI's service objective could be determined.

PROBLEMS

10-1. For a single-server queueing system where $\mu = 4$ and $\lambda = 3$ per hour, define and find L, L_q, W, W_q, $P(O)$, $P(n \geq 2)$, and U. Assume Poisson processes.

10-2. Ocean-going tankers arrive at a docking facility where they are loaded with oil. Various sizes of tankers arrive randomly according to a Poisson process at a rate of two per day. The docking facility can service an average of three tankers per day. Find
  (a) The average number of tankers waiting to dock in the harbor. *4/3 TANKERS*
  (b) The average time a tanker spends waiting to dock. *2/3 DAYS*
  (c) The average amount of time it takes from the entrance of the tanker in the harbor to its departure from the dock. *1 DAY*
  (d) The proportion of the time the dock will be busy. *2/3 OF THE TIME*
  (e) The probability that three or more tankers will be in the queueing system (harbor and dock). *8/27*
  (f) Answer parts (a) through (e) if the dock facility could handle an average of four tankers per day.

10-3. In a big economy move the governor of New Jersey has ordered that there be only one toll booth open during the evenings at each toll

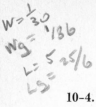

station on the Garden State Parkway. If automobiles arrive according to a Poisson process at an average rate of 150 per hour, and if Osvaldo the human octopus can process cars through the toll booth at an average rate of 180 per hour, find L, L_q, W, and W_q.

10-4. Airplanes arrive according to a Poisson process at a rate of 30 per hour at the Phoenix Sky Harbor airport. The controllers can safely land planes at the rate of 40 per hour. If the average plane expends $500 of fuel per hour of flight, how much fuel will be spent in a typical four-hour period by planes waiting to land?

10-5. Crawford Manufacturing of Rochester has a small clinic at its production facility which is staffed by a single physician and a nurse. Dr. Anderson can treat workers at a rate of 8 per hour. Workers enter the clinic randomly at a rate of 6 per hour. Assuming Poisson processes,

(a) What is the average number of workers in the clinic (either waiting or being cared for by the physician)?
(b) What is the average number of workers waiting for the physician?
(c) What is the average amount of time per worker spent in the queueing system? in the queue?
(d) What is the probability the physician will be idle?
(e) If workers get paid an average of $5 per hour, how much money is Crawford losing in an 8-hour day by workers in the clinic?
(f) If another nurse were added to the staff, Dr. Anderson could treat patients at a rate of 9 per hour. Should another nurse be added at wages of $6 per hour? **NO**

10-6. The plant manager of Welder Inc. must decide whether to purchase one High Speed piece of machinery or two Low Speed pieces. The total maintenance and purchase costs are the same for both alternatives. The jobs, which are processed on this type of machinery, arrive according to a Poisson process at a rate of 12 per hour. The High Speed machine can process these jobs at an average of 20 per hour. One Low Speed machine can process these jobs at the rate of 11 per hour. Which alternative, one High Speed or two Low Speed machines, will yield the least average time for a job in the system and hence be preferable?

10-7. Trucks from Scott Motor Lines arrive according to a Poisson process at the depot at Tuscaloosa. The depot has two unloading docks. The trucks arrive at a rate of five per day and they can be unloaded at a dock at the rate of three per day. Find
(a) The probability that no trucks are in the docks.
(b) The average number of trucks waiting in the yard.
(c) The average number of trucks waiting in the yard or actually at a dock.
(d) The average amount of time a truck spends waiting in the yard (in the queue).
(e) The average amount of time a truck spends in the queueing system.

10-8. Alilosi Airlines has a large maintenance hangar in which many mechanics are at work servicing aircraft. Within the hangar is a tool & parts crib which carries an inventory of rarely used tools and various aircraft replacement parts. Mechanics arrive at the tool crib randomly at the rate of 10 per hour seeking a tool or part. These mechanics get paid $8 an hour, thus each hour spent waiting or being served at the tool crib is $8 lost to Alilosi. Alilosi is interested in staffing the tool crib. Tool crib attendants would be paid at the rate of $4 per hour and a single attendant can process 12 requests per hour on the average. Should Alilosi use one or two attendants in the tool crib? Perform the analysis on the basis of an average eight-hour day.

10-9.   With regard to the Fairbanks North illustration of Section 10.6,
        (a) Simulate another 40-day season with two teams of expediters. Then describe the economic implications of this simulation run.
        (b) Simulate another 40-day season with three expediters. Then describe the economic implications of this simulation run.

10-10. With regard to the Inspector Colosse Incorporated illustration of Section 10.7,
        (a) Simulate an 8-hour day with two inspectors on duty.
        (b) Simulate an 8-hour day with only one inspector on duty.
        (c) Simulate an 8-hour day with three inspectors on duty.
        In each part, give the average waiting time per vehicle and the proportion of vehicles which must wait more than five minutes.

10-11. The VCU computer center allots a different amount of computer time for student use each day depending on how much time the university administration needs the computer in the day. The more the administration uses the computer, the less the students get to use it. The probability distribution below gives information as to the maximum number of student programs the computer center can handle in a day.

Daily Capacity for Student Programs	Probability
100 programs	.1
120	.2
140	.4
160	.2
180	.1

The number of programs that students submit in a day also varies. The next distribution indicates how many student programs are submitted in a day.

Number of Student Programs Submitted in a Day	Probability
90 programs	.1
110	.3
130	.2
150	.2
170	.2

Simulate a period of 30 successive days for the purpose of determining the average number of student programs per day which must be delayed till the next day. (Hints: Let each row in the simulation work sheet equal a day. There is only one server.)

10-12. The Port of New Orleans has two docks. Dock A can only handle small freighters while dock B can handle small or large freighters. The inter-arrival time for the freighters has the following probability distribution:

Interarrival Time in Weeks	Probability
1 week	.3
2	.4
3	.1
4	.1
5	.1

The probability that a freighter is large is .30 and the probability that it is small is .70. Remember that large freighters can only dock at B. When a ship enters the dock the Port Authority officer may order a search for contraband. The probability that a freighter will be searched is .2. It takes one week to search a freighter; the freighter may not be loaded or unloaded while being searched. A freighter can be serviced (loaded and/or unloaded) at either of the docks in the times dictated by the following distribution:

Service Time per Freighter in Weeks	Probability
1 week	.2
2	.3
3	.2
4	.3

Remember that if the ship had to be searched, an extra week at the dock would be required.

Simulate the operation of the Port of New Orleans for a period of 40 weeks. What proportion of the freighters must wait in the harbor before docking? What is the average wait in the harbor (not including the time at the dock) per freighter. (Hint: Each row of the simulation work sheet will represent a freighter.)

11 Bidding, Purchasing, and Replacement Models

11.1 BIDDING STRATEGY

In many businesses it is not unusual that contracts are awarded by competitive bidding. Contracts to build highways, office buildings, missiles, and radar systems, as well as contracts to provide paper, food, and laundry service, are only a few examples where competitive bidding is used to determine who gets the work. Not only is bidding common in the situations just listed, where the goal is to get the work done at a minimum cost, but it is also used as a means of obtaining the highest price through the medium of an auction. Thus, for example, many Treasury obligations are sold by means of competitive bidding.

In this chapter the bidding situation where the competitors submit sealed bids for a contract and where the lowest bidder receives the job will be considered. It will also be assumed that all the bids submitted will be made public upon the award of the contract. It is in such a context that an optimal bidding strategy will be developed.

11.2 HISTORICAL COSTS AND ESTIMATES

A company interested in bidding on a job should initially have some idea as to the reliability of its estimating department. In the past when the company won contracts, were the actual costs close to the estimated costs? Because of so many uncertainties it would be unlikely that actual costs would be identical to the estimates made beforehand. Some of the time the estimates might be quite close to the actual costs yet in other cases there might be a considerable difference. Before designing a bidding strategy the reliability of cost estimates or forecasts will be considered.

Taylor Construction Company was involved in the construction of forts for the U.S. Government in the last century. Taylor, along with a couple of other companies, would bid for the contracts to construct forts in various places in the old west from the Mississippi River to the Pacific. Taylor was contemplating the

311

submission of a bid on the proposed Fort Bozeman. Before bidding Taylor decided to compare the actual costs it incurred with the estimates it had made for the forts already constructed. Taylor had built ten forts of varying sizes. Table 11.1 shows Taylor's cost estimates made prior to construction and then the actual costs of these ten forts. In the last column of Table 11.1 the ratio of the cost estimate to the actual cost for each fort is given. In only two cases, Yuma and Custer, did the estimates exceed the actual costs. In six cases the actual costs ran higher than the estimates. A study of these E/A values reveals something about two distinct aspects of Taylor's estimating department. First of all, it appears that Taylor's estimates are biased. Most of the time the cost estimates are below the actual costs. Each time this occurs an E/A ratio of less than 1 appears. Secondly, the estimates are not reliable in the technical sense of the word in that the estimating department is not consistent in how much the estimates miss the actual costs.

TABLE 11.1
Costs for Ten Contracts

Fort	Cost Estimate, E	Actual Cost, A	Ratio, E/A
Yuma	$48,400	$44,000	1.1
Collins	81,000	90,000	0.9
Custer	55,000	50,000	1.1
Torres	56,000	70,000	0.8
Worth	58,500	65,000	0.9
Hays	25,600	32,000	0.8
Kearney	41,000	41,000	1.0
Broda	38,000	38,000	1.0
Miller	37,800	42,000	0.9
Gilbreath	40,600	58,000	0.7

Before attempting to measure the bias and reliability of Taylor's estimates, one might wonder what Table 11.1 would look like if there were no bias but still a lack of reliability. In such a case the ten E/A ratios might be 1.2, 1.1, 1.1, 1.0, 1.0, 1.0 1.0, .9, .9, and .8, or 1.3, 1.3, 1.3, 1.3, 1.3, .7, .7, .7, .7, and .7. On the other hand, if there were perfect reliability yet bias existed, the ten E/A ratios might be .8, .8, .8, . . . , .8. If there were perfect reliability and no bias the cost estimates would always equal the actual costs yielding an $E/A = 1.0$ in every case. Generally speaking bias is easier to correct, since this correction may be accomplished by a simple mathematical operation. Problems with reliability are best treated by using a decision model under risk.

Returning to the Taylor case, a random variable R can be defined which equals the ratio E/A. Let the historical data of Table 11.1 be the basis for the probability distribution of R, which appears in Table 11.2 Referring to this distribution, if Taylor's estimating procedures continue as they have in the past, the probabililty is .3 that the E/A ratio for the next contract received will be 0.9, that is, $P(R=0.9) = .3$. With the distribution for E/A or R determined from past experience, bias and reliability may be easily measured. The expected value of

TABLE 11.2

**The Probability Distribution
of the Ratio of Estimated Costs to Actual Costs**

R	P(R)
0.7	.1
0.8	.2
0.9	.3
1.0	.2
1.1	.2
	1.0

R, designated as $E(R)$, is 1.0 when there is no bias. If the mean or expected value of R deviates from 1.0 then bias is present in the estimating process. In Taylor's case the expected value of R is

$$E(R) = (0.7)(.1) + (0.8)(.2) + (0.9)(.3) + (1.0)(.2) + (1.1)(.2)$$
$$= .92$$

An expected value of .92 indicates that on the average Taylor's estimates run 92 percent of actual costs, so Taylor tends to underestimate costs. Now suppose that Taylor's estimating department has just estimated the costs for Fort Bozeman to be $80,000. From past experience one would guess that this estimate would be too low. In order to correct it for bias it should be divided by .92 thus yielding the unbiased estimate of $86,956.

Reliability may be measured by the standard deviation of the distribution of R. A standard deviation of zero means that there are no deviations of R from $E(R)$. This is the case of perfect reliability. As the standard deviation of R increases, the estimating procedure is shown to be less reliable. In Taylor's business it is unlikely that the estimating department will ever produce perfectly reliable cost estimates. Unanticipated changes in materials costs, bad weather, Indian attacks, oversights, and the like make the estimating process unreliable. Thus in Taylor's case the standard deviation of R would not be expected to be zero. Based on the distribution of R as given in Table 11.1, the variance of R is (see Section 2.9 of Chapter 2 for a review)

$$\sigma_R^2 = \Sigma (R - \text{Mean})^2\, P(R)$$
$$= (.7 - .92)^2(.1) + (.8 - .92)^2(.2) + \ldots$$
$$\ldots + (1.1 - .92)^2(.2)$$
$$= .0156$$

The square root of the variance yields the standard deviation which is the measure of reliability

$$\sigma_R = \sqrt{.0156} = .125$$

11.3 BIDS AND PROFITS

In the context of a bidding decision situation the decision maker must determine the bid to be submitted. If an unusually high bid is submitted there is little chance that it will win. Of course if it does win there will be a substantial profit. As the bidder reduces the bid there is a better chance that it will win; however, not as much profit will be made if the contract is won. How large a bid then should be sumbitted? Before answering this question the profit associated with a given bid must be considered.

Returning to the Taylor Construction example, Taylor's unbiased estimate of the cost to construct Fort Bozeman is $86,956. Let C denote the unbiased cost estimate for a job, hence in this case $C = \$86,956$. Letting B equal the actual bid to be submitted, then the profit to be derived if B is the winning bid will be $B - C$. (It will be assumed that Taylor's estimates are reliable.) Suppose Taylor bids $94,782 for the Fort Bozeman contract. If this is the winning bid Taylor would make a profit of $94,782 - \$86,856$ or $7,826. If this bid does not win Taylor will make no profit in this case. Letting G equal the gain or profit, the expected gain is

$$E(G) = (B-C)(\text{Probability of Winning})$$
$$+ (0)(\text{Probability of Not Winning}) \qquad (11\text{--}1)$$

If the probability of winning with a bid of B is denoted by $P(W|B)$, Equation 11-1 may be expressed symbolically as

$$E(G) = (B-C)\,P(W|B) \qquad (11\text{--}2)$$

Taylor would like to find that bid B which will maximize the expected gain or profit. In order to do so attention must first be focused on the determination of the probability of winning the contract with a bid of B.

11.4 WINNING AGAINST ONE COMPETITOR

Assume that there is only one other company which competes with Taylor for the contracts to build western forts, namely, the James Brothers Construction Company. Something must be known about the James Bros. bidding behavior before Taylor can expect to determine the probability of winning the Fort Bozeman contract with a bid of B. The policy of the U.S. Government has been to give public notice of all the bids submitted at the time of the announcement of the winning bid. Eighteen forts have been constructed so far, the nineteenth is to be Fort Bozeman. Table 11.3 displays the history of the bids on these eighteen forts by Taylor and the James Bros. The boxed bids are the winning bids. The columns in this table giving Taylor's bids, B, and the James Bros.' bids, J, are public information; added to these is a third column containing Taylor's cost estimates for the eighteen forts. This cost information is not public knowledge. Finally, in the last column Taylor has computed the ratios of the James Bros. bids to Taylor's own cost estimates. This ratios, J/E, is denoted by the random variable X.

It might be noted in Table 11.3 that in the case of Fort Brindley the James Bros. submitted a bid which was less than Taylor's cost estimate. This is quite possible. There is no reason to suppose that the James Bros.' bid of $39,615 was based on the same cost estimate that Taylor used. This bid may well have been submitted with the intention of making a profit and in fact may have yielded a

TABLE 11.3
Bids on Eighteen Forts

Fort	Taylor's Bid B (Winning Bid is Boxed)	James Bros. Bid J (Winning Bid is Boxed)	Taylor's Cost Estimate E	X = J/E
Davis	$34,000	$30,000	$30,000	1.00
Yuma	49,900	53,240	48,400	1.10
Collins	89,000	93,150	81,000	1.15
Canavos	102,000	93,450	89,000	1.05
Brindley	46,000	39,615	41,700	.95
Custer	60,000	60,500	55,000	1.10
Torres	66,000	67,200	56,000	1.20
Worth	60,000	64,350	58,500	1.10
Robertson	71,000	66,360	63,200	1.05
Hays	30,000	30,720	25,600	1.20
Kearney	42,000	43,050	41,000	1.05
Casey	83,000	75,600	72,000	1.05
Coleman	80,900	78,225	74,500	1.05
Broda	41,000	41,800	38,000	1.10
Miller	43,000	43,470	37,800	1.15
Umberger	66,600	66,550	60,500	1.10
Spinelli	55,000	50,400	50,400	1.00
Gilbreath	41,000	42,630	40,600	1.05

profit for the James Bros. Sometimes a contractor may be willing to take a loss on a job in order to gain expertise which will result from performing a particular job. In the case of Fort Brindley it was the contention of some observers that the James Bros.' eagerness for the contract was related to the matter of gaining expertise in the installation of the Musler Minuteman Multialarm Safe. Contractors are also willing under certain circumstances to bid under their estimated cost for the sake of maintaining employment for their work force.

As was done with the $R = E/A$ column of Table 11.1, Taylor next summarized the $X = J/E$ column of Table 11.3. The distribution of X is presented in Table 11.4, page 316. This distribution describes the James Bros. bidding behavior in terms of Taylor's unadjusted cost estimates. For example, eleven percent of the time James Bros. submits a bid equal to what happens to be Taylor's cost estimate E; such is the case when X equals 1.00. The probability is .28 that James Bros. will submit a bid which is 10 percent higher than Taylor's estimated cost; such occurs when $X = 1.10$. With this distribution Taylor can determine the

TABLE 11.4
Distribution of the Ratio
of James Bros. Bid to Taylor's Cost Estimate

X	Frequency	Probability	Cumulative Probability
0.95	1	.06	.06
1.00	2	.11	.17
1.05	6	.33	.50
1.10	5	.28	.78
1.15	2	.11	.89
1.20	2	.11	1.00
	18	1.00	

probability of winning a contract with a particular bid if Taylor has first estimated the cost to construct the fort. For example, Taylor has estimated the cost of construction for Fort Bozeman to be $80,000 (this is the estimate before adjusting for bias). Now if Taylor submits a bid 9 percent above this cost estimate, the bid would be $B = \$87,200$, and the probability is .50 that Taylor will win the contract. Why? The probability that James Bros. will win in this case is the probability that James Bros. submits a bid which is 95, 100, or 105 percent of Taylor's cost estimate. Considering the X distribution it is seen that this probability is .50 which is derived from .06 + .11 + .33. Hence if the probability of the James Bros. winning is .50, the probability that Taylor would win the contract is $1 - .50 = .50$. The same conclusion is reached if it is realized that Taylor will win with a bid which is 9 percent above his cost estimate if James Bros. submits a bid which is 10, 15, or 20 percent above Taylor's cost estimate. The probability of this is .28 + .11 + .11 = .50.

Instead of thinking in terms of bids as percentages of Taylor's cost estimates, one can convert everything into dollars. Since Taylor's cost estimate for Fort Bozeman is $80,000, if the James Bros. bid 5 percent above this it would mean that their bid is ($80,000)(1.05) = $84,000. Table 11.4 indicates that the James Bros. will bid 5 percent above Taylor's cost estimate about .33 of the time, therefore the probability that the James Bros. will bid $84,000 is .33. Table 11.5 gives the distribution of James Bros. bids where these bids are expressed in dollars. It is apparent that Taylor stands a .50 chance of winning with a bid of $87,200 when the probability distribution of the James Bros. bids is as given in Table 11.5. If Taylor submitted a bid 4 percent above estimated costs, $B = \$83,200$, the chance of getting the Fort Bozeman contract would be .83; the probability of losing the contract would be .17.

11.5 OPTIMAL BIDDING AGAINST ONE COMPETITOR

It has already been noticed that James Bros. always seems to bid at 95, 100, 105, 110, 115, or 120 percent of Taylor's cost estimate E. This example has been arranged in this manner to permit a simple distribution of X; in a later section the more realistic situation where James Bros. might have bid at say 107.3 percent of E will be considered. In keeping with the motif of simplicity, let it be

TABLE 11.5
Distribution of James Bros. Bids for Fort Bozeman

X	James Bros. Bid J = $80,000 X	P(J)
0.95	$76,000	.06
1.00	80,000	.11
1.05	84,000	.33
1.10	88,000	.28
1.15	92,000	.11
1.20	96,000	.11
		1.00

further assumed that Taylor has a policy of bidding at 104, 109, 114, or 119 percent of estimated cost E. In the Fort Bozeman case this means that Taylor is only considering the following bids: $83,200 (104 percent of $80,000), $87,200, $91,200, and $95,200. By referring either to the distribution of X or J, the probability of winning the Fort Bozeman contract with each of these bids is easily determined. Table 11.6 displays the probabilities of winning with each of these bids; these probabilities are determined from Table 11.5

TABLE 11.6
Probabilities of Winning with Bids of B

B	P(W|B)
$83,200	.83
87,200	.50
91,200	.22
95,200	.11

With the probability of winning with various sized bids having been determined, Taylor can now find the optimal bid by selecting the bid which has the maximum expected gain. The expected gain or profit was previously given to be

$$E(G) = (B-C) \, P(W|B) \qquad (11\text{--}3)$$

where B is the bid, C is the adjusted cost estimate which is equal to $E/.92$ in this case, and $P(W|B)$ is the probability of winning with a bid of B against the James Bros. This means that the expected gain for a bid of $83,200 is

$$E(G_{83,200}) = (83,200-86,956)(.83)$$
$$= -\$3,117$$

The expected gains associated with the remaining bids are

$$E(G_{87,200}) = (87,200-86,956)(.50) = \$122$$
$$E(G_{91,200}) = (91,200-86,956)(.22) = \$934$$
$$E(G_{95,200}) = (95,200-86,956)(.11) = \$907$$

Therefore, the optimal bid is $B = \$91,200$ as it yields the maximum expected gain or profit. Upon submission of this bid Taylor should realize that the probability of winning the Fort Bozeman contract is only .22.

11.6 COMPLICATIONS

In Table 11.3 the last column gave the values of X where X is the ratio of the James Bros. bid to Taylor's cost estimate. The only values for X which appeared in that column were .95, 1.0, 1.1, 1.15, and 1.2. A simple discrete distribution of X was then derived and given in Table 11.4. In a real case one would not expect X to be limited to these five ratios. For example, suppose that the X values in the last column of Table 11.3 had been, after arranging them in ascending order, .96, .99, 1.00, 1.03, 1.03, 1.05, 1.06, 1.06, 1.07, 1.08, 1.08, 1.10, 1.10, 1.12, 1.14, 1.17, 1.19, and 1.21. Taylor could summarize these data by means of a grouped frequency distribution as in Table 11.7.

TABLE 11.7
Distributions of X

NONCUMULATIVE DISTRIBUTION		CUMULATIVE DISTRIBUTIONS		
X	Frequency	X	Cum. Freq.	Cum. Prob.
.925 — .975	1	.925	0	0
.957 — 1.025	2	.975	1	.06
1.025 — 1.075	6	1.025	3	.17
1.075 — 1.125	5	1.075	9	.50
1.125 — 1.175	2	1.125	14	.78
1.175 — 1.225	2	1.175	16	.89
	18	1.225	18	1.00

Also given in this table is a cumulative frequency distribution and a cumulative probability distribution. It may be seen from Table 11.7 that, for example, there were three cases where the X ratio was less than 1.025, and in fourteen cases X was less than 1.125.

From the cumulative probability distribution of Table 11.7 the graph of Figure 11.1 was derived. The dots in Figure 11.1 were taken from the cumulative distribution and then a smooth line was run through or near these points by eye yielding the continuous cumulative distribution of X. Now suppose that Taylor is considering the submission of a bid which is 10 percent above the cost estimate of $80,000, that is, $B = \$88,000$. Figure 11.1 reveals that for an X of 1.10 the cumulative probability is .66. What does this mean? Since X is the ratio of the James Bros. bid to Taylor's cost estimate, Figure 11.1 indicates that the probability that the James Bros. will win the Fort Bozeman contract is .66 since this is the probability that their bid will be less than Taylor's. Another way to look at it is to realize that in about 66 percent of the bidding competitions the James Bros. submit a bid which is *less than* 10 percent above Taylor's cost estimate. From Figure 11.1 it also appears that if Taylor submitted a bid which was 25 percent above the cost estimate, then the probability of the James Bros. winning is 1.0 since it is certain that the James Bros. will bid less than Taylor in this case.

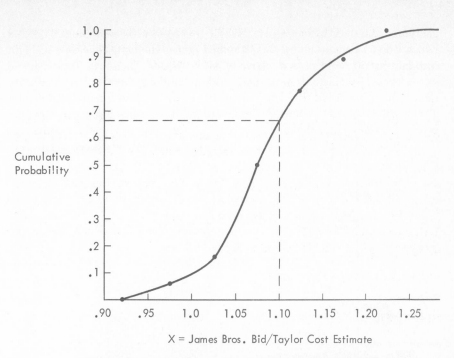

CHAPTER 11

X = James Bros. Bid/Taylor Cost Estimate

FIGURE 11.1 Continuous Cumulative Distribution of X

The distribution of Figure 11.1 which gives the probability of the James Bros. winning in the face of a bid by Taylor can easily be used to determine Taylor's probability of winning. The probability that Taylor will win with a given bid is simply one minus the probability that the James Bros. will win. In view of the situation as presented in Figure 11.1 an optimal bid for Taylor may be determined in a manner similar to that outlined in Section 11.5. A systematic trial-and-error technique can be applied to find the optimal bid. Initially Taylor might select a few representative bids to analyze. For example, suppose bids of 5, 10, 15, and 20 percent above the cost estimate of $80,000 are selected. Table 11.8 gives the expected gains for each of these bids; these expected gains are

TABLE 11.8
Evaluation of Four Bids

Taylor's Bid as a Proportion of Estimated Costs	B Actual Bid	C Estimated Cost adjusted for bias	B—C Profit if Contract Won	Prob. of James Bros. winning	P(W|B) Prob. of Taylor winning	E(G) = (B—C)P(W|B) Expected Gain
1.05	$84,000	$86,956	—$2,956	.30	.70	—$2,069
1.10	88,000	86,956	1,044	.66	.34	355
1.15	92,000	86,956	5,044	.83	.17	857
1.20	96,000	86,956	9,044	.95	.05	452

computed exactly as in Section 11.5. Of the four bids considered, the $92,000 bid which was 15 percent above the estimated cost is the best. However, it might turn out that 17 or 14 percent above would be better. Therefore, Taylor should select several possible bids in the neighborhood of the $92,000 bid in an effort to isolate the optimal bid. By determining the expected gain for these other bids Taylor will be able to systematically determine the optimal bid. By plotting the expected gains against the bids, as in Figure 11.2, one can visually approximate the optimal bid. Such a graph also reveals how sensitive the expected gain is to changes in Taylor's bid.

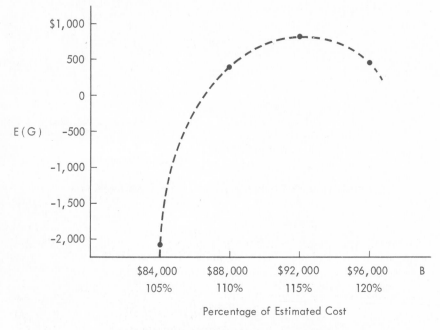

FIGURE 11.2 Expected Gains for Bids

11.7 OPTIMAL BIDDING AGAINST TWO OR MORE COMPETITORS

In the situation where Taylor might be facing not only the James Brothers but also the Daltons, the optimal bid would be determined by again examining the expected gain for several possible bids and systematically eliminating the suboptimal bids. The expected gain for any bid remains equal to $(B-C)P(W|B)$, the only modification concerns the probability of winning $P(W|B)$. For the new competitor, the Daltons, Taylor should carry out an analysis of bidding behavior similar to that which was done for the James Bros. Just as J denoted the James Bros. bid (see Section 11.4), let D represent the Daltons' bid and then form the random variable $Y = D/E$ which is analogous to the $X = J/E$ where E was Taylor's estimated cost. Then as was done in the James Bros. case, a distribution of Y could be determined. Let the cumulative distribution of Figure

11.3 represent the fruition of this process. From Figure 11.3 it is seen that the Daltons have never submitted a bid which was any lower than 10 percent above Taylor's own cost estimate. Also, the Daltons have never bid more than 20 percent above Taylor's cost estimate.

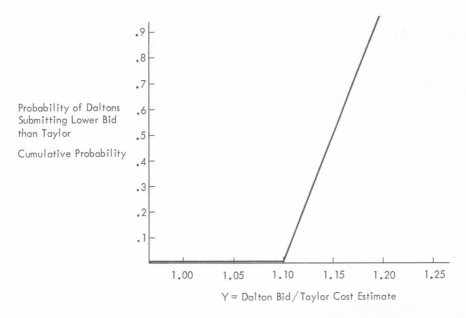

FIGURE 11.3   Continuous Cumulative Distribution of Y

With Taylor facing these two competitors, what is the probability of winning the Fort Bozeman contract with a bid of B? Suppose Taylor's bid is 15 percent above the estimated cost of $E = \$80,000$. It has already been shown that the probability is .83 that the James Bros. will bid lower. Figure 11.3 indicates that there is a .50 probability that the Daltons will bid lower than Taylor if Taylor's bid is 15 percent above their estimated cost. Thus the probability that Taylor would win with this bid against the James Bros. is $1 - .83 = .17$, and the probability is $1 - .50 = .50$ that Taylor would win against the Daltons. To win the contract Taylor must underbid *both* competitors. Assuming that the James Bros. and the Daltons are acting independently, the probability that Taylor will simultaneously beat both is the product of .17 and .50 or .085. This is merely an application of the multiplication law for independent events. The expected gain then for this bid of $92,000 which is 15 percent above estimated costs is

$$E(G) = (B-C)\,P(W\,|B) \tag{11-4}$$
$$= (92,000 -86,956)(.085)$$
$$= \$429$$

By systematically evaluating the expected gain for a number of bids Taylor could again determine the optimal bid.

If there were three or more competitors the only change in the analytic procedure would be to further modify $P(W|B)$. The probability that Taylor would win with a bid of B would be the probability of winning against the first times that of winning against the second times that of winning against the third and so on.

11.8 INTRODUCTION TO TRANSISTORY PURCHASING OPPORTUNITIES

In certain types of business a company may have to purchase some commodity in a market where the price changes quite frequently on a periodic basis. For example, the prices of wheat, corn, oats, beef, and pork fluctuate markedly in certain commodity markets. Other products like steel and coal also fluctuate in price but the price changes are typically slow in coming. Not only is the purchasing manager of a company involved in the procurement of product in a market where prices are changing, but financial and investment managers also may be "buying" money where interest rates fluctuate or they may be buying bonds and stocks whose prices vary. In all of the above cases a decision must be made in the present. The alternatives are "Buy Now" or "Wait;" the decision to wait to make the purchase is founded on the hope of getting a better price in the future. When it comes to a decision of selling rather than buying, we instinctively realize that if there is considerable time before the sale has to be made we can hold out at first for a good price. Such is the case when one sells a home. However as the selling horizon or deadline approaches one considers selling the home for less. In the next few sections a formal model will be developed for guiding the decision maker toward an optimal purchasing or selling strategy when the purchase or sale deadline lies somewhere in the future. It will be assumed further that the purchase or sale opportunities are transitory, that is, once an opportunity to purchase or sell in the current period has not been taken, that particular opportunity is gone forever.

Taylor of the foregoing sections on bidding models submitted a bid on the Fort Bozeman contract. The James Bros. and Daltons also submitted bids but this time Taylor received the contract. Taylor must now start assembling the construction materials in St. Louis. Taylor must transport the materials and equipment across the prairie to get to the construction site in Wyoming. In four weeks the prairie will be dry enough to move out with the wagons. Taylor must leave then in order to finish the fort by autumn and return to St. Louis. (In Chapter 13 Taylor's construction timetable and planning are discussed in detail.) By the end of this four-week period Taylor must purchase a hundred mules which will be used to transport equipment and material to the Fort Bozeman site. Now in St. Louis there is a very volatile mule market with prices changing weekly. It is in this market that Taylor must purchase the 100 mules within four weeks. Before dropping out of Hahvad Business School Taylor learned one thing: "If you're gunnin' for the big one, put all your eggs in one saddlebag." Taylor rightly concluded that this principle implies that all 100 mules should be bought at once in order to attempt to reduce costs to their lowest rather than buying some this week, some next week, and so forth. For this reason, a *single procurement* strategy will be developed for Taylor in the section to follow.

11.9 A TRANSITORY PURCHASING MODEL

In the purchasing situation Taylor faces there are 4 periods (weeks) in which to purchase the 100 mules where the price of a mule may change once each week. Taylor also wishes to purchase all 100 mules at the same time as such a strategy will lead to a minimum expected cost per mule. Taylor has subjectively assessed four price distributions corresponding to the four weeks before the deadline. These distributions are given in Table 11.9. From these distributions it is seen that the price of a mule will be in the $80 to $95 range over the next four weeks. For the first week the probability that M will be $80 is .1, and the probability that M will be $85 is .4 where M is the random variable denoting the price of a mule. Also for the first week, $P(M=90) = .4$ and $P(M=95) = .1$. The distribution of M changes for the second week; this distribution reflects Taylor's subjective appraisal of the mule market.

TABLE 11.9
Weekly Price Distributions
for Mules

| Price per Mule | Week | | | |
M	1	2	3	4
$80	.1	.1	.2	.2
85	.4	.3	.3	.3
90	.4	.4	.3	.3
95	.1	.2	.2	.2
	1.0	1.0	1.0	1.0

Looking at Taylor's situation intuitively, some suggestions could be made. For example, if the price during the first week turns out to be $95 there would be no point in buying the mules then as there is no possible way that Taylor could do worse by waiting. Also, if the price is $80 in the first week the mules should be purchased then as there will never be a better deal and Taylor may not be able to get as good a deal later. The same kind of advice could be given if the second week arrives and a purchase has not been made. Only if Taylor comes to the fourth week without a purchase must the prevailing weekly price be accepted. Such is the case because the mules must be purchased by the end of the fourth week.

Returning to the first week, if the market price for a mule turns out to be $90, what would seem to be the best decision in this case? Most people would rightly conclude that "Wait" would be a better decision than "Buy" as it seems quite likely that the price will be lower sometime in the following weeks. Continuing the line of thinking established, Taylor wishes to determine a series of four *critical prices*. Let the critical price for Week 1 be denoted by C_1 and defined as follows: The critical price for Week 1 is that price such that if the price of a mule is less than the critical price, the decision maker should make the purchase; if the price of a mule equals or exceeds the critical price then the decision maker should not purchase but rather wait. Alternatively, in Week 1 if $M < C_1$ then purchase, but if $M \geq C_1$ then wait. Finding a purchasing *strategy* simply consists of determining the optimal critical price for each week. A somewhat appealing strategy would be defined by $C_1 = \$82$, $C_2 = \$82$, $C_3 = \$92$, and $C_4 = \$100$ or infinity. Such a strategy is appealing because it enables Taylor to "hold out" for a low price initially. Only if a low price is not forthcoming early in the four weeks is Taylor willing to buy at a higher price realizing that a purchase must be made; hence the critical price increases with the passing of time. If Taylor adopted this strategy the mules would be purchased in the first week only if the price per mule were below \$82, or in this case only if they were \$80 each. In the second week the mules would be purchased only if they had not been previously purchased and only if the price were below \$82. In the third week the mules would be purchased only if there had been no prior purchase and if the price were less than \$92. In the fourth week the mules would have to be purchased at the prevailing market price regardless of its level if there had been no previous purchase.

Having considered the nature of a single procurement purchasing strategy, the discussion may now turn to the matter of determining the optimal strategy. For period i three values must be computed; these are

C_i = The critical price for period i

E_i = The partial expected price paid in period i assuming no previous purchase has been made (see Section 2.10 of Chapter 2 for the definition of a partial expected value).

P_i = The probability of not making a purchase in period i assuming no previous purchase has been made

These values are computed starting with the last period or week. Once the C_i for a period is found, the E_i and P_i are easy to determine. Consider now how Taylor would compute the C, E, and P for each week.

C_4 must equal any value higher than \$95 because if a purchase has not been made by the fourth week Taylor must buy regardless of price which may be anywhere from \$80 to \$95. For this reason in any purchasing situation the critical price for the last period may be assigned a value of positive infinity. With $C_4 = \infty$ what is E_4? E_4 is the partial expected price paid in the fourth week which is computed as follows

$$E_4 = (\$80)(.2) + (85)(.3) + (90)(.3) + (95)(.2)$$
$$= \$87.50$$

Actually in this case E_4 is the expected price, not a partial expected price since every price is a possible purchase price in the last week because each is below $C_4 = \infty$. Finally P_4, which is the probability that a purchase will not be made in the fourth week if Taylor gets that far without having already purchased, is 0.

The C, E, and P for Week 3 must next be computed. Through the use of calculus it can be shown that C_3 will equal E_4, therefore C_3 must equal \$87.50. From this it follows that

$$E_3 = (\$80)(.2) + (85)(.3)$$
$$= \$41.50$$

which is the partial expected price paid in Week 3, and, $P_3 = .5$ which is the probabililty of no purchase in Week 3 realizing that $C_3 = \$87.50$.

Subsequent values for C, E, and D will now be determined. As the rigorous reasoning behind the formulas to be used to accomplish the computation of C, E, and P is somewhat complicated, no attempt will be made to formally justify these formulas. A brief intuitive explanation as to their origin will follow later in this section.

For Week 2, the critical price C_2 may be computed according to the formula

$$C_2 = E_3 + P_3 {\cdot} E_4 \qquad (11\text{--}5)$$

Notice that C_2 is derived from values taken from later periods (weeks) which have already been computed. Therefore

$$\begin{aligned} C_2 &= \$41.50 + (.5)(87.50) \\ &= \$85.25 \end{aligned}$$

Also,

$$\begin{aligned} E_2 &= (\$80)(.1) + (85)(.3) \\ &= \$33.50 \end{aligned}$$

and

$$P_2 = .4 + .2 = .6$$

Finally for Week 1,

$$\begin{aligned} C_1 &= E_2 + P_2 {\cdot} E_3 + P_2 {\cdot} P_3 {\cdot} E_4 \qquad (11\text{--}6) \\ &= \$33.50 + (.6)(41.50) + (.6)(.5)(87.50) \\ &= \$84.65 \end{aligned}$$

Thus an optimal purchasing strategy has been mechanically derived in that the critical price for each week has been found, that is, $C_1 = \$84.65$, $C_2 = \$85.25$; $C_3 = \$87.50$, and $C_4 = \infty$.

To summarize the approach utilized, the critical prices for each period where the purchasing strategy covers four periods are found as follows

$$\begin{aligned} C_4 &= \infty & (11\text{--}7) \\ C_3 &= E_4 & (11\text{--}8) \\ C_2 &= E_3 + P_3 {\cdot} E_4 & (11\text{--}9) \\ C_1 &= E_2 + P_2 {\cdot} E_3 + P_2 {\cdot} P_3 {\cdot} E_4 & (11\text{--}10) \end{aligned}$$

where for any period i, E_i is the sum of the products of the prices below C_i and their respective probabilities, and P_i is the sum of the probabilities associated with the prices greater than or equal to the critical price C_i.

Though the optimal critical prices were determined through certain mathematical processes involving calculus, they are capable of being intuitively understood. For example, imagine a game where a die may be rolled no more than two times. After the first roll you can take a dollar for each dot which turns up. If 3 dots turned up you could take \$3; if 5 dots turned up you could take \$5. However, you are also given the choice of passing up the first roll with its payoff and instead taking the payoff determined by the second (final) roll. The payoffs associated with the second roll are computed as in the case of the first. In this game if you take the payoff of the first roll the game is then terminated. If the payoff of the first roll is passed up and the die is rolled the second time, the payoff will be that which is determined by the second roll. What sort of strategy would you use in approaching this game?

With reference to a strategy for the game set forth above, if 1, 2, or 3 turned up on the first roll you would be inclined to wait for the second roll thereby forfeiting the $1, $2, or $3 associated with the first roll. Why? You might reason that the expected gain from the second roll is $E = (1/6)(\$1) + (1/6)(\$2) + \ldots + (1/6)(\$6) = \$3.50$ and this exceeds the $1, $2, or $3 you would get on the first roll. On the other hand, by the same sort of reason you might choose to take the $4, $5, or $6 if that were the opportunity on the first roll. The essence of the strategy is based on what the decision maker can expect from the future; if $3.50 can be expected, then accept nothing less now but accept any payoff which is more than that if presently available. In the Taylor example the critical prices were determined according to such reasoning. C_3 was the expected price if Taylor waited out the third week and took what came in the fourth, hence $C_3 = E_4$. Likewise all the other critical prices are merely Taylor's expected prices if a purchase were not made in the current period.

If a purchasing manager were faced with a transitory purchasing situation of other than four periods the critical prices could be determined in a manner similar to that illustrated for Taylor. In general, for a situation with a deadline N periods off, the critical prices are

$$
\begin{array}{ll}
C_N \;\;= \infty & (11\text{--}11)\\
C_{N-1} = E_N & (11\text{--}12)\\
C_{N-2} = E_{N-1} + P_{N-1}{\cdot}E_N & (11\text{--}13)\\
C_{N-3} = E_{N-2} + P_{N-2}{\cdot}E_{N-1} + P_{N-2}{\cdot}P_{N-1}{\cdot}E_N & (11\text{--}14)\\
C_{N-4} = E_{N-3} + P_{N-3}{\cdot}E_{N-2} + P_{N-3}{\cdot}P_{N-2}{\cdot}E_{N-1} + P_{N-3}{\cdot}P_{N-2}{\cdot}P_{N-1}{\cdot}E_N & (11\text{--}15)\\
\quad \text{etc.}
\end{array}
$$

As before, the critical price for the last period is computed first, then for period N–1, and so on till C_1.

11.10 A SELLING MODEL

Having considered the purchasing model of the previous section, an analogous selling model will now be hastily presented. In the selling model let the following be defined

c_i = The critical price for period i. If an offer
 exceeds c_i accept the offer, if the offer
 is less than or equal to c_i reject it and
 wait to sell at a later period.

e_i = The partial expected price received in period i
 assuming no previous sale.

p_i = The probability of not making a sale in period i.

A selling strategy consists of specifying the critical prices for each period. As each period comes, the seller should only accept an offer above the critical selling price. These critical prices are determined by the expressions

$$c_N = 0 \tag{11-16}$$
$$c_{N-1} = e_N \tag{11-17}$$
$$c_{N-2} = e_{N-1} + p_{N-1} \cdot e_N \tag{11-18}$$
$$c_{N-3} = e_{N-2} + p_{N-2} \cdot e_{N-1} + p_{N-2} \cdot p_{N-1} \cdot e_N \tag{11-19}$$
$$\text{etc.}$$

These critical prices are identical in form to those of the purchasing model; the only difference lies in the redefinition of C, E, and P. An example will now be given to demonstrate the application of this model.

A Navajo silversmith has purchased a quantity of the world's most expensive turquoise, Bisbee Blue Spider Web, from the Laevendor open pit near Bisbee, Arizona. The silversmith has fashioned an exquisite squash blossom necklace from the turquoise and plans to sell it. Three wealthy tourists have made appointments to see the squash blossom; a week separates each of their visits. The first potential buyer, Willa Krahn, will offer either $2,000, $3,000, or $4,000 for the necklace. The silversmith assesses a probability of .3, .4, and .3, respectively, for each of these offers. The second buyer, Anna Smith, and the third, Toni Chapman, will also make offers of two, three, or four thousand dollars; the probabilities of .3, .4, and .3 also apply in each of these last two cases. What should be the selling strategy of the silversmith if it is assumed that each of the wealthy tourists must have an immediate acceptance or rejection of their offers?

The critical price for the third and last tourist must be anywhere between 0 and $1999 as the silversmith is planning to take a vacation after this last appointment and must sell the necklace to finance the vacation. Since Chapman's offer is sure to be at least $2,000, the silversmith will be assured of having at least $2,000 for the vacation.

The critical price for the second tourist may be found after first finding e_3. By definition,

$$e_3 = (\$2,000)(.3) + (3,000)(.4) + (4,000)(.3)$$
$$= \$3,000$$

Therefore from Equation 11-17, $c_2 = e_3 = \$3,000$. The critical price for the first tourist will be

$$c_1 = e_2 + p_2 \cdot e_3 \tag{11-20}$$
$$= \$1,200 + (.7)(3,000)$$
$$= \$3,300$$

since $e_2 = (.3)(\$4,000) = \$1,200$ and $p_2 = .3 + .4 = .7$. The silversmith now has an optimal strategy for the disposal of the squash blossom. With the first tourist only an offer above $3,300 should be accepted, with the second the offer must exceed $3,000, and with the third any offer must be accepted if a sale has not already been made.

11.11 REPLACEMENT POLICY

Occasionally management is faced with a decision involving the development of a policy for replacing certain types of equipment or parts therein which may fail in service. Some types of equipment perform satisfactorily till a failure occurs which renders the equipment completely dysfunctional. Such is the case when a light bulb burns out, a tire blows out, or a vital component of some piece of machinery breaks. In other kinds of situations the equipment might not abruptly fail but instead slowly deteriorates. An automobile begins to burn oil, minor parts break, its body rusts, and so forth as age increases. Ultimately the owner deems it too expensive to keep the automobile running and trades it in for a newer model.

Attention will first be directed toward the development of an optimal replacement strategy in the case where there are abrupt and irreparable failures. An example at the outset will be helpful for the sake of identifying the critical elements of the decision situation where such a strategy is applicable.

Suppose a company lights its factories with mercury vapor lamps. Initially all the lamps are new and few failures are experienced. As time wears on lamps begin to burn out. When a lamp burns out a supervisor calls for a maintenance worker who replaces the burned-out lamp. Replacing lamps in this manner can be expensive, because to the cost of the lamp must be added the labor cost of the maintenance worker who brings the single new lamp from the shop, installs it, and then returns to the shop. As the lamps burn out more frequently this relatively high replacement cost (it is relatively high because of the labor component) is incurred too often. It is likely that a decision will then be made to replace all of the lamps, good or bad, in order to eliminate the frequent replacements of individual lamps. This replacement of all the lamps at one time is known as the *renewal*. Since all the lamps are replaced at the renewal, the labor cost per lamp is substantially reduced. However, many operative lamps are replaced at this time and therefore a relatively high equipment cost is incurred. A replacement policy where renewals of the entire system are rarely made will yield relatively high inter-renewal costs and low renewal costs. This means that labor costs will be high but equipment costs will be low. A policy where renewals are made frequently will have low inter-renewal replacement costs as not many lamps will burn out between renewals; however, renewal costs will be great. An optimal replacement policy will minimize the sum of these two kinds of costs in finding the optimal renewal frequency.

In the section to follow a model for the determination of the optimal renewal period will be presented. In the section after that a replacement model dealing with slow failures will be considered.

11.12 A PROBABILISTIC RENEWAL MODEL

Our friend Taylor has now purchased 100 mules and also 25 wagons to carry material and equipment out to the Fort Bozeman construction site. Taylor will be moving out along the Oregon Trail and is concerned with wagon wheel failures. Taylor must decide how many wheels to take as broken wheels along the Oregon Trail are inevitable. If a wheel breaks while a wagon is being drawn there will be time delays and damage to the cargo. Taylor figures that a broken wheel will cause $5 of damage. About the only way Taylor can guarantee no broken wheels in transit is to replace all the wheels (renew the system) every morning as a wagon wheel has never been known to fail in its first day of use. Wagon wheels cost $2 each, hence with 25 wagons it will cost $200 to renew the system. Taylor feels that the best way to go is not to renew the system every morning. This intuition is based on Taylor's knowledge of the mortality table for a wagon wheel on the Oregon Trail. Table 11.10 gives the mortality table along with some random number classifications which will be used and explained later. It is evident that a wheel has never failed during its first day of service, ten percent of the wheels fail during the second day, ten percent during the third day of use, and so on.

TABLE 11.10
Mortality Table for a Wagon Wheel

Day of Failure, d	P(d)	Random Number
1	0	——
2	.1	00 – 09
3	.1	10 – 19
4	.2	20 – 39
5	.4	40 – 79
6	.2	80 – 99
	1.0	

Taylor judges that the optimal replacement strategy will be one of the following:

a_1: Renew every 2 days

a_2: Renew every 3 days

a_3: Renew every 4 days

Which of these is optimal? There is an analytic method of determining the optimal strategy,[1] but Taylor has decided upon a simulation technique in order to find the optimal strategy.

Taylor's trip to the Fort Bozeman site will take 40 days. What kind of costs could be expected if strategy a_2 were selected? After every 3 days Taylor will renew the system, that is, replace every wheel regardless of its condition. This renewal will cost $2 per wheel, and under a_2 will be accomplished 13 times before getting to Bozeman. Taylor would renew the system in the morning of the fourth day, in the morning of the seventh day, in the morning of the tenth day, et cetera. But what if a wheel fails between renewals? When wheels are replaced between renewals there will be a cost of $7, $2 for the wheel and the remaining $5 for the time delay and cargo damage. The results of the implementation of a_2 may be simulated by a Monte Carlo technique. As was explained in Chapter 5, a simulation work sheet must be first constructed.

---

[1] David Heinze, *Statistical Decision Analysis for Management* (Columbus, Ohio: Grid, Inc. 1973) pp 199–202.

In Table 11.11 a work sheet is presented. Taylor can use this work sheet to simulate the effects of adopting a_2.

Before performing the simulation several clarifications should be made. First, it will be assumed that renewals take place at 6 a.m. Soon after 6 a.m. the wagons hit the trail. Next, it will be assumed that wheels fail early in the morning, 7 a.m., on the day of failure. This means that the distribution of d as given in Table 11.10 refers to failures in the mornings only. If at 7 a.m. in the morning of May 20 a wheel fails, it is replaced immediately and the probability that it will fail during the rest of May 20, its first day of service, is zero. However, the probability that it will fail in the morning of May 21 is .10 since $P(d=2) = .10$.

The simulation is to be carried out with respect to one wheel only. If strategy a_2 is optimal for one wheel, then it will be optimal to use a_2 for all 100 wheels simultaneously. Since only one wheel is considered in the work sheet the total renewal cost will be $2. Also, due to the nature of the d distribution as found in Table 11.10, there will never be more than one failure in a day if the simulation is confined to one wheel only.

Taylor is now ready to run through one Monte Carlo simulation of the trip using strategy a_2. Each row in the work sheet of Table 11.11 represents the experience with one wheel. Column (1) identifies the wheel. Column (2) shows the date, I, of the respective wheel's installation. The date of the installation of the first wheel is Day 1. For this wheel, the anticipated date of renewal is the morning of Day 4 which is 3 days later, $I + 3$. But will this first wheel fail before Day 4? A random number taken from Appendix I appears in Column (4); when comparing this number 96 to the distribution of d as given in Table 11.10 it is found that the day of failure, d, for this wheel is 6. That is, this wheel will fail at 7 a.m. on the morning of its sixth day of use. Therefore, this wheel would fail on Day 6 if not renewed earlier. This date of failure if not renewed earlier is given in Column (6). The date of failure may conveniently be calculated as $I + d - 1$. The actual date of the renewal or replacement of the wheel is recorded in Column (7). The date here will be the earlier of the two dates as found in Columns (3) and (6). Since this first wheel would last to Day 6 if given a chance, it will make it to the renewal on Day 4. Hence Column (7) records 4 as the actual date of the changing of this first wheel. Since it is renewed a renewal cost of $2 is recorded in Column (8).

The second wheel (see the second row of Table 11.11) was installed on Day 4. The entry in Column (2) is the same as the entry in Column (7) of the previous row since this is the wheel which took the place of the first wheel. The anticipated date of renewal is Day 7. This wheel would last 5 days before failing which means it would fail at 7 a.m. on Day 8. Since the renewal date comes first, the second wheel is renewed on Day 7 and thus a $2 renewal cost is recorded.

The third wheel was installed on Day 7. The renewal would come on Day 10 which is three days hence. However, the random number 12 indicates that this wheel fails on its third day which is at 7 a.m. on Day 9. It is therefore replaced on Day 9 at an expense of $7.

The fourth wheel which was installed on the morning of Day 9 has a renewal due on Day 10 at 6 a.m. which is the day that all Taylor's wheels are

TABLE 11.11
Renewal Policy Simulation
(Renewal Every Three Days, a_2)

Wheel (1)	Date of Installation I (2)	Anticipated Date of Renewal (at 6 a.m.) (3)	(RN) (4)	Day of Failure d (5)	Date of Failure if not renewed earlier (at 7 a.m.) I + d − 1 (6)	Actual Date* of Renewal or Replacement (7)	Renewal Cost (8)	Replacement Cost (9)
1	1	4	(96)	6	6	4	$ 2	
2	4	7	(64)	5	8	7	2	
3	7	10	(12)	3	9	9		$ 7
4	9	10	(07)	2	10	10	2	
5	10	13	(06)	2	11	11		7
6	11	13	(03)	2	12	12		7
7	12	13	(63)	5	16	13	2	
8	13	16	(35)	4	16	16	2	
9	16	19	(86)	6	21	19	2	
10	19	22	(65)	5	23	22	2	
11	22	25	(69)	5	26	25	2	
12	25	28	(19)	3	27	27		7
13	27	28	(24)	4	30	28	2	
14	28	31	(20)	4	31	31	2	
15	31	34	(96)	6	36	34	2	
16	34	37	(77)	5	38	37	2	
17	37	40	(72)	5	41	40	2	
						Total:	$26	$28

*The actual date of renewal or replacement will be
I + 3 if (I + 3) ≤ (I + d−1), and I + d−1 otherwise.

renewed. The random number indicates that this wheel would fail in its second day of service, $d = 2$, which would be at 7 a.m. on Day 10. However, a renewal has taken place at 6 a.m. on Day 10 so the wheel is not replaced at 7 a.m. The renewal cost is $2.

The fifth wheel, which was installed on Day 10, fails on its second day, $d = 2$, or on Day 11. It is replaced costing $7.

The replacement, the sixth wheel, being installed on Day 11 also fails before the renewal date which is Day 13. It fails in its second day, $d = 2$, which is Day 12. Another $7 replacement cost is incurred.

The seventh wheel being installed on Day 12 is renewed on Day 13. (Again, remember that a renewal of all Taylor's wheels comes every three days regardless of the experience of any one wheel.) The cost is $2.

The eighth wheel is installed on Day 13 and lasts to Day 16 when it is renewed.

In this manner the work sheet of Table 11.11 is completed. The simulation ends when the seventeenth wheel is renewed at 6 a.m. on Day 40 which is the last day of travel.

Having completed the simulation, the costs are tallied. Columns (8) and (9) are summed. The result of this single Monte Carlo simulation of one wheel is

Total Renewal Costs	$26
Total Replacement Costs	28
Total Costs	$54

As long as a_2 is simulated the total renewal costs will be $26 since there will of necessity be 13 renewals in a 40 day period. Since renewal costs will be $26, total costs for a single wheel simulation will never fall below this figure. Taylor should repeat this simulation of the trip. Taylor did so nine more times getting the following total cost figures: $33, 33, 33, 40, 40, 40, 47, 47, and 47. These figures are arrayed in the form of a frequency distribution in Table 11.12. The average cost over these ten simulated trips is $41.40. By simulating a number of trips using a_1 and a_3 in a similar manner and then computing the respective average costs, Taylor can select the optimal strategy. (Refer to Section 5.7 of Chapter 5 for a discussion of the determination of an adequate number of simulation trials.)

TABLE 11.12
**Frequency Distribution of Total Cost
for Strategy a_2**

Total Cost	Frequency
$33	3
40	3
47	3
54	1
	10

The simulation procedure outlined above not only gives an estimate for average costs, it also gives the decision maker a picture of the variability of the outcomes. Taylor would conclude, for example, that by using a_2 costs are likely to fall between \$33 and \$54 per wheel. An analogous range of costs could be determined for a_1 and a_3 also. Thus Monte Carlo simulation is shown to be a powerful technique for the evaluation of alternative renewal strategies.

11.13 A DETERMINISTIC REPLACEMENT MODEL

The second type of replacement policy deals with equipment which does not need to be replaced upon failure but may be repaired. Eventually this type of equipment is replaced either because the repair and maintenance expenses become prohibitive or because of obsolescence. Typically construction equipment, for example, is replaced because it wears out while computers are replaced because of obsolescence. The problem of replacing equipment which becomes obsolete will not be broached in this text, rather the situation where equipment wears out and is replaced by similar new equipment will be considered.

Another one of the problems Taylor Construction faces is the replacement of some of its heavy construction equipment. Taylor keeps quite busy drilling wells in the prairie and plains. Taylor uses the Platte River Drilling Rig which is replaced every few years as maintenance expenses mount quickly with a few years of use. Table 11.13 gives pertinent data of the Platte River Rig which when new costs \$4,000. It will be assumed that though maintenance and repairs may take place at any time during the year, these expenses will be paid at the end of each year of operation of the rig.

TABLE 11.13
Values and Costs
for Platte River Drilling Rig

Years of Use	Trade-in Value	Maintenance Cost
1	\$2,000	\$ 100
2	1,500	500
3	1,100	1,000
4	900	1,500
5	700	2,100

Taylor's particular problem concerns the frequency with which the rig should be replaced. The appropriate alternatives are

a_1: Replace at the end of every year
a_2: Replace at the end of every two years
a_3: Replace at the end of every three years
a_4: Replace at the end of every four years
a_5: Replace at the end of every five years

Initially the technique for deciding on the optimal replacement alternative will be carried out with no regard for the time value of money, that is, the interest rate will be 0 percent. This assumption implies that an expense of \$100 to be paid two years from now is just as bad as one which must be paid today. In other words, the value of money to the decision maker is not dependent upon the time at which it is to be received or paid.

With the foregoing assumption it is quite easy to determine which replacement alternative is optimal. Consider first a_1. Over the period when Taylor would use the drilling rig, namely one year under a_1, the cash flows are

Initial cost	$ 4,000
Maintenance expense in first year	100
Trade-in value	−2,000
Net cost	2,100
Net cost per year	$ 2,100

For act a_2 under which the rig is replaced every two years:

Initial cost		$ 4,000
Maintenance expense,	year 1	100
	year 2	500
Trade-in value		−1,500
Net cost (over two years)		3,100
Net cost per year		$ 1,550

For a_3

Initial cost		$ 4,000
Maintenance expense,	year 1	100
	year 2	500
	year 3	1,000
Trade-in value		−1,100
Net cost (over three years)		4,500
Net cost per year		$ 1,500

In a similar manner the net cost per year for a_4 could be found to be $1,550 and the yearly net cost for a_5 is $1,700. Thus it appears that Taylor ought to adopt a_3 thereby replacing the rig every three years. This strategy will minimize annual expenses.

Taylor must now incorporate the time value of money into the analysis. Taylor would definitely prefer to pay $100 a year from now over paying it immediately. Assuming Taylor has $100 now, it could be invested for the year at an interest rate of 8 percent, for example. Then at the end of the year Taylor would have the $100 to pay off the debt but could keep the $8 interest. According to the compound interest formula, if P dollars are invested today at an annual interest rate of i, then it will grow to $P(1+i)^n$ in n years. Letting S equal the value of a future sum or payment to be received n years hence, the relationship between P and S is given as

$$S = P(1+i)^n \tag{11-21}$$

This expression may be algebraically converted to give the present value of a future sum:

$$P = S \frac{1}{(1+i)^n} \qquad (11\text{-}22)$$

For example, the present value of a payment of $100 to be received two years hence is

$$P = 100 \frac{1}{(1 + .08)^2}$$

if the annual interest rate is 8 percent, Appendix Table 3 gives the value of $1/(1.08)^2$ to be .8573, therefore $P = \$85.73$. A decision maker working with an 8 percent interest rate considers a payment of $100 to be received two years from now to be of equal value to an immediate payment of $85.73.

Incorporating the time value of money in Taylor's replacement model is relatively simple. For a_3, instead of summing up all of the costs over the three year horizon, Taylor must sum up the present value of all of these costs. Thus the present value of the costs under a_3 is

$$
\begin{aligned}
P_3 &= 4{,}000 + 100/(1.08) + 500/(1.08)^2 + 1{,}000/(1.08)^3 - 1{,}100/(1.08)^3 \\
&= 4{,}000 + 100(.9259) + 500(.8573) + 1{,}000(.7938) - 1{,}100(.7938) \\
&= \$4{,}441.85
\end{aligned}
$$

Notice that each of the future cash flows was discounted (their present values found) and that the $4,000 has not been discounted at all since it represents the immediate cash outlay for the drilling rig. The present values for the other four acts are

$$
\begin{aligned}
P_1 &= \$2{,}240.79 \\
P_2 &= 3{,}235.29 \\
P_3 &= 5{,}766.04 \\
P_5 &= 7{,}370.38
\end{aligned}
$$

No decisions can be made by directly comparing these present values as they represent the use of the rig over differing time periods. Neither can P_2 be divided by 2 years to get a per year figure nor can P_5 be divided by 5 years to get an annual cost figure as was done in the model where no interest rate was incorporated. However, something logically analogous to this can be done in order to put the five strategies on a comparable basis. In particular, the "equivalent annual cost" for each strategy must be determined.

The equivalent annual cost for a_3 is a uniform cost payable at the end of each of three years which has the same present value as the costs actually incurred over the three year period under a_3. Earlier it was determined that the present value of the costs under a_3 is $4,441.85. In this case the equivalent annual cost is $1,723.57 which means that a cost of $1,723.57 payable at the end of the first, second, and third years has the same present value as a_3 which has an immediate cost of $4,000, a cost of $100 at the end of the first year, a cost of $500 at the end of the second year, and a net gain of $100 at the end of the third year. Mathematically this may be expressed as follows:

$$\$4{,}441.85 = (1{,}723.57)/(1.08) + (1{,}723.57)/(1.08)^2 + (1{,}723.57)/(1.08)^3$$

and

$$\$4{,}441.85 = 4{,}000 + (100)/(1.08) + (500)/(1.08)^2 + (-100)/(1.08)^3$$

Once the equivalent annual cost for each strategy is determined the optimal strategy may be found by comparing the equivalent annual costs and selecting the act with the minimum EAC.

The equivalent annual cost may be found if the present value P of a strategy is known. The relationship is given by

$$EAC = (P)\left(\frac{i(1+i)^n}{(1+i)^n-1}\right) \tag{11-23}$$

where n represents the number of periods in the horizon of the replacement cycle and i is the interest rate. The value of the right hand factor of Equation 11–23 may be evaluated by using Appendix Table 3. For example, the EAC for a_3 may be determined as

$$\begin{aligned} EAC_3 &= (P_3)\left(\frac{.08(1+.08)^3}{(1+.08)^3-1}\right) \\ &= (4{,}441.85)(.38803) \\ &= \$1{,}723.57 \end{aligned}$$

where the factor .38803 was read from Appendix Table 3. The equivalent annual costs for all of the acts are

$$\begin{aligned} EAC_1 &= (2{,}240.79)(1.08) = \$2{,}420.05 \\ EAC_2 &= (3{,}235.29)(.56077) = 1{,}814.25 \\ EAC_3 &= (4{,}441.85)(.38803) = 1{,}723.57 \\ EAC_4 &= (5{,}766.04)(.30192) = 1{,}740.88 \\ EAC_5 &= (7{,}370.38)(.25046) = 1{,}845.99 \end{aligned}$$

From a comparison of these equivalent annual costs it is seen that a_3 is optimal; Taylor should replace the Platte River Drilling Rig at the end of every three years. This happens to be the same strategy as that determined when no interest rate was used earlier in this section. Such need not be the case; there will be differences in the optimal strategy in many problems encountered depending on the interest rate used. As the interest rate i which is used in the discounting process is increased the effect is to minimize the importance of costs and gains which lie further out in the future. Low interest rates and no interest rate ($i=0$) have the opposite effect of giving equal weight to all costs and gains regardless of their timing. Though ignoring interest rates in the analysis of short term projects or policies may not result in poor decisions, certainly i should be incorporated in the analysis of situations extending more than two years into the future.

PROBLEMS

11-1. Paxton Gyro has had ten government contracts. Following is a summary of Paxton's estimated costs and the actual costs of performing the contracts. Measure the bias and reliability of Paxton's estimating department.

Estimated	Actual Cost	E/A
$134 thousand	$155 thousand	.865
105	112	.938
69	56	1.232
96	104	.923
89	100	.890
102	98	1.041
143	143	1.000
154	165	.933
97	106	.915
70	75	.933

(handwritten: $\mu_R = .967$, $\sigma_R = .10$, $\bar{E} = 105.9$, $\bar{A} = 111.4$, $\frac{\bar{E}}{\bar{A}} = .951$ NOT SAME, $\frac{E}{A}$ 9-67)

11–2. Vernon Paper Co. is going to submit a bid to supply all of the paper forms used by Hubble Intl. Vernon has only one competitor, McPeters Inc. The following table summarizes past bidding competitions:

Contract	Vernon's Cost Est.	Vernon's Bid	McPeter's Bid	Vernon's Actual Cost	M/E
GE	$ 80,000	$ 88,000	$ 84,000	—	1.05
Textrin	40,000	41,000	44,000	40,000	1.10
IBXX	120,000	140,000	132,000	—	1.10
Mericle	38,000	41,000	43,700	38,000	1.15
PIC	50,000	54,000	55,000	50,000	1.10
LoneStar	69,000	76,000	79,350	69,000	1.15
Bigal	100,000	111,000	110,000	—	1.10
Abus	87,000	93,000	91,350	—	1.05
Timmons	54,000	60,000	62,100	54,000	1.15
Anamax	70,000	75,000	77,000	70,000	1.10

(a) Is Vernon's estimating department biased? reliable? *NO, YES*

(b) Vernon estimates the cost on the Hubble contract to be $100,000. What should Vernon's bid be? (Assume that Vernon is limited to bids of $104,000, $109,000, $114,000, and $119,000.)

(handwritten table:)

X	P(x)	E·X
1.05	.2	105,000
1.10	.5	110,000
1.15	.3	115,000

(handwritten: $E(B_1) = 4,000$, $E(B_2) = .8 \cdot 9000$, $E(B_3) = .3 \cdot 14,000$ $E(B_4) = 0$)

11–3. Buzzard Built is competing against Big Mope Co. and Torres Inc. to build a guano processing plant. Buzzard Built's estimating department tends to underestimate costs by about 5 percent. Considering past bidding competitions, an analyst for Buzzard Built has constructed the following two frequency distributions: the first is for the ratio of Big Mope's bids to Buzzard Built's estimates, the second is for the ratio of Torres' bids to Buzzard Built's cost estimates. Letting W equal the ratio of Big Mope's bid to Buzzard Built's cost estimate, and T equal the ratio of Torres' bid to Buzzard Built's cost estimate:

W	Relative Frequency	T	Relative Frequency
.90– .95	.10	1.00–1.05	.10
.95–1.00	.10	1.05–1.10	.10
1.00–1.05	.20	1.10–1.15	.40
1.05–1.10	.20	1.15–1.20	.20
1.10–1.15	.30	1.20–1.25	.20
1.15–1.20	.10		

Buzzard Built's cost estimate for the guano plant is $400,000.

(a) What should Buzzard Built's bid be if only Big Mope is a competitor?

(b) What should Buzzard Built's bid be if both Big Mope and Torres are competitors? (Assume Big Mope and Torres act independently.)

11-4. (This problem requires knowledge of the normal distribution.) Do Problem 11-3(a) assuming that the random variable W has a normal distribution with a mean of 1.15 and a standard deviation of .10.

11-5. The Old Ranger Co. produces a variety of leather goods. The purchasing agent must make a purchase of leather for Old Ranger within the next 3 weeks. Leather prices fluctuate weekly; the purchasing agent subjectively assesses the following distribution for leather prices over the next 3 weeks:

Price of Leather	Week 1	Week 2	Week 3
40	.2	.2	.25
50	.3	.2	.25
60	.3	.3	.25
70	.2	.3	.25
	1.0	1.0	1.00

Design an optimal purchasing strategy for this situation.

11-6. Specific Mills must make a large purchase of corn within the next five days. The price per bushel and five daily price distributions are given below. Determine the optimal purchasing strategy.

Price per bushel	Day 1	Day 2	Day 3	Day 4	Day 5
3.00	.2	.2	.2	.2	.2
3.20	.2	.2	.2	.2	.2
3.40	.2	.2	.2	.2	.2
3.60	.2	.2	.2	.2	.2
3.80	.2	.2	.2	.2	.2
	1.0	1.0	1.0	1.0	1.0

11-7. An employee of Welder has been transferred and must sell her home within 4 weeks. Assuming that she can expect to get one offer per week over the next four weeks, and the distributions of offers for each week are as given, what should the employee's critical price be each week? (The asking price of the home is $62,000).

Offer	Week 1	Week 2	Week 3	Week 4
$60,000	.2	.2	.3	.4
61,000	.5	.5	.5	.4
62,000	.3	.3	.2	.2

11-8. Kadko has a film-cutting machine in which a certain critical component is subject to failure. If the component fails while a roll of film is being cut there will be a cost of $400 incurred as a good deal of film (a roll) will be wasted. This $400 includes the cost of installing a new component in the machine at the time of failure. If the component is

338

replaced between rolls (a renewal), the only expense will be the cost of replacement as there will be no loss of film. The replacement at renewal time costs $80. By Monte Carlo simulation, evaluate the replacement policy which would automatically replace (renew) the cutting component after two rolls of film have been cut. (If the component failed *during* the first roll, for example, then it would be replaced at a cost of $400. This new component would be renewed after the second and third rolls have been cut assuming that it does not fail during the cutting of these two rolls.)

The mortality distribution for the component is given as

R	P(R)
1	.10
2	.20
3	.30
4	.40

where R is the random variable denoting the "roll of failure," that is, the probability that the component will fail while cutting the first roll is .10, while cutting the second is .20, et cetera. Simulate the cutting of 40 rolls of film, and on the basis of this simulation find the average cost associated with the cutting component per roll. Instead of using a simulation work sheet similar to that of Table 11.11, use the work sheet below. This work sheet is purposely sketchy; however, with some study you should be able to understand it and then continue to use it through the 40th roll of film.

Roll	Cost of Installing Component	Roll During Which Component Will Fail Unless Replaced Earlier (RN)	R	Failure of Component?
	$ 80	( )	4	
#1				No
#2				No
	$ 80	( )	3	
#3				No
#4				No
	$ 80	( )	4	
#5				No
#6				No
	$ 80	( )	2	
#7				No
#8				Yes
	$400	( )	3	
#9				No
#10				No
	$ 80	( )	1	
#11				Yes
	$400	( )	4	
#12				No

11-9. After every 10,000 miles of travel every truck in the Pancon fleet comes in for a maintenance check. It is Pancon's policy to replace all of the tires on a truck simultaneously during one of the maintenance checks. (Tires which are in good shape at the renewal are resold.) A new tire costs $200 to install (labor and tire) at renewal time, however, if a tire fails while on the road the cost is $500 due to extra labor expenses and lost time. By means of Monte Carlo simulation, evaluate a replacement policy which calls for the automatic replacement of the tires at 0 miles, 40,000 miles, 80,000 miles, 120,000 miles, et cetera. The distribution of the failure of a truck tire is as given below. Assume that the tires fail at 11,000 miles, 21,000, 31,000, ... miles of use. Also assume that a tire removed at X miles has a trade-in value of $T = 1,000,000/X$ where X equals the miles it has travelled. If the tire is replaced because of failure (blow-out), it has no trade-in value.

m	P(m)
11,000	.10
21,000	.00
31,000	.05
41,000	.10
51,000	.15
61,000	.25
71,000	.30
81,000	.05

m = mileage at which time failure occurs.

Simulate the truck till its odometer reaches 800,000 miles. In so doing assume the truck has only one wheel. Use the simulation work sheet below to perform this simulation. The work sheet as given is purposely sketchy, thus you will have to study it in order to see the rationale behind it.

Odometer Miles	Action	Cost	Trade-in Value	Miles till Tire would fail (RN)	m
0	Tire installed	$200		( )	51,000
40,000	Tire installed	$200	$ 25	( )	31,000
71,000	Failure (blowout)	$500	0	( )	11,000
80,000	Tire installed	$200	$111	( )	61,000
120,000	Tire installed	$200	$ 25	( )	11,000
131,000	Failure (blowout)	$500	0	( )	31,000
160,000	Tire installed	$200	$34.50	( )	71,000

11-10. Do Problem 11–9 with the added condition that when a tire fails there is a .30 probability that there will be damage done to the truck in the amount of $600 in addition to the $500 for the replacement of the tire. In the other 70 percent of the failures only the $500 cost is incurred.

11-11. Considering the simulation of Section 11–12, simulate one trip using a_1 and one trip using a_3 where the trips are the 40-day trips to Fort Bozeman as described.

11-12. Mother and Dad have to decide how often to replace the family car. If the cost of a new car is $5,000 and if the trade-in values and maintenance costs are as given, what is the optimal replacement policy without considering the time value of money?

Year	Trade-in Value	Maintenance/Repair
1	$3,200	$50
2	2,600	100
3	2,000	200
4	1,500	300
5	1,100	500
6	800	900

11-13. Using an interest rate of 6 percent, is it better to replace the family car every 2 years or every 3 years (see Problem 11–12)? Assume that the maintenance/repair expenses occur near the end of the year.

11-14. Travis Manufacturing must decide on a policy respecting the replacement of a piece of equipment. The equipment costs $30,000. The salvage value of the equipment for the year y is given by the linear function $S = 30,000 - 6,000y$ and the maintenance cost for the yth year of service is given by $M = 1,000 + 1,000y^2$. Find the optimal replacement policy disregarding the time value of money.

11-15. In Problem 11–14, is it better to replace the equipment every year or every two years if the interest rate is 8 percent? Assume that the maintenance expenses occur near the end of the year.

11-16. Letting $i = .10$,
  (a) Find the equivalent annual cost of a machine which is purchased at time 0 for $1,000, has a repair expense of $200 at the end of one year, has a repair expense of $300 at the end of the second year at which time it is scrapped.
  (b) Find the EAC for the situation as described in (a) except that at the end of the second year another identical machine is purchased for $1,000 and it has a repair expense of $200 after its first year (3 years from time 0) and has an expense of $300 at the end of its second year (4 years from now) and is scrapped. In other words, find the EAC for a sequence of two identical machines.
  (c) Compare your answers in (a) and (b).

12 Forecasting

12.1 INTRODUCTION

The importance of forecasting to managerial decision making cannot be overemphasized. It is through forecasting that management steps into the future. Nearly every decision depends on some sort of forecasting for its resolution. It is ultimately on the basis of the sales forecast, for example, that product decisions, staffing decisions, transportation decisions, and finance decisions are made. Forecasts play an important role in the construction and solution of many of the models which have been considered in this text. For example, demand and cost forecasts are extremely important in inventory models. The forecasts of arrival and service rates as well as the forecasts of various costs play an important role in queueing decisions. Even in linear programming applications which do not contain a probabilistic element, forecasts may be important in the determination of various constants in the constraints and objective function.

Forecasts and forecasting techniques can be categorized or classified in many ways. They can be categorized with regard to the actual form of the forecast. Some forecasts are probabilistic as in the case where the sales manager sees next year's sales as being normally distributed with a mean of 1 million units and a standard deviation of .1 million units. On the other hand, a forecast may be one of assumed certainty where the single best estimate is given. For example, the engineering department may forecast that it will cost $325 to build a particular electronic component.

Forecasting techniques may also be categorized according to the amount and type of information which is available for forecasting purposes. When a company is introducing a new product unlike any other product on the market, management may be forced to rely on the subjective forecasts of those who would most likely understand the market for the new product. Even though market research might be conducted before the introduction of this new product, there is still a lack of historical data which is required by many of the mathematical forecasting techniques. On the other hand, forecasting the sales of a product which is well along in its life cycle might best be achieved by a mathematical technique with relatively little subjective input.

Forecasts may also be classified as to the term of the forecast. Forecasting may be divided into short-term, intermediate-term, and long-term forecasting. Short-term forecasting commonly refers to forecasts no further than a year or two into the future while long-term forecasting usually refers to periods five or more years away. Different techniques become relatively more useful depending on the term or time horizon being considered. In short-term forecasting there may be considerable attention focused on matters of seasonality and the effect of business cycles. In long-term forecasting these factors are less important.

In selecting a forecasting technique the analyst should not only be cognizant of the type of forecast desired (probabilistic or single estimate), the availability of information, and the term, but also the purpose of the forecast. A fairly rough forecast might be quite adequate to guide a company regarding the advisability of entering a new market. On the other hand, a forecast upon which a budget is to be based might need to be quite accurate.

Several forecasting techniques will be presented in this chapter as they apply to certain special forecasting situations. Subjective forecasting will be considered first, followed by discussions of mathematical forecasting techniques. In presenting the mathematical techniques the applications will be confined to short-term forecasting. Short-term forecasting is very important to the various operational decisions confronting management. As many of the models considered in this text are concerned with situations where short-term forecasts are needed, a focus on short-term techniques would be appropriate. Though forecasting is considered more an art than a science, it could be argued that it comes closest to being a science in the realm of short-term forecasting. For this reason and because of its relevance to operational decisions, this chapter is limited to the coverage of short-term forecasting.

12.2 SUBJECTIVE FORECASTS

In many forecasting situations, historical quantitative data which would be useful for prediction purposes are sparse, unavailable, or even nonexistent. In these situations an "objective" forecasting technique, which relies primarily on a given set of historical data upon which to base a forecast, cannot be used. In these instances the forecast must be a subjective forecast. Such a forecast consists of the subjective judgment of the forecaster and has its roots in the perspectives of the forecaster who has acquired all sorts of information through experience. Consider now some examples where the subjective type of forecast comes into prominence.

QQQ Markets, Inc., is a chain of small fast-service grocery stores which are strategically placed in various parts of the city. QQQ is considering a new location for their second market in Cincinnati and is attempting to forecast annual sales for the new location. Based on the experience with the first QQQ market, it is management's judgment that sales volume will stabilize about six months after the store is opened. QQQ Markets, Inc., anticipates sales of $200,000 for their first market. This forecast is based on the sales experience at that location for the past three years. Can QQQ Markets therefore conclude that sales, after six months or so, at the proposed second location will be at about the same level? Even though the stores themselves are identical, the locations in the community are different, meaning that the competitive environment is likely to be different as well as the population of customers. These kinds of differences may cause management to forecast sales at some value other than the $200,000 which was forecasted for the first QQQ market. Perhaps the forecast for the new location will be $170,000; how did this forecast come to be $30,000 less then that for the first location? There is no mathematical forecasting technique which would have dictated this difference for the second location, rather it is due to the subjective evaluation of management. Here then is a case where subjective judgment was used to modify a forecast ($200,000) which may have originally been made very formally on the basis of historical data (three years of experience at the first location). In other cases there may be no historical data which is of significance in the forecasting procedure. In such a case management cannot proceed by subjectively modifying some partially relevant forecast which was based on historical data. Consider now an example at this extreme.

Suppose Kodak is contemplating the introduction of a small machine which the amateur photographer can use at home to automatically develop super-8 movie film. Management estimates that it would take at least ten to fifteen years to develop and produce such a unit which would sell, in terms of today's prices, for $200. What annual sales level could Kodak expect ten or fifteen years down the road? The uniqueness of this product, the distant time horizon, the plans of other competitors, and so forth make obvious that any historical data Kodak presently has could only be expected to be loosely related to the future sales of this hypothetical product. Having sampled present-day consumer interest in such a product, and being conversant with projected camera usage and sales, Kodak's management would undoubtedly make a subjective forecast. Being a subjective forecast does not mean that management will not consider actual data concerning consumer interest, for example, in the planned product. However, this data would not be used in a formal mathematical model. Also, being a subjective forecast does not imply that management would not use a mathematical technique to forecast camera sales, for example, as a means of gaining insight into the state of the world ten years hence. Though mathematical techniques might be used along the way, the ultimate forecast in such a case as the super-8 developer would be the result of that indescribable analysis and synthesis of human minds apart from a formal mathematical forecasting model.

In the next sections subjective forecasting by individuals and then by groups will be considered. After this several mathematical or so-called objective forecasting techniques will be presented.

12.3 SUBJECTIVE FORECASTS BY INDIVIDUALS

Individuals, whether managers or not, make many forecasts or predictions of the subjective variety. Predictions abound at Super Bowl time as to which team will win and by how much. People make predictions or forecasts concerning inflation, unemployment, interest rates, weather, grades, jobs, and so on.

These subjective forecasts result from a seemingly inscrutable mental process where the amount and kind of information the individual has plays an important, though not exclusive, role. It is not the purpose here to hypothesize as to how the mind functions in generating a forecast like "I think the Cowboys will win by 9 points," or, "Ford will never sell the Edsel," or, "This country will be bankrupt in ten years." Rather it is the intent of this section and the next to outline some guidelines or techniques by which an individual can convert subjective judgments, whatever they may be, into a probabilistic forecast.

Making "best guess" or point forecasts comes quite natural to the human mind. What is your best guess for the road mileage from New York City to Houston? Everyone can answer that question even though the answers will differ from person to person. What is your best guess as to the mileage between the two American settlements of Chicago and Beardsley? Everyone can answer that question also! But you say that you have never heard of Beardsley! Nevertheless, you can guess even though you might have little confidence in your estimate. Suppose that you estimated the mileage from New York City to Houston as 1500 miles and the mileage from Chicago to Beardsley as 1500 miles also. Even though the term "forecast" has a connotation of predicting something in the future, it could be said that you have made two forecasts of 1500 miles each in answering the questions above. Subjective estimates of mileage and subjective future forecasts are logically similar. These subjective estimates of 1500 miles each must now be scrutinized more closely. You, most likely, feel much more confident with the New York City to Houston forecast. However, by looking at the "1500" in each case, an outside observer could never tell that in fact you were more comfortable with the first forecast. We do not give our first forecast as "1500_{wcc}" and the second as "1500_{wmc}" where the first subscript reads "with considerable confidence" and the second reads "with minimal confidence." Putting this kind of subscript on forecasts would be helpful, yet it is open to too much misunderstanding. It is therefore desirable to state mathematically the degree of confidence one has in one's forecasts.

A probabilistic forecast, in contrast to a best guess or point forecast, gives information as to the confidence of the forecaster. How can such a subjective, probabilistic forecast be made? Perhaps the best way to explain this sort of forecasting is by example.

Suppose I, as a manager, am interested in the price of natural gas five years from now. I have looked at the history of natural gas prices, I've talked to suppliers and other large users, I've attempted to keep abreast of the political moods which might have an impact on the price regulation of this resource, and I've read some predictions of price trends by both producers and regulators. After saturating my mind with all of this information and with my notes before me which include some sketchy mathematical calculations, I want to forecast the price of natural gas. My best guess or point forecast for the price five years hence is $.70 per hundred cubic feet. After making this forecast I readily admit that I could be way off. In other words, I would prefer to submit the forecast as $.70$_{wmc}$ where the subscript reads "with minimal confidence." Better yet, I would like to make a probabilistic forecast.

I can make a probabilistic forecast by asking myself a series of questions. First, what according to my personal judgment is the probability that the price will be equal to or under $1.50 per hundred cubic feet? After some reflection I conclude that I am certain that the price will be equal to or under $1.50 and thus assign a probability of 1 to this. That is

$$P(N \leq 1.50) = 1$$

where N refers to the price of natural gas five years hence. Then I ask myself, what is the probability that N will be $1.00 or less five years hence? After pondering this question I give the probability of .90. That is, in my judgment there is a ninety percent chance that the price will be $1.00 or less.

$$P(N \leq 1.00) = .90$$

If I had a bag of ten marbles where nine were blue and one was red, I consider that having gas prices of $1.00 or less is just as likely as selecting a blue marble from the bag with my eyes closed.

The next question is, what is the probability that N will be $.70 or less? My feeling is that there is a 50–50 chance or a probability of .50 that this will happen. Hence,

$$P(N \leq .70) = .50$$

Finally, what is my subjective probability that N will be equal to or below $.50? After some thought I give the probability of .20, or,

$$P(N \leq .50) = .20$$

That is, as I see it there are two chances in ten that the price would be $.50 or lower. More questions like these could be asked; however, the thoughtful answering of just these four will enable me to construct a probabilistic forecast for natural gas prices five years hence. For the sake of assessing a subjective forecast, four questions are sufficient assuming that the questions are "reasonably spaced." It would not have been acceptable to ask, in this particular case, for the probabilities of the price being $.80, $.75, $.70, and $.62 or lower; these values are too close to each other given the state of my beliefs concerning prices five years hence. I have subjectively assessed the following four probabilities

$$P(N \leq 1.50) = 1.00$$
$$P(N \leq 1.00) = .90$$
$$P(N \leq .70) = .50$$
$$P(N \leq .50) = .20$$

where N equals the price of natural gas five years hence. These should now be plotted on graph paper as is illustrated in Figure 12.1(a). The vertical axis denotes the cumulative probabilities, that is, it gives the probability that N will be less than or equal to the prices given on the horizontal axis. After plotting these four points I should smooth a curved line through them as is accomplished in Figure 12.1(b) in order to form a continuous cumulative probability distribution. (See Section 2.12 of Chapter 2 for a review of cumulative distributions).

Sometimes the points do not fall on a smooth line which may mean that individuals were not consistent in preparing their subjective probability assessments. If after more thought the individual is convinced that these points accurately reflect personal thinking, then the smooth line will not be so smooth.

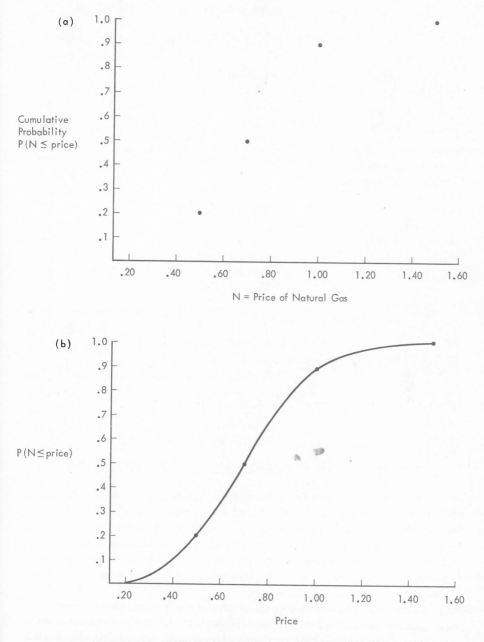

FIGURE 12.1   **A Subjective Distribution for Natural Gas Prices Five Years Hence**

As stated, the graph of Figure 12.1(b) is nothing more than a continuous probability distribution. Furthermore it is a subjective distribution because it was generated directly from my judgments or subjective probabilities. From this distribution the following probabilities, for example, may be read: $P(N \leq 1.40) = 1.00$, $P(N \leq 1.00) = .90$, $P(N \leq .80) = .68$, $P(N \leq .60) = .35$, $P(N \leq .40) = .10$, and $P(N \leq .20) = 0$. If the probability that N is \$1.00 or less is .90 and the probability that N is \$.80 or less is .68, then the probability that N is between \$.81 and \$1.00 must be .90 − .68 or .22. In like manner the probability that N will be between \$.61 and \$.80 is .68 − .35 or .33. In this fashion a discrete probability distribution for natural gas prices can be determined as given in Table 12.1. I, the manager, have therefore converted my thoughts and judgments into a probability distribution which now, in the form of Figure 12.1(b) or Table 12.1, can be used in a model for the sake of decision making.

TABLE 12.1
Probability Distribution of Natural Gas Prices

Price, N	P(N)
\$ .21– .40	.10
.41– .60	.25
.61– .80	.33
.81–1.00	.22
1.01–1.40	.10

Notice that the distribution of Table 12.1 has considerable variability. It is quite apparent that even though my best guess was \$.70 per hundred cubic feet, I have relatively little confidence that the actual price will be within a dime of this figure. That is, I see only one chance in three that the price will be between \$.61 and \$.80. Another manager following the same process might have a more diffuse or more compact distribution depending on the manager's knowledge and subjective evaluation of the situation. The manager who might have a more compact distribution, a smaller standard deviation, is the manager who is more confident in personal beliefs regarding the object of the forecast.

12.4 SUBJECTIVELY ASSESSED NORMAL DISTRIBUTION

In the realm of subjective probabilistic forecasting, the normal distribution is commonly used because it often seems appropriate as a vehicle to express a person's beliefs concerning some unknown quantity. A further reason for the pervasiveness of the normal distribution in subjective forecasting is the fact that it is easy to assess or construct. Before proceeding with the use of the normal distribution in the context of subjective forecasting, this distribution should be reviewed (see Section 2.13 of Chapter 2).

Managers who forecast the price of natural gas five years hence might feel that a distribution in the form of a normal distribution would adequately express their feelings. In Figure 12.2 an example of a normal distribution for natural gas prices is given which might have been the result of the manager's subjective judgment. Notice that the most likely price is $.70. Not only is this the most likely price or mode, but there is a .50 probability that the price will be greater than this and a .50 probability that the price will be less than $.70. Hence $.70 is also the median of the forecast. The distribution is symmetrical and this, it is assumed, is in accord with the thinking of the manager who has assessed this distribution. How can such a normal subjective distribution be determined?

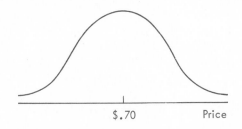

$.70   Price

FIGURE 12.2   Normal Distribution of Prices

It must be remembered that there is a family of normal distributions all with different, though similar, shapes. A particular normal distribution is determined once its mean and standard deviation are known. In other words, if it is known that a given distribution is normal and that its mean is .70 and its standard deviation is .10, then there is no longer any question as to which normal distribution it is. The distribution is perfectly known. It therefore follows that if a manager is going to subjectively assess a normal distribution which is to constitute a subjective forecast, only the mean and standard deviation of that distribution must be determined.

Assuming the manager is convinced that a normal distribution will be adequate for the subjective forecast, the procedure for determining the mean and standard deviation will now be outlined. Suppose, for example, that I as a manager am attempting to forecast sales in the first year of a new compact automobile called the Tudor which my company will introduce in the European market. My best point forecast is 50,000 units. This best guess or forecast will serve as the mean of the normal distribution expressing my subjective forecast; it also happens to be the mode and median of the normal distribution. Though 50,000 is my best forecast, I would not be surprised if actual sales strayed considerably from this figure. At this point I could proceed using the technique of the previous section to determine a probability forecast for sales. Instead I have recognized that a normal distribution would be adequate as an expression of my beliefs concerning first year sales of the Tudor.

There are an infinite number of normal distributions with a mean of 50,000. Which one of these mirrors my feelings? In order to determine the standard deviation of the normal distribution which reflects my beliefs, I must only answer the following question: "Between what limits, lower and upper, am I exactly 50 percent sure that actual sales will fall?" After pondering this question I come out with this statement: "There is a 50–50 chance that sales will be between 40,000 and 60,000 units." Coming up with such a declaration is not as difficult as it may seem; toward the end of this section this matter will be discussed in detail. For the moment, assume that this is my statement which accurately reflects my beliefs concerning Tudor sales.

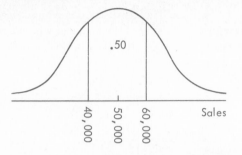

FIGURE 12.3   Subjective Normal Distribution

If I assert that there is a .50 probability that actual sales will be between 40,000 and 60,000 units, then I can accept the normal distribution of Figure 12.3 as being descriptive of my beliefs. Notice that the area between 40,000 and 60,000 is .50 and the area between 50,000 and 60,000 is necessarily .25 since the distribution is symmetrical about its mean. What is the standard deviation of this particular distribution? With *any* normal distribution, fifty percent of the area (or probability) lies within ± .67 standard deviations of the mean (see Appendix Table 2). Equivalently, twenty-five percent of the area under the curve is between the mean and a point which is .67 standard deviations above it (see Figure 12.4). Since twenty-five percent of the area under the curve in the subjective distribution of Figure 12.3 lies between 50,000 and 60,000, 60,000 *must* be exactly .67 standard deviations above the mean since it is a normal distribution. That is,

$$60,000 = \text{Mean} + (.67)(\sigma)$$

or,

$$60,000 = 50,000 + (.67)(\sigma)$$

where σ represents the standard deviation. Now this last equation may be solved for the standard deviation yielding

$$\sigma = \frac{60,000 - 50,000}{.67}$$

$$\sigma = 14,925$$

Thus the standard deviation of the normal distribution of Figure 12.3 must be 14,925 units. I can therefore state that my subjective forecast for Tudor sales is represented by a normal distribution with a mean of 50,000 and a standard deviation of 14,925 units.

To summarize this procedure, suppose a person is forecasting the value for X where, for example, X may refer to some quantity like sales or costs. If the person feels that a distribution which is symmetrical and whose mode is the same as its median is appropriate, then the normal distribution would be a good choice for the subjective distribution. To actually determine this normal distribution,

1. Forecast the most likely value for X. Call this value M.
2. Make a thoughtful statement like "I am 50 percent sure that X will fall between L and U." Alternately you should be 50 percent sure that X will fall outside the interval from L to U.
3. The subjective forecast will then be: "My forecast for X is normally distributed with a mean of M and a standard deviation of σ where

$$\sigma = (U-M)/.67$$

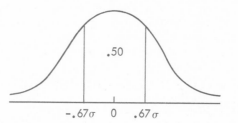

FIGURE 12.4   Area Within .67 Standard Deviations of the Mean

In conclusion focus on the statement where the manager states that there is a .50 probability that X will fall between some lower value of L, like 40,000, and upper value of U, like 60,000, as in the Tudor example. The making of such statements is an art and thus best learned by practice. Answer this: What is your best guess for the distance between Oklahoma City and Atlanta? Write down your answer. Now make a statement of the sort "As far as I am concerned, there is a 50–50 chance that the true distance between Oklahoma City and Atlanta is between 100 and 5000 miles." Write down *your* limits. Now, if you live in the USA and have gotten this far in school, your limits should not be on the order of "between 100 and 5000 miles." You should be 100 percent sure, not just 50 percent sure, that the distance between these two cities is between 100 and 5000 miles! On the other hand, if your limits were "between 900 and 901 miles," you made them too narrow since no reader happens to know the indicated mileage that accurately. In this situation, for example, the author's .50 interval is from 850 to 1000 miles. I am equally sure that the distance lies outside this interval as it lies within. Your interval would undoubtedly be different depending on your knowledge of geography. However, if you are giving a 50–50 interval it should not be something like "100 to 5000" or "900 to 901."

How can it be determined if a person is getting the hang of assessing these .50 subjective intervals? The only way is to try assessing a number of them and see how things go. Therefore, twenty forecasts will be requested from the reader in a moment. In each of these situations take a few seconds of thought and then *write down* a .50 subjective interval in each case. If you have a relatively large amount of information on the matter, your interval will be relatively narrow. If you are ignorant about the subject, your forecast or 50–50 interval will be very wide. After you have constructed a .50 subjective interval for each of the twenty situations, the answers will be given and a diagnosis made of your personal ability to construct or make these 50–50 statements. Again, be sure to write down your interval (lower and upper limit) in each case.

Give a .50 subjective interval for each of the following:

1. The number of square miles in Wisconsin.
2. Percentage of land in Norway which is agriculturally unproductive.
3. Total popular vote Nixon received in North Carolina in 1968. (Do not express as a percentage.)
4. The number of points that James Taylor scored in 1962.
5. The number of auto deaths in New York in 1969.
6. Percentage increase in population in the USA from 1850 to 1860.
7. The number of Psalms in the Bible.
8. The year of the death of Edgar Allen Poe.
9. Average January temperature in Albuquerque.
10. Closing price of VEPCO stock on January 28, 1976.
11. Total dollar sales of Eastman Kodak in 1970.
12. The number of cubic feet of natural gas sold in 1966.
13. Average speed of the Indianapolis 500 winner in 1940.
14. John L. Sullivan's weight on September 7, 1892.
15. The year that Al Hodges was U.S. Chess Champion.
16. Distance between Tau Ceti and the north pole.
17. Area in square miles of Lake Superior.
18. Percentage of the popular vote Abe Lincoln got in 1860.
19. Amount Old Hickory spent refurbishing the White House.
20. The amount of money the USSR owed the USA in 1965.

The actual values for these twenty cases are given in Problem 12–1 at the end of the chapter. Check to determine how many of the actual values fall within your stated intervals. If you have the right idea in constructing these subjective intervals you will find that in approximately ten cases the actual value was within your interval. If your intervals contained the actual value in fifteen or more cases, it can be said quite dogmatically that you are not assessing .50 or 50–50 intervals. It is extremely rare that a reader will make this kind of error. If you happen to be a person who did get considerably more than ten actual values in your intervals, in the future you should consciously reduce the size of your intervals and rethink what it means to be exactly 50 percent sure that the value is within your interval.

By far the most common tendency is getting too few of the actual values in your interval. If you got five or fewer in your intervals it can be stated quite dogmatically that you do not have the hang of this process. The diagnosis is that you know less than you think you do. In the future you should widen your intervals. The majority of readers will get between five and ten of the actual values in their intervals. This means that on the whole there is a propensity for people to make the intervals too narrow which, again, is another way of saying that most people know less about what they are forecasting than what they think. If you fall in this category, especially between five and seven, you should consciously be aware of this bias in your behavior with the objective of compensating for it.

With the development of the ability to assess .50 subjective intervals, the manager becomes capable through the technique presented earlier in this section of accurately converting mental judgments into a subjective normal distribution. This forecast can then be used in the decision making process.

12.5 SUBJECTIVE FORECASTS BY GROUPS

In many instances a number of managers may have an interest in some forecast. Take the example of Kodak's supposed interest in developing and marketing a machine which will develop home movies. Decisions and forecasts associated with such an endeavor would come from all quarters of the company. In order to obtain a sales forecast, inputs would be desired from the marketing and sales divisions as well as from engineering, finance, and production. Typically a committee or panel of experts from within the organization would be assembled and this committee would be the vehicle through which information was exchanged and a forecast made. The forecast would be some sort of composition of the individual subjective forecasts of the committee members.

Such committees have advantages and disadvantages. On the positive side, valuable information is exchanged along with useful insights. With the accumulation of relevant information and the contribution of various perspectives, it might be expected that the forecast would be better. However, there are disadvantages to the committee approach. In the committee setting, face-to-face confrontations too often develop which are counter-productive. Dominating personalities take over, .members feel constrained to defend their previously stated opinions, and junior managers are reluctant to disagree with senior members. For these reasons the possible benefits of group forecasting are often never actualized.

Cognizant of the disadvantages and advantages of committee forecasting, a research group of the Rand Corporation devised a group forecasting technique which capitalized on the advantages of the committee approach but which circumvented the disadvantages. This technique, known as the Delphi method, consists in constructing a short questionnaire which is sent to the would-be committee members. The questions are brief and pointed. "Can we develop a home movie developer in ten years which would cost $200?" "What is the probability that one of our competitors would develop one in less than ten years?" "How many could we sell?" The respondent is encouraged to briefly give reasons for the answers and relate information which might be foreign to the other managers.

These questionnaires are then collected and summarized. From the results a new questionnaire is prepared which carries with it important information and perspectives collected from the respondents' first questionnaire. In this manner the ideas of the various managers are shared. With the sharing of the new information and forecasts of the other managers, the manager is encouraged to reevaluate ideas and come to a better position. This kind of thing continues for up to five or six rounds by which time a consensus is often reached. Thus a forecast is achieved which represents the subjective belief of a group of experts.

It should be noted that the subjective forecasting techniques for individuals as presented in the foregoing sections can be incorporated into the group approach. For example, instead of asking "How many can we sell," the questionnaire could request a .50 subjective interval for sales. In this way more information can be communicated by the respondents.

12.6 TIME SERIES AND AN OVERVIEW

A time series consists of the values of some variable which are associated with successive units of time. For example, in Figure 12.5 a time series is given where sales is represented on the vertical axis and time is represented by the horizontal axis. It is seen from this time series that sales in 1950 were 220 and the number of units sold in 1964 was about 240. The series continues up to the point where the last available sales value is plotted in 1976. Typically the values in a time series are considered to indicate the presence of a trend which is a long-term gradual movement covering at least fifteen or twenty years. The dotted line in Figure 12.5 depicts this trend. The time series given seems to exhibit cyclical characteristics in that the series remains above the trend for several years and then dips below. These cycles may correspond to alternate periods of boom and recession in the economy. The cycles themselves exhibit erratic tendencies so that the time series appears to be somewhat jagged in places. These little movements are called random or irregular fluctuations.

If the sales data were given for each quarter of each year, the time series might exhibit yet more jaggedness due to the existence of seasonality. The sale of air conditioners and snow shovels as well as fertilizer are quite seasonal. A time series depicting the sales of snow shovels on a quarterly basis, for example, would show sales to be relatively high each fall and winter quarter from year to year.

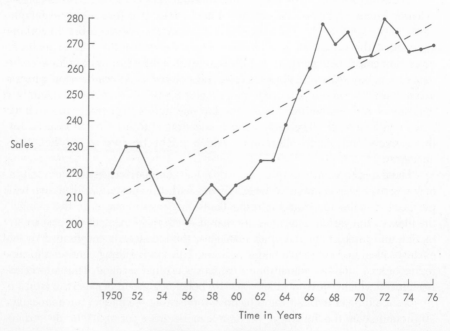

FIGURE 12.5   A Time Series

In the remainder of this chapter several forecasting techniques will be presented and applied to one special kind of forecasting situation. Specifically, the forecasting situation that will be considered is that where

1. The object is to make short-term forecasts. That is, the forecasts required will not be for more than a year or two in the future.
2. There is a relatively short history. That is, the time series does not begin decades ago.
3. There is no seasonality in the time series. The situation where, for example, quarterly or monthly data have a seasonal pattern will not be considered.
4. There is no marked trend of growth or decline in the time series. Time series with strong trends will not be considered.

It is not to be inferred that situations other than the type to be considered present difficult forecasting problems. This is not necessarily the case. Rather this discussion is confined to this particular type of forecasting situation because of the limitations on space in this book. The forecasting techniques to be used can be modified for the sake of dealing with forecasting situations other than the ones alluded to. It should also not be inferred that the type of forecasting situation that will be considered is rare. The forecasting techniques to be studied have practical relevance in managerial decision making. Furthermore they represent a sample of the so-called "objective" or mathematical methods of forecasting and thus give some insight into the form and capability of this type or category of forecasting techniques.

12.7 A SHORT-TERM PROBABILISTIC FORECAST

The banks in each of the Federal Reserve cities have formed their own clearinghouse associations. Each day the twelve banks in the Richmond area, for example, exchange all the checks which are drawn upon each other. In addition to these, the Federal Reserve returns all of the out-of-town checks to the banks. As a result each bank has a pile of checks each day which it must process within a short period of time. The Metropolitan National Bank is daily faced with the task of processing such a pile of checks and is concerned with the assignment of personnel to this task. If the same number of checks needed processing each day the bank could easily determine personnel requirements and schedules. However, there is considerable variability not only from day to day within a week, but from week to week. Figure 12.6, page 356, displays the time series showing the number of clearings required on Thursdays for the past twenty-four Thursdays at the Metropolitan National Bank. From this historical data the bank wishes to forecast clearings for future Thursdays.

Examining the time series of Figure 12.6, one is impressed with the lack of any regular pattern. If a best guess or point forecast were required, it would make sense to forecast 6000 bank clearings for future Thursdays since the time series appears to be fluctuating about the 6000 level. However, many of the models that have been developed in this text, whether they be simulation or mathematical models, utilize a probability distribution for the forecasted quantity rather than a point forecast. Witness many of the examples in the decision theory, inventory, bidding, simulation, and queueing chapters which are

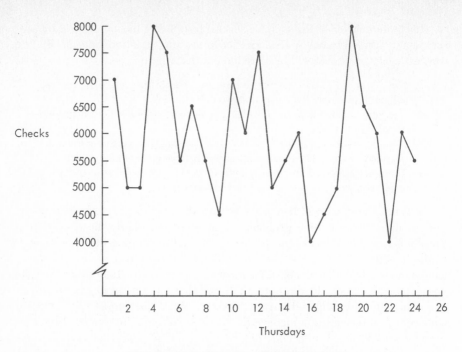

FIGURE 12.6   Thursday Bank Clearings

probabilistic. Let it be assumed that the Metropolitan bank is prepared to utilize a probabilistic forecast. How can a probability distribution be distilled from the time series of Figure 12.6?

As there is no discernible recurrent pattern in the time series and no upward or downward trend, the Metropolitan might proceed by counting how many Thursdays of the last twenty-four had 8000 clearings. It is seen that on two occasions there were 8000 clearings. Following this procedure, there were two occasions when there were 7500 clearings, there were two occasions with 7000 clearings, and so on. All of these frequencies are recorded in Table 12.2(a), page 357. Now since there is no apparent reason to suppose that the immediate future will differ from the experience of the past twenty-four Thursdays, the Metropolitan can convert this frequency distribution into a probability distribution which will serve as a probabilistic forecast for ensuing Thursdays.

Each of the frequencies of Table 12.2(a) is divided by 24 yielding the probability distribution of Table 12.2(b). The Metropolitan can now predict that the chance of there being 8000 clearings next Thursday is .08. This distribution may be formally incorporated into a decision model or it may be used directly by management in making decisions. For example, if one bank clerk is required for the prompt processing of 1000 checks, the Metropolitan Bank would take only a 17 percent chance (.083 + .083) of not having enough clerks if seven clerks are assigned to the Thursday check processing task. Such is the case because seven clerks can process 7000 checks, and according to the distribution of C in Table 12.2 there is a .166 probability that the number of checks to be cleared will exceed 7000. Thus the forecast is used in assigning personnel.

TABLE 12.2
**Frequency and Probability Distributions
for Bank Clearings**

(a)	Clearings, C	Frequency		(b)	Clearings, C	P(C)
	4,000	2			4,000	.083
	4,500	2			4,500	.083
	5,000	4			5,000	.167
	5,500	4			5,500	.167
	6,000	4			6,000	.167
	6,500	2			6,500	.083
	7,000	2			7,000	.083
	7,500	2			7,500	.083
	8,000	2			8,000	.083
		24				1.00

12.8 EXPONENTIAL SMOOTHING

In many situations management needs merely a point forecast or best guess forecast. For example, many inventory models are deterministic in nature and thus probabilistic forecasts are not needed. For the sake of the preparation of a budget or the determination of a production schedule, a point forecast may be adequate, especially when there is relatively little variability in the variable being forecasted. Exponential smoothing is one method of making point forecasts based on data from a time series. This method of point forecasting is gaining popularity because of its flexibility, computational simplicity, and adaptability to the computer. In this section the most elementary form of exponential smoothing will be introduced. As this elementary form will only be presented, the applications must be confined to those which fit the four assumptions of Section 12.6.

JP Chem must predict its chlorine sales for the next quarter. Sales data for the last twelve quarters have been assembled and a time series has been constructed as shown by the solid line in Figure 12.7, page 358. It is seen that chlorine sales were 960 in the first quarter of the time series. Sales in the last quarter were at 970. What is JP Chem's best point forecast for the next quarter?

There are a couple of ways an analyst could view a time series like that of Figure 12.7 in attempting to make a point forecast for the next period. At one extreme the analyst could pay attention to only the most recent data, say from the eighth quarter on. Considering this data only, a point forecast of about 965 might be forthcoming since the most *recent* data (since the eighth quarter) seem to roughly center around 965. At the other extreme, the analyst might feel that there is no reason to consider the most recent data as being the more important. Thus if all the data from the twelve quarters were given equal weight in the forecasting process, a forecast of about 945 might result because overall the time series data average at about this level. Which of these two approaches is better? Unfortunately there is no universal answer to this question.

If a time series will have distinct cycles, that is, protracted periods of higher than normal or lower than normal sales, then basing a forecast on the more

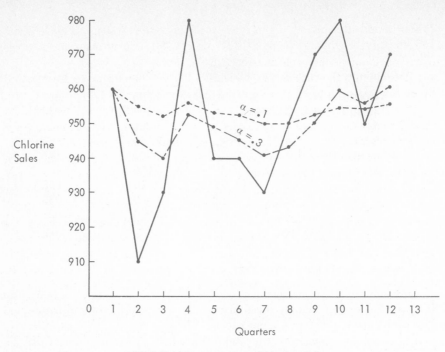

FIGURE 12.7 Quarterly Chlorine Sales

recent data would make the most sense. A forecast which is based on giving all the data equal weight would essentially be ignoring the existence of the current cycle making such an approach inferior. On the other hand, if the time series were composed chiefly of random movements, then it would make more sense to consider all of the data equally in order to get an average which would serve as a forecast. Sometimes a time series which is composed of merely random movements will look like a cycle is beginning. In these cases the supposed beginnings of a cycle is due purely to chance. A sequence of high (or low) values just happened to get bunched together giving the illusion of the start of a cycle. A forecaster who gives too much weight to recent data can get fooled by these chance movements which look like the beginnings of a cycle and hence make forecasts which are too high (or low) because of the supposed presence of a cycle.

Distinguishing between the beginning of a real cycle and a set of purely chance movements which look like the beginnings of a cycle is not an easy matter. The forecaster should be aware of other information which might indicate that a cycle may be starting. For example, if there have been recent upturns in construction, automobile sales, and steel production, the forecaster might surmise that a very recent increase in chlorine sales might be the beginnings of a cyclical upturn. This would especially be the case if chlorine were used in construction, automobile manufacturing, and in the production of steel. For each period thereafter that chlorine sales continue to increase, the forecaster would become more certain that a cyclical upturn was in fact occurring. The "law of averages" makes it unlikely that chance movements alone will continue to cluster period after period in a manner which gives the illusion of a cycle. Even with these sorts of things being considered, it is still difficult many times to detect the beginnings of a cycle at an early date.

Returning to the time series of Figure 12.7, JP Chem must decide whether to use the approach to forecasting which gives most weight to the recent data, or whether the approach which takes more of an overall perspective should be used. The first of these two approaches is prone to follow the beginnings of a cycle whether the cycle be real or due to chance. The purpose at hand is to forecast sales for the thirteenth quarter. From the fifth quarter on there seems to be a general rise in sales. Is this the beginning of a cyclical upturn or is it a purely random phenomenon? In light of the discussion of the previous paragraph, the answer to this question is important for forecasting. The forecaster in an actual management setting will not be working in a vacuum having this time series and absolutely no other information or experience. Conversations with other managers, acquaintance with the chemical industry and the economy, and a knowledge of past forecasting failures and successes should enable the forecaster to come to some position in this matter. The forecaster should have some notion regarding the nature of the time series for chlorine sales and thus be able to conclude that it is essentially random or that it is prone to exhibit successive periods of higher or lower than usual levels. With this background consider exponential smoothing.

Exponential smoothing is a forecasting tool which is merely a mathematical way of averaging the data in a time series for the sake of producing a point forecast. For each period represented in the time series an average is computed which is based on the value for that period and all of the data which precedes it. As such an average is computed for each period, this sequence of averages forms a time series itself. The method of computing these averages will now be presented. Subsequently the interpretation and use of these averages will be considered.

An exponential average, as it is called, is computed according to the following relationship

$$\text{Current Exponential Average} = (\alpha) \begin{bmatrix} \text{Current} \\ \text{Value} \end{bmatrix} + (1 - \alpha) \begin{bmatrix} \text{Previous Exponential} \\ \text{Average} \end{bmatrix}$$

where alpha, α, is a number between 0 and 1 and is called the smoothing constant. The "current value" will be seen to represent the value plotted in the actual time series. The selection of a value for α will be considered later, presently assume that α has a value of .1. Thus the current average will be computed according to

$$\text{Current Exponential Average} = (.1) \begin{bmatrix} \text{Current} \\ \text{Value} \end{bmatrix} + (1 - .1) \begin{bmatrix} \text{Previous} \\ \text{Exponential} \\ \text{Average} \end{bmatrix}$$

This equation will now be used to compute an exponential average for each of the twelve quarters in the JP Chem situation.

For the first quarter the current value, which is the actual sales figure for that quarter, is 960. Since the time series begins with the first quarter there is no previous exponential average. In order to get started, it is acceptable to let the first value in the time series represent the previous exponential average as well as the first current value. Therefore, let 960 be the previous average and

$$\frac{\text{Current}}{\text{Average}} = (.1)(960) + (1 - .1)(960)$$
$$= 960$$

This current average for the first quarter appears in Table 12.3. For the second quarter, the current value is 910 as indicated in both Figure 12.7 and Table 12.3. The previous average as just completed is 960, hence the current average associated with the second quarter is

$$\frac{\text{Current}}{\text{Average}} = (.1)(910) + (1 - .1)(960)$$
$$= 955$$

For the third quarter, the current sales value is 930, the previous exponential average is 955, thus the current average is

$$\frac{\text{Current}}{\text{Average}} = (.1)(930) + (1 - .1)(955)$$
$$= 952.5$$

For the fourth quarter the chlorine sales value is 980, the previous exponential average is 952.5, and the current average is

$$\frac{\text{Current}}{\text{Average}} = (.1)(980) + (1 - .1)(952.5)$$
$$= 955.2$$

This process is continued through the last quarter. In the last quarter the current sales figure is 970 and the previous average as seen from Table 12.3 is 954.4. This means that the current exponential average for the twelfth quarter is

$$\frac{\text{Current}}{\text{Average}} = (.1)(970) + (1 - .1)(954.4)$$
$$= 956.0$$

These exponential averages where $\alpha = .1$ are plotted in Figure 12.7 and are connected by a dotted line. Notice that these exponential averages follow the general drift of the time series while not following the erratic ups and downs which are usually random fluctuations. The erratic ups and downs of the actual time series are therefore smoothed out by the exponential smoothing process. Having computed the exponential averages, what is the forecast for the next quarter? In exponential smoothing the current exponential average for the last period, the twelfth quarter in this case, becomes the forecast for the next period in the future. Therefore, when $\alpha = .1$ the forecast for chlorine sales in the thirteenth quarter is 956 which is merely the average for the twelfth quarter.

Of critical importance in exponential smoothing is the choice of alpha. Look again at the equation by which the exponential average is computed

TABLE 12.3
Exponential Smoothing

Quarter	Sales	Exponential Average When $\alpha = .1$	Exponential Average When $\alpha = .3$
1	960	960.0	960.0
2	910	955.0	945.0
3	930	952.5	940.5
4	980	955.2	952.4
5	940	953.7	948.6
6	940	952.4	946.1
7	930	950.1	941.2
8	950	950.1	943.9
9	970	952.1	951.7
10	980	954.9	960.2
11	950	954.4	957.1
12	970	956.0	961.0
13	Forecast =	956.0	961.0

$$\begin{array}{c}\text{Current}\\\text{Exponential}\\\text{Average}\end{array} = (\alpha) \begin{bmatrix}\text{Current}\\\text{Value}\end{bmatrix} + (1 - \alpha) \begin{bmatrix}\text{Previous}\\\text{Exponential}\\\text{Average}\end{bmatrix}$$

The current average is composed of two inputs which are the current value of sales and the previous average which incorporates all of the previous values of sales in the time series. If α were .5, then the current value and the previous average would be equally weighted in determining the current average. When α tends toward 1 the current value becomes much more important at the expense of the previous average. On the other hand, as α approaches 0 the current value becomes relatively less important in the determination of the current average. Therefore, when α is high the exponential averages will give relatively more weight to the more recent data. This produces a tendency for the exponential averages to follow or "track" the up and down movements of the time series quite closely. The use of a low value for α, on the other hand, forms exponential averages which are not as dependent on recent data. These averages do not follow the ups and downs like those based on a high α.

The fact that a relatively large alpha causes the exponential averages to more closely follow each movement of the time series is demonstrated by the use of $\alpha = .3$ in the JP Chem case. Table 12.3 gives the resulting exponential averages. The first average is based on the current sales value of 960 which as before is also taken to be the initial previous average

$$\begin{array}{c}\text{Current}\\\text{Average}\end{array} = (.3)(960) + (1-.3)(960)$$
$$= 960.0$$

For the second quarter,

$$\frac{\text{Current}}{\text{Average}} = (.3)(910) + (.7)(960)$$

$$= 945.0$$

When all of these are plotted they yield the dot-dash line of Figure 12.7. Notice that these averages track the movements of the time series more closely than those of the $\alpha = .1$ variety. In the end the use of $\alpha = .3$ yields a forecast for the thirteenth period of 961. This forecast is higher than that derived from the $\alpha = .1$ series because it is more sensitive to the upswing in sales that occurred in the last quarters.

What forecast should JP Chem accept? 956, 961, or some other based on another alpha? Recalling the earlier discussion in this section, if the forecaster thinks that the sales are prone to follow a cyclical pattern, then the choice would be for a forecast based on a higher alpha. If the forecaster sees the quarterly sales values as being primarily a series of random movements, then a low alpha forecast would be preferable. It is therefore the judgment of the forecaster which determines the alpha to be used. Practically speaking, the forecaster should try an assortment of alphas in order to see how each responds to the particular time series under observation. That alpha is chosen for future use which does the best job of tracking real changes while overlooking random movements. An example follows.

Suppose JP Chem wanted to make a judgment in favor of $\alpha = .1$ or $\alpha = .3$ for the sake of forecasting chlorine sales. Table 12.3 gives all the exponential averages based on these two alphas. It has earlier been pointed out that the exponential average corresponding to the last period of the time series becomes the forecast for the next period in the future. Consider now only the $\alpha = .1$ exponential averages. If the time series consisted of only the first quarter datum, then the corresponding exponential average, 960, would serve as the forecast for the second quarter. The second quarter sales turned out to be 910, therefore this forecast missed by 960—910, or 50. Now supposing the time series consisted of only the first two quarters, the last exponential average would be 955 (which corresponds to the second quarter). Thus 955 would be the forecast of third quarter sales. Third quarter sales turned out to be 930, hence this forecast missed by 955—930 or 25. If the time series had extended only through three quarters, then the forecast for the fourth quarter would be 952.5 when using an alpha of .1. This forecasts misses actual fourth quarter sales by 952.5—980 or −28.5. This process could be continued through the eleventh quarter. Based on a time series of eleven quarters of data, the forecast for the twelfth quarter would be 954.4. The actual sales in the twelfth were 970 and therefore the forecast missed by 954.4—970 or −15.6. In each quarter the following deviation has been computed

$$\frac{\text{Forecast}}{\text{Deviation}} = \text{Forecast} - \text{Actual Sales}$$

The use of these forecast deviations in evaluating a particular alpha will now be considered.

The performance of forecasting with alpha equal to .1 can now be summarized by computing the standard forecast deviation

$$\begin{array}{l} \text{Standard} \\ \text{Forecast} \\ \text{Deviation} \end{array} = \sqrt{\frac{\Sigma\,(\text{Forecast} - \text{Actual Sales})^2}{n}}$$

where n is the number of periods where forecasts have been made and where actual sales are known. The standard forecast deviation measures how far the forecasts have deviated from the actual sales figures. In the JP Chem case where alpha is .1,

$$\begin{array}{l} \text{Standard} \\ \text{Forecast} \\ \text{Deviation} \end{array} = \sqrt{\frac{(960-910)^2 + (955-930)^2 + (952.5-980)^2 + \ldots + (954.4-970)^2}{11}}$$

$$= \sqrt{\frac{(50)^2 + (25)^2 + (-28.5)^2 + \ldots + (-15.6)^2}{11}}$$

$$= 23.04$$

In like manner, the standard forecast deviation when alpha is .3 may be computed

$$\begin{array}{l} \text{Standard} \\ \text{Forecast} \\ \text{Deviation} \end{array} = \sqrt{\frac{(960-910)^2 + (945-930)^2 + \ldots + (957.1-970)^2}{11}}$$

$$= 24.50$$

Since the standard forecast deviation corresponding to $\alpha = .1$ is less than that for $\alpha = .3$, it may be concluded that forecasting with $\alpha = .1$ would have been better in the past. It is therefore plausible that $\alpha = .1$ should be favored in the future forecasting of chlorine sales. Other alphas could also be tested; the one yielding the least standard forecast deviation would be optimal.

It has been indicated that the use of a high alpha value results in the exponential averages being quite sensitive to the most recent data. What values for alpha are considered to be high? Typically any alpha from .3 through .5 would be considered as high; rarely would an alpha greater than .5 be used. Small alphas are those of .1 or smaller.

In conclusion, exponential smoothing is flexible because of the control of alpha permitted. It is computationally simple and is especially adaptable to the computer because only the previous average must be stored (not the entire previous time series) for the sake of computing the new current average which serves as the forecast. With regard to the limitations of the form of exponential smoothing that has been presented, the following should be noted. If the time series has a distinct trend, a modified form of exponential smoothing must be used. Otherwise the forecast will be too low if the trend is upward, or too high if the trend is downward. Even when distinct cycles exist it would be advantageous to use the more sophisticated form of exponential smoothing which has been developed. This more sophisticated form will not be presented here.[1]

[1] For a more extensive treatment of exponential smoothing, see N. Siemens, C. H. Marting, & F. Greenwood, *Operations Research* (New York: The Free Press, 1973), pp. 15–36.

12.9 REGRESSION ANALYSIS

Finally, forecasting by means of a causal model will be considered. In the time series analyses that have preceded there was no attempt to incorporate any variable other than time. Forecasts were made by merely extrapolating the time series. In forecasting a quantity like sales, there may be a distinct relationship between the variable and time. Often, however, time is not highly related to sales. For example, in the JP Chem case the chlorine sales seemed to exhibit little relationship to changing time (see Figure 12.7). Likewise in the Metropolitan Bank example there was little or no connection between time and clearing volume. In this section a forecasting model which takes into account other variables beside time will be considered. If one were forecasting sales, for example, variables such as advertising expenditures, interest rates, and unemployment might be good predictors of sales. Consider now an example where simple time series analysis proves to be of limited value in comparison to another technique which incorporates causal variables.

Sitting Bull (Section 6.7) had set up a small business on the Bright Angel trail in the Grand Canyon and was selling sopaipillas. Sitting did not want to prepare too many or too few sopaipillas. In constructing his inventory model it was stated that attention would be later devoted to the forecasting of sopaipilla demand; that time has come. Having kept records for twenty days, Sitting wisely

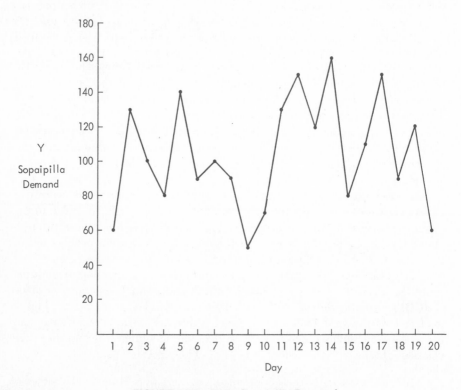

FIGURE 12.8   Daily Sopaipilla Demand

decided to plot a time series in order to ascertain the relationship of demand to time. Figure 12.8 presents this time series. From this it appears that the daily demand is quite erratic. If Sitting utilized exponential smoothing with an alpha of about .1, the forecasted demand for the twenty-first day would be approximately 100 sopaipillas. Seeing the great fluctuations in the time series, Sitting could not be very confident that the actual demand would be at this particular level. He could easily expect demand to be just about anywhere between 60 and 140. Sitting wanted a more reliable forecast than this and so began to search for some other variable or factor which when introduced into the forecasting procedure might enhance his ability to forecast demand.

What factors, which could be measured the day before, might Sitting consider as being influential on sopaipilla demand for a given day? Reflecting upon this matter. Sitting first thought that the weather forecast might be a factor in the determination of how many hikers took the trip down the canyon (remember that Sitting sells an average of one sopaipilla per hiker). In the summer when this business is in operation, there is actually little variation in weather forecasts at the canyon. Unlike the Midwest and East, weather in the arid regions is quite similar from day to day. The weather forecast might be a significant factor in forecasting the number of hikers on Mt. Washington in New Hampshire, but not in forecasting the number of summertime hikers at the Grand Canyon. Then Sitting hit on another idea. Perhaps the number of persons entering the park the day before might be valuable information. Sitting went to the ranger and was given the daily number of park admissions for each day. Table 12.4, page 366, gives a listing in the first three columns of the day, the admissions the day before,

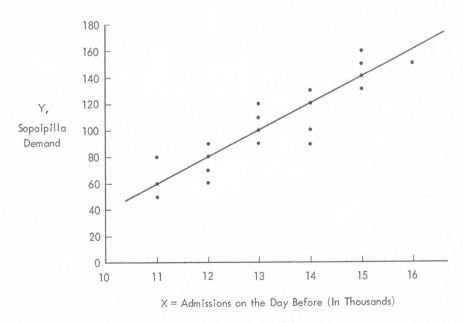

FIGURE 12.9 Scattergram and Regression Line

and the sopaipilla demand for the day. (Notice that by plotting the data in the third column against that of the first yields the time series of Figure 12.8).

Sitting plotted the data from the second and third columns of Table 12.4 letting the vertical axis represent demand and the horizontal represent park admissions the day before. Figure 12.9, page 365, depicts this scattergram. One point is plotted for each day, thus there are twenty points in the scattergram. Quite obviously Sitting has uncovered a relationship between prior admissions, X, and demand, Y. As admissions increase the day before, sopaipilla demand increases. As the data points are clustered quite closely around the line (the origin of this line will be discussed later), Sitting can materially increase the reliability of his forecasts. For example, if admissions the day before were 13,000, Sitting can be quite certain that demand will be between 80 and 130. This is a much narrower interval than that interval which could have been achieved on the basis of an analysis of the time series of Figure 12.8. If admissions were 11,000, Sitting could be fairly certain that demand would be between 40 and 80.

TABLE 12.4
Sitting Bull Data

Day	Admissions the Day Before X (Thousands)	Demand Y	X²	XY	Y²
1	11	60	121	660	3600
2	14	130	196	1820	16900
3	13	100	169	1300	10000
4	11	80	121	880	6400
5	15	140	225	2100	19600
6	12	90	144	1080	8100
7	14	100	196	1400	10000
8	13	90	169	1170	8100
9	11	50	121	550	2500
10	12	70	144	840	4900
11	15	130	225	1950	16900
12	15	150	225	2250	22500
13	13	120	169	1560	14400
14	15	160	225	2400	25600
15	12	80	144	960	6400
16	13	110	169	1430	12100
17	16	150	256	2400	22500
18	14	90	196	1260	8100
19	14	120	196	1680	14400
20	12	60	144	720	3600
	265	2080	3555	28410	236600
	ΣX	ΣY	ΣX^2	ΣXY	ΣY^2
	$\bar{X} = 13.25$	$\bar{Y} = 104$			

In Figure 12.9 Sitting has demonstrated that a relationship exists between demand and admissions. Sitting next desires to pinpoint the mathematical nature of this relationship. A straight line, as in Figure 12.9, could be fitted through the data by inspection. Because different people might fit different lines through the same scattergram, it is desirable to determine such a line more objectively. There exists a technique known as the least squares technique for mathematically fitting this line to the data. The line will henceforth be referred to as the regression line. The essentials of determining this regression line will first be outlined, then the regression line will be used for forecasting purposes.

If the data of the scattergram is arrayed so that a straight line would fit it best, the technique that follows is applicable. If the data exhibits a pattern which would be best fitted by a curved line, then another mathematical technique must be used to determine the curved regression line. The mathematical equation for any straight line has the general form

$$Y = a + bX$$

Once the constants a and b are specified, the line becomes known. The straight line passing through the scattergram of Figure 12.9 must have this mathematical form. The regression line's values for the constants a and b may be found by

$$b = \frac{\Sigma XY - n\bar{X}\bar{Y}}{\Sigma X^2 - n\bar{X}^2}$$
$$a = \bar{Y} - b\bar{X}$$

where n equals the number of data points in the scattergram, ΣXY equals the sum of all the products of the X and Y values for each data point, ΣX^2 equals the sum of the squared X values for each point, $\bar{X}$ equals the average X value, and $\bar{Y}$ equals the average Y value. The required calculations to find a and b will now be clarified by the Sitting Bull example.

The X and Y values for each data point (or day) are listed in Table 12.4. The sum of the X values is 265, hence $\Sigma X = 265$. The sum of the Y values is 2080. Dividing each of these by $n = 20$ yields $\bar{X} = 13.25$ and $\bar{Y} = 104$, respectively.

Next form another column which contains the square of each X value for each day. The entries in this column are 11^2 or 121, 14^2 or 196, et cetera. The sum of this column is $\Sigma X^2 = 3555$. Similarly the entries under the XY column are found by multiplying the respective values from the X and Y columns. The product of 11 and 60 is the first entry of 660, for example. The sum of this column is $\Sigma XY = 28,410$.

The values computed from Table 12.4 may now be substituted into

$$b = \frac{\Sigma XY - n\,\bar{X}\,\bar{Y}}{\Sigma X^2 - n\,\bar{X}^2}$$

yielding

$$b = \frac{28,410 - (20)(13.25)(104)}{3,555 - (20)(13.25)^2}$$
$$b = 19.43$$

Then,

$$a = \bar{Y} - b\bar{X}$$
$$= 104 - (19.43)(13.25)$$
$$= -153.45$$

This means that the regression line equation is:

$$Y = -153.45 + 19.43\,X$$

This equation gives a value for Y corresponding to any value of X. It is the equation of the regression line in Figure 12.9.

Sitting can use this equation to make a point forecast. If he has just learned that the admissions to the park today are 12 thousand, then the best forecast for tomorrow's sopaipilla demand is

$$Y = -153.45 + (19.43)(12)$$
$$= 80 \text{ sopaipillas}$$

Suppose a probabilistic forecast was desired. If the following conditions hold, Sitting can make such a forecast.

1. n is about 20 or more.
2. The data points are most dense near the regression line.
3. The spread of the points about the regression line is symmetrical and similar all along the line.

Before looking at the probabilistic forecast which can be derived, consider these conditions one by one. The first states that there must be at least twenty data points in the scattergram. In the second, the data points are to be most dense near the regression line. A violation of this condition is presented in Figure 12.10(a). The scattergram should rather look something like that of Figure 12.10(b). With the third condition a situation like that of Figure 12.10(c) is ruled out; both Figure 12.10(a) and 12.10(b) are acceptable in regard to the third condition.

With these conditions satisfied in the case of a straight regression line, the forecast when a value for X is given is

Y is normally distributed with a mean
of $\bar{Y}_x = a + bX$ and a standard deviation
of S where

$$S = \sqrt{\frac{\Sigma Y^2 - a\,\Sigma Y - b\,\Sigma XY}{n - 2}}$$

Can such a probabilistic forecast be made in the Sitting Bull example? Looking at the scattergram of Figure 12.9, certainly the first and third conditions are satisfied. One might hesitate in regard to the second condition since the data points are not really concentrated about the regression lineas in Figure 12.10(b). However, since the violation of this condition is not substantial, Sitting proceeds. He has just learned that today's admissions are 12 thousand. With $X =$

12, the probabilistic forecast for sopaipilla demand, Y, on the morrow is

Y is normally distributed with a mean
of $\bar{Y}_{12} = -153.45 + (19.43)(12) = 80$
and a standard deviation of

$$S = \sqrt{\frac{236,600 - (-153.45)(2080) - (19.43)(28,410)}{20 - 2}}$$
$$= 14.5$$

Notice that ΣY^2 was computed in Table 12.4.

Sitting can use this probabilistic forecast in his inventory model. He in fact did use such a normal forecast in Section 6.7 where he determined the optimal

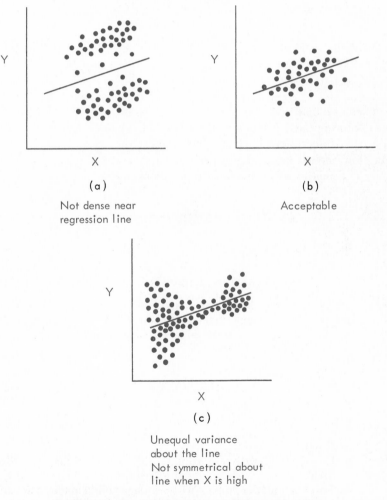

(a)

Not dense near
regression line

(b)

Acceptable

(c)

Unequal variance
about the line
Not symmetrical about
line when X is high

FIGURE 12.10   Scattergrams and Regression Lines

number of sopaipillas to take with him down the Grand Canyon. In completing this example a warning should be given. Since the scattergram of Figure 12.9 was based on days where admissions varied from 11,000 to 16,000, Sitting should be reluctant to use the regression equation for forecasting when admissions are outside this range. This is because Sitting has no historical data for such situations.

In this section a so-called causal forecasting model has been presented. The variable being forecasted, Y, is called the dependent variable and the causal variable, X, is known as the independent variable. Oftentimes a forecaster may be aware of several causal variables. In these cases "multiple regression analysis" is used which bases a forecast for Y on these several causal variables.

For example, a university may wish to forecast the total enrollment, Y, for an upcoming school year. Appropriate causal variables might be

X_1 = This year's enrollment
X_2 = Number of high school seniors this year
X_3 = Number of advance applications for admission

By collecting data on Y, X_1, X_2, and X_3 for the past ten years, the university might construct a regression model like

$$Y = .8\,X_1 + .05\,X_2 + 2\,X_3$$

Then suppose that in the present year, $X_1 = 10{,}000$, $X_2 = 50{,}000$, and $X_3 = 700$. By substituting these values into the regression equation the university would get a point forecast of 11,900 students for next year. Such multiple regression forecasting models have often proved to be excellent aids in short-term forecasting in a multitude of managerial applications.

PROBLEMS

12-1. Answers to 1–20, page 352: True values are: 54,464; 72%; 627,192; 114; 3,164; 35%; 150; 1849; 35 degrees; 14; 2.78 billion, 17,207 billion; 114.27; 212; 1894; 11.8 light years; 31,820; 39.79%; $50,000; $195.4 million.

12-2. Follow the procedure of Section 12.3 to construct your probabilistic forecast for the annual inflation rate for the U.S.A. next year. (Assume that the annual inflation rate is measured by the consumer price index).

12-3. A forecaster working for Niagra-Hohawk is making a subjective forecast for electricity usage in 1990. The forecaster makes these statements: "As far as I am concerned, there is a .90 probability that usage will be below 410 bkwh, there is a .70 probability that usage will be below 380, there is a .40 probability that usage will be below 360, and there is a .10 probability that usage will be below 330." From these judgments,
(a) Graph a cumulative probability distribution of electricity usage in 1990.
(b) From (a) find the probability that usage will be under 340, 350, 360, 370, 380, 390, and 400, respectively.

12-4. Construct your own subjective normal forecast for the year in which people will first stand on Mars.

12-5. A manager for U.S. News states that her best guess for the circulation of that magazine in 10 years is 8 million copies. The manager further says that there is a 50–50 chance that circulation will be outside the 6 to 10 million range. Assuming that the normal distribution mirrors the manager's beliefs, find the normal distribution which could serve as a probabilistic forecast for circulation 10 years hence.

12-6. An executive states that there are two chances in three that earnings per share next year will be between $1.20 and $1.40. Assuming a normal distribution is appropriate, find the subjective normal distribution for earnings per share next year.

12-7. California Raisin wishes to predict the rainfall in the month of October for the vicinity where the raisins will be dried. October rainfall for the past 20 years are (in inches): .8, 0, .2, .4, .2, .3, .4, .5, .5, .3, .2, .7, 0, .1, .1, .5, .4, .2, .7, and .3. Construct a probabilistic forecast for rainfall in next October. What is the probability of .5, .6, and .7 inches, respectively? Often in following the procedure of Section 12.7, the resulting probability distribution will seem unnatural in places because of sparse historical data. In such a case it is legitimate to "move some of the probability around" in order to achieve a reasonable distribution. In this case some probability should be given to .6 inches. Do so! Another alternative is to make the rainfall categories larger, that is, combine classes. Do this also to get a probability distribution.

12-8. The number of defects produced daily by an assembly operation for the past five days are 20, 26, 14, 21, and 16. Use exponential smoothing with alpha equal to .1 and then with alpha equal to .4 to predict the number of defects for tomorrow. Also compute the standard forecast deviation corresponding to each alpha. Which alpha yields the lower SFD?

12-9. Florida sales of Johns-Brooks insulation for the past 25 quarters were 120, 150, 130, 140, 160, 140, 160, 130, 140, 130, 140, 120, 100, 140, 110, 100, 120, 90, 110, 140, 150, 120, 140, 120, and 100. Plot the resulting time series. Then,
(a) Use exponential smoothing with alpha equal to .1 to forecast sales for the next quarter.
(b) Use alpha equal to .3 to forecast sales for the next quarter.
(c) Plot the exponential averages from parts (a) and (b) and comment on their abilities to track the actual time series.

12-10. Amtruck is attempting to predict the number of meals which will be demanded on the Washington to Florida run. For each of the last 20 days Amtruck has recorded the number of meals demanded. This information is given on page 372.
(a) Plot a time series for meals demanded and guess what the point forecast would be for tomorrow if exponential smoothing with alpha equal to .1 were used. Within what range would you be fairly certain that tomorrow's demand would fall? (Make this judgment from looking at the time series.)

Day	Meals Demanded	Early Reservations
1	230	450
2	200	390
3	180	360
4	240	495
5	200	395
6	160	320
7	200	405
8	210	430
9	240	470
10	220	440

(continued)

Day	Meals	Reservations
11	160	315
12	220	445
13	160	325
14	220	450
15	220	440
16	210	420
17	240	480
18	190	365
19	180	355
20	220	430

(b) Amtruck next collected date on early reservations for each run. These data are also given for each day. Incorporate the early reservations into a forecasting model for meals demanded. If there are 400 early reservations for the next run, what should Amtruck's point forecast for the number of meals be?

(c) In order to use the regression model for a probabilistic forecast, three conditions (as elaborated in the text) must be satisfied. Comment on whether the Amtruck data meets these conditions. Then assume that they are met and make a probabilistic forecast for meals if there are 400 early reservations.

13.1 INTRODUCTION

The manager in charge of a large project like the construction of the Alaskan pipeline is faced with a monumental task. There are a multitude of activities which must be accomplished if the project is to be completed. Some activities may only begin upon the completion of others while some may be performed simultaneously. In a project where hundreds or thousands of distinct activities must be performed, some formal method of planning and coordinating these activities is needed. CPM (critical path method) and PERT (program evaluation and review technique) are two formal planning methods by which the varied activities of a project can be coordinated. Through these methods management can estimate the total time it will take to complete the project. Furthermore, the starting times for each of the distinct activities may be determined as well as the sequencing of these activities. These techniques also isolate potential bottlenecks in the project as well as activities which are not particularly critical to the completion of the project on time. Hence CPM and PERT can be viewed as techniques important in the control of projects.

CPM and PERT are quite similar, the primary difference between them being the fact that CPM is deterministic while PERT is probabilistic. In this chapter CPM will be emphasized leaving the discussion of PERT until the end. However, because of the similarity of these two planning methods, much of what is presented in connection with CPM is applicable to PERT.

13.2 SYMBOLS AND DEFINITIONS

At the heart of CPM and PERT is the network diagram. In Figure 13.1, page 374, a simplistic network diagram for a house construction project is given. The network consists of a logical array of *activities* and *events*. An activity is merely one phase of the construction process and thus always takes some amount of time to complete. Events, as will be seen later, mark the beginnings and endings of activities.

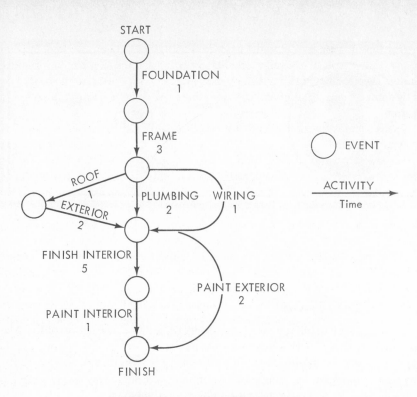

FIGURE 13.1   CPM/PERT Network

Activities are denoted by arrows. Notice that the first activity is "Pour the foundation." The second is "Put up the frame." After the frame of the house has been constructed, three other activities may begin. In each case the activity is denoted by an arrow. Below each activity arrow the time in weeks it takes to complete the activity is given. For example, it will take 1 week to put on the roof, 2 weeks to put up the exterior siding, 5 weeks to finish the interior, and 1 week to paint the interior of the house.

Each activity is separated by a circle which denotes an event. An event is a moment in time which marks the beginning or ending of an activity. The first circle (to the left) marks that instant in time when the project began with the pouring of the foundation. The second circle marks the event or moment when the foundation has been completed, and when the framing begins. That event will take place one week after the project began. The third circle marks the completion of the frame and the earliest moment when the roof, plumbing, and electrical wiring may begin. The event denoted by the third circle takes place four weeks after the start of the house.

Some of the activities in the network of Figure 13.1 are performed in series. For example, the framing can begin only after the foundation has been completed. Likewise the interior can be finished only after the wiring has been completed. Other activities may be performed in parallel. The roofing, plumbing, and wiring, for example, can all be performed at the same time. Likewise the interior finishing work can be done while the exterior is being painted. It is important that the network reflect reality. If two activities can be performed in parallel, then the network must show this. The network must also show what activities must precede a given activity—there must be a logical flow to the diagram.

Within the network of Figure 13.1 several paths exist. A path is a connected series or sequence of activities which extends from the beginning of the project to the end. For example, one path is "Foundation-Frame-Roof-Exterior-Paint Exterior." Another path is "Foundation-Frame-Plumbing-Paint Exterior," and yet another is "Foundation-Frame-Wiring-Finish Interior-Paint Interior." Notice that the activities which constitute a path are always performed in series. That is, each activity can only begin upon the completion of the preceeding activity.

The longest path, in terms of time, is called the *critical path*. The critical path in Figure 13.1 can be found by inspection. The "Foundation-Frame-Roof-Exterior-Finish Interior-Paint Interior" path consumes $1+3+1+2+5+1$ or 13 weeks. This path is the critical path because no longer path exists in the network. Since the critical path is the longest path from start to finish, it represents the length of time it will take to complete the project. Thus it will take 13 weeks to construct this house. What if one of the activities on the critical path took more time than anticipated? For example, suppose it took 2 weeks instead of 1 to complete the foundation. If this happens the critical path is lengthened and thus the entire project will be delayed by a week. Whenever a critical path activity is lengthened, the completion date for the entire project is delayed. Management should therefore pay special attention to the activities which compose the critical path. These activities are referred to as the *critical activities*.

Activities that are not on the critical path may be delayed to some extent with no adverse effects on the project completion date. Suppose, for example, that the wiring took 2.5 weeks instead of 1 week. This extra time would not cause the entire project to be delayed. The exterior painting and interior finishing would still be held up by the roof-exterior work. Of course if the wiring took 6 weeks, then it would delay the entire project. In the analysis to follow the noncritical activities will be examined to determine how long any of them can be delayed with no adverse effect on the total project time. These potential delays in noncritical activities are called *slacks*. There will be a slack or slack time associated with every noncritical activity in the network.

13.3 CONSTRUCTING THE NETWORK

Lanter Laboratories has just received FDA approval to market Tetranil which is Lanter's new broad spectrum antibiotic. All of the research for this drug and the laboratory testing have been completed. In order to introduce the drug, Lanter Laboratories must yet deal with matters relating to production and marketing. Production and marketing managers have listed eleven activities which must be performed before Tetranil is introduced. (The drug is "introduced" when Lanter's medical detail personnel or salespeople begin to call on physicians for the sake of describing Tetranil.) These eleven activities have been listed in Table 13.1, page 376, along with other information.

TABLE 13.1
Activities for Tetranil

Activity	Immediate Predecessor	Time (weeks)	Time Saved by Crashing	Cost of Crashing
A (Quality Control System)	None	12	3	$6000
B (Raw Material Acquisition)	None	6	2	2000
C (Production Facility Set Up)	None	8	3	7500
D (Compile Drug Sales Information)	None	5	3	3000
E (Test Manufacture)	B,C	7	3	6000
F (Full Manufacture of a Batch)	A,E	10	4	12000
G (Prepare Advertising Copy)	D	3	1	1000
H (Update Salespeople)	D	9	7	21000
I (Advertising Contracts)	A,E,G	3	1	1000
J (Initial Advertising)	I	8	0	—
K (Ship to Pharmacies)	F	5	2	4200
Z (Call on Physicians)	H,J,K			

For each activity the immediate predecessor(s) is listed. For example, the test manufacture of Tetranil cannot begin till the raw materials have been acquired and the production facility set up. Symbolically, activity E cannot begin till activities B and C have been completed. The anticipated time for each of the activities A through K is also given. Activity Z, which is to call on physicians, represents the actual introduction of the drug and hence is the first activity of the next phase of Lanter's operations. Z will not enter into the present analysis and therefore no time is attached to it.

Having listed the activities, their predecessors, and their times, a network must now be constructed. Figure 13.2, page 378, presents the network. The network begins with a circle which denotes the event or moment when the project begins. This event is circle a. Since activities A, B, C, and D have no predecessors, they all may begin immediately with the start of the project at event a. Therefore the arrows representing A, B, C, and D emanate directly from event circle a which marks the beginning of the project. (The numbers found in the event circles will be discussed later. Presently the logical ordering of the activities and events is being considered.) Focusing attention on the list of activities given in Table 13.1, it is apparent that the first four, A, B, C, and D, have now been accounted for by arrows in the network of Figure 13.2. The next activity of concern is E. Activity E has two immediate predecessors, namely B and C. Therefore the E arrow may begin only when both B and C have been completed. Event b marks the completion of both B and C and therefore event circle b also marks the moment when E can begin. The next activity in Table 13.1 is F which has A and E as its immediate predecessors. Thus F can begin no sooner than the moment when both A and E have been completed. The A and E arrows must precede the F arrow. Event circle d identifies the moment when A and E have both been completed. Hence the F arrow emanates from d. Activity G has D as its only predecessor and therefore it can begin at event circle c which is the event representing the completion of activity D. Likewise, H emanates directly from c since its only predecessor is D also. H and G can be performed simultaneously or in parallel. As this process of constructing a network is continued, the arrows representing the activities are chronologically ordered. Under each arrow the time to perform the activity is given; these times are taken from Table 13.1.

The remainder of the network diagram is self-explanatory when one understands the meaning of the symbols and can refer to Table 13.1. Every activity (arrow) begins with an event (circle) and ends with an event. A complication does exist in one place, however. Near the center of the network a dotted arrow labeled "Dummy" and bearing a time of 0 may be found. What is the purpose of this? From Table 13.1 it is seen that activity I can only begin after A, E, and G have been completed. Also, activity F can only begin when A and E have been finished. Attempting to diagram these requirements becomes somewhat difficult. For example, the network section of Figure 13.3, page 379, is not adequate to express these relationships since it would make the beginning of activity F dependent on the completion of G. In order to draw an adequate diagram, an artificial or dummy activity is drawn which consumes no time but is used solely for the sake of maintaining the correct logical relationships between the activities.

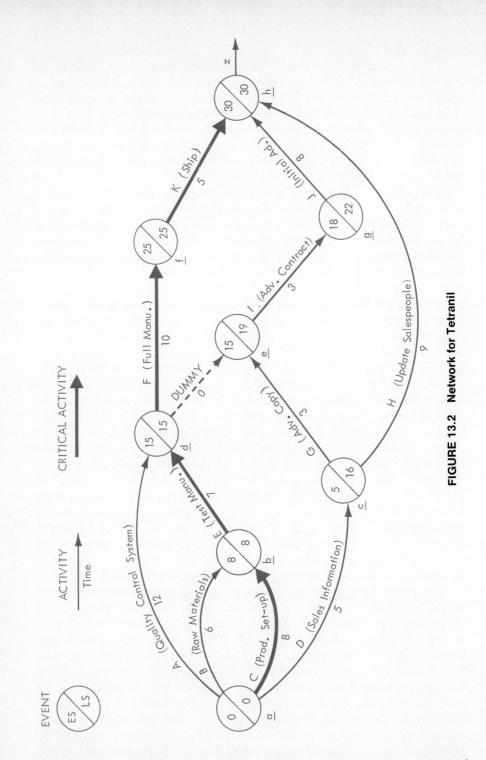

CRITICAL ACTIVITY

ACTIVITY

Time

EVENT
ES / LS

FIGURE 13.2   Network for Tetranil

The use of the dummy activity permits F to begin upon the completion of A and E (with no reference to G), and holds back the start of activity I until A, E, and

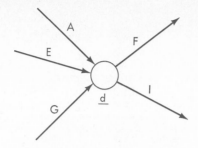

FIGURE 13.3   Incorrect Diagram

G have all been completed. The incorporation of the dummy activity with a time of zero presents no particular analytic difficulties as will be seen.

The last circle (to the right) denotes the termination of the project at which time Tetranil may be introduced. Activities *H, J,* and *K* must be completed before event h occurs, therefore these three arrows lead to circle h.

Finally it should be noticed that some activities such as *A* and *E* may be performed in parallel while others such as *F* and *K* must be performed in series.

13.4 FINDING THE CRITICAL PATH

The network of Figure 13.2 is small enough so that the critical path can be found by inspection. However, when a project involves hundreds of activities and hundreds of paths, then a formal method of finding the critical path is required. Such a method will now be presented.

In each circle representing the events of the network, two numbers will be placed. In the upper left a number representing the earliest starting time for all the activities emanating from the circle will be given. The second number will be discussed later. Event a represents the start of the project. The starting time of the project will be given as zero, thus a zero is placed in the upper left of event circle a. Four activities, *A, B, C,* and *D,* can begin immediately. Thus the earliest start, *ES,* for these four activities is time 0. This earliest start, *ES,* is recorded in Table 13.2, page 380, for these four activities.

What is the earliest possible start for activity *E*? From Figure 13.2 it is seen that both *B* and *C* must be completed before *E* can commence. *B* takes 6 weeks and *C* takes 8 weeks. This means that the earliest *E* can start is at time 8. An 8 is placed in the upper left of event circle b and in Table 13.2 under *ES.*

What is the *ES,* earliest start possible, for activity *F*? Both *A* and *E* must be completed before *F* can begin. *A* can be completed after 12 weeks but *E* is not completed till 15 weeks have elapsed. This is because *E* requires 7 weeks and begins only at event b. As event b occurs after 8 weeks, *E* is finished at 8 + 7 or 15 weeks. The earliest that *F* can begin is therefore at time 15. 15 is placed in the upper left of event circle d and is recorded in Table 13.2 under the *ES* column.

What is the earliest time at which *G* can start? *G* is preceeded by *D* which is completed at time 5. Thus both *G* and *H* can begin as early as, but no earlier than, time 5. 5 is recorded in event circle c and in Table 13.2 under the *ES* column across from both *G* and *H.*

TABLE 13.2
Slacks for Activities

Activity	Earliest Start ES	Latest Start LS	Slack LS-ES
A	0	3	3
B	0	2	2
C	0	0	0
D	0	11	11
E	8	8	0
F	15	15	0
G	5	16	11
H	5	21	16
I	15	19	4
J	18	22	4
K	25	25	0
Z	30	30	—

Activities with zero slacks are critical
path activities.

What is the earliest time that activity I can start? As originally indicated in Table 13.1 and as displayed in the network, I can begin only after A, E, and G have been finished. The fact that A and E must precede I is shown by the use of the dummy activity which itself requires no time. Both A and E are completed by time 15 as shown by the entry in the upper left of event circle d̲. G can be completed as early as time 8 which is the sum of the ES value in event circle c̲ and the time, 3 weeks, it takes to finish G. Even though G can be finished by time 8, activity I can begin no sooner than time 15 because of event circle d̲. Thus the earliest possible starting time for I is time 15 which should be recorded in event circle e̲ and under the ES column in Table 13.2.

Following this type of approach, the earliest possible start for K will be 25 and the earliest start for J will be 18. These values are recorded in event circles f̲ and g̲, respectively, and in Table 13.2.

Event h̲ represents the moment at which all the activities have been completed. When h̲ occurs, Tetranil may be actually introduced to the physicians. The time of event h̲ is 30 which is the earliest time when H, J, and K are all completed. H could be completed as early as 14, J could be completed as early as 26, but K can be completed no earlier than at time 30. 30 is therefore recorded in the upper left of event circle h̲.

The first step in finding the critical path has now been completed, namely, finding the ES for each activity. The next step requires that the latest possible start, LS, for each activity be found such that the entire project can be completed at time 30. The latest start, LS, for each activity is recorded in Table 13.2 and in some cases is recorded in the lower right portion of the network event circles. A 30 is initially recorded in the lower right of event circle h̲. This means that the latest time and earliest time for the occurrence of event h̲ are both 30.

For the sake of finding the critical path, the *LS* for the last event is automatically made equal to the *ES* for that event. By backing through the network the latest time that each activity can start can be determined.

For example, the latest that *K* can start is at time 25. *K* must be completed by 30 and *K* requires 5 weeks. Hence the *LS* value for *K* is 25. 25 should be placed in the lower right of event circle f as well as under the *LS* column in Table 13.2. In like manner the latest time that *J* can start is 22 since *J* takes 8 weeks. The latest that activity *I* can start is at time 19. *I* must be completed by time 22 so that *J* can start by then.

When is the latest that *H* can start? Since *H* takes 9 weeks and leads directly to event circle h, *H* can begin as late as 21. This is recorded in Table 13.2 but not in the lower right of event circle c. The reason why it is not recorded in event circle c will now be seen. The latest that *G* can start is 16. *G* must begin no later than time 16 in order to be completed by time 19 which is the latest that activity *I* can start as indicated by event circle e. Both *G* and *H* emanate from event circle c and it has just been shown that these two activities have latest starts of 16 and 21, respectively. The lesser of these two is recorded in event circle c, namely 16. If 21 were recorded there it would give the impression that *G* and *H* could both start as late as time 21 and the whole project could still be completed at time 30. Although *H* could be done if started at 21, the *G-I-J* subpath would never get completed by time 30 if *G* started as late as 21.

Continuing this process, the latest possible start for *E* is time 8. Since *E* takes 7 weeks, a later start would carry *E* beyond time 15 which is the latest that *F* can start. In Table 13.2 it is further seen that the latest start for *A* is time 3, for *B* is time 2, for *C* is time 0, and for *D* is 11. These are found in the same manner as the other *LS* times were found.

With *ES* and *LS* recorded for each activity in Table 13.2, the final step in the determination of the critical path may be undertaken. It is required that the slack for each activity be computed. The slack for an activity is defined as

$$\text{Slack} = LS - ES$$

The slack measures how much leeway there is between the earliest and latest start for an activity. The slacks for each activity in the Tetranil case are shown in Table 13.2. Every activity which has a zero slack is a critical activity. With critical activities there is no room for a delay in starting them because the *LS* is the same as the *ES*. The critical activities in the Tetranil case are *C*, *E*, *F*, and *K*. These critical activities when placed in series form the critical path in the net- · work. Thus *C-E-F-K* is the critical path. (The analyst should be aware that two or more critical paths may exist in some networks.) This critical path is denoted by the bold arrows in Figure 13.2. Looking at the network, it is seen that the *ES* and *LS* are equal for the event circles a, b, d, f, and h which connect the critical activities. This will always be the case if the *LS* and *ES* for the last event, event h, are identical. By adding the times for *C*, *E*, *F*, and *K*, the total project time of 30 weeks can be confirmed: $T = 8 + 7 + 10 + 5 = 30$.

Having identified the critical activities, Lanter Laboratories has isolated the activities which must be especially watched. If any of the critical activities consumes more time than anticipated, then the total project time T will be increased beyond 30 weeks. These activities along the critical path represent the bottlenecks in the project.

13.5 SLACKS

It has been shown that the activities with zero slacks are the critical activities which require the close attention of management if the project is to be completed on schedule. Of what use are the slacks for the noncritical activities? Activity A, for example, has a slack of 3 weeks. This means that if the time required for A increased by no more than 3 weeks, no delay in the final completion of the project will be experienced. If A were extended more than 3 weeks, then the total project time will be affected. Thus by knowing the slacks management can judge the seriousness of delays in completing noncritical activities.

Sometimes the slacks are actually shared among activities. For example, D has a slack of 11 and H has a slack of 16 as indicated in Table 13.2. If D were lengthened from 5 to $5+11$ or 16 weeks and if H were lengthened from 9 to $9+16$ or 25 weeks, then the $D–H$ path would require $16+25$ or 41 weeks. Thus it is obvious that the full slack of every activity cannot necessarily be utilized with no adverse effect on the total project time. Care must be taken to determine how the slack of one activity is affected by the lengthening of the time for another noncritical activity. Activities performed in series may share slacks.

Thus for control purposes the slacks are valuable to management as they enable the project manager to determine whether a delay in the completion of a noncritical activity will have adverse effects on the total project time. Suppose, for instance, that everything has gone according to plan for Lanter Laboratories until activity I. Management had anticipated that it would take three weeks to sign the advertising contracts. However, a delay has just been encountered and it will take five weeks to finish I. By noting that the slack for I is four weeks, management need not be concerned with this unanticipated delay of two weeks.

13.6 A TIME-SCALED NETWORK

It is sometimes helpful to convert the earliest start, ES, and latest start, LS, information into time-scaled networks. A time-scaled network has essentially the same logical design as the original network. However, the movement from left to right is scaled by elapsed time. In the top of Figure 13.4 a time-scaled network is given where each dot represents the earliest time an activity can start. This network is nothing more than that of Figure 13.2 placed on time-scaled paper. The advantage is that the project manager can visually see more readily that the ES for both F and I are, for example, at time 15. The manager can also ascertain more readily which activities may be performed simultaneously.

At the bottom of Figure 13.4 is presented a time-scaled network where the dots represent the latest time an activity can begin. At a glance it can be seen, for example, that I cannot be started any later than time 19. It can also be seen that B can start no later than time 2 and the latest that H can start is 21. This information, of course, is also available in Table 13.2. Finally, the manager who is presently standing at time 22 can see that *H* better have started at least a week ago, *J* better start immediately, and *F* ought to be completed in three more weeks if the project is to be completed by time 30.

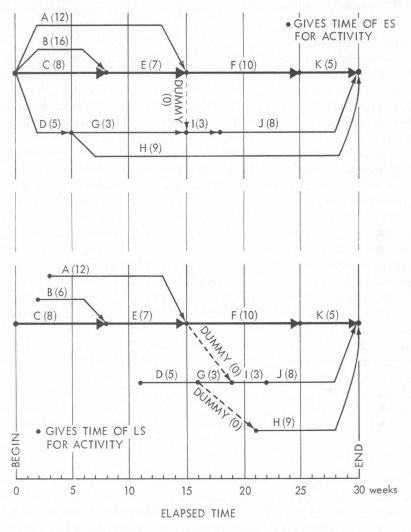

FIGURE 13.4   ES and LS Time-Scaled Networks

13.7 CRASHING

Lanter Laboratories has identified the critical activities for the project of getting Tetranil ready for introduction. The critical path composed of *C-E-F-K* consumes 30 weeks which means that the total project will take 30 weeks. Management was hoping to be able to introduce Tetranil within 25 weeks after FDA approval. In order to achieve this shorter project time, Lanter will have to institute a crash program. With a crash program some of the activities are shortened in order to complete the entire project sooner. In Table 13.1 the time that can be cut or saved by crashing each activity is given. For example, the quality control system can be developed in 3 weeks less than the normal 12 weeks. The time required for the shipment of the drug to the pharmacies can be cut by up to two weeks. One activity, initial advertising, cannot be accomplished in less than 8 weeks and thus no time can be saved by crashing.

Whenever crashing occurs there will be added expenses. Shipping raw materials by air instead of by truck will cost more. Using production workers on overtime runs up wages, and so forth. In the last column of Table 13.1 management has estimated the cost of crashing for each activity. For example, to expedite the development of the quality control system by 3 weeks will cost an additional $6,000.

Management has indicated that the drug should be introduced in 25 weeks rather than in 30 weeks. Which activities should be crashed or expedited in order to effect this time savings of 5 weeks? The noncritical activities are not currently holding up the project, thus by expediting them no savings in the total project time will be realized. For example, by cutting the length of activity A to 9 weeks from 12, the total project time will not be reduced. Why? Activity F cannot begin till E is completed also and E is completed at 15. The only way the total time will be reduced is by reducing the time of activities which are on the critical path. Hence activities C, E, F, and/or K must be shortened or crashed if the total project time is to be reduced. This follows because the total project time is the same as the critical path time.

TABLE 13.3
Economics of Crashing

Critical Path Activities	Crash Cost	Crash Time Savings	Cost per Week
C	$ 7500	3	$2500
E	6000	3	2000
F	12000	4	3000
K	4200	2	2100

Table 13.3 gives the critical path activities along with information pertinent to crashing. Consider activity C. 3 weeks can be saved by crashing at a total cost of $7500. This amounts to a cost of 7500/3 or $2,500 per week. E can be crashed at a cost of only $2,000 per week. For each critical activity the crash cost per week should be computed. It then becomes apparent that the most economical way to reduce the length of the critical path is by crashing activity E. By reducing activity E from 7 to 4 weeks, the ES of event $\underline{d}$ would decline to 12 (see Figure 13.2). This savings of 3 weeks would ultimately mean that the ES and LS for event $\underline{h}$ would be 27. Thus the total project time would be reduced by 3 weeks. In reducing the length of a particular activity, the analyst must keep in mind that other activities can become critical. For example, if E could have been

384

symbolically designated as t_o, t_m, and t_p, respectively. Fron
probabilistic statement can be made concerning the complet
ect. For example, it might turn out that the total project ti
tributed with a mean of 30 weeks and a standard deviation
tinguishing features of PERT will now be amplified by means

Taylor Construction is presently concerned with plannii
the activities necessary for the construction of Fort Bozemar
to use a probabilistic technique (PERT) because weather ai
stantially affect the amount of time it takes to complete an ac
ployees are also something of an unknown quantity and thi
the uncertainty associated with each activity.

Table 13.4 gives all of the information relevant to Taylor
From the list of the five activities and their immediate prede
structs a network diagram just as was done in earlier section

TABLE 13.4
Fort Bozeman Construction

Activity	Immediate Predecessor	t_o	t_m	t_p
			(In Weeks)	
A (Stables)	None	3	5	9
B (Stockade)	None	4	5	9
C (Adobe Quarters)	A	5	6	8
D (Furniture)	A	2	4	7
E (Interior Work)	B,C	1	3	6
F (Occupy Fort)	D,E			

$$\text{where } t_e = \frac{t_o + 4t_m + t_p}{6} \quad \text{and } \sigma = \frac{t_p -}{}$$

the Fort Bozeman site, work can immediately commence
(which will at first serve as sleeping quarters for the workers
Figure 13.7, page 388, shows the complete network. Taylor
optimistic, most likely, and pessimistic time for each activi
time is one such that there is only one chance in a hundre
would be completed in less time. The pessimistic time is one
about one chance in a hundred that a longer time would be n
the activity. For the stables, Taylor believes that the most like
Taylor further believes that there is only one chance in a
stables could be completed in less than 3 weeks, and that there
only .01 that it would take more than 9 weeks to finish the sta
estimates for each activity are listed in Table 13.4.

From t_o, t_m, and t_p the average or expected time is compu
ity according to the definition

$$t_e = \frac{t_o + 4t_m + t_p}{6}$$

and the standard deviation for the activity is computed accord

reduced by 4 weeks, such an extra reduction of 1 week would not help since A
still takes 12 weeks and hence the ES and LS for event $\underline{d}$ would yet be 12 even
though E could be finished at time 11.

Lanter still needs to trim two weeks off the total time if the goal of 25 weeks
is to be reached. Crashing activity E has now resulted in the presence of two
critical paths: C-E-F-K and A-F-K. Figure 13.5(a) depicts these two critical

(a) Activity E Crashed:

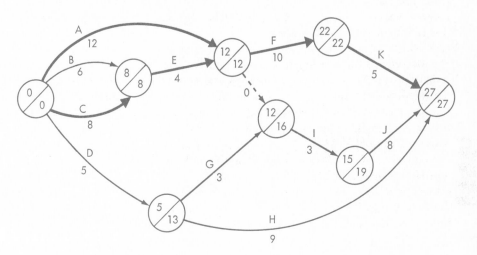

(b) Activities E and K Crashed:

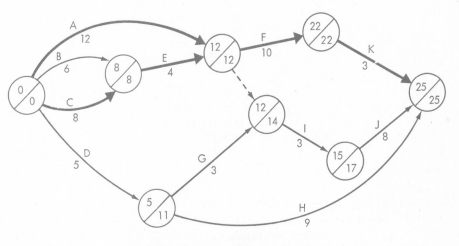

FIGURE 13.5   The Effects of Crashing

paths. Since activity A is parallel to C and E, a reduc
companied by a reduction in C in order to reduc
Table 13.3 it can be seen that it costs $2,500 to redu
13.1 it can be seen that the per week crash cost for
simultaneously reduce A and C by a week would c
pensive way of reducing the length of both critical p
reduce K by a week and K is common to both criti
crashed since that is the most economical way to re
hence the total project time. K can be reduced by 2
ect time of the desired 25 weeks. The total cost to
weeks is 6,000 + 4,200 or $10,200. Figure 13.5(b),
work with both E and K crashed.

If more time were to be saved, the same process
be careful to recognize that a new path may become
cal path is reduced. As more time is shaved from th
and higher costs will result because the relatively c
undertaken as the activities which are most ine
shortened. Figure 13.6 depicts the general relations
for a given project. Management may decide that th
the desired time is prohibitive and thus will settle wi
carries an acceptable cost.

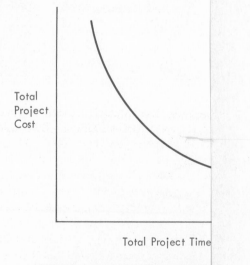

Total
Project
Cost

Total Project Time

FIGURE 13.6 Time and Cost Rel

13.8 PERT

In many projects the activity times may vary wi
CPM or deterministic variety as has been described
not be adequate. In PERT the manager makes three
tivity: an optimistic time, a most likely time, and a

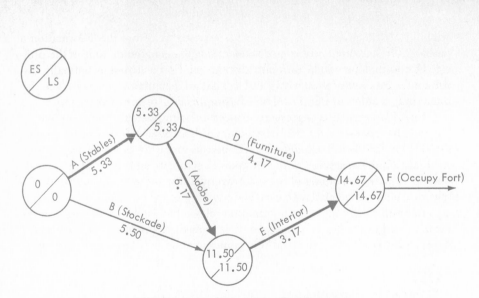

FIGURE 13.7   Network for Fort Bozeman

$$\sigma = \frac{t_p - t_o}{6}$$

Thus for the stables the expected time is

$$t_e = \frac{3 + (4)(5) + 9}{6}$$
$$= 5.33 \text{ weeks}$$

and the standard deviation for the stables, activity A, is

$$\sigma_A = \frac{9 - 3}{6}$$
$$= 1.00 \text{ week}$$

The expected times for the activities are then used for the sake of finding the critical path. The expected times have been attached to each of the arrows in Figure 13.7. By inspection, the critical path for Taylor construction is A-C-E. The total expected project time is therefore $5.33 + 6.17 + 3.17$ or 14.67 weeks. This total project time could also be found by examining the ES, earliest start, for the last or terminal event. If the times for the various activities along the critical path are independent, then the standard deviation of the total project time is equal to the square root of the sum of the variances of the critical activity times. In the Taylor case, the standard deviation of the total time will therefore be

$$\sigma_T = \sqrt{\sigma_A^2 + \sigma_C^2 + \sigma_E^2}$$
$$= \sqrt{(1.00)^2 + (.50)^2 + (.83)^2}$$
$$= 1.39 \text{ weeks}$$

Finally, if there are about five or more activities along the critical path, then the total project time will be normally distributed. There are only three critical activities in the Taylor case, nevertheless Taylor goes ahead (for pedagogical reasons) and assumes that the total project time is about normally distributed.

Figure 13.8 shows the normal distribution for total time for the Fort Bozeman project. It has a mean of 14.67 weeks and a standard deviation of 1.39 weeks. With this distribution Taylor can make probabilistic statements concerning the total project time. For example, only ten percent of the area in any normal distribution lies beyond 1.28 standard deviations above the mean. Thus in Taylor's case there is a ten percent chance that the total construction time T will go beyond

$$\text{Mean} + 1.28 \,(\text{Standard Deviation})$$
$$= 14.67 + 1.28 \,(1.39)$$
$$= 16.45 \text{ weeks}$$

Because all of the activities are subject to variable performance times, it is conceivable that the path which in the end proves to be the longest is not the same as the path which was originally identified as the critical path. For example, if A, C, and E proved to take times of 3, 4, and 3 weeks, respectively, and B took 8 weeks, then $B\text{-}E$ would have been longer than the original critical path of $A\text{-}C\text{-}E$. This sort of thing can easily complicate PERT. CPM is often used even when there is uncertainty in the activity times since PERT can become quite complex and makes more assumptions than CPM. Software packages exist for the solution of PERT networks on the computer. If these did not exist it would be extremely difficult to handle large PERT networks.

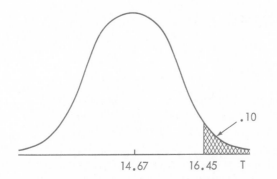

FIGURE 13.8   Normal Distribution of Total Project Time

PROBLEMS

13-1.   List all of the paths in the network shown on page 390, along with the time for each path. Which is the critical path?

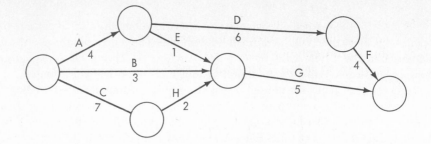

13-2. Construct a network based on the following information:

Activity	Immediate Predecessor
A	None
B	None
C	A
D	C,B
E	D
Finish	E

13-3. Construct a network based on the following information:

Activity	Immediate Predecessor
A	None
B	None
C	None
D	B
E	A
F	A
G	B
H	C,G
I	F,D
J	F,D
K	E,I
L	H,J
Finish	K,L

13-4. Construct a network based on the following information:

Activity	Immediate Predecessor	Activity	Immediate Predecessor
A	None	H	C
B	None	I	E
C	None	J	E
D	C	K	I
E	B,D	L	F,G,K
F	A,B,D	Finish	H,J,L
G	A		

13-5. For the following network (times are in weeks)
  (a) Find the *ES*, *LS*, and slack for each activity.
  (b) Find the critical path.
  (c) Draw *ES* and *LS* time-scaled networks.

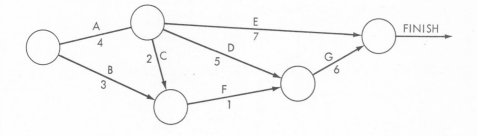

13-6. Referring to Problem 13–5, the amount of time that can be saved by crashing each activity and the cost thereof is given below. What activities should be crashed if the total project time is to be reduced by four weeks? What is the cost of this?

Activity	Time Saved by Crashing	Cost of Crashing
A	2 weeks	$800
B	1	500
C	.5	300
D	2	760
E	2	820
F	0	—
G	1	430

13-7. For the following network (times are in months)
  (a) Find the *ES*, *LS*, and slack for each activity.
  (b) Find the critical path.

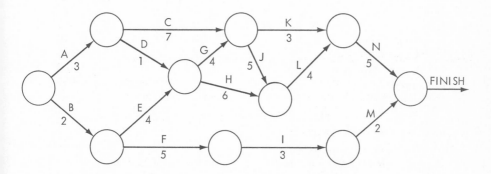

13-8. Referring to Problem 13–7, the amount of time that can be saved by crashing each activity and the cost thereof is given on page 392. What activities should be crashed if the total project time is to be reduced by one month? What is the cost of this one-month reduction in total time?

Activity	Time Saved by Crashing	Cost of Crashing
A	1 month	$230
B	.5	200
C	2	500
D	0	—
E	0	—
F	2	210
G	1	180
H	2	600
I	.5	300
J	1	500
K	0	—
L	.8	480
M	0	—
N	1	400

13-9. A foreign country has invited Krahn International to build a manufacturing plant within its territory. Krahn has responded positively to the country's invitation and is now in the planning stage for this endeavor. The primary activities and related information is given below.

Activity	Immediate Predecessor	Time in Months	Time Saved by Crashing	Cost of Crashing
A Government Permission	None	2	0	—
B Plant Site Selection	None	3	1	$2000
C Gov't. Tax Decision	A	3	0	—
D Plant Design	B,C	2	1	800
E Construction Permit	B,C	1	0	—
F Employment Advert.	B,C	1	0	0
G Solicit Bids	D,E	2	.5	1000
H (Dummy)	D,E	0	0	—
I Transportation	G	3	1.5	1500
J Plant Construction	G	8	3	4800
K Hiring & Training	F,H	9	1	2100
L Supplier Contracts	I	3	1	1600
M Sales Contracts	I	2	0	—
Finish	K,J,L,M	—	—	—

(a) Draw the network.
(b) Find the slack for each activity and the critical path.
(c) Draw an *ES* time-scaled network.
(d) Draw an *LS* time-scaled network.
(e) If the total project time were to be reduced by one month, which activity should be crashed?

13-10. For the following network (time is in months)
   (a) Find the critical path by inspection.
   (b) Find the probability distribution of the total project time.
   (c) There is a .90 probability that the project will be completed in how
       many months or less?

Activity	t_o	t_m	t_p
A	1	3	7
B	2	3	6
C	2	4	6
D	5	6	8
E	1	2	4
F	2	3	5
G	2	3	5
H	2	3	5
I	1	2	4
J	2	4	6
K	2	4	6
L	1	2	4
M	1	2	4

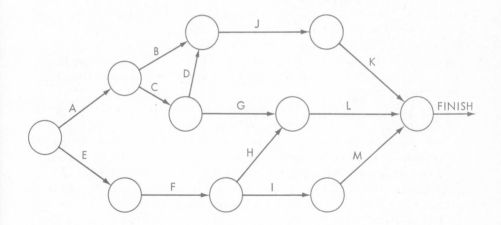

14 Game Theory

14.1 INTRODUCTION

Decision theory can be viewed as a decision making procedure for non-competitive decision situations. These situations are non-competitive in the sense that a competing participant does not select the state or event which occurs. Rather, "nature" (or "chance"), which is undauntedly stable in its ways and mindlessly indifferent to the decision maker's affairs, is said to control which state occurs. Decision theory, as described in Chapter 3, begins with a complete description of the situation, the decision model, and ends with some rational choice being made based on the probability of certain events or states occurring in the future.

Competitive situations differ from this type situation in that some of the events or states which will occur are actually choices made by other decision makers. Seat-of-the-pants analysis of such situations usually begins and ends with the approach: I think I'll do this; but *they* think I'll do this, so I'll do this other; but then they'll think that I think that they think I'll do this, therefore I think that they think that I think. . . . This is the well-known problem of infinite regress, and, among other shortcomings, does not yield quick results.

Each decision maker in a competitive situation may be referred to as a competitor. Each competitor faces a decision problem which includes the possibility of the occurrence of particular events, knowledge of the payoffs, and alternative acts or choices. If the competitor is assumed to be a "rational" (to be defined later) decision maker, then an estimate or prediction can be made of what action will be taken by estimating the decision problem facing the competitor. Then for future events in which our competitor is involved, we can analyze our own decision problem by substituting our best estimate of what we think the competitor will do. What we are actually doing is analyzing the competitor's decision problem and our decision problem at the same time.

This chapter was written by Daniel G. Brooks, Indiana University.

394

This simultaneous mathematical analysis of all competitors' decision problems for situations in which there is a conflict of interests is referred to as *game theory*. These competitive situations in which there are several sets of opposing interests are referred to, whether appropriately or inappropriately, as *games*.

14.2 TYPES OF GAMES

Games can be categorized in several ways. Three basic ways in which competitive situations, or games, may be classified are now given.

The Number of Competitors

The number of competitors is probably the most basic way to categorize competitive situations. In game theory a competitor is characterized as being a distinct set of interests and is usually referred to as a *person*, whether this distinct set of interests is held by an individual or by a larger body such as a group, corporation, gang, or army. The smallest number of competitors is two. This situation is usually referred to as a *two-person game*. If there are more than two competitors, the resulting many-person competitive situation is referred to as an *n-person game*.

The two-person conflict situation is a common one. A classic example comes from the early American and British tradition of dueling. Differences in sets of interests were resolved by having the two persons fire at one another. That there are two distinct sets of interests is clear, since Mssr. A does not share Mssr. B's interest in putting his projectile through Mssr. A's head, thus giving rise to this competitive game. Each duelist knows the other's shooting accuracy, and as the two approach each other, each with a single bullet to shoot, the probability of hitting the other increases but so also does the probability of being hit. The "game" is deciding when to shoot.

When there are more than two conflicting sets of interests, the situation becomes much more complex. First of all, it is necessary to keep track of more participants. What really makes for increased complexity, however, is that with more than two parties, there is now a possibility for competitors to form coalitions to aid them in eliminating other competitors. This situation is well-known. Suppose you and six of your friends each have quite a bit of oil. In fact, the seven of you together have almost all the oil there is and other people would like to buy some. Although the seven of you may not have exactly the same interests, one approach to help maximize your individual returns would be to form a coalition to set a single policy for oil pricing. This coalition is known in economics as a cartel. Similarly, workers form unions, countries form treaty groups or trade agreements, and criminals form gangs. The problem of solving *n*-person games will not be considered in this chapter.

The Degree of Opposition between Competitors

At one extreme in the degree of opposition is the situation of pure conflict or competition. These situations are referred to as *strictly competitive* games. As an example, remember that a frequent reason for dueling was to avenge one's honor, with the winner of the duel achieving that purpose. Notice that the gain of one is the loss of the other, and thus the sum of the winnings is zero. This is referred to as a *zero-sum game* for the reason that the sum of the winnings is zero. More examples of this type game will be given later. The duel is also just a special case of the two-person zero-sum game, and the "fast-guns" of the old West were revered for their expertise in these zero-sum competitive situations.

The other extreme is a situation in which the competitors' individual interests are best served if they cooperate with each other. In these instances the competitors can communicate with each other, and realizing that either they all win or all lose together, they agree on some cooperative strategy. One of the more notable examples of a cooperative game is the situation in which two people who committed a crime are apprehended and questioned separately. The criminals best serve their interests in not going to jail by cooperating with each other and not telling what they know, in which case both may be released. This is best accomplished by rehearsing their story together before they are caught.

In between these two extremes of pure competition and pure cooperation are varying mixtures of the two. Most situations of human interaction involve certain common, as well as opposed, interests. All these situations are referred to as *non-strictly competitive* or *non-zero sum* games. For example, if the officials offered, independently, a light sentence to each of the criminals apprehended as inducement to turn "State's evidence," as opposed to "throwing the book" at both of them on some minor trumped-up charge, there might be some motivation for each to double-cross the other, especially since they have no chance to communicate during the questioning.

The Amount of Information the Competitors Have

Games can be categorized according to the amount of information available to the players. There are two basic aspects of the game about which the players need some information in order to play: (1) what their competitors can do, and, (2) how the outcomes of the game depend on the actions taken by the participants. Both of these aspects will be expanded later in the chapter but an illustration here may help show their importance.

For example, Wells Fargo sends a shipment of gold dust across the Badlands by stagecoach. The Badlands were so called because they were inhabited by Bad Guys, and it was in their interest to make sure the stagecoach did not make it through that area. This conflict of interest is an example of a strictly competitive game, and when the Bad Guys attempted to relieve the stage of the strongbox holding the shipment, the payoff was the contents of the strongbox, namely, x pounds of gold dust where x is unknown. The outcome or payoff may not be the only unknown. The Bad Guys may be unaware that Wells Fargo has on the stage the feared Gatling gun, so not only is the outcome of the game unknown, but the possible actions of the competitor are unknown as well. Games lacking full information on what competitors can do or on what the outcome of the game will be in certain situations are said to be games with *incomplete information*.

Suppose now that the Bad Guys know exactly what Wells Fargo can do: that they have only two agents at most to ride the stage and they have no money to buy a Gatling gun. Further, suppose that the exact contents of the strongbox are known. The Bad Guys know that if no agent is on the stage they will get the strongbox, but if one or both agents ride with the stage the gold dust will make the journey safely. This is a game with complete information because what the competitors can do is known and the outcomes or payoffs of the game are known. There is still something unknown, however, because the Bad Guys know what Wells Fargo *can* do but they do not know what Wells Fargo actually *decided* to do. Likewise, Wells Fargo knows that the Bad Guys can either go after the stage or not, but they do not know for sure which action they have chosen to take. This is an example of a game with complete but *imperfect information*.

Games in which each participant knows the payoff for winning, knows who the competitors are, and knows all the moves the competitors make as soon as they make them are referred to as games with *perfect information*. For example, if Wells Fargo knows the Bad Guys are going to try to hold up the stage and the Bad Guys know that Wells Fargo has sent two agents and 150 pounds of gold dust on the stage, both sides are playing a game with perfect information and the outcome is known even before the game is played. A more common example of a perfect information game is checkers in which each player knows exactly what an opponent has done before making a move, and knows, in theory at least, the outcome of every possible move.

In this chapter the normal form of a game will be defined, the notion of the solution of a game will be introduced, and techniques to solve two-person, zero-sum finite games with perfect or imperfect (but complete) information will be shown. An example of an n-person, non-zero-sum game is given at the end of the chapter to illustrate some of the problems encountered in finding solutions to these more complicated competitive situations.

14.3 PAYOFFS, STRATEGIES, AND THE GAME MATRIX

A sequence of moves made by the participants which continues until the game is terminated is referred to as one *play* of the game. An *outcome* occurs at the end of a play of the game and depends on the particular moves made during the play. These outcomes might be anything. Considering previous examples, it is seen that there is a different set of possible outcomes for each of the different games. This is true in general. For the duel, the set of possible outcomes might be

$$\{A \text{ hits } B; B \text{ hits } A; \text{ Both miss and start again}\}$$

For the cooperative game played by the prisoners, the outcome set can be reduced to

$$\left\{ \begin{array}{l} \text{Both squeal; Neither squeals; The first squeals and the second does not;} \\ \text{The second squeals and the first does not.} \end{array} \right\}$$

It must be assumed that each of the players has a preference with regard to the possible outcomes and, in fact, can order the outcomes according to preference. It must also be assumed that there is a utility function for each player which assigns to each outcome a number representing the utility of an outcome to each player. The amount of utility a player receives at the end of a given play of a game is the *payoff*. It will be assumed that in games with a monetary payoff the number of dollars is the amount of utility a player receives from a particular outcome. For example, an outcome of winning $5 is a payoff of 5. Note that this implies that $5 has the same value for everyone playing the game.

For the Bad Guys holding up the stage, the outcomes might be simplified to the basic set

$$\text{Outcomes} = \{\text{Get the strongbox; Don't get the strongbox}\}$$

If the strongbox contained $5000 in gold dust, the payoffs would be the set

$$\text{Payoffs} = \{5000, \ 0\}$$

Because each player has preferences about the outcomes, and since it is assumed that the players are "rational" and know what the outcomes are (two assumptions), it makes sense that the individual players would actually plan what moves to make in a play of the game. Imagine a player making a list before a play of the game, and in this list specifying every possible situation which could arise in the course of playing the game and a corresponding move to be made in each situation. This list is referred to as a *strategy*. It is simply a plan which tells the player what to do no matter what other participants do. Just because this plan is referred to as a strategy, do not infer from this that it is always a good plan. Strategies can be bad as well as good.

As an example, one possible plan for holding up the Wells Fargo stage is

If there is a six-horse team pulling the stage and one Wells Fargo agent riding shotgun, don't chase the stage.
If there is a four-horse team and one agent riding shotgun, chase the stage.

However, this plan is not a strategy, and for several reasons. First, this plan does not specify what action to take for all possible actions by the competitor. For instance, what if the stage is spotted and it has a five-horse team and no agent aboard? The Bad Guys will lose valuable time deciding what to do in this unexpected, and unplanned for, situation. Second, the plan does not take into account that there may be a lack of knowledge in some areas, that is, that there is imperfect information. For instance, it is usually unknown how many agents are aboard until the gang actually begins chasing the stage, and sometimes unknown right up until the stage is caught.

To make this plan a strategy, it could be greatly simplified to the following:

1. Chase the stage.

This plan specifies what to do in all possible situations. It matters not at all what the opposition does—they could send the stage pulled by a steam locomotive on a track if they like—the Bad Guys' plan tells them what to do. Any plan, then, which specifies what to do in every possible eventuality of the game is a strategy. Other examples of strategies are:

2. If there are fewer than three agents aboard, chase the stage; otherwise, do not chase the stage.

3. If there are fewer than eight horses pulling the stage and it is raining, chase the stage. If either of these conditions do not hold, refrain from giving chase.

It is easy to think of other strategies of varying degrees of complexity, depending on how specific the planner wishes to be.

A game matrix can now be defined by combining the ideas of a payoff and a strategy. Suppose a particular game has two players, making it a two-person game, and each player has available three possible strategies. These two players are referred to as *Row* and *Column*. Row has three different strategies called Row 1, Row 2, and Row 3. Likewise, Column may use any of three strategies designated as Column 1, Column 2, and Column 3.

Now it is easily noticed that there are nine different combinations of strategies that might be employed by the two players in this game. There is Row 1 and Column 1, Row 1 and Column 2, and so on. To fully describe the game, the payoff to each of the players for each possible combination of strategies must be specified. The arrangement of Table 14.1 is often used to help keep track of all this information. The matrix, of course, is the rectangular array of boxes. The payoff corresponding to the use of a particular combination of strategies is written in the appropriate box in the matrix, and this specification of payoffs is continued until the game matrix is full. Usually the payoff to the Row player is written first and the payoff to the Column player second. To help distinguish between strategies, Row's strategies are denoted by R1, R2, and R3 while Column's are C1, C2, and C3.

Considering the incomplete game matrix in Table 14.1, if Row uses strategy R2 and Column uses C3, the resulting payoff is found by looking at the square in the matrix at which Row's strategy R2 and Column's strategy C3 intersect. The payoff specified there is that Row receives $500 and Column pays $500 (in fact, in this two-person game, Column pays Row $500). In the same manner, if Row uses R1 and Column uses C1, then Row loses $100 and Column gains $100 from Row.

TABLE 14.1
Game Matrix
(Incomplete)

		Column's Strategies		
		C1	C2	C3
Row's Strategies	R1	(−$100, $100)		
	R2			($500, −$500)
	R3			

Notice that in these two cases Row's gain is Column's loss, and vice versa. The sum of the payoffs for the given strategy combinations is zero in both cases since

$$-\$100 + \$100 = 0$$
$$\$500 + (-\$500) = 0$$

If this summing to zero holds for every square in the matrix, then the game is said to be a zero-sum game. Why is it necessary to specify both numbers in each square if they are always negatives of each other? The answer is that it is not necessary. In fact, for zero-sum games, the matrix contains only one number in each square, and that number represents the amount paid *from* Column *to* Row. Therefore, Table 14.1 could be rewritten as Table 14.2. To completely define the game the payoff from Column to Row must be specified in the same way for each possible combination of strategies (each square) in this matrix.

TABLE 14.2
Game Matrix for
Zero-sum Game
(Incomplete)

	C1	C2	C3
R1	−100		
R2			
R3			500

The following example will help illustrate how to set up a game matrix. Recall the Wells Fargo stage traveling across the Badlands. The Bad Guys, as it happens, actually have four possible strategies they might employ. These are: (1) Send no one after the stage, (2) Send one Bad Guy after the stage, (3) Send two, or (4) Send three after the stage. Wells Fargo, on the other hand, has only three strategies available: (1) Send no agent riding shotgun on the stage, (2) Send one agent, or (3) Send two agents.

Suppose it is well known that in an attempted stage holdup, one agent is the equal of two Bad Guys. Also, by Badlands' rules all ties, as when there is one agent against two Bad Guys, result in the payload being split. Suppose also that if the agents are superior in force to the Bad Guys (i.e., more than one-to-two), the agents rob the Bad Guys. The outcome set can be specified by arranging the outcomes in matrix form as shown in Table 14.3(a). The "pot" refers to the payload of gold dust. To determine the exact payoffs, it is assumed that there is $5000 in the strongbox (pot) and that the Bad Guys normally carry $500 each. The resulting game matrix is then given in Table 14.3(b).

To summarize, the game matrix above shows that there are two players or competitors and that the Row player has four possible strategies and the Column player has three possible strategies. Because the gain of the Row player (Bad Guys) is the loss of the Column player (Wells Fargo) and vice versa, it is necessary to specify only one number in each square. The numbers in the squares represent the payoffs to the Bad Guys or Row player. This game matrix is the so-called normal form representation of a two-person zero-sum game with a finite number of strategies. In the next section the idea of solving this type of game will be discussed so that the best strategies for each player to use may be found.

TABLE 14.3
Badlands Game Matrix
(Two-Person Zero-Sum)

(a)

		Wells Fargo's Strategies		
		Send 0	Send 1	Send 2
	Send 0	No one robbed	No one robbed	No one robbed
	Send 1	Bad Guys get pot	Agents rob Bad Guys	Agents rob Bad Guys
Bad Guys' Strategies	Send 2	Bad Guys get pot	Split pot	Agents rob Bad Guys
	Send 3	Bad Guys get pot	Bad Guys get pot	Agents rob Bad Guys

(b)

		Wells Fargo		
		Send 0	Send 1	Send 2
	Send 0	0	0	0
	Send 1	5000	−500	−500
Bad Guys	Send 2	5000	2500	−1000
	Send 3	5000	5000	−1500

14.4 SOLUTION BY DOMINANCE

In game theory, *rational* behavior is defined as behavior aimed at securing as much as possible from the game while taking into consideration the fact that the other competitors in the game are behaving likewise. The idea of a *solution* to a game—in terms of a strategy to use which maximizes the return from playing the game—must be considered. Only two-person zero-sum games with a finite number of strategies will be dealt with here. The following two assumptions are basic to obtaining a solution concept:

1. Both players play the game so as to maximize their own payoffs. This is the assumption of rationality defined earlier.
2. Both players know everything in the game matrix, i.e., both sets of strategies and all the payoffs. This is the assumption of complete information.

The convention that game matrices represent money paid by the column player to the row player will be followed.

Consider the game represented by the matrix of Table 14.4(a), page 402. Remember that these numbers represent amounts paid by Column to Row so that Row wants a strategy which brings a large payment and Column wants a strategy that yields a low payment. Looking at the payoffs with this in mind, notice that Row's strategy R2 brings a payoff higher than strategy R3 no matter what strategy Column uses. The payoff from R2 is at least as great as the corresponding payoff from R3 in each of the four cases where C1, or C2, or C3, or C4 is used by Column. R2 is said to *dominate* R3 because it is always the superior strategy and thus R3 would never be used.

TABLE 14.4
Game Matrix
and Solution by Dominance

(a)

Column's Pure Strategies

		C1	C2	C3	C4
	R1	2	9	2	1
Row's Pure	R2	7	8	6	7
Strategies	R3	3	4	3	2
	R4	10	5	5	1

(b)

	C3	C4
R1	-2-	-1-
R2	6	7
R4	-5-	-8-

Notice also in Table 14.4(a) that strategy C3 is superior to strategies C2 and C1 for Column. C3 is at least as small or smaller than the corresponding amounts paid out under C1 and C2, no matter what strategy Row uses. Since C1 and C2 are dominated by C3, they will never be used by Column and can be eliminated from the game matrix along with strategy R3 for Row which is dominated by R2. This leaves the reduced game matrix of Table 14.4(b). With these strategies eliminated it is seen that R2 now dominates R1, which can now be eliminated. With R1 eliminated (draw a dotted line through it), C3 dominates C4 because C3 results in a smaller payoff whether Row uses R2 or R4. Finally, with C4 eliminated (draw a dotted line through it), R2 dominates R4. Every strategy for Row has been eliminated but R2 and every strategy for Column has been eliminated except C3. In this particular game, Row should therefore use R2 and Column should use strategy C3. The payoff when these two strategies are used is 6 to Row. This method of successive elimination is known as *iterated dominance*.

Something of interest about these two strategies should be noted. Given that Row plays strategy R2, Column's best response strategy is C3 since 6 is the least Column can get away with paying (see Table 14.4(a)). Also, given that Column used strategy C3, Row's best response is strategy R2 because 6 is the most Row can get paid. Because each of these strategies is a best response to the other and because neither player has any reason to want to switch strategies given the other stays put, these strategies are said to be in *equilibrium*. Because neither player can do better by switching strategies, both should stick with their respective best response strategies if they want to maximize their return (or equivalently, minimize their loss). This equilibrium pair of strategies represents a solution to this game.

Don't stop reading yet. This method of iterated dominance is easy enough, but will it always find an equilibrium point? The answer is no. Another solution technique of broader application will now be presented. In learning a new approach it is possible to see more clearly what this equilibrium point represents, and the principle that lies at the heart of game theory.

14.5 PURE STRATEGIES AND SADDLE POINTS

There can be but little doubt that Daniel Boone was a well-known man. What is not so well known is that Dan's diminutive cousin "Minnie" was a horseback rider with few equals. Every third Thursday, right after morning bingo, Minnie Boone was off to the hills for some friendly horseraces with her friends, the Shawnees. The problem centered around where the races were to be held. The Indian ponies were mountain ponies and the higher the elevation, the greater their advantage. Minnie's trusty steed was a lowland animal and was better suited to low elevation races. The way the problem was solved, by tradition, was for Minnie to set out from the valley and Chief Max (Chief Maximillian, but to his friends, Chief Max) and his group to set out from the mountains and wherever their paths crossed, that was where the races were held.

There were, in those days before mass transit, only four trails leading up toward the mountains from the valley, and there were four trails from the mountains heading downward. Topographically speaking, the situation is represented by Figure 14.1. The trails are labeled as Mountain Trails M1, M2, M3, and M4. The Valley Trails are V1, V2, V3, and V4. Kentucky, the Boones' home state then, is a land of thick vegetation and only the intersections of these trails afforded the room necessary for those magnificent beasts to reach full speed. By each intersection, to be viewed as a possible race sight, is a single digit representing the elevation of that intersection in thousands of feet.

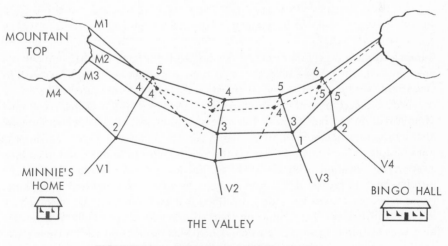

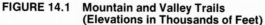

FIGURE 14.1   Mountain and Valley Trails
(Elevations in Thousands of Feet)

Pondering this map for only an instant, Minnie knew immediately what she must do. If she took V2, the very highest race would be a race at 4000 feet, and if Chief Max did not take M2, she would get to race at an even lower elevation. She immediately resolved to take no trail but V2 for as long as she lived to race. Though Minnie was clever, Chief Max was equally crafty, and after quick council noticed that if he took M2 the very lowest elevation at which he would be forced to race would be 4000 feet. Furthermore, a slip-up by Minnie Boone in choosing one of the higher trails would let him race at an even higher elevation. He forthwith determined that M2 would always be taken so long as he was chief.

Minnie stuck to V2 and Max to M2 and many third Thursdays were spent racing at 4000 feet. Both were happy with this location realizing they opposed a wily adversary and could do no better. This intersection, being in between the two mountains as it was, came to be known as the saddle point.

The game just presented which pitted Minnie against Chief Max could be solved by dominance. That is, V2 dominates all of Minnie's other strategies and M2 dominates all of the Chief's other strategies. This game, however, will be used to describe a more general mode of analysis which yields optimal strategies in cases where there is no dominance as well as in cases where dominance exists. After this more general approach to games is developed, it will be applied to a two-person zero-sum game where dominance does not exist.

When the elevations at the intersections of the trails, as depicted in Figure 14.1, are put in matrix form, the game matrix of Table 14.5 is obtained. To begin

TABLE 14.5
Minnie & Chief Max
Game Matrix

		Minnie's Trails			
		V1	V2	V3	V4
Chief Max's Trails	M1	4	3	4	5
	M2	5	4	5	6
	M3	4	3	3	5
	M4	2	1	1	2

thinking through a general approach leading to the selection of M2 and V2, remember that Chief Max's objective is to race at as high an altitude as possible and Minnie's is to race at as low an elevation as possible. How should Chief Max proceed to select a strategy (trail) under these circumstances realizing that Minnie will do her best to keep the race at a low elevation? Chief Max might first determine what each of his strategies can guarantee in terms of elevations. For example, if the Chief selected M1 there is the possibility of being forced into a race at an elevation as low as 3000 feet. The lowest elevation the Chief would possibly have to race at if M2 were selected is 4000 feet. Continuing, the minimum elevation associated with M3 is 3000 feet and the minimum elevation of the M4 trail is 1000 feet. Cognizant that Minnie will act shrewdly to keep the race at as low an elevation as possible, Chief Max should select M2 which guarantees an elevation of at least 4000 feet. No other mountain trail can guarantee as high a minimum.

In selecting M2 Chief Max has utilized the *maximin* principle of choice which was introduced in Section 3.4 of Chapter 3. Recall that the maximin principle calls for the selection of that act or strategy which maximizes the minimum payoff. In other words, the strategy with the greatest minimum payoff (elevation) is selected.

Now looking at the game matrix from Minnie's perspective, Minnie should select V2 since V2 guarantees that the race will never be held above 4000 feet. If V1 were selected, the race might be held at 5000 feet, if V3 were selected the race might be held at 5000 feet, and if V4 were selected the race might be held as high as 6000 feet. As Minnie fears that if she selected any trail other than V2 the Chief would capitalize on the situation and force the race at an elevation above 4000 feet, she selects V2 in order to guarantee that the race be held no higher than 4000 feet. Minnie in actuality has applied the *minimax* principle of choice, which was introduced in Section 3.4 of Chapter 3. In particular, the maximum elevation for each valley trail is noted and the valley trail which has the minimum of these maximums is selected.

In Table 14.5 the Chief's maximin strategy, M2, and Minnie's minimax strategy, V2, have been enclosed in dotted lines. As a result of the use of these strategies the race will be held at an elevation of 4000 feet. Notice that 4000 feet is the minimum elevation on the M2 trail and it is the maximum elevation on the V2 trail. This point, as mentioned earlier, is called the *saddle point*. Whenever the minimum value for Row's maximin strategy equals the maximum value under Column's minimax strategy, then a saddle point is said to exist in the game. Again, the saddlepoint in the game of Table 14.5 is an elevation of 4000 feet which occurs at the intersection of M2 and V2.

When a saddle point exists there is great stability in the game. If Chief Max uses his maximin strategy, M2, there is no advantage to Minnie in switching away from V2. If the Chief uses M2, any change of trails by Minnie will only force the race to a higher elevation and thus work to the Chief's advantage and to Minnie's detriment. Likewise, if Minnie holds to V2, the Chief cannot reap advantage by switching to another trail from M2. A change to another mountain trail would work to the Chief's detriment and to Minnie's advantage. The reason why neither of the competitors would want to abandon the original strategies lies in the fact that the saddle point or 4000 feet is the minimum elevation for M2 and the maximum elevation for V2. Because there is no incentive for either competitor to switch strategies when a saddle point exists, the maximin and minimax strategies can rightly be designated as the solution to the game. Their use results in equilibrium, hence these two strategies are called the *equilibrium pair*.

In the foregoing example the optimal strategies (equilibrium pair) could have easily been found by dominance as pointed out earlier. Thus the use of the maximin and minimax principles was not necessary to solve this particular game. Nevertheless, the maximin-minimax sort of analysis can be successfully used in games where dominance does not exist. This mode of analysis will now be demonstrated in a game where there are no dominant strategies. It will be apparent that the analysis proceeds in the same manner as when dominating strategies existed.

The game matrix in Table 14.6 has no dominant strategies. In this situation, however, the maximin and minimax strategies can still be determined and the game will also be shown to have a saddle point.

TABLE 14.6
A Game with No Dominant Strategies

		C1	C2	C3	C4	Row Minima:
	R1	6	3	4	2	2
Row	R2	5	(4)	5	6	(4)
	R3	4	2	8	7	2
	R4	1	3	1	8	1
Column Maxima:		6	(4)	8	8	

The row player, Row, looks at each strategy and notices the smallest or minimum return possible with each strategy. These values are sometimes called the *security levels* for each strategy. For example, in using R1 Row is sure to make at least 2, and in using R2 Row is sure to make at least 4. With R3 the security level is 2 and the security level with R4 is 1. The column player, Column, on the other hand looks at the largest or maximum amount that would have to be paid with each column strategy. With C1 Column would at most have to pay 6. If C2 were used the maximum payment would be 4 and so on. These values are written on the border of the game matrix. Remember once again that the numbers in the matrix represent payments to Row from Column.

Row, by being smart and assuming that Column is smart, will pick the strategy providing the highest possible security level (in terms of income). Strategy R2 does this; it yields the maximum value of all the row minima. Using R2, Row is guaranteed at least 4. Likewise, Column picks the strategy providing the lowest possible security level (in terms of payout). Strategy C2 is the one which gives the minimum value of all the column maxima. That is, the most Column might be forced to pay if C2 is used is 4. This 4 is less than the maxima for the other available column strategies. R2 is therefore the maximin strategy and C2 is the minimax strategy.

As noted before, when the maximum of the row minima equals the minimum of the column maxima, the maximin and minimax strategies are in equilibrium. In other words, a saddle point exists. This means that Row has no desire to change to a different strategy as long as Column stays with C2, and Column has no incentive to switch strategies if Row stays with R2. The payoff from this equilibrium pair of strategies is called the *value* of the game.

It has been shown that certain games have saddle points and that when a saddle point exists, the players would find the use of the maximin and minimax strategies to result in equilibrium. Thus two-person zero-sum games which have saddle points are fairly easy to solve and there can be little disagreement as to how the competitors ought to behave in these games. But, do all games have a saddle point? It will be shown that they do not. A more complex sort of analysis is required in these cases. Attention will now be turned to this type of game which has no saddle point.

14.6 MIXED STRATEGIES

Is it possible for a game to have no equilibrium pair or saddle point? If such a situation did exist, how could the game be analyzed? These questions will now be considered.

Suppose the game of Table 14.7 is to be analyzed. According to the maximin principle, Row should select R2 which guarantees a payoff of at least 1. Applying minimax, Column would select C2 which guarantees that Column's loss will be no more than 3. Immediately it should be noticed that this game has no saddle point since the security level for R2 does not equal that of C2. (The security levels for the maximin-minimax strategies will be marked with an asterisk.) Hence the game has no equilibrium value or equilibrium pair of pure strategies. What does this mean?

TABLE 14.7
Game with No Saddle Point
(Asterisk Denotes Security Levels of
Maximin-Minimax Strategies)

		Column	Column	Row Minima
		C1	C2	
	R1	-2	3	-2
Row				
	R2	4	1	1*
Column Maxima		4	3*	

Well, suppose to start the game, Row uses the maximin strategy R2 and Column uses the minimax strategy C2. But knowing that Column expects Row to use R2, Row's position can be improved by not playing R2 but rather R1, and receiving a payment of 3 instead of 1. But Column can see the matrix as well, and thinking that Row might try this trick, knows it would be profitable not to play the minimax strategy C2, but rather C1 thus lowering the payment to -2 (a gain). But Row, realizing Column might reason this way . . ., and so on. The strategies are not in equilibrium because both players have some incentive to switch, given that the other player does not. How can such a game be solved? The following example illustrates the approach to such games.

In the early 1900s the streets of New York City saw the rise and fall of many small businesses. Probably none of these businesses was so small, however, as the operations of Ronald and Tracy, two cousins, each in the vegetable push-cart business. The two push-carts come out early each morning and take their positions across from each other on 37th Avenue. Having an appreciation for the benefits of specialization, each of the cousins carries only one commodity. Ronald carries tomatoes and Tracy carries squash. However, the times are changing and the cousins see the trend to the larger, one-stop shopping facilities, so each is considering expanding their line to include the item on which their rival now has a monopoly. Ronald might add squash to his display and Tracy is considering adding tomatoes to provide a full line of products. Each knows that the other is considering expanding, and this influences each of their decisions. They each sign a one-season contract with a supplier at the beginning of the vegetable season and in that contract must specify what vegetables they want delivered.

Ronald figures that if he does not expand his service and his cousin does, it will hurt his trade by a dollar of profit per day. If neither of them expand their inventory to include the extra vegetable, Ronald thinks it will boost his net by one dollar a day, due to the slightly superior location of his cart. If he expands and his cousin does also, he believes the combination of location and expanded inventory will increase his profits by two dollars per day. However, if he alone expands and his cousin does not, he is afraid a customer sympathy move to help his cousin with the poorer location and smaller inventory will result in no net increase in business. This information, in terms of daily losses or gains to Ronald in dollars, is summarized in Table 14.8.

TABLE 14.8
Push-cart Game Matrix
(Asterisk Denotes Security Levels
of Maximin-Minimax Strategies)

		Tracy's Strategies		
		Do Not Expand	Expand	Row Minima
Ronald's Strategies	Do Not Expand	1	−1	−1
	Expand	0	2	0*
	Column Maxima	1*	2	

Since neither one knows how the other will negotiate their supply contract for the new season, each must determine the best strategy in deciding whether to expand or not without knowing the other's plans. Ronald realizes at once that there is no equilibrium strategy. In fact, because there is no equilibrium strategy, and the circuitous reasoning considering "what if she thinks that I think that she thinks" tires him, he decides he is actually indifferent between the two strategies. He could as well flip a coin to decide then, if he is truly indifferent. But would this help? Suppose he pulls a coin from his pocket and flips it telling himself that if a head comes up he will expand, otherwise (a tail) he will not. That means that there is a 50 percent chance of expanding and a 50 percent chance of not expanding. A strategy, such as this one, which is a probabilistic mixture of pure strategies is called a *mixed strategy*.

Using a coin toss, if his cousin does not expand, then the profit Ronald will make using his mixed strategy is $1 a day with probability 1/2 and 0 with probability 1/2. Thus, the expected profit to Ronald given that Tracy does not expand is $(1/2)(\$1) + (1/2)(0)$ or $.50. Well, this is certainly better than making nothing for certain using his maximin strategy of expanding. If his cousin does expand her product line, then Ronald's profit is $2 per day with probability 1/2 and a loss of a dollar with probability 1/2. This gives an expected profit of $.50 since

$(1/2)(-\$1) + (1/2)(\$2) = \$.50$. Is an expected profit of $.50 better than nothing for certain (the result of Ronald using his maximum strategy and Tracy using her minimax strategy)? The answer is yes.

What is interesting is that Ronald seems to be better off by flipping a coin than he is by following strictly his maximin strategy. This new mix of strategies or mixed strategy can be treated as a third option for him as shown in Table 14.9. By mixing the two pure strategies using a coin, the wise Ronald has actually raised his security level from 0 to .5. There is still no equilibrium, however, since .5 does not equal 1 which is the optimal security level of Tracy.

TABLE 14.9
Push-cart Game Matrix
with Extra Mixed Strategy

		Do Not Expand	Expand	Row Minima
			Tracy	
Ronald	Do Not Expand	1	−1	−1
	Expand	0	2	0
	1/2 Do Not + 1/2 Do	$.5 =$ $(1/2)(1) + (1/2)(0)$	$.5 =$ $(1/2)(-1) + (1/2)(2)$	.5*
	Column Maxima	1*	2	

This approach of mixing strategies worked for Ronald so perhaps it should be tried by Tracy. Suppose Tracy decides to not expand with probability 3/4 and expand with probability 1/4. (The reason why Tracy uses these two probabilities rather than 1/2 and 1/2, for example, will be discussed later in the section.) Using this probabilistic mix of strategies, Tracy's expected payout given that Ronald does not expand is $(3/4)(1) + (1/4)(-1)$ or $.50. But if Ronald expanded, what would Tracy's expected payout be? It would be $(3/4)(0) + (1/4)(2)$ or $.50 since if Ronald does not expand, the payout from Tracy will be either 0 or 2 depending on what Tracy actually does. Thus it has been shown that regardless of what Ronald does, Tracy's expected payout using the mixed strategy is $.50. But what if Ronald uses his coin to determine what he will do? In this case (see Table 14.9), there would be a 3/4 probability that Tracy would pay out .5 and a 1/4 probability of a payout of .5 (which is associated with the utilization of "Expand" assuming Ronald is using his mixed strategy). Thus the expected payout would be $(3/4)(.5) + (1/4)(.5)$ or $.50 if Tracy used the mixed strategy and Ronald did also.

Table 14.10, page 410, shows Tracy's new alternative along with Ronald's. Notice that a saddle point exists in this game where the mixed strategies are permitted. The equilibrium value of .5 is the saddle point and Ronald's equilibrium strategy is "1/2 Do Not + 1/2 Do" while Tracy's is "3/4 Do Not + 1/4 Do." Both Ronald and Tracy share the security level of $.50 which is an improvement over each of their initial security levels (see Table 14.8) of 0 and 1, respectively.

TABLE 14.10
Push-cart Game Matrix with Mixed Strategies Admitted

		Tracy			
		Do Not Expand	Expand	3/4 Do Not + 1/4 Do	Row Minima
	Do Not Expand	1	−1	.5	−1
Ronald	Expand	0	2	.5	0
	1/2 Do Not + 1/2 Do	.5	.5	(.5)	.5*
Column Maxima		1	2	.5*	

Thus a game has been given where no saddle point existed initially. However, when mixed strategies were admitted, the game proved to have an equilibrium pair of maximin and minimax mixed strategies. These two mixed strategies constitute the solution to the game.

This brings up the most central and famous theorem of game theory, the *minimax theorem* of John von Neumann which says:

1. If mixed strategies are permitted, every two-person zero-sum game, no matter how many strategies are available to the players, has a unique equilibrium value obtained by playing the equilibrium pair of strategies.
2. The equilibrium pair of strategies is made up of one maximin strategy and one minimax strategy. Either or both of these strategies may be mixed strategies.

Now that it is known that an equilibrium value always exists, the next problem is to determine the mixed strategies which achieve this value when it cannot be reached by pure strategies. In general, how are these optimal mixed strategies found?

Consider again the game matrix of the previous example in the more general form of Table 14.11. Because it is a two-person zero-sum game, an equilibrium value must exist. Because there is no equilibrium point or saddle point using pure strategies, this indicates that mixed strategies must be used. Denote the mixed strategy which uses R1 with probability p_1 and R2 with probability p_2 by $(p_1 R1, p_2 R2)$. For example, the mixed strategy $(.3R1, .7R2)$ would mean that R1

TABLE 14.11
Game Matrix

		Column	
		C1	C2
Row	R1	1	−1
	R2	0	2

is used with probability .3 and R2 with probability .7. The problem is to find the probability mix or mixed strategy for Row which yields the equilibrium value or saddle point. Let $S°$ represent the equilibrium value.

If Row uses the probability mix (p_1, p_2), then the expected payoff can be calculated by considering what Column might do. There are two cases. First, if Column uses strategy C1, it can be seen from Table 14.11 that Row's expected payoff is the payoff from using R1 times the probability R1 is used plus the payoff from R2 times the probability of using R2, or,

$$\text{Expected Payoff to Row if Column uses C1} = (p_1)(1) + (p_2)(0)$$

In the same way Row's expected payoff can be calculated if Column uses C2:

$$\text{Expected Payoff to Row if Column uses C2} = (p_1)(-1) + (p_2)(2)$$

Because the equilibrium value $S°$ is fixed no matter which strategy Column uses (notice that in Table 14.10 the payoff to Ronald is $S° = .5$ no matter what strategy Tracy uses), it follows that

$$\text{Equilibrium Value} = \text{Expected Payoff to Row if Column Uses C1} = \text{Expected Payoff to Row if Column Uses C2}$$

if Row is using the maximin mixed strategy. Converting the above to symbols yields

$$S° = (p_1)(1) + (p_2)(0) = (p_1)(-1) + (p_2)(2)$$

assuming (p_1, p_2) is Row's maximin strategy. Note that $p_2 = 1 - p_1$ since $p_1 + p_2 = 1$. Hence by substitution,

$$S° = (p_1) + (1-p_1)(0) = (p_1)(-1) + (1-p_1)(2)$$

Through simplification the latter equation becomes

$$p_1 = -p_1 + 2(1-p_1)$$

which may be solved for p_1

$$4p_1 = 2$$
$$p_1 = 1/2$$

Finally, since $p_2 = 1-p_1$,

$$p_2 = 1 - (1/2)$$
$$p_2 = 1/2$$

Therefore, the optimal mixed strategy for Row is (1/2 R1, 1/2 R2). This is, of course, the maximin strategy Ronald found to be optimal in Table 14.10. By substituting the optimal values of p_1 and p_2 into $S° = (p_1)(1) + (p_2)(0)$ or into $S° = (p_1)(-1) + (p_2)(20)$, the equilibrium value of .5 is found.

Analogous equations can be found for Column in order to determine an optimal mixed strategy. Let q_1 be the probability with which C1 is used and q_2 the probability of using C2. Then for the minimax strategy of (q_1C1, q_2C2),

$$\begin{array}{ccc} \text{Equilibrium} \\ \text{Value} \end{array} = \begin{array}{c} \text{Expected Payout from} \\ \text{Column if Row Uses R1} \end{array} = \begin{array}{c} \text{Expected Payout from} \\ \text{Column if Row Uses R2} \end{array}$$

$$S^* = (q_1)(1) + (q_2)(-1) = (q_1)(0) + (q_2)(2)$$

Since $q_2 = 1 - q_1$

$$(q_1)(1) + (1-q_1)(-1) = (q_1)(0) + (1-q_1)(2)$$
$$4\,q_1 = 3$$
$$q_1 = 3/4$$

Finally,

$$q_2 = 1 - q_1$$
$$q_2 = 1 - 3/4$$
$$q_2 = 1/4$$

Thus the optimal or minimax mixed strategy for Column is (3/4 C1, 1/4 C2). This, of course, is the mixed strategy Tracy employed in Table 14.10 which was her optimal strategy guaranteeing the security level of .5.

In this manner, then, the equilibrium value and optimal maximin and minimax strategies may be determined for any two-person zero-sum game. This mixed strategy approach is only utilized if a saddle point does not exist with the use of pure strategies.

14.7 GRAPHICAL SOLUTIONS

The games for which mixed strategy solutions have been found have had only two pure strategies available to each player. These are referred to as 2 x 2 (read "two-by-two") games or as two-person zero-sum 2 x 2 games. If the row player has not two but n strategies available against two for the column player, this is referred to as an n x 2 game. If the column player has m strategies and the row player has two, it is called a 2 x m game. As one might suspect, if the row player has n strategies and the column player has m strategies, that is an n x m game. In this section graphical interpretations of 2 x 2 games will be considered. Then some comments will follow concerning the solution of larger games.

Consider the following problem as an example. The oil workers in Oklahoma work hard keeping all the oil rigs running and expect to be paid well for their effort. They expect, in fact, to be paid better than they are currently being paid by the huge oil concern OK Oil, for whom they work. To impress this expectation on the management of OK Oil, the workers have formed a union, Oklahoma Crude, and are beginning to threaten to strike if something is not done soon about their wages. The union has settled on two basic strategies, namely, (1) a full strike, and, (2) no strike at all. Each has advantages and disadvantages. If a full strike is called, there is a good chance of finally settling for higher wages but interim pay is sacrificed. On the other hand, no pay will be lost if no strike is called, but the renegotiated wage level may not be as high either. OK Oil, for its part, is fully aware that things are not OK with the oil workers.

The two strategies they have decided to consider are quick acquiessence to the union's demands, or a stall. From past dealings with strikes, the payoffs from OK Oil to the oil workers as depicted in Table 14.12 are expected by both sides.

TABLE 14.12
Union-Company Game Matrix

		OK Oil Company		
		C1 Stall	C2 Give In	Row Minima
Oklahoma Crude Union	U1 Do Not Strike	−3	4	−3
	U2 Strike	2	−1	−1*
	Column Maxima	2*	4	

Note that this game has no saddle point in pure strategies. That means mixed strategies must be employed. First, consider what mix of striking or not striking is healthiest for the union, i.e., its maximin mixed strategy. In order to graphically depict the situation, draw two vertical axes and a horizontal axis as in Figure 14.2(a), page 414. The vertical axes represent the payoff to Row (the union) and the horizontal axis gives values for p_2 which is the probability that Row uses strategy U2. Recall that a mixed strategy for Row (the union) would be designated by $(p_1 U1, p_2 U2)$.

For the time being, assume that Column (the company) uses strategy C1. If the union were to use the pure strategy U1, the payoff to the union would be −3 according to the game matrix. When the union uses the pure strategy U1, this in essence is the same as a mixed strategy where $p_1 = 1$ and $p_2 = 0$. Since the horizontal axis gives the value for p_2 only (the value for p_1 is always $1 - p_2$), place a point representing the payoff of −3 below the $p_2 = 0$ value. This point will fall on the left vertical axis which is labeled "Pure U1." Still assuming that the company uses C1, the payoff to the union for the pure strategy U2 is 2 according to Table 14.12. Of course, a pure strategy of U2 is the same as a mixed strategy where $p_2 = 1$. Place a point at the payoff of 2 above the place where $p_2 = 1$ in Figure 14.2(a). This point falls on the right vertical axis which is labeled as "Pure U2." Now connect these two points with a straight line. The result is the line of Figure 14.2(a).

The line of Figure 14.2(a) gives the payoff to the union (Row) corresponding to every possible mixed strategy the union can use assuming the company sticks with C1. For example, if the union uses (.5U1, .5U2), then the union will receive a payoff of −3 with probability .5 and a payoff of 2 with probability .5. The expected payoff would be $(.5)(-3) + (.5)(2) = -.5$. It can be confirmed by the graph of Figure 14.2(a) that the line is at a height of −.5 when $p_2 = .5$. In general, the payoff to the union when a mixed strategy of (p_1U1, p_2U2) is employed, assuming the company uses C1, is

$$\text{Payoff} = (p_1)(-3) + (p_2)(2)$$

Since $p_1 = 1 - p_2$, this can be rewritten as

$$\text{Payoff} = (1-p_2)(-3) + (p_2)(2)$$

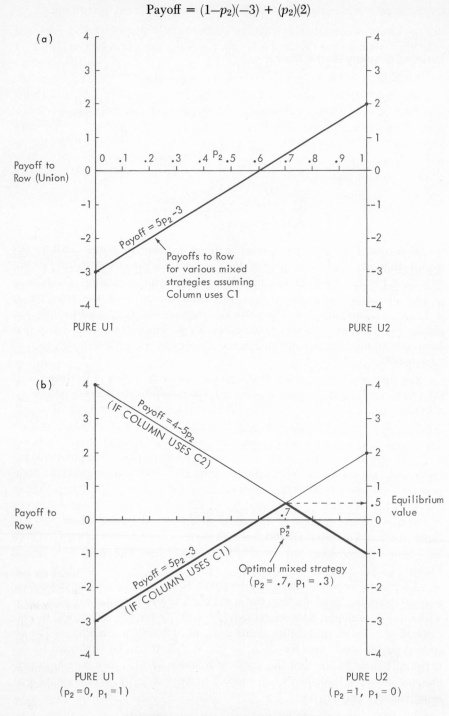

(a)

Payoff to
Row (Union)

Payoff = 5p₂−3

Payoffs to Row
for various mixed
strategies assuming
Column uses C1

PURE U1   PURE U2

(b)

Payoff = 4−5p₂
(IF COLUMN USES C2)

Payoff to
Row

.7
p₂*

Equilibrium
value

Payoff = 5p₂−3
(IF COLUMN USES C1)

Optimal mixed strategy
(p₂ = .7, p₁ = .3)

PURE U1   PURE U2
(p₂ = 0, p₁ = 1)   (p₂ = 1, p₁ = 0)

FIGURE 14.2   Row's Analysis (Maximin)

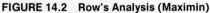

Then simplifying,

$$\text{Payoff} = 5p_2 - 3$$

This equation is actually the equation of the line in Figure 14.2(a). Again, it gives the payoff to the Oklahoma Crude Union for all probability mixes of U1 and U2 when OK Oil uses pure strategy C1.

A similar line can be drawn for payoffs to the union in the case where the company uses strategy C2. The union will make 4 by using the pure strategy U1 and will make -1 using pure strategy U2, assuming the company sticks with C2. These two points are plotted in Figure 14.2(b) and a straight line is drawn connecting them. This line gives the expected payoff to the union for each of its potential mixed strategies from $p_2 = 0$ to $p_2 = 1$. The equation of this line which gives the payoffs to the union assuming the company uses C2 is

$$\begin{aligned}
\text{Payoff} &= (4)(p_1) + (-1)(p_2) \\
&= (4)(1 - p_2) + (-1)(p_2) \\
&= 4 - 5p_2
\end{aligned}$$

Putting the two payoff lines on the same graph, as in Table 14.2(b), trace over the bent line which is the lowest line going across from the point at which $p_2 = 0$ to where $p_2 = 1$. This gives all the minimum payoffs possible for the union which correspond to the possible mixed strategies. The union should then pick the mixture, which is defined by p_2, which gives the *maximum* of all these minimums. This is the maximin strategy introduced long ago; it is the strategy which determines the equilibrium value of the game. That value of p_2 which yields the maximum of all the minimums can be read from the graph of Figure 14.2(b) if the two payoff lines have been drawn accurately. In particular, $p_2 = .7$ is the value which represents the optimal mixed strategy. The union should use the mixed strategy of (.3 U1, .7 U2). Reading to the vertical axis, the equilibrium value for this mixed strategy is .5. With this strategy the union can guarantee itself an expected payoff of .5. No other mixed strategy can guarantee as high an expected gain.

The optimal value for p_2 could also have been found realizing that it occurs at the intersection of the two payoff lines. By setting each of these equations equal to each other, the p_2 of the intersection can be found:

$$\begin{aligned}
5p_2 - 3 &= 4 - 5p_2 \\
p_2 &= .7
\end{aligned}$$

This same type of graphical analysis can be used to find the optimal mixed strategy for OK Oil Company. In this case, the vertical axes show the payoff to Row or, in other words, the payout from the company (Column). The horizontal axis represents the various mixed strategies from (1 C1, 0 C2) or $q_2 = 0$ to (0 C1, 1 C2) or $q_2 = 1$. Remember that q_1 denotes the probability of using C1 and q_2 the probability of the company using C2.

If the union uses U1, then the company would pay out -3 if it used the pure strategy C1 and would pay out 4 if it uses a pure strategy of C2. The -3 is plotted on the left vertical axis, below $q_2 = 0$, in Figure 14.3 and 4 on the right vertical axis, above $q_2 = 1$. A line is then drawn connecting these two points.

This line shows the expected payout for every mixed strategy from $q_2 = 0$ to $q_2 = 1$ assuming the union uses U1. This line has the equation

$$\text{Payout} = (q_1)(-3) + (q_2)(4)$$

which may be simplified to

$$\text{Payout} = 7q_2 - 3$$

since $q_2 = 1-q_1$.

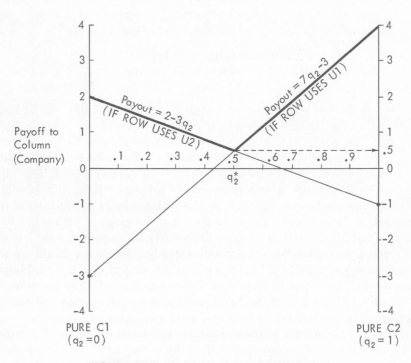

FIGURE 14.3 Column's Analysis (Minimax)

Likewise, if the union uses U2, the company would pay out 2 if a mixed strategy of $q_2 = 0$ were employed and -1 if a mixed strategy of $q_2 = 1$ were used. The line connecting these two points also appears in Figure 14.3. The equation of this line which gives the payout corresponding to every company mixed strategy assuming the union uses U2 is

$$\begin{aligned}\text{Payout} &= (q_1)(2) + (q_2)(-1) \\ &= 2 - 3q_2\end{aligned}$$

The heavy boundary shows the maximum payout the company might have to make corresponding to each mixed strategy. By the minimax criterion, the

416

company wishes to minimize the maximum possible payout and thus should select the mixed strategy where $q_2 = .5$. With the mixed strategy (.5 C1, .5 C2), the equilibrium value for the game is .5 as is seen in Figure 14.3. This is necessarily the same equilibrium value as was determined in Figure 14.2(b) since it is the same game.

The optimal value for q_2 could also have been determined algebraically by solving the two intersecting payout lines simultaneously

$$7q_2 - 3 = 2 - 3q_2$$
$$10q_2 = 5$$
$$q_2 = .5$$

The equilibrium value may then be found by substituting $q_2 = .5$ into either of the payout equations.

In conclusion, the optimal mixed strategy for the union is (.3 U1, .7 U2) and for the company is (.5 C1, .5 C2). The value of the game is an expected payoff of .5 thousand ($500) to the union.

A useful thing about the graphical approach is that it can be used to solve two-person zero-sum games of the n x 2 and 2 x m varieties. The approach, though a little more complex, is analogous to the analysis that has been demonstrated for 2 x 2 games. n x m games are more difficult to solve partly because it is difficult to visualize what is taking place. Although these games cannot be graphed, they can be solved. Linear programming can be used to solve such games.

14.8 OTHER GAMES

There are two large classes of games which have not been considered. These are non-zero-sum games and games with more than two players, or *n*-person games.

Consider the game of Table 14.13. This game is a three-person non-zero-sum game. In this game, Row picks the row, Column picks the column, and the third player picks the matrix. The first number in each box is the payoff to Row,

TABLE 14.13
A Three-person Non-zero-sum Game

	C1	C2		C1	C2
R1	1,4,1	3,3,3	R1	1,1,1	3,3,3
R2	2,2,2	1,1,1	R2	2,2,1	4,1,1
	I			II	

the second is the payoff to Column, and the third is the payoff to the third player. Can such a game have an equilibrium? Consider the strategies R2, C1, and Matrix I. Row has no reason to change to R1, Column has no incentive to switch to C2, and the third player has no reason to switch to Matrix II. This strategy triplet seems to be stable and thus constitutes equilibrium. Thus the definition of an equilibrium is one which can be used in certain more complex games.

This game illustrates well the fact that more involved competitive situations become very complex very quickly. Such games will not be further considered.

14.9 OTHER APPLICATIONS

Operating a business in a free enterprise system means that many decisions faced by the operators arise from situations which are, to differing degrees, competitive. While the exact outcomes or payoffs of certain actions might not be known, a game-theoretic approach may be of considerable value in lending structure and organization to the competitive situation. This section indicates very briefly some examples of areas in which the theory of games might be usefully applied to help decision makers view certain situations more analytically.

Corporate advertising for different products is definitely a competitive game. Consider a situation in which two firms are advertising similar products. Each firm might have several strategies available subject to a fixed advertising budget. Say, for example, that in a certain community Pepsi and Coke are both deciding whether to buy advertising space in the morning or evening paper. The results of the ad campaign might be viewed as in Table 14.14.

TABLE 14.14
Advertising Competition

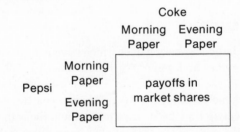

If advertising budgets are not fixed, then the strategy might be the size of the budget itself. Often these conflicts can be viewed as either a zero-sum or non-zero-sum game. Suppose Wilson Sporting Goods and Spalding are considering the athletic equipment market in some region. The strategies for the two companies can be structured like the game in Table 14.15. The payoffs are in millions of dollars. The first number in each box represents the return to Wilson and the second number the return to Spalding under the relevant strategy mix.

Marketing decisions are often of a competitive nature. Pricing decisions are the most direct form of competition. If Texaco and Exxon decide to engage in price competition in a given locality, the results in profit can be viewed as a function of the price per gallon set by each company. The game of Table 14.16 might depict such a competitive situation.

Another form of market competition is fought using product design, as is illustrated annually by the automobile industry. An example of such a game is given in Table 14.17.

TABLE 14.15
Advertising Budget Competition

		Spalding	
		Low Ad Spending	High Ad Spending
Wilson	Low Ad Spending	1,1	2,7
	High Ad Spending	7,2	−3,−3

TABLE 14.16
Gasoline Price Competition

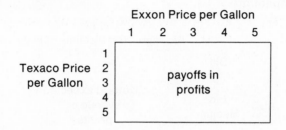

TABLE 14.17
Model Change Competition

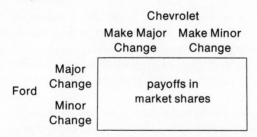

Companies must also consider advantages and disadvantages associated with different research and development programs. For example, a company might be aggressive and invest heavily in order to develop a new product to increase its market share, or it might take a "wait and copy" strategy thereby saving money on research. Table 14.18, page 420, shows a situation of this type.

Firms must also consider strategies to use in bidding to obtain certain projects. The television networks, for example, often must bid for coverage of certain events like the Olympics. Because there is some joint work, the network losing the bid may still make some money from that project. This is illustrated in Table 14.19, page 420.

Even business decisions in the area of personnel are all too often competitive. The example earlier in the chapter showed a simple case of company-union competition. In some cases the decision of the workers to become

TABLE 14.18
R & D Competition

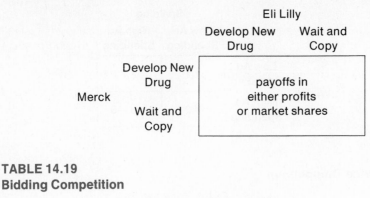

Eli Lilly

		Develop New Drug	Wait and Copy
Merck	Develop New Drug		payoffs in either profits or market shares
	Wait and Copy		

TABLE 14.19
Bidding Competition

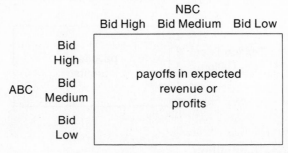

NBC

		Bid High	Bid Medium	Bid Low
ABC	Bid High		payoffs in expected revenue or profits	
	Bid Medium			
	Bid Low			

unionized causes a confrontation of labor and management over certain key issues. If, for example, a vote is to be taken among the employees on unionization and there are several major issues being discussed both by management and the union organizers, then strategies might be formulated in terms of stands on these issues. The payoffs in such a confrontation might include percentages of the vote.

These examples should make more apparent the value of game theory as a model for representing many situations involving competition.

PROBLEMS

14-1. Solve each of the games represented by the following payoff matrices.

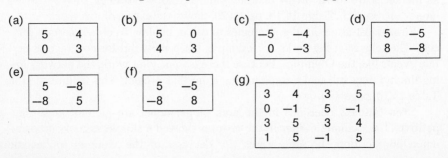

(a)

5	4
0	3

(b)

5	0
4	3

(c)

−5	−4
0	−3

(d)

5	−5
8	−8

(e)

5	−8
−8	5

(f)

5	−5
−8	8

(g)

3	4	3	5
0	−1	5	−1
3	5	3	4
1	5	−1	5

14-2. Sharon Graham has a monopoly on the non-stop transportation (Sharon's Shuttle) between the two moons of Mars. However, it is rumored that there is possible competition in the future from her old rival Jan Ross (Ross's Rocket). Graham is considering two approaches to ward off the loss in business from this competition. The two alternatives are to do nothing and to hold an advertising campaign. Taking into account the cost of advertising and its anticipated effect on revenues, the following payoff table is determined in terms of the net payoff to the Shuttle.

		Ross	
		Do Not Introduce Rocket	Introduce Rocket
Sharon	No Advertising	400,000	800,000
	Advertising Campaign	700,000	600,000

Use the graphical method to find the solution to this problem.

14-3. Suppose you have just sold the family jewels and are looking for a place to invest. Your friend Andrea Burns suggests to you to consider either stocks, bonds, or a mutual fund. The economy can be in either of two states next year, recession or inflation. The return to you in percentage is given in the matrix below. What should you do with your money?

	Recession	Inflation
Stocks	4	5
Bonds	5	6
Mutual Fund	3	4

14-4. One of the long-running feuds of the prairie days involved the cattle ranchers and sheepherders of the Midwest. The Amalgamated Sheepherders Union, Local 35, was responsible for two very large flocks. The Cattle Ranchers Association in that area decided a raid was in order as an expression of their feelings of comradeship. There are enough people in the Association to attack one flock or the other, but not both. Local 35 has only enough members to maintain one defense force which it assigns to either of the flocks on a daily basis. If the Association raids where there is no defense they will get 12 sheep. They get no sheep if they hit Local 35's defense. If they attack the larger of the two flocks, they will get an additional four sheep before the sheepherder defense will know they are there. This is in addition to the number of sheep they will get after meeting (or not meeting) the flock defenders.

Set up the payoff matrix and decide what the best strategy is for the Association in deciding which flock to attack, and for Local 35 in deciding how to assign the defense force each day. On the average, how many sheep do the cattle ranchers get per day?

14-5. The new miners buying ore wagons for their diggings in northern Colorado seem to be a fickle lot. It is difficult to predict which type wagon will be stylish each year, the Luxury Liner or the Compact. John Duke is strained to decide what stock to buy for his OK Wagons franchise in Denver. When the Luxury Liner is in style, Duke can sell 100 Luxury Liners and zero Compacts. When the Compact is in style, Duke can sell 50 Luxury Liners and 200 Compacts. In preparing for the uncoming year, Duke can select either of two acts:

a_1: Purchase 100 Luxury Liners and 0 Compacts

a_2: Purchase 50 Luxury Liners and 200 Compacts

A Luxury Liner costs $200 and sells for $400, Compacts cost $80 and sell for $200. Whatever Duke does not sell is a total loss.

Set up the payoff matrix and find a mixed strategy that can stabilize Duke's profit despite changing fashions. Should Duke keep the franchise?

14-6. There are three sizable towns in southern Indiana. Their relative locations and the percentage of the total population of that region living in each town are shown in the map below. M. Mag Binkley is considering opening a quick-food business (Binkley's Burgers) but is not sure where to build. She can build in any one of the three cities and will attract customers from all three spots. The problem is that there is competition to face. Long's Wieners will be opening a new branch in the very same area, but neither knows where the other will locate. The pertinent data obtained by interviewing the inhabitants of the region suggests that

1. If Binkley is closer to a city than Long, she will get 75% of the business in that city.
2. If Long is closer to a city than Binkley, Binkley will get only 30% of the business from that city.
3. If the two establishments are equally distant from a city or in the same city, Binkley will get 60% of that city's business.

Set up the game matrix for this location decision. Find the strategies Binkley and Long should follow in locating their businesses.

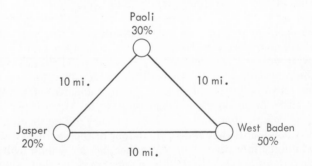

Markov Processes

15.1 INTRODUCTION

Suppose you are about to flip a "fair" coin. What is the probability of heads? You correctly answer, .5. Suppose that you flip the coin and a head turns up. What is the probability of a head now if you flip the coin again? Is it still .5? The answer is yes, of course, because the result of the first flip does not change the shape of the coin or anything else that would influence the outcome of the second flip. In fact, the outcomes of the two flips are independent (see Section 2.6 of Chapter 2 for a discussion of statistical independence). A sequence of experiments, such as repeated flipping of a coin, in which the outcome of each experiment is independent of the outcomes of all the other experiments is called a *Bernoulli process*.

Situations are not always so happily arranged that what happens at a particular time is totally independent of what has just preceded. To change examples, consider the pond of Figure 15.1 with the assortment of lily pads shown.

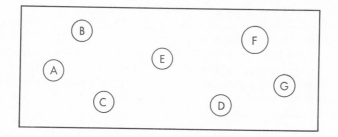

FIGURE 15.1   Lily Pond

Assume a frog is resting on one of the pads. Knowing that the frog makes a jump to a different pad once each hour, and that it can jump only to adjacent pads

This chapter was written by Daniel G. Brooks, Indiana University.

423

because it is unable to leap completely over a pad to another one, what is the probability that the frog is on pad C after the next jump? Before you would be willing to answer this, you would ask where the frog is presently located. If the previous jump had landed the frog on pad F, then there is no chance of the next jump taking it to pad C whereas if it is currently on pad A then there is a high probability of ending up on C with the next jump. In this kind of situation, the outcome of a jump is influenced by the outcomes of previous jumps. Therefore, the current outcome is not independent of previous outcomes. A *Markov process* is a sequence of experiments, such as repeated leaps by this frog, in which the outcome of each experiment is dependent on the outcome of the experiment immediately preceeding it.

In this chapter some of the mathematical characteristics of a Markov process will be explored and the usefulness of Markov processes in solving managerial decision problems will be illustrated. The next section begins with a simple example.

15.2 STATES AND TRANSITIONS

Transportation for crops and other vendibles was basic to life in the Arizona Territory in the late 1800s, and the wagon was basic to transportation. J. E.'s Wagon Works, Inc., supplied wagon buyers in northern Arizona from its three production sites located in Prescott, Flagstaff, and Winslow (P, F, and W, respectively). To spur worker morale and motivation, each summer from June to October, J. E. himself travels from plant to plant each week, spending a week at the plant he visits and then traveling to a new plant on the weekend. He assumes that if this visitation schedule were predictable so that workers knew when to expect him, much of the benefit would be lost. Therefore, he uses the following scheme to decide which plant to visit each week:

1. If he visited Prescott last week, he flips a fair coin and if a head comes up he goes to Flagstaff; otherwise, he goes to Winslow.
2. If he visited Flagstaff the preceeding week, he draws a card from a deck; a heart sends him to Winslow, a diamond to Prescott, and a club or spade means he will visit Flagstaff again.
3. If he visited Winslow the week before, he puts the numbers one through ten on pieces of paper and puts these in a hat, drawing one piece of paper out at random. Numbers one through four mean a visit to Prescott next, numbers five through eight a visit to Flagstaff, and a nine or ten means another week in Winslow.

The plant J. E. starts with the first week of June is determined by which area has the nicest weather at that time. After that, the scheme above determines all subsequent visits. This rather lengthy description of the process by which J. E.'s visits are determined is given to illustrate these points:

1. The choosing of a plant to visit each week is a "chance" event.
2. The probability that a particular plant is visited next week depends on the plant that was visited this week.

3. To know the probabilities of the different plants being visited next week, it is sufficient to know which plant is being visited this week. It is irrelevant which plants were visited on past weeks so long as the plant visited this week is known.

The outcome of the experiment J. E. performs each week is dependent only on the outcome of the experiment immediately preceeding it. This is called the *Markov property* and it is described in points 2 and 3 above.

The probabilities associated with the outcomes of the experiments described are portrayed in the map of Figure 15.2. The plant sites in this diagram are referred to as *states*. It will be seen later that "state" has a more general meaning. In this example there are three states. The arcs represent *transitions* from state to state, the passing from one state to another. The numbers in the diagram represent the probability of making the associated transitions given that the current state is the one from which the arc originates. The probabilities are determined by the experiments performed by J. E.

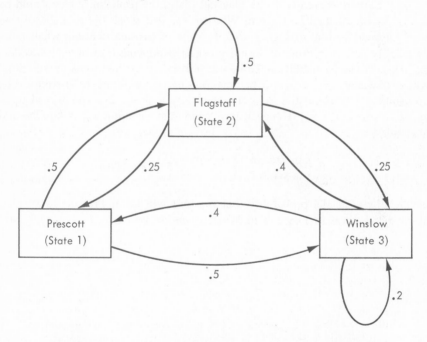

FIGURE 15.2   States, Transitions, and Transition Probabilities

15.3 PROBABILITY TREES AND TRANSITION MATRICES

Suppose it is known that the boss (J.E.) is in Prescott. The probabilities associated with the plant (state) he next visits are represented using the *probability tree* in Figure 15.3, page 426. Note that the probabilities sum to 1. This makes sense because he either has to go some place or stay where he is, so the probability tree accounts for all possible moves.

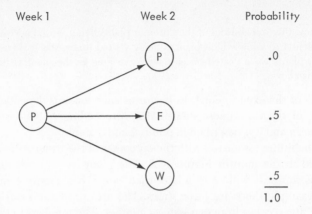

Week 1   Week 2   Probability

                   P   .0

   P   F   .5

                   W   .5
                                   ———
                                   1.0

FIGURE 15.3   Probability Tree

If J. E. were currently at the Flagstaff plant, the probability tree would be that of Figure 15.4; if he were in Winslow the first week the probability tree would instead be that of Figure 15.5. In view of this information, what is the probability J. E. is in Prescott during Week 2? It depends on where he was during Week 1. The probability is 0 if he was in Prescott the first week, it is .25 if he was in Flagstaff, and it is .4 if he was in Winslow in Week 1. Therefore, the probability of being at the Prescott plant during Week 2 is conditional upon where he was in Week 1. Hence, it is referred to as a *conditional probability* and is written as

$$P \left(\begin{matrix} \text{In Prescott} \\ \text{in Week 2} \end{matrix} \; \middle| \; \begin{matrix} \text{In Flagstaff} \\ \text{in Week 1} \end{matrix} \right) = P(P|F)$$

which represents the probability that the boss will be in Prescott in Week 2 *given* that he was in Flagstaff in Week 1 (see Section 2.5 of Chapter 2 for a

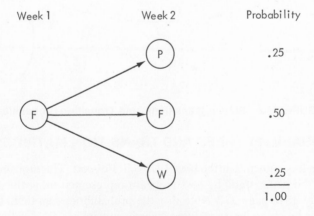

Week 1   Week 2   Probability

                   P   .25

   F   F   .50

                   W   .25
                                   ———
                                   1.00

FIGURE 15.4   Probability Tree

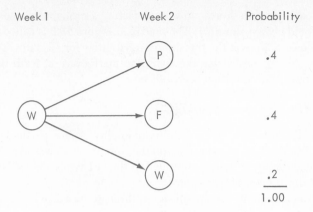

Week 1	Week 2	Probability
	P	.4
W	F	.4
	W	.2
		$\overline{1.00}$

FIGURE 15.5   **Probability Tree**

review of conditional probability). Using the state notation, this conditional probability can be written as

$$P \left(\begin{matrix} \text{In State 1} \\ \text{in Week 2} \end{matrix} \middle| \begin{matrix} \text{In State 2} \\ \text{in Week 1} \end{matrix} \right) = .25$$

This probability can be read from either Figure 15.2 or 15.4.

This conditional probability, representing the chance of passing from one specified state to another, is called a *transition probability*. The probabilities associated with each of the transition arcs in Figure 15.2 are transition probabilities. The transition probabilities associated with Winslow are shown in Figure 15.5.

There is another way to keep track of these transition probabilities that is easier than drawing probability trees. This is done by arranging the values in matrix form and properly labeling the rows and columns as shown in Figure 15.6.

(a)

	Prescott	Flagstaff	Winslow
Prescott	P(P|P)	P(F|P)	P(W|P)
Flagstaff	P(P|F)	P(F|F)	P(W|F)
Winslow	P(P|W)	P(F|W)	P(W|W)

(b)

		To		
		P	F	W
	P	0	.5	.5
From	F	.25	.50	.25
	W	.4	.4	.2

FIGURE 15.6   **Transition Matrix**

Notice that each row is a shorthand way of writing a probability tree. Therefore each row should always sum to 1. The matrix in Figure 15.6 is called the *transition matrix* because it gives the transition probabilities for all states. The analyst, therefore, in having constructed the transition matrix has set forth the relevant states, transitions, and transition probabilities.

15.4 OTHER CHARACTERISTICS

It should be clear that the probability of ending up in a particular state in a given week, say week K, depends only on the state the boss was in at Week K−1 so long as he sticks to the scheme outlined in the last two sections. Notice three · things about this process of transitions.

First, there are a finite number of states; three, to be exact.

Second, it is assumed that J. E. switches from plant to plant using the same three techniques (coin, cards, and numbers) every week so that the transition probabilities stay the same whether it is the first week, the tenth, or the hundredth. The transition matrix, therefore, remains unchanged. When this is true the transition probabilities are said to be *stationary* in time. That is, they do not change from transition to transition, and therefore depend only on the prior state and not on the time of the transition.

Third, when the transitions can come only at specified times, that is, only at discrete points in time and not at *any* time, then the process is referred to as a *Markov chain*. The current example is a Markov chain because the boss can switch to another plant only once per week, so there is only one transition per week. If he visited another plant only when lightning struck, for example, then the changes from state to state could take place at any point in the continuum of time and the process would not be called a "chain."

In the remainder of this chapter, the case of stationary Markov chains with a finite number of states will be considered.

15.5 MATRIX ALGEBRA SURVEY

For the reader already familiar with the basic manipulations of matrices, this section can be skipped with no loss in continuity. For those rusty in this art, this section will provide a brief review of certain computational techniques with matrices.

A rectangular array of numbers

$$\begin{bmatrix} 6 & 5 & -2 \\ 2 & 3 & 4 \\ 9 & 6 & 1 \end{bmatrix}$$

is referred to as a *matrix*. Each number in the array is referred to as an *element* of the matrix. As can be seen, a matrix has *rows* and *columns*. A very common example of a matrix with rows and columns is a wall calender. When the number of rows is the same as the number of·columns, the matrix is said to be *square*. The matrix above is a square matrix having three rows and three columns.

A matrix is often denoted by a single capital letter, such as

$$A = \begin{bmatrix} 2 & 4 \\ 3 & 1 \end{bmatrix}$$

A single number, not a matrix, is referred to as a *scalar*. Addition of a scalar to a matrix is defined by the process illustrated below.

$$A = \begin{bmatrix} 2 & 4 \\ 3 & 1 \end{bmatrix}$$

$$A + 6 = \begin{bmatrix} 2 & 4 \\ 3 & 1 \end{bmatrix} + 6 = \begin{bmatrix} 2+6 & 4+6 \\ 3+6 & 1+6 \end{bmatrix}$$

$$= \begin{bmatrix} 8 & 10 \\ 9 & 7 \end{bmatrix}$$

The scalar value is added to each element of the matrix.

Addition of two matrices is performed by adding corresponding elements. Let

$$C = \begin{bmatrix} 2 & 4 & 8 \\ 3 & 1 & 2 \end{bmatrix} \text{ and } D = \begin{bmatrix} 1 & 1 & 9 \\ 2 & 4 & 4 \end{bmatrix}$$

Then,

$$C + D = \begin{bmatrix} 2+1 & 4+1 & 8+9 \\ 3+2 & 1+4 & 2+4 \end{bmatrix}$$

$$= \begin{bmatrix} 3 & 5 & 17 \\ 5 & 5 & 6 \end{bmatrix}$$

To add two matrices, the two must have the same number of rows and columns. If this is true they are said to be *conformable for addition*. Note that $C + D = D + C$.

A matrix is multiplied by a scalar by multiplying each element of the matrix by the scalar. Let

$$a = 3 \text{ and } A = \begin{bmatrix} 2 & 4 & 8 \\ 3 & 1 & 2 \end{bmatrix}$$

Then,

$$a \cdot A = 3 \begin{bmatrix} 2 & 4 & 8 \\ 3 & 1 & 2 \end{bmatrix} = \begin{bmatrix} 3 \cdot 2 & 3 \cdot 4 & 3 \cdot 8 \\ 3 \cdot 3 & 3 \cdot 1 & 3 \cdot 2 \end{bmatrix}$$

$$= \begin{bmatrix} 6 & 12 & 24 \\ 9 & 3 & 6 \end{bmatrix}$$

Multiplying a matrix by another matrix is not quite so intuitive as the definitions given up to now. The definition of a product of two matrices is illustrated below.

Let

$$A = \begin{bmatrix} 2 & 4 \\ 6 & 8 \end{bmatrix} \text{ and } B = \begin{bmatrix} 1 & 3 \\ 5 & 7 \end{bmatrix}$$

then

$$C = AB = \begin{bmatrix} 2 & 4 \\ 6 & 8 \end{bmatrix} \begin{bmatrix} 1 & 3 \\ 5 & 7 \end{bmatrix} = \begin{bmatrix} 22 & 34 \\ 46 & 74 \end{bmatrix}$$

How is this multiplication performed? Let us consider how the 22 in matrix C is determined. The 22 in matrix C occurs in the *first row* and the *first column* of C. Hence the entire first row of A and the entire first column of B will be used to find this 22. The first row of A is (2 4) and the first column of B is $\begin{pmatrix} 1 \\ 5 \end{pmatrix}$. Corresponding elements in these two are then multiplied yielding

$$2 \cdot 1 + 4 \cdot 5 = 2 + 20 = 22$$

It is not a fair question here to ask, why?! This is the definition of matrix multiplication. How can the 34 in C be found? It occurs in the first row of C and the second column, thus the corresponding elements of the first row of A, (2 4), and the second column of B, $\begin{pmatrix} 3 \\ 7 \end{pmatrix}$, are used, that is,

$$2 \cdot 3 + 4 \cdot 7 = 6 + 28 = 34$$

To find the 46 in C, which occurs in the second row and first column of the matrix, the second row of A and first column of B are used, that is,

$$\begin{bmatrix} 2 & 4 \\ 6 & 8 \end{bmatrix} \begin{bmatrix} 1 & 3 \\ 5 & 7 \end{bmatrix}$$

or,

$$6 \cdot 1 + 8 \cdot 5 = 46$$

Finally, the 74 in C is found by

$$\begin{bmatrix} 2 & 4 \\ 6 & 8 \end{bmatrix} \begin{bmatrix} 1 & 3 \\ 5 & 7 \end{bmatrix}$$

$$6 \cdot 3 + 8 \cdot 7 = 18 + 56 = 74$$

In general, to find the product of A and B where

$$A = \begin{bmatrix} a & b \\ c & d \end{bmatrix} \qquad B = \begin{bmatrix} w & x \\ y & z \end{bmatrix}$$

the product matrix $C = AB$ is found element by element where

$$AB = C = \begin{bmatrix} C_1 & C_2 \\ C_3 & C_4 \end{bmatrix}$$

For example, because C_1 is in the first row and first column of C, it represents the product of the first row of A and the first column of B

$$C_1 = (a)(w) + (b)(y)$$

Performing this operation for each of the elements in C yields the product matrix

$$AB = C = \begin{bmatrix} (a)(w)+(b)(y) & (a)(x)+(b)(z) \\ (c)(w)+(d)(y) & (c)(x)+(d)(z) \end{bmatrix}$$

Each element in C is the product of the corresponding row of A and column of B.

To be able to multiply the row times the column there has to be as many elements in the row of A as there are in the column of B. But each element in the row of A is in a separate column, so the number of elements in a row of A is actually the number of columns of A and, likewise, since each element in a column of the second matrix is in a separate row, the number of elements in a column of B is exactly the number of rows in B. From this it follows that two matrices cannot be multiplied unless the number of columns of the first matrix is equal to the number of rows of the second matrix. When this condition holds (number of columns in first equals number of rows in the second matrix), the two matrices are *conformable for multiplication*. As an example, if

$$A = \begin{bmatrix} 2 & 3 & 1 \\ 3 & 4 & 2 \end{bmatrix} \qquad B = \begin{bmatrix} 6 & 3 \\ 2 & 2 \\ 1 & 2 \end{bmatrix}$$

then,

$$AB = \begin{bmatrix} 2 & 3 & 1 \\ 3 & 4 & 2 \end{bmatrix} \begin{bmatrix} 6 & 3 \\ 2 & 2 \\ 1 & 2 \end{bmatrix}$$

$$= \begin{bmatrix} 2 \cdot 6 + 3 \cdot 2 + 1 \cdot 1 & 2 \cdot 3 + 3 \cdot 2 + 1 \cdot 2 \\ 3 \cdot 6 + 4 \cdot 2 + 2 \cdot 1 & 3 \cdot 3 + 4 \cdot 2 + 2 \cdot 2 \end{bmatrix}$$

$$= \begin{bmatrix} 19 & 14 \\ 28 & 21 \end{bmatrix}$$

It is important to note that in general $AB \neq BA$. In fact, in the example just finished BA is not even the same size as AB (you might want to check this).

To summarize, two matrices are conformable for multiplication only if the number of columns in the first matrix is equal to the number of rows in the second matrix. The resulting product matrix will have the same number of rows as the first matrix and the same number of columns as the second matrix.

If a matrix is multiplied by itself, it must be conformable with itself for multiplication. This means the number of columns in the first matrix must be equal to the number of rows in the second. Since A is both the first and second matrix, the number of rows of A must equal the number of columns of A. Therefore, the only type of matrix which can be multiplied by itself is a square matrix. For example, if

$$A = \begin{bmatrix} 3 & 2 \\ 1 & 4 \end{bmatrix}$$

then,

$$A^2 = AA = \begin{bmatrix} 3 & 2 \\ 1 & 4 \end{bmatrix} \begin{bmatrix} 3 & 2 \\ 1 & 4 \end{bmatrix}$$

$$= \begin{bmatrix} 3 \cdot 3 + 2 \cdot 1 & 3 \cdot 2 + 2 \cdot 4 \\ 1 \cdot 3 + 4 \cdot 1 & 1 \cdot 2 + 4 \cdot 4 \end{bmatrix}$$

$$= \begin{bmatrix} 11 & 14 \\ 7 & 18 \end{bmatrix}$$

With this definition any power of a matrix can be calculated. For example,

$$A^3 = AA^2$$

and

$$A^4 = AA^3$$

and so on in the same pattern.

In the sections to follow some of these techniques are used in analyzing Markov chains.

15.6 PROBABILITY TREES FOR MULTI-STEP TRANSITIONS

A *step* is a move or transition from one state to another. In the example of the Wagon Works, the conditional probabilities of switching from one plant in Week 1 to another plant in Week 2 were called transition probabilities. This could be made more specific by noticing that these are transitions to be made in a single move, namely, from one plant in Week 1 directly to another in Week 2. These probabilities could therefore be referred to more accurately as *1-step* transition probabilities. In this section a procedure will be defined by which the probability of moving from one specified state to another specified state in some finite number of steps can be determined. If this idea is not too clear yet, read the next example.

There was only a single union steward, Stu, for the workers in the three Wagon Works plants. It was his job to try and be at the same plant J. E. is visiting even though he is not privy to J. E.'s plans. Stu was on vacation the second week of June, however, and upon returning does not find out which plant J. E. visited that week although he knows that Prescott was the plant visited in Week 1. The problem then is to figure out the probabilities of the boss visiting the various plants on Week 3, given he was in Prescott during Week 1. This corresponds to the probability tree in Figure 15.7. The numbers in the "probability" column represent the probability the boss is in the associated state on Week 3, starting from Prescott on Week 1 and taking the exact path leading to the associated state. Also, the appropriate 1-step transition probabilities, as taken from Figure 15.2 or Figures 15.3–15.5, are shown on the branches of the tree. By means of the multiplication law of probability (see Section 2.7 of Chapter 2) these 1-step transition probabilities are multiplied in order to find the probabilities in the "probability" column. In particular, the probabilities along each distinct path

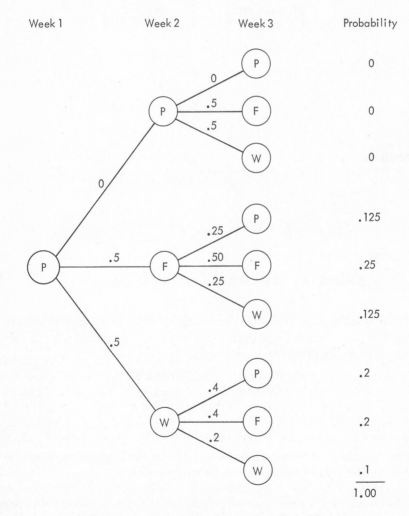

FIGURE 15.7   Probability Tree — Two Transitions

are multiplied to find the resultant probability as found in the "probability" column. For example, the .125 at the end of the *P-F-P* path is found by multiplying .5 by .25.

If the steward would like to know the probability that J. E. will be in Prescott again in Week 3, this can be found from the tree of Figure 15.7. There are three ways of ending up at Prescott on Week 3. These are shown in Figure 15.8 which is a sort of subtree of Figure 15.7. Each of the three possible paths has a certain probability of being followed. The boss might go to Flagstaff and back or to Winslow and back. It is not possible that he stay put for all three weeks in Prescott. The path taken depends on the outcomes of the experiments each week. However, the total probability of being in Prescott two weeks after the start is the sum of all possible paths, .325. This is written as

$$P \begin{pmatrix} \text{In Prescott} & \text{In Prescott} \\ \text{on Week 3} & \text{on Week 1} \end{pmatrix} = .325$$

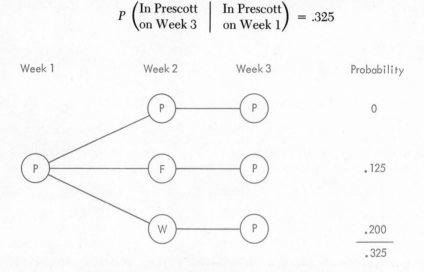

FIGURE 15.8   Ways to Return to Prescott in Week 3

It is plain that this is the probability of ending up at the Prescott plant after two moves. For this reason it is called a *2-step* transition probability. Doing the same computation for the other two states yields

$$P \begin{pmatrix} \text{In Flagstaff} & \text{In Prescott} \\ \text{on Week 3} & \text{on Week 1} \end{pmatrix} = .450$$

$$P \begin{pmatrix} \text{In Winslow} & \text{In Prescott} \\ \text{on Week 3} & \text{on Week 1} \end{pmatrix} = .225$$

It is most probable therefore that the boss will visit the Flagstaff plant on Week 3 given that he was last spotted in Prescott two weeks ago.

In the same way the 2-step transition probabilities can be determined for the cases in which J. E. was in either Flagstaff or Winslow in Week 1. Using abbreviated notation, these are

$$P(\text{In P on W3} \mid \text{In F on W1}) = .225$$
$$P(\text{In F on W3} \mid \text{In F on W1}) = .475$$
$$P(\text{In W on W3} \mid \text{In F on W1}) = .300$$

and,

$$P(\text{In P on W3} \mid \text{In W on W1}) = .180$$
$$P(\text{In F on W3} \mid \text{In W on W1}) = .480$$
$$P(\text{In W on W3} \mid \text{In W on W1}) = .340$$

15.7 MATRICES FOR MULTI-STEP TRANSITIONS

It can be tedious drawing probability trees for each possible initial state. A more direct method is afforded by the use of matrix algebra. The transition matrix for the Wagon Works case has already been shown (see Figure 15.6) to be

To

$$
\begin{array}{c}
 & & \text{P} \quad \text{F} \quad \text{W} \\
 & \text{P} & \begin{bmatrix} 0 & .5 & .5 \\ \end{bmatrix} \\
\text{From} \quad \text{F} & \begin{bmatrix} .25 & .5 & .25 \\ \end{bmatrix} \\
 & \text{W} & \begin{bmatrix} .4 & .4 & .2 \end{bmatrix}
\end{array}
$$

This transition matrix gives all the 1-step transition probabilities. To find the 2-step transition probabilities merely multiply the transition matrix by itself.

$$
\begin{bmatrix} 0 & .5 & .5 \\ .25 & .5 & .25 \\ .4 & .4 & .2 \end{bmatrix}
\begin{bmatrix} 0 & .5 & .5 \\ .25 & .5 & .25 \\ .4 & .4 & .2 \end{bmatrix}
=
\begin{bmatrix} .325 & .450 & .225 \\ .225 & .475 & .300 \\ .180 & .480 & .340 \end{bmatrix}
$$

This product matrix is the matrix of 2-step transition probabilities. Properly labeled it appears as in Figure 15.9. Note that Row 1 contains the probabilities

		State at Week 3		
		Prescott	Flagstaff	Winslow
State at Week 1	Prescott	.325	.450	.225
	Flagstaff	.225	.475	.300
	Winslow	.180	.480	.340

FIGURE 15.9   2-Step Transition Matrix

calculated earlier from the probability tree giving the probability of being in each of the three plants in two moves assuming the boss started in Prescott in Week 1. This indicates how the values can be read from the matrix. For example, the number .340 in the last row and column represents the probability of being in Winslow after two transitions given that the initial location was also Winslow.

This condenses the calculations quite a bit. The general result is this: If P denotes the 1-step transition matrix, then the 2-step transition probabilities are found by multiplying P by itself. In other words, P^2 is the matrix of 2-step transition probabilities.

The technique for finding the 3-step transition probabilities is completely analogous. The transition matrix is multiplied by itself three times:

$$P^3 = P \cdot P^2 = \begin{bmatrix} 0 & .5 & .5 \\ .25 & .5 & .25 \\ .4 & .4 & .2 \end{bmatrix} \begin{bmatrix} .325 & .450 & .225 \\ .225 & .475 & .300 \\ .180 & .480 & .340 \end{bmatrix}$$

$$= \begin{bmatrix} .2250 & .4775 & .3200 \\ .2388 & .4700 & .2912 \\ .2660 & .4660 & .2780 \end{bmatrix}$$

These values represent the 3-step transition probabilities. Therefore the value .2250 in the first row and column of P^3 is the probability J. E. is in Prescott in Week 4 given that he started in Prescott at Week 1, that is, three moves ago. Note also that since it is assumed that the transition matrix is stationary in time, .2250 would also represent the probability of being in Prescott on Week 10 given that Prescott was visited in Week 7,

$$P(\text{In P on W4} \mid \text{In P on W1}) = P(\text{In P on W10} \mid \text{In P on W7}) = .2250$$

In general, for the period t

$$P(\text{In P at Time } t+3 \mid \text{In P at Time } t) = .2250$$

The general 3-step transition matrix therefore appears as shown in Figure 15.10.

		State at Time $t + 3$		
		State 1	State 2	State 3
State at Time t	State 1	.2250	.4775	.3200
	State 2	.2388	.4700	.2912
	State 3	.2660	.4660	.2780

FIGURE 15.10   3-Step Transition Matrix

It is probably obvious by now how this procedure is expanded to any finite number of moves. The k-step transition probabilities are found by multiplying the transition matrix P by itself k times and is denoted by P^k. This may be a lot of work if k is very large, but it is certainly much simpler, and easier to remember, than trying to draw a k-step probability tree.

In conclusion, suppose the steward was on vacation the week of J. E.'s first visit and returned seven weeks later. To determine the probability of the boss being in a given plant after seven moves from the initial one, the steward need only have a Markov chain specialist multiply the original transition matrix by itself seven times, P^7, and read directly from this product matrix.

15.8 STEADY STATE AND A BRAND SWITCHING EXAMPLE

Jes-Tilla, a manufacturer of roto-tillers, has its main factory in Michigan. The production manager has encountered considerable difficulty in keeping the factory running smoothly. In particular, if the factory is running smoothly one week, then the probability it will be out of whack the next week is .7 (the workers relax too much) while if the factory is not running smoothly one week, the probability it is still off the next is only .5. The transition matrix is therefore that of Figure 15.11.

		State at Time $t+1$	
		State 1 "Smoothly"	State 2 "Not Smoothly"
State at Time t	State 1 "Smoothly"	.3	.7
	State 2 "Not Smoothly"	.5	.5

FIGURE 15.11   Jes-Tilla Transition Matrix, P

Letting State 1 represent "running smoothly" and State 2 represent "not running smoothly," the probability of being in State 2 in one transition from the initial state is .7 if the initial state was State 1 and .5 if it was not. After three transitions the probability of being in State 2 is given by the matrix of Figure 15.12; this matrix is P^3. The probability, therefore, of being in State 2 after three

		State at Time $t+3$	
		State 1	State 2
State at Time t	State 1	.412	.578
	State 2	.420	.580

FIGURE 15.12   Jes-Tilla 3-Step Transition Matrix, P^3

moves from State 1 is .578, and in three moves from State 2 is .580. It does not seem to matter quite as much which state was the initial state. In fact, the more transitions that are made, the less the influence of the initial state. Using this same example,

$$P^4 = \begin{bmatrix} .4176 & .5824 \\ .4160 & .5840 \end{bmatrix}$$

$$P^5 = \begin{bmatrix} .4165 & .5835 \\ .4163 & .5837 \end{bmatrix}$$

The initial state matters less and less.

$$P^6 = \begin{bmatrix} .4165 & .5835 \\ .4164 & .5836 \end{bmatrix}$$

And, after a while,

$$P^{15} = \begin{bmatrix} .41666 & .58333 \\ .41666 & .58333 \end{bmatrix}$$

These matrices seem to say that after about six or seven transitions, it does not really matter what the initial state was. The probability of being in State 1 is .41666 and the probability of being in State 2 is .58333 regardless of the initial state. As the number of transitions goes to infinity, the probability of being in State 1 goes to .416666... and the probability of being in State 2 goes to .583333.... These are called the *steady state* (or long-run, or equilibrium) probabilities. They might be viewed as representing the percentage of time the factory spends in each of the two states in the long-run. Also, if the factory has been operating for a long time and the initial state is not known, a reasonable approximation of the probability that the factory is not running smoothly this week is .583.

It would be very painful to calculate steady state probabilities if the only method were multiplying a matrix by itself again and again. Fortunately, there are less painful methods. Such a method is introduced by way of a brand switching example.

Dodge City in 1890 was a city of excitement and danger. In those days before gun control, folks bought firearms at the drop of a friend, so the hardware business was brisk. Ned Buntline came out to Dodge City from the East and immediately invented two things: the dime novel and the Buntline Special. The Buntline Special was a handgun, suitable for wearing on your hip, which had a barrel eighteen inches long. According to Ned, it combined the best parts of a rifle and a pistol, being lighter than a rifle but more accurate than a pistol. The only drawback was that it looked a little strange, especially on your hip. The only serious competition in Dodge was the Colt 45 and the Winchester rifle.

Ned, entrepreneur that he was, started holding turkey shoots every Saturday to show off his weapon. He knew that of the folks who bought the Special, 60 percent would buy it again on the next purchase while 20 percent would switch to the Colt and 20 percent to the Winchester. Of those who first bought a Colt 45, 50 percent repeated while 25 percent changed to the Winchester and Buntline each. The buyers of the Winchester were only 40 percent faithful, 20 percent switching on the next purchase to the Colt and 40 percent to the Buntline. For the sake of the example, assume that Dodge city residents needed to buy a new shooter every six months. The behavior of gun purchasers is summarized in the transition matrix of Figure 15.13. The question on Ned's mind, understandably, is what percentage of the market he will capture after he has been in Dodge long enough for the market to stabilize.

The matrix of information in Figure 15.13 makes some sense if each of the states is thought of as a type of gun. It is possible to analyze the movement of a purchaser from state to state. To say that a customer is in state Colt means that the customer purchases the Colt 45 as a weapon. What do steady state probabilities mean then? If a single purchaser is considered, they represent the probabilities that that person will buy each of the different brands of guns after a very

		Gun Bought Next Purchase		
		Buntline	Colt	Winchester
Gun Bought This Purchase	Buntline	.6	.2	.2
	Colt	.25	.5	.25
	Winchester	.4	.2	.4

FIGURE 15.13   Dodge City Transition Matrix

large number of previous purchases. However, if these steady state probabilities are considered as representing the buying habits of the total purchasing population, then they represent the percent of the market buying each type of gun. Individuals may switch from purchase to purchase, but the switches at steady state occur in such a way that the total percentages buying each brand remain the same. Thus the steady state percentages represent the respective market shares of the competing brands.

Before calculating these steady state probabilities, think for a minute. It is known that in steady state the number of people switching *to* a particular gun must be the same as the number of people switching *away* from that gun if the percentage of the (unchanging) total market is to remain the same. Let B be the steady state probability of a purchaser being in state Buntline, or in other words, the steady state probability that a purchaser will buy a Buntline Special. Let C and W be the steady state probabilities (market shares) for the Colt and Winchester.

Using the fact that the number switching out of a given state must equal the number switching in when the market is in steady state (or equilibrium), it holds that,

$$\text{Number Switching Away} = \text{Number Switching To}$$

for each state or brand of gun. This means that in Ned's case, 40 percent will be switching away (20 percent to Colt and 20 percent to Winchester) from his product, but he will be gaining 25 percent of Colt's customers and 40 percent of Winchester's customers on the next purchase. This yields the equality

$$\frac{\text{Number Switching Away}}{\text{from Buntline}} = \frac{\text{Number Switching To}}{\text{Buntline}}$$

$$.4B = .25C + .4W$$

For the other two brands the corresponding equalities are,

$$.5\,C = .2\,B + .2\,W \qquad \text{(for Colt)}$$
$$.6\,W = .2\,B + .25\,C \qquad \text{(for Winchester)}$$

if steady state prevails. There are now three equations and three unknowns. Unfortunately, the last equation does not tell anything new; it is only a special combination of the first two. Therefore, leave that equation out and use another piece of independent information. That is the fact that Buntline, Colt, and Winchester account for the entire market, thus their shares must add to one.

$$B + C + W = 1$$

There are now three independent equations and three unknowns

$$.4B = .25C + .4W \qquad (1)$$
$$.5C = .2B = .2W \qquad (2)$$
$$B + C + W = 1 \qquad (3)$$

It is now necessary to solve these three linear equations simultaneously in order to find B, C, and W. Rearranging Equation (3) yields

$$W = 1 - B - C \qquad (4)$$

Now substitute Equation (4) in Equation (1) for the sake of eliminating the W

$$.4B = .25C + .4(1 - B - C) \qquad (5)$$

Simplify this

$$.8B + .15C = .4 \qquad (6)$$

Now go back and substitute Equation (4) into Equation (2) for the sake of eliminating the W

$$.5C = .2B + .2(1 - B - C) \qquad (7)$$

Simplify this

$$.7C = .2 \qquad (8)$$

Following this sort of procedure will result, typically, in two equations, Equations (6) and (8), expressed in two unknowns.

Equation (8) may now be solved for C

$$C = .2/.7 = .286$$

Substituting this value for C into Equation (6) yields

$$.8B + (.15)(.286) = .4 \qquad (9)$$

This may now be solved for B

$$B = .446$$

Finally, the values for C and B are substituted in Equation (4) in order to determine W

$$W = 1 - .446 - .286 = .268$$

The solution then is

$$B = .446$$
$$C = .286$$
$$W = .268$$

These results mean that in the long run, after "enough" switches from brand to brand, the transition matrix will be that of Figure 15.14. No matter what the initial market shares are, the Buntline Special will end up with about 44.6

percent of the purchasers in Dodge City. This, of course, assumes that the switching probabilities as given in Figure 15.13 remain stationary.

		n^{th} Purchase (large n)		
		Buntline	Colt	Winchester
First Purchase	Buntline	.446	.286	.268
	Colt	.446	.286	.268
	Winchester	.446	.286	.268

FIGURE 15.14   Dodge City Steady State Probabilities

In summary, the general solution technique is to set up as many independent equations as there are states. These equations are obtained by using the fact that at steady state the number of transitions into a state is equal to the number of transitions out of a state. This is used for every state but the last state, which will be a special combination of the preceding states, and will contain no new information (or, in other words, is not independent). The last equation used is the one that says the probabilities of being in the individual states in steady state must sum to one. Then in solving these simultaneous equations the steady state market shares are determined.

There are times when it might be of more interest to know the next period's sales than to know the ultimate shares of the market in the long run. The transition matrix can be used to this end also. Let the vector, which is a matrix having only one row or one column,

$$(.5 \quad .3 \quad .2)$$

represent the market share this six-month period for Buntline, Colt, and Winchester. In other words, this period Buntline has 50 percent of the gun market in Dodge, Colt has 30 percent, and Winchester has 20 percent of the market. The probable market shares for next period's buying are found by multiplying the current market shares by the 1-step transition matrix, that is,

$$
\begin{array}{ccc}
\text{Market Shares} & \text{Transition} & \text{Next Period's} \\
\text{This Period} & \text{Matrix} & \text{Market Shares}
\end{array}
$$

$$(.5 \quad .3 \quad .2) \begin{bmatrix} .6 & .2 & .2 \\ .25 & .5 & .25 \\ .4 & .2 & .4 \end{bmatrix} = (.455 \quad .290 \quad .255)$$

(Note that .455 is found by $(.5)(.6)+(.3)(.25)+(.2)(.4)$, for example.) Thus Buntline can expect 45.5 percent of the market in the next period, Colt can expect 29 percent, and Winchester is expected to capture 25.5 percent of the market.

If the analyst using this model is interested in prospective market shares three periods from now, given these current market shares, then the vector giving the current market shares must be multiplied by the 3-step transition matrix, P^3. In the case at hand,

$$
\begin{array}{cc}
\begin{array}{c}\text{Current Market}\\ \text{Shares}\end{array} & P^3 \\
\end{array}
$$

$$
\begin{array}{c}\text{Current Market}\\ \text{Shares}\end{array} \quad P^3 \qquad\qquad \begin{array}{c}\text{Market Shares}\\ \text{Three Periods from Now}\end{array}
$$

$$
(.5 \quad .3 \quad .2) \begin{bmatrix} .460 & .278 & .262 \\ .425 & .305 & .270 \\ .455 & .275 & .270 \end{bmatrix} = (.449 \quad .285 \quad .266)
$$

Therefore, Buntline could expect to have 44.9 percent of the market in three periods, Colt could expect 28.5 percent, and Winchester could expect to capture 26.6 percent of the gun market.

It has been demonstrated that the transition matrix enables the analyst to make both short-run and long-run or steady state predictions of market shares for the competing products. The transition matrix also permits certain valuable insights into the nature of the competition. For instance, the Buntline-Colt-Winchester matrix of Figure 15.13 indicates something about the loyalty of buyers to the competing products. Sixty percent of Buntline's purchasers remain loyal, fifty percent of Colt's remain loyal from period to period, but only forty percent of Winchester's customers return to Winchester in making their next purchase. Winchester should, for example, seek to determine why its customers do not remain loyal. Is it because of a poor quality product? Does the product have some unattractive features which become apparent to the purchaser only after the product has been used? Do the competitors have especially strong advertising programs? Obviously, if Winchester can increase the loyalty of its customers it can then capture a larger share of the market. Also, through an examination of the transition matrix a company can see where its unloyal customers are going and where their new customers are coming from. Such information may point to certain factors (price, advertising, quality, packaging, etc.) which either enhance or detract from the company's competitive position.

Not only can the transition matrix be used to locate problems, the elements in it can be altered in order to see the market share effects of such changes. For example, Winchester could compute short- and long-run market shares based on a transition matrix where the bottom row of Figure 15.13 is replaced with (.35 .15 .50). In other words, the effect of increasing its loyalty rate from 40 percent to 50 percent and decreasing its contribution to Buntline and Colt by .05 points each can be determined by working with the new transition matrix. Thus the effects of various marketing policies can in some measure be evaluated by simulating with altered transition matrices.

15.9 GEOMETRIC CALCULATION OF STEADY STATE

There is a method of computing the steady state probabilities which is simpler, though sometimes more limited, than the simultaneous linear equation approach of the last section. Return once again to the Wagon Works case. The boss, J. E., continues switching plants weekly. Suppose the steward takes four months off and on returning would like to know which plant J. E. is currently visiting. In four months there have been enough switches from plant to plant so that the initial plant makes little difference. The steward needs to know the probability of finding the traveling boss in each of the plants, which means the steward needs to know the steady state probabilities. The transition diagram of the Markov chain is redrawn in Figure 15.15. Normally, calculating the steady state probabilities would not be a pleasant thought, but the following approach makes it "almost fun."

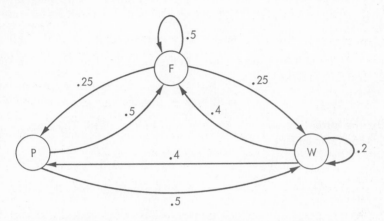

FIGURE 15.15 Wagon Works Transition Diagram

First of all, it is not necessary to consider the cycles, such as the probability of staying at Flagstaff again, so the two loops, one at F and one at W, can be ignored. Now, consider all the ways the boss can get to Prescott. There are three of them, and each is diagrammed in Figure 15.16. These can be called *intrees*.

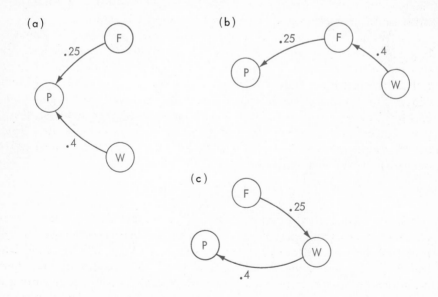

FIGURE 15.16 Intrees for State P

An intree for state P, for example, is a subtree of the transition diagram in which every state has *only one* arc leaving it except state P which has none, and all arcs point "toward" the state P. There are, as was said, three such subtrees for state P: (a) go directly from F or W, (b) go from W to F to P, or (c) go from F to W to P. There are not any others. The *weight* of an intree is defined to be the product of the arc probabilities, so that the three weights for intrees (a), (b), and (c) of Figure 15.16 would be $(.25)(.4) = .1, .1,$ and $.1$. The sum of the weights for state P is

$$wP = .1 + .1 + .1 = .3$$

For state F the intrees are pictured in Figure 15.17. The weights for state F are $.2$, $.2$, and $.2$, and the sum is

$$wF = .2 + .2 + .2 = .6$$

Finally, the intrees for state W are shown in Figure 15.18. The corresponding weights and their sum are

$$wW = .125 + .125 + .125 = .375$$

The steady state probabilities are found by normalizing these three values as follows

$$P(\text{In State P}) = \frac{wP}{wP + wF + wW} = \frac{.3}{.3 + .6 + .375} = .2353$$

$$P(\text{In State F}) = \frac{wF}{wP + wF + wW} = \frac{.6}{.3 + .6 + .375} = .4706$$

$$P(\text{In State W}) = \frac{wW}{wP + wF + wW} = \frac{.375}{.3 + .6 + .375} = .2941$$

(a)

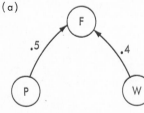

(b)

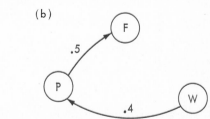

(c)

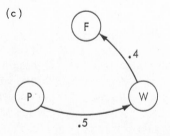

FIGURE 15.17   Intrees for State F

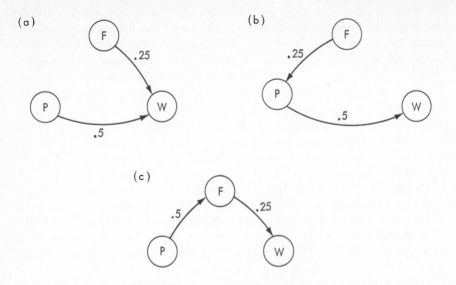

FIGURE 15.18   Intrees for State W

The resulting steady state matrix is given in Figure 15.19. In the long run, the boss spends about 24 percent of his time at the Prescott plant, 47 percent of his time at Flagstaff, and 29 percent of his time at Winslow. Therefore, the steward's best strategy would be to check the Flagstaff plant first upon returning from vacation.

| | | Plant on Week n (large n) | | |
		Prescott	Flagstaff	Winslow
Initial Plant	Prescott	.2353	.4706	.2941
	Flagstaff	.2353	.4706	.2941
	Winslow	.2353	.4706	.2941

FIGURE 15.19   Wagon Works Steady State Matrix

This technique of weighting intrees, summing the intrees for each state, and then normalizing gives a quick and (it is hoped) easily remembered way to find the steady state probabilities if there are not so many states that the trees are too hard to draw.

15.10 SUMMARY AND OTHER APPLICATIONS

At the beginning of this chapter the difference between a sequence of independent trials and a sequence of dependent trials was considered. While at first dependence seems to complicate analysis, if the dependence is Markovian it can be handled. Markovian means that the outcome of the next trial is dependent on the outcome of the present trial, and none before it. This chapter was concerned only with Markov processes which could have transitions only once per time period, that is, at discrete points in time, which had only a finite number of states, and which had transition probabilities which did not change over time. Although this limits the extent to which the model might be used, the breadth of application is still large and Markov chains are an important aid in decision-making.

Some of the techniques in this chapter can be extended to chains with an infinite number of states, or even to processes which operate in continuous time. The transition probabilities can be allowed to vary over time to further extend the ability of Markov processes to model actual situations. This chapter only touches on the usefulness of Markov processes.

While it is clearly impossible to even approximate a list of possible applications of Markov chains, it might be of some help to consider several areas in which their use might be of help in making decisions. In general, any situation in which a relatively small number of states can be isolated and in which a probabilistic transition from state to state over time can be identified is a situation which might be modeled by a Markov chain. Some possible examples are now listed, while others are presented in the problems following this chapter.

A business might be interested in estimating future losses from bad debts. If accounts are classified as paid up, overdue, and bad debt, then the transition probabilities from state to state can be estimated from past data. By calculating the steady state probabilities based on the transition matrix of Figure 15.20, the percentage of bad debt accounts at some future date, the end of the year for instance, can be estimated. From this a "loss expectancy ratio" of expected bad debt to paid debts can be calculated.

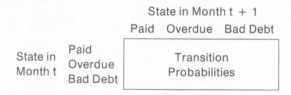

FIGURE 15.20   Debt Status Transition Matrix

In order to plan for future financial needs and orderly expansion of service facilities, it is necessary that counties attempt to forecast future land use. The county can list the major types of land uses, including vacant land, single-family dwellings, multi-family dwellings, commercial, industrial, agricultural, etc. Based on past demographic studies, the probability of the transition of land from one use to another can be estimated. Representing this information in a transition matrix like that of Figure 15.21, the county can then predict future land use. As in Section 15.8, the land use one period in the future could be forecasted by multiplying the vector which represents the current land use by the transition matrix of Figure 15.21. In the same manner forecasts further in the future could also be made.

Suppose there are population movements among three closely situated cities: Timbuckone, Timbucktwo, and Timbuckthree. Each city sends a certain fraction of its population each year to itself and to the other two cities. The

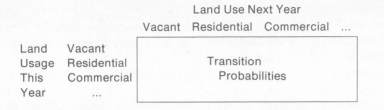

Land Use Next Year
Vacant   Residential   Commercial   ...

Land Usage This Year		Transition Probabilities
	Vacant	
	Residential	
	Commercial	
	...	

FIGURE 15.21   Land Usage Transition Matrix

cities are the "states" and the transition probabilities reflect the movement of a typical individual (see Figure 15.22). Such analysis would be important in determining tax rates, city services, and other population-based decisions.

Location in Year t + 1
Timbuckone   Timbucktwo   Timbuckthree

Location in Year t		Transition Probabilities
	Timbuckone	
	Timbucktwo	
	Timbuckthree	

FIGURE 15.22   Population Transition Matrix

The same analysis would apply to occupational mobility of workers on a yearly basis where the states might be job levels in terms of income. This would facilitate the prediction of expected income level for specific sections of the city several years in the future, or long-run income distribution of a city's population.

PROBLEMS

15-1. The weather in Phoenix changes a little, but is somewhat predictable. "Bug" Jestila, the weather watcher, has compiled the following data. There are three types of weather: hot and damp, fair and warmer, and hot and dry. If it is hot and damp, the probability of being hot and damp the next day is .7, and of being fair and warmer is .3. If it is fair and warmer, there is an 80% chance of being hot and damp the next day, and a 20% chance of being fair and warmer again. Finally, if it is hot and dry, it will be hot and dry the next day eight times out of ten, and fair and warmer two times out of ten.
   (a) Set up the transition matrix for daily weather changes.
   (b) Bug sees that it is damp (and hot) today and wonders what the weather will be like for the big family picnic the day after tomorrow. What are the chances it will be a nice day for a picnic, that is, not damp?

15-2. Freda Gruner, the fearsome physics teacher, has two moods: neutral and angry. Her mood varies hourly according to the probabilities on page 448. What percentage of the time during the school year is Freda angry?
   (a) Solve algebraically.
   (b) Solve geometrically using intrees.

| | | Mood Next Hour | |
		Neutral	Angry
Mood This Hour	Neutral	.6	.4
	Angry	.2	.8

15-3. The notorious Taylor Gang, led by dirty Dick Taylor, finances its operation by periodically robbing the daily stagecoach out of Golden. There are three routes the stage can take. For convenience, call these A, B, and C. The gang can watch only a single route. If the stage takes route A one day, there is a 50% chance it will take A the next day and 25% chance each of taking B and C the next day. If the stage takes B, there is a 20% chance of taking A the next day, and an 80% chance of taking C. If the stage travels route C, it travels route A the next day with probability .4, route B with probability .4, and route C with probability .2.

(a) Set up a transition matrix describing the behavior of the stage.

(b) Suppose Taylor's gang robs the stage on Tuesday on route A. They decide to rob it again on Thursday. On which trail are they most likely to find the stage then?

(c) Of the three trails, which is traveled the most? (Solve algebraically.) If the gang, after their three-month winter stay in Florida, shows up in the Spring, on which route are they most likely to find the stage?

15-4. Nomi and Tracy, two good friends, started a Livery Stable and Rental Service, renting horse and buggy or buckboard for trips between the three towns in the area. Chubby's Buggies (as this precursor of U-Haul was called) has a rental and livery building in each of the three towns, Big, Up, and Down. Renters return the rented buggies to the three different livery stables according to the probability pattern below.

| | | Returned To | | |
		Big	Up	Down
Rented From	Big	.6	.0	.4
	Up	.0	.2	.8
	Down	.2	.3	.5

The two founders of Chubby's are considering building a blacksmith's shop to service the buggies. Which town would be the best location for the shop? Why? (Solve geometrically using intrees.)

15-5. There is more than one way to skin a cat. There are, in fact, three different efficient ways. Earl Bertram, catskinner, has developed a new three-in-one kit which he will offer for sale in his little taxidermy shop beginning next month. However, two others have preceded him in skinning kits: Universal Catskinners and Catskinners Unlimited. The market is now evenly divided between these two. Earl has found out the following information. On a monthly basis, Universal retains 75% of its customers, and gains 5% from Unlimited and probably will gain 10% from Earl. Unlimited retains 85% of its monthly customers, and gains 10% from

Universal and expects to gain 10% from Earl. Earl expects to retain 80% of his customers, gain 15% from Universal, and 10% from Unlimited. If buying habits continue to follow this pattern, what will Earl's market share be after the first two months of business? In the long run, how much of the market should he expect to control?

15-6. The Big University has four levels of teachers in its faculty: Instructor, Assistant Professor, Associate Professor, and Full Professor. The yearly pay is $5,000, $10,000, $15,000, and $20,000, respectively. A new agreement with the teachers union requires 20% of the teachers at each of the three lower levels to be promoted each year. Currently there are 400 Instructors, 300 Assistant Professors, 200 Associates, and 100 Full Professors. It is certain that due to retirement and job changing, 20% of the Full Professors, 25% of the Associates, 15% of the Assistants, and 10% of the Instructors leave the school yearly. If the agreement is implemented this year, what will be the school's total payroll after two years if no new teachers are hired during the two years?

15-7. Suppose that before Ned Buntline actually sets up his factory to produce the Buntline Special, he hires a market research firm to check out the two most likely markets: Dodge City and Tombstone. The firm returns with the brand switching information below.

Dodge City	B	C	W
Buntline	.7	.2	.1
Colt	.2	.7	.1
Winchester	.1	.1	.8

Tombstone	B	C	W
Buntline	.8	.1	.1
Colt	.2	.7	.1
Winchester	.3	.1	.6

If both cities are the same size, which is the preferrable location? (Use an algebraic procedure for Dodge City and use intrees in the analysis of Tombstone.)

Appendix

TABLE 1

Table of Random Numbers

73310	60288	63577	73455	37934	03129	40925	78395
01847	56844	08198	78401	86756	77247	92110	36216
11415	60919	37282	58414	17041	46406	65948	33433
59904	14566	17560	01207	08524	78466	54385	85977
91949	26871	24194	23557	03087	73521	57892	17521
23508	00921	41837	91474	02823	54046	60816	30407
61959	24468	29867	28336	58566	06874	55020	32109
25331	71533	13363	41962	63996	22425	74337	00253
65397	87789	17863	13223	14485	51935	12155	86530
57357	84246	35832	75425	99208	67379	66887	58634
56889	70257	45315	41428	50166	32962	71446	73229
75802	24387	52183	02935	94143	68424	94263	64390
04778	93048	51135	28714	25696	22690	52141	68005
37211	67903	49585	32749	97035	53820	29382	38981
57133	17416	19555	22474	42718	33142	59996	52763
86062	21176	37823	47127	36676	07243	23397	43173
61226	03677	00086	22723	57463	63959	59465	49627
40075	12613	09780	87206	90447	41887	06312	83332
61073	58323	59741	70270	18884	85794	32504	47781
34624	10187	80102	91149	12205	67151	39922	78558
79690	31099	40885	50813	00054	21900	36653	86715
28587	24620	72831	08156	79211	70752	59096	84209
07064	91427	16180	21018	46865	04522	36743	07116
77293	08441	51742	74868	06431	77105	90106	01449
42198	42693	14800	25939	84468	48466	06070	94096

TABLE 2

Areas (Probabilities) for the Standard Normal Distribution

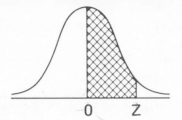

Example: The area from the mean to Z = 1.25 standard deviations above the mean is .3944, that is, P(O ≤ Z ≤ 1.25) = .3944.

Z	.00	.01	.02	.03	.04	.05	.06	.07	.08	.09
0.0	.0000	.0040	.0080	.0120	.0160	.0199	.0239	.0279	.0319	.0359
0.1	.0398	.0438	.0478	.0517	.0557	.0596	.0636	.0675	.0714	.0753
0.2	.0793	.0832	.0871	.0910	.0948	.0987	.1026	.1064	.1103	.1141
0.3	.1179	.1217	.1255	.1293	.1331	.1368	.1406	.1443	.1480	.1517
0.4	.1554	.1591	.1628	.1664	.1700	.1736	.1772	.1808	.1844	.1879
0.5	.1915	.1950	.1985	.2019	.2054	.2088	.2123	.2157	.2190	.2224
0.6	.2257	.2291	.2324	.2357	.2389	.2422	.2454	.2486	.2517	.2549
0.7	.2580	.2611	.2642	.2673	.2704	.2734	.2764	.2794	.2823	.2852
0.8	.2881	.2910	.2939	.2967	.2995	.3023	.3051	.3078	.3106	.3133
0.9	.3159	.3186	.3212	.3238	.3264	.3289	.3315	.3340	.3365	.3389
1.0	.3413	.3438	.3461	.3485	.3508	.3531	.3554	.3577	.3599	.3621
1.1	.3643	.3665	.3686	.3708	.3729	.3749	.3770	.3790	.3810	.3830
1.2	.3849	.3869	.3888	.3907	.3925	.3944	.3962	.3980	.3997	.4015
1.3	.4032	.4049	.4066	.4082	.4099	.4115	.4131	.4147	.4162	.4177
1.4	.4192	.4207	.4222	.4236	.4251	.4265	.4279	.4292	.4306	.4319
1.5	.4332	.4345	.4357	.4370	.4382	.4394	.4406	.4418	.4429	.4441
1.6	.4452	.4463	.4474	.4484	.4495	.4505	.4515	.4525	.4535	.4545
1.7	.4554	.4564	.4573	.4582	.4591	.4599	.4608	.4616	.4625	.4633
1.8	.4641	.4649	.4656	.4664	.4671	.4678	.4686	.4693	.4699	.4706
1.9	.4713	.4719	.4726	.4732	.4738	.4744	.4750	.4756	.4761	.4767
2.0	.4772	.4778	.4783	.4788	.4793	.4798	.4803	.4808	.4812	.4817
2.1	.4821	.4826	.4830	.4834	.4838	.4842	.4846	.4850	.4854	.4857
2.2	.4861	.4864	.4868	.4871	.4875	.4878	.4881	.4884	.4887	.4890
2.3	.4893	.4896	.4898	.4901	.4904	.4906	.4909	.4911	.4913	.4916
2.4	.4918	.4920	.4922	.4925	.4927	.4929	.4931	.4932	.4934	.4936
2.5	.4938	.4940	.4941	.4943	.4945	.4946	.4948	.4949	.4951	.4952
2.6	.4953	.4955	.4956	.4957	.4959	.4960	.4961	.4962	.4963	.4964
2.7	.4965	.4966	.4967	.4968	.4969	.4970	.4971	.4972	.4973	.4974
2.8	.4974	.4975	.4976	.4977	.4977	.4978	.4979	.4979	.4980	.4981
2.9	.4981	.4982	.4982	.4983	.4984	.4984	.4985	.4985	.4986	.4986
3.0	.4987	.4987	.4987	.4988	.4988	.4989	.4989	.4989	.4990	.4990
3.1	.4990	.4991	.4991	.4991	.4992	.4992	.4992	.4992	.4993	.4993
3.2	.4993	.4993	.4994	.4994	.4994	.4994	.4994	.4995	.4995	.4995
3.3	.4995	.4995	.4995	.4996	.4996	.4996	.4996	.4996	.4996	.4997
3.4	.4997	.4997	.4997	.4997	.4997	.4997	.4997	.4997	.4997	.4998

Reprinted by permission from William Stevenson, *Business Statistics: Concepts and Analysis,* New York; Harper & Row, Publishers, 1977.

TABLE 3

Compound Interest Tables
$i = .04$

n	$(1+i)^n$	$1/(1+i)^n$	$\dfrac{i(1+i)^n}{(1+i)^n-1}$
1	1.0400	.9615	1.04000
2	1.0816	.9246	.53020
3	1.1249	.8890	.36035
4	1.1699	.8548	.27549
5	1.2167	.8219	.22463
6	1.2653	.7903	.19076
7	1.3159	.7599	.16661
8	1.3686	.7307	.14853
9	1.4233	.7026	.13449
10	1.4802	.6756	.12329
11	1.5395	.6496	.11415
12	1.6010	.6246	.10655
13	1.6651	.6006	.10014
14	1.7317	.5775	.09467
15	1.8009	.5553	.08994
16	1.8730	.5339	.08582
17	1.9479	.5134	.08220
18	2.0258	.4936	.07900
19	2.1068	.4746	.07614
20	2.1911	.4564	.07358

$i = .06$

n	$(1+i)^n$	$1/(1+i)^n$	$\dfrac{i(1+i)^n}{(1+i)^n-1}$
1	1.0600	.9434	1.06000
2	1.1236	.8900	.54544
3	1.1910	.8396	.37411
4	1.2625	.7921	.28859
5	1.3382	.7473	.23740
6	1.4185	.7050	.20336
7	1.5036	.6651	.17914
8	1.5938	.6274	.16104

Compound Interest Tables

$i = .06$

n	$(1+i)^n$	$1/(1+i)^n$	$\dfrac{i(1+i)^n}{(1+i)^n-1}$
9	1.6895	.5919	.14702
10	1.7908	.5584	.13587
11	1.8983	.5268	.12679
12	2.0122	.4970	.11928
13	2.1329	.4688	.11296
14	2.2609	.4423	.10758
15	2.3966	.4173	.10296
16	2.5404	.3936	.09895
17	2.6928	.3714	.09544
18	2.8543	.3503	.09236
19	3.0256	.3305	.08962
20	3.2071	.3118	.08718

$i = .08$

n	$(1+i)^n$	$1/(1+i)^n$	$\dfrac{i(1+i)^n}{(1+i)^n-1}$
1	1.0800	.9259	1.08000
2	1.1664	.8573	.56077
3	1.2597	.7938	.38803
4	1.3605	.7350	.30192
5	1.4693	.6806	.25046
6	1.5869	.6302	.21632
7	1.7138	.5835	.19207
8	1.8509	.5403	.17401
9	1.9990	.5002	.16008
10	2.1589	.4632	.14903
11	2.3316	.4289	.14008
12	2.5182	.3971	.13270
13	2.7196	.3677	.12652
14	2.9372	.3405	.12130
15	3.1722	.3152	.11683

Compound Interest Tables

$i = .08$

n	$(1+i)^n$	$1/(1+i)^n$	$\dfrac{i(1+i)^n}{(1+i)^n-1}$
16	3.4259	.2919	.11298
17	3.7000	.2703	.10963
18	3.9960	.2502	.10670
19	4.3157	.2317	.10413
20	4.6610	.2145	.10185

$i = .10$

n	$(1+i)^n$	$1/(1+i)^n$	$\dfrac{i(1+i)^n}{(1+i)^n-1}$
1	1.1000	.9091	1.10000
2	1.2100	.8264	.57619
3	1.3310	.7513	.40211
4	1.4641	.6830	.31547
5	1.6105	.6209	.26380
6	1.7716	.5645	.22961
7	1.9487	.5132	.20541
8	2.1436	.4665	.18744
9	2.3579	.4241	.17364
10	2.5937	.3855	.16275
11	2.8531	.3505	.15396
12	3.1384	.3186	.14676
13	3.4523	.2897	.14078
14	3.7975	.2633	.13575
15	4.1772	.2394	.13147
16	4.5950	.2176	.12782
17	5.0545	.1978	.12466
18	5.5599	.1799	.12193
19	6.1159	.1635	.11955
20	6.7275	.1486	.11746

Index